CW00819856

SPITFIRES
OVER
MALTA

THE EPIC AIR BATTLES OF 1942

BRIAN CULL
WITH FREDERICK GALEA

GRUB STREET · LONDON

Published by
Grub Street
4 Rainham Close
London SW11 6SS

Copyright © 2005 Grub Street, London
Text copyright © 2005 Brian Cull

British Library Cataloguing in Publication Data
Cull, Brian
  Spitfires over Malta
  1. World War, 1939-1945 – Campaigns – Malta
  2. World War, 1939-1945 – Aerial operations, British
  3. Spitfire (Fighter planes)
  I. Title II. Galea, Frederick
  940.5′421585

ISBN 1 904943 30 6

All rights reserved. No part of this publication may be reproduced,
stored in a retrieval system, or transmitted in any form or by any means,
electronic, mechanical, photocopying, recording or otherwise,
without the prior permission of the copyright owner.

Typeset by Pearl Graphics, Hemel Hempstead

Printed and bound in Great Britain by
Biddles Ltd, King's Lynn

CONTENTS

ACKNOWLEDGEMENTS

First and foremost the authors thank their respective wives, Val and Val, as without their support, encouragement, understanding and tolerance, a happy life while researching/writing would have proved very difficult. Thanks girls!

Jochen Prien and Gerhard Stemmer are thanked for permission to use quotes and material from their *History of JG53* and *History of JG77*, and to Gerhard for supplying additional information. Thanks also to Chris Shores and Nico Malizia, co-authors of *Malta: The Spitfire Year 1942*; Mr James Churchill, son of Grp Capt Walter Churchill DSO DFC for information; Colin Attewell (grandson of Flg Off Paudrick 'Paddy' Schade DFM) for information and photographs; Mr Nigel Stephens, son of Grp Capt Mike Stephens DSO DFC for a copy of his father's logbook; Gus Mansfield (nephew of Riversdale 'Barny' Barnfather) for information and photographs; Alan Johnson (son of Sqn Ldr W.J. 'Johnny' Johnson DFC) for information and photographs; Robin Bush (son of Flt Lt Cyril 'Joe' Bush) for information and photographs; Nick Keyes, son-in-law of Sqn Ldr John Mejor DFC; Flt Lt Ray G. Smith DFC; J. Scott Kinghorn of New York for information and photographs regarding John 'Willie' Williams DFC RCAF; the late Wg Cdr Laddie Lucas DSO DFC for permission to use material from his many excellent Malta-orientated books; Norman Franks for permission to use material from *Buck McNair*; Dan McCaffery for permission to use quotes from *Hell Island*; David Ross, author of *The Greatest Squadron of Them All*; the late Leo Nomis, co-author of *The Desert Hawks*; Barry Baddock MA and Bjorn J of Malta (translations); Bruce Lander, a good friend, ever helpful and responsive; Hugh A. Halliday for information on RCAF pilots and author of the unique RCAF website; Kevin Mifsud of the NWMA for assistance with the compilation of Appendix VIII; Mrs Susan Dickinson and staff at AHB (RAF) MoD; the lovely ladies at Bury St Edmunds Public Library; Ray and Mary Rose Polidano at Takali Air Museum, Malta; Jack Lee, gentleman and scholar. Last but not least, our thanks to Mr John Davies of Grub Street, not only for his support, but his expert editing of the draft.

For first-hand accounts we have leaned heavily on Denis Barnham's excellent *One Man's Window*, a classic of the period; *Tattered Battlements* by Tim Johnston; Paul Brennan and Ray Hesselyn's *Spitfires over Malta* (the original), and Screwball Beurling's ghosted *Malta Spitfire*. Also *Air War over Malta* based on Sqn Ldr Lord Douglas-Hamilton's diary.

PREAMBLE

Following the declaration of war by the Italian Fascist Government in June 1940, Malta had stood alone as Britain's outpost in the vast Mediterranean Sea. For eighteen months the island defences had held out against the might of the Regia Aeronautica, which had been joined by elements of the Luftwaffe in January 1941 and again towards the end of the year. Apart from the impressive array of heavy and light AA guns that had been assembled on the island, the aerial defence had relied solely upon varying numbers of Hurricanes flown to the island from aircraft carriers, although the initial defence when war broke out had depended on a handful of ex-FAA Sea Gladiators based at Hal Far, and flown by RAF volunteers.

The Hurricanes had fared well against the Italians but the Luftwaffe's all-conquering Messerschmitt Bf109Fs had proved too much for the mainly inexperienced RAF pilots, and losses mounted accordingly, particularly in December 1941. By the turn of the year the situation was becoming desperate, with very few Hurricanes remaining serviceable*. Help was urgently required if Malta was to hold out – and the threat of invasion had become real. Across the 60-mile stretch of water, in Sicily, the Axis commanders were finalising plans to take the island out of the war for good. Such a move would aid Rommel and his Afrika Korps in his effort to push British and Commonwealth forces out of North Africa, but supplies and manpower were limited. Hitler and Mussolini could not invade Malta and aid Rommel simultaneously.

In Britain, Malta's plight at last finally became a priority and Prime Minister Churchill personally intervened to ensure reinforcements reached the island. First priority was aerial defence – Spitfires. By early 1942, the United Kingdom had a plethora of Spitfire squadrons, yet none had as yet been sent to the Middle East or elsewhere, where modern fighters were desperately needed. Under pressure, the Air Ministry decided to commence the release of Spitfires, the first batch – albeit just 18 aircraft – being earmarked for delivery by sea, in crates, to Gibraltar for onward distribution. The pilots selected to fly these aircraft were to accompany the crated machines.

To bolster this meagre force, a small party of experienced Spitfire pilots was flown directly to Malta by Sunderland flyingboat on 16 February 1942: Sqn Ldr Stan Turner DFC, an aggressive and successful Canadian fighter pilot[1] was placed in charge of this group, which comprised Flt Lt Laddie Lucas and Plt Off Raoul Daddo-Langlois (a Channel Islander) from 66 Squadron – both of whom were under the impression they had volunteered for service in the Far East – together with Plt Offs Harry Fox, Bob Sergeant and Tex Putnam, the latter an American volunteer in the RCAF and former Eagle Squadron pilot. Also on board were two Australian NCO pilots, Sgts Tim Goldsmith and Tom Freeman. During the early hours of 21 February, another Sunderland arrived with a further batch of Spitfire-trained pilots including Canadians Flt Lt Bud Connell and Flg Off Buck McNair, Flg Off Buck Buchanan and Plt Off Jimmy James from Rhodesia, Flg Off Ron West, Plt Off Jeff West DFM, a New Zealander[2], Plt Off Sandy McHan, another American, Plt Offs D'Arcy Milburn and Dennis Kelly, and Sgts Charlie Broad and Gordon Tweedale, the latter an Australian.

This generally happy and cheerful bunch of pilots, confident that they and their Spitfires would soon restore air superiority in the skies over Malta, could not have known the strength, experience and ability of many of the German fighter pilots based on the south-eastern coast of Sicily. The Messerschmitts – some 100 Bf109Fs – of all three Gruppen of the illustrious JG53, plus the Stab (Staff) Flight, were divided between Comiso, Gela and San Pietro, with II/JG3's 30 Bf109Fs also based at Comiso. Various Staffeln of JG53 would intermittently operate from the neighbouring outpost island of Pantelleria. There were also five Gruppen of Ju88s, plus two coastal strike units also equipped with Ju88s, plus two Gruppen of Ju87s. The Regia Aeronautica had on strength about 100 fighters: seven squadriglie equipped with MC202s, MC200s, CR42s and RE2000 fighter-bombers; and approximately 50 bombers and torpedo-bombers – SM79s and Z1007bis.

* See the authors' companion volume *Hurricanes over Malta* for a comprehensive account of this turbulent period.

To Malta's Spitfire Pilots

Malta, Mediterranean gem
Set in an azure sea;
Guarded by an Empire's sons
Who fight to keep you free.

By day, by night, when you're beset
These sons obey your call
They gladly give their life for you
They sacrifice their all.

High in the firmament above
On speedy wings they soar;
Seeking to protect the island
Keep in safe for evermore.

R.A. Willis, Malta resident 1942[3]

CHAPTER I

IN THE NICK OF TIME

7 March 1942

The Spitfires had been expected for some time. A party of 17 Spitfire pilots under the command of newly promoted Sqn Ldr Stan Grant, a Battle of Britain veteran, had departed England, on 10 February 1942 aboard the 5,000-ton *Cape Hawke* bound for Gibraltar. The pilots had been briefed they were to fly their Spitfires, which were currently in crates aboard the vessel, from an aircraft carrier to Malta – a 700-mile flight across open water. These pilots had earlier forgathered at Portreath, Cornwall, where they had all gained some air experience of flying Spitfires fitted with a 45-gallon slipper tank beneath the fuselage. However, the aircraft they were to fly from the carrier were each fitted with a newly designed 90-gallon slipper tank, never before used on operations, to enable it to complete the long flight to Malta.

On arrival at Gibraltar on 22 February, after a very rough crossing of the Bay of Biscay, one of the junior pilots, Australian Sgt Jack 'Slim' Yarra, wrote in his diary:

"Arrived today after the worst sea trip I've ever done in my life. The conditions are not fit for animals to live in. The beds are lousy and all the condensation from the roof falls on us when we sleep. It was absolutely shocking and after this war is over there are going to be some pretty stories told of how the invincible [*sic*] British Government looks after their troops. How in hell do they ever expect to win a war when they treat their fighting men like cattle? The Government spares no expense on machines of war, but when it comes to the men who run the machines the cheapest is too good for them, in the eyes of the crowd who are running this war. This may seem rather hard but it is perfectly right, and I am getting sick of seeing Churchill stick his bowler hat up on his cane so the populace hail him as their saviour, and think we are winning the war. The sooner the people of England realise that we are losing this damned war so far, the better it will be for everyone."

Shortly after their arrival at the famous Rock, the group went aboard the carrier HMS *Eagle*, where they found their cannon-armed Spitfire Vbs in the hangar, hidden from the eyes of potential Axis agents and sympathisers in nearby Spain. These aircraft had been hoisted aboard the ship partly assembled – with wings attached and undercarriage lowered for final assembly[4]. Comfort aboard the carrier for the NCO pilots was again noticeable by its absence, as Flt Sgt David Ferraby recalled:

"At least on *Cape Hawke* we had our wooden bunks, but on *Eagle* the crew and us had to doss down wherever we weren't in the way. The spot I picked for my bedding was on top of a wire mesh lock-up store in the hangar, with blokes assembling Spits all night long."

At this stage, Sqn Ldr Grant was introduced to Flt Lt Norman Macqueen and Flg Off Norm Lee, both of whom had been flown to Gibraltar from Malta, and who were to join his party at the expense of two of the less-experienced pilots in the party, Sgts Maurice Irving Gass and Harry Fox RCAF[5]. The final 17 selected for this epic flight now comprised:

Sqn Ldr S.B. Grant[6]	Flt Sgt D.W. Ferraby
Flt Lt P.W.E. Heppell DFC	Flt Sgt I.M. Cormack
Flt Lt N.C. Macqueen	Flt Sgt V.P. Brennan RAAF

Flg Off N.W. Lee   Flt Sgt C.F. Bush
Plt Off P.A. Nash   Sgt J.L. Tayleur
Plt Off K.N.L. Murray RAAF   Sgt J.W. Yarra RAAF
Plt Off J.J. Guerin RAAF   Sgt R.B. Hesselyn RNZAF
Plt Off J.A. Plagis (Rhod)[7]   Sgt R.J. Sim RNZAF
Plt Off D.C. Leggo (Rhod)

After four days at Gibraltar the carrier sailed on the night of 26 February, escorted by the Royal Navy's Force H – a battleship, a cruiser, nine destroyers and the elderly training carrier *Argus*. The latter had embarked nine Fulmars from 807 Squadron to provide air cover, and nine ASV-equipped Swordfish for anti-submarine purposes, while *Eagle* also carried two Sea Hurricanes of 813F Squadron for Combat Air Patrol duties, as well as a few ASV Swordfish. But all was not well, as Grant later recalled:

> "We were well clear of land. Hughes [Sqn Ldr Hughes, the senior engineer officer] brought the aircraft up on deck to run the engines and, above all, to test the functioning of the long-range tanks without which the operation was not on. These first 90-gallon tanks had evidently been produced in a great hurry and were a bit of a lash-up. The fuel was drawn up into the main tanks by suction and if there was the slightest air leak in the seal between the tank and the fuselage, there was no transfer. Hughes soon found that the seals were not satisfactory and although he and his team strove hard all that day and well into the night he could not make them work properly. Accordingly, around midnight, with our take-off due the next morning, Hughes sent a message to the Admiral via Wg Cdr John McLean, saying that the aircraft could not be allowed to take off without further extensive tests. And since his men had now been working for over 20 hours without rest, they could not continue without some sleep.
>
> "We heard later that the Admiral nearly exploded, and sent back the message that under no circumstances could his ships hang around in daylight in the middle of the Mediterranean, within easy range of enemy bombers. The Spitfires had to take off the next morning – at all costs. But Hughes was adamant. The aircraft were, in his view, not serviceable and he would not agree to their take-off until he was certain that the tanks would work. So the Admiral had to give in, and the whole fleet turned around and steamed back to Gibraltar."[8]

On arriving back there, the Spitfire servicing team promptly got to work and soon the problem was located – faulty suction valves – but it would take precious time to remedy. The designer of the system was immediately flown from Supermarine's head office in Southampton to oversee the work, and by the evening of 4 March the modifications were complete. *Eagle* put to sea the following morning. She was to launch the Spitfires at a predetermined point, some 700 miles west of Malta. On the morning of the launch (**7 March**), on running up the engines, two of the Spitfires were found to be unserviceable, and thus only 15 aircraft lifted off the deck and set course for the four-hour flight to the besieged island. Sgt Yarra was one of the two left behind:

> "When the time came – 7am – on the second day out everyone was keyed up and expectant and most of us were wondering if the Spitfires would really get off the deck quite OK ... All the aircraft were lined up waiting and everyone was in their cockpits half an hour before the first Blenheim, which was to lead us there, arrived. The Blenheim was sighted and the ship turned into wind. The first motor started and was run up. Suddenly the naval controller gave 'Chocks Away' and Sqn Ldr Grant opened his throttle and went roaring down the deck. He lifted off the end, sank slightly below the level of the deck, and sailed away, gaining altitude, proving that a Spitfire can take

off an aircraft carrier. All the aeroplanes got off within the hour and we turned back to Gibraltar. I was not going, as my aircraft [AB333] was u/s. I was to go back to Gib and come out with the next lot of Spitfires."

The other pilot left behind, Flt Sgt Cyril Bush (known to his friends as Joe), formerly of 603 Squadron, recalled:

"Unfortunately, I could not take off as my Spit [AB263] had a glycol leak. On returning to Gibraltar, my Spit was flown off the carrier by the AOC – it was flown to North Front for repair. I remained at Gibraltar while my aircraft was repaired."[9]

Although there had been much anticipated apprehension amongst the pilots, all the launches had gone smoothly, but such take-offs were not straightforward, as related by one pilot:

"On a Spit, unlike a Hurricane, you could not use partial flap for take-offs or landings. To overcome this and to facilitate take-offs from the carrier, small blocks of wood were cut to make an angle of about 150 degrees, so before we took off we dropped our flaps and as mechanics held the blocks of wood in place – I think there were two on each flap – we closed our flaps which wedged the wood between the flaps and the wing. After take-off, we lifted our undercarriages and climbed to a couple of thousand feet, then dropped our flaps to allow the blocks of wood to drop out, and then quickly raised our flaps again."

As the Spitfires[10] – in two flights, one of eight and the other of seven, led by Sqn Ldr Grant and Flt Lt Norman Macqueen respectively – droned towards the island which was to be their new base, guided by four Blenheims of 1442 Flight from Gibraltar, a number of Ju52/3m transports were seen in the distance, and one or two pilots broke away and gave chase, but without result, as Flt Sgt Paul Brennan, a 22-year-old Australian from Queensland, noted:

"Not knowing what to expect, we felt nervous and apprehensive, and immediately started to weave, keeping a sharp look-out. We saw nothing of the Hun fighters. Flt Lt Macqueen called for a homing. Chasing some Ju52s we had seen some distance from Malta, he had become separated from the squadron. We dropped down lower, rather fearfully wondering where the Me109s could be, but still seeing nothing of them. Grand Harbour now stood out very sharply, as also did the yellow-sandstone Mosta dome. Third largest in the world, it dominated the huddle of white buildings. Away to the north, 60 miles off, we could see Sicily, the base from which all air operations against Malta are conducted. It was faintly outlined as a flat beach, with a bank of cumulus cloud."

Towards the end of the four-hour flight, the Spitfire pilots were welcomed by the soon-to-be-familiar voice of Grp Capt A.B. Woodhall – 'Woody' to all on Malta – the senior controller, calling over the R/T: "Keep your present course. Watch out for Me109s below", as he gave them clearance to land at Takali. On approaching Malta, they found Hurricanes in the air, patrolling to cover their arrival and landing, but of the Luftwaffe there was no sign. Among the thousands watching their arrival was Flt Lt Laddie Lucas:

"The sight of the first Spitfires landing at Takali acted as a fillip for the pilots who had been waiting for weeks, with increasing exasperation, for their arrival. Like small boys delving excitedly into their stockings at dawn on Christmas Day, so we rushed down the hill from Mdina to the airfield to touch and stroke our new toys. No Christmas or birthday morning in our short lives had ever produced such genuinely longed-for presents. Nor was Stan Turner slow in exerting his substantial influence to acquire the new aircraft for the Squadron. 'If it's the last goddam thing that I do, I'm going to see that 249 is re-equipped with these airplanes first.' Stan was true to his word."

An RAF sergeant who manned a fire-tender at Takali throughout the battle described their arrival in these words:

"The Spitfires came waggling their wings as if to say 'OK boys, we're here.'"

At long last one reporter at Malta was able to file his copy with joyous news:

"There seemed to be a new sound in the air, and it did not take the people long to identify the new aircraft which were zooming and hissing and whistling through the air. There they were, silvery streaks, skimming over the roof tops, climbing higher and higher and then diving straight to the earth, vanishing behind the buildings, only to rise again, at a speed never imagined possible before. Their magic name was whispered from group to group, those who knew anything about them were showing off their knowledge. The men in the skies seemed conscious of their audience as they went all out to show their prowess with this new machine. Young and old lifted beaming faces to the skies. There was fresh hope in their eager looks – and pride. The Maltese talk about nothing else."

The same Takali RAF sergeant later added, ominously:

"But that very same evening the gen went round that a big plot was building up over Sicily and within half an hour or so we were to see that Jerry really meant business. Standing at a vantage point in the village of Zurrieq, I saw the first waves of 88s coming all the way over the island. They dived down on Takali where the whole batch of Spits had landed. We tried to count them as they came in, but it was an utter impossibility. Straight down they went, and one could see the stuff leave the kites before it really got dark. The guns were belting rounds up like nothing on earth; tracers filled the sky, and if things weren't so serious one could have called it a lovely sight. The din was terrific and Takali seemed to be ablaze from end to end. The lads would shout that some gun or other had stopped firing, the crew had been knocked out. But no – they've started again pushing up rounds harder than ever. The Jerry seemed to be under orders to finish the place and, by hell, he tried his best."[11]

In preparation for this historical and much-anticipated event there had been considerable movement of pilots between the resident squadrons, following the recent spate of new arrivals. 249 Squadron was to be promptly resurrected and re-equipped, and in consequence those recently arrived pilots with Spitfire experience were concentrated in this unit under the command of Sqn Ldr Turner, and included Flt Lts Buck McNair and Laddie Lucas, both of whom had arrived with Turner aboard the Sunderland. The arrival of the Spitfires was literally in the nick of time, for the island's defences had almost ceased to exist – current availability being just 21 serviceable Hurricanes.

Following their arrival, the Spitfires were immediately stripped of their long-range fuel tanks and full servicing began in preparation for their introduction to operations; the aircraft and their pilots were absorbed into 249 Squadron. Sqn Ldr Turner now found himself not only with Sqn Ldr Grant as his supernumerary, but with no less than five relatively experienced flight lieutenants when Flt Lt Lucas was given command of A Flight and Flt Lt McNair took over B Flight. Other pilots already on the island were posted to fly the Spitfires and the Squadron now comprised 29 pilots with Spitfire experience.

The day also saw the arrival at Malta of a long-range PR Spitfire IV (AB300), which had been flown from Gibraltar by Plt Off Harry Coldbeck, a New Zealander and former fighter pilot with 66 Squadron, who had volunteered to ferry it to the Middle East. He landed at Takali to refuel and refresh, before undertaking the final leg:

> "Landing at Takali, I found the two smiling faces welcoming me to be Laddie Lucas and Raoul Daddo-Langlois. There were several others from 66 Squadron in evidence, which made it something of a reunion, before I began the third leg of my journey to the Middle East. I wallowed in the warmth of my welcome."

His plans to continue eastwards were promptly dashed when he found himself and his aircraft 'shanghaied' by the AOC and advised that he was to be attached to 69 Squadron at Luqa. This unit was currently operating a variety of aircraft in the reconnaissance rôle including Hurricanes, Beaufighters, Marylands and a Mosquito. A number of losses had been suffered in recent months and the addition was most welcomed.

Since it would be two or three days before the Spitfires were ready for action, some of the newly arrived NCO pilots – Paul Brennan, Ian Cormack, Ray Hesselyn, Bob Sim, and Junior Tayleur – decided to explore Valetta the following morning; Brennan noted:

> "As we wandered through Valetta we noticed that on many of the walls the Maltese had scrawled 'Bomb Rome!' That surprised us, as the Maltese are deeply Roman Catholic, but it was characteristic of the people's morale. Everybody was pleased to see us. A crowd of children quickly gathered on our heels. They followed us everywhere, and it was impossible to get rid of them. They made buzzing noises to represent aeroplanes, tried to loop the loop, fell over constantly, and generally indulged in every kind of antic. We had expected to find the Maltese looking lean and hungry, and with their nerves shaken. We thought they would be rather anti-British. Instead the people looked well fed, were cheerful, and were markedly pro-British. Food seemed plentiful enough, and after a drink of very bad beer we had an excellent meal of a pork chop, sausages and chips, with two eggs each. About four o'clock, rather to our surprise, some buses started to run, and we caught one to Mdina.
>
> "That evening we attended our first picture show. The cinema at Rabat looked as if it had been a house from which the interior walls had been removed in order to convert it into one large hall. The screen was grimy, and the house half full with the dirtiest, rowdiest children I have ever seen or heard. Every now and then the film would break, the manager would step on the stage to announce that the show would resume in a few minutes, and the children would stamp their feet, whistle, and yell at the top of their voices. It reminded me of a bush cinema in an outback Queensland town."

The new arrivals spent the next couple of days getting to know their surroundings, the veterans sparing no time in letting them know what to expect.

CHAPTER II

SPITFIRES INTO ACTION

March 1942

On the morning of **10 March** came the moment for the Spitfires' debut over Malta. This occurred at 1020 when seven aircraft (wearing 249 Squadron's newly painted GN code markings, which had been hurriedly applied in white paint) took off from Takali in company with eight 126 Squadron Hurricanes, together with four more from 185 Squadron from Hal Far. A pilot of the latter unit noted in his diary:

> "The Spitfires have arrived and are now doing top cover for us, which is a great help.
> It rather shakes you up to see one on your tail because they look so much like a Me109."

The objective of the scramble was to intercept an incoming raid of nine Ju88s, of which three crossed the coast to bomb Luqa, where a Wellington was destroyed. The Spitfires climbed to 19,000 feet, three led by Sqn Ldr Turner and four by Flt Lt Heppell. On reaching altitude, Heppell's section saw the bombers and their escorts – Bf109s from both II/JG3 and III/JG53 – below them, and at once bounced the unsuspecting Messerschmitts. Heppell (AB262/GN-B) fired a long burst at one, which was seen to crash in the sea; this was Fw Heinz Rahlmeier's Black 11 (7600) of 8/JG53, in which the pilot was killed. Other Messerschmitts were attacked by Plt Offs Pete Nash (AB335/GN-F) and Johnny Plagis (AB346/GN-K), both of whom claimed probables, the latter having attacked one on Nash's tail. Meanwhile, Flg Off Daddo-Langlois (AB343/GN-D) claimed one damaged, having knocked pieces off its tail, and Flt Lt Lucas (AB337/GN-A) chased another without success. None of the bombers was shot down, but one Hurricane was lost and another damaged. Uffz Hans Schade of 8/JG53 claimed a Spitfire (his 13th victory) during this action, but was probably responsible for shooting down a Hurricane that crash-landed at Takali. Plt Off Nash wrote in his diary:

> "I was No.2 to Heppell with Plagis and Leggo three and four. We scrambled about 10.30am, got up to 21,000 and saw three 88s and some 109s about 4,000 feet below. A lovely bounce. Heppell got one. Plagis and I got a probable each. Leggo missed his. I think we shook them up a bit. Plagis did well to knock one off my tail!"

Among the many thousands on the island peering into the blue sky to witness the historic event were a number of reporters, one of whom wrote:

> "The siren went, but for some reason the people did not immediately go to their shelters. There was an air of expectancy. The more venturesome went on to the high ramparts that give a commanding view of the island. They were soon to be rewarded. High overhead, flashing in the sunlight, could be seen the Spitfires. They weaved about the sky as they headed out to sea to meet the invaders. A little below them were the Hurricanes this time destined to tackle the bombers while the Spitfires above protected them from Messerschmitts jumping on their tail. On they flew, majestically. Those on the bastions waited in the hope of seeing the dogfights. Alas! They took place out at sea. But the watchers saw the Spitfires come home triumphantly and in the middle distance do their victory rolls before landing."

Attempts to intercept two more raids during the mid-part of the day failed, but at 1632 an estimated 40 'hostiles' were plotted approaching to attack Luqa and Hal Far, Ju88s of I/KG54, II and III/KG77 and LG1 taking part. Eleven Hurricanes and four Spitfires were scrambled. Both Flt Lt Macqueen and Flg Off Buck Buchanan (AB262/GN-B) claimed damage to bombers, but the aircraft flown by Plt Off Ken Murray (AB343/GN-D) was attacked by Bf109s and shot down, apparently by Hptm Karl-Heinz Krahl, Gruppenkommandeur of II/JG3 (his 19th victory), the first of the Spitfires to be lost. Murray baled out at high altitude, but his parachute failed to open properly. He sustained severe injuries on hitting the ground and the 20-year-old Australian from Toorak, Victoria, died in hospital that evening. Initially his colleagues believed that he had been shot whilst descending, although this was not the case. His Spitfire crashed at Ta'Zuta near Rabat.

Since it was first believed that Murray had come down in the sea, three Spitfires went out to cover him while a launch was despatched to pick him up. During the subsequent search, Buchanan (AB262/GN-B) was attacked by Messerschmitts and suffered superficial wounds to his right leg when his aircraft was hit, necessitating an emergency landing at Takali. Nash wrote:

"I was off this afternoon. Murray shot down in flames. He baled out, but a 109 gave him slipstream and collapsed the chute. He died in hospital. Flg Off Buchanan crash-landed on drome. A little shrapnel in right leg. Plane badly shot up."

During the raid only one Ju88 had actually been hit, a 4/KG77 machine returning with two wounded on board; however, this was probably a victim of the Hurricanes. Additionally, a Ju88 from 2/KG54 crash-landed at Gerbini on return, but reportedly due to undercarriage malfunction.

There was only one raid during **11 March**, when at 1135 two Ju88s of 5/KG77 escorted by six Bf109s approached the coast. The Ju88s turned back without bombing, one of which crashed on landing at Comiso and was completely destroyed. Sixteen Hurricanes and four Spitfires scrambled, the latter in pairs led by Sqn Ldr Grant (AB262/GN-B) and Flt Lt Connell (AB335/GN-F), and a number of dogfights took place. Grant attacked two Messerschmitts at 10,000 feet over Grand Harbour and one was seen going down inverted towards the sea; he was credited with its probable destruction. Connell and Sgt Hesselyn (AB346/GN-K) engaged the escorting fighters, with the former claiming damage to one. Flt Sgt Ferraby (AB341/GN-E) also engaged a fighter but observed no result. Flt Sgt Brennan also had his first taste of action:

"The signal to scramble came at about eleven o'clock, after an uneventful morning at dispersal. Eight or nine Hurricanes were already airborne. We rushed to our aircraft, and in less than two minutes were off the ground. Sqn Ldr Grant was leading, and I was flying No.2 to Flt Lt Bud Connell, a Canadian, being Red 4 in the section. Climbing at a steady 140mph we joined the Hurriboys from Hal Far above St Paul's Bay, and orbited the island, gaining still more height. Woody, who, as usual, was controlling, told us some 'big jobs', with fighter escort, were coming south about 30 miles north of St Paul's Bay. We were at 12,000 feet when my reflector sight, which I had already switched on, began to dim, and the various cockpit and undercarriage lights commenced to fade. My electrical system had packed up. It was not a pleasant start to my flying career over Malta. I realised that I had no R/T and should have returned to base, but I decided to remain aloft and see what happened.

"We climbed out to meet the Huns. Three Me109s came towards us at about our height. Bud Connell and I saw them at the same time, and pulled round together. With a quick deflection shot Bud damaged one. I fired at another, without reflector sight, pointing my nose in his general direction. I am sure I did not hit him. The Huns climbed above us, and we started turning inside them in an effort to get on their tails. They obviously had a healthy respect for the Spitfire, for although we gave them plenty of invitations they refused to come down and engage. Stan Grant and his No.2, who were ahead of us, had a similar experience. They mixed it with a number of 109s, but without result. We landed at Takali after having been 40 minutes in the air, and although we had merely exchanged shots with the Hun we thought the fight had been a good pipe-opener. There was plenty of nattering in dispersal after we landed. The four of us could talk of nothing but our sortie. Stan Grant said the 109s were fairly fast and nippy. He had had a squirt, but didn't know if he had scored any hits. Bud felt certain he had hit one, and I also was convinced he had."

Brennan later reflected on his first action:

"The most vivid impression I gained that morning concerned the Me109. It struck me as a very sinister and lethal-looking aircraft. It flew over Malta with a brownish-bluish camouflage, and its big airscrew revolved very slowly. The spinner was painted yellow, and in its centre was a single cannon with a high rate of fire. The 109, smaller than the Spitfire, had remarkably clean, clear-cut lines.

"We found a bullet hole about two feet behind Bud's cockpit, on a level with his head, and spent the rest of the morning wondering whether in my excitement and inexperience I had put it there. Never before had I fired my guns at the enemy. My feelings were curious and mixed, as I suppose are those of all pilots who go into action for the first time. On the climb up I knew I did not have the score weighed up. I was extremely nervous and excited, but the thought flashed across my mind that if the worst came to the worst, my leader was bound to look after me. I had complete confidence in him, and tried to create a favourable impression on him by maintaining good formation. Once the Hun was sighted, however, all nervousness and excitement left me. I was surprised to find myself cool and calm, my mind being occupied solely with the business of shooting him down and not getting shot down myself. When I first fired my guns I had a remarkable feeling of aloof detachment. I felt no personal animosity, no anger. My sole thought was whether I was in range and shooting straight."

Later, three Spitfires were scrambled and ordered to climb to 25,000 feet since Bf109s were reported to be in the area. Plt Off Bob Sergeant recalled that none were sighted but two Hurricanes mistaken for Messerschmitts narrowly escaped being attacked.

Takali was raided twice on **12 March** and neither raid was intercepted. During the second attack at 1635 by three Ju88s, one Spitfire was slightly damaged on the ground, as was a Hurricane and a Blenheim. Plt Off Nash noted in his diary:

"Takali bombed this morning. I was on drome defence with Sgt Hesselyn this afternoon. Four readiness Spits operated from Luqa. Bombed again this afternoon. They knock out 11 Hurricanes. Did not fly. Murray's funeral this morning. I was present but I think it is a bad thing for pilots to go to funerals. It kind of rubs it in!"

AB300 was flown on its first reconnaissance sorties from the island in the hands of 69 Squadron's Plt Off Phil Kelley, who had been engaged flying the Mosquito. On his return from a flip over Sicily, Plt Off Reg 'Johnny' Walker, normally a PR Beaufighter pilot, took it over for a similar trip in the afternoon. Plt Off Coldbeck, AB300's rightful owner, was instructed to carry out a sortie next day (**13 March**):

"I think it was Johnny Walker who had said to me in conversation, that it would not be a good idea to climb to operating height straight over Sicily. I hope it would have occurred to me anyway, with Sicily only 60 miles away. I therefore went away from Malta at 0700 over the sea to about 12,000 feet then on up to 25,000 feet on my second leg, on the way to the east coast of Sicily – Mt Etna, snow-covered, in the clear air, that day, provided a great pivot to swing around. Over Catania airfield, at the foot of Mt Etna, I was startled by the black puffs, which appeared alongside and behind me after a slight noise belatedly awakened me to their presence. This unwelcome attention of the heavy anti-aircraft fire continued right across Catania and over Gerbini as well, as I photographed the airfields with hundreds of aircraft down there. To photograph Catania I flew slightly to one side until I found I was almost level then made a steep turn over the field turning the cameras on as I went. I turned the cameras off when I thought I would have covered it. Another steep turn to check.

"The control of the cameras during a photo run was through a grey metal box, which was placed under the windscreen where the reflector sight is located in a fighter Spitfire. Two knobs controlled exposure interval rate and start and finish respectively. Another window on the box showed the number of exposures made. Approaching Luqa after this, my first PR operational sortie [the first of 153 operational sorties he would fly from Malta], there was little activity, either friendly or enemy. Anyway, I had photographed Catania and Gerbini then made my way to the Italian naval and seaplane base of Augusta further south on the east coast taking one hour 50 minutes flying time."

The airfield was raided again during the day, when a Hurricane and a petrol bowser were burnt out. **14 March** heralded not only further action for the Spitfires of 249 Squadron, but a change in command as Sqn Ldr Turner handed the reins to Sqn Ldr Grant, when the Canadian was promoted to take command of the Takali Wing. Flt Lt McNair noted:

"There was an uncomfortable situation in 249 Squadron at this time. Stan Turner, an extremely good pilot and fighter leader, was CO, but Stan Grant had been told as he left for Malta that he would be CO. There remained a feeling of embarrassment until it became known that Turner was to be promoted to Wing Commander Flying. Grant was a good type of Englishman, quite a good flyer, but his personality was of far greater value to him as CO than his flying ability."

The first intrusion of the morning, at around 0830, by a reconnaissance Ju88 and two escorting Bf109s of 3/JG53 was not countered by fighters; however, AA gunners on Gozo claimed the reconnaissance aircraft damaged and one of the escorts shot down. Indeed, it would seem that their fire hit Yellow 8 (7392) flown by Uffz Heinrich Blum, the Messerschmitt careering into Ltn Walter Seiz's aircraft (7301); Seiz was able to bale out but the unlucky Blum crashed to his death. Ltn Jürgen Harder of 7/JG53 wrote:

"I had to fly early this morning after a big birthday party thrown by Wilcke [Hptm Wolf-Dietrich Wilcke]. Once again two comrades came down in the drink near Malta. Then we had to protect the air-sea rescue aircraft. Unfortunately the seas were too high and we could not land. As well the Spitfires kept raging about. There was no time to effect a rescue."

Four Spitfires were sent off at 1030 on the approach of three Ju88s of II/KG77 escorted by about 20 Bf109s. A trio of Messerschmitts was seen orbiting Gozo, apparently part of a search party looking for the two pilots missing from the early morning sortie. Flt Lt Macqueen dived on one, attacking from 275 down to 50 yards and fired all his ammunition, reporting strikes along its fuselage. The Messerschmitt pilot took no evasive action, continuing a slow climbing turn as the Spitfire broke away in front of it. Macqueen believed that it dived into the sea and this would seem to have been an aircraft of 7/JG53, from which Uffz Adolf Jennerich baled out. The skipper of ASR launch *HSL107* was refused permission to go out when the Messerschmitt was seen to fall in flames a mile outside Kalafrana Bay, owing to the threat posed by the large numbers of other Bf109s at low level. Plt Off Nash recorded:

> "On this morning with Macqueen, Sgts Sim and Hesselyn. Scrambled for three Me109s. Macqueen's R/T was duff so I took over. Operations gave us 16,000 as height of the 109s. Sighted them at 6,000 feet and went down on them from 18,000 feet. They were circling the dye patch from an 88 shot down by flak this morning. Ops said there was one above us. On looking round for it I lost the other three 109s in the mist. Macqueen went straight in and gave one all he had and saw strikes. Later confirmed."

The downed pilot, Jennerich, was however rescued from the sea by an Axis ASR craft in the afternoon, cover to this operation being provided by more Messerschmitts; two of these were seen orbiting Gozo at about 1535 by Flt Lt Lucas (GN-G) and Flg Off Daddo-Langlois (AB332/GN-N), the former reporting strikes on the fuselage and tail of the one he attacked before others drove him away. Fw Josef Kröschel of 8/JG53 claimed a Spitfire at 1610 for his first victory, possibly believing that he had shot down either Lucas or Daddo-Langlois as they dived away. Between 1550 and 1750 an estimated 16 Bf109s were reported patrolling to the west and south-west of the island. Taking off again, Lucas and Daddo-Langlois initially escorted a Maryland departing on a reconnaissance sortie before encountering two Messerschmitts. Lucas fired all his ammunition and saw hits on the fuselage of one, reporting a trail of black smoke as it dived away; again he could claim only a damaged. Daddo-Langlois noted:

> "Scramble to intercept two 109s off Gozo. Ran into 16 more escorting Do24s. Running fight with six 109s. Safely home not a scratch. Bags of confidence. Laddie damaged one."

At about 1835, Ltn Seiz was finally picked up by a rescue launch from Sicily.

On 15 March, three Ju88s with close escort provided by 4/JG53 raided Luqa and Valetta shortly before lunchtime; eight persons were killed, including two soldiers. Four Spitfires led by Flt Lts Connell and Heppell, together with seven Hurricanes, were up and intercepted the raid in low cloud. Heppell claimed a Bf109 damaged after seeing his cannon shells strike the underside of its fuselage, and from which his No.2 saw pieces fall off into the sea; he then attacked a second Messerschmitt and a Ju88, but without result. One of the bombers was attacked by Plt Off Jeff West and Sgt Junior Tayleur (AB334/GN-J), who jointly claimed some damage before being driven away by the escort. The escorting top cover Messerschmitts of III/JG53 claimed two Spitfires shot down during this engagement, one apiece by Oblt Helmut Belser (his 19th) of 8 Staffel and Obfw Werner Stumpf (his 31st) of 9 Staffel, although none of the defending fighters was lost on this occasion. At 1320 three Ju88s and seven Messerschmitts raided Zabbar, and were met by four Spitfires. Connell (AB346/GN-K) claimed one bomber, and it seems likely that this was an aircraft of 3/KGr806 (M7+ML) which failed to return from an operational sortie over Malta, Uffz Rudolf Max and his crew being reported missing.

Between 0730 and 0945 on **17 March**, 23 Ju88s struck at Luqa, where four Wellingtons were destroyed and five other aircraft damaged, including a Spitfire. A petrol bowser was burnt out, two civilians killed and three injured. Bombs also fell on Sliema, Tigne and Cospicua, where 23 more civilians and two policemen were killed and 40 civilians seriously injured. Four Spitfires led by Flt Lt Heppell and 11 Hurricanes were scrambled, the 249 quartet climbing to 20,000 feet, where six Ju88s and a number of Bf109s (from II/JG53) were seen 10,000 feet below. Flt Sgt Brennan and Sgt Tayleur were approached by two of the Messerschmitts, but the latter's aircraft (AB337/GN-A) went into an uncontrollable dive as the seat had come off its hinges and jammed the control column; the aircraft fell to 8,000 feet before Tayleur was able to get it back into place and pull out. Brennan (AB346/GN-K) meanwhile engaged a Messerschmitt from dead astern:

"I started turning with them. One was in front, the other behind. Round and round we went. Suddenly the one in front decided to go up sun. Luckily for me, he was not quite certain where I was. As he straightened up, I was 100 feet below and 200 yards behind him, dead astern. I pulled a bead on him at once, tracer from the other 109 whipping past my port wingtip as I did so. I could see my explosive cannon shells and machine-gun bullets bursting along the front 109's fuselage, behind his cockpit and on his port wing root. I gave him six seconds – a long burst. For a moment or two the 109 seemed to hang, then it dived straight down. I had no time to watch it crash into the sea 20,000 feet below. The second 109 was still firing although his bullets were not hitting me. I glanced over my shoulder, and saw that he was breaking away. At this moment Hep called up, saying he was being attacked by five 109s and asking if anybody could help him. I told him I was having a good fight with two myself, and I would see him later, but not then.

"As he broke away, the 109 behind me followed his friend towards the sea. I was 300 yards behind him. Deciding to give chase, and convinced I could not get closer, I gave him a short burst at that range. In my excitement I pressed the wrong gun button and fired only my machine-guns. I did not notice my mistake, and imagined my cannon ammunition must be exhausted. I broke away to return to base, but called up Hep and asked him how he was doing. He replied: 'The Huns think they can shoot me down. Not bloody likely!' Ten minutes later I landed, and was screaming to all and sundry about my terrible battle. Everybody must have been bored to tears during the next few days with my oft-repeated story of my first Hun. Hep, Junior and Ian Cormack, the fourth member of the section, landed. All three were disgusted. I was the only one who had scored a victory."

At 0955 seven more Ju88s and four Bf109s crossed the coast, a further four Spitfires led by Flt Lt Heppell attempting to intercept. Unable to gain position, Heppell instructed the others to dive for home, which they did, but 21-year-old Flt Sgt Ian Cormack from Elgin in Scotland failed to pull out and was killed when his aircraft (AB330/GN-C) crashed straight into the sea off Filfla. Of the incident, Flt Sgt Ferraby recalled:

"Why they didn't just turn towards the 109s, I don't know. Cormack blacked out and spun in. He was a black-haired, slightly built chap from Scotland, and another good buddy."

It seems probable that Oblt Gerhard Michalski of 4/JG53 shot down Cormack's aircraft, since he claimed a Spitfire (his 28th victory) shot down at about this time. Of the day's action, Plt Off Nash commented:

"Off today. More raids. Did very little of interest. Flt Sgt Ian Cormack killed this afternoon. Ops are pinning too much faith in the Spits. They sent four against fifteen 109s and five 88s. Crazy!"

During the afternoon and early evening an estimated 56 raiders approached Malta at intervals, including 25 bombers, which attacked all three airfields. A dozen Hurricanes, with two Spitfires as top cover, were scrambled. While the Hurricanes engaged the bombers, Sqn Ldr Grant and Plt Off Plagis (AB335/GN-F) each claimed damage to Messerschmitts they encountered.

18 March proved to be another day of heavy combat, which began around 0900 when two Bf109s crossed the coast at low level, covered by more higher up. This marauding pair strafed the Gozo ferry boat *Royal Lady*, which had just docked at Marfa with 209 passengers aboard although only one civilian and two soldiers were wounded. The Messerschmitts were away again before Malta's fighters could be scrambled. Lunchtime was interrupted by four Spitfires scrambling to intercept five Messerschmitts patrolling off the coast, while another four took off to escort a returning reconnaissance Maryland, but instead engaged two of the German fighters at sea level south of Delimara. Flt Lt McNair (AB262/GN-B) attacked one at which Wg Cdr Turner also fired, reporting strikes, while McNair then attacked and damaged the other.

The bombers were back during the early evening, two dozen Ju88s of I/KG54, KüFlGr606 and KGr806 – in five waves with large fighter escort – bombing the airfields, with in excess of 14 tons of bombs being dropped. At Hal Far an Albacore was destroyed and several others hit by debris, and at Luqa three damaged Wellingtons were now destroyed. Four Spitfires and six Hurricanes were scrambled, but at 12,500 feet the 249 quartet were jumped by four Bf109s of III/JG53 and Plt Off Harry Fox's aircraft (AB334/GN-J) was hit; the 20-year-old Liverpudlian baled out into the sea, but was lost. Plt Off Sergeant (AB336) noted:

> "Ju88s with escort. Four of us mixed up with several 109s east of Gozo. I also met two 109s near Filfla and squirted, one 109 damaged. Harry Fox went straight in. Two bullet holes in my machine."

Flt Lt Macqueen attacked a Messerschmitt which he believed had just shot down Fox, opened fire from 100 yards, whereupon it smoked, shed pieces and dived into the sea close to where Fox's Spitfire had splashed, about three miles off Wied iz-Zurrieq. The other two 249 pilots, Flg Off Norm Lee and Sgt Johnny Berchamps, claimed damage to a Ju88 and a Bf109 respectively. Immediately following this action, ASR launch *HSL107* was sent out to search for the missing pilots (two Hurricanes had also been shot down into the sea), escorted by two Spitfires. More Messerschmitts were encountered, one of which was claimed probably destroyed by Plt Off Sergeant (AB336) who reported:

> "Mac and I out over launch and picked up Plt Off Lester [a Hurricane pilot of 185 Squadron]. Seven 109s over, which took no notice. Jumped by two. Got on tail of one about to attack Mac and dogfought. Last seen heading out to sea with slight white smoke. One bullet in my machine."

Ltn Ernst Kläger of 7 Staffel claimed a Spitfire (his 10th victory) shot down in this action, but so did Ltn Kurt Lauinger of Stab III/JG53, who baled out of Black <2 (7590) wounded and had also suffered a broken leg. He was plucked from the sea by *HSL107* from Kalafrana, subsequently telling his interrogators that he had shot down a Spitfire in this action:

> "[We] were flying over Malta at 12,000 feet in two pairs stepped up in an echelon when [we] sighted three Spitfires below and dived to attack. [I] fired a burst at one of the Spitfires and then did a climbing turn in order to keep at the same height as section leader. By this time one of the other Spitfires had turned inside [me] and attacked, shooting away [my] rudder. [I] baled out, landed in the sea and was picked up after dark by a rescue launch."

This was probably the action witnessed by Carmel Grech, a young Maltese, who was watching Spitfires at Takali:

"The Spitfires soon took off in quick succession and swiftly climbed in the direction of Delimara. Some 20 minutes later, I again heard the noises of low-flying aircraft. For a moment I thought that our fighters were returning to the airfield and therefore, I emerged from my cover. But, on stepping out, there was a sudden burst of machine-gun fire from an aeroplane strafing the fields around the hut. I identified it as a Messerschmitt 109 about to attack Takali airfield. Two others quickly followed it in. A column of thick, black smoke rose from a structure on the airfield but it was not a bomb as no explosion had preceded it. Afterwards I learnt that a petrol bowser, that was standing by to refuel the Spitfires upon landing, had been hit and caught fire. Then, two Spitfires swooped down out of the clouds like hawks onto the Messerschmitts and opened fire on them. I saw part of a Messerschmitt's wing fly off as if it had been sawn off and spin down to the ground. The aircraft flipped on its back and plummeted down. The pilot took to his parachute which looked like a big, white silk umbrella and the wind carried it in the direction of Naxxar, while the aircraft appeared to have crashed in the sea beyond Dingli cliffs."[12]

Plt Off Nash noted:

"On [duty] this afternoon. Again we stayed on the ground and were bombed to hell and back. My beloved F [GN-F/AB335] was holed. Macqueen and a few others went to hospital to see the Hun [Lauinger] he had shot down. Nice lad apparently. First trip and very pleased to have got Harry Fox. Belongs to crack squadron of which he is very proud. Does not give a damn who wins the bloody war."

On **19 March** there was just a single raid by an estimated 15 Ju88s and a dozen Bf109s on Takali, which destroyed a Beaufighter and damaged four other aircraft including another Spitfire. 249 was rapidly running short of aircraft; of the 15 Spitfires delivered, three had been shot down and a further two damaged on the ground, all within the space of ten days. Another was lost next day (**20 March**), when four Spitfires and a dozen Hurricanes were sent off at 0805 to intercept an incoming raid. Flt Lt McNair (AB341/GN-E) encountered Messerschmitts from 7/JG53 led by Ltn Hermann Neuhoff, at one of which he fired, reporting that pieces fell off as it went down in a spiral dive:

"We four got our scramble call and soared up to 10,000 feet. We were just turning down into the sun, when Daddy called on the R/T that there were Me109s at 6 o'clock – behind and above. We had time to turn around and break into them and I screamed round to the right and found I had turned too quickly and the Huns were still some distance away. I eased up a bit on my turn, for if I had continued it I would have put my belly to a 109, so I straightened up and he would have to turn his belly to me. He did, and I let off a great squirt at him. The 109 went into a spiral dive, and looking round and finding no other Huns about, I went down after it, having no trouble in following. I waited my chance to fire again, and got a good burst into it. I saw hits on the starboard wing, pieces came off, but he still didn't take any evasive action, just continued with the spiral dive. Down to 3,000 feet I started clobbering the 109 all over. I emptied my cannon and continued with the machine-guns. Oil and glycol from its cooling system poured out. The white glycol looked beautiful streaming out into the clear air; it was a really lovely day."

This was undoubtedly Uffz Josef Fankhauser's White 4 (7586); of his loss, an official

Luftwaffe report stated:

"Mission: free chase over Malta. Uffz Fankhauser was a member of Ltn Neuhoff's *Schwarm* [section of four] during the free chase over Malta. The *Schwarm* became involved in a dogfight with enemy fighters. During the dogfight the flight leader, Ltn Neuhoff, saw four Spitfires diving after a Messerschmitt. Three of the Spitfires pulled up, one continued the pursuit. The Messerschmitt was not seen to crash as the flight was engaged in combat. Afterwards Ltn Neuhoff saw Uffz Fankhauser swimming in a patch of dye. The flight was low on fuel and was forced to return to base. The subsequent search was unsuccessful, Fankhauser could not be found and the dye patch was also not seen again. It is to be assumed that Fankhauser was picked up by the English and is a prisoner of war."

However, the German pilot did not survive and his body was washed up on the coast of Sicily some seven weeks later. Flg Off Daddo-Langlois later commented:

"I fired all ammo at 109 and missed. Buck nearly shoots down all three of pilots with him while trying to get 109 at sea level. We laugh about that."

Meanwhile, Plt Off Doug Leggo was lagging behind when another Messerschmitt came out of the sun and shot him down from 50 yards range. Flt Lt Lucas witnessed his demise:

"In my section, we spotted, far away to port, a single Spitfire obviously looking for a mate. As we turned to go to his aid, a 109, diving steeply and very fast out of the sun, pulled up unseen under the Spitfire. From dead astern the pilot, who plainly knew his business, delivered a short, determined burst of cannon and machine-gun fire, sending his victim rolling on to his back and spiralling down to earth or sea. It was a clinical operation. Relieved, we saw a parachute open. As we watched the silk canopy floating down in the distance, with the pilot swinging on its end, another single 109, diving out of broken cloud, made a run at the chute, squirting at it as he went and collapsing it with his slipstream as he passed by. The canopy streamed, leaving the pilot without a chance. The next thing we knew, the 109 was diving away for Sicily with never a hope of catching it."

The Rhodesian was killed and his Spitfire (AB337/GN-A) crashed in a field near Qrendi. The incident was also witnessed by many on the ground including a gun crew of the 4th HAA Regiment located near Hagar Qim[13], including the senior NCO[14]:

"The pilot of a Spitfire which had sustained bad damage ejected from his plane but was too low for his chute to open properly. He dropped between the gun-position and a line of hills, known to us as Gebel Ciantar. Several of us ran to see if we could be of assistance. On arriving at the scene it was obvious the young man was quite dead. On his shoulders was the word RHODESIA."

Another member[15] of the gun crew wrote in his diary:

"Before breakfast we witnessed a dogfight above our site, which resulted in a rather sickening start to the day's activities, for one of our Spitfires had one of its tail fins practically shot off and the pilot lost control of the plane. It fell like a falling leaf, describing small circles, with its nose downwards, and several times it seemed as though the pilot had managed to straighten out into a glide, but no – on it came until, just over 100 feet from the ground, the pilot baled out. He was too late; his parachute just billowed until the cords were taut when he reached the ground about the same time as the plane, which just pancaked in the next field only a couple of hundred yards from our camp. When we picked the pilot up he was grasping the harness of the parachute with both hands – dead; we placed him on a stretcher covering him up with the parachute, and carried him into our MI room. I thought at the time of his family in Rhodesia somewhere, just having breakfast maybe, oblivious of the horrible shock which awaited them, depriving them of the pride which they felt, in having a son so young, in his early twenties, and a pilot officer in the RAF."

A third gunner[16] commented:

"His body was brought in on a stretcher by our medical orderly and placed on the floor of the MI hut. I saw him there and noticed he was dressed in blue battledress with one shoe missing and a large hole in his sock, which somehow seemed to make the whole incident more tragic. Later, the RAF came and took him away."

Claims for Spitfires in this engagement were submitted by Ltn Neuhoff (his 38th) and Ltn Ernst Kläger (his 11th). It seems likely that both fired at Leggo's aircraft. A German journalist's report pertaining to Neuhoff's combat later appeared in print:

"Pilots are sitting in the standby hut, above us a bright blue sky. Everybody knows that today, with such weather, the air will be full of action. Our proud Messerschmitts are at dispersal waiting to fly their destructive sorties against Malta – to the terror of the Hurricanes and Spitfires. Now message is received: we are escorting the bombers, which are to lay their eggs on the airfields of Malta. Already the first Messerschmitts are up; the air is filled with the thunder of their motors. Above us the bombers, with us close and on course. Everything is going according to plan. We have half the trip behind us already, when my *Katschmarek* [wingman] reports engine trouble and has to return home. I am alone – now what? Turn back too? No, I don't feel like doing that, especially as enemy fighters have been reported. I am going to rely on my experience acquired in over 400 missions against the enemy and continue flying as a blind *Rotte* [pair]. Already we are over Malta. The bombers are preparing to dive. They dive very calmly because they know their Messerschmitts keep a lookout. Everything seems to be going well when, at the beginning of the dive, there, overhead – the Tommy! Shooting wildly they dive into our group. Behind me are three Spitfires wanting to sniff my pants! Now I have to watch out – first let them come close, then go hell for leather and turn! It has worked. The Spitfire is no longer in a position to fire. On the other hand, I have got dangerously close to the last one. They are immediately aware of the situation and dive straight down.

"I am just about to return to the bombers when I discover a Hurricane [it seems likely this was Leggo's Spitfire; no Hurricanes were lost] 100 metres below me. Now with the stick forward I dive swiftly towards the Tommy. He sees me coming and wants to escape. But too late, I have already pressed the buttons and my machine-guns and cannons bark hoarsely. He sees that there is no escape and has to engage in an air battle with me. Now things are really hotting up. Ten times I was unable to get into position, the sweat pouring from my head. Then I was successful. I curved around and managed to get behind him and filled him so full of lead that he momentarily flew straight and level. It was enough – once more let him fill my sights and fire with all barrels. I was 50 metres behind that Tommy when I saw him break up. Half of the left wing broke off, so that the bird spun twice on its own axis right in front of my nose and disappeared into the water like a U-boat [the aircraft seen crashing into the sea was presumably Fankhauser's Messerschmitt]. Now one more turn around the spot, but nothing else showed. There was nothing more I could do, so I turned back and went home in order to announce my 38th air victory to my comrades. On the return flight I met up with three more comrades, who had seen the air battle and could positively confirm the shooting down."[17]

A heavy raid on Takali at dusk, when in excess of 60 Ju88s pounded the airfield and rendered it temporarily unserviceable, prompted 249 Squadron's Sgt Alf Branch (temporarily attached to 126 Squadron) to write in his journal:

"I was on watch and I must say Jerry is getting to be a nuisance. The drome was dive-bombed by Ju88s and He111s [*sic*], making the fourth day in succession. Approximately 30 bombs dropped in one go during one raid. The mess had a near shave; at the same time an amusing thing happened. The two bombs dropped close to the mess were approximately 1,000lbs each. These bombs were very close to an old well and the blast sucked all the mud and water out of it – and poured it down on the building, shaking the occupants who thought the lot was coming down on top of them!"

Not all the bombs aimed at Takali fell on the intended target, some dropping on nearby Mosta town, as revealed in a police report:

"Mosta. Bombs fell and exploded at Wata Street, five houses totally demolished and another 20 badly damaged. Four persons killed, two are still buried under the debris, eight other persons were admitted to hospital, three of whom were seriously injured."

The dusk raid was followed next morning (**21 March**) by an even heavier attack by over 100 Ju88s. Neither of these fighter-escorted raids was opposed by the handful of Hurricanes and Spitfires remaining, although relatively little long-term damage resulted from the first example of carpet-bombing the island had experienced. Soon after the bombers had departed, eight Bf110s of III/ZG26 appeared overhead to bomb and strafe Hal Far, under an umbrella of Bf109s. Amongst the four aircraft damaged on the ground was one of the Spitfires; there were now just two serviceable Spitfires – but more were on their way. Bombs again fell on Mosta:

"Several bombs fell and exploded in different streets in Mosta and 35 houses were demolished. A bomb exploded on a shelter in Gafa Street and a large rock fell from the ceiling by blast. 27 dead (10 unidentified), 68 injured. Several bombs fell on Internment Camp area and in different streets at Rabat. 11 persons were killed (five of whom were RAF personnel and two internees). Another 11 persons are still buried under the debris and believed to be dead."

Ground personnel at Takali immediately got to work clearing the rubble and in-filling bomb craters, ready to receive the Spitfires winging their way in from the west, nine aircraft having been launched from *Eagle*; it had been the intention to fly off 16 Spitfires, but the Blenheim escort for the second flight failed to arrive. Led by Sqn Ldr Jumbo Gracie DFC[18] (BP844), the new pilots were Flt Lt Tim Johnston (BP850), Plt Offs Mike Graves, Don McLeod RCAF[19] and Jimmie Peck, the latter two both US citizens, and Sgts Gordon Bolton RNZAF, Dusty Miller RNZAF, Wally Milner, and Slim Yarra RAAF (AB333), who had been aboard *Eagle* when the first Spitfires had flown to Malta but whose aircraft had gone unserviceable and was therefore left behind. He wrote in his diary:

"The weather was lousy. Foggy and raining with a ceiling of 1,000 feet. However we decided to take off and attempt the trip if the Blenheims found us. At 9am the first Blenheim arrived and we started to get off. I was the third man off. When my turn came I taxied into position. I was rather keyed up and my nerves were taut as stay-wires, but as soon as I opened the throttle I lost all my tautness and got that queer kick one always gets when opening up on the world's best fighter aircraft. The old Merlin sounded very sweet that morning as I raced down that little deck and lifted off the end. At that moment the fact that we had 700 miles to travel over water, and hostile water at that, mattered not the slightest. All that mattered was that I was in the air again after nearly three weeks on the ground. We formed up on the leader and began our 700-mile trip. We were right down on the deck all the way, flying through rainstorms and patches of thick mist. We made one attempt to get above the overcast, but as this was unsuccessful we remained on the deck for the remainder of the way. I had trouble with my air pressure all the way. The release valve was not working and I had to keep the pressure down.

"As we were passing Pantelleria we sighted a squadron of CR42s (Italian biplane fighters) but, as they did not interfere, we were quite happy to let them alone. We could not afford to use up vital petrol dogfighting. After three hours flying I was very much in need of a cigarette but, as I could not find any matches, I had to forego the pleasure. I could see smoke coming from various other cockpits as the boys were enjoying theirs. When we were 30 minutes from Malta we tightened up our formation a little and began to keep a good lookout for hostile aircraft. Suddenly Malta showed up on the horizon dead ahead. I, for one, was very pleased, as we had been flying for four hours and we were very tired. Just then I happened to look around and spotted a twin-engined machine approaching from the starboard quarter astern. I immediately thought Me110 and broke away to do a head-on attack. Just as I was about to fire I recognised it as a Beaufort. I very nearly squirted at that guy. He would have been a little brassed if I had! We landed at Takali and put the aircraft away. I then went up to the mess to get a drink and find out how the rest of the boys were. I learned that Mac, Fox, Leggo and Murray were all dead and that, out of the 15 Spitfires they had brought, only two were left."

At 1435, the third major raid to be centred on Takali within 24 hours began when the first of 70 Ju88s (with a large fighter escort) bombed the airfield, while wayward bombs also fell on Rabat, Mosta, Gzira, Boschetto, Tigne, Attard and Birkirkara. At Rabat, a large bomb fell just outside the front door of the Point de Vue Hotel, which had been requisitioned to billet RAF officers stationed at nearby Takali, where a number of officers had gathered to watch the raid; six were killed outright and another died in hospital. Among the dead were two of the Squadron's pilots, Flg Off John Booth (who had joined 249 at Malta) and Plt Off Jimmy Guerin. Flt Lt McNair had just entered the building with Flt Lt Connell and Flg Off Ron West (126 Squadron) when the bomb exploded:

"When I came to I didn't know where I was. I didn't feel I was dead, but I didn't feel whole. My eyes were open, but my jaw and chest didn't seem to be there. There was no pain. As I became more conscious, I found I was upstairs. Then I realised I had been blown upstairs either through a door or through an opening at the turn of the staircase. I'd been blown up 20 or 30 feet. I went down the main staircase, which was barely hanging in place. I saw the bodies lying at the foot of it. They were in a heap. Heavy dust covered the bodies. One was headless. I heard a moan and I put my hand gently on the bodies to feel which of them was alive. One of them, I noticed, had a hole, more than a foot wide, right through the abdomen. Another's head was split wide open into two halves, from back to front, by a piece of shrapnel. How the man managed still to be alive, I don't know. I thought of shooting him with my revolver. I heard Bud Connell's voice behind me. Ronnie West appeared. We decided to get drunk. When we got over to the Mess, the orderly refused us anything to drink and wouldn't open the bar. We broke our way in and each took a bottle of White Horse [whisky]. We drank gulps of it straight."

On the airfield, Spitfire AB331, four Hurricanes and three other aircraft had been destroyed, while five more Spitfires and 15 Hurricanes were damaged in this latest attack. However, many of the damaged Hurricanes had previously been written-off as a result of earlier raids and were thus non-operational. Takali appeared to have been so severely bombed that returning Luftwaffe bomber crews reported that the base looked as if it had been subjected to a volcanic eruption! Air Vice-Marshal Hugh Pughe Lloyd, the AOC, had to admit that it resembled a WWI battlefield, and it was feared that it would remain unserviceable for at least a week. However, troops worked throughout the night and all next day and, by the evening, all serviceable Hurricanes and Spitfires were flown to Luqa.

The new Spitfires and their pilots were intended to re-form 126 Squadron under the command of Sqn Ldr Gracie, in a similar manner to that which had occurred with 249 Squadron. Because of the losses of Spitfires to date, however, the two squadrons were now going to have to share the remaining aircraft. This left the two units with a preponderance of pilots to aircraft, while the remaining Hurricane unit, 185 Squadron, was very low on pilots. Consequently after about a week, a trawl was made of Spitfire pilots to establish who had Hurricane experience. Hence, newly arrived Sgt Yarra, having initially been posted to 249, was one of those soon to be transferred to fly Hurricanes, together with Flt Sgt Ferraby, Sgt Berchamps (another who had joined 249 at Malta) and Sgt Sim. The arrival of the new Spitfires and new faces brought with it a debate on tactics, instigated by Wg Cdr Turner. Initially, it had been the policy to send 249 up as cover to the Hurricanes; their task being to hold off the Messerschmitts while the latter sought to deal with the Ju88s. But experience had shown that the Hurricane IIBs were too slow and too lightly armed to have great effect against the swift, heavily-armed bombers. Few cannon-armed Hurricane IICs now remained, and of those that did, most had two of their four cannons removed to increase their speed although thereby reducing their firepower by half. 249's initial experience had been to lose as many of their own aircraft to the Bf109s as they were able to claim – hardly a profitable ratio given the dire circumstances prevailing. It was agreed, therefore, that in future both Spitfires and Hurricanes would concentrate their efforts against the bombers and avoid the escorting fighters wherever possible.

The two-day period 22-23 March witnessed much action out to sea, east of Malta, as convoy MW10 from Alexandria fought its way to the island. A cruiser and a single destroyer from Malta set out to escort the four merchant vessels, once its naval escort had turned back, aircraft from Malta providing cover. Initially long-range Beaufighters attempted to keep the Axis bombers at bay, but once within appropriate range, Spitfires and Hurricanes took over protection of the valiant ships, one of which had already been lost. All available FAA torpedo-bombers on the island had been ordered to prepare to attack Italian warships assembling to engage the convoy.

At 1755 on **22 March** therefore, five Albacore biplanes took off, escorted for the initial part of their flight by three Spitfires that had been made serviceable, flown by Sqn Ldr Gracie, Flt Lt Macqueen and Plt Off Jimmy James. No sooner were they on their way than two Bf109s attempted to intercept out of the setting sun, one diving on Gracie's tail; this was possibly Ltn Rudolf Müller of 8 Staffel, who claimed a Spitfire at 1815 for his first victory. Macqueen turned towards him, but then saw the other Messerschmitt firing at an Albacore and attacked this instead, sending it down in a shallow dive. James reported that he saw the aircraft turn on its back at 50 feet above the sea, and Macqueen then observed a splash; on the basis of this circumstantial evidence he was credited with its destruction. By now low on fuel the Spitfires turned back, leaving the biplanes to their fate, but after a further two hours these were recalled and the operation cancelled.

There were several skirmishes over and around Malta on **23 March**, as the two surviving merchant vessels reached the island. Fourteen Spitfires and 11 Hurricanes had been made ready by daybreak, and these were split between defence of the island and convoy protection. Operating in pairs at approximately half-hourly intervals, encounters were reported throughout the day. A pair of Hurricanes made the first contact, inflicting damage on a Ju88 two miles south of Kalafrana, Spitfires flown by 126 Squadron pilots Flt Lt Tim Johnston and Plt Off Mike Graves observing another at about the same time. As they approached, the Ju88 fired a recognition flare of three red stars – presumably the crew thought the approaching fighters were Messerschmitts. Johnston engaged:

"I followed him in his turn and opened fire with a one-and-a-half-seconds burst of cannon and machine-gun at 80 yards; deflection was for 60 degrees so he was actually under my nose and I couldn't see the results until I'd broken; pleased to find that his starboard engine was giving off a stream of white smoke. He continued to climb, and take evasive action, making for the great banks of cloud above. I fired three more two-seconds bursts with cannon and machine-guns at 200 yards from quarter astern, but without seeing any results; knew it wasn't good attack for an 88, but with cloud-cover so near it was a race against time, and to get him at all I had to get him quickly. Starboard engine was still smoking, leaving a thin white stream of glycol vapour, but he appeared to be flying strongly. Suddenly he pulled up very steeply in a final effort, with me still hanging on to his flanks, and managed to reach the first patch of cloud; he disappeared, reappeared, disappeared again. He had been twisting and turning this way and that and I realised that I had lost all sense of direction and that we were probably far out over the sea. The cloud was more solid here and I thought I'd lost him for good; one part of me was cursing like hell for letting him slip away, while another was wondering whether my R/T was working, where I was, whether I should ever be able to find the island again in such poor visibility, and whether I'd been hit by his return fire.

"Continued to hunt about for him in the broken cloud and had almost given up, when spotted him below and slightly ahead, running from one piece of cloud-cover to the next; came in dead astern this time, took careful aim and finished off my cannon ammunition in him; broke away and found that both his motors were now giving off white smoke. As I watched three objects suddenly fell away from the fuselage; thought at first that the aircraft was beginning to break up, and felt surprised that this should happen so long after my burst, then realised it was probably the crew jumping out. Three little black specks had been silhouetted for a moment against the cloud, before they disappeared into it; wondered what it was that had made them exchange their cabin for the almost certain death of a rough sea 20 miles from land. The aircraft fell away in a right-hand spiral dive and disappeared into cloud; I followed, emerged underneath and at first saw only an expanse of dirty grey sea, with endless white horses; then looking round picked out a patch of burning petrol. Felt none of the exultation I'd experienced last year with my first kill, just satisfaction at having completed the job."

This was almost certainly Obgfr Hans Spix's F6+CH of 1(F)/122, which failed to return. There were no survivors. Another Ju88 fell to Hurricanes shortly thereafter. There were several skirmishes in the early afternoon when, shortly after 1300, small formations of Ju88s attempted to reach the ships, being met by sections of patrolling Hurricanes and Spitfires. One pair of Spitfires flown by Flt Lt Macqueen and Plt Off Sergeant (AB344) joined two Hurricanes in engaging a trio of Ju88s, claiming damage to all three bombers before they escaped in cloud. Sergeant noted:

"Exceedingly low cloud. Mac and I attacked an 88 and set both engines on fire. Will most probably be confirmed."

One of the bombers attacked – B3+LL of 3/KG54 flown by Ltn Hermann Janzik – was indeed shot down, returning crews reporting that it fell victim to four Spitfires [*sic*]. Following debriefing it transpired that the two Hurricane pilots of 185 Squadron had attacked the same aircraft as Macqueen and Sergeant, and the two squadrons shared the victory. Two other Spitfires patrolled four miles east of Grand Harbour, where a further pair of Ju88s was intercepted, one of which was claimed damaged by Plt Off Plagis (BP846). Flt Lt Johnston was up again during the early afternoon, once more with Plt Off Graves. They spotted three Ju88s of 3/KGr806 about five miles off Kalafrana, and chased these southwards out to sea. Graves carried out a quarter attack on one:

> "While I was weaving behind and slightly below Blue One, I spotted a Ju88 about 3,500 feet below. I immediately half-rolled and went into attack. The Ju88 was approaching the convoy from the north-east. My first attack was from the starboard quarter and above. I opened fire at about 400 yards and fired about a six-seconds burst, closing to somewhere between 50 and 100 yards. I observed strikes on the starboard engine wing root and cockpit. The starboard engine immediately began to let out black and white smoke and then stopped. I saw parts come off the cockpit also. The bomber also jettisoned its bombs on the commencement of the attack. I then climbed and started another attack from the front quarter with my remaining machine-gun ammunition. At the commencement of the attack I noticed two people bale out. I then finished up by giving it a final very short burst from the rear starboard quarter, the 88 then flying about 500 feet above the water. I then noticed a red glow round about the starboard engine wing root. The Ju88 suddenly turned over onto its back and went into the sea at a steep angle and seemed to disappear. The sea was very rough."

Just as the bomber rolled over and dived into the sea, six Beaufighters approached from the east, having been dispatched from Gambut to provide cover for the convoy, which they had been unable to locate. One of these promptly shot down another of the Ju88s. M7+DL and M7+GL, flown by Ltn Hermann Damaske and Fw Herbert Augustin respectively, were lost in this engagement. There were no survivors from either aircraft.

On Malta at the end of this hectic day, although no losses had been suffered, only five fighters remained fully serviceable. A fierce resumption of attacks could be expected on the morrow, particularly on Grand Harbour where the two freighters now lay at anchor. By a tremendous overnight effort, the hardworking ground crews had a total of 18 Spitfires and Hurricanes airworthy by dawn next day, aided during the night by the unloading of a number of Merlin engines and other aircraft spares from the two ships, mainly by the efforts of RAF personnel, including aircrew. A spell of bad weather helped protect the ships from sustained assault. A pilot of 7/JG53, Ltn Jürgen Harder, sarcastically wrote:

> "Since yesterday there has been a fantastically heavy storm which made heavy attacks on the island almost impossible. But we have to fly in fog, storm and rain, as the convoy is now sailing into Valetta, having been lost by the courageous Italian fleet in spite of its better position and contact. And so with 100kph squalls and visibility of four kilometres, our crews and bombers have to attack and if possible sink the ships. We have already sent two to the bottom, and the next attack will come in two hours. Hopefully the last merchant ship will be hit and sunk then too. And all this in the land of our brave ally."

The Luftwaffe launched a determined raid against the berthed ships in Grand Harbour on the morning of **24 March**. The first interceptions were reported soon after 1040, when two Spitfires of 126 Squadron flown by the American pair, Plt Offs Jimmie Peck and Don McLeod, attacked two Bf109 Jabo as they approached Kalafrana Bay. McLeod reported:

> "First sighted two e/a at 8,000 feet below going in direction of Kalafrana Bay. Immediately dived to attack and taking one on the left – P/O Peck the one on the right – opened fire with five-seconds burst from dead astern. The 109 was enveloped in white smoke (apparently glycol) and started in gliding turn to left. E/a on my right did sharp turn in front of me. I used rest of my ammo on beam attack. On breaking from this attack I saw first e/a attacked by me diving straight into the sea, a mass of flames and black smoke."

Peck's victim gave him some trouble before it, too, went down. Apparently McLeod called on the R/T to the effect:

> "Hello Peck, Mac here, I've knocked mine down, do I have to come and help you with yours?"

Peck's reply, not surprisingly, was said to be unprintable! The identities of their victims, possibly pilots from II/JG3, has not been established. Some 40 Ju88s and a strong fighter escort arrived over the island at 1140. Six Hurricanes and three Spitfires including two flown by 249 pilots were scrambled, but only Flg Off Buchanan was able to make a claim when he damaged a Messerschmitt. An accompanying Spitfire, flown by Sgt Gordon Bolton of 126 Squadron, was shot down and crash-landed at Luqa. At least three Hurricanes were damaged in combat during the day, leaving just nine serviceable fighters – Spitfires and Hurricanes – to meet what the morrow had in store for them. Between 1420 and 1800, 30 more Ju88s, 30 Ju87s and 25 Bf109s again approached, four Spitfires and four Hurricanes being scrambled. At about 1510, the 126 Squadron pair, Flt Lt Johnston and Plt Off Graves, were engaged by Bf109s and became separated. Evading his assailants, Johnston then saw bombs exploding on Hal Far, which was under attack by Ju87Ds of III/StG3. He attacked one of these:

> "...opened on the nearest Stuka from 100 yards with both cannon and machine-guns. Can remember promising myself something spectacular – small fragments or sheet of flame – but all that came were some vivid flashes from exploding cannon shells and a stream of white smoke from his belly. I was so over-confident that I pulled out to one side, instead of breaking away properly, and sat there watching him; it was probably then that I got hit, if not by him then by one of his nearer friends. By this time we were out over the sea, and I knew the Me109s wouldn't be far away, so I quickly gave him another three-seconds burst from the port quarter; think I allowed too much deflection, because he still kept flying, though he was beginning to lag behind the others and there was more glycol streaming out than before. I knew he couldn't get home, so broke off and flew back to the island; a last look showed him farther behind the formation than before and still trailing his white plume."

On entering the circuit at Luqa, Johnston lowered his wheels and was about to lower flaps when he noticed light AA bursting above him. He looked around and saw a Bf109 at 500 yards on his port beam.

> "I whipped my wheels up and stuffed my nose down at the same time; as I did so he opened fire, but I felt fairly certain he wouldn't hit me. He flashed past, did a stall turn and came back towards me, but didn't attack again. I followed him north-west; knew I couldn't catch him, and that I hadn't much ammunition left, but thought I might be able

to jump him later if he decided to go ground-strafing; possibly I was feeling bloody-minded at being attacked over my own base. I was about 1,000 feet below him and half a mile astern, heading for some cloud cover from which to watch him, when he returned and started a diving head-on attack; seeing it coming, I pulled up hard, in something between a loop and a climbing turn, towards a cloud to port. I continued to watch him over the side of the cockpit and knew he'd opened fire when the sinister blue tendrils shot out of his wings towards me; saw him follow me round in my turn and the deflection looked about right. This time I didn't feel a bit confident of not being hit. The aircraft had lost so much speed that the evasive action I tried to take as I saw him firing was sluggish and ineffective."

Johnston's aircraft was hit three times in the leading edge, one bullet puncturing a tyre. Two Spitfires were claimed at this time, one by Obfw Rudolf Ehrenberger of 6 Staffel at 1503 (his 18th victory), and the second by Oblt Kurt Brändle of 5 Staffel (33rd) just five minutes later. Johnston's No 2, Mike Graves, had landed earlier, not having seen the Stukas. Witnesses on the ground stated that two Ju87s had been shot down during the raid, but records indicate that only Uffz Hans Bretschneider of 7 Staffel, in T6+BM, failed to return. AA gunners claimed two Stukas shot down and it seems likely that Bretschneider's aircraft was hit by ground fire. Johnston was credited with a probable. On the ground Sgt Tim Goldsmith, currently flying Hurricanes with 185 Squadron, had a grandstand view of the dive-bombing of Hal Far, as he was sheltering with others in the entrance to the operations room:

"We leaped down the ops burrow like a couple of rabbits just as two terrific explosions above indicated a very near miss. The raid continued for 15-20 minutes, winding up with some strafing by three enemy fighters. We came forth blinking in the sunlight to survey the results. The officers' mess had been flattened altogether with part of the airmen's quarters. On the other side of the drome a Swordfish blazed furiously inside its dispersal bay. The wreckage of a Stuka [T6+BM] smouldered in the centre of the field, the pilot smouldering with it. The gunner [Uffz Ferdinand Burger] had managed to bale out, I learned later, and was taken prisoner by the crew of a Bofors gun, near which he had landed. It was not until we had looked around and taken all this in that we noticed two craters where the nearby air raid shelter had been. Apparently the two 'eggs' which landed just after we leaped for shelter had caused the damage. Together with the others, we raced for spades and shovels and set to work excavating, or rather exhuming. Several hours later, when the job was completed, 23 bodies had been recovered. In addition, five badly injured airmen had been transferred to hospital. Three of these later died."

Shortly after this raid a formation of eight Ju88s from III/KG77 approached the island, four Hurricanes being scrambled to intercept. In the ensuing engagement, three of the bombers were claimed damaged, one of which failed to return. Three of the Hurricanes were also damaged by return fire although all three landed safely. By the end of the day Malta was down to just nine serviceable fighters.

Rather surprisingly there was little hostile activity over Malta until the afternoon of **25 March**, but then at least 30 Ju88s, 25 Ju87s (from III/StG3) and 13 Bf109s were reported over the island between 1540 and 1725. To meet these raids eight Hurricanes and six Spitfires (four flown by 249 pilots and two by 126) got into the air, and a number of claims were made, primarily against the Ju87s, with Sqn Ldr Grant and Plt Off Plagis reporting shooting down one apiece. The Rhodesian then claimed strikes on a second before his aircraft (BP850/F) was attacked and damaged by Fw Max Fischer of Stab II/JG3. Fischer's joy was short-lived however, for Grant was soon on the tail of the Messerschmitt and shot it down into the sea off Gozo. The German pilot managed to bale out and was rescued later by a Do24 from Sicily. Meanwhile, Flg Off Lee gained strikes on another Ju87, while Plt Off Nash (AB264/GN-H) initially claimed one as a probable, only to have this upgraded later to a confirmed victory.

Although four Ju87s were claimed shot down, with two more probables, records suggest that only one was lost, Ltn Klaus Heemann's T6+CC falling into the sea about five miles east of Marsaxlokk; a second aircraft returned to Sicily with a wounded gunner. The two 126 Squadron Spitfires were flown by the inseparable American duo, Peck and McLeod, the former claiming a Ju87 damaged, while the latter believed he had shot down another Bf109:

> "Six Spitfires took off on interception; while flying at 16,000 feet in vicinity of Grand Harbour, several Me109s were spotted below. We dived to attack; Me109s were in line astern and turning to left. I opened fire at about 200 yards, closing to 150, with three-seconds burst. E/A suddenly did violent down snap. At this time I was engaged by another 109, which opened fire on me from my right front quarter. I did a head-on attack on this e/a, finishing my ammo. Pete Nash, who was in the attack with me, saw first 109 attacked going straight into the sea."

It seems likely that McLeod had actually attacked a Messerschmitt of 4/JG3 flown by Ltn Rudolf Wicklaus, who was wounded but succeeded in returning to Sicily, and that the aircraft witnessed by Nash falling into the sea was that shot down by Sqn Ldr Grant. The two freighters in harbour escaped damage during the assault. That night, Nash confided to his diary:

> "We first bounced five Me109s. Grant got one and McLeod beat me to another and got that one. We then sighted the raid – and what a raid! 30-plus Ju87s. I dived behind the first one to dive. Overshot him but managed to get in a short squirt that made him smoke white. Then bounced by a 109 so did not get another crack at him. Grant damaged one, Plagis one destroyed and one probable – 87s, Peck one damaged 87, Lee one damaged 87. A great party. Bloody good show!"

The first bomber raid on the morning of **26 March** was intercepted by seven Hurricanes, inflicting negligible damage. At 1355 four Spitfires – the only fighters then available – scrambled to engage the second formation, which comprised an estimated 15 Ju87s of III/StG4 and three Ju88s of I/KG54, with escorting Bf109s. Flt Sgt Brennan (AB335/GN-F) attacked the trio of Ju88s as they dived in formation, seeing cannon strikes on one, which turned away. Flt Lt Connell (GN-L), who was leading the formation, claimed to have shot the tail off another, but this was probably the same aircraft as that attacked by Brennan, which Flt Lt McNair (AB264/GN-H) then attacked, reporting that it went down disintegrating into the sea half a mile off Xlendi Bay, Gozo. Brennan later wrote:

> "Bud decided to attack the 88s. They seemed to be everywhere, and there were so many I could not decide which to attack. After a few seconds hesitation I turned on one, opening fire when well out of range. It was the first 88 I had attacked, and it seemed much closer to me than it was. The 88's rear gunner also opened fire. I thought I had hit him. Just then I had a quick look behind. Two 109s were coming down on me. I had to leave the 88 and turn towards the fighters, but instead of engaging, they rolled on their backs and went down. I turned back to my 88, which, travelling parallel with the coast, was streaking over Filfla.
>
> "Buck McNair also gave chase. He was about 200 yards ahead of me and 500 yards from the bomber. The 88's throttles were wide open, and a streak of brown smoke was

pouring from each exhaust, due to the pilot's heavy demand on his motors. Buck caught the bomber south of Gozo, and gave him a short burst. I could see spent cannon shells falling out of Buck's wings and the black smoke coming from his guns. He gave the fleeing bomber a second and longer burst. Its starboard wing root and motor caught fire. The 88 commenced to disintegrate and, as Buck broke off his attack, crashed into the sea. Buck and I joined up and, without further incident, returned to base."

McNair added:

"I selected one, decided it was going too fast and that I couldn't catch it. I saw another and went full out at it. Brennan was above me, and had a go, too, and he thought he'd hit it, but then he saw another Spit going for it – me – so pulled off to give cover. I was 800 yards behind the 88 and could scarcely gain on it. He nipped into cloud 1,000 feet thick. I followed on course and when I came out he was still ahead of me. If he'd had any sense he would have turned and foxed me, but he just tried to out-run me; the Spit didn't have that much speed advantage over a fleeing Ju88. I chased him full out, and had a difficult time catching him, so I fired short bursts at various sights, first up, then down with the nose of the Spit. Brennan staying behind and above, called to me: 'Spitfire chasing an 88 – it's a Spitfire behind you', in case he thought I might think him a 109. I said OK.

"One of my bursts hit the 88; glycol came out of one engine, which then burst into flames. I started to gain on him now – I knew I had him. The rear gunner kept firing at me, I could see smoke from his bursts. I put my face right behind the sight. Even if a bullet hit my windscreen and shattered it, the glass would be deflected by the gunsight. I fired another short burst and he dived down towards the water, but the rear gunner was still firing at me when the bomber 'woomped' into the water. The machine seemed to disintegrate. I flew over the spot, circled and could see a rubber tyre and odd bits of wreckage floating about. Two or three fellows were hanging on to bits and pieces, then I saw a fourth. They managed to get out a dinghy which they held on to."

Connell, meanwhile, had attacked the Ju87s, claiming one of these probably destroyed, this subsequently being upgraded to a confirmed victory. The pilot of the shot down Ju88, Ltn Johann Rottmann, told his captors:

"We were attacked by two Spitfires off Gozo. The first attacked from above and was driven off by fire from the top rear gunner; the second attacked from slightly below, the bottom rear gun jamming. The starboard engine was set on fire and there was a probability that this would reach the petrol tanks, so I decided to land on the sea."

Amazingly all members of the crew survived including the gallant gunner and scrambled into their dinghy before the aircraft sank; local police rescued them later and one crewmember was taken to Victoria Hospital, suffering nothing more serious than a strained knee. Meanwhile, the fourth member of the section, Flt Lt Johnston of 126 Squadron, having missed an opportunity to engage the Ju88s, found himself entangled with several Ju87s:

"Bud [Connell] swung us north-eastward; at the same time I noticed that the Grand Harbour barrage had suddenly appeared from nowhere, but couldn't see any aircraft yet. As we approached I saw two 88s break south-west out of the barrage a long way below us. The other three Spits half-rolled and went after them, I decided to wait for the Stukas; flew on till I was right over the barrage at 10,000 feet and then sat waiting for them to emerge and hoping no 109s would pick me up before they did so. A minute or two passed and nothing happened. I began to think I must have missed them, perhaps they had gone out before the 88s. What a fool I'd been not to take that chance while I had it, now I probably wouldn't even fire my guns, and so on, when suddenly the first Stuka pulled up out of the smoke-puffs and headed north. He was a long way below me, so I had to get rid of my surplus height without gaining too much speed. I pulled throttle right back and swish-tailed down, while 87s popped up out of the barrage, one after the other, like tumblers coming up through a trap-door in the stage.

"There seemed so many I hardly knew which to take. Was manoeuvring behind one when another overtook me and passed within 30 yards so that I could see every detail of his camouflage. The Intelligence people had thought the last lot might have been Italians, but there was no doubt about this swastika; decided he was a better target than the other, and was about to attack when he suddenly seemed to stand on his head. I tried to follow, but couldn't compete with so sudden a dive and passed over the top. As I did so I noticed his bombs leaving his belly. That was rather puzzling; I thought they'd already released all their bombs; possibly this one had shied at the barrage and chosen an easier target north of the harbour. No time for speculation; they were flying out among the big, scattered, cumulus clouds which usually build up over the island, and if I wasn't quick I should lose them.

"Chose the nearest and attacked dead astern with a two-seconds burst of cannon and machine-guns from 150 yards; he escaped into cloud before I could see any result. Picked the next – they seemed to be on all sides – and gave him a four-seconds burst from 200 yards. He began to dive for cloud, but before he reached it streams of black smoke were pouring from his belly; I followed him into it, hoping to pick him up on the other side and finish him off, but decided there was no need, so pulled up and looked for another. Stukas were scurrying on all sides across the gaps between the clouds and I had begun to feel pleasantly like a wolf. I chose another and got in a short burst before he reached cover, but with no observed result, so looked round and found a fourth, in which I finished my machine-gun ammunition from close range; saw what looked like several jets of white vapour, spurting from round his radiator and coming back in a substantial stream; hauled out of range of his return fire to see what would happen, and noted the last of clouds had been left behind. Sea and sky stretched away unbroken to Sicily. Checked my gauges as a precaution and was horrified to find that the oil pressure, instead of standing at 90°, was at 80° – and falling as I watched. Hell! Ten or fifteen miles offshore with no ammo, and a failing engine."

At that stage a Messerschmitt, probably flown by Ltn Joachim Kirschner of 5/JG3, appeared and opened fire:

"… suddenly I saw a bright flash on the top of my port wing, outward of the cannon. I was still wondering what had happened, when the 109 overshot me and disappeared at once into the cloud ahead. I followed and was gratefully swallowed."

Johnston promptly set course for Takali but, as a Messerschmitt was overhead as he approached, he went instead to Luqa and landed safely. His aircraft, BP850/F, had suffered a machine-gun strike below the spinner, which had made a jagged hole in the oil tank, there was another strike in the spinner, and a third in the leading edge of the starboard wing. In addition, a cannon shell had exploded in the port wing and had blown a hole about four inches square through both the outer skin and the top of the main spar below it, while another cannon shell had exploded at the root of the starboard elevator. He was lucky to have got back. Of the day's fighting, Plt Off Nash commented:

"Off [duty] today. Grand Harbour very heavily blitzed. All from ships of the convoy and a destroyer sunk or on fire. The boys had a lot of fun this afternoon. Buck McNair got one 88 destroyed and one 88 probable. Bud Connell got two 88s destroyed [sic]. Tim

Johnston shot up again – he will buy it soon. The Luftwaffe is taking a bashing from 'The Few'".

The survivors of Ltn Rottmann's Ju88 were fortunate to have been rescued. Fate was less kind to another Ju88 crew, as Laddie Lucas recalled:

"…a few of us saw a Canadian pilot, in a gesture of calculated revenge [of Plt Off Leggo, whose death it was believed was caused by a Messerschmitt pilot collapsing his parachute] dive on the dinghy of a ditched Ju88 crew as it bobbed up and down on the waves, six or eight miles south-west of Delimara Point at the southern end of the island. The three occupants must obviously have reckoned they had a good chance of being picked up by air-sea rescue. A short, ruthless burst of fire and their hopes were at an end. None of us who saw the first act forgot it, but those of us who witnessed the second, set our faces against it, and said no more."

The next major series of assaults came in between 1630 and 1857, when 24 Ju88s and 18 Ju87s, with fighter escort, were reported over Grand Harbour and Kalafrana, while three Messerschmitt-escorted ASR Do24s searched near Gozo for the crew of the missing bomber. Four Spitfires and six Hurricanes were scrambled to meet these latest raiders. As the Spitfires approached a formation of Ju88s, Plt Off Sandy McHan – an American former Eagle Squadron pilot – found himself targeted by the AA guns, his aircraft (AB346/GN-K) being peppered by shrapnel. He managed to reach Takali and land safely. The other three engaged the bombers, four of which were claimed damaged – one each by Flt Lt Connell and Flg Off Buchanan, the other two being credited to Flt Lt McNair (AB264/GN-H) – before the escorting fighters forced them away. It was later decided that all three had attacked the same bomber and were jointly credited with its destruction and, in fact, Ju88 (M7+AA) of 3/KGr806 crash-landed at Comiso on return, having been damaged by fighter attack, during which the rear gunner (Obfw Güstav Reimers) was killed. Sqn Ldr Gracie led four more Spitfires to intercept another Ju88 raid but the sortie was disorganised, as noted by Flt Lt Daddo-Langlois:

"Interception. Shambles. R/T failure. Sqn Ldr Gracie got a damaged Ju88 and was shot up himself."

Gracie may have been the target of Ltn Max-Bruno Fischer of 4/JG3, who claimed a Spitfire as his first victory. Flt Sgt Brennan, who was feeling depressed by his lack of success, wrote:

"We held a post-mortem after we landed, frankly swapping our impressions. The mass raids promised to be a piece of cake, and we anticipated taking a heavy toll of the raiders. The German fighters, determined and skilful when attacked, did not display the same efficiency in their escort work. Bud Connell, I think, aptly summed up our impressions at seeing the big formations of Ju88s diving across the island when he remarked: 'I'm glad I was above, and not beneath, them.' I felt I had not done well, and told Bud so. He cheered me up, and gave me some worthwhile tips for the future. 'Make your decisions quickly,' he advised me. 'Don't be confused by numbers. You can't shoot them all down. Pick one out, and give him everything you've got. If you hang about up there the 109s will certainly get you.' It was good advice.

"Our discussions in the mess, over a pint of unpalatable Maltese beer, were long, animated and profitable. We learnt a great deal about the Hun's tricks. I listened attentively, and somewhat enviously, to these chaps who knew it all. Those talks in the mess taught us all, I think, how little we did know and how much we had to learn. A real knowledge of Hun tactics, of course, comes only with personal experience, but many lessons may be learnt in the mess. It was there, for example, that I began to appreciate the prime necessity for maintaining a careful look-out at all times, so as to guard against being jumped from behind."

Following a relatively quiet 36 hours, during which ten reinforcement Hurricanes arrived from the Middle East, a quartet of Spitfires flown by 249 pilots engaged a reconnaissance Ju88 just after midday on **28 March**. Although all four – Sqn Ldr Grant, Flg Off Lee, Plt Offs Plagis (AB346/GN-K) and Nash (AB335/GN-F) – attacked the aircraft some 20 miles north of Grand Harbour, they were unable to shoot it down despite using all their ammunition. Nash noted:

"Single unescorted 88 raided Grand Harbour out of 11,000 feet cloud so we were scrambled. We spotted one but he was a long way away and got into cloud jettisoning his bombs. We then spotted another which all four of us attacked. He also jettisoned his bombs. We gave him all we had but he would not go down. I saw both engines smoking. Lee followed him down to 1,000 feet and got a shell through his engine for it. So Grant, Plagis, Lee and I get $1/4$ probable apiece."

The remaining seven Spitfires arrived from *Eagle* on **29 March**, the balance of the earlier delivery, although so few were obviously not going to save Malta from the onslaught. Flt Lt Tony 'Sailor' Barton DFC, a Battle of Britain pilot[20], led the flight which comprised Plt Offs John 'Bill' Bailey, Frank Jemmett and John Bisley RAAF, and three Canadian sergeants, Wilbert Dodd, Jack Ryckman, and Eric 'Junior' Crist (AB418), who recalled:

"It was pretty scary. And the *Eagle* had a pretty short flight deck, only 390 feet. There were no flaps to assist you on take-off. Spitfire flaps were either fully up or fully down, there was no in between. The first one off was our CO. He disappeared over the bow and finally staggered into view about a half a mile ahead. That didn't inspire any confidence. I remember the flight crews on the carrier removed the chocks. There was a sailor on each wingtip and a sailor on the tailplane to hold her down. I got her revved up pretty good. She was just jumping. And I'm of slight stature. I was only about 126 pounds. I got airborne before I got to the end of the flight deck. I had a pretty fair wind off the deck. I think I caught her just right."[21]

Canadian Plt Offs Winston McCarthy and Stan Brooker arrived at the same time and is assumed to have been flown to Malta aboard a transport aircraft. The arrival of the latest delivery did not go unnoticed by the Germans and soon after midday nine Ju88s approached the island, crossing the coast singly or in pairs to attack and depart under cover of heavy cloud, but failed to inflict any damage on the airfields. Four Spitfires and four Hurricanes were scrambled, Flt Lt Johnston and Plt Off Peck of 126 Squadron climbing to 17,000 feet, then being vectored onto an intruder 2,000 feet below:

"Kept well above him, so that we should have a background of blue sky behind us, but unfortunately we were down sun and he appeared to see us, because we saw him drop his bombs – tiny specks against the cloud – and swing away to the east. Had plenty of height and speed, so soon cut him off; came in very fast on his port beam and was about to lay sight on him when suddenly thought: 'My God, it's the Mosquito.' This had been flying earlier in the day[22]; I'd quite forgotten about the bombs. I was coming in so fast that this momentary check spoilt the attack and I had to pull up over the top of him, cursing like hell.

"Watched Jimmie come in behind me, quarter astern, and saw streams of tracer flying past him as the 88 opened fire; noticed it was painted in desert camouflage. As soon as Jimmie broke away, I dived on him from above and fired until I was dead astern. Could see his tracer getting too close for comfort so pulled up hard and then dropped a wing to watch; he was just entering cloud and a thin stream of white smoke was coming from his starboard motor. This must have been Jimmie's work, not mine, because I discovered afterwards that I had pressed the wrong button and that only my machine-guns had been fired. Was furious with myself; with so much cloud-cover I doubt whether we could have got him anyway, but I'd managed to do everything wrong and spoilt what chance we had."

During the hours of darkness a BOAC Catalina from Gibraltar alighted on the calm waters of St Paul's Bay. Among its passengers was another fighter pilot, for whom there had not been an available Spitfire aboard *Eagle*, hence he arrived in somewhat luxury aboard the flyingboat. This was Flt Sgt Paudrick 'Paddy' Schade[23], of Dutch/Irish ancestry, who would make his mark in the coming weeks. He was immediately posted to 126 Squadron.

There were no raids on Malta next day (**30 March**), although a reconnaissance Ju88 was intercepted by Flt Lt Macqueen and Flg Off Daddo-Langlois (GN-A) just after 1400. Having chased it to within a few miles of the Sicilian coast, both pilots attacked, Daddo-Langlois using all his ammunition, but they did not see it crash. Macqueen claimed it damaged. However, a Ju88 of 5/LG1 ditched in the sea east of Catania with engine damage, Uffz Heinz Pfeiffer and his crew of two being killed, and may have been their victim, although Luftwaffe records put the loss down to an accident. It was left to the Hurricanes to operate on the last day of the month, since only small numbers of Ju88s and Bf109s appeared over Malta. One Hurricane was shot down, as was the PR Mosquito, although the latter was crash-landed at Luqa, where it burnt out; the crew survived.

During the course of the 20 days since their operational debut over Malta, the Spitfire pilots were credited with 20 enemy aircraft shot down, including one shared with two Hurricanes, which, when compared with the handful of victories achieved by the Hurricane pilots since the beginning of the year, emphasised the combat superiority of the Spitfire V over the Hurricane II. But, in return for these successes, four Spitfires had been lost together with their pilots. Meanwhile, 69 Squadron's PR Spitfire (AB300) had notched up a total of 54 hours flying time. Of his third and last flight of the month, Plt Off Coldbeck recalled:

"Messerschmitt 109s began to manoeuvre for an interception over Palermo but I saw them before they became dangerous and made my escape out to sea. For the solo pilot, alone over enemy territory, eternal vigilance was the price of survival."

As March drew to a close, British intelligence revealed that Hitler had issued orders for Malta to be seized during April, to safeguard the sea lanes for supplies to Rommel's Afrika Korps preparing for the North African offensive. Malta was thus forewarned of imminent invasion.

CHAPTER III

ON THE BRINK OF DEFEAT

April 1942

1 April was 249 Squadron's day to man the Spitfires and, at 1315, six were scrambled to intercept four Bf109s apparently on a reconnaissance flight. One broke away as the Spitfires turned towards them, Plt Off Plagis (AB335/GN-F) giving chase and shooting it down south-east of Grand Harbour. It would seem that his victim was one of III/JG53's leading pilots, Fw Hans Schade of 8 Staffel, a 13-victory ace; his aircraft (7535) crashed into the sea and he was posted missing. Thirty-five minutes later, just as the flight landed, four were immediately scrambled again. This time they encountered escorted Ju88s of I and II/KG77, diving through the AA barrage to get at them. Some way behind followed six Hurricanes. Plagis noted:

> "Shot down Ju88 bomber quarter mile north-west of Grand Harbour. Also shared a probably destroyed Ju88 with Hurricane."

In fact, two Hurricane pilots reported sharing a Ju88, so presumably all three attacked the same bomber. Meanwhile, Plt Off Nash (GN-Z) attacked another of the bombers, which he claimed to have hit in the fuel tanks and reported that it flicked onto its back in flames and spiralled into the sea, and Sqn Ldr Grant damaged another. On the ground at Takali, other pilots of 249 were watching including Sgt Hesselyn:

> "Stan, Johnny and Pete shot down an 88 each [*sic* – Sqn Ldr Grant claimed a damaged only]. We saw Pete's [victim] burst into flames and head straight for the sea, sending up a column of water as it crashed. The other two also fell into the sea, but from where we stood we could not follow them all the way down. Norman [Lee] was unlucky. He was attacking an 88 when he was shot-up by 109s. He force-landed [AB418] on the aerodrome with a cannon shell in his wing. A shell splinter had entered his ankle and he had to be packed off to hospital."

Lee's victor was probably Maj Günther von Maltzahn of JG53, who claimed a Spitfire at 1445 as his 60th victory, although Oblt Walther Dahl of 4/JG3 also claimed a Spitfire, but at 1530. At 1630, a Do24 flyingboat was seen five miles north-east of Grand Harbour, under an umbrella of Bf109s, apparently searching for missing aircrew. Four Spitfires and a Hurricane were sent off to investigate. Plagis – on his third sortie of the day in AB335/GN-F – claimed one of the Messerschmitts shot down into the sea six miles north of Grand Harbour. Sgt Hesselyn also claimed a fighter shot down, the CO and Flg Off Buchanan each claiming one damaged. Hesselyn wrote:

> "Stan [Grant] led us down until we were directly behind the enemy and about 5,000 feet above. Then he told us to go in and take our pick. I chose the one on the extreme right, and as I dived on him I could see the rest of the boys going in, line abreast. I quickly caught my 109, but I was coming in too fast and overshot him. However, I got a good bead on the one ahead. It was a lovely break. This 109 was turning at the time and I had him dead in my sights. Opening fire from about 50 yards, I gave him a four-seconds burst. He flipped on his back immediately and went straight in. I was as excited as hell. I told everybody, including Woody, that I had shot down my first, screaming over the R/T."

Hesselyn began circling the Messerschmitt down in the sea, but was attacked by two more, streams of tracer just missing his port wing. On landing he discovered that in his excitement he had pressed the wrong firing button, using only his four machine-guns to shoot down the German fighter, rather than his cannons. It would seem that he or Plagis, or more likely both of them, had shot down Uffz Gerhard Kitzenmaier's Black 5 (7270) of 5/JG53, the only Messerschmitt lost on this sortie.

No sooner were the Spitfires down than another raid approached, some 70-plus aircraft including 54 Ju87s making for the dockyard and Hal Far. Two Hurricanes had been sent up at 1700 to cover the returning Spitfires, and these were joined by five more at 1800, and then by five Spitfires half an hour later. The Ju87s were encountered over Grand Harbour, six of which were claimed shot down (two by the AA defences), five more as probables and three damaged. Of these, Plt Off Nash (BP844/GN-W), Plt Off Plagis (AB335/GN-F) and Sgt Hesselyn claimed one apiece, Sqn Ldr Grant a probable and a damaged and Flg Off Buchanan a probable. Plagis reported setting his opponent's engine on fire, whereupon it spun down in flames, while Nash saw his target blow up and fall into the sea. Of the action, Hesselyn wrote:

> "We each got onto a bomber's tail. Pete [Nash] was slightly ahead of me and I could see him firing before I opened up. His shells were striking and suddenly his 87 blew up. I had no time to see any more. I was within 100 yards of my 87 and, pressing the right gun button this time, I gave him everything I had. In a couple of seconds he burst into flames and dived into the drink."

Hesselyn was jumped by a Bf109 as he approached to land with wheels and flaps down, but was able to retract these and turn steeply, the attacker missing his opportunity. The Messerschmitt climbed away after overshooting, allowing the New Zealander to land safely. Oblt Helmut Belser of 8/JG53 was awarded his 20th victory after submitting a claim for a Spitfire at about this time, which may have been Hesselyn's aircraft. Watching the action from the ground was Sgt Tim Goldsmith:

> "In the excitement of screaming bombs, bursting flak, only one or two spectators noticed the two Spitfires streaking down from the direction of Luqa. There was a flock of 109s after them, and one was attacked and had to break away before reaching the Stukas. The other, who I later heard was Hesselyn, joined the bombers and, attacking from the rear quarter, blew one to pieces. He then moved in behind another and fired a long burst at it. This one flicked over and spiralled earthwards, but both of the crew baled out."

It seems likely that the AA gunners claimed the same aircraft as those attacked by the fighters. Two Ju87s were actually lost, T6+FN of 8/StG3 crashing on the seashore at Delimara Point with the loss of the gunner, Gfr Wilhelm Neubauer. The pilot, Uffz Winfried Günther managed to bale out and was blown out to sea. Luckily, he was soon picked up by ASR tender ST331. A second Ju87 from this unit came down in the sea five miles north-east of Valetta, the pilot, Oblt Kühn, being rescued later by an Axis ASR craft, although his gunner (Gfr Helmut Süchlich) was lost. A third aircraft, from 7 Staffel, was hit during this operation and its pilot, Obfw Kurt Auer, was wounded. There was a tragic sequel to this action. While RAF and military personnel were inspecting the wreck of T6+FN at Delimara Point, a bomb aboard the aircraft exploded and killed a number of those present. Among the many claims submitted by the guns, at least one was confirmed when a II/JG3 Messerschmitt flown by Uffz Hans Pilz crash-landed in a wheat field near Paola, the aircraft flipping over and trapping the pilot. Locals rushed to free the injured pilot, who was taken away for medical treatment following the arrival of a doctor. Pilz was fortunate; many other

German and Italian aircrew who reached Malta *sans* their aircraft were greeted by hostile Maltese civilians and some did not survive the experience. One member of a KG77 Ju88 who managed to reach the shore after having baled out off Sliema Point was lucky to have been met by soldiers rather than locals:

"When the swimmer was near to the shore calls for help were clearly audible and then the bobbing head appealed for mercy, mercy which is never denied a stricken, enemy by the British. Soldiers lined the beach, ready to help the swimmer, and soon a lifeline was thrown out. To which the man clung for dear life. He was ashore. As rifles were pointed at him he lifted his arms to surrender, and then fell back in a heap on the cold, bare and hard rocks. Two soldiers assisted him to his feet and in their strong grasp he moved off, with little trace to show for his exhausting swim of at least over two miles. As the prisoner was blindfolded, the watching crowd booed with all its might, whistling and booing, and calling upon the soldiers to hand the prisoner over to them. When Maltese anger is once roused it is not easily cooled, and only at bayonet point did the people desist. The soldiers (Lancashire Fusiliers) laid the prisoner on a stretcher and carried him into the fort at Ghar-id-Dud (Sliema)."[24]

It was the turn of the 126 Squadron pilots to be on duty next day (**2 April**), four Spitfires being scrambled between 0930 and 0940, together with two Hurricanes. Flt Lt Johnston, the Spitfire leader, was unable to start his aircraft and was delayed taking off while he transferred to another. As he caught up with his section, which was led by Plt Off McLeod, Bf109s came flashing down on them and Johnston saw one Spitfire go down in flames. He managed to evade the attackers and, now alone, saw many Ju88s:

"Flew towards the barrage, slightly downhill, weaving gently and keeping a look-out behind and above all the time; picked out some 88s among the bursts, they were well above cloud and must have been bombing through it. Thought at first they were going out westward, away from me, until the first one had almost passed; even then it did not occur to me until afterwards that I'd missed a chance of delivering head-on attacks on the whole bunch of them. Instead I did a stall-turn and dived after the nearest one. Opened fire from astern and above, with machine-guns at 300 yards; closed to 100 yards, firing short, savage bursts until my cannon ammunition was exhausted. At first I had seen no results, but later there had been a large flash and an impression of smoke from his starboard motor; noticed no return fire. Pulled up out of range, and then dropped a wing to have a look; was almost directly above him and expected to see some kind of damage, but there was nothing, no fire, no smoke, no glycol, only noticed that his props were turning very slowly, but this might have been bravado, not injury. Didn't approve in theory of the attack I'd made, firing everything into his armour, but I'd known I shouldn't be left alone long enough to attempt anything artistic.

"No time for disappointment, immediately found myself attacked by a 109. Avoided him, but as I did so, my scarf, which had been working looser and looser ever since I changed machines on the ground, came completely undone and almost flew out of the cockpit; grabbed it in time and began to wedge it under my seat. As soon as it was firmly stowed I looked back behind me, and sure enough there was a 109 sitting on my tail, firing. As I evaded him another flew across in front of me and began a left-hand climbing turn, offering a lovely shot. I'd just pushed my bead out in front of him, when I saw something in the corner of my right eye; still don't know whether it was a burst of flak or a 109, but I wasn't taking any more chances and half-rolled down to cloud-cover."

Two of the four Spitfires failed to return. The American McLeod had been hit and slightly wounded, with shrapnel wounds to his left arm and leg; despite weighing a hefty 16-stone, he succeeded in rapidly evacuating AB335/GN-F east of Kalafrana when it started to burn:

"Four of us went up to meet 24 Messerschmitts escorting bombers on a daylight attack. I thought I was all right until I saw stuff flying around me like a horizontal hailstorm. Then I knew I was in for it. I said to myself, 'So this is how it feels to die.' My Spitfire was shot up so badly that the right aileron was sticking up vertically, and the elevators were disabled. The only thing to do was to hold the plane in a 200mph glide. I was at 21,000 feet when the attack started. I saw the machine being torn apart as Jerry after Jerry attacked. I kept looking over my right shoulder. I'd see two of them coming at me. Then I'd skid some and they would miss. Then I'd skid again. I felt something burn my left arm and leg, and saw blood. But it didn't hurt. I skidded again. That was all I could do. The radio was shot out from in front of me. I couldn't talk to anyone, so I decided to get out of there."

McLeod baled out at between 500 to 800 feet. When the parachute snapped open, the straps struck his chin so hard that his thyroid cartilage was fractured. He came down in the sea just off the coast. Having gained the comparative safety of his dinghy, he felt inclined to abandon this when a Messerschmitt pilot persisted in 'buzzing' him, but was soon picked up four miles east of Delimara Point by *HSL128*. Despite his broken neck and the cannon shell fragments in his left arm and leg, McLeod was back flying again within two months. However, Plt Off Winston McCarthy (BP844), who had also been shot down in flames – the Spitfire Johnston had seen going down – was presumed killed. It seems that the Spitfires had fallen to Hptm Wolf-Dietrich Wilcke of Stab III/JG53 (his 35th victory), Ltn Joachim Louis of Stab I/JG53 (4th), and/or Oblt Gerhard Michalski of 4 Staffel (29th), who each claimed one during this sortie. Flt Lt Johnston later reflected:

"Went out to look at my machine, feeling terribly tired and dispirited. The fuselage was smothered in oil and I counted more than 20 holes, some made by machine-guns and some by cannon. An oil pipe in the port wing root had been severed by a slug that came in from astern; that was probably the work of the 109, which had jumped me when I was fumbling with the scarf. A cannon shell had passed horizontally through the fuselage from port to starboard five feet behind my seat, and two others had hit the rudder and starboard elevator; these three were beam shots and were probably inflicted in the first attack. I was glad to see that the shot, which damaged the oil system was the only one to enter from astern: at any rate I hadn't made it easier for them. Don't like the way the number of hits I receive is increasing. The first time it was two strikes, the next time three, then five, now 20 something – there's no future in it!"

McLeod was transported to hospital where he was visited by his friend Jimmie Peck and others, as Johnston noted:

"Mac is found to have pulled a cartilage in his throat and has been grounded. Jimmie of course insists that this is not the result of having to bale out, but of inability to stop talking about it afterwards; in any case he for one can't see what Mac is so proud about – if he'd been bloody careless and got himself shot down in a 25,000 dollar ship he wouldn't go bragging all over the place about it!"

Twenty-six Ju87s and 29 Ju88s were back at 1625, bombing Grand Harbour, Hal Far and Luqa, where an unserviceable Wellington was burnt out. At Kalafrana a hangar and a repair shop were hit and badly damaged, an Albacore under repair being destroyed and another damaged. Six of the escorting Bf109s strafed the schooner *Anna Dacoutros* on her way to Gozo and she sank. Seven 185 Squadron Hurricanes and four Spitfires were scrambled. The Spitfire leader, Sqn Ldr Gracie, led his trio after a formation of Ju88s, one of which he claimed probably destroyed. Plt Off Graves similarly claimed the probable destruction of a second, while Flt Lt Barton damaged a third. Ju87s were engaged by the Hurricanes but there was only time for a brief clash before the escort came down. Meanwhile, at Takali airfield, Sgts Tim Goldsmith and Dusty Miller were waiting for a lull between raids to ferry four Spitfires over to Luqa, the Australian later writing:

> "I cautiously rang the controller to see if the coast was clear before taking off. Everything was OK and a few minutes later we had landed at Luqa and dispersed our machines. A car picked us up and drove us with our chutes back to Takali for the remaining two machines. Again I rang the controller and was told to make it snappy and keep low. He rang off before I could get any further particulars. Once more we raced across without wasting time. I landed second (in AB340), and was just turning off the main runway when I saw those nasty grey streamers sizzling across my starboard wing and immediately afterwards a series of flashing explosions on the ground ten yards away. I twisted my neck around just as a 109 flew over not 20 feet above me. I opened the throttles, and ignoring the taxiway, taxied across the rough stuff with my tail up, till I reached the dispersal bay. Dusty raced across from the next bay, laughing his silly head off, but I was unable to see any humour in the situation for quite some time!"

A Spitfire was claimed shot down during this action by Hptm Walter Spies of Stab II/JG53, his third victory. Some of the off-duty pilots of 249 Squadron made the most of their brief respite, including Plt Off Nash:

> "Went to Valetta with Norm Lee this afternoon. Sent three cables. Usual orgy. Pretty drunk. Came back this evening driving a gharry!"

That evening Sqn Ldr Gracie departed Malta aboard a Hudson. His destination was London where he was to plead Malta's case for more Spitfires. Lord Gort, the Governor-General, had ordered Gracie to carry out this mission on his behalf, and Gracie was obviously chosen for his no-nonsense attitude to most matters. Flt Lt Lucas wrote:

> "Jumbo Gracie was the man for the job, a blunt and thick-skinned officer, whose methods bordered on the ruthless, but whose resource and ability were never in question. I was personally in no doubt that Jumbo, with his tenacity and pungent views was the man to bear the harsh tidings. He had the courage to do it. If things were bad this determined character could be relied upon to make them sound a damned sight worse. If there were sensitive toes to tread on, Gracie's heavy foot would find the sorest spot. He would have no compunction whatever about employing any subterfuge designed to increase the impact of his message. If a senior officer's door was shut, he would put his stocky, medium-sized frame against it and give it a shove. For one who had been a serving officer in peacetime, he was surprisingly insensitive to protocol. In a phrase, Gracie was now 'The Man for the Hour.'"

Good Friday (**3 April**) of Easter weekend found the island with few serviceable fighters available. Three major raids were suffered. In the first a Blenheim and a Beaufighter, both under repair at Takali, were damaged, as was a petrol bowser; AA guns claimed one Ju88 shot down and one damaged. At midday a Hurricane was destroyed at Hal Far, and the officers' quarters damaged; AA claimed damage to another Ju88. Four hours later Spitfire AB418 was destroyed at Takali and AB419 and AB420 badly damaged and at Hal Far another Albacore was damaged and two soldiers killed. Spitfires of 249 were required to scramble after one raid, Sgt Slim Yarra engaging a Ju88 without tangible success. During this sortie Obfw Rudolf Ehrenberger of 6/JG53 claimed his 21st victory, another Spitfire.

Due to the surplus number of Spitfire pilots over actual Spitfires available, several transfers were made at this time. Sgt Yarra found himself posted to 185 Squadron. Also joining the Hurricane force was 126 Squadron's Canadian Flt Sgt Dodd, who was considered to be too inexperienced on Spitfires to be thrown into the battle. At the same time Plt Off Tex Putnam and Sgt Goldsmith were posted from 185 Squadron to 126 Squadron, due to their earlier Spitfire experience in the UK.

For more than three months Malta had been almost entirely a Luftwaffe reserve by day, but this situation was about to change. At sunset, 4°Stormo CT began returning to Sicily, where it had been based the previous November and December, 10°Gruppo flying into Castelvetrano from Rome/Ciampino with 26 new MC202s, led by Cap Franco Lucchini, Italy's top fighter ace who was credited with 14 victories including one shared. It was followed shortly by the similarly equipped 9°Gruppo. In preparation for the latest assault on Malta, the Aeronautica della Sicilia could now call upon a quite substantial force.

On **4 April**, Ju87s and Ju88s targeted a damaged cruiser in dock in Grand Harbour, but she suffered only minor damage. An evening raid by 60 Ju88s was intercepted by four Spitfires and six Hurricanes, Flt Lt Macqueen leading a stern quarter attack on one of the bombers, seeing its starboard engine catch fire. He then shot at the port engine and the bomber turned on its back and dived vertically. Another bomber was claimed damaged by Plt Off Sergeant (AB500), who reported an apparent dead rear gunner following his attack, with the aircraft last seen rolling onto its back; however, this may have been the aircraft under attack by his leader, a Ju88 of 5/KG77 belly-landing at Comiso on return, having been badly damaged by fighters. A third bomber was claimed damaged by Flg Off Daddo-Langlois, whose own aircraft (GN-U) sustained one bullet strike from the rear gunner; he wrote:

> "Four Spits jump 88s. Mac gets one, Bob and I damage one each. Bullet in filter from rear gunner. Rather hasty landing. The aerodrome was bombed incessantly, we landed among bomb holes, with 109s in circuit. But no one shot up in the circuit. Mac has a near one. Bob lands with one elevator after being beaten up out to sea. Norman shot up, flaps down full of holes, attacked by 109s."

During one of the day's raids, two Bf109 fighter-bombers of 10(Jabo)/JG53 crashed into the sea, Uffz Heinrich Bross (White 9) and Obfw Günther Fronhöfer (White 2) being lost. It was presumed that they had collided.

When 40 Ju88s – including aircraft from KGr806 – and 15 Ju87s of III/StG3 attacked under a large fighter escort during the early afternoon of **5 April**, four Spitfires flown by 126 Squadron pilots, and four Hurricanes were scrambled. Plt Off John Bisley, an Australian, claimed a Ju87 and a Ju88 as probably destroyed, but both were later upgraded to confirmed victories, presumably as a result of the Y Service. Bisley's report of the action read:

> "I was east of Grand Harbour and followed a Ju88 line astern. I got within 300 yards about three miles out to sea and was not gaining, so I gave a one-second burst with cannons and observed no results. Turned port back to Grand Harbour at 6,000 feet and saw about ten Ju88s in the flak, line astern, and as they came out I went in to attack the nearest from beam, turning to quarter and astern, closing to about 150 yards; rear

gunner did not return fire. I broke to port and noticed black smoke from port engine. I did not follow because about six 109s above. I returned in circles to Grand Harbour and asked control if there were any more bombers coming in, and they told me there were some Ju87s coming in. I saw two Ju87s, which had pulled out of their dives, on my port at same altitude. I turned towards the nearest at 3,000 feet and attacked from quarter to astern. Rear gunner fired but ceased after my first burst. I closed to about 50 yards, firing the whole time, and set his engine on fire. He dived to starboard with smoke coming from underneath his engine. I then broke to port and saw a large number of 109s at 3,000-4,000 feet, about five miles out to sea, above me. I made for sea level and two 109s dived and attacked me. Had a burst in cockpit, which struck right leg (shrapnel wounds to right leg and hand). Shook off 109s after crossing the coast and came in and landed wheels up at Takali, with cockpit full of smoke."

There is little doubt that the Ju87 was an aircraft of 9/StG3, which crashed in the sea about five miles north of Malta. The pilot baled out and was later rescued, but the gunner (Fw Christoph Würzer) was lost. Meanwhile, Flt Lt Johnston, the Spitfire leader, had sighted what he believed were four Bf109s, but which on investigation turned out to be the four Hurricanes. He then saw Messerschmitts below:

"As I was waiting for suitable target, I looked up and saw eight or ten 109s in ragged line astern, flying north; they didn't seem to notice me, thank goodness. Next moment spotted an 88 pulling out of its dive and heading north-east; chased it flat-out and at first seemed to make no impression whatever; remembered I'd been climbing, he diving, so hung on and gradually the range began to close. It had almost done so when I saw two 109s of the protective cordon heading towards me; knew it was useless to go on, since they had clearly spotted me, therefore turned towards them and both went past without firing. But another, which I hadn't seen at all, came diving out of the sun at me almost head-on; as I saw him open fire I pushed the stick forward hard and saw a torrent of tracer fly over my head. Imagine the Huns must have tracers at every tenth round; as the aircraft flies over the old tracers you can watch new ones appearing in their place – they don't form or grow, they simply appear. Often the new ones seem to be slightly out of line with the old – probably because an aircraft at high speed is an unstable firing platform – and are more sharply defined in colour and outline. Sometimes seeing an aircraft open fire gives the impression that it has suddenly shot its tentacles out at you, or that it has grown some curious light-blue antennae since last you looked; occasionally the eye is quick enough to follow the making of a trace, and then it may seem a little frightening because of its speed, but normally they are not sinister for what they appear, but what they are.

"Having avoided this 109, I saw a Stuka climbing out of the barrage towards me; headed for him and prepared to attack, when more 109s appeared from nowhere and rode me off; didn't see any of them firing, but I was forced to lose height to evade them, and lost the Stuka, too. Flew in over Grand Harbour; everything seemed to have disappeared, until I picked out a lone 88 going north; began to chase him, but he had altitude and I realised that I shouldn't catch him this side of Sicily, so gave it up. For first time I'd failed to fire at a bomber. Reached Takali and entered the circuit warily. Took a good look round before dropping my wheels and noticed two aircraft above and behind me. I'd just decided they were Hurricanes when I noticed red tracer flying all round them; I whipped round so fast I almost spun and they both passed overhead; heard afterwards they were 109s and had fired a quick, wild burst at me. That was the second time I'd almost been jumped on the circuit; still find it difficult to be as vigilant there as one should be.

"Landed and found that both Tex [Putnam] and Australia [Bisley] had got back safely, though Australia had been shot up and had had to land with his wheels up; he had splinter wounds and had been taken off to hospital. He had shot down a Stuka and claimed an 88 probably destroyed as well; this was confirmed later. Tex had secured an 88 destroyed and I claimed my 109, after hearing that a single parachute had appeared some miles off shore, as a probable; moreover for the first time from a big raid I'd brought my machine back unscathed."

The single parachute observed was almost certainly that of the pilot of the Stuka shot down by Bisley. One Ju88, M7+JL of 3/KGr806, crash-landed one mile west of Catania on return, Uffz Hugo Paul and two of his crew sustaining injuries, but they reported having been hit by AA fire. Plt Off Nash noted in his diary:

"If this goes on much longer Valetta will be nothing but a shambles. Raids seem to consist of 109s sweeping first, then wave number one of about 20-30 Ju88s, then another wave about the same. Sometimes varied by Ju87s. I watched them from the bastions today. 109s embarrassed the boys landing this afternoon. The weather is getting pretty hot, too!"

There was only one major raid – unopposed by fighters – on Easter Monday, **6 April**. At least 20 Ju87s and up to 55 Ju88s attacked Grand Harbour, the dockyard and the airfields. Luqa came under heavy attack and five Hurricanes and two Spitfires (AB338 and AB454) were damaged beyond repair. 126 Squadron recorded that nearly all its former Hurricane pilots had now departed, including those transferred from 249 earlier, although Flg Off Ron West (who had previously flown Spitfires) now joined 249. However, a flight of nine Hurricanes arrived from Gambut to help bolster the defences, although the need was for more Spitfires not Hurricanes.

One Spitfire airborne during the day was AB300 of 69 Squadron flown by Plt Off Coldbeck, who had been briefed to carry out a reconnaissance over Lampedusa. On his return, he took the defences at Luqa by surprise:

"While in the vicinity of Lampedusa, there was heavy AA fire each time I approached the island but fortunately, no damage was done to my aircraft so I continued with my surveillance. I had calculated my arrival back at Malta to be at dusk and as it happened, it coincided with the tail end of an Axis bombing raid with a lot of fighter activity both Axis and our own. My approach to Luqa was signalled by red tracer coming up and, fortunately, past me in the failing light. I had checked my IFF was switched on, so my only recourse was to call up fighter control on the VHF and tell them I was being fired on by our own guns and request them to inform the gunners. This was immediately followed by a fighter Spitfire making a pass at me – obviously taking his cue from the Bofors firing at me. I turned into him, with more tracer passing me from behind until I spoke to him on the VHF channel which fortunately he was apparently tuned to and using. After this encounter, I landed and handed my aircraft over to the groundcrew and made my report to Intelligence and the Met Office".

He later added:

"The gunnery officer in charge of the Bofors gun firing at me, came to the mess afterwards and declared to me he was just about to switch his gun to automatic before my complaint on the radio. 'We'd have got you if we'd done that!' he said matter of factly. I didn't hear from the Spitfire pilot."

Of this period of heavy air attack, LAC Metcalf at Takali confided to his diary:

"This Easter has been one that I'll remember (should I be one of the lucky ones to get away with it!). From dawn to dusk wave after wave of 88s, 87s and other gash kites to make weight have bombed and better bombed. During one lull I bobbed my head above the slit trench and suddenly spotted a fresh wave of 88s coming in over St Paul's. I counted 27, but when the leader put his nose down and started a power-dive straight for my slit trench – what a sensation – I could neither speak nor move! Luckily he came a few feet too low and the bombs went over the top of the trench. And still they come, in all their might. God in Heaven alone knows what's going to happen next or where this is all going to end. It's a pity we haven't some fighter protection, but what we do have, have done wonderful work and each pilot deserves a VC at least. To send the last few up alone would be murder in the first degree. The ack-ack boys too are great and I hold my hand out to each of them."

Despite the ferocity of the continuous and seemingly never ending air raids, many of those on the receiving end managed to keep their sense of humour – perhaps indicative of the British soldier under fire. Although not the originator[25], Flt Lt Connell penned an irreverent but topical doggerel in his logbook, entitled 'Luftwaffe Hymn for Easter':

> This Holy Thursday let us snooker
> All the bloody Spits at Luqa;
> Fill the air with every Stuka!
> Hallelujah!
>
> Hail Good Friday! Hal Far's turn
> Watch the bloody Swordfish burn
> Won't the buggers ever learn?
> Hallelujah!
>
> Easter Saturday, that's damn fine
> Make Takali toe the line.
> Here's a rocket, here's a mine!
> Hallelujah!
>
> Christ the Lord is risen today!
> Bomb the harbour, bomb the bay
> Bomb the bloody place all day!
> Hallelujah!
>
> Easter Monday, let 'em rip
> God we'll give those boys the pip
> And tear them off a Safi strip!
> Hallelujah!

Raids on **7 April** found the fighters grounded again. The first raid concentrated on Grand Harbour and the airfields. At Kalafrana an ASR Swordfish floatplane and a Walrus amphibian were damaged, while a Spitfire (AB262/GN-B) under repair at Takali was seriously damaged. At the end of the day Flt Lt Johnston, who had been in Valetta with Mike Graves during the raids, wrote in his journal:

"The first of the 88s came in from the south-east and seemed to be very high. Mike and I went down to the shelter, which must have been 35 feet deep, and stood at the foot of the steps. We could hear the guns firing and then without any warning there was a tremendous bang, followed by darkness; thought at first that the mouth of the shelter had been hit, because the blast-wave had been very heavy, but two soldiers came stumbling down the steps, smothered in white dust and badly shaken, said it had caught them outside and bowled them over. Was impressed with the way the Maltese accepted the bombing: the older people all appeared quite phlegmatic and talked of their chores and shopping, the small boys seemed to find it exciting and rather enjoyable, only a girl opposite us began to cry when the raid was at its height. We smiled reassuringly and said something trivial which seemed to comfort her; I suppose she thought that as we were in uniform we knew.

"The all clear sounded at about 7pm. We found the bomb which had shaken us so much had fallen fully 80 yards away in front of the Public Library, making an immense crater; forgot to notice how Queen Victoria had taken it, must remember to look next time. Strada Reale was a shambles; there seemed to be almost as much new damage as old from all the previous raids, and it was clear that this time the town, not the docks, had been the objective. Every few yards there were obstructions where houses had collapsed across the street. The Opera House had received a direct hit and half of it had been demolished – no great loss, perhaps, architecturally; the Castile had been damaged and outside the city hardly a bus seemed to have escaped. The rock shelters are so effective that we only saw a single stretcher-case; the ARP people were behaving extremely well, but some of the other civilians seemed rattled. The local stone is so soft that houses collapse easily; even when the walls stand, the floors commonly fall through; mercifully there is little wood in their construction and they never seem to burn.

"Floriana and Hamrun were both heavily damaged. Felt very gloomy, both the last raids had obviously been directed at civilian morale; there had been rumours that Berlin had announced that since Malta was impregnable to invasion by sea or air, their only remaining course was to bomb us out, and it began to appear that the new policy had started. With so few aircraft, I couldn't see what we could do to stop it; the only possible answer as things were now would be the threat of reprisals on, say, Cologne. Felt very strongly that we ought to defend our outposts better. Admittedly the Huns still have the initiative and move on interior lines, and I suppose this makes all the difference in the world. Told myself I ought to be angry or defiant, but found myself numb and depressed: both these raids had been 150-plus, what could we do against such numbers with four Spits and a couple of Hurricanes? Both glad to get away from Valetta; had begun to feel we were witnessing the beginning of a Warsaw or Rotterdam."

An airman[26] who happened to find himself present during the raid noted:

"I was at Kalafrana reporting sick when twenty-two 87s dive-bombed us. That was the first time Kalafrana had been heavily bombed and I had to be there. Today I had a day off and had a wizard sleep but woke up to hear Kalafrana's overhead siren. Went to the entrance of shelter and saw thirty-one 87s dive-bombing Kalafrana, then eighteen 88s bombing Sliema. After that about fifty 109s bombed and strafed Hal Far and then circled the island at about 2,000 feet. Talk about air supremacy!"

A few days later, back at Hal Far, the same airman wrote:

"Several raids last night but stayed in bed all the time. Brassed off with bombs and shelters. This morning at 12.00 noon, 75 bombers and 109s dive-bombed Grand Harbour, Luqa and Hal Far. They hit one Hurricane here at Hal Far and it burned out."

At the end of the following day he wrote:

"After several raids last night, the warning went this morning at 0630. All day long 88s have been bombing us at Hal Far and 87s dive-bombing Grand Harbour. The All Clear went at 2000, that's a 13$^1/_2$-hour raid, the record for Malta. The last record was 11 hours 50 minutes. I can feel my nerves gradually going now and I hope I get off the island before they completely go. A lot of our blokes are in hospital with their nerves completely gone."

It was not long before sickness overtook him:

"I went sick yesterday morning with sandfly [fever] and all last night I lay in bed shivering and sweating at the same time. My mate has got a dose of Malta Dog [a severe form of diarrhoea] that's about 20 times worse than dysentery. On average one visits the lavatory about 50 times a day for six days and nights. After that you are a complete physical wreck."

Plt Off Nash noted in his diary:

"Went to St Paul's Bay with Don McLeod. Managed to wrangle the last two beds. Eat at Harbour Bar, asparagus omelettes! The blitz still continues with unabated savagery. Saw 109s flying at 0 feet beating up boats and homes. We can do absolutely nothing about it. All because of the dumb foolishness of people at home who will not send us aircraft. It passes human understanding."

One of 249's chief sufferers at this time of Malta Dog was Plt Off Jeff West, who went down with a bout every ten days or so, but was ever keen to fly as soon as he was feeling better. According to Flt Lt Lucas, the well-rehearsed dialogue went something like:

Sqn Ldr Grant: "And how are you today, Jeff?" Plt Off West: "Better sir, thank you. I could do a trip of 40 minutes, no more." Sqn Ldr Grant: "But Jeff, can you fart yet without danger? That's always the test." Plt Off West: "Not yet sir, but I don't want to." Sqn Ldr Grant: "Right then, you're still stood down."

Apparently Plt Off West was feeling somewhat better by **8 April**, since he was one of a trio of pilots ordered off at 1330 on the approach of another raid. Following desperate efforts by groundcrew, a handful of Spitfires had been made serviceable overnight and three of these joined seven Hurricanes to intercept six Ju88s at 14,000 feet over Kalafrana. West attacked one bomber head-on and saw strikes on the cockpit. He then turned on the tail of a Messerschmitt and closed, firing all his ammunition and causing black smoke to appear; this may have been a 6/JG53 aircraft (7460) flown by Ltn Hans-Jürgen von Möller, which crashed into the sea off Valetta; Möller was picked up later by an ASR craft from Sicily, when he reported that he believed he had been hit by AA fire.

Meanwhile, Flt Lt Heppell attacked another bomber, seeing strikes on wings and fuselage, then fired at a second, hitting the cockpit, fuselage and starboard engine, which gave off smoke. He fired a further six-seconds burst from astern and then broke away due to the attentions of another. A splash was seen in the sea, convincing Heppell that his victim had gone in. A Hurricane pilot also claimed a Ju88 in similar circumstances and it would seem that both had attacked an aircraft of KüFlGr606, which ditched after having been hit by fighters, the crew later also being picked up by an Axis ASR aircraft. The third member of the trio, Plt Off Dennis Kelly, claimed damage to yet another bomber.

A larger raid developed at 1500, no fewer than 57 Ju88s and 26 Ju87s being reported, together with many fighters. Grand Harbour and Luqa were apparently the main targets. Flt Lt Heppell again led off three Spitfires, which were joined by nine Hurricanes. Heppell attacked a bomber over the harbour at 8,000 feet; he wrote later of his experience:

"I recall registering strikes in the wing roots and the tail unit of the 88... and the next thing I remember was falling head first towards the harbour *sans* aircraft. When my parachute opened it seemed that I was on some sky-hook, and not apparently losing height, with bombs falling past, ack-ack exploding and a continuous rattle of machine-guns all around. I crashed into a bomb hole, still conscious but unable to move. I was given a shot of morphia by a MO and taken to Mtarfa hospital. Shortly afterwards I was on the operating table about to have the gashes in my head and legs sewn up."

Although initially it was believed that Heppell's aircraft (AB346/GN-K) had hit an 'aerial mine', it was established later that it had received a direct hit from an AA shell and that he had been blown out of the aircraft, the remains of which fell near Sliema. Meanwhile, the bomber attacked by Heppell – possibly an aircraft of 6/KG77 that crash-landed at Comiso on return – was probably the same as that engaged by Flg Off Ron West and a pilot of 185 Squadron. The explosion of Heppell's aircraft was probably what caused Oblt Ernst Kläger to submit a claim for a Spitfire shot down at 1515 for his 12th victory.

With the approach of dusk, three of 249's Spitfires were again scrambled, this time after an ASR Do24N of 6 Seenotstaffel, which was operating offshore under a screen of Messerschmitts, obviously searching for survivors of missing aircraft. The flyingboat KK+UQ (0012) was seen taxiing on the water with six Bf109s overhead and six Ju88s in the general area, Flg Off Ron West at once diving to attack the Dornier. Strikes were seen all along the fuselage and the rescue craft caught fire. The crew escaped unhurt and were themselves later rescued. Among those watching the action was Flt Lt Johnston:

"At dusk three Spits took off to attack the Huns just offshore; they found a big Dornier flyingboat on the water with an escort of two 88s and about a dozen 109s and waded straight into them. Ron West saw the Dornier had ordinary camouflage and black, not red, crosses; it rather foolishly opened fire on him with a cannon, so he attacked it with a short burst and it at once exploded. From the roof of the mess we could see it burning furiously on the sea."

Plt Off Kelly meanwhile had attacked one of the Ju88s from quarter astern, claiming strikes on the port engine and cabin, before following West down to attack the flyingboat. As West pulled up from his attack, he was bounced by some of the escorting fighters, but succeeded in getting a deflection shot along the fuselage of one as it overshot. A patrolling Hurricane pilot apparently reported that he had seen both the Messerschmitt fired at by West and the bomber attacked by Kelly, hit the water; consequently both were credited as having been shot down. In his diary Plt Off Nash wrote:

"Three Spits and four Hurricanes up. By 3 o'clock three 88s and one 109 confirmed. At about 6 o'clock the Spits went out and shot down a Dornier rescue aircraft, one 88 and one 109. Many people yelling about a bad show shooting down the Dornier. By God, if they want total war then give it to them."

The famous Mosta Church was damaged by bombs at 1640 on **9 April**, during a raid by Ju88s, one bomb penetrating the nine-feet thick dome before bouncing twice off the interior wall, but it failed to explode. It then skidded along the floor of the nave and came to a standstill. There were some three hundred of the congregation present, although most had scattered to the side chapels and corridors for shelter as the bombs began falling, and none was hurt, even by flying debris. LAC Jim Somerville of 249 Squadron and two or three soldiers entered the church and proceeded to roll the bomb outside, from where it was taken away on an army pick-up truck. Seconds later Somerville was wounded in the leg by shrapnel from another bomb, which exploded nearby. Luqa village was also badly hit, as a contemporary police report reveals:

"Several HE bombs exploded on Luqa village demolishing several houses. An entrance to a public shelter at St Joseph Street was blocked, but the persons taking cover thereat went out through another exit. One male dead, one female dead (buried under debris), one female seriously injured (admitted to hospital). Another public shelter in Pope Innocent Street had one of its entrances blocked [in all 23 people were killed, only nine were rescued alive]. The parish church was extensively damaged. Two bakeries, one in Carmel Street and the other in St George's Street were also demolished."

Over 60 Ju88s and a dozen Ju87s featured in this raid, in addition to two Bf109 Jabo of 10/JG53 and a formidable escort from III/JG53. One of the Messerschmitt fighter-bombers fell to AA gunners, who also claimed a Ju88 and two Ju87s. To combat this heavy raid two Spitfires, one flown by Flt Lt Barton, and ten Hurricanes were scrambled. For the loss of one Hurricane, claims were submitted for nine Ju88s damaged by the returning pilots including two by Barton.

The first raid on **10 April** came at 1245 and met no defenders. The bombers returned in greater strength at 1645, an estimated 65 Ju88s and 20 Ju87s attacking Grand Harbour, Hal Far and Takali. Four Spitfires flown by 249 pilots scrambled to join two more Spitfires from 126 Squadron and ten Hurricanes, meeting ten Ju88s of III/KG77, one of which Flt Lt Macqueen and Flg Off Lee jointly claimed shot down; two of the crew appeared to bale out, but in fact, the gun position had been blown off the cabin of 3Z+HS, this and the body of the gunner, Uffz Paul Boger, falling on Takali airfield. The 8 Staffel machine was also claimed by AA gunners. Of the incident, LAC Metcalf wrote:

"The rear gunner of an 88 was shot out of his kite complete with turret and landed roughly 50 yards from our trench. He wasn't greatly disfigured although his neck was broken."

Flt Lt Johnston was among the many who had witnessed the raid:

"Mac and Geoff [sic] West agreed that the first one to run for a shelter should buy the other a beer, but when a wave of 88s, which no one had noticed in the general excitement, appeared almost overhead they cancelled the bet by mutual agreement and only one man reached the shelter before Mac. We had watched him before, he was a priest. At the first sign of imminent danger he would not stampede; while the others drew ahead he would pause to cram his beaver over his eyebrows, pick up his skirts from ankle to hip and then, setting off at an astonishing pace with a high-kneed action, he would outstrip the whole field and always win. Mac called him the midnight express, and acknowledged his mastery. These 88s bombed Takali; one of them was hit and three men appeared to bale out, though only one chute opened. Learnt later that it was two men and part of the aircraft; the rear gunner and most of his gun-position had been blown off the rest of the machine. Johnny Plagis, who inspected the body, said he wasn't wearing a chute or harness. The 88 crashed farther on; it was at first attributed to the ack-ack, but later claimed by Norman, who appeared that night wearing the dead gunner's cap."

Meanwhile, Flg Off Buchanan dived out of the sun on a Messerschmitt over St Paul's Bay as it was pulling up after firing at a Hurricane. He fired from long range and, to his surprise, the aircraft burst into flames and the pilot baled out; he was credited with its destruction, although a pilot of 185 Squadron claimed a Bf109 in similar circumstances and was also credited with a victory. Only one Messerschmitt was lost, the pilot none other than III/JG53's leading *Experte*, Ltn Hermann Neuhoff in Yellow 1 (7375), who now became a prisoner. Only the previous evening he had been promoted to lead 6 Staffel. Neuhoff subsequently asked to meet his victor, and was introduced to Buchanan. However, the returning pilots of JG53 believed that Neuhoff had been shot down accidentally by Ltn Werner Schöw, a pilot of 1 Staffel, who had apparently admitted firing at a Messerschmitt in error during the heat of the battle. Neuhoff told his captors:

> "I sighted a Hurricane below and dived to attack, leaving my No.2 to protect my rear. This, however, he failed to do and, when diving on to the Hurricane, I was attacked by a Spitfire from behind."

Retrospectively, he revealed:

> "I was flying with my *Schwarm* over Malta. Suddenly, my second *Rotte* [pair] disappeared. Instead, three Spitfires appeared. I shot at one aircraft as it flew in front of me. At the same time, I was hit. Leutnant Schöw reported his first victory – unfortunately it was me! He had mistaken me for a Hurricane. I stayed in my aircraft because I knew that if I came down in the drink I would be fished out again. However, when the fire spread I jettisoned the cockpit hood. Shortly afterwards the 109 exploded. It was lucky for me that I had released my harness and got rid of the cockpit hood. I ejected from the aircraft at 2,500 metres altitude and deployed my parachute at about 400 metres and belly-landed [*sic*] near Luqa."[27]

Neuhoff's aircraft crashed between Luqa and Safi airstrips. Other claims were submitted by Flg Off Lee for a Ju88 probably destroyed and one damaged, and by Plt Off Nash (GN-X) for a Ju87 probable, who later recorded:

> "On this afternoon just managed to get four Spits on the line with 12 Hurricanes. Terrific balbo. Scramble at twenty to six and had 120-plus on own hands. More 109s than I have ever seen before in one mass. They bombed Grand Harbour, Takali and Hal Far. The Hurricanes had a terrible time there, being shot up the whole time on the circuit. Buchanan led the Spits. He got a 109 when we were first bounced. I came down to the deck and Lee joined up. We went to Grand Harbour and I got an 87 with smoke pouring out of it. Was then well and truly bounced by six 109s. Managed to get a damaged when they thinned out a little. Landed while 109s were shooting the joint up. Not sorry to get down again today! Frantic time shoving the kites into bays with the help of two very game airmen who were above ground. Hesselyn landed early with oil over windscreen. Lee claims an 88, which the AA also claim. Hurricanes lost three kites and one pilot missing. Both Buchanan and Hesselyn's kites hit by shrapnel just as they got out on landing."

Nash's attack on the Ju87 would seem to have been successful, for one Ju87 of 8/StG3 crashed into the sea north of Valetta after being attacked by a fighter, both Uffz Gerhard Bode and Gfr Josef Seidl, the gunner, being wounded although both were later rescued. Flt Sgt Paddy Schade was flying one of the two 126 Squadron Spitfires – his first operational flight over Malta – and noted in his logbook:

> "First flip in three months! Got mixed up with about 15 Me109s. Was really scared!"

In his combat report he added:

> "Two Spitfires took off at 1655. Patrolled south-west coast of island, climbing up.

Formations of Hurricanes below us. Enemy bombers reported ten miles north. The two Spitfires were at a height of approximately 17,000 to 19,000 feet. Six 109s swept in from St Paul's Bay. Chased these e/a to south-west, but they climbed up and we broke away to port, coming back to the island. We then met some Ju88s coming in from the north. These e/a passed us and we turned to Grand Harbour. I was caught up in some of our own AA so broke away to port, climbing up into the sun. I then received reports that bombers were attacking our drome (Takali). So I did a stall-turn and came down out of the sun. When I got about 400 yards from the leading 88, I opened fire with my cannons for about three seconds, closing up to 200 yards. I saw the 88 going through my line of fire but could not observe any hits as I was, at the same time, being attacked by three 109s. I did some violent weaving – and then shook them off by doing aileron turns down to 1,000 feet. I was attacked by four more 109s after this but their attempt was half-hearted. I circled around for a while then landed. One Ju88 damaged."

One Spitfire was damaged in the action but two Hurricanes were shot down and three more crash-landed. The victorious German pilots from JG53 claimed ten victories including seven Spitfires, two of these being credited to Obfw Rudolf Ehrenberger of 6 Staffel, raising his score to 23; others were claimed by Ltn Joachim Louis Stab I (his fifth), Oblt Friedrich-Karl Müller 1 Staffel (25th), Ltn Jürgen von Möller of 6 Staffel (eighth), Oblt Wilfried Pufahl of 7 Staffel (also his eighth), Fw Alfred Seidl of 8 Staffel (10th).

During the next few days the defending fighters were not able to achieve much against raiders that targeted the airfields. At Takali on **11 April**, two Spitfires (probably including AB451/GN-T) and a Hurricane were damaged on the ground, the other two airfields suffering similar losses to dispersed aircraft; AB300, the PR Spitfire, sustained minor damage to its canopy while at Luqa, but was soon repaired. Of this period, Plt Off Coldbeck remembered:

"Air HQ had ordered PRU Spitfire early take-offs to be an hour before first light for convoy and similar naval location and confirmation sorties. Because our aircraft had no cockpit night flying equipment this entailed rigging up torches with rubber bands to odd fittings in the cockpit to cope with the night flying aspect of pre first light take-off and early course setting. It was also a good idea to take the torch for the last light sortie as well, because of the possibility of being caught out by darkness.

"On the way across the airfield [in darkness], one would sometimes be confronted by an airman with a rifle who would demand: 'Halt, and come forward to be recognised, Sir!' Obviously I was a familiar figure. These incidents usually used to pass off quickly, except for one night when the station commander, inexplicably, used his distinctive but on this night somewhat slurred voice to refer to me by name, to reinforce the sentry's order for me to drop my cycle, which I was wheeling, and to stand with my hands above me in the torchlight. Perhaps he got a kick out of it, but all I could think of was getting some sleep in anticipation of a long flying day beginning at four in the morning."

Next day (**12 April**) Spitfire AB347 and a Hurricane were destroyed at Takali. The island received a visit from Air Marshal Sir Arthur Tedder, AOC Middle East, during the day, and he was at Hal Far when strafing Bf109s II/JG53 put in an appearance. A Hurricane pilot recalled:

"Air Officer Commanding Middle East gave us a pep talk and told us we were doing a magnificent job, but we all wished he would go up in one of our Hurricanes against Messerschmitts that outnumbered us at least ten to one! There was a raid just after the talk and then the 109s started ground strafing. One was firing on its way over the aerodrome when it was hit by ack-ack and it went straight in. There was a terrific explosion and huge sheet of flame. The engine rolled at least two hundred yards away from the wreckage. The pilot was more or less swept up."

The luckless pilot, Gfr Horst Gisy (White 2), was from 4/JG53. Another of the bewhiskered, oil and sweat-stained pilots assembled to meet the AOC laconically recalled:

"When Tedder passed this way we shook him rigid. I thought he was going to get out his wallet and give us ten bob each to buy a new shirt!"

During this period Plt Off Nash and Flg Off Lee took the opportunity to visit some of their colleagues in hospital:

"[Day] off. Two heavy raids on Grand Harbour and Luqa. Fighters stand down. Went up to Mtarfa hospital with Lee to see Heppell. Also saw Bisley and Bloody Kurt [Ltn Kurt Lauinger]. Big raid on Takali while we were there. No Spits serviceable."

Another to visit the wounded, including Ltn Lauinger, was Flt Sgt Brennan:

"I talked for some time with a 109 pilot Norman Macqueen had shot down. His sole interest in life seemed to be to fly a 109 and have plenty of squirts. Indeed, flying was in his blood, and outside flying he had little interest in the war. He told me he did not think it would make much difference who won the war. I asked him what he and his fellow pilots thought of the Spit, and he answered unhesitatingly that it was a very good aircraft. He considered the 109 faster, but admitted it did not have the Spit's manoeuvrability. Then we became engaged in a technical argument on the relative merits of the Spitfire and the 109."

As if the constant threat of death in the air was not of sufficient strain and stress, on the ground the pilots not only had to put up with constant bombing but also a lack of decent food, as Brennan noted:

"Meals appeared at irregular hours, and the quality of the food deteriorated. In the sergeants' mess, which had been one of the best on the island, bully beef appeared more frequently. Often there was no bread. Breakfast in particular was much disorganised. The sirens which heralded the early morning raid generally sent the cooks and waiters scurrying to shelter, and the mess would be deserted when we arrived. Each pilot cooked his own breakfast, scrounging round the kitchen and selecting whatever he could find. Frequently there were no lights, and the radio was silenced. We missed the daily news bulletins of the BBC. The news sheet, printed in English and published daily, sometimes got through to us, but more often arrived several days late. We began to feel almost completely out of touch with events outside Malta. Both cinemas in Rabat closed down.

"Even worse was the plight of the civilian population. The Maltese were in and out of the shelters throughout the day and, although the bombers were not coming over at night, slept in them each evening. Food distribution was erratic, and the problem of cooking acute. Hot meals made an ever less frequent appearance. Casualties, although still light, were mounting. The schools, however, were not closed. I often watched the children being marched to shelter when danger was imminent. They seemed cheerful and unworried, and whenever they spotted a pilot would break ranks and run across to him, crying at the top of their youthful voices, 'Spitfire! Spitfire! Pilot! Pilot!' They seemed to be able to stand up to the nerve-racking strain of the bombing better than the older people. The latter looked tired, nervy."

Only reconnaissance flights bothered the radar operators and controllers at Malta on **13 April**, allowing urgent maintenance and repairs to be carried out on the remaining Spitfires and Hurricanes. Plt Off Nash and Flt Lt Johnston paid another visit to Valetta:

"Today was practically raid free. Amazing phenomenon. It lasted until about 8.30 last night when BR20s bombed Takali, Luqa and Hal Far in the dusk light. Incidentally, Johnston and I went into Valetta this morning. The damage there is frightful. Practically every street is blocked with tons of stone and rubble. Sent two cables. The Hun has evidently wearied of bombing a mere harbour and has vented his spleen on the surrounding district. Of course it's just too bad that civilians happen to live there. In the same way it is unfortunate that fishermen happen to be in the boats they shoot up!!"

The first raid on Malta on the morning of **14 April** was by six Ju88s, which targeted Takali. Immediately thereafter, three Spitfires of 249 took off to provide protection for a returning reconnaissance Maryland of 69 Squadron, but were promptly engaged by Bf109s. Plt Off Kelly claimed one damaged before being shot down himself by Maj Günther von Maltzahn of JG53, for his 62nd victory. Kelly baled out of AB342 from about 800 feet, three miles west of Hal Far, but his parachute failed to open properly and he hit the water very hard, suffering severe bruising. He also became entangled in the shroud lines, and lost his dinghy whilst freeing himself. Two more Spitfires were at once scrambled to search for him, the two Wests (Ron and Jeff) locating him and circling overhead, some two miles offshore. Kelly was seen to be swimming strongly and even found the strength to raise two fingers to his colleagues as they passed low overhead. *HSL128* was despatched to the rescue, covered by a pair of Hurricanes. Coxswain Flt Sgt George Head wrote:

"Two Hurricane pilots warded off Messerschmitt 109s who were attacking the launch whilst proceeding to base at Kalafrana after rescuing a Spitfire pilot, Plt Off Kelly. One can only speculate on Kelly's thoughts – to be attacked and brought down in his plane and then to be attacked in the rescue boat after being pulled out of the sea. He must have wondered whether the Gods were being unkind to him particularly bearing in mind the fact that Plt Off Kelly's parachute failed to open when he baled out of his crashing Spitfire."

Another two Spitfires were off at 1300 to cover the returning Maryland, which was being pursued by two Bf109s. Flt Lt Macqueen and Plt Off Sergeant (AB340) attacked at once; the latter wrote:

"Cover for Maryland. Attacked by two Messerschmitts with three below. A good squirt at one 109 and a quick squirt at another. A 109 went in so Mac and I split the bag – half destroyed, half damaged."

An aircraft of III/JG53 crashed into the sea as a result of this combat, the pilot – believed to have been Uffz Paul Gläser of 7 Staffel – subsequently being rescued by the Axis ASR service. In return, Fw Erich Schmidt of 7 Staffel claimed a Spitfire, raising his score to five. During the day the AA defences submitted claims for two Ju88s, two Ju87s and two Bf109s, although their only confirmed victim was none other than the Kommandeur of II/JG3, Hptm Karl-Heinz Krahl, who was killed when his Messerschmitt crashed into a stone wall north-east of Hal Far.

Adverse weather – heavy cloud and high winds – brought flying over Malta and Sicily for both sides, to a virtual standstill for the next three days. This did not, however, prevent uninterrupted reconnaissance by small groups of Bf109s each day.

Plt Off Nash noted in his diary:

"Thursday, April 16. Weather again very overcast and windy. No raids. Our two serviceable [Spitfires] were today put u/s by bad luck. McNair and Connell were taking them up on test. McNair took off and in doing so, he hit a bomb crater and tore half a leg off and had to belly land it. Connell's plane got so oiled up he had to jettison the hood to see out of it at all!

"Buchanan went to St Patrick's Hospital in Sliema to see the Hun [Ltn Neuhoff] he shot down on the 10th. He is the flight commander of the one [Ltn Lauinger] in Mtarfa, who Macqueen shot down. He says he has 38 victories among them Doug Leggo. Doesn't speak English, but can understand Buchanan's Afrikaans. Says he shot down 22 in Russia, some in Battle of Britain over London and some in Libya. He did not see Buchanan at all [when shot down]. First he knew, his hands were knocked off the controls."

He added:

"Johnny Plagis got the DFC so did Macqueen. Damn good show to both of them. McLeod and Heppell are both getting sick leave and are hoping to get to USA."

The Luftwaffe was back with a vengeance on **18 April**, making raids against the airfields, but no fighters were available to engage the estimated 139 Ju88 and 53 Ju87 sorties. Only the AA gunners were able to continue the fight, claiming one Ju88 and two probables. Nash:

"Today was fine and warm, therefore, of course, Valetta, Hal Far and Luqa heavily bombed, particularly Hal Far. There were three raids today. In the last one, Luqa had the biggest bomb explosion I have ever seen. The smoke climbed straight up to 2,000 feet or more. An enormous bang. The official cameraman was on the mess room with us and got it all. No fighters up at all today."

The shortage of Spitfires and consequent lack of flying started to dampen spirits, as Brennan noted:

"Among the pilots a wave of depression set in. We felt impotent and helpless. There were so many targets and practically no aircraft with which to shoot at them. Most of us had to watch from the ground instead of fighting in the air, and we did not like it. The 126 Squadron boys, operating from Luqa, had a few Spitfires left, and scrambled on every possible occasion. So also did the Hurriboys from Hal Far, but again it was the same story of too few aircraft. Whenever the boys flew, they spent at least half-an-hour getting beaten up on the circuit by the 109s while attempting to land. The numerical odds against our fighters were overwhelming. They could only nibble, when what was needed was a large-sized bite.

"But shortly after this intensified blitz broke over Malta we received cheering news. All the pilots were summoned to a meeting at the officers' mess, Woody told us that the AOC would speak to us later. While we were waiting for him we discussed the position, and decided that it was a hell of a business when fighter pilots were sitting on the ground while the Hun was doing what he liked above our heads. Lloyd arrived about nine o'clock. He spoke very briefly, but he gave us what we needed most – hope. 'It's as hard for me not to be able to give you aircraft as it is for you not to have them,' he declared, 'but, believe me, you will have them soon. When you get them, I know what you'll do to those devils.' Nobody could tell us when the new Spits were due, but a whisper went round that the 20th was the day."

*   *   *

The numbers of serviceable Spitfires and Hurricanes had by now dwindled to a mere handful. When seven more Hurricane reinforcements arrived from North Africa on **19 April**, it had been four days since Malta's fighters had been able to operate, and the situation was truly desperate. While the delivery of the two initial batches of Spitfires to the island had brought some relief, it was obvious that the small numbers involved would not allow sustained operations to be maintained for long – as indeed had been the case. But help was on its way. Prime Minister Churchill had pressed US President Roosevelt for the use of the US Navy's aircraft carrier *Wasp* to deliver the next batch of Spitfires to Malta; his cable to the President read:

1: Air attack on Malta is very heavy. There are now in Sicily about 400 German and 200 Italian fighters and bombers. Malta can now muster only 20 or 30 [*sic*] serviceable fighters. We keep feeding Malta with Spitfires in packets of 16 loosed from *Eagle* carrier from about 600 miles west of Malta. This has worked a good many times quite well, but *Eagle* is now laid up for a month by defects in her steering gear. There are no Spitfires in Egypt. *Argus* is too small and too slow, and moreover she has to provide fighter cover for the carrier launching the Spitfires and for the escorting force. We would use *Victorious*, but unfortunately her lifts are too small for Spitfires. Therefore there will be a whole month without any Spitfire reinforcements.

2: It seems likely, from extraordinary enemy concentration on Malta, that they hope to exterminate our air defence in time to reinforce either Libya or their Russian offensive. This would mean that Malta would be at the best powerless to interfere with reinforcements of armour to Rommel, and our chances of resuming offensive against him at an early date ruined.

3: Would you be willing to allow your carrier *Wasp* to do one of these trips provided details are satisfactorily agreed between the Naval Staffs? With her broad lifts, capacity and length, we estimate that *Wasp* could take 50 or more Spitfires. Unless it was necessary for her to fuel, *Wasp* could proceed through the Straits at night without calling at Gibraltar until on the return journey, as the Spitfires would be embarked in the Clyde.

4: Thus, instead of not being able to give Malta any further Spitfires during April, a powerful Spitfire force could be flown into Malta at a stroke and give us a chance of inflicting a very severe and possibly decisive check on the enemy. Operations might take place during the third week of April.

The President replied in the affirmative two days later, and while the manner of delivery of more Spitfires was thus being organised, pilots had to be selected. The first two batches, whilst effectively forming existing squadrons upon arrival, had been no more than collections of available pilots brought together in England for the purpose. On this occasion it was decided to send two complete units – 601 and 603 Squadrons, commanded by Sqn Ldr John Bisdee DFC and Sqn Ldr Lord David Douglas-Hamilton, respectively. Few of the pilots embarked were combat experienced. Thus it was that the USS *Wasp* arrived on the Clyde at Glasgow, where she berthed in King George V docks. The majority of her bomber and scouting aircraft had been flown ashore to make room in her hangars for the 52 Spitfires, which she began lifting aboard during 12 and 13 April. One of 603's more senior pilots, Flg Off Tony Holland, recalled:

"As a flight commander at a flying school, I had been happy to drop rank when the opportunity came my way to join a famous auxiliary fighter squadron, commanded by Lord David Douglas-Hamilton. I had been posted direct to the squadron from the flying school without attending a fighter OTU course, and found myself pitched in at the deep end, along with several other pilots who like myself, had little or no operational experience. When we stepped aboard USS *Wasp* bound for Malta, we little realised that we would be required to fly our Spitfires off the carrier, something none of us had ever done or even contemplated!"

The Spitfires had been flown from Prestwick to the small grass field at Renfrew – which had not previously been used by Spitfires – during the past few days. To allow maximum space below decks, the 19 F4F Wildcats of her resident USN fighter squadron (VF-71) were secured on deck. The laden carrier sailed on the 14th, escorted by a battle cruiser and by four British and two US destroyers. Subsequently, as the vessels approached the Straits of Gibraltar, two RN anti-aircraft cruisers joined what became Force W, the armada passing through the Straits in darkness during the early hours of the 19th, and commenced steaming eastwards into the Mediterranean. The Spitfire pilots travelled in well-appointed *Wasp*, and were looked after with typical hospitality and generosity by their American hosts. Aware of the tradition of rum and gin in the Royal Navy, most were surprised to find the USN vessel 'dry' – although, to many, ice cream and Coca-Cola proved an acceptable alternative.

Aboard the carrier to brief the pilots on their forthcoming flight was Wg Cdr McLean, aided by Sqn Ldr Gracie, who had been flown to Gibraltar from London following his special and successful mission. He was to lead the Spitfires to Malta. The aircraft in the ship's hangars were all Mark Vcs armed for the first time operationally with the maximum possible armament of four 20mm Hispano cannons and four .303 Browning machine-guns. Each was also fitted with a 90-gallon overload fuel tank, and like the earlier deliveries, also featured a Vokes air filter beneath the nose – all of which added to the weight and to the air resistance which inevitably reduced the overall performance. All were painted in the RAF's 'sand and stone' desert camouflage scheme, with blue undersides, but were now to be sprayed dark blue to make them less obvious during the long sea flight; the application of the blue paint was still underway in the hangars as the carrier sailed. It seems probable that the blue paint was USN issue as used on the Wildcats. 601 Squadron aircraft all featured a number '1' painted on one side of each fuselage roundel, and an individual letter on the other side, while 603 Squadron aircraft sported a number '2' and similar individual letters. This was a most unusual departure from normal RAF identification codes, particularly for squadrons that had carried two-letter codes – UF for 601, and XT for 603 – that had been in use since the outbreak of war.

Thus at 0400 on **20 April**, Operation Calendar began as 11 Wildcats from VF-71 took off to provide air cover while the RAF pilots breakfasted and received their final briefing from Wg Cdr McLean. It was decided that the Spitfires would form roughly into four groups – to be led by Sqn Ldrs Gracie, Bisdee and Douglas-Hamilton, and Flt Lt Bill Douglas, the senior flight commander – and that they would proceed in pairs or individually. Hence, at 0545 precisely, Gracie's Spitfire rolled down the deck, dipped out of sight off the bows, and climbed laboriously into the sky; within 61 minutes 47 aircraft[28] were on their way. As if to test their taut nerves even more, a number of the tense pilots – strapped into their cockpits awaiting the launch – witnessed a horrific incident as an RAF mechanic backed into the turning propeller of Sgt Fernando Farfan's 601 Squadron aircraft, and was killed outright. The shocked Trinidadian pilot was only allowed to stop his engine long enough to inspect the propeller for damage; finding none, he soon took off but, according to his CO, "he was never quite the same man again." Of the flight, South African Archie Bartleman[29] recalled:

"No time to think about take-off – off, and terrible sinking feeling as off the end of the deck; only one circuit of the carrier permitted, when we were to switch over to the long-range tank – and we were ordered to fly on pre-set courses, either singly or in pairs. I flew on my own, as I didn't see any other Spits. About halfway to Malta, off Cap Bon, when flying at about 12,000 feet, I saw at about 2,000 feet below, possibly 12 Ju52s flying singly towards Tunisia. Although two machine-guns were loaded, these were purely for defence if attacked – we were ordered not to become involved in combat. When Pantelleria came into view, a new course was set for Malta, and I arrived at about 1030. I had about ten minute's fuel left. About eight Spits had already landed safely."

With the successful departure of the last of the serviceable Spitfires, *Wasp* and Force W turned back towards Gibraltar, while patrols of four Wildcats were maintained for the rest of the day. At 1117, a message was received from Malta that 46 aircraft had arrived safely and that one was missing. This was the aircraft flown by one of 603 Squadron's Americans, Sgt Bud Walcott, who had been with the unit for only a month. He had apparently confided to Canadian pilot Sgt Dick Buckley, with whom he shared a cabin, that he had no intention of flying to Malta. Consequently, as the Spitfires began their long flight, he turned for Algeria, some 55 miles to the south, where he force-landed BP958 in the area to the south of the Atlas mountains[30].

Such a large number of aircraft flying from the west had not gone unnoticed by the Axis on this occasion, their presence having been plotted on radar and picked up by radio intercepts, although the flight to Malta proved uneventful for the majority of the Spitfire pilots. The Luftwaffe decided to attack immediately after the new Spitfires had landed, rather than try to intercept the armed fighters as they flew in. Nevertheless, Messerschmitts were intruding over and around the island as the new arrivals approached, and as American Plt Off Reade Tilley noted:

"Me109s picked up the last flight of the group just before they reached the coast of Malta. Nobody had enough petrol to do more than run some 109s out of the pattern."

There were no casualties. 601 Squadron landed at Luqa and 603 Squadron at Takali without further incident. Sqn Ldr Douglas-Hamilton wrote:

"Malta came into sight as a small speck when still about a hundred miles away. Gradually it came nearer. We put our noses down and gathered speed. Over the R/T we began to hear the voice of the controller at Malta giving instructions to the earlier arrivals about landing. We also heard him talking to a section of Spitfires, which was covering our approach to the island. There were Messerschmitts about, but we never saw any. Malta did not look very big, but it was a most gratifying sensation to be over British soil once more. I led my group to Takali aerodrome and circled it to see what sort of condition it was in: for we were warned that it would probably be bombed before we arrived. Not knowing the form, we did not notice the landing-run on which we were supposed to land singly. Instead we did a formation landing into wind in sections of four across the landing-run. Some of us finished up a matter of inches from bomb craters, but fortunately no aircraft was damaged. We never landed like that again. After taxiing away and putting our Spitfires into blast pens dispersed round the aerodrome, we stopped the engines, jumped out, and drank in the silence and pleasant warm atmosphere of the morning. How nice it was to be on dry land again. In spite of obvious bomb damage all round everything seemed peaceful, and I thought subconsciously, 'What a lovely place for a holiday!' This innocent dream was rudely shaken two hours later."

* * *

The pilots of the 46 aircraft to arrive at Malta, in addition to Sqn Ldr Gracie, were:

601 Squadron
Sqn Ldr J.D. Bisdee DFC[31]
Flt Lt D.W. Barnham (BP969/1-R)
Flt Lt H.L. Parry (Rhod)
Flg Off C.M. Hone (Rhod) (BR125/1-P)
Plt Off. K.W. Pawson
Plt Off R.P. Johnson (BP977)
Plt Off M.H. Le Bas (Anglo-Argentinean)
Plt Off W.J.E. Hagger (Rhod)
Plt Off W.R.P. Sewell RCAF
Plt Off W.E. Cripps RCAF
Plt Off R.F. Tilley RCAF (US)
Plt Off T.W. Scott RAAF
Plt Off G.M. Briggs RAAF
Plt Off M.R.B. Ingram RNZAF
Plt Off. W.A. Caldwell RNZAF
2/Lt A. Bartleman SAAF (BR176/1-N)
Wt Off F.H. Belcher RCAF
Flt Sgt A.B. Cleaveland RCAF (US)
Sgt J.W.L. Innes
Sgt E.G. Shea RCAF
Sgt J.N. McConnell RNZAF
Sgt G.R. Dickson RNZAF
Sgt F.S. Howard (Rhod)
Sgt F.W. Farfan (Trinidadian)

603 Squadron
Sqn Ldr Lord D. Douglas-Hamilton (BR190/2-A)
Flt Lt W.A. Douglas (BR124/2-U)
Flt Lt J.W. Buckstone
Flt Lt L.V. Sanders
Flg Off A.C.W. Holland (BR184/2-C)
Plt Off L.W. Watts (BR120/2-T)
Plt Off J.W. Forster
Plt Off J.G. Mejor (Anglo-Belgian[32])
Plt Off N.S. King
Plt Off J.W. Slade
Plt Off O.R. Linton RCAF
Plt Off C.B. MacLean RCAF
Plt Off G. Murray RCAF (US)
Plt Off D.E. Booth (US)
Plt Off F.E. Almos (US)
Plt Off H.R. Mitchell RNZAF
2/Lt C.J.O Swales SAAF
Flt Sgt J. Hurst
Flt Sgt A.W. Otto RCAF
Flt Sgt J.D. Rae RNZAF
Sgt L.F. Webster

* * *

With the arrival of the Spitfires, a major effort was at once prepared by the Luftwaffe and, during the remainder of the day no fewer than 272 bomber sorties were flown against Malta's airfields. The first of the new Spitfires had arrived at around 1000, but it was 1230 before the first raid was plotted coming in, comprising 32 Ju88s and 20 Ju87s. These hit all three airfields but without causing undue damage. At Takali one newly arrived Spitfire (BP956) was badly damaged, three others and a Hurricane slightly damaged. Six Spitfires flown by 249 pilots had been scrambled and were joined by three Hurricanes, these soon becoming entangled with the escort. Flt Lt Lucas, leading the flight, wrote:

> "Around 1300 hours, six of we old hands really got stuck into what turned into one of the heaviest raids to date. There were pickings all round, although Junior Tayleur had the cockpit canopy of his aircraft [AB465] shattered by cannon fire from a 109 which had attacked him from head-on. Despite being badly cut about the face and bleeding freely, Junior had carried doggedly on, probably destroying an 87 before landing his Spit, with wheels and flaps down, at Takali and immediately being carted off to hospital at Mtarfa[33].
>
> "Raoul [Daddo-Langlois] had a similarly unnerving experience – he saw one coming straight at him, head-on, with guns blazing. Returning the fire, he held his bead on the German. Each refused to give way and, with a closing speed of some 500 or 600mph, neither broke in time. They collided, the tip of Raoul's starboard wing

catching the root of the 109's wing, severing it completely and sending the aircraft spiralling earthwards. Only the outer section of the Spitfire's wing had been severed. Bringing the aircraft in with excess speed, Raoul had let it run down the strip until he saw he was going to overshoot. Then, as the undercarriage was whipped smartly up, the run was brought to a halt with the pilot leaping from the cockpit just as four 109s were beginning an aggressive run across the airfield, all guns firing."

The Messerschmitt (10038) which collided with Daddo-Langlois' aircraft (GN-C) had apparently been hit first by Flt Lt McNair (GN-K); the unidentified I/JG53 pilot was seen to bale out south of Delimara and was later picked up by an Axis ASR craft. McNair recalled:

"Junior Tayleur was my No.2 and we climbed to 10,000 feet south of the island. We flew back over to the north side and were turning back into the island as some 109s attacked us. We'd seen Huns around, but hadn't the opportunity to get into position to attack them. I went after one of the Huns and it went into a vertical dive. The German pilot pulled away from me and then he thought he had lost me. He throttled back to come out of the dive and I shot at him from 400 yards before he realised he hadn't lost me. He went into a steep dive again. I fired a long burst at him and hit him around the wing roots and pieces started to come off. He kept on going. We were going so fast I couldn't steer the Spitfire straight. Suddenly he pulled up, much tighter than I would try because I didn't want to black out. I couldn't chance blacking out because there were probably other Huns about. I pulled out to one side to come out of my dive with less strain – on me and the aircraft. If I had stayed right behind him there would have been a danger of collision. In the very middle of his pull-out, where the worst strain or most was, pieces started to come off his aircraft, then more and more pieces came off. Then his aircraft flicked over and dived straight into the sea. I went down in a great spiral dive to watch him go in – nothing came up. If he was conscious when he tried to pull out, he was certainly unconscious when his machine started falling to pieces and still unconscious when he hit the water. I made my pull-out much shallower and was almost blacking out all the time. He may have been unconscious before he started to pull out or he may have been wounded while in the dive and relaxed on the stick which he had pushed forward to dive."

McNair then pursued a Ju88 as it was heading back towards Sicily:

"I chased this Ju88 at full speed and we headed north for Sicily, throttles wide open. The 88 started a 20° gentle dive and I was doing everything to get more speed. I didn't want to go to Sicily – I wanted to shoot him down long before we got there. We had never left the island area before this, there was too much danger from roaming 109s. I went into a steep dive to get speed, then levelled out. The 88 pilot kept in his gentle dive until he was down to my level; he was only 400 yards ahead of me, but we were more than halfway to Sicily. I started firing and great chunks started coming off and it caught fire. A body came out, either he jumped or had been blown out, but there was no parachute. The 88 slowed down a bit and there was an explosion and it spiralled down towards the sea on fire. I was making a wide orbit looking for my No.2 but I was too close to Sicily to stay around and watch the 88 go in."

Meanwhile, a Ju87 was attacked by Flg Off Ron West, which turned over and was seen to go down five miles south of Delimara; he also claimed damage to a second Ju87 before gaining strikes on a Ju88, another of which Plt Off Sergeant (1-L) damaged:

"Dived on two Me109s which I lost due to oiled windscreen. On my own, so attacked

Ju88 over Grand Harbour but cannons jammed. Ju88 damaged."

Hurricanes attempted to provide cover for the Spitfires as they came in to land in the face of strafing Messerschmitts, as recalled by LAC Somerville of 249 Squadron:

"Airmen were encouraged to fire at low-flying enemy aircraft. It had become a habit for enemy aircraft to follow our Spits into Takali when they [the Spitfires] had run out of fuel and/or ammo, with the object of shooting up an easy target. Drill was to collect from the armoury a rifle and belts of .303 machine-gun ammunition – ammo supplies unlimited. Imagine the effect when the Me109s saw tracer bullets converging on them from all round Takali – tracers, armour-piercing, incendiaries, the lot! It was not haphazard banging away with guns – the task was taken seriously as the airmen had been advised they were the first line of defence should there be an invasion! As a matter of fact two enemy aircraft destroyed were credited to small-arms fire at Takali."

One of the damaged Spitfires attempting to evade the strafers was that flown by Flg Off Daddo-Langlois. Sgt Hesselyn was watching from the ground:

"I noticed one Spit with its wingtip sheared off. He was flying low down with a bunch of 109s above, and was whistling around the circuit, waiting for a favourable moment to come in and land. His damaged wing was plainly visible from the ground. About 18-inches of it was missing, and instead of the usual elliptical section of a Spit wing, it looked rather like the square-cut wing of a Me109E. Eventually the Spit came in, but was hit. It went running past dispersal when the pilot whipped up his undercart, and skidded the aircraft along on its belly. It came to rest in a cloud of dust. Brennan ran towards it, but the 109s swooped down and started to beat up the aerodrome. Brennan dodged behind some sandbags, and Buck [Buchanan] and I ran towards a slit trench. Before we could reach it, the 109s were overhead and we had to fling ourselves on the ground. As we did so I saw Raoul Daddo-Langlois leap from the cockpit of the Spitfire and make a bee-line for dispersal. Machine-gun bullets ploughed into the ground all round us, and a cannon shell burst within a few yards of Buck, but luckily we were not hurt."

Sqn Ldr Douglas-Hamilton wrote:

"For us new arrivals the sight of a first-class bombing raid from a ringside seat was the most staggering thing we had ever experienced. Many of us, including myself, had never even heard the whistle of a bomb before. Some of us had not till now even seen any enemy aircraft, and few of us had seen them in such large numbers, or been able, unmolested, to watch aerial combats from the ground."

At 1400, the Italians put in an appearance when 19 MC202s of 10°Gruppo CT undertook their first mission – a fighter sweep over Malta. Led by Cap Giovanni Guiducci of 90^Squadriglia, they were half-an-hour into their flight when Guiducci and his No.2 (Serg Magg Giambattista Ceoletta) collided, both aircraft falling into the sea off Porto Empedocle. Although Ceoletta managed to bale out and was picked up by a fishing boat, Guiducci's aircraft fell in flames and he was killed; the mission was at once aborted. Subsequently Cap Ranieri Piccolomini was posted in to take over 90^Squadriglia.

As evening approached radar warned that another big raid was brewing. At 1700, two Spitfires flown by Flg Off Buchanan and Sgt Hesselyn of 249 took off to provide airfield defence, flying out to sea to enable them to offer cover when the main interception force returned to land.

"About four o'clock a plot of 88s was reported, and a dozen Spits scrambled at once.

Buck and I were very brassed off. We had been put on aerodrome defence, and took off a quarter of an hour after the boys had scrambled. Our job was to go out to sea, and wait there to give the boys cover when they came in to land. There were a lot of 109s about, but they gave us no trouble until we had got up to about 10,000 feet. We were by then some distance from the island, and could see neither the bombers nor the Spitfires. Four 109s began making passes at us. Being on a specific job, we were supposed to ignore them, and to avoid getting into a mix-up. They were very persistent, however, and Buck finally decided that we would have to mix it, whether we liked it or not. We turned into them, and for perhaps five minutes all six aircraft went round and round in tight circles, the 109s trying to get on our tails and we on theirs. We drifted steadily closer to the island, and eventually two of the 109s climbed away. We concentrated on the remaining two.

"I got on the tail of one, and almost simultaneously Buck got behind the other. We were almost over Filfla by now, and the two 109s headed for Sicily, putting their noses down to gain speed. We chased them across Malta, and caught them as they crossed the coast at St Paul's Bay. I gave mine a four-seconds burst. Very gently, his nose starting to dip down, he hung poised for a second; then suddenly went into a vertical dive, crashing straight into the drink. A few seconds later I saw Buck's also crash into the sea. We started to turn, intending to regain our position south of the island so as to cover in the boys when they returned to land, but were jumped by four 109s. They succeeded in separating us. I dived and turned towards the ground, and when 1 pulled out at 1,000 feet the two 109s which had attacked me were no longer on my tail. Hardly had I made certain of this when I found myself amongst some 88s going out over Filfla. I got a quick, two-seconds deflection shot at one before my cannons jammed but although I could see some strikes along his fuselage, he kept going and was only damaged. Buck had already landed when I came in. He had got in a few squirts at the other 109s, but had done no damage."

An aircraft of I/JG53 did, in fact, crash into the sea off Valetta, from which the unidentified pilot was later rescued by an Axis ASR craft. No other losses appear to have been recorded, but one of their opponents may have been an aircraft of 3 Staffel, in which Ltn Walter Seiz was hurt when he crash-landed on return, although reportedly due to engine failure; a second aircraft, from 5 Staffel, also crash-landed at Comiso, less seriously damaged.

The evening raid came in at 1715 and was, indeed, a major affair, including an estimated 64 Ju88s, 25 Ju87s and more than 30 Bf109s, accompanied by an ASR Do24 from 6 Seenotstaffel. At 1720 six Spitfires from Takali flown by 249 pilots and six from Luqa manned by 126 Squadron were scrambled, meeting Messerschmitts south-west of Gozo at between 15,000 and 17,000 feet, covering Ju88s that had just bombed Takali, where two Spitfires were destroyed on the ground and three others damaged. One of the escorting fighters was claimed by Flt Sgt Brennan (BR192/2-W):

"We scrambled, climbing south of the island and getting to 26,000 feet, with the sun behind us. Woody called up and said: 'Hullo, Mac. There's a big plot building up, but it's taking a long time to come south. Keep your present angels, and save your gravy. I'll tell you when to come in.' We stooged round until Woody gave us the word. Then we sailed in. Buck and I went to Comino Channel, between Gozo and Malta. Buck reported 20 Me109s and told me to break left, but to stay with him. I could not see the 109s, and when I asked where they were Buck told me they were all around us. We had lost some height, and suddenly, glancing behind me, saw four 109s coming down on me, I pulled round, and blacked out. When my vision cleared I saw them again, and also another bunch about 2,000 feet above me. Three of the four 109s overshot me. The fourth made his turn too wide, and I got inside him. I was slightly below him when I attacked from 200 yards. I allowed some deflection, firing perhaps 20 feet ahead of him in the hope that his aircraft and my bullets would arrive at that spot simultaneously. They did. The 109 and my shells met. He spurted glycol. I kept on firing, as I was determined to make certain of him. He caught fire. Black smoke poured out of him. He rolled on his back, and went into a vertical dive. I followed him down in case he was foxing, but he went straight into the drink.

"As he crashed, it struck me suddenly that there might be something on my tail. In my excitement I had forgotten to look, but, luckily, none of the other 109s had dived down on me. Woody reported that the 88s were diving on Takali, and I pulled up to 10,000 feet. The next instant the 88s were diving past my nose, with Mac and the other boys coming down from above to attack them. I picked out one 88, and went for him. Macqueen, 100 yards to my left, was also attacking an 88, and I could see his guns firing. Indeed, for a moment I thought the black smoke from his cannon meant he was on fire, and it gave me a sudden shock until I realised he was firing. I got within 200 yards of my 88, and as I pressed my gun button his rear gunner opened fire. Although I was flying one of the new four-cannon Spits, only one cannon on each wing was loaded. I had fired for about a second when my port cannon packed up. Luckily I was travelling fast. This prevented my aircraft from slewing from the recoil of my starboard cannon, as I was able to correct with rudder. I concentrated my fire on the 88's starboard motor and wing root, and I could see my shells hitting. After perhaps six seconds, by which time I had fired all my ammunition, the 88 caught fire. Bits were flying off him, and the flames were spreading as he continued in his dive, and he was well ablaze when he crashed."

A second Messerschmitt was claimed probably destroyed by Flt Lt McNair, who believed he had shot away most of its tail, in addition to the probable destruction of a Ju88, while Flt Lt Lucas gained strikes on a third. Flt Lt Macqueen reported shooting down another bomber, which he believed crashed into the sea, while Plt Off Sergeant (1-L) claimed a second north of Grand Harbour:

"Hell of a dogfight with 109s over Gozo, one squirt. Attacked an 88 over Grand Harbour and set port engine on fire. Last seen diving down flaming and smoking. Ju88 destroyed."

It seems that the bombers were from KüFlGr606 and KGr806. One aircraft from the former unit was crash-landed at Catania in a badly damaged condition by Fw Winfried Böhlen, two of the crew having been wounded, while an aircraft from the other Gruppe also crash-landed at Catania.

Meanwhile, the 126 Squadron Spitfires led by Flt Lt Johnston had become engaged with Messerschmitts, and suffered badly. Two pilots were lost – the 28-year-old American Plt Off Tex Putnam was wounded by a cannon shell and then collided with a radio mast near Siggiewi, being killed when his aircraft (AB336) crashed in the Ta'Kandja valley. He may have been hit by Ltn Karl-Heinz Quaritsch of 8/JG53, who claimed a Spitfire shot down for his first victory. The second fatality was Canadian Flt Sgt Jack Ryckman from Ontario, who was thought to have followed a Ju88 out to sea, where he was jumped by a Bf109; watchers saw a splash in the sea just off the coast where it was believed his aircraft (BP969) had fallen. Oblt Klaus Quaet-Faslem of 2/JG53 reported:

"After meeting several Spitfires at a height of 3,500 metres, I saw a few Ju88s flying towards Valetta, but these disappeared north. To cover them I got between a group of

Spitfires and the Ju88s. I heard a report of a Spitfire behind a Ju88 over the sea, and spotted this, but it disappeared in a right turn behind another Ju88 before I could get close enough to open fire. I fired from long range and the Spitfire broke away from the bomber. After I had passed above the Spitfire, I saw it turning towards the Ju88 again. At the same time Ltn Zellot attacked the Spitfire, which did a left turn and flew off south towards the island. Ltn Zellot fired at the Spitfire whilst in a turn and hit the fuselage and the top of the right wing. Very soon the plane started swinging and before the pilot could escape, went down into the water leaving a white and blue smoke trail. The aircraft was the latest model of Spitfire with four cannons."

Ltn Walter Zellot, the successful pilot, added:

"I fired at the Spitfire and it tried to escape by doing a left turn towards Valetta. I followed and fired so that pieces of the fuselage flew off. Shortly afterwards I saw a small flame and a light trail of smoke coming from the right side of the motor. Swinging violently from left to right, the Spitfire lost height, fell sideways and crashed down vertically into the water from a height of 300 metres. I couldn't see anything apart from an oil slick where the aircraft had hit the sea."

Clearly Ryckman's aircraft had been Zellot's victim, his 14th victory. Flt Lt Johnston had become separated from the other four due to an oil leak partly obscuring his vision. Nonetheless, he pursued a Ju88 over Takali, and skirmished with several other aircraft before he saw:

"... two 109s dive across my bows not more than 300 yards ahead. They were obviously going to shoot up the aerodrome and I felt sure they hadn't spotted me, so I turned hard left and went through the cloud after them. Re-emerged over the field at 50 feet and knew they must be a short distance ahead, but couldn't see them anywhere; was in the act of cursing my oily windshield, when suddenly, without warning, there was a vivid flash and I felt rather than heard a tremendous bang."

It transpired that the damage to his aircraft had been caused by an explosion of a bomb from a Ju88 that was attacking the airfield, although Ltn Herbert Soukop of 6/JG53 reported shooting down a low-flying Spitfire near Luqa at about this time; Johnston continued:

"The stick, which had felt taut and sensitive in my hand, seemed to sag and become quite limp; knew at once that the aircraft had been vitally hit and was out of control, knew too that this must be the end – it might fly on another couple of hundred yards, but then it would keel over one way or the other and take me into the ground with it. I remember feeling surprised and thinking rather bitterly that my belief that I should survive had been a myth after all. At that time I had no hope whatever, it was as if I'd been in a racing car doing about 100mph when the steering-gear had failed; I was so close to the ground that it felt rather like that; the only difference was that I was 50 feet up and doing 200mph. But instead of going down, the aircraft began to climb very steeply, and as the nose went up so the port wing went down, as if we had begun to do a climbing roll to the left. I jammed the stick into the forward right-hand corner of the cockpit, and this seemed to prevent the machine from making its climb a vertical one, or executing rolls in the course of it, but we were still both tilted and banked at about 60°; however, there was hope. I had to hold the stick forward with my right hand, and with my left I began to undo my harness and extracted the pin successfully. I'd decided that I couldn't risk being held to the machine by the R/T cable and oxygen-tube as I tried to jump."

The Spitfire was at a height of about 900 feet, well below the minimum safety, when Johnston finally emerged:

"I was turning over and over so fast that the movement seemed to confuse my arms, and when my hand reached for the rip-cord it wasn't where it should have been; I had to make three separate grabs before I found it. As the chute opened the sensation was as if a giant was swinging me round his head by the scruff of the neck, then suddenly the world, which had been whirling round, came right side up. I looked up and made sure that the canopy had opened properly and then wondered whether 109s would shoot me up before I reached the ground, but immediately realised how silly that was, I was only 150 feet up and seemed to be falling astonishingly fast; just had time to see my machine hit the deck a couple of hundred yards away on the other side of a small ravine when I was bracing myself for my own landing. I wasn't swinging at all and dropped straight on to a rocky terrace and immediately fell forward on my hands and knees; luckily the chute collapsed at once, so I just lay where I was, panting and sweating as if I'd run a quarter, but profoundly thankful to be alive. I could see the aeroplane blazing furiously and could hear the ammunition exploding in the heat; that was the only sight and sound; the bomb dust seemed to have drifted away, and everything else was calm and normal. One of the first thoughts that occurred to me was that this was what came of leaving my little elephant behind.

"After a few minutes I heard voices and I thought I'd better stand up and declare myself; a group of Tommies appeared, and I shouted 'British' and then felt rather foolish, because they never seemed to have been in any doubt of the fact. They took me to the mess of ack-ack headquarters, where I was given a drink and a wash and allowed to telephone. I was surprised and rather pleased to find how unmoved I was by what had happened; pouring myself out a beer I noticed my hand was quite steady, only hoped there wouldn't be a reaction later. No one turned up to take me home, so I stayed with the soldiers and had quite a party; one of these later drove me back to the mess in the colonel's car."

The stricken Spitfire (AB344) crashed at Wied Hanzir near Qormi. The blast from this bomb also bowled over 126 Squadron's Sgt Junior Crist, who was on the airfield taking pot-shots at strafing Bf109s with his revolver. The only claim the 126 Squadron could make was for a single Messerschmitt damaged by Plt Off Stan Brooker. Five Hurricanes were despatched to patrol over an ASR launch searching for the missing Ryckman, but these ran into a number of Ju88s, making several claims, but of Ryckman there was no sign. At Takali, during the raids, two Spitfires had been destroyed and three others slightly damaged, while two more were damaged at Luqa.

Air Vice-Marshal Lloyd, the AOC, had been delayed getting to Takali to welcome the new arrivals due to a bomb splinter puncturing a tyre on his car, but when he did arrive he found many of the new pilots almost speechless at the exhibition of concentrated bombing. However, the gist of his welcoming speech to the new arrivals was positive, as noted by Flt Lt Denis Barnham of 601 Squadron:

"I think, gentlemen, that the Germans have welcomed you in a far more striking manner than I could myself. I know the Germans. I fought against them in the last war. I'm fighting them again in this; they're the same lot, cowardly and bullies – and incredibly foolish. The manner in which they are conducting their offensive against the island shows us that you are here to shoot down his bombers. To make it easier for you we are going to hit the Hun where it hurts him most. Ten Wellingtons will arrive here after dark tomorrow evening. They will go out twice or three times every night for the next three months and bomb their fighters on the ground. We will not see any great results at once, the effect will be cumulative. You must remember Malta's main rôle is an offensive one, to destroy the enemy shipping and to cut his supply lines. You must remember that in Malta we are all one team. Our bombers, torpedo-carrying planes and our submarines are our striking power, like Achilles' sword. Our sword has been blunted but we will sharpen it. Until then Achilles must rely on his shield. The anti-aircraft defences and you pilots flying your Hurricanes and Spitfires are that shield; Malta relies on you.

"The odds are very great over the island for the Germans have more than 500 machines in Sicily and you have considerably less than 50. You must, however, achieve air superiority. Sooner or later, and probably much sooner than you think, we must bring in another convoy. You know what happened to the last one. Only three merchant ships got through. Of these one was sunk at the entrance to Grand Harbour and the other two were sunk before they could be unloaded. This must not happen again. Not only are supplies for our war machine critically low, but the remaining stocks of food on the island are very short indeed. Without another convoy we will starve. Whether or not we achieve this convoy is up to you. One last word: in the future you will look back on your time spent on Malta and you will feel proud you were here. Good luck."

One of the new arrivals, Flg Off Holland of 603 Squadron, recalled:

"When we had arrived at Takali, our reception had been somewhat loose and slightly casual. Our AOC, a most excellent commander, but perhaps more orientated to the manner of Coastal than Fighter Command, told us he planned to hold half of our newly arrived Spitfires on the ground in reserve, and put half on the line. Our assailants had other ideas, and it was with dismay that we watched Ju87s dive on Takali, bombing with great accuracy so that before nightfall on that first day, plumes of black smoke arose from many of the sandbagged or stone-walled pens in which the reserve, and front line Spitfires, had been parked. This was catastrophic."

The assembled pilots were then given a no-holds-barred lecture by Sqn Ldr Gracie of what they were to expect, and what he expected of them. The gist of his welcome, mainly for the benefit of the pilots new to Malta, was revealed by an account written by another new arrival, Canadian Plt Off Chuck MacLean[34]:

"When I first spoke to you pilots back on the carrier I said that aircraft on this island are much more valuable than pilots. We have many pilots and so few Spitfires. No matter what predicament you find yourself in, even if completely surrounded by enemy fighters, you should not panic, nor give up. Your first and last duty on Malta is to get that aircraft back safely. And now I can tell you what very few of you know and what most of you must be wondering about. I was chosen by the Military Governor of the island to go to Whitehall to present the horrible and true picture of Malta before the Chiefs-of-Staff; to paint the real picture of our terrible lack of planes and what it could mean; to describe to them the incredible odds we have been facing. The decision to send a plenipotentiary [ambassador] to London was reached sometime back at the end of that three-week period … a period those of us who survive will never forget when we pilots sat here with not a single aircraft. Now I know what really happened during those three weeks. I told them when an operational pilot lands on this island he can escape one of four ways. One. He can be wounded so that he is no use to us here. Two. He can surrender. Three. He can die. And four, he can go on to victory. I made it emphatically clear to the Chiefs-of-Staff that we fighters here on Malta will never surrender."

Gracie obviously had in mind the imminent threat of invasion when he referred to 'no surrender', but then by way of encouragement made further, although disguised references, to imminent relief when he continued:

> "There is something big coming in the near future. I do not know exactly what it is myself or, by God, I would tell you. Not even the Military Governor knows, for it was I who brought the word back to him and he wanted to withhold even this amount of information. But, when I suggested that if any people needed encouraging news it was those men who were defending the island, he changed his mind. All I can say, is, have courage and do your job to the limit, for the vital stage that might well be the turning point in all this misery is nearer than most of you would dare to hope."

Following the latest pounding, AOC Lloyd feared that Takali would be unserviceable for three or four days, so severe appeared the damage. But soldiers and airmen again worked through the night and by first light next morning the runways had been cleared, filled and rolled, allowing Spitfires that had landed at Luqa or Hal Far to return. However, nine Spitfires remained trapped in their pens by debris and could not be moved for the time being. Following inspection, the condition of many of the new Spitfires left much to be desired. Even after being worked on all night, most were still not ready by morning. Guns were dirty and had not been synchronized and most had not been fired since they had been installed. Many radios were not working. The AOC was furious and made his feelings known to those responsible. He also complained of the lack of experience of most of the new pilots, his subsequent cable to the Air Ministry emphasising:

> "Only fully experienced operational pilots must come here. It is no place for beginners. Casualties up to now have been the beginners."

To help fill the gaps in 249 Squadron's ranks, four of the new arrivals – Plt Off Les Watts, Canadian Plt Offs Ossie Linton and Chuck MacLean, and Plt Off Fred Almos, an American – were posted in from the 603 Squadron contingent, while Plt Off D'Arcy Milburn moved across from 185 Squadron, where he had been flying Hurricanes. 126 Squadron also received some new pilots from the latest influx including two Americans, Plt Off Doug Booth (known as 'Tiger') from 603 and Flt Sgt Artie Cleaveland from 601. It had been decided that a few of the pilots assigned to the Spitfire squadrons were too inexperienced to be risked to fly operations in such a hostile environment, and these were sent back to the UK, although New Zealander Sgt Bolton[35], who had arrived with the first contingent, went to the Middle East.

The initial intention had been that half the new aircraft would go to reinforce the existing Spitfire units on the island (126 and 249 Squadrons), but events over the next 48 hours soon put an end to these plans. Despite all efforts, only 27 Spitfires could be made serviceable by dawn on **21 April** to oppose the anticipated onslaught on the airfields, the first raid approaching at 0730 when an estimated 37 Ju88s and 34 Bf109s began a series of attacks on Grand Harbour, the docks, Luqa and Takali. Ten Spitfires and five Hurricanes were scrambled shortly after 0830. Six Ju88s that had just bombed Luqa were encountered, and one of these was engaged jointly by Sqn Ldr Grant and Plt Off Plagis (AB263) of 249; the bomber was last seen diving steeply towards the sea with both engines pouring black smoke and they were credited with its destruction. Plagis also claimed damage to a Messerschmitt, as did Sgt Hesselyn, while Flg Off Buchanan gained strikes on another Ju88. Two of the Spitfires were flown by Sqn Ldr Douglas-Hamilton and Flt Lt John Buckstone of 603 Squadron, on their maiden operational flights from the island, but due to their inexperience of the unique fighting conditions over Malta, they had become separated from the others and failed to make contact with the bombers. 603's CO noted in his journal:

"We had not long to wait. 'Scramble!' Up we climbed to about 30,000 feet, joining up with another party of Spitfires and Hurricanes from the other aerodromes. From that height Malta looked about the size of a penny. It was easy to lose sight of it under one's wingtip. Sicily, however, seemed very large and hostile with Mount Etna sitting up at the back of it. For the rest, there was nothing but miles and miles of unfriendly sea all round. Then we saw AA bursts below, and dived down towards them. Aircraft suddenly started whirling all round, and I and another of my pilots got separated from the others. Not knowing the 'Malta form' we dived down in the wrong direction and missed the bombers. So we tried an abortive chase after some 109s, but were too far behind them and could not catch up. We did not fire our guns at all that time."

Sqn Ldr Gracie (BR125/1-P) led his quartet to the north of the island, waiting for departing bombers. His patience was rewarded when he spotted a section of three Ju88s below, speeding out to sea. Diving onto them from above and astern, he claimed two shot down into the sea in quick succession:

"I took off with four Spitfires with instructions to cover Hurricanes. Owing to R/T failure I flew as No.4. The section was split up at 18,000 feet and owing to lack of R/T and no companions, I orbited Filfla at 4,000 feet suspecting that e/a would come out that way. I was correct and as Ju88s turned out to sea, I attacked one from quarter astern with three-seconds burst, seeing black smoke from starboard engine. I then attacked another from astern and below with eight to ten-seconds burst. White smoke from starboard engine appeared. Owing to lack of ammunition I then flew out to sea and saw both the aircraft pancake with one another on the water. The apparent damage was not sufficient to warrant any claim until after they were seen to pancake."

Plt Off Peck (BR192/2-W) gained strikes on another before it, too, evaded, and the escorting fighters intervened, one of which Sgt Goldsmith (BP964/1-X) claimed shot down:

"I was flying No.2, Wombat White Section, to Plt Off Peck, when we were jumped by four Me109s at 18,000 feet. I took evasive action, aileron turning down to about 6,000 feet, and about seven miles north of Grand Harbour. Here, one of the four e/a, which had followed me down, crossed my nose in a climbing turn to the left, at a range of about 150 yards. I followed him round, opening fire with the four cannons, observing strikes along the top of mainplane and fuselage. After about two seconds, port cannons ceased firing, and I continued firing with starboard guns for two-three seconds. I then saw a large splash on the surface, and the e/a was seen for a few seconds just under the water before disappearing."

It is likely that the splash the Australian had seen was caused by Plt Off Stan Brooker's Spitfire (BP977), who was shot down in this engagement – probably the victim of Obfw Rudolf Ehrenberger of 6/JG53 (his 25th victory) – since no Messerschmitt losses were recorded. Goldsmith continued:

"A little later another 109 attacked me from astern. I turned sharply starboard, and then when he overshot, I turned back and opened fire with starboard cannon as he climbed. Fired for about six seconds and saw strikes along bottom of fuselage, range 150-200 yards, before breaking off. I was attacked again from behind, and struck in the port wing with a cannon shell, partially jamming my ailerons. I took evasive action, and the remaining e/a broke off the engagement as I crossed the coast at about 1,500 feet near Sliema. I made my report to the IO, and was later credited with a 109 destroyed and another damaged. Luckily a gun crew had seen my 109 hit the sea. First blood for the Goldsmiths!"

One of the Hurricane pilots was also lost. Of this action, Flt Lt Johnston recorded:

"Goldie opened his score today with a 109, one of four which attacked him and Jimmie, and the CO entered into double figures with a brace of Ju88s. Apparently he became separated from the others, so he flew to Filfla and circled there at 5,000 feet hoping the bombers would come out his way. His R/T would receive, but not transmit; he heard someone call up and say: 'Look out, Wombat aircraft, there's something over Filfla', and later the voice of one of his own sergeant pilots came through with: 'Keep your eyes open, Wombat, that little bastard's still mucking about over Filfla'; this put him in such a good mood that when the 88s came out he got two of them in quick succession and watched them go down close to each other in the sea. The 109s didn't so much as come near him. His Guardian Angel must be a four-cannon job; think he knows it too; he has twice been shot up here, his neck after his accident – it was slightly broken in the Battle of Britain – only allows his head to turn one way, and he's short-sighted, but he remains cheerfully intrepid and his attitude to the Hun is expressed in his invariable: 'Me109s? Of course I never see 'em!' He reckons this is tougher, if anything, than the Battle of Britain. Afraid Brooker is missing; this was his first flight here [sic], but he had a lot of experience at home; no one saw anything of him after they split up to attack the 88s."

At Takali the returning pilots were greeted by many of those yet to fly at Malta, including Flt Lt Barnham, who wrote:

"Sqn Ldr Gracie appears in the narrow entrance at the end of the cavern: he and his parachute seem to be stuck there: bursting through he tosses his chute on to one of the wooden benches, then turns and glares at us. 'Just shot down two 88s,' he snaps; 'they fell in the sea in formation.' Gracie's machine will have to be repaired before it flies again. On our aerodrome there are three [Spitfires] left. The CO and I, as the two most experienced pilots of our Squadron and anxious to get going, ask Gracie to take us up on the next raid. He agrees.

"Overwhelmed by my ignorance of how to fight against odds of 40 to 50 to one, I stare at Gracie for he is obviously brilliant at air fighting. 'Sir,' I ask him, 'what are the best tactics to use?' Gracie stares at me: I shrivel inside for I'm aware that my question is hopelessly broad and vague. 'You'll learn,' he replies 'but don't go chasing the bastards all the way to Sicily. If you're by yourself weave around at nought feet all over the island, or better still do steep turns in the middle of Takali aerodrome, inside the ring of Bofors guns, but don't take any notice of their fighters, it's the big boys we've got to kill.' I attract his attention again: 'With the Ju88s in heaped formation their return fire must be pretty concentrated – what's the best way through it? 'Return fire? Ignore it. Come on, let's get out there.'"

A Do24 of 6 Seenotstaffel escorted by seven Bf109s was soon on the scene, obviously searching for the missing bomber crews. At 1210, a second raid approached: 20 Ju88s, 15 Ju87s and 36 Bf109s being reported making for Takali, Hal Far and the Grand Harbour. Plt Off Nash, who had returned early from the scramble when his electrics failed and the gun panels fell off, ran across to see if he could help extinguish his burning Spitfire (BP963) in its pen:

"After first wave spotted burning Spit. Went out to see what I could do and ran into next wave. Knocked out and blown 15-20 yards. My plane was smashed in its bay and I lost my kit. 109s causing chaos on the circuit. Off flying for 48 hours."

As a result of the attack on Takali two more Spitfires (BP849 and BP874) were destroyed and one damaged. Four Spitfires were scrambled by 126 Squadron, two of these flown by Sqn Ldr Bisdee and Flt Lt Barnham of 601 Squadron. They were followed ten minutes later by eight more from 249 Squadron. The experienced pilots of 249 Squadron enjoyed some success when they got amongst the Stukas. Sgt Hesselyn:

"We climbed to 20,000 feet, and there the 109s tried to break us up, so as to prevent us going for the incoming bombers. We refused to mix it with them for a while, but eventually I was compelled to turn into twos. I turned to what I imagined was the rear enemy fighter, but it proved to be the leading 109. I was surprised to find him in my sights, as I had turned so quickly, but had the presence of mind to press my gun button. I caught him with a lucky climbing deflection shot. The Hun disintegrated in the air. Pieces of the 109 flew in all directions, and the pilot, literally blown out of his aircraft, shot out on the right-hand side and hurtled towards the earth. His parachute did not open. I had fired all four cannons, and although it was only a snap shot, 30 to 40 of my cannon shells must have ripped into his fuselage.

"The fact that I had turned into the leader by mistake gave the other Hun his opportunity. He got on my tail, and in my mirror I could see him behind me, firing for all he was worth. I broke down promptly, and aileron-turned to about 2,000 feet, with the Hun following all the way. Johnny Plagis [AB263] was on the 109's tail, but we were all so close together that he could not fire for fear of hitting me. At 2,000 feet, however, the Hun gave up the chase, and climbed away out to sea. Johnny followed him, and probably destroyed him. I began to climb to regain height, and was over Gozo when I spotted six to eight 87s diving on Takali. I waited until they came out of their dive, by which time I had gained a good, tactical position, 4,000 feet above them. Making the most of this advantage I dived on the rear 87, opening up on him from dead astern. I gave him a four-seconds burst, and he went down in flames, straight into the drink. A bunch of 109s jumped me, but I evaded them by diving and turning, and by the time I was over Mdina I had shaken them off. A 109, low down, was shooting up Takali. I dived on him and followed him as far as Kalafrana Bay, but could not get closer than 300 yards. I fired all the way, but could only see strikes near his tailplane. He climbed away, shaking me off without difficulty. I returned to Takali and landed."

Flg Off Buchanan claimed a second Ju87 shot down. One of the new pilots, Plt Off Watts (BR190/2-A), reported strikes on the Messerschmitt he attacked. The flight from 126 Squadron was less successful. A formation of Ju88s was sighted and engaged, Sqn Ldr Gracie (BR125/1-P) inflicting damage on one, while Barnham later wrote:

"I take one near the bottom. My Spitfire shudders as I fire two bursts of cannon into a cluster of bombers that get in the way. May have hit one. Can't stop to look. My target is wheeling nicely into position. A huge part of a Ju88, nose and engines, flashes out from under my left wing: must have been right on top of him! Gone now. Target's wing overlapping my windscreen – I fire. A flash and a burst of smoke from his port engine. He rears up in front of me, steep turning left. Fire again. He's swerving to the right. Try for his starboard engine. Fire again and again."

Two Bf109s then appeared and opened fire on Barnham's aircraft (BP976), but failed to score. Then more appeared and he managed to get onto the tail of one:

"Drop on to his tail. I'll get him all right. A gigantic shape, all rivets and oil streaks, the underside of another Messerschmitt blots out the sky! Gone. But I'm still on a 109's tail, it's right there in front of me, pointing very slightly downwards. My aircraft shudders and shudders as I pour bullets and shells into it. It bursts with black smoke and topples over sideways. Bang! An explosion from my engine – smoke bursting back into my cockpit. Upside down, spinning again. Cliffs very close. Controls don't answer. All gone slack. Can't stop spinning… Spitfire burning… out of control. Too low to bale out? Might just make it. Bale out quickly.

"But everything is going so slowly. The scene is strangely peaceful, for unconcerned and apparently unimplicated. I am outside my aeroplane, looking back at my body. In front of me is the wingtip, but my attention is drawn back along the upper surface of the wing, back over the painted roundel, to the wing root where the light is shining; above the wing root is the cockpit; within the perspex canopy I can see my own helmeted head with my arms encircling it in such a strange manner! I'm so interested in watching my body over there that I have but a feint impression of the aeroplane's long nose trailing horizontal smoke against a background of dark sea. Pressure! Controls do respond. Hope. Not going to be killed after all. Smoke's not bad."

Following his strange but not unique out-of-the-body experience, Barnham regained control of the situation and was able to nurse the crippled aircraft (1-J) down to a crash-landing at Hal Far, where a flight lieutenant congratulated him on the unintentional flick rolls he carried out to escape his assailants. On his return to Takali, Sqn Ldr Gracie was not so generous with his greeting, as he had written-off his aircraft. Gracie also announced that Sqn Ldr Bisdee was missing. However, it transpired that Bisdee was safe, having baled out into the sea. He had also attacked a Ju88, damaging its starboard engine, and it was confirmed to have crashed by the crew of an AA battery. So intent on shooting down the bomber was Bisdee that he failed to notice a Messerschmitt closing on his tail. Ltn Walter Zellot of 1/JG53 was part of the escort to the bombers, and he spotted Bisdee's aircraft (BP954/1-D):

"I noticed a Spitfire firing at a Ju88 from long range. I was flying with Oblt Tedler about 1,000 metres above it. I went down right behind the Spitfire and tried to chase it away with my machine-guns. It would not break away and stayed behind the Ju88, which kept shooting back. I could see that the Englishman was not hitting the bomber hard. I was close enough to fire at the Spitfire from a shallow left turn. At once pieces flew off the aircraft. As he now saw me, he tried to get away by doing a very sharp left turn, but while he was doing so, I had the whole upper side of the aircraft in my sights. I did a right turn and was ready to fire again when I saw a parachute opening. The Spitfire tumbled over and crashed down into the sea. I then saw the parachute floating close to the oil slick which appeared in the water."

This combat – Zellot's 15th victory – was witnessed by Oblt Friedrich-Karl Müller and Oblt Udo Padior of the same unit. Sqn Ldr Bisdee later recalled:

"I'd attacked a Ju88 and I hung around a bit too long. I thought I saw in my mirror an aircraft behind me, my No.2. It wasn't, it was a Messerschmitt! I was only about a thousand or twelve hundred feet up, and luckily had my hood open. The aircraft was totally out of control, going round like a whirligig, and I was more or less blown out of the cockpit. I pulled the ring and found myself hanging in my harness upside down by one leg! I only had about ten seconds on the parachute, before splash, I was in the water. I was very lucky to get away with it. If I'd had to open the hood I wouldn't have made it. It was difficult to get out of a Spitfire cockpit because of the airstream directly you got up. Under your bottom you had this bulky pack of your dinghy and your parachute – the dinghy was folded in the form of a cushion, so you sat on that, and underneath that was the parachute. You could catch on an awful lot of things on the way out. The airstream was pushing you backwards against the top of the cockpit, where the hood was, so it wasn't all that easy, but it's remarkable what you can do if you know you bloody well must!"

Bisdee fell into the sea head first, freed himself from his harness and scrambled into his dinghy. Searches were made throughout the rest of the day for him. He, unbeknown to the searchers, was paddling towards the island three or four miles to the north. After about six hours he eventually reached the rocky shoreline beneath the cliffs not far from Hal Far. By chance, he was spotted from the cliff top by an FAA airman, Air Fitter Monck, who scrambled down the rocks and dragged the grateful semi-conscious pilot to safety. Spitfires were also claimed in this action by Oblt Kurt Brändle of 5 Staffel (his 34th victory) and Hptm Helmut Belser, Staffelkapitän of 8 Staffel (his 22nd).

The third and final raid began at 1559, with an estimated 60 Ju88s, 20 Ju87s and 40 Bf109s approaching to attack the airfields and Grand Harbour yet again. Nine Spitfires of 249 scrambled at 1645, and two of these dived on a formation of Messerschmitts but were then attacked by other fighters, possibly MC202s of 10°Gruppo CT, as a pilot from this unit claimed a Spitfire shot down although none was lost. At 1720, the Spitfires encountered a number of Ju88s and their escorts as they were diving in line astern from 12,000 feet, heading for Filfla after attacking Takali, one of which Flt Sgt Brennan (BR192/2-W) claimed probably destroyed. As the Spitfires attempted to return to Takali, low-flying Messerschmitts did their utmost to shoot them down. Brennan later wrote:

"At the end of half-an-hour, when I was feeling exhausted and ill, Laddie called up [to Flt Lt Macqueen]: 'Look, Mac, this is a hell of a bloody do. We must get in. We'll cover each other in.' Mac replied that we were to go in, and he would cover us. I started a normal circuit, about 300 feet above the aerodrome, put my wheels and flaps down, did a weaving approach, and as my wheels touched ground felt a sigh of relief. I taxied to my pen, forgetting to put up my flaps. All I could do when I got there was to lie back in the cockpit and gasp for breath. The groundcrew had to help me out of my aircraft, and, dazed and dizzy, I groped my way along the wing out of my pen. I met Laddie as I was wandering over to dispersal. He was taking off his Mae West. I noticed his tunic was soaked with perspiration. I pulled off my Mae West, and was surprised to find my tunic in the same condition. We both looked up to see how Mac was getting on. He was making his approach, about 50 feet up. Suddenly two 109s darted out of sun. I said to Laddie; 'Mac's had it.' The 109s were dead astern of him, firing at a range of 50 yards. Their shooting, however, was poor, and they had not hit him. Whipping up his wheels, Mac turned sharply into them. The 109s overshot him, carried on, and beat up the aerodrome. Mac made a quick dart, put down his wheels and managed to get in."

A much-relieved Macqueen joined his colleagues and reported that he had shot down a Bf109 and damaged a bomber. Another Junkers was claimed shot down into the sea by Flg Off Buchanan, but his aircraft was shot-up in the circuit as he was endeavouring to land; despite the damage he, too, got down safely. Plt Off Sergeant's Spitfire (1-L) was also hit when six Messerschmitts attacked:

"Chased 109 but was jumped by six others and badly shot-up with cannon [shell] in empennage – landed OK but very frightened. More 109s than ever."

Among 249's opponents in this clash was Oblt Kurt Brändle of 5/JG53, who claimed his second Spitfire of the day at 1739, to raise his score to 35, while Fw Erich Schmidt of 7 Staffel claimed another as his sixth, and Ltn Rudolf Müller of 8 Staffel, a third. Two Spitfires flown by Flt Lt Barton (BR190/2-A) of 126 and Flt Lt Parry (BR125/1-

P) of 601 were also scrambled, meeting a Ju88, which they jointly claimed damaged.

On the ground the evening attack had taken a heavy toll. Some 150 bombs had struck Takali, and while not rendering the airfield completely unserviceable, had destroyed two more Spitfires (believed to have been AB333 and BP974) and damaged four others. At Luqa the situation was even worse, with no fewer than seven Wellingtons being destroyed or damaged beyond repair. A transit Wellington departed that evening for Cairo carrying on board seven pilots who were to collect Hurricanes from El Ballah airfield and ferry them to Malta. These included Flt Lt Connell and Flg Off Lee of 249 Squadron, three Americans – Plt Offs Sandy McHan, Tiger Booth and Don McLeod – and two Malta-based Hurricane pilots.

When the first raid approached the island at 0930 on the morning of **22 April**, no more than 17 Spitfires could be made ready for operations. The raiders again headed for the airfields and, as a result of the attack on Takali, one Spitfire (BR129) was destroyed; in addition, two soldiers were killed and six wounded. First off at 0915 to meet the raiders were four Spitfires with Flt Lt McNair (BP968/2-N) leading three inexperienced new arrivals – Plt Offs Max Briggs (BP969/1-R) and Bill Hagger (BP975/1-K) with Sgt Len Webster (BP973/2-J). They gave chase to a lone Ju88 – Uffz Wilhelm Schreiber's 3Z+FM of 6/KG77 – at which all fired. McNair observed many strikes during his attack and was probably responsible for its destruction. There were no survivors. Sgt Webster then engaged one of the two escorting Messerschmitts, which he claimed to have damaged. At 1010, seven more Spitfires led by McNair were scrambled, including four flown by 603 Squadron pilots, intercepting 20 Ju88s approaching St Paul's Bay. Flg Off Ron West claimed two bombers damaged and Flt Sgt Brennan (BR192/2-W) another:

"We were at 25,000 feet south of the island when the 88s came in. It was one of the biggest raids on Malta, over 150 bombers and fighters crossing the coast. The first wave attacked the harbour, but we left them alone. The second lot raided Luqa, and Woody brought us in. They were below me, moving towards Filfla at between 8,000 and 10,000 feet. With the others, I dived down on them. As I started to close on one, I looked behind and saw two 109s on my tail. I judged them to be too far away to open fire, and I decided I had a good chance of getting my 88 before the 109s could get properly on my tail. I did not break away, but continued my dive, and at 300 yards opened fire. I gave him a three-seconds burst, but my port cannon then packed up. I stopped firing and took a quick look behind. The 109s were closing faster than I had expected. I decided to risk another squirt at the 88 as I was very close to him. I gave him two-seconds. The 109s were now firing. Their tracers were whipping past my starboard wing, and their shells exploding five or six feet away from me.

"I broke violently left, and as I did so saw six more 109s coming down at me from above. I pulled up and fired at one. My speed was too low, however, to fire with only one cannon, and my aircraft slewed violently away, sending my shots wide. I decided Filfla was too hot a spot. I dived away. Woody reported more 88s diving on Takali and, believing I had shaken off all the 109s, I headed for there. I picked out an 88 that was diving, intending to follow him down to get some speed, so that I could attack him with my one gun. I had a quick look behind, and could see nothing. I started a stall-turn down with the bomber. Suddenly there was a flash between my legs and a loud bang in the cockpit. A cannon shell from a 109 had joined me in the cockpit. I was paralysed with fear. For a few seconds I just sat there, doing nothing. I was fascinated by my flying boots, which had been ripped to ribbons. Then, as I looked down, I became aware of a big hole in my aircraft, close to my right foot. It struck me that I had better do something."

Bringing his aircraft under some sort of control, Brennan was eventually able to make a creditable landing having again successfully evaded marauding Messerschmitts over the aerodrome. Only 603 Squadron's experienced Flt Sgt Johnny Hurst reported any tangible success when he shot down Obfw Franz Kaiser of I/JG53, who ditched his crippled machine (White 6/10028) about six miles south of Marsaxlokk. Kaiser was picked up by a rescue vessel and became a prisoner. Another new pilot, Plt Off Gordon Murray (one of 603's Americans), was seen to break away to pursue a Ju88. He failed to return and his Spitfire (BP970) was presumed shot down into the sea by Bf109s; he was killed, the likely victim of Fw Wilhelm Budke of 2/JG53. On returning to Takali, Plt Off Linton's Spitfire (BR180) ran through the boundary fence and tipped on its nose, while Flg Off Holland, observing this accident, attempted to land short in BR184/2-C and ran into a bomb crater.

A further big raid at midday was not intercepted, although AA claimed two Ju88s. Takali was again heavily cratered and a number of Spitfires under repair were further damaged. When 50 Ju88s and 20 Ju87s appeared at 1730, however, six 126 Squadron Spitfires and two Hurricanes were up to meet them. The Spitfire leader, Flt Lt Barton, claimed one Ju87 shot down with a second as a probable, plus a Bf109 damaged, before his own aircraft BR120/2-T was hit. Plt Off Bailey's BR125/1-P was also hit but he claimed a Ju88 probably destroyed first. His victim was almost certainly an aircraft of II/LG1 that returned damaged following fighter attack:

"Four Me109s were sighted. This number later increased to about twelve. We continued to circle inside and below the enemy aircraft. On hearing that Ju88s were diving on Hal Far and were leaving low down over the sea, I dived towards that area, into the middle of the AA bursts and several Ju88s. I was about to attack one when another suddenly appeared in front of me, and much closer, presenting a good deflection target. I opened fire from approximately 200 yards and closed to about 50 yards. I saw pieces fly off the port wing and a cloud of black smoke emerge from the port engine. The 88 turned to starboard and I was able to get in another burst. I saw a flash of flame from the rear part of the fuselage in front of the cockpit. No return fire was seen from this second attack. When I broke away the 88 was losing height and still smoking. Turning back towards Hal Far, I met other 88s coming towards me and I gave a very short burst head-on, when my guns stopped firing. Returning to base I found my starboard cannons had not fired."

603 Squadron's Flt Lt Douglas (BP850/F) engaged three Ju88s without visible success before his aircraft was thrown into a spin by AA bursts aimed at the bombers. Plt Off Frank Jemmett was attacked from the beam by two Messerschmitts from II/JG53 flown by Fw Walter Recker of 4 Staffel and Obfw Rudolf Ehrenberger of 6 Staffel, and he was severely wounded. He belly-landed BR180 near Rabat, where the aircraft slithered into a stone wall at Tal-Virtu and caught fire. Flt Lt Johnston, who was not flying on this occasion, wrote:

"Bart got two Stukas and Old Bailey an 88, all probable; there was too much opposition for either to confirm them as destroyed. Frank Jemmett crash-landed after being badly shot-up by 109s and died in hospital. We'd seen two 109s make a beam-attack on a lone Spit flying just below the brow of the hill behind Verdala Castle; they had each fired a longish burst and we could make out the puffs of their self-destroying ammunition, but the Spit hadn't appeared to be hit and we'd thought no more about it. But Jeff West had happened to be there, he said Jemmett had put it down very prettily on its belly but it had slithered on into a stone wall and the engine had caught fire. Tommies [soldiers from 11/Lancashire Fusiliers] got there almost at once and tried to drag him out, but they hadn't understood the harness and made no headway until Jeff arrived and pulled the pin out for them. If a wall between him and the aircraft hadn't delayed him Jeff thinks they might have saved him, but the doc says it was the wounds, not the burns, which were fatal. He was a charming boy and very young; I'd had a premonition, but it was probably more rational, because it was his first flight here, than intuitive. A girl in the house where Jemmett was billeted also had a premonition; apparently at the moment when he had come into the room this morning, very pleased because he was to fly for the first time here, a bead had come off the rosary in her hand."

One of the Hurricanes was also shot down and its pilot killed. Bored with the lack of his own activity, Wg Cdr Turner decided to fly an offensive sortie over Sicily. He asked Plt Off Sergeant to accompany him. Spitfires were at a premium so Turner requisitioned two Hurricanes. Sergeant recalled:

"Stan Turner and I went down to the flights and Stan said 'Come on, we'll go up.' I said I'd never flown a Hurricane before and he said, 'Well, it's a bloody good chance to learn!' And it was an operational trip! He didn't brief me or tell me what we were doing. We went out at low level halfway to Sicily, pulled up and looked around, saw nothing and came back."

An evening raid on Takali, which was not contested by the fighters, saw the destruction of three more Spitfires (AB263/GN-B, BR188 and BR204) on the ground. During the afternoon, at 1645, four Spitfires were scrambled, three of which were flown by 603 Squadron pilots Plt Offs Chuck MacLean, Bert Mitchell, and Flt Sgt Jack Rae. Both Mitchell and Rae experienced gunsight failure, despite which the former fired at a Ju88 and a Bf109, albeit with no observed effect, while McLean's aircraft was badly shot-up by a Bf109, which damaged its rudder. All three, however, landed safely.

23 April opened with a small, early morning fighter-bomber attack by Messerschmitts from 10(Jabo)/JG53, followed at 1035 by a major raid by an estimated 42 Ju88s and 15 Ju87s, directed against the usual targets. At Takali a number of aircraft pens were damaged and two unserviceable fighters – a Spitfire and a Hurricane – were destroyed; a second Hurricane was destroyed at Hal Far. Half-a-dozen Hurricanes and two Spitfires were scrambled to oppose this raid, the Hurricane pilots shooting down a Ju87 and damaging two others, for two of their own damaged, while Plt Off Tilley's Spitfire (BR120/2-T) was also shot-up. Gunners claimed four Ju88s shot down, at least two of these sustaining serious damage. Plt Off Nash, who was not flying, noted:

"An 87 was shot down off Kalafrana this afternoon. One of the crew baled out and two 109s shot him up in his brolly, then four 109s killed him in his dinghy. This time they blundered. I saw a Spit bounced by four 109s over Dingli. My word! He nearly bought it! One 109 attacked with two on one side and one on the other. The Spit boy saw him at 50 yards and turned left and down. Lucky he did not turn level. I have just learned this was Tilley of Texas [sic]."

The bombers were back at 1555, an estimated 50 Ju88s and 16 Ju87s attacking the airfields and dockyard. A Spitfire was destroyed at Takali, where three others and three Hurricanes were damaged, and an unserviceable Wellington was destroyed at Luqa and another slightly damaged by debris; an Albacore was destroyed at Hal Far, another and a Hurricane sustaining damage. AA claimed a Ju88 shot down and another damaged. Four Hurricanes and two Spitfires were scrambled, but only the latter managed to intercept on this occasion, Sqn Ldr Gracie (BR120/2-T) and Flt Sgt Schade (BP850/F) of 126 Squadron being credited with two Ju87s destroyed – one jointly, the other by Schade. Gracie reported:

> "I took off with another Spitfire and climbed to 26,000 feet, 25 miles south of the island, with orders to intercept final wave of attack when told this was coming. When ordered we dived on to island and arrived at Grand Harbour at 4,000 feet as Ju87s started to dive. Owing to fierceness of enemy fighters and cloud at 6,000 feet it was not possible to keep higher. I fired at a Ju87, which passed right through my sight at approximately 400 yards. No claim made. I then made an attack from underneath on another Ju87, observing hits. I stalled machine as I pulled out. This aircraft emitted lots of black smoke from starboard wing roots. This must have been after F/Sgt Schade's attack on same aircraft. This was confirmed as destroyed from the ground. We returned to Luqa, dodged a number of 109s and landed intact. One Ju87 destroyed (shared with F/Sgt Schade)."

Schade's subsequent report added:

> "Climbed up sun to the south of the island, about 26,000 feet and about 15-20 miles out to sea. Called in by Ops about 1605. Dove down onto Takali, passing about 15 Messerschmitts at about 20,000 feet to our starboard (six of these peeled off and followed us). We missed the Ju88s at Takali so made off to the Grand Harbour with the CO. We dove onto the 87s as they were just pulling out of their dive. I was a little behind the CO and to the right. I saw him attack an 87, pulling up at the same time and stalling. As the CO broke away to port I was just in the right position to attack the same 87. I opened fire at about 200 yards, closing in to about 70 yards. I fired about a two-seconds burst and saw hits then black smoke come out from underneath the e/a. I broke away to port after this and went into a tight, steep turn, coming back at the 87s just in time to catch the second lot diving. I engaged an 87 from quarter-stern from about 200 yards closing to about 50 yards. Hits were observed on the e/a (the plane shook) and black smoke came out of the wing roots. I broke away to port again and joined up with the CO, who made off towards Takali. We dodged a couple of 109s by going in and out of cloud. We eventually landed with Hurricanes as cover. $1^1/_2$ Ju87s destroyed."

During the early evening nine Ju88s and 21 Bf109s made another unopposed raid on Luqa, where another Spitfire was destroyed on the ground. This was the thirteenth Spitfire to be destroyed in this manner in the last four days, with at least another dozen sustaining debris and blast damage, while a further nine had been shot or had crash-landed. The situation was again becoming very serious for the defenders. Since there were more pilots than Spitfires, some of the new arrivals felt somewhat under-employed, one such being 603 Squadron's Flt Lt Douglas, who confided to his diary:

> "There's not a lot to do but watch the raids from a safe vantage point. Actually the latter is quite an occupation, as it is very useful to be able to study the Hun's technique from the ground, and to see how the chaps and the guns are getting on."

In a letter to his parents, he wrote:

> "This would be a really wonderful spot in peacetime. At the moment the climate is just right. A nice warm sun, a pleasant breeze off the sea usually to keep us cool, and an occasional white cloud to break the intensity of the blueness of the sky. It's jolly comfortable being able to go about in shorts and a shirt – just the thing – and we get quite a lot of time off. We get quite a lot of exercise, too, as we have to walk practically everywhere. Life on the whole is quite enjoyable – never a dull moment, and getting on with the war."

A few days later he wrote:

"We have quite a lot of time off, though there's not much to do, transport being pretty strictly rationed. Sandy Sanders, a supernumerary flight lieutenant in my flight, and I and Paul Forster and Jack Slade went for a swim the day before yesterday. We had to walk ten miles into the bargain, which is quite a lot in the heat of the sun. However, it was well worth it. The climate really is ideal just now, and I haven't felt so fit for a long time. There's a grand crowd of chaps here, and I'm really beginning to enjoy myself here. We go to bed early, and get up fairly early, and there's not a lot to do..."

Next day (**24 April**), Grand Harbour and the airfields bore the brunt of the morning raid by at least 30 Ju88s, with 20 Bf109s as escort. At Luqa two Hurricanes were destroyed, as was a Wellington, while yet another Spitfire was damaged. Four Spitfires of 126 Squadron were scrambled at 0730, followed five minutes later by six Hurricanes, but these could not prevent the Gozo ferry boat from being strafed by the Messerschmitts; five civilians aboard the vessel were wounded. Flt Lt Johnston led his quartet of Spitfires to engage a formation of bombers over Grand Harbour:

"Suddenly an 88 with its nose down and its tail right up in the air went past within 100 yards of me. I knew the wave was on its way, because of the flak, but he seemed to have appeared from nowhere; I dived after him flat-out, cut the corner as he pulled out and caught him halfway between Luqa, where he had dropped his bombs, and Valetta. I waited until I'd closed to 200 yards and then opened fire with a longish burst from dead astern, five-six seconds. I could see the high-explosive incendiary shells exploding as they hit him and what looked like a mixture of black and white smoke began to pour from both motors; he turned right-handed very sharply until he was almost standing on his starboard wing-tip. For a moment I hoped he was going to roll over on to his back and dive into the ground; in any case I felt certain he was finished, so pulled away and began to look for another. The other 88s had come out of their dives higher than mine, and I couldn't get up to their height before they reached safety, so turned back and landed without further incident."

Sgt Junior Crist (BP850/F) also claimed a bomber probably destroyed:

"I was Red 2. We scrambled and climbed up to 15,000 feet south of the island. We dove down on the 88s attacking Grand Harbour. I closed in on one Ju88 about one-and-a-half miles off Grand Harbour, and opened fire at 300 yards, closing to about 250 yards. I fired about a four-seconds burst using both cannons and machine-guns from dead astern. Hits were observed and pieces flew off the port engine and wing root. Fire from the rear gun ceased. The e/a was last seen very nearly on its back. I was then forced to abandon the attack as I was attacked and fired at by four 109s."

Sgts Dusty Miller and Wally Milner (BR176/1-N), both on their first operational sorties, claimed damage to two more Ju88s. The Hurricanes also claimed damage to two bombers and two fighters. One of the Hurricanes was shot-up by a Messerschmitt, probably that flown by Obfw Herbert Rollwage of II/JG53, who reported shooting down a Spitfire.

The next raid came in at just after 1000, when 26 Ju88s and 14 Ju87s accidentally dropped most of their bombs on Valetta, although the dockyard was the intended target; St Luke's Hospital was hit, where one person was killed and three injured. Two shelters were also struck, killing four civilians and injuring 13 others; two RCAF airmen from the Wellington unit were also killed. Flt Lt Barton (BP973/2-J) led off four Spitfires of 126 Squadron to meet the raiders, encountering a number of bombers near Takali. Barton and his No.2 Sgt Milner (BR176/1-N) jointly engaged a Ju88 and claimed it shot down, while Sgt Crist (BP850/F) severely damaged a Ju87:

"I was Yellow Leader in a section of four. We dove as Ju88s attacked Takali but I was unable to close to attack. I then saw 87s diving on Grand Harbour and attacked one as it was going out from the harbour. I opened fire from line astern at 400 yards, closing to 300 yards. The 87 began to dive with smoke pouring from it. I broke off the engagement as I was attacked by six Me109s, who opened fire. The 87 was seen by P/O Scott and others diving steeply towards the sea with smoke pouring from it. I did not experience return fire. One Ju87 awaiting confirmation."

As the Spitfires attempted to land, half-a-dozen Bf109s tried unsuccessfully to strafe but the ground defence gunners drove them away, claiming two damaged. One of these may have been the aircraft (8646) flown by Ltn Josef Einsinger of 5/JG53, which crash-landed at Comiso on return; the aircraft was totally destroyed. Of this period, Crist wrote:

"The worst part was trying to land because the Germans would try to shoot you up while you were landing. The All Clear would sound because the bombers had gone, but the fighters would still be around. Landing was always a chore. We had a guy on the ground watching with a radio. You'd zip in quickly, sometimes even downwind. Sometimes they would chase you even when you were on the ground. If they were on our tails when we were coming in we would try to lead them over flak nests. There was a little valley over Rabat with lots of anti-aircraft guns there, if they were foolish enough to chase us that far."

The last raid of the day was made by 34 Ju88s and 15 Ju87s on the three airfields, a single Spitfire being burnt out at Takali. Three Spitfires of 601 Squadron, led by Plt Off Nash of 249 Squadron, and four Hurricanes scrambled. However, immediately after getting airborne, Nash's aircraft suffered engine failure and crash-landed on the cliff tops near Rabat; although understandably shaken, he was not injured. The others headed for the Stukas. Flt Lt Barnham (BP975/1-K) attacked two:

"Low over the rooftops, bombs bursting up towards us, shells bursting among us, while from high above us Stukas are plunging straight down, pulling out of their dive at our level. On my own now, pulling my Spitfire up on its tail, a head-on Stuka is charging towards me, the 'W' structure of its wings perfectly distinct, larger and larger, bombs falling away from its belly disappearing under my aircraft's nose. I fire into its gigantic shape; its unfolding shadow broods for an instant over my head. This is mad, crazy but wonderful."

There was no shortage of targets. Another Stuka came into his sights:

"… already huge, much closer, winged, round, pregnant with twin bombs hanging there; head-on detailed beyond the red circle of my gunsight. Firing steadily I pull my nose carefully upwards so that the enemy machine disappears beyond my engine cowlings, so that it must pass through my close grill of bullets and cannon shells; a monstrous scarlet shape, a mass of flames, flashes overhead. Another plunging towards me. I pull my aircraft up until it too disappears behind my Spitfire's nose."

Out of ammunition, Barnham called Luqa to advise that he was coming in to land, two Hurricanes providing cover. Despite their presence, four Messerschmitts followed the returning Spitfires and while attempting to avoid their attack, Barnham crash-landed:

"Dust and silence. Sitting there I realise with awful horror what I've done; I don't think any bullets struck me. I've crashed a Spitfire through sheer bloody carelessness. I don't care about the 109s now. Through my blur of tears I'm aware of 109s streaking across the aerodrome making another attack. I'm too ashamed to care."

It is possible that his attacker was Ltn Karl-Heinz Quaritsch of 8/JG53, who reported shooting down a Spitfire for his second victory. Barnham was credited with one Ju87 destroyed and a second as damaged. Claims for damage to Stukas were also made by the other two Spitfire pilots, Plt Offs Tommy Scott (BP973/2-J) and Pancho Le Bas (BR125/1-P), while another was claimed by a Hurricane pilot. Le Bas (who was born in Argentina, hence the nickname) recounted:

> "Led by Plt Off Peter Nash, three of us were scrambled and told to climb to 20,000 feet to engage an incoming formation of Ju87s escorted by 109s. Almost from the beginning things began to go wrong. Nash had engine trouble and had to turn back. Then the controller took us up too high with the result that when we dived to attack we came in much too fast and two of us overshot the dive-bombers. The third pilot managed to get in a good burst at an 87 but then a horde of escorting Messerschmitts got on to us and we were lucky to escape with our lives."

AA gunners claimed two Ju88s shot down and two damaged.

Up to 85 Ju88s and 15 Ju87s were reported attacking Luqa on the morning of **25 April**, a raid that was not opposed by the fighters. The building commonly known as the Poor House (formerly an old peoples' home now in use to billet airmen and soldiers) was hit and an RAF officer seriously injured. Bofors gunners scored a hit on a low-flying Bf109 (Black 8/7373) of 5/JG53, from which Fw Alexander Kehlbuth baled out and landed in a nearby field to become a prisoner. Soon after midday a further 80 Ju88s and Ju87s returned, Luqa's Poor House now being totally destroyed, and a Wellington badly damaged. St George's Barracks were also hit and 14 soldiers killed, with over a dozen more seriously injured. Bombs also fell on the 4.5-inch HAA gun battery at Spinola, where a dozen British gunners and one Maltese signalman lost their lives. On this occasion six Hurricanes and three 601 Squadron Spitfires were scrambled at 1225, followed half an hour later by two more of 249 Squadron and two of 603 Squadron; all became heavily engaged.

First in the air were the 601 Squadron trio, who attacked Ju87s near Luqa. Plt Off Ken Pawson (BP973/2-J) failed to return, but when the other two pilots – Plt Off Bill Hagger and Sgt Stan Howard – landed, they reported that they believed Pawson had probably shot down two Ju87s and had then seen him being pursued out to sea by four Bf109s. They were later to learn that he had attempted to get back to the airfield but had crashed his damaged aircraft on a hilltop just east of Burmarrad near Naxxar; he subsequently died from his injuries. It would appear that he had been shot down by Obfw Josef Kronschnabel of 9/JG53, as his ninth victory. Of his loss, Flt Lt Barnham – now effectively in command of 601 Squadron – wrote:

> "Pawson was the first of our party to be killed – on his first flight. Parry and I were walking back across Naxxar market place, and talking of the last raid, 'The dreaded Pawson may be an ace by now', he said. 'Things happen so suddenly here – he may have shot four down.' Then we reached the doorway of the mess just as the B Flight car drew up and we learned the news – yes, he may have destroyed four; he stayed with the bombers too long and was attacked mercilessly by the 109s as he tried to get back to the island. He most certainly destroyed one Ju88 [sic]. He crash-landed and died on his way to hospital from wounds and injuries."

Hagger and Howard each claimed a Ju87 damaged. The Hurricane pilots also claimed several of the bombers damaged but similarly lost one of their number. The other four Spitfires, meanwhile – again led by Flt Lt McNair – had been ordered to join the 601 Squadron section in the attack on the Ju87s, following which Flt Sgt Brennan (2-E) engaged a Ju88 over Naxxar but was in turn attacked by six Bf109s. He pulled up into these, and all bar one overshot:

"I pulled up 30 or 40 feet underneath him. It was point-blank range, and every detail of his machine stood out vividly. I could see his markings, his twin radiators, his retracted wheels, even the rivet heads on his fuselage. I gave him a second-and-a-half with all four cannons. The result gave me a terrible fright. His starboard wing snapped off near the fuselage. It folded back, and banged against the fuselage. For a moment I thought it was going to tear away from his machine and come hurtling into my aircraft."

The Messerschmitt pilot, Uffz Heinrich Becker of 8/JG53, managed to bale out of Black 7 (7531) into the sea from where he was later rescued by an Axis ASR craft. Brennan then attacked a Ju88 from dead astern at 200 yards:

"I opened fire with all four cannon. The rear gunner stopped firing. I concentrated my fire now against the 88's two motors and the pilot's glasshouse. I could see my shells crashing into him, and in a few seconds he started to smoke. I was acutely conscious of the 109s diving on me, and knew that if I waited to check my aim I would be cold meat for them. The thought went through my mind that I must get my 88 quickly. I kept on firing. It was only for a matter of seconds, but seconds in air combat seem like minutes. He caught fire and started to disintegrate. That was enough for me. I turned on my side and skidded violently."

Brennan headed back to Takali but, there, Bf109s were in the circuit and he heard the controller call for Spitfires to cover Hurricanes as they attempted to land at Hal Far. In response to the call for help, both he and McNair (GN-P) arrived over Hal Far to keep the Messerschmitts at bay, but as two Hurricanes tried to land simultaneously, one apparently took the other for a Bf109 and pulled away, while the other mistook the Spitfires for Messerschmitts and also hesitated. An irate McNair called over the R/T that he would shoot down the over-cautious pilots himself if they did not land quickly! After finally landing at Takali, he reported that he had damaged two Messerschmitts, plus a Ju88 and a Ju87.

The Luftwaffe was back again in mid-afternoon when an estimated 57 Ju88s and 24 Ju87s were reported attacking Takali and Luqa from 1740 onwards, further damaging airfield buildings. Four Hurricanes were scrambled at 1705 to meet the incoming raid, followed 25 minutes later by three more Hurricanes and four Spitfires, two each flown by 126 and 603 Squadron pilots. As the two 126 Squadron machines got airborne, Sgt Goldsmith's cockpit hood flew off:

"It was my 21st birthday, which I considered would be a good opportunity for some solid shine bashing, followed by a quiet pub crawl – certainly not the sort of day to go picking fights with bull-headed Germans. I was therefore disgusted when I found I was on afternoon readiness. We were scrambled just when a mug of afternoon tea was coming up. As soon as I was airborne, I found that my prop was throwing a lot of oil on my windscreen, and my forward visibility rapidly became nil. Then my hood came adrift when I attempted to close it. This looked like divine providence to me, and a hint from the patron saint of fighter pilots that he didn't want to see me killed on my 21st birthday, so I returned and landed at Luqa, having called Jimmie [Peck] to tell him."

Seeing Goldsmith return, Flt Lt Johnston immediately scrambled in BR125/1-P to join Plt Off Peck, but was unable to catch up with him. After sighting several enemy aircraft, Johnston dived to attack some Ju88s but was then set upon by several of the escort and became embroiled in a series of dogfights:

"I saw two 109s pass a long way below me, and next moment the R/T said 'Look out, lone Spitfire over Grand Harbour, two 109s below you, two 109s below you'; someone on the ground had been pretty spry. I orbited and kept a very sharp lookout. Presently six 109s, in pairs, swept round from the south-west, below me; two of them were directly underneath and I could have jumped them beautifully, but decided to keep my ammunition for the 88s. Later a couple – possibly the same ones – pulled up and attacked, both fired wide and flew away north; decided they would probably shadow me and try again when they thought I wasn't looking. Felt the peculiar agitation and petulance that comes when you think you are going to miss a train; wouldn't those bloody bombers ever come? Made another orbit, and at last saw flak bursting to the north-west at the same height as myself; flew that way and spotted a wave of 88s coming through it towards me, rather difficult to distinguish among the black bursts. Thought of making a head-on attack, but decided it would be better to dive with them. As I reached them the 88s began to stuff their noses down, one after the other, in their bombing-dives; I could see a couple of 109s away to the south, but didn't think they'd worry me, hoped perhaps they hadn't seen me. I turned round to join the stream, picked up my 88 and tucked myself in behind him, following him in his 60° dive; was just laying my sight on him when a 109 came in from the south, firing hard, and I had to break towards him.

"My memory of the next minutes is very blurred; I had the impression of at least four, I think six, attacking in the most determined way I'd ever experienced, from every direction; most 109s make off after delivering one attack, but these came back repeatedly and I should say each fired once at least. I managed to take them all head-on or on the beam and felt no hits in the aircraft. If they had synchronised their attacks I think they must have got me, but they seemed to come down in turn and this just gave me time to deal with each individually; as soon as one had been evaded I'd look round and there would be another one attacking, sometimes already firing. It was a non-stop performance and I've no idea how long it lasted, it might have been five minutes, it might have been fifteen. At the start I lost height by design, hoping the barrage would make them shy, but soon this became sheer necessity; at first I could catch glimpses of the tail end 88s diving past and there was a good deal of flak, later both disappeared and left me alone with the 109s.

"There was no chance to look at the clock, but I must have been doing 300 or more most of the time, to judge by the weight of the controls. I had my feet on the G-pedals and was kicking the aircraft about with all my strength whenever they fired; from first to last I was too hard pressed to get a shot back at any of them. Gradually I began to tire and wondered how much longer I could keep it up; remember thinking they were bound to get me if they persisted and speculated whether I should have any chance of jumping out at that speed. As I tired, the controls seemed to grow heavier and heavier, and the physical effects of the g more and more crushing. I can remember I heard myself saying 'God!' once and later 'Christ!' but the words were wrung out of me and sounded more like groans than oaths. I felt no exaltation in hard fight, had no time to think romantic thoughts of fighting to a finish. I didn't even realise consciously that I was fighting for my life, but must have known it subconsciously. All I felt was an increasing desperation as I tried. At last I must have grown too ham-handed in a turn and the machine spun; it wasn't intentional, but it was the best thing that could have happened. Normally I hate it, but this time I felt rather smug, knowing that I made a hopeless target; it occurred to me that anyone watching from the shore would probably believe me shot down. Pulled out at 2,000 feet, looked all round carefully and found I was alone, so flew inland towards Luqa. Now that it was all over I felt absolutely exhausted; there was no hope of climbing up to bomber height again in time to do any good; decided I'd better land quickly before the circuit-strafers arrived."

Having evaded his attackers he received a call to cover Sgt Webster of 603 Squadron, who had also damaged a Ju88, as he prepared to crash-land his damaged Spitfire at Takali. He was followed in by his leader, Flt Lt Douglas (BP962/2-R), who reported shooting down a Ju88, as did a Hurricane pilot; one Hurricane and its pilot were lost; this was possibly the victim of Oblt Friedrich Below of Stab III/JG53, though Maj von Maltzahn (63rd) and Hptm Walter Spies (his sixth) each claimed a Spitfire in this action. Two Ju88s of KGr806 were hit during this sortie, Ltn Werner Schrader's 3 Staffel machine (M7+LL) crashing near Vittoria on returning to Sicily due to damage, the crew all suffering wounds or injuries. In the second bomber – M7+FK of 2 Staffel – the rear gunner was killed. A third Ju88, from 5/LG1, crashed on returning to Catania, possibly due to battle damage. Of its crew Ltn Wolfgang Herkner and one other survived with injuries, the other two being killed. Flt Lt Johnston later wrote in his journal:

> "So far this week to earn one five-seconds burst at an 88 I've twice been the target for half-a-dozen 109s and once been blown up by a bomb. However [on this occasion] it was cheering to find that the machine hadn't a hole in it anywhere."

He added, profoundly:

> "I keep wondering what sort of mood I should wake up in if I was to be killed later in the day, whether morose or over-confident, nervous or expectant, with foreboding or at peace. I wonder how much longer I could continue to see every 109 which attacked me in time to evade and spoil his shot, and how many more times I could be shot-up without being shot down."

At the end of the day Sqn Ldr Douglas-Hamilton found time to write to his wife:

> "I have now been on this island for five days, and I must say it is a somewhat different life from any I have known before. You will have gathered from the press and news that we have raids every day and pretty heavy ones at that, but this place still holds out and it will continue to hold out. For the first time I have heard the whistle and explosion of a bomb so clearly that I will never forget it! The boys here are simply marvellous – they have shot down masses of Huns for virtually no loss – it is a real honour to be with such chaps. We too are lacing into them and one of the Squadron, Bill Douglas, got a Hun today. My respect for the German pilots has gone down considerably – they are scared stiff of Spitfires! I have lived through many adventures already, but it has been great fun really and I must say I have enjoyed it all greatly. England seems very far away just now, and so does the life I used to lead."

That evening the AOC sent a very strongly worded signal to the Air Ministry:

> "Regret that the quality of the pilots from Operation Calendar is not up to that of previous operations. In No. 601 Squadron, seven pilots out of 23 have had no operational experience and a further four have less than 25 hours flying on Spitfires; 12 pilots of the 23 have never fired their guns in action. The Commanding Officer of No. 601 Squadron (Sqn Ldr John Bisdee) also reports that seven of his experienced pilots were posted away from the squadron just before they left. Only fully experienced operational pilots must come here. It is no place for beginners. Casualties up till now have been the beginners."

On **26 April**, the AOC was advised that an intercept of Luftwaffe Enigma traffic indicated that some units of Fliegerkorps II were preparing to leave Sicily. There was little obvious evidence of this immediately however, as 55 Ju88s and some 15 Ju87s arrived from 1430 onwards to attack Kalafrana and Valetta, the telephone exchange being amongst other buildings demolished in the city. Six Spitfires (three/601, three/249) and four Hurricanes were scrambled. The 601 Squadron trio engaged Ju87s, the New Zealand pair Sgt Reg Dickson (BP964/1-X) and Sgt Jack McConnell (BR192/2-W) claiming one damaged between them, but their Canadian section leader, Plt Off Pip Cripps, was hit by fire from a Bf109 – possibly Oblt Helmut Belser of 8/JG53, who claimed his 24th victory – and was seriously wounded in the foot by a cannon shell. Cripps managed to bale out, but his parachute only partially opened and he broke his other foot on landing, later dying in hospital from spinal concussion and shock. His Spitfire (BR125/1-P) crashed in Qormi's main street. Flt Lt Barnham and Flg Off Cyril Hone watched the battle unfold and of 601 Squadron's second fatality, Barnham wrote:

> "Over came the waves of bombers, the noise of the shells shrieking out into space was the same as before, the barrage of black smoke smeared as the planes passed. Clouds of dust and smoke had risen from where the bombs had burst near Valetta and were drifting westwards towards Luqa when we saw something. Hone saw it first. 'There's a parachute coming down', he remarked quietly. 'Where?' I shouted. He pointed it out to me, about 4,000 feet and above the drifting dust. It seemed to be coming down very fast – was it going to pass behind the smoke or fall in front of it? But it was already there, a white silhouette against the drifting redness. It was falling appallingly fast, something must be wrong. Yes, one side of the chute was flapping loosely but the man hanging there was not struggling; as far as I could see he was just suspended looking down at his feet, or perhaps past them at the earth, which must be rushing up to meet him, 'Oh God, he won't survive that', I said to Hone. His parachute appeared suddenly in front of a sunlit square house and he disappeared from sight behind one of the stone walls in the valley beneath us. Sorrowfully, Cyril and I turn back towards Naxxar."

The four 249 Squadron aircraft had scrambled five minutes after the 601 Squadron section had departed, but Plt Off Nash had returned with an electrical systems failure, leaving Sgt Hesselyn to lead Plt Off James into action against a number of Bf109s over St Paul's Bay, as Hesselyn later recalled:

> "Thirty-five 109s were already over the island when we received word to scramble. I was pretty worried and expecting to be jumped by the 109s before we gained much height. I was worried still more after we had taken off. Pete's electrical system packed up. With his R/T useless, he signalled me to take over by waggling his wings and pointing downwards. As he went down to land, I called up Jimmy and told him to come a little closer and stay with me. Woody told us to get as much height as we could and wait, so we climbed up into sun. We could see the 109s above us. Some were behind, some in front, some on either side – I counted 20 in all. Woody kept calling up, telling us to watch the small jobs. We managed to get up to 16,000 feet without trouble. Then four 109s began making a pass at us, with others following in behind them. I felt bloody awful, and wondered what I should do.
>
> "I was afraid that if we attacked these we should become separated. However, I decided that if we attacked we might bluff our way out of it. It seemed the only thing to do. I told Jimmy we were going in at the four in front and that he was to take the rear one while I took the leader. I tackled the leader at about 200 yards range from the port quarter, and I could see Jimmy going in from the same angle on the rear 109. I had a chance for only a snap shot, but even so I saw one of my shells strike on the 109's starboard wing. The others were too high and missed. Straightening out for a second to take a squirt at a 109 in front, I was attacked head-on by about six others. I could see the shells and bullets coming from their noses and wings. One bullet hit my aircraft and flicked it over slightly,

so that I was flying half on my side and half on my back. I straightened up, and the 109s came at me again, some head-on and others from astern. I felt scared stiff, and thought that I was for it. I called up Jimmy, telling him to go back on his own.

"I climbed up and away from them to about 8,000 feet. Then Woody announced that 87s were diving on Takali. I caught one as he was going down in his dive, and went down after him, trying to get a bead on him. Not until he was pulling out of his dive did I finally get him in my sights. The rear gunner was firing, but he didn't worry me, as I knew he could not hit me. I opened fire at 300 yards, but could see only a few shells strike him on the starboard wing. I straightened my aircraft after this two-seconds burst and let him have four-seconds. He burst into vivid flames, and a second or two later two chutes came out. Both opened, and I could see them drifting lazily downwards. I went towards Takali, looking for Jimmy. A Spit was over the aerodrome, and I recognised it by its markings as Jimmy's aircraft. It jettisoned its hood and, realising that he was in trouble, I covered him while he landed. He force-landed on the aerodrome, landing on his belly with his wheels up. More 109s were coming in and strafing the drome. I saw Jimmy get out of his aircraft [BR199] and run towards a bomb hole, into which he slithered."

James suffered wounds to his neck and one leg from cannon splinters, but escaped further injury during the crash-landing. This may have been the incident witnessed by the Maltese teenager Carmel Grech:

"I heard the drone of aircraft engines, high up, coming from the direction of the sun. I tried to spot them but the blinding glare of the sun prevented me from seeing anything. I tried to shield my eyes with my hands but it was to no avail. From the sound of their engines, I could tell these were small fighter planes. I strained my eyes almost to the point of tears but still could not see a thing. Shortly afterwards I heard machine-gun and cannon fire, high up in the sky. It was obviously a dogfight between the Spitfires I had seen taking off and enemy aircraft. Still, there was nothing to be seen in the sun's blinding glare. I jumped into a field nearby, where there was a country hut, and took the wise precaution of taking cover from stray shells, bullets or empty cartridges that might have fallen from the sky. I still continued to search the sky and finally, I made out a thin line of smoke. This enabled me to locate where the dogfight was taking place. The aircraft were very high up, probably about 30,000 feet. They looked like small mosquitoes and I was unable to identify friend or foe. Then there was a loud wail and an aircraft fell from the sky, spinning out of control. Initially, I thought it was going to crash close to where I was but, when it descended to 5,000 feet, the pilot seemed to have regained control and levelled out. The sound from the engine was still very erratic and I could hear it spluttering and cutting out a number of times.

"It was one of our Spitfires and it glided down to land in the direction of Takali. When it lowered its undercarriage, only one wheel locked into place and the other remained retracted. The pilot circled the airfield hopefully but it was to no avail, as one of his wheels would not come down. The engine kept spluttering all the time, cutting out and coming to life again. I prayed to God to bring the pilot down safe and sound. He then made a final attempt. It seemed that he did not want to lose his precious Spitfire. Indeed, losing a Spitfire was just not on, even if the pilot had to risk his own life to bring it in safely. The aircraft was now at the end of the runway. It levelled out and glided in gently, engine cut. It touched down on one wheel and after about 50 yards, this wheel folded in and the plane skidded on its belly for another 100 yards, until it came to a stop and disappeared in a cloud of dust, off the runway. Three vehicles sped up to the crashed Spitfire. The outline of a man could be seen emerging from the dust cloud. It was the pilot who had escaped unhurt [sic]. I thanked God for hearing my prayer and sparing that poor pilot. When the dust cloud subsided, I saw the Spitfire lying on one side, with its nose dipped into the ground and its tail pointing skywards. Meanwhile, the dogfight, high above, was still raging on, although, by this time, it had moved onwards beyond Rabat and I could neither hear nor see any signs of the battle above. I decided to move on and proceed up the road to Rabat. When I had crossed the field and come to the road, the other two Spitfires came in over Takali. One of them performed a victory roll over the airfield."[36]

Remaining fighter strength was now so reduced that little resistance could be offered to two raids on **27 April**. During the morning 46 Ju88s and 16 Ju87s were counted in the sky over Luqa, where a Wellington was destroyed and another damaged. Gunners blazed away at the raiders and successfully accounted for two Ju88s, one of which fell into the sea and the other crashed on land. Mid-afternoon saw another 35 Ju88s and 21 Ju87s accompanied by five Z1007bis and 27 MC202s. Again, only the guns were able to put up a defence. Plt Off Nash and others took the opportunity to visit a few of the hospital cases:

"Went up to Mtarfa to see James [Plt Off Jimmy James]. He is quite OK. Also saw Sgt Tayleur. He is very rough. His eyes are bad and his nerves very shaky. Shocked at the difference between the officers and NCOs wards. It's a terrible scandal. Tayleur's ward resembles an extremely shabby barrack room and his food is very bad, while the officers [ward] is very good indeed."

There was a slight improvement for the fighters next day (**28 April**). The first scrambles of the day came early, two Spitfires of 126 Squadron and one of 601 going off at 0740. They were followed ten minutes later by four Hurricanes, to counter an estimated 43 Ju88s, 20 Ju87s and a large fighter escort. Three bombers were seen to detach themselves from the last wave, dive low over Floriana and release their bombs. One struck the dome of the picturesque church of St Publius. The miracle of Mosta was not to be repeated, for the bomb penetrated into the crypt and exploded, killing about a dozen persons taking shelter, including the priest.

The three Spitfires made initial contact with the raiders and dived after the Ju87s, but the 601 Squadron pilot had to break away with engine trouble, and returned to land. Flt Lt Johnston (BR190/2-A) got on the tail of one Stuka, but was attacked by another; he later wrote:

"Chris [Sgt Junior Crist] and I began to orbit and presently sighted Stukas, diving in a stream, all perpendicularly, and pulling out towards the east. Chose my man, manoeuvred to a position astern and underneath, took a last look round while waiting for the range to close, more from habit than in expectation of seeing anything, and was surprised to find an aircraft behind me firing. Thought, My God, 109; then saw its Stuka undercart and thought, well, it can't be firing; yet it undoubtedly was, so I thought. Perhaps it's a 109 after all; looked again and made sure of both the tracer and the undercart and finally admitted that it was a Stuka and that it was attacking me. Pulled out of line, feeling rather as if I'd been charged by an outraged ewe. Was amazed to find him following me round in the turn; not very perturbed, perhaps, because I could see that his deflection was far too small, but I kept thinking 'the intrepid bastard.' I should like to hear the line he's shooting in his mess tonight; feel he's justified, too.

"Returned to the procession, placed myself below and astern another one and opened fire with two cannon at 250 yards in an interrupted five-seconds burst. I saw strikes and he began to take most violent evasive action; I closed right in until I'd lost him under my nose. Dropped a wing to look at him and thought I saw a thin white stream of glycol vapour, but wasn't certain. I'd found him halfway between Luqa and Valetta at 6,000 feet, and we were now off Grand Harbour at 1,500. I dived on him again and repeated the attack with the same result, before two 109s left the offshore patrol and made me break off; it was no use going on, I could see others behind them. Landed without incident. This was a lesson to me in how effective really violent evasive action can be; normally I shouldn't have fired while the target was being thrown about, but waited my opportunity, but here the time-element is too important for such refinements and it's essential to fire quickly to fire at all. All the same felt bitterly disappointed in my shooting, after all the time I've spent in practice."

Crist did not make any claims but the Hurricane pilots claimed damage to two Ju87s and a Ju88 but lost another pilot. A little later, as the raid was clearing the island, three Spitfires of 603 Squadron were sent off, Plt Off Jack Slade claiming damage to one of four Bf109s engaged. Flg Off Holland of 603 wrote:

"In between devastating raids on our airfield, Takali armourers were still rearming the last of our Spitfires, which had just returned from a scramble. The sirens wailed yet again and anti aircraft bursts appeared in the sky over St Paul's Bay. One of the armourers started to slide off the wing and a few of us pilots made a move in the direction of the dispersal point slit trenches. We halted in our tracks when the sergeant in charge let the armourers know in no uncertain terms that they must finish the rearming. Shamefaced, we waited alongside as the Ju88s put their noses down, fortunately for us, at Luqa rather than Takali on that occasion. This was typical of the quality of our groundcrew NCOs to whom we owed the means to hit back."

Another raid at midday was not intercepted, a Wellington being destroyed at Luqa and a damaged Spitfire – BR124/2-U of 603 Squadron – was written off on the ground at Takali. The guns claimed two bombers damaged during the raid. A flight of five Z1007bis – in perfect formation – with fighter escort was sighted over the island at 20,000 feet during the afternoon, Luqa being their target. No interception was made. The fighters were up again to meet the evening raid when 37 Ju88s and 15 Ju87s, escorted by many Messerschmitts and Macchis, arrived to attack the usual targets. Six Spitfires and four Hurricanes scrambled, Flt Lt Barnham leading four of 601 Squadron to attack some of the bombers. He reported seeing one of his flock – 2/Lt Bartleman (BR116/1-V) on his first operational flight – knock pieces off a Ju88. He then became engaged with several Messerschmitts, almost colliding with one, but returned safely. The American Plt Off Tilley (BR185/2-Q) attacked a Bf109 on the tail of a Spitfire (possibly Barnham's aircraft) and claimed to have shot it down in flames. Of the action, ever self-critical, Barnham wrote:

"We're both down safely, and well done Baby Face! [Bartleman] Although his formation was hopeless – nearly pranging me in turns, passing low over the top of my cockpit instead of underneath – he can shoot straight. Saw puffs streaming back over his wings and huge lumps flying off the black 88 in front of him. Wasn't much good myself – over careful, watching for a precise moment to break. Baby Face followed me at once – downwards in direction of sun – best way – can see if one's being followed – 109s lost us. But did I break too early? Not much good getting amongst bombers without destroying any – one's shooting must be perfect – three or four seconds should be enough. Perhaps I should have stayed – my chosen 88 was large and staring at me through my gunsights – Oh! I'm a fool."

The guns claimed a further Ju88 shot down; on the ground an Albacore, two Spitfires (AB341/GN-E and AB348) and a Hurricane were damaged, and considerable further damage inflicted on airfield buildings. This was probably the raid referred to by Flg Off Holland:

"Slit trenches were certainly effective. Ordered to return from a late evening scramble, we were followed in by enemy aircraft. We had barely landed and climbed out of our cockpits, excitedly discussing the scraps in which we had just been involved, when an airman gave a warning shout. Eight diving Ju88s were releasing their loads directly at our dispersal point, the bombs consequently appearing round in shape. Pilots and groundcrew together leapt for a slit trench, as a 500kg bomb landed about twenty feet away. The explosion created a vacuum, which prevented any intake of breath for a few very uncomfortable seconds before the dust-laden air could be breathed in. Two of our precious Spitfires, still outside their blast-proof pens, and a steamroller, were riddled with shrapnel. Miraculously there were no human casualties."

With only four Spitfires immediately available, Grp Capt Woodhall refused to send them up to meet the next raid. Flt Lt Barnham recorded:

"Woody says there are only four fighters serviceable on the whole island. He says he must hold them on the ground – and the reason: lest Kesselring sends in his airborne invasion – we've got to stand by! I suppose this means that if we are sent off we attack gliders. In my apprehension I've been asking the Wingco how he'd operate against them. He just laughs."

Raids on **29 April** proved to be much smaller affairs, but brought heavy fighting nonetheless. Seven Ju88s and eight Bf109s raided Hal Far at 1445, four 126 Squadron Spitfires being led off by Sgt Goldsmith (BR187/2-O), followed somewhat later by four Hurricanes. The Australian wrote:

"I took my four machines, grabbing for as many angels as possible before the bombers arrived. At 20,000 feet we levelled off and came back towards the island with the sun behind us, from the south-west. Nearing the coast, ten 109s crossed us ahead and above but did not see us. Near Kalafrana we could see the flak, and then at once the bombers. These were about 30 Ju88s at 15,000 feet, with a close and medium cover of Messerschmitts. More 109s weaved about, 3,000 feet above us. As we saw them, the bombers started their dive towards Luqa. We stuffed our noses down and went after them, but we were unable to reach them to shoot anything until they had released their bombs and were heading out to sea. I closed on one and, at about 150 yards, opened up. My port cannon fired a couple of rounds, my starboard gun one, and then both chucked it in. Cursing violently, I broke away as the rear gunner's tracer came snaking after me. At the same time a Ju88 plummeted down, burning from Junior's guns.
    "Then there were 109s on us from all directions and independent dogfights raged furiously. A 109 started a head-on attack at me, but I wasn't in a condition for such frivolity, so dived for the waves and raced home on the deck. Preparing to land, I heard the controller call: 'Hullo all aircraft, cover a Spit landing at Luqa.' Climbing up, I saw it come in with its wheels up, so switched on the R/T and said: 'Wheels! Wheels!' Junior's voice came back in very heated tones, 'wheels be buggered', said as only a Canadian can say it, and his machine slithered to a stop in a cloud of dust. Having landed, we found Junior's machine had been shot-up quite a bit and he really was in a hurry to get down. He himself had been hit, too, his hands and forearms having been laced with splinters when a couple of shells had burst in the cockpit. Junior had been our only casualty, but he had knocked down an 88, and Jimmie got a 109."

Plt Off Peck (BR116/1-V) was credited with one probable and one damaged, while Crist's aircraft (BR190/2-A) had probably been hit by Fw Alfred Seidl of 8/JG53, who claimed a Spitfire as his ninth victory. The young Canadian later recalled:

"We were always badly outnumbered. You didn't have time to stick with one aircraft for any more than a second or two. If you damaged a bomber there were always fighters on you. You'd like to take a second shot at it but you had to look after yourself. It was difficult to finish them off because you were always under attack. It was a dog-eat-dog kind of affair. I remember one time I saw enemy fighters coming in but I thought I had enough time to line up a bomber for another shot. I cut it too fine and they got a pretty good burst into my aircraft. A big chunk of one wing came off, plus I was hit myself, although not seriously. The Spitfire went into a dive and by the time I recovered I was too low to bale out. I flew into the airstrip with my wheels up. I came in at 160mph but I made a pretty successful landing. Still, the plane was a write-off [not so, it was later flown to the Middle East], which was unfortunate because we were under unwritten orders to bring the plane in safe at all cost. I got out and an ambulance took me to hospital, where I was to remain for the next six weeks."[37]

A Ju88 of 1/KG54, B3+DH flown by Ltn Martin Krickl, was reported shot down by a fighter, apparently Crist's victim; there were no survivors. The Hurricanes returned safely, although two were damaged, the pilots in turn claiming damage to three Ju88s. Among those watching the action from the ground were pilots of 601 Squadron, who were awaiting breakfast, including Flt Lt Barnham:

"There was the sound of heavy engines rising to a crescendo as the German bombers, hidden from sight behind our palace roof, plunged towards us … a lone Spitfire was attacking. 'Don't shoot them down on top of the palace, you fool, we haven't had breakfast yet,' yelled Pancho [Le Bas]. My balcony was shuddering with each crash of anti-aircraft fire but, leaning out as far as I dared, I stared upwards to the palace parapet behind which the action was hidden; a wingtip, an engine, then the whole formation of about 30 Ju88s swept into view. I saw the elliptical flash of the Spitfire and heard the stutter of machine-guns, but incongruously I was intrigued by the Maltese crowds below; gesticulating with excitement, they surged and swayed – all except one huge fellow who stood like a breakwater with his arms folded, only his head turned, following the released bomb load over the rooftops."

Six more Ju88s and six Bf109s returned at 1720 to attack Luqa, where a Spitfire was damaged. AA claimed a bomber shot down. An hour later, five Macchi-escorted Z1007bis raided the same target but their bombs fell wide. Although six Spitfires were scrambled they failed to make an interception. Plt Off Peck came close, but could not gain altitude in time. However, an intense AA barrage greeted this raid, the gunners inflicting severe damage to Cap Aldo Gon's 53^Squadriglia MC202. Despite severe wounds, Gon successfully flew his damaged fighter back to Sicily and carried out a forced-landing at Agrigento.

April ended with two Luftwaffe raids on **30 April**, the first by 20 Ju88s, 18 Ju87s and a number of Bf109 Jabo, which attacked Hal Far and Luqa just after 1100, a Beaufighter being destroyed at the latter airfield. Four 603 Squadron Spitfires scrambled, followed by four more from 126 Squadron, the former quartet led by Sqn Ldr Douglas-Hamilton attacking Ju88s over Hal Far:

"Down we went at about 400mph into the middle of the 88s, just as they finished their dive. We rapidly closed with them head on and squirted one after another. Johnny Hurst destroyed one and John Buckstone damaged another. I squirted three 88s and a 109. Others had been shot at and quite possibly damaged, but we had not time to wait and see. One of my cannon had jammed and both Neville King's refused to fire. One of John Buckstone's had also jammed. We found later that some of the ammunition was faulty. Then the 109s came down on us, and we pulled this way and that. I remember being shot at on five occasions as I turned around, each time being thankful I had seen the Hun in time and watching the tracer passing behind me."

Douglas-Hamilton continued:

"We became split up, but reformed over the aerodrome, and then we had the longest part of the fight waiting to land. Round and round we went, a few feet above the ground, watching the 109s circling above and waiting for the unwary. I seized what I thought was a propitious moment for landing, having looked carefully all round and seen nothing. Lowering my wheels and flaps I concentrated on the landing. I throttled back a little earlier than usual as I straightened up on the glide, and to my surprise heard the rattle of musketry coming from the ground. Forthwith I started to turn, but barely had time to look behind me when I saw the large round nose of a Messerschmitt pass just a few feet behind me. Luckily for me he was a bad shot, as I did not get a single bullet hole in my aircraft. But his bullets had surprised several people on the ground as much as he had surprised me, and some of them had narrow escapes. We all got down without a scratch, though Johnny Hurst had been shot-up and we were all perspiring freely. I felt as if I had just played a strenuous rugger match."

Help for the vulnerable Spitfires came from an unusual source, as Wg Cdr Jack Satchell, Takali's station commander, recalled:

"I was manning a pair of Vickers K guns (which I did most days in company with others, who helped with the loading etc), when a 109 came in behind one of our remaining Spitfires (flown by David Douglas-Hamilton), who had wheels down for landing. I aimed the gun directly at Lord David's aircraft; the deflection of the speed was just right. I fired and had the satisfaction of seeing the 109 pull straight up, stall, and crash on the far side of the airfield. It was very spectacular indeed."

His victim, Fw Josef Kröschel of 8/JG53, managed to bale out of Black 5 (10104) just before it crashed and was taken prisoner. This brought Jack Satchell's tally with his twin-Vickers to one confirmed, two probables (a Bf109 and a Ju87) and a dozen damaged (five Bf109s, four Ju88s and three Ju87s) in the previous two weeks. The 126 Squadron Spitfires also attacked the Ju88s, Flt Lt Barton (BR116/1-V) and Plt Off Bailey (BR122/2-O) each claiming one damaged:

"On hearing that 88s were approaching the island from Zonqor Point direction we dived to meet them. At about 14,000 feet I had to take evasive action from 109s during which I lost the other two aircraft in the section. Finding myself in the centre of Ju88s, though slightly below at about 6,000 feet, I climbed and attacked one, which was pulling out of a dive after it had released bombs. Coming in below and astern, I fired cannons for four-five seconds, closing from 250 yards to about 50 yards. I saw several strikes underneath starboard wing and fuselage before I spun away. Coming out of spin I suddenly found myself on tail of a 109, the No.2 of a pair. He did not see me, so that I was able to get within firing range. Pressing the button, nothing happened (on landing I found that both cannons had jammed through faulty ammunition). I broke away and flew over Takali where I was again presented with a 109 as a target, unable to take advantage of it. I landed at Luqa."

In addition to his claim for a Ju88 damaged, Flt Lt Barton also claimed a Bf109 probably shot down. During the morning's action, two Spitfires were claimed shot down by Ltn Jürgen Harder (his 12th) and Ltn Erich Beckmann (his seventh), both of 7/JG53, although no losses were suffered by the defenders on this occasion.

The Regia Aeronautica was back at 1620, five Z1007bis of 50°Gruppo BT, escorted by almost two-dozen 4°Stormo Macchis, bombing in the Mellieha Bay area, causing Douglas-Hamilton to comment:

> "There were five of them in beautiful vic formation, and we all wondered when they would start their dive and what place they would bomb. But they did not dive at all, and presently we heard a sort of warbling, hissing sound that turned out to be their bombs falling – quite unlike the usual whistle of German bombs. The general consensus of opinion decided that they were Eyeties. Their escorting fighters flew in a very close but unwarlike formation. To keep such formation they obviously had to concentrate rather hard to keep position, which precluded their looking about them for our fighters."

Again six Spitfires took off, led by Plt Off Pete Nash – and again no interception resulted, the blame on this occasion being directed at poor controlling. An hour later, ten Ju88s and 23 Bf109s hit Luqa and Safi, finishing off a damaged Spitfire. AA gunners claimed another Bf109 shot down and one damaged, as well as a Ju88. They were successful in the case of the Messerschmitt, hitting an aircraft from JG53's Jabostaffel, the pilot of which baled out into the sea. Within the hour an escorted Do24 arrived to pick him up from under the very noses of the defenders.

The cause of the cannon jamming experienced by the Spitfire pilots was later ascertained to be faulty 20mm ammunition of American manufacture. Problems with cannons jamming were becoming ever more frequent, and on investigation it was discovered that one third of all cannon rounds in the armouries were misfits. Flt Lt McNair later wrote:

> "We wanted to take out two of the four cannons. The two additional guns were cutting down the performance of the aircraft and we were simply having twice as much gun trouble. Partly this was due to faulty ammunition, partly to weak recoil springs and partly to sloppy maintenance. Sloppy maintenance was because the work was so heart-breaking. It was becoming progressively more difficult to keep the aircraftmen under control. Some of them were most exemplary, showing in many instances more of the qualities of officers than some of the officers themselves. But it was heartbreaking work for them. They would work for weeks and weeks, without proper tools and equipment, making tools in many cases to do a job, and then a bomb would drop on the Spitfire before it had a chance to fly. It was most discouraging for them, and quite a number simply walked away, going absent without leave for several days ... "

He added:

> "There was little relaxation for either officers or men. The pilots weren't getting results. Time after time we would get into position to fire at the enemy only to find our guns jammed. This would lead to words between the pilots and armourers, although generally speaking the pilots and groundcrew got along amicably. The erks did an amazing job on the whole. All the fellows were amazingly good. Everyone pitched in to help the others. Pilots, officer or NCO, were glad to help the airmen. We had no bowsers to carry the fuel. All petrol had to be lugged by hand to refuel every Spitfire dispersed all around the airfield – we could not spare the gasoline to truck it around. And it takes a lot of petrol to fill even a fighter when you have to manhandle every drop. But there was a great spirit among those who stayed on Malta. Everyone was proud to be in the service with men who were carrying on under such miserable privations without any recognition. Officers and men felt like brothers to each other – we all shared work, foul food, poor lodgings, filth – and we all shared each other's worries."

By way of stark contrast, across the way in Sicily, German and Italian aircrews lived like kings, with batmen, cooks and orderlies waiting on them hand-and-foot.

Mealtime there was unforgettable. Describing one of his dinners, a German pilot wrote, "... the *pièce de résistance* consisted of two large dishes of scrambled eggs mixed with Italian tinned meat. Besides this, there were dishes and plates piled with tunnyfish, tinned sardines and anchovies, liver sausage, tinned ham, Italian saveloys [a type of sausage] and tomatoes and fresh fish." The pilots washed it all down with litres of wine that "glowed like amber" in the gentle lamplight. At nearby Italian air force bases, the airmen gorged themselves with fresh fish purchased from open-air markets. There was so much food available that, when flying, they often brought along hampers stuffed with wine, cheese, cake, king-sized loaves of homemade bread, sausages and fruit. Some bomber crews even had classical music pumped in over the radio and had curtains put on their side windows.[38]

By the end of the month no more than seven Spitfires and a handful of Hurricanes remained serviceable. It was estimated that Takali alone had been on the receiving end of 841 tons of bombs during April, compared to 482 tons in March and 120 tons in February; the other two airfields had received similar tonnages. 339 civilians and 208 servicemen had been killed during the April assault; in addition, some 550 civilians and many servicemen were injured. Defending fighters were credited with 53 victories during the month, of which Hurricane pilots claimed a few but these were generally categorised as probables rather than 'confirmed' victories. Actual German losses were substantially fewer than this, however. During the month a second PR Spitfire had arrived, BP885 flown by Sgt Les Colquhoun, who had previously served as a fighter pilot with 603 Squadron. The two Spitfires, in the hands of Plt Off Coldbeck and Colquhoun, had carried out 23 sorties during the month, totalling almost 64 hours flying time.

Several personnel changes occurred during the month, the most notable being the departure of Wg Cdr Turner, his place as Wing Commander Flying at Takali being taken by newly promoted Wg Cdr Gracie. Command of 126 Squadron passed to Sqn Ldr Barton. Others on the move included the pilots from both 126 and 601 Squadrons, as Sgt Goldsmith recalled:

> "The pilots of our squadron and of 601 Squadron were moved from our comparatively comfortable billets at Mdina to a village on the outskirts of Takali/Naxxar. Here we were settled into a building that was originally a palace. The walls and ceilings were covered with paintings and practically every room sported a chandelier. After the officers had selected the best rooms for sleeping and messing, we sergeants moved into what was left, and found that they hadn't left much. The rooms proved to be in a filthy state, as was the kitchen and mess hall. Flies swarmed on everything and when eating it was necessary to continually move one hand over the food, while using the other to transfer portions of it swiftly to the mouth. The effect of the dirt on us was soon shown by the increased number of cases of Malta Dog."

249 Squadron saw the departure of the injured Flt Lt Nip Heppell[39] and the sick Plt Off Jeff West, while Sqn Ldr Grant, Flt Lt Lucas, newly promoted Flt Lt Ron West, Flt Lt McNair and Flg Off Daddo-Langlois were flown to Gibraltar aboard a Hudson to assist with the next Spitfire delivery. The AOC had decided that it was essential for the next reinforcements to be led in by experienced Malta pilots.

CHAPTER IV

BATTLE FOR SURVIVAL

May 1942

May opened with a number of small Axis fighter sweeps. The first of these was intercepted at around mid-morning on **1 May** by two Spitfires flown by Flt Lt Macqueen and Plt Off Les Watts (BP962/2-R), who, while on an air test near Filfla, were advised of the presence of Messerschmitts nearby. Four Bf109s of 6/JG53, all carrying long-range tanks, were spotted. Giving chase at once, Macqueen and Watts jointly shot down one Messerschmitt (10076), the pilot of which carried out a successful ditching in the sea off Cape Scaramia. Watts also reported strikes on a second Messerschmitt. Later, while searching for the downed pilot, a Do24T CH+EZ of 6 Seenotstaffel from Sicily was obliged to force-land on the sea, but the Messerschmitt pilot was picked up safely by another Axis craft.

Late afternoon saw the appearance of five 50°Gruppo BT Z1007bis over the island, escorted by 19 MC202s of 9°Gruppo CT, two of which were slightly damaged by AA fire. 603 Squadron scrambled four Spitfires at 1700 to intercept the Italian bombers, but these encountered instead a number of Bf109s, two of which attacked Flt Lt Buckstone and Flt Sgt Rae. The latter's Spitfire (BP962/2-R) was hit by cannon fire, apparently from the Messerschmitt flown by Ltn Herbert Soukop of 6/JG53. Rae later related:

> "Suddenly I heard a scream over the radio from Mitch: 'Break left, Jack! Break, break, break, Jack!' With that first yell I began to turn immediately. That's what saved me from being blown to pieces as the 109 had come up under me and fired at short range. But for Mitch's warning it would have been a direct hit. As it was my control column was blasted out of its base, cannon shells exploded into my flying boot, most of the instruments were shattered and to add to the problems my instinctive action when breaking into the turn had been to give full throttle. The throttle was now hanging useless and the aircraft was in a spiralling power dive. I was thrown to the floor of the cockpit with the g-force and for what seemed an eternity lay pinned there by the force of gravity. Clawing my way up the side proved impossible then all of a sudden the stricken aircraft gave a sudden jolt and I was hurled right out of the cockpit ... it was a lucky day for me that my hood was open and I was thrown out."

Meanwhile, Sqn Ldr Douglas-Hamilton and Plt Off Bert Mitchell fired at Soukop's aircraft, following which Buckstone saw a cannon shell apparently hit the Messerschmitt's tail. It was later reported to have crashed into the sea but, in fact, Soukop returned safely, and it is believed that this report referred to the aircraft shot down that morning by Macqueen and Watts. Despite abandoning his aircraft some seven miles out to sea, the wind blew Rae back over the island, and he eventually came down near Rabat:

> "The landing was far from a textbook example of how to do it but it was wonderful to be back on mother earth. I was grateful to be able to just lie there next to a stone wall and wait for help. So much for my fond expectations. Instead of help, a shotgun appeared over the stone wall, followed by a very excited and hostile Maltese. He approached me muttering in Maltese with his finger white on the trigger. He either did not speak English or did not want to understand me and his excitement was increasing.

Then the most wonderful sight of all appeared, a group of British army boys from the 4th Buffs. One lesson all fighter pilots in Malta learned from my confrontation with that Maltese. We stopped recording our victories with swastikas painted on our Mae Wests. That was where my problem arose. The swastikas had acted like a red rag to a bull. In the future, large roundels of red, white and blue appeared as added insurance."

Sqn Ldr Bisdee, who had returned to 601 Squadron from convalescence, decided to lead a dawn readiness patrol of four Spitfires on **2 May**. He and two others flew to Takali, from where they were to operate but Flt Lt Barnham was delayed, as his aircraft required further work to render it fully serviceable. He followed a little later, landing at Takali just as a lone Ju88 swept in. As Barnham climbed from his Spitfire he was surprised to see everyone else running away from him. He looked up to see the raider diving in his direction:

"I began to dash for cover when – snap-crack; a ringing blow seemed to have stretched all the membranes within me. It must have been only a few minutes later, the dust was falling back, some airmen were running to help me, there was a ringing, ringing, ringing in my head – staggering to my feet I must have started running, running in the same direction as before. Overwhelmed by a single desire to bury myself deep and safe in the rock, I found myself jolting down a steep rocky incline into a kind of pit… ashamed, I turned round at once and walked back."

This raider's other three bombs had been released elsewhere, one falling on the main square at Zejtun, which was crowded with people and 21 were killed and 29 seriously injured. The afternoon saw a raid by a dozen Ju88s on Luqa and Safi, with escort provided by Messerschmitts and Macchis, 18 of the latter from 10°Gruppo CT, which had transferred to Gela airfield only the previous day. A Maryland was damaged and an unserviceable Wellington burnt out, although two Spitfires of 249 Squadron managed to scramble. Sgt Hesselyn was on this sortie:

"Buck [Buchanan] and I were scrambled. This time a fairly big party was reported coming in. As we broke cloud we saw six Ju88s about 1,000 feet below us. They had a heavy escort of 109s, and on the starboard side of the bombers what was to us a new type of machine and formation. At first glance we didn't know what they were, but later recognised them as Italian fighters – Macchi 202s. There were 13, and they were flying tightly packed in echelon formation. However, we had little time to devote to them, and started to go in at the bombers. I chose the rear one, which was lagging slightly. I was getting nicely within range, and considered I had him dead in my sights, when I was attacked head-on by four 109s. At the same moment other 109s, which I had not previously seen, broke cloud behind me and came down, trying to get on my tail. I had no chance of getting my 88. I turned and climbed for the cover of the cloud. As I went up I saw Buck doing precisely the same thing."

After some time playing hide-and-seek among the clouds, the Messerschmitts eventually turned and headed back towards Sicily, leaving the two relieved Spitfire pilots to land safely at Takali, where Flg Off Buchanan reported that he had gained strikes on one of the Messerschmitts.

Next morning (**3 May**) the Ju88s were back, seven bombers raiding Hal Far shortly before midday. Five of 249 were scrambled while two others covered the aerodrome. Plt Off Nash (BR184/2-C), who was flying with Plt Off Milburn, noted:

"D'Arcy and I were drome defence section. Came in at 2,000 feet just under 9/10th cloud and jumped four 109s over Hal Far. D'Arcy lost me during subsequent manoeuvres. Chased two and shot the No.2 down at sea level. Was then jumped by two more so came home five miles west of Kalafrana. Only had port cannon working."

Milburn claimed a second Messerschmitt as damaged. Plt Off Watts (GN-N) also claimed one damaged. Sqn Ldr Bisdee (BR964/1-X) was also airborne in company with Sgts Jack McConnell (BR122/2-O) and Ernie Shea (BR185/2-Q), similarly engaging the Messerschmitts. No claims were made but one Spitfire suffered two bullet holes through one wing. On a later sortie Plt Off Peck landed heavily in BR185/2-Q, the Spitfire being damaged beyond repair. When five Cants bombed at 1355, the raiders found no defending fighters up. Bombs fell close to Naxxar where 601 Squadron pilots were now billeted. Flt Lt Barnham and 2/Lt Bartleman, with Plt Offs Max Briggs and Tommy Scott, rushed to give aid. Finding a bomb-damaged house, the four pilots began digging with their bare hands. Barnham subsequently wrote:

> "The last rocks removed, the old man is freed, and we lift him on to a stretcher that has been squeezed through to us ... now I'm walking alongside the stretcher for he talks to me and I hold his hand. We pass red-eyed neighbours, who, peering from their doorways, cross themselves as we approach the square where an ambulance is surrounded by an excited crowd. In the ambulance the old man talks to me for a few moments, then, relaxing his grip on my hand, he dies."

Almost two dozen Ju87s from III/StG3, a dozen Ju88s, bomb-carrying Bf109s, and a strong fighter escort including 16 MC202s of 9°Gruppo CT, approached the island at 1740 to attack Hal Far and Luqa yet again. One Hurricane was slightly damaged at the former field, a PR Spitfire (AB300) and a Wellington suffering damage on the latter. Five Spitfires were again scrambled, this time flown by pilots of 603 Squadron. Flt Lt Douglas (BR198) attacked a Ju87, shooting off the cockpit canopy and seeing the gunner slump, apparently dead, over his gun. To his chagrin, he was credited with only a 'damaged'. However, Plt Off Jack Slade succeeded in shooting down another Ju87 with his machine-guns only, when his cannons refused to fire. Gfr Karl Haf's S7+JP crashed near Zonqor, his gunner (Gfr Fritz Weber) surviving to be taken prisoner. The Canadian Flt Sgt Allan Otto, on his first operational flight over Malta, noted in his logbook: "Intercepted Ju88, 87 and 109s. Short squirt at 88, nil."

At 1015 on the morning of **4 May**, six Ju88s and nine Bf109s, some carrying bombs, raided Luqa and Safi, AA gunners claiming one Messerschmitt shot down. Shortly afterwards, the usual formation of five Z1007bis – aircraft of 211^Squadriglia – covered by five Macchis of 9°Gruppo and ten Bf109s – came over and bombed Grand Harbour. The Italians reported that three Spitfires attempted to attack the bombers, and that two of these were shot down by Sottoten Alvaro Querci and Serg Teresio Martinoli of 73^Squadriglia, one of which they believed crashed into the sea. They may have attacked Sgt McConnell's BR187/O, one of four 601 Squadron Spitfires that had been scrambled. McConnell crash-landed his aircraft at Luqa after its radiator had sustained damage – though reportedly following an attack by a Messerschmitt. Four Spitfires of 249 Squadron led by Flt Lt Macqueen had also been scrambled to counter the raid. Flt Sgt Brennan wrote:

> "Caught as we head up sun, a little south of Gozo. The 109s were everywhere. Linny [Plt Off Linton] and I were at once separated from Mac and Almos [Plt Off Fred Almos, an American newcomer]. The last I saw of Linny was when he was in a vertical dive, skidding and twisting like blazes, with four 109s hotly pursuing him. It seemed to me as if I had been throwing my aircraft about for an hour when a Hun blundered. He made

a belly attack on me, missed and overshot. He was a sitting target. I gave him four-seconds. He went into a spin, pouring glycol. Almos called up that Mac was in trouble and wanted to land."

Having arrived too late to catch the bombers, Flt Lt Macqueen had apparently suffered an R/T failure and, consequently, was unable to hear warnings of approaching danger. Watchers on the ground saw a Bf109 bounce him, but miss and overshoot. The German No.2, Uffz Walter Manz of 9/JG53, then pulled up underneath and gained strikes on Macqueen's aircraft (BR226). As he approached Takali, Brennan saw it gliding across the airfield at 5,000 feet:

"As I watched his aircraft gave a sudden lurch, side-slipped about 1,000 feet, and then seemed to come under control again. I did not like the look of things. I called up: 'Mac, if you're not OK, for God's sake bale out. I will cover you.' There was no reply. A couple of seconds later his aircraft gave another lurch, went into a vertical dive, and crashed at Naxxar, a mile from the aerodrome."

Many on the ground including the CO of 601 Squadron, Sqn Ldr Bisdee, also witnessed Macqueen's demise:

"Several of us saw it happen from the mess verandah. We saw the 109's tracer going right into Norman's machine. His Spitfire lurched and gave out a thin smoke trail. For some time it seemed to be under control and circled downwards as if he hoped to land. Then suddenly the nose went forward, and the machine dived like a stone into the ground, bursting into flames as it hit. I felt a lump come into my throat."

It was assumed that Macqueen had been seriously wounded, if not killed, when attacked. Witnesses were of the impression that the inexperienced Almos had been too close to protect his leader's tail from this attack. The luckless American was soon transferred to 126 Squadron in which an all-American flight was to be formed.

At 1225, Flg Off Buchanan and Sgt Hesselyn were scrambled to provide cover for a returning photo-reconnaissance Spitfire being pursued by Italian fighters. The reconnaissance pilot evaded his attackers but crashed on landing, though escaping injury. No sooner were the 249 Squadron duo airborne than they were warned of two low-flying Bf109s over Hal Far. Unable initially to find these, they saw a pair, probably the same, being fired upon by AA over Grand Harbour. Catching up with one, Hesselyn opened fire for two seconds before his cannons jammed. The Messerschmitt dived steeply for Takali and at first appeared about to crash, but at the last moment pulled up and flew off northwards. Hesselyn was credited with damaging the fighter, but as it sped away it passed over a bus full of Maltese civilians, which was trundling down the Rabat to Takali road. Thinking they were about to be strafed, the passengers piled out of the bus, seeking cover. One man dived through a window, cracked his skull on the road and died shortly afterwards from the resultant fracture.

On Sicily, a new fighter unit arrived from mainland Italy. This was 2°Gruppo Aut CT equipped with the new Reggiane RE2001, powered by the German Daimler-Benz DB601A engine. Three squadriglie – 150^ (Cap Roberto Fassi), 152^ (Cap Salvatore Teia) and 358^ (Cap Annibale Sterzi) – eighteen aircraft – under the command of TenCol Aldo Quarantotti flew into Caltagirone airfield, in preparation for operations over Malta. The Reggiane was untried and untested in combat, but its pilots were keen and confident. The unit was soon to be in action.

Further respite from constant action followed on **5 May**, a day of no reported engagements. With the arrival at Malta of the new Hurricanes from Egypt, four of these were scrambled on the morning of **6 May**, accompanied by four Spitfires flown by 603 Squadron pilots, to intercept a raid comprising ten Ju88s and ten Bf109s. Three of the bombers were claimed damaged by Flt Lt Sanders, Plt Off Slade and Sgt Webster, but the fourth man of the quartet, Flt Sgt Otto, had returned early. On his first attempt to land, he overshot, tried to go round again but crashed and sustained head injuries including concussion and severe bruising. His aircraft, AB340, was damaged beyond repair. One Hurricane pilot failed to return and a second crash-landed having been hit by return fire. Two Spitfires from 126 Squadron had been despatched to cover the returning fighters, Flt Lt Johnston (BR116/1-V) and Plt Off Booth meeting four Bf109s over Hal Far. Johnston reported gaining strikes on one with one cannon only working, then attacked another:

"Next instant, without warning, bang, bang, bang, I could hear and feel three cannon shells exploding in the bottom of my machine. I remember instinctively kicking on the rudder after the first explosion and feeling how futile it was as the other two followed in quick succession, as quickly as you can say three words, and then experiencing that sensation of insignificance and resignation that comes when you are suddenly overtaken by fate; I remember also that I realised that the aircraft was on fire. Then there is a gap in my memory which I still don't fully understand; it can't have lasted more than two or three seconds, and the most likely explanation seems to be that when it was hit the machine did something of its own accord so violent that I was momentarily blacked out. Alternatively my head may have hit part of the cockpit – a deep gash was afterwards found under my hair – and I may have been knocked out. My only recollection is a hazy one of putting the stick forward and correcting a spin, but the speed must already have been 270-300mph and the nose was down, so it can't have been that. When full consciousness returned, I found myself still in the seat, squirming this way and that against the straps, but making no effort to undo the harness and get out, with a great flame rushing up from the bottom of the cockpit and being drawn past my face by the suction of the slip-stream. My first thought was that this time it was certainly the end and that there must have been some mistake, because I wasn't supposed to die. The fire prevented me from seeing anything outside the aircraft, but I could tell by feel that it was diving very steeply and fast and, after being blacked out for those few moments, I must have imagined I was nearer the ground than I actually was. After the last experience I never thought I should be able to escape this time.

"I can remember I noticed a curious smell; I don't know whether it was something burning, or me being burnt; it was not so much unpleasant as entirely strange to me, and it was this, not heat or pain, which was the most forcible physical sensation. I found afterwards that my legs had been peppered by cannon splinters, but I never felt them at the time. No past life flashed before me, I think things happen too quickly in the air for this to be possible; I only remember that everything was red, that I felt this terrible flame was robbing me of the power to think, and that I knew that if I lost my head it would destroy me. I thought of what was waiting a few hundred or a few thousand feet below, I didn't know which, that terrible crash and burst of flame. In the meantime I'd very deliberately pulled out the locking-pin of the harness; I knew I couldn't afford to fumble with it and remember I shaded my eyes with my left arm and looked down so as to make sure; then half stood in the cockpit, decided there was no time to try to take my helmet off and it would have to be risked, kicked the stick forward as far as I could, felt the helmet and mask parting, and was shot forward into the air. The aircraft was diving so fast that I might have been an arrow and it a tautened bow. I must have passed out at once, I don't even remember pulling the ripcord and have no memory of the chute opening or of the descent, only hitting the ground, then more oblivion.

"I began to come round as the first Tommies arrived; they helped me to unbuckle the chute and soon had me on a stretcher. I don't know where they took me, I had a cloth over my head and was taking little interest; I remember hearing the sympathetic wailing of a crowd of Maltese and a voice saying: 'Is he dead?' I wanted to say, 'No bloody fear!' – or something like that, but shirked the effort, it was so much easier to keep absolutely still; my right leg was numb now, and face and arms had grown pretty painful. We arrived at some sort of barrack room and a medical orderly put a dressing on my left knee, which was bleeding from a splinter wound. After what seemed a long wait an ambulance arrived; by this time I had begun to suffer from violent shivering-fits and my face and arms were growing hotter and hotter and steadily more painful. I lay there wondering whether I should lose my eyesight, and how much my face would be disfigured."[40]

It would seem that Johnston was shot down by the combined fire of Obfw Rudolf Ehrenberger of 6/JG53 and Ltn Hans Langer of Stab II/JG53, each of whom claimed a Spitfire shortly after 1000. Johnston's No.2, the American Booth reported, to quote his hand-written combat report:

"Scrambled with my section leader on airdrome defense. Climbed to west until we were told to come back, at which time we were about 12,000 feet. We then flew around over the island until my leader started down on an attack. I followed and saw two 109s. My leader seemed to be heading for the 109 leader, so I went for the second. That was the last I saw of my leader. I close in on the 109 from the rear on a quarter attack until I was close enough to plainly see the black cross on it. I fired for about two seconds, and then looked all around behind me. As the 109 had apparently taken no evasive action I proceeded firing again for about two seconds. I observed a little black smoke, not enough to be sure what it meant, and broke away. The 109, as I left, was still making the gentle turn it was in when I attacked, and had still taken no evasive action. I then proceeded to Takali at very low altitude, waiting for permission to land."

Italian intelligence had received information – presumably from one of its spies – that a further reinforcement of Spitfires was imminently due, but had got the date wrong. Hence, throughout the daylight hours of **7 May**, pairs of MC202s patrolled off the coast of Malta to prevent the landing of new arrivals but, of course, none were seen. Although six Spitfires flown by 603 Squadron pilots were scrambled during the afternoon, together with eight Hurricanes, only the latter made contact with the incoming raid, one Hurricane pilot claiming a Bf109 shot down. There were no losses.

After several days that had been much quieter than those recently, **8 May** heralded the start of another intensive Luftwaffe offensive against the island. Early morning saw two Spitfires of 126 Squadron intercept a reconnaissance intrusion – a Ju88 escorted by two Bf109s. Plt Off Tilley reported an engagement with one of the escort some 30 miles north of the island, returning safely to claim its destruction. The next raid came in at 0900, six Ju88s of KGr806 and 15 Ju87s of III/StG3 with a large fighter escort that included MC202s from 97^Squadriglia attacking Hal Far, Kalafrana and Luqa. Seven Hurricanes and four Spitfires flown by 126 Squadron pilots engaged, Plt Offs Tilley and John Mejor each claiming a Bf109; of his first combat, the latter noted in his logbook:

"Me109 destroyed. Yellow-nose. Got burst at his No.2. Was jumped at 17,000 feet by four 109s. Had no ammo, was forced to do dummy attacks."

Several of the Macchi pilots reported combats with Spitfires, two of which were claimed by Ten Luigi Giannella and two more by Cap Roberto Dagasso and Ten Ado Bonuti. There were, however, no losses of Spitfires or Hurricanes in this action. The raiders were back at 1325. Five Ju88s and 18 Ju87s attacked Luqa and Takali, while five Cants bombed Hal Far. Only a dozen Hurricanes and Spitfires remained serviceable, and as these were being preserved to support the imminent Spitfire delivery, no fighters rose to intercept. When the raiders hit Takali, Flt Lt Connell and Flg Off Buchanan of 249 Squadron found themselves caught in the open, the Canadian being wounded by shrapnel or debris.

Help for the beleaguered island was not far away. The USS *Wasp*, with 50 Spitfires embarked, had departed Gibraltar on the night of 7/8 May, and was joined by *Eagle* carrying a further 17 Spitfires for Malta. Sqn Ldr Grant and Flt Lt Ron West were on board *Wasp* and were to lead the first two flights to Malta; the other three 249 pilots sent to Gibraltar for similar duty were held back to assist with a second operation, planned for 18 May. That decision did not go down well with Flt Lt McNair, as recalled by Flt Lt Lucas:

> "Buck McNair nearly did his nut: he was a restless, aggressive Canadian who wanted to be in the thick of the fighting all the time. He could be rude – even to a wing commander! And he was certainly rude to Mac [Wg Cdr McLean, in charge of the Spitfire delivery] in Gib. 'Goddam, Sir, are you really asking Laddie, Daddo and me to sit on our arses here in Gib for another ten days while they'll be the hell of a party going on over the island? Sir, Goddam, I'm brassed right off.' He got no change out of Mac who was surprisingly calm with him. Daddo-Langlois and I (and Mac) had nearly ten days of Buck's bitching and binding before we went aboard *Eagle* to lead in the next 17 Spitfires to Malta."

More than half the pilots aboard the two carriers were from Commonwealth countries, of whom 28 were members of the RCAF, and included five Americans. The pilots embarked on *Eagle* were, in fact, a complete flight from 611 Squadron; these were:

Flt Lt J.P. Winfield	Plt Off J.W.P. Baril RCAF
Plt Off E.L. Hetherington	Plt Off A.S. Yates RAAF
Plt Off R.H. Turlington	Flt Sgt D.A.Bye
Plt Off A.R. Boyle	Flt Sgt H. Haggas
Plt Off W.J. Johnson (BP870)	Sgt J.W. Patterson
Plt Off D.E. Llewellyn (BP953)	Sgt C.E. Graysmark BP871
Plt Off C.A.McC. Barbour	Sgt L.J. Morsheimer RCAF (US)[41]
Plt Off R.O. Jones (US)	Sgt F.R. Johnson RAAF

Plt Off J.A.W. Gunn was also earmarked for this flight, having been posted to Gibraltar with the rest of 611 Squadron, but was then considered too inexperienced even to make the onward journey[42]. Aboard *Wasp* were 50 pilots from assorted squadrons; these are believed to have included:

Sqn Ldr S.B. Grant (flight leader)	Flt Sgt J.E. MacNamara RCAF
Flt Lt R. West (flight leader)	Flt Sgt J.V. Rounsefell RCAF
Flt Lt R.H.C. Sly RAAF (BR348)	Flt Sgt D.G. Reid RCAF
Flg Off J.R. Stoop	Flt Sgt C.N. Valiquet RCAF
Flg Off R.A. Mitchell	Flt Sgt B.W. Andrews RCAF (US)
Plt Off O.W.H. Berkeley-Hill	Flt Sgt M.W. Vineyard RCAF (US)
Plt Off J.R.S. Halford	Flt Sgt L.A. Verrall RNZAF
Plt Off R.R. Barnfather (BR345/3-Z)	Flt Sgt W.C. Conway RNZAF
Plt Off E.S. Dicks-Sherwood (Rhod)	Flt Sgt W.R. Irwin RAAF
Plt Off L.G. Barlow (SA)	Flt Sgt E.L. Mahar RAAF
Plt Off N.R. Fowlow RCAF	Sgt J.I. Williamson
Plt Off J.A. Smith RCAF (BR126/3-X)	Sgt R. Downing

Plt Off D.W. Kent
Plt Off G.W. Northcott RCAF
Plt Off A.A. McNaughton RCAF
Plt Off F.J. Sherlock RCAF
Plt Off C.A. King RCAF (BR248)
Plt Off B.C. Downs (US)
Flt Sgt J.C. Gray
Flt Sgt F.D. Schofield
Flt Sgt G.H.T. Farquharson RCAF
Flt Sgt B. Butler RCAF
Flt Sgt T. Parks RCAF
Flt Sgt R.H. Brown RCAF
Flt Sgt J.W. Williams RCAF

Sgt G. Allen-Rowlandson
Sgt A.A. Toller
Sgt J.C. Gilbert
Sgt K.J. Lusty
Sgt R.D. Sherrington RCAF
Sgt W.N. Shepherd RCAF
Sgt E.D. Moye RCAF (US)
Sgt V. Willie RCAF
Sgt H.J. Fox RCAF (US)
Sgt R. Buckley RCAF
Sgt C.S.G. de Nancrède RCAF
(BR300)
Sgt E.J. Shaw RNZAF
Sgt C.D. Bell RAAF

The Canadian pair Bob Brown and Dick Buckley were 603 Squadron pilots whose aircraft had become unserviceable for an earlier flight to Malta; they had returned to Gibraltar with Wasp, and were now able to rejoin their squadron. Bert Toller, Bob Downing and the Australian Colin Bell were members of 601 Squadron who had also failed to make the earlier ferry flight.

*   *   *

First off from *Wasp* at dawn on the morning of **9 May** were eleven of her own F4F Wildcats, to provide cover for the departing Spitfires. Sqn Ldr Grant was airborne at 0643 and set course for Malta at the head of his flight, which was to land at Takali. The pilots of Flt Lt West's flight, who were to follow, were briefed to fly to Luqa. All was going well until one Spitfire (possibly BP972) failed to gain sufficient flying speed and crashed into the sea. The carrier, unable to alter course, passed over the ditched aircraft, splitting it in two; its Canadian pilot Bob Sherrington, a 20-year-old from Toronto, did not survive. A second Spitfire, BR126/3-X flown by fellow Canadian Jerry Smith, returned with a faulty long-range fuel tank. Against orders, but having waited for all aircraft to take off and for any unserviceable Spitfires to be cleared from the deck, he made an approach to land, only to be waved off by the Deck Landing Officer, Lt Cdr David McCampbell USN, as he was too high:

> "Smith had lost his 90-gallon belly tank on take-off. There was, therefore, no way that he was going to have enough fuel to reach Malta; nor could he make it back to Gibraltar. He had two choices – climbing up and baling out and being picked up by a destroyer, or going for a landing back aboard ship with no tailhook to check him.
>
> "Fortunately I had given all the Spitfire pilots a briefing before take-off to acquaint them with the operations aboard ship. One of the things I told them was that during landing operations if anyone saw me jump into the net alongside my platform he would know the plane coming in to land was in trouble and it was the signal for the pilot to go round again and make a new approach. When Pilot Officer Smith decided to make his attempt at a landing without the tailhook, all our planes were in the air, so we could give him the whole length of the flight deck.
>
> "On the first approach he was much too high and too fast and when I found I couldn't bring him down or slow him down enough for a landing, I simply jumped into the net. He got the news real fast and went round for a second approach. As I got him to slow down and make his approach a little lower, I decided to give him the 'cut' signal. He landed safely with his wheels just six feet short of the forward part of the flight deck."

Although his performance was frowned upon by the British authorities, he was heartily congratulated by his amazed American audience. In his diary Jerry Smith wrote:

"We took off today. One of our lads went in off the end, and ship cut him in two. He never came up. I took off and found wing tank out of commission, so after others had finished I landed back on carrier – the first Spit ever to do it. The Americans made a terrific fuss and presented me with US Navy wings and a cake. Had great time that night."

Malta was ready for the Spitfires this time. Pilots at Takali were advised that every new Spitfire was to be back in the air within 15 minutes of its arrival. Five men were to be allocated to each aircraft pen, plus an experienced pilot to take over the aircraft. Long-range tanks would be removed first, and each pen would contain all that was necessary to rearm and refuel the fighters, the fuel being kept in four-gallon cans protected by sandbags. Every incoming Spitfire from *Wasp* had a large number ('3' or '4') and letter combination painted on its fuselage. Each aircraft pen was allocated a specific aircraft so identified, which had to be led in regardless of the situation at the time. Whatever the rank of the new arrival, the Malta pilot in the pen was in command, and was to take over the aircraft at once and get it back into the air with all speed. If the aircraft happened to be damaged, it was to be taxied to repair pens at the rear. The pilot, if not wounded, was to return to the airfield to take over a more junior pilot's aircraft. All available Hurricanes and Spitfires were to be airborne to provide cover for the incoming fighters. The welcome for the Spitfires upon the ground was worked out to the last detail by Wg Cdr Jumbo Gracie, who described the preparations for the operation:

"We went to our pilots and groundcrews and administrative staffs and told them we were going to give them, we hoped, an organisation which would enable us to win the battle of Malta, which at that time we were in grave danger of losing. We then told them it would mean the hardest possible work under very difficult conditions, that we were going to enlist the aid of the army, both in men and materials, but that the battle was lost unless they all pulled their weight one hundred per cent. The response was tremendous. Every man felt himself an important item in the battle and not merely an insignificant unit. So magnificently did the ground staffs work that our half-hour service became an absolutely outside limit, and the official records show that six Spitfires of one squadron took off to engage the enemy within nine minutes of landing on the island. What a change in thirty-six hours! Within half-an-hour every serviceable Spitfire was in the air. I shall never forget the remark of one airman who, coming out of a slit trench, and seeing two or three squadrons in the air, said; 'Heavens, look at the fog!'"

First enemy activity over Malta had occurred at 0720, when a reconnaissance Ju88 and five Bf109s crossed the coast, only the AA guns engaging them. When another Ju88, five Cants, 16 Macchis and up to 45 Messerschmitts appeared two hours later, however, nine Hurricanes took off to provide some protection for the first batch of Spitfires, which were then imminently due. They were followed by six Spitfires flown by 603 Squadron pilots, both formations seeking to provide maximum cover for Takali. From near Pantelleria, Sqn Ldr Grant advised Malta of his flight's imminent arrival, and 30 minutes later the 16 fighters arrived over Takali. They went in to land at once, the Hurricanes endeavouring to hold the Messerschmitts at bay. As one Spitfire lowered its wheels and went in slow and straight, a Bf109 raced onto its tail, but a Hurricane was at once on to it, turning violently with it as it attempted to avoid his fire; the Hurricane pilot claimed some damage and succeeded in driving it away. This may have been Plt Off Bill Johnson's aircraft BP870, who noted: "Attacked by 109 on landing in circuit. Down OK."

As the 603 Squadron formation climbed to the south of the island, led by Flt Lt Buckstone (BP872), they were attacked by Bf109s and the leader's No 2, Flg Off Holland (BR184/2-C), reported:

"As they passed us, we all fired at them, and John was either hit in their attack or, I think more likely, followed one down too far and too fast. I saw the 109 go into the water with a great dirty splash and John Buckstone's Spitfire hit the water seconds later with a big clean white splash."

On the strength of Holland's report, a Messerschmitt was credited jointly to Buckstone, Plt Off Bert Mitchell and himself, while Flt Lt Sanders also claimed one shot down. Only one was actually lost – Yellow 6 of 6/JG53 flown by Uffz Helmut Schierning – while Buckstone was probably shot down by Obfw Herbert Rollwage, who claimed a Spitfire at 1105 south-east of Luqa. Another Messerschmitt was claimed by Takali Bofors gunners. Meanwhile, all the first batch of Spitfires had got down safely, although harried by the Bf109s. A few of the new arrivals were refuelled and rearmed in four minutes, the last in seven minutes, with pilots strapped in the cockpits ready to scramble, including Wg Cdr Gracie. Of his flight and arrival at Malta, one of the new pilots, Flg Off Richard 'Mitch' Mitchell, recalled:

"Took off from *Wasp* at 0645 hrs. Landed at Takali at 1030 hrs. The formation leader flew too fast and got his navigation all to hell, so I left them 40 miles west of Bizerta, five miles off the North African coast, and set course for Malta, avoiding Pantelleria and Bizerta owing to fighters and flak being present there. Jettisoned the long-range tank 20 miles west of Bizerta with 20 gallons to spare in main tank. On landing at Takali, I immediately removed my kit, and the machine was rearmed and refuelled. I landed during a raid and four Me109s tried to shoot me up. Soon after landing the airfield was bombed but without much damage being done."

Plt Off Pancho Le Bas of 601 Squadron was one of the pilots ready at Luqa to meet the incoming Spitfires:

"I guided one Spitfire in and, even before the pilot had shut down, men were clambering on to the wings to load the cannon with their full complement of ammunition and the soldiers had started a human chain to pass up the petrol cans. The pilot pulled off his helmet and shouted to me: 'That's jolly good. Where's the war?' I told him: 'The war hasn't started for you yet, mate. Get out and be quick about it!' Within fifteen minutes of landing the Spitfire was ready to fight and shortly afterwards I received the order to scramble."

All went well with the initial refuelling, and at 1055 eleven of the new Spitfires took off, now flown by 249 Squadron pilots and led by Sqn Ldr Grant, who had only just arrived. The formation almost immediately encountered Messerschmitts, as Plt Off Nash (BR108) recorded:

"I was leading D'Arcy [Milburn], Almos and Linton. Sent to Hal Far to deal with 109 trouble. We bounced them at 3,000 feet from 15,000 feet. Mine went into the sea off Hal Far. Formed up again and attacked by three 109s. One stuck around above us. Got up to him and gave a short burst. Spun down, lots of black smoke, five miles east of Malta."

Nash was credited with one confirmed and one probable, but 19-year-old Plt Off Harold Milburn from Sunderland – known to his friends as D'Arcy – was shot down and killed as he attempted to land. Jumped by four Bf109s at 1,000 feet, his Spitfire (BP845) crashed in a field near Safi. He was possibly the victim of Ltn Herbert Soukop of 6/JG53, who claimed a Spitfire (his fifth victory) at 1041. Meanwhile, Flg Off Buchanan engaged a Bf109 at 10,000 feet, five or six miles south-east of Kalafrana, claiming a probable when it dived away streaming glycol but then lost sight of it near the sea. On the ground, waiting for 'his' Spitfire to arrive, was Sgt Goldsmith:

"Just before 1030 they started to come in, splitting up to approach their various dromes and land. The 109s had thickened considerably so that there were well over 60, ranging from 15,000 feet down to 500 feet. Takali's Spitfires were having a tough do upstairs while the lower 109s were strafing the Spits with their weary pilots as they circled or approached to land. The ack-ack was doing its best, firing everything from 4.5 heavies down to .303 machine-guns. One Spit [that flown by Milburn] circling our drome had just lowered its undercarriage when a 109 bounced it from behind. After a long burst of cannon fire, the Spit fell away into a dive and crashed in flames near the boundary of the drome.

"As our Spits landed, we met them on the runway and directed them to the dispersal bays. Mine [BP871] was piloted by an RAF sergeant, Ted Graysmark, and as soon as it was in the bay, the erks leapt onto it, whipped off panels, loaded guns, refuelled, checked radio, oil and glycol, while I stowed my chute aboard and told Ted the score on what had happened in Malta. Ten minutes later we were scrambled and as we climbed steadily, the R/T told us that a big party of bombers was approaching from Catania, with a large fighter escort. The controller estimated 100-plus. At 18,000 feet we were directly above Luqa when we were bounced by about 20 Huns. The squadron split up and independent dogfights became the order of the day. After twisting round for about five minutes with some Me109s who obviously wished me no good, I heard Woody call up to say 88s were bombing Valetta, so I rolled over in an aileron turn and chucked away 14,000 feet to see what was going on. I attacked a Ju88 and left it with its starboard engine smoking."

Plt Off Graves (BP877) of 126 Squadron also claimed a Ju88 damaged.

At 1115, Spitfires were again scrambled as Flt Lt Ron West's flight approached Luqa, having attempted to formate on a patrol of Bf109s over Grand Harbour by mistake. A Messerschmitt promptly attacked West's aircraft and shot a large piece out of its fuselage, although he was able to force-land safely. At least 28 of the new arrivals were still in the air when AA bursts indicated another swarm of Bf109s approaching at 12,000 feet, shepherding a dozen Ju88s and five Z1007bis. Their target was Hal Far, which disappeared under a cloud of dust and smoke. Two soldiers and three civilians were killed and nine more men wounded, while the airfield was rendered unserviceable for several hours. Two Spitfires were claimed about this time by 5 Staffel pilots Fw Herbert Rollwage (his 16th victory) and Fw Walter Kneur (his first), and they may have jointly been responsible for the attack on West's aircraft. Just prior to the attack on Hal Far, Flt Lt Ray Sly, an experienced Australian with three victories who was due to take command of a flight of 185 Squadron, had landed safely when he saw others of his flight being attacked; he immediately attempted to take off again down-wind to go to their aid, his Spitfire (BR348) striking the top of a dispersal pen and blowing up. Sly was dragged alive from the wreck but died later the same afternoon. Amongst those struggling to avoid the Messerschmitts over Hal Far was

Canadian Plt Off Jo Sherlock, who recalled:

"As we neared Malta, and which we could see some distance away, we could hear lots of natter on the R/T and we knew the Jerries were waiting for us over the island. We started a shallow dive some distance west of Malta. We could see flak all over the island and by now some of the pilots were yelling that they were out of petrol and were gliding in. In other words, anybody with any petrol was to get the hell out of their way and to cover them as they glided in. Cy King and I were together and he called that he was out of gas and he dropped his wheels and flaps. A 109, also with wheels and flaps down, flew in front of Cy and he lifted the nose of his plane, took a squirt, and continued to land. I had my wheels and flaps down and when I went around in the circuit I realised many of the planes in the circuit were not Spits. It seemed to me that there were as many 109s in the circuit as there were Spits. Everybody was yelling: 'Spit, break! Break! Watch out behind you! Break,' and with that every Spit over the island would break sharply and practically spin in. I imagine the German R/T was just as hectic. Two or three Spits were on the field or landing path at Hal Far – there was no runway other than a dirt strip and which was marked by flags and empty petrol cans as most of the field was bomb-cratered and u/s.

"I recollect seeing a Spit which appeared to me to have landed, speed up and try to take off again, and then hit a pen and crash [obviously Flt Lt Sly]. A 109 was shooting at me at the time and there was so much going on at the same time, your main consideration was to get down safely. Several 109s were shooting up the field and anything that moved was a target. About the same time I saw another Spit touch down and saw puffs of dust running up to the Spit but a little off to one side. Two 109s, going flat out, roared along the field, one of them obviously shooting at the Spit. The Spit slowed down but before it came to a stop, the pilot climbed out onto the wing and jumped off, falling arse over tea kettle. The Spit came to a stop, swerving slightly, the engine stopping. The pilot had obviously chopped the switches. The pilot of this plane was Sgt Tex Vineyard, a US citizen in the RCAF. He had filled every space on his plane with bottles of Coca-Cola. After a few seconds Tex, who was possibly thinking more about his Coke than the plane, started out to his plane with the intention of taxiing it into the safety of his pen. He had proceeded only a short distance when a D/A [delayed-action bomb] went off and Tex, thinking another raid was in progress, scurried back to the pen. He waited a short time longer and then started out again when several D/As went off very close together. The Coke, however, was finally retrieved intact."

Only two of this latest batch of Spitfires failed to arrive, and were initially reported to be down in the sea near Lampedusa, where it was believed the pilots had ditched, presumably due to exhaustion of fuel. It later transpired, however, that Flt Sgt Charlie Valiquet from Montreal, an experienced and aggressive 21-year-old French-Canadian fighter pilot whose middle name was Napoleon, and his friend Flt Sgt John Rounsefell (23) from Vancouver, had encountered an Italian floatplane en route. They both attacked the Fiat RS14, a machine from 170^Squadriglia RM flown by Sottoten Luigi Arco, which sustained two bullet strikes before the dorsal gunner AvScArm Piero Bonannini saw his return fire strike one of the Spitfires, whereupon it was reported that it collided with the other and both Spitfires (possibly BP965 and BP971) crashed into the sea. Both pilots were lost. However, it is probable that, unseen by the Italian crew, the Spitfires had been shot down by two Messerschmitts from Stab II/JG53 flown by Ltn Ewald Schumacher and Ltn Hans Langer, both of whom claimed Spitfires shortly after 1100.

Throughout the remainder of the day the Axis air forces returned repeatedly in an effort to catch the new arrivals on the ground. At 1315, some 15 Ju88s and 18 escorting Bf109s approached, making for Hal Far and Takali. A strong formation of 24 Spitfires took off, eight of which were flown by 249 pilots, ten flown by 126 and six by Hurricane pilots of 185 Squadron. The 249 flight was scrambled too late to catch the bombers and became engaged with the escort off Dingli, one of which Plt Off Nash claimed damaged.

Some of the new Spitfires were allocated to pilots of 185 Squadron, who had been struggling to survive with the island's few remaining Hurricanes. The unit's diarist Slim Yarra wrote:

"At two o'clock the first scramble [with Spitfires] took place and a section of four took off, led by Flt Lt Lloyd. The boys got in amongst the bombers, Ju88s and 87s, and there was a lot of squirting and carrying on for a while. Plt Off Broad [BR294/GL-E] got one Ju87 probably destroyed and an 87 damaged. For once the sky seemed to be full of friendly aircraft. There were Spitfires everywhere. Plt Off [Ron] Noble, flying a Spitfire [BP980] for the first time, was unfortunately jumped by a very nasty Mc109 and managed to crash-land at Takali. Ron got a couple of pieces of Jerry lead in his carcase but these injuries were only superficial. Sgt Tony Boyd, also flying a Spitfire for the first time, squirted at the odd Hun but did not make any claims."

Noble's assailant was possibly Ltn Erich Beckmann of 9/JG53, who claimed a Spitfire shortly after midday. Noble recalled:

"Scramble to cover other Spits landing. Ops said Me109s at 8,000 feet but one jumped me at 3,000 feet. Pierced side of cockpit with cannon shell and crashed on trying to land at Takali with no flaps, brakes or ASI. Aircraft written off – slight shrapnel wounds in leg and shoulder. He very nearly got me!"

Meanwhile, Plt Off Phil Wigley, another of those selected to fly Spitfires, noted:

"Most of the pilots had never flown Spitfires before and it had been originally intended that they should not fly them immediately on operational flights. However, the few survivors of 185 were not prepared to accept this decision without protest, and an appeal to Air Vice-Marshal Lloyd soon reversed it – those without Spitfire experience had been shown the cockpit drills by Plt Off McKay, who had; the wrecked fuselage of one of the March contingent of Spitfires was used for this purpose."

Although it was an understandable decision at the time – with the desperate circumstances prevailing – to allow Malta-experienced pilots the opportunity of flying the new machines into action, it would ultimately prove to be a tragically unwise one although Sgt Tony Boyd (3-J), one of the six chosen for this initial sortie, noted in his logbook:

"First trip in Spit. Two minutes after take-off was squirting at 88s. No claims. Got on well, wizard machine. Six of us covered remainder in landing at Takali."

A reconnaissance Ju88 with two Bf109s as escort, which appeared at 1530, caused four 249 Squadron Spitfires to be scrambled, but they did not engage and patrolled instead off Sicily. As they departed, a dozen 603 Squadron aircraft took off at 1550, followed 30 minutes later by six more flown by 185 Squadron pilots. They were all up to intercept 18 Ju87s and 20 Messerschmitts that approached to raid Luqa and Grand Harbour. 603 Squadron made initial contact with the raiders but became engaged with the escort, Plt Off Bert Mitchell and Flt Sgt Johnny Hurst each claiming Bf109s damaged. The latter's Spitfire was shot-up as he came in to land. The 185 Squadron flight then engaged the Ju87s over Grand Harbour, Flt Lt Keith Lawrence attacking one, which Denis Barnham witnessed from the ground, reporting that it burst into flames and crashed into a field. A probable was claimed by Plt Off Wigley (BR306). Sgt Boyd again:

> "Six of 185 Squadron set off late. Fired at two Ju87s and one 109, windscreen oiled up. Covered the others again while they landed. Pretty hot time. Lost Sgt Tweedale. No claims."

Flt Sgt Gordon Tweedale, the successful Australian pilot with nine victories under his belt was shot down in BR248. The Spitfire crashed in St Saviour Street, Lija, killing both the pilot and a Maltese soldier, Gunner Seraphim Cauchi, on the ground. One of the new arrivals, Plt Off Cy King, recalled briefly meeting Tweedale, who had been allocated his aircraft:

> "Tweedale and I stayed in or close to the dispersal pen and I gave him all the gen I could on the Spitfire, as all his time had been on Hurricanes. Going over how it handled on the ground, in the air, controls, critical speeds, cockpit drills, everything, getting him to sit in the cockpit while I sat beside him on the wing, then I would get in and show him, as he watched. About 2.30 or 3pm all the serviceable Spits were scrambled and Tweedale took off. There were many enemy planes all over the island, the object to destroy as many of the new arrivals as possible, as was done in April. After a time the Hal Far aircraft began to come back and land in ones and twos and taxied to the widespread dispersal pens. Tweedale did not appear. I waited a long time at the pen with the airmen but no more aircraft landed. So, within hours of arriving off the *Wasp*, my aircraft, and the personable Aussie who flew it, were gone."

Meanwhile, returning from the sortie to Sicily, the 249 Squadron quartet met the Stukas over Grand Harbour as they headed home, Plt Off Nash (BR108) claiming a probable:

> "Chased recco 88 but unable to find him even over Sicilian coast. Stuck around at 27,000 feet for big raid. Bounced 87s over Grand Harbour. Only one cannon (working) again. He went on his back belching black smoke."

Shortly after the 603 Squadron aircraft had landed and were being refuelled, six Ju88s swooped on Takali. Pilots leapt from cockpits and headed for slit trenches; one large bomb exploded 20 feet from one trench crammed with pilots and groundcrew, but no one was hurt, although two Spitfires were riddled with shrapnel. Flt Sgt Brennan of 249 Squadron twice tried to take off between raids, but was prevented on the first occasion by a flat tyre, just reaching a trench before the bombs fell. On the second, he was fully strapped in as the Ju88s appeared. He ripped off his straps although in the panic forgot the dinghy cord, which jerked him back and for a few seconds had him suspended on the wing root of the Spitfire! Once more he just reached cover before the first bombs exploded. At Luqa another unserviceable Wellington was burnt out and a Spitfire damaged, but aircraft losses on the ground remained low.

It was now the turn of the Regia Aeronautica, and at 1745 the usual formation of five Z1007bis approached – aircraft of 210^Squadriglia BT on this occasion – escorted by 16 Macchis, eight from each Gruppo. To meet this threat, 33 Spitfires were scrambled, and 11 of these from 126 Squadron intercepted led by Sqn Ldr Barton. Barton's single section engaged the escort while Plt Off Mike Graves (BP877) led the rest to attack the bombers. Three Cants were claimed shot down, two by Flt Sgt Paddy Schade and one by Sgt Tim Goldsmith (BP871). Schade also claimed a Macchi damaged, as did Barton, Graves and Plt Off Tilley, while Plt Off John Bisley

– recently returned to operations on recovery from his wounds – claimed one shot down. On this occasion enthusiasm seems to have overcome the Spitfire pilots, for only a single Cant was hit. Although badly damaged, it did return, one member of Serg Giovanni Dal Ponte's crew being killed and two slightly wounded. One of the latter was the dorsal gunner, AvScArm Francesco Melpignano, who claimed one fighter – identified as a P-40 – shot down in return and a second as a probable. The Macchis also all returned, although Ten Luigi Giannella's aircraft had been hit by a 20mm shell. The Italian pilots were no less optimistic in their claims, Cap Franco Lucchini (his 15th victory), Serg Ambrogio Rusconi and Serg Teresio Martinoli all claiming Spitfires shot down, while Magg Larismo di Pergameni claimed one damaged; in fact all Spitfires returned safely although Plt Off Mejor's aircraft (BP850) suffered slight damage: "Got behind five Cants. Could not see to fire – good rear gunners. They bloody well hit me!"

The last raid of the day occurred during the evening when seven Ju88s and a dozen Bf109s attacked Takali from 1840 onwards. Nine Spitfires of 601 Squadron, eight of 603 and three of 249 had all been ordered into the air towards the end of the previous Italian raid, and were still up, several of these making contact with the escorting Messerschmitts. Plt Off Briggs of 601 claimed a Bf109 shot down as it was strafing, and Plt Off Scott another damaged. Similar claims were submitted by 603 Squadron, with Flt Lt Douglas (BR251/4-S) claiming one shot down, and Plt Off Slade one damaged. Only one of the bombers was successfully attacked, 601's Plt Off Percy Sewell and Sgt Stan Howard gaining strikes before being forced away. Hptm Helmut Belser claimed a low-flying Spitfire near Qrendi. Bombers were over during the night, two or three falling to prowling Beaufighters. With the end of the day, reporters worked through the night to produce copy for the morning's newspapers, one account noting:

> "In the early and dark hours of the morning enemy planes were already being shot down from the sky during attacks which were far from as long, heavy or effective as the civilian population had been accustomed in the past … This latest enemy adventure did not even succeed in awaking from their beds the greater numbers of Malta's population – an apt reflection upon the manner in which Malta looks upon the frustrated exertions of the enemy across the Sicilian channel."

The day had been almost the success planned for. A total of 61 Spitfires had arrived safely although three others had been lost during the operation. In the frantic fighting over Malta during the day, four more had been shot down and six damaged to some extent on the ground. Nonetheless, counting those already on the island, nightfall saw the defenders with at least 50 undamaged Spitfires to hand, with another dozen or so repairable, together with a handful of Hurricanes. The defences had never been in better shape. As a back-up to the successful delivery of Spitfires, the fast minelayer-cruiser HMS *Welshman* had made an unescorted run from Gibraltar carrying quantities of AA ammunition, smoke-making canisters, aircraft engines, powdered milk, canned meat and dehydrated foodstuffs, as well as 100 RAF technicians to aid in servicing the additional fighters[43].

However, an inquest on Operation Bowery held at Malta considered that the new arrivals did not contain sufficient flight leaders and experienced pilots; in fact, there were only two officers of flight lieutenant rank included – Phil Winfield and Ray Sly – one of whom (Sly) had already been killed. More than half of the new arrivals were NCOs, and many of the others were newly commissioned pilot officers. It was agreed that briefing aboard *Wasp* had not been thorough – pilots did not know the names of others in their sections, and had very little instruction on methods of joining up and flying to Malta. Many did not know the names of the Malta airfields and had no maps of the island. One section leader had taken his formation to the North African coast before setting course, then followed the coastline towards Malta. Indeed, 601 Squadron's Flt Lt Barnham recorded that he was given the job of interviewing many of the new pilots, the intention being that all with 50 hours or less of operational flying experience would be sent straight back to the United Kingdom, and it does appear that a number of pilots may indeed have been disposed of in this way. Nonetheless, Prime Minister Churchill was jubilant and cabled his appreciation to the US President, exulting: "Who says a *Wasp* can't sting twice?"

With the arrival of more Spitfires, a new era began for 185 Squadron – the former Hurricane unit – which also received its share of new pilots, and was now commanded by Flt Lt (Acting Sqn Ldr) Rhys Lloyd, who had effectively commanded the dwindling Hurricane force since February. The new arrivals were divided among the existing squadrons where needs applied, but Sgt Colin Bell[44]; a former Whirlwind pilot, was soon returned to the UK due to his lack of experience, as were other new arrivals American Sgt Leroy Morsheimer and Sgt John Patterson, both from the 611 Squadron contingent, and Sgt John Williamson. The AOC repeated that Malta was no place for beginners.

10 May 1942 – a turning point

On 10 May, the defenders were ready for the Axis raiders as never before. Two early morning reconnaissance sorties caused Spitfires to be scrambled, during which Plt Off Plagis (3-N) claimed damage to a Messerschmitt. However, it was 1020 before a major raid approached, some 20 Ju87s and ten Ju88s, under a heavy fighter escort, making for Valetta to attack the *Welshman*. A smoke screen helped prevent the vessel from being hit, while 37 Spitfires and 13 Hurricanes rose to challenge the raiders – an unprecedented reception. First off were 11 Spitfires flown by 601 Squadron pilots and nine from 126, Flt Lt Peck's section of four from the latter unit breaking away to patrol off the Sicilian coast to await returning stragglers. With Sqn Ldr Bisdee called away to Valetta and Flt Lt Parry still in hospital suffering badly from the effects of Malta Dog, Flt Lt Barnham was to lead 601 but, at the last moment, he too went down with a bout of dysentery, so he asked Plt Off Briggs to lead instead. This initial force of 20 Spitfires was followed at 1048 by eight flown by 185 Squadron pilots, and five minutes later by seven more from 603 and five of 249 Squadron. Barnham watched the battle from the ground:

> "Something very strange is happening over towards Valetta. Over Grand Harbour a grotesque fog of greeny-grey smoke is spreading wider and wider; the harbour smoke screen is vomiting upwards from huge canisters to cover the target area and shield the ammunition ship. The guns have started to erupt, spattering the blue with shell-burst – a procession of enemy bombers has started to arrive; five, ten, sixteen, seventeen, twenty-three Stukas, with more emerging; forty now, fifty, their pilots obviously straining their eyes downwards trying to get a glimpse of the target ship through the smoke cover. One after one they are beginning their dive. Hundreds of enemy aircraft are diving into this inferno with Spitfires, appearing suddenly in the blue, following down behind them; black dots dropping like stones behind the Spitfires: 109s! What an aerial monument of courage this scene is."

The inexperienced and leaderless pilots of 601 Squadron soon found themselves caught up in the action, as 2/Lt Bartleman (4-A) recalled:

"We were ordered to get to about 30,000 feet into sun – unable to reach this height before raid arrived; on about same level as about 40 Ju87s as they reached the island. Attacked from abeam – bombs jettisoned and formation broke up. Selected one and fired from about 200-300 yards and closing. No return fire; black smoke seen and it went down vertically. Onto tail of second 87 – again black smoke and it went spinning down; attacked a third and saw pieces fly off, and it fell away."

He was credited with two probables and one damaged, while his colleague Sgt McConnell was credited with one Ju87 destroyed and a Ju88 damaged. Flg Off Hone (4-K) and Plt Off Le Bas took off as a section, but both returned early when the latter's R/T failed. The casualties in this action were not confined to the raiders and 601 lost two aircraft and one pilot. Barnham witnessed the loss of one Spitfire without being aware that it was flown by one of his own pilots, Sgt Reg Dickson:

"High up in the blue sky still more enemy planes are appearing, searching, plunging downwards. More Spitfires are after them. There goes a Spitfire – leaping on to its prey – it's hit by a bursting shell – Oh! God! Snapping in half, the Spitfire gyrates violently and disappears. A parachute has opened in the middle of the holocaust, it's floating, floating, slowly floating through the dark luminous layers of bursting shells, slow down towards the bomb-bursts."

On being hit, Dickson's seat straps snapped and he was thrown through the perspex hood of BP960; nonetheless, he managed to pull his ripcord and fell into the sea about a mile offshore in Marsamxett harbour. Rescue was soon on the way to the downed pilot, whose leg had been badly gashed as he was blown out of his aircraft. Despite the presence of many enemy fighters in the vicinity, three small boats put out to pick him up, one crewed by brothers Emanuel and Vincent Nappa, another by Joseph Camenzuli, but it was that of Gunner Joseph Azzopardi of the Royal Malta Artillery and Tony Saliba, which reached the wounded pilot first. Barnham later met some Maltese who witnessed the incident and knew the rescuers; he wrote:

"All the guns were firing, all the sea was splashing with pieces from the sky, all the people were cheering when someone called out, 'fighter coming down' – and there was a parachutist. He goes into the sea about a mile away, so Joseph and Tony push out in the boat. David Angus and Joseph Camenzuli take another boat in case the first one sinks. There are lots and lots of people, a thousand, watching, perhaps more, and when they see the pilot isn't hurt they all cheer. Carmel Palmier brings down whisky from his bar as they put the pilot, all laughing, on a door from a broken house as a stretcher."

Sgt Dickson was soon on his way to hospital[45]. Plt Off Max Briggs did not return. He was shot down into the sea in BR282.

The 249 flight led by Sqn Ldr Grant climbed steeply and were attacked by Bf109s over Filfla. While the CO and Flg Off Buchanan engaged the Messerschmitts, the other three went after the dive-bombers, as Flt Sgt Brennan (3-U) graphically recounted:

"We climbed steeply, endeavouring to gain height rapidly. There were already many 109s above the island, and the bombers were due to arrive any minute. We managed to reach 14,000 feet when 109s attacked us over Filfla. As they came in we could see more 109s above, waiting the opportunity to jump us. All five of us started turning with the 109s attacking us. Woody called up and told us the 87s were diving the harbour. While Buck and his pair held off the Hun fighters, Johnny and I beetled over the harbour. The barrage was the heaviest I had seen so far in Malta. The smoke puffs were so numerous that they formed a great wall of cloud, contrasting oddly with the Bofors shells shooting up like huge, glowing match heads. We dived through the barrage to get at the 87s on the other side. I looked down as we went through the flak, and the ground seemed to be on fire with the blaze of guns. My aircraft was not hit, but it rolled and yawed, and almost got out of control. We came out of the barrage suddenly. The whole sky seemed to be filled with aircraft. The first thought that struck me, so numerous were the aircraft, was that there was great risk of collision, and that I would have to watch out carefully. Spitfires were coming in from all points of the compass, and there were plenty of 109s about as well. Three thousand feet below me, sharply silhouetted against the blue sea, a couple of fellows in parachutes were floating downwards. The thought occurred to me that I might be joining them shortly. As I watched a 109 crash into the sea I thought that at any rate there was one less with which to contend.

"Tracers started to whip past my port wing. I turned to starboard. An 87 was right in front of me. It was in the act of pulling out of its dive. I gave it a quick squirt, but overshot it, and found a 109 dead ahead of me. I had a quiet squirt at him, but again overshot. Buck was yelling: 'Spits over the harbour, for Christ's sake climb! They're up here.' I pulled up my nose to gain height, giving the motor all she had. As I shot up, climbing 5,000 feet in a few seconds, I had another quick squirt – this time into the belly of an 87. I saw cannon shells go into his motor, but had no time to see what effect they had on him. Then I was above the 87s, and went into a steep climbing turn, waiting to pick out one. Spits seemed to be everywhere, weaving beside the barrage, to pounce on the 87s as they pulled out of their dive. It was not long before the Spits were getting on the tails of the 87s. Wherever I looked I could see only 87s with Spits already on their tails. It was several seconds before I saw one, which I reckoned was my meat. Diving on to his tail, I opened fire, noticing an 87 crash into the sea and start to burn as I did so. My fellow went into a hell of a steep turn, and, I followed him round, firing all the time. I had given him three seconds when the thought flashed through my mind, 'this damn 87 should blow up.' But, to my surprise, he didn't, so I kept firing. There came no return fire; either the barrage or my fire had got the rear gunner. The 87 continued in his steep turn, climbing all the time. I hung to him grimly, and kept on firing. I could see all my stuff going into his cockpit and motor. Suddenly he went to pieces. He literally flew apart – an awesome but satisfying sight for a fighter pilot. His radiator fell off, the air scoop broke away, the pilot's hood whirled off in one piece, and bits of fuselage scattered in every direction. Black smoke poured from him. Rather dumbfounded, I was watching him spinning down when Johnny [Plagis] called up: 'Spit attacking 87. There's something firing at you.'

"I looked round quickly. I saw the big yellow spinner of a 109 about 50 yards from my tail. Flashes were coming from his guns. I got a hell of a fright, and pulled the stick back to turn. By this time my speed had fallen away. My aircraft gave a hell of a shudder and flicked over on its back, and started to spin. The suddenness of events so confused me that I did not realise I was spinning. I imagined the 109 had got me and I prepared to bale out. Subconsciously I must have applied corrective control. My Spit stopped spinning to the left, and I was so surprised that I almost let it go into a spin to the right. The 109, probably deciding that he had shot me down, had left. Johnny told me later that the Hun had been firing at me for about ten seconds. I put my nose down to gather speed. Right beneath me, about 100 yards from the bomber I had seen crash earlier, my 87 was plunging into the sea. Having no ammunition left, I went home. I was very excited and elated when I landed, and told everybody how we were pasting hell out of the Hun over the harbour. Stan Grant, who had landed before me, was very brassed off. He had been up to 30,000 feet turning with 109s, and had not been able to have a crack at the 87s."

Plt Off Nash (BR108) was also in the thick of the action and claimed two Ju87s shot down:

> "Terrific party over Grand Harbour. All the Ju87s missed the target (two cruisers). Everyone got something. The Stukas stuck! Starboard wing came off one, the other disappeared into smoke screen at 200 feet!"

Flg Off Lee claimed a probable, and Plt Off Plagis (3-N) claimed yet another Stuka shot down north-east of Grand Harbour, but had initially experienced difficulty in finding a suitable target, having to fly seven miles out to sea to find a Ju87 which didn't have a Spitfire on its tail.

Led by Sqn Ldr Douglas-Hamilton, the pilots of 603 Squadron also engaged the mixed force of bombers, as Flg Off Holland later recalled:

> "David, as the leader of 603, was a calm pillar of strength at the head of the squadron. With more understanding of humanity than most, he combined enthusiasm with an unrivalled patriotism and a thorough knowledge of, and flair for, the job at hand. His concern for those serving with him was paramount. If conditions were favourable in combat, he never hesitated to attack, and he had the knack of positioning his formation so that all might have an opportunity to fire. During a 35-minute sortie [on 10 May], he led me and others on a hectic scramble, intercepting a massive Luftwaffe attack on Grand Harbour. We arrived over Valetta at about 18,000 feet as the first wave of Stukas, and their escort, were starting their dive and the fierce harbour barrage was opening up. David led us straight through the barrage, giving everyone a chance to score hits on the enemy..."

Most, however, could not claim any conclusive victories. Only Flt Sgt Johnny Hurst was credited with a Ju87 shot down, and a second damaged, while Flt Lt Douglas claimed a probable and a damaged. Meanwhile, Flg Off Holland found himself in a battle royal with the escort, though he returned claiming damage to three. Holland (BR184/2-C) and Hurst each had their own aircraft slightly damaged by AA shrapnel as they entered the barrage over Grand Harbour. Sqn Ldr Douglas-Hamilton did not enjoy any personal success:

> "An almost solid cone of AA bursts rose over the harbour. From ground level to about 7,000 feet. Into this the Huns were diving. Into it, too, the Spitfires dived, chasing the Huns. It never occurred to any of us that we might just as easily get hurt. In fact, it was with some irritation that I watched an 87 I was making for in front of me blown to pieces by a direct hit. It turned out that two of the squadron's pilots received slight gashes in their machines from shell splinters."

He then closed on a Bf109 only to have all his four cannons jammed, which remained so when he subsequently attempted to attack a Ju87. As he approached to land, a Bf109 attacked him from astern but failed to hit his aircraft:

> "He must have been a very bad shot, for I had not a scratch on my aeroplane. He had been firing at me, a sitting target going straight and level, but I was in luck again."

Sqn Ldr Barton led his flight of five from 126 Squadron to attack the bombers, Flt Sgt Schade claiming one Ju88 destroyed, which burst into flames. Plt Off Bailey claimed a Ju87 destroyed and Plt Off Graves (BP877) a Ju88 shot down and a Ju87 probably destroyed. Barton personally engaged a Bf109, which he claimed shot down, while the American Flt Sgt Artie Cleaveland damaged another. Meanwhile, Flt Lt Peck's section off the Sicilian coast also achieved success, engaging a number of Messerschmitts; Sgt Goldsmith (BP871) recalled:

"Four of us jumped two 109s, but had cannon trouble. I fired 20 rounds at one, saw strikes on wing and fuselage. He dived away. Confirmed as destroyed."

Sgt Wally Milner claimed a probable, Peck and Plt Off Tilley reporting damage to both Messerschmitts. As the section returned to Malta, Ju87s were sighted and engaged and Peck was able to claim one shot down and one damaged. Plt Off Mejor (BP850/F) claimed a Ju88 probable:

"Killed gunner. Range about 50 yards. Large pieces came away. Many strikes. Port engine on fire. Heavy smoke. Went down steeply towards sea. Bursts at Ju87 and Me109. No results."

The former Hurricane pilots of 185 Squadron were also enjoying the experience of flying the new Spitfires. Sgt Boyd (BR350/3-J) had an exciting time:

"Most terrific air battle ever seen here – astounding – plus an appalling barrage. There were about 25 Spits, eight Hurris, 30 Stukas, 15 Ju88s, 20 Me109s all mixed up in one enormous milling fight. 30 e/a destroyed or damaged in this raid. We lost one Spit. I got 88 probable, 88 damaged. First at 2,000-3,000 feet over Grand Harbour in five-seconds burst, 300-200 yards on 88, and large explosion rear of cabin – black smoke poured out and it nosed down in shallow dive three miles north of Grand Harbour."

He was credited with one probable and one damaged. His colleague Plt Off Ian McKay (BR306), following a successful attack on the Ju88s, commented: "Four cannons certainly blow hell out of an aeroplane!"

He claimed one destroyed and a second damaged, while Ju88s were also claimed by Flt Lt Lawrence and Plt Off Broad (BR294/GL-E), and Flt Sgt Dodd (BR291/GL-H) shot down a Ju87. With the guns also claiming two Ju87s and a Bf109 destroyed, the total claims for this raid was estimated as 17 destroyed and eight probables, for the loss of two Spitfires and one pilot. Obfw Herbert Rollwage of 5/JG53 claimed one Spitfire just south of Valetta, and two more were credited to Ltn Rudolf Müller and Ltn Karl-Heinz Quaritsch of 8 Staffel, at about the same time. Observers on the ground also reported seeing a Stuka apparently shoot down a Spitfire, the pilot of which was intent on downing another of the dive-bombers. Of the battle, the diarist wrote:

"At 1030 five aircraft took off and sailed straight into 30 Ju87s, after dealing first with some Ju88s. The 88s were just the appetiser, however, for when the 87s came down they were met by about 20 Spitfires. The Spits really got to work and, out of the 30 Ju87s which were misguided enough to attempt to bomb the harbour, only two [sic] escaped scot-free. The number destroyed amounted to ten [sic]. Old Joe Kesselring is reputed to be jumping up and down in one spot at the rate of 75 bars to the minute!"

Flt Lt Barnham, although sick, was on readiness to meet the next call:

"The bus has arrived with lunch so I join the queue of airmen. Old Greg, the catering officer, and several of his helpers are handing out plates of food and mugs of tea through the splintered window frames; there's also free beer and free cigarettes, but I cannot face the food; a cup of tea is all that I need. As I sip the tea I notice an Austin car, very square and upright, drawing up in a cloud of dust; out gets the CO. I quickly tell him [of the loss of Plt Off Briggs]. Hearing it he withdraws into sudden silence. I've got to tell him more, although to mention my own trivial troubles in the same breath of the death of a gallant comrade overwhelms me with self-disgust."

Sqn Ldr Bisdee was sympathetic and ordered Barnham not to fly again until he was well. He was given the job of interviewing new arrivals to find out how many operational hours they had, since it had been decided that only those who had flown in excess of 50 hours in action were to be retained. One of these, a young sergeant, was about to climb out of his aircraft:

"I was shocked by what he tells me; another babe with no operational hours at all. Of all the pilots I have so far seen, only two qualify to remain here. It looks as though we'll have to keep some of these babes as replacements. As the young pilot looks at me, he glances furtively up at the sky; a formation of enemy bombers, high up over Grand Harbour, is heading towards us. I know he wants to get into the shelter but for both of our sakes I want to appear indifferent to the immediate situation. Then, giving him a broad, mischievous wink, and hoping not to spoil the impression, I accelerate vigorously down the perimeter track."

After a minor alert at midday, the Luftwaffe returned at 1400, seven Ju88s covered by at least 30 Bf109s again raiding Grand Harbour, but again all bombs missed their target, the *Welshman*. Twenty Spitfires scrambled and were accompanied by six Hurricanes. Only 249 Squadron reported decisive engagements, Sqn Ldr Grant claiming one bomber shot down in flames, while a probable was credited to Flg Off Buchanan. Sgt Hesselyn dived on the Ju88s:

"There were 20 bombers strung out in a great gaggle. We started to go down. I waited for a couple of seconds to take a good look behind, and then went down to cover Buck's tail. I could see Stan [the CO] getting on to the tail of an 88. He was 5,000 feet below me, but I could see plainly the white stuff coming from his wings as he fired. A few seconds later his 88 was crashing in flames. I took another hurried look behind, but could still see nothing. Buck went in on the tail of an 88. I was preparing to go down on to the tail of another when there was a terrific explosion in my cockpit. Simultaneously, I felt a slight jerk at my helmet. An explosive bullet had hit the hood and, nicking my helmet, had exploded against the instrument panel. At the same time a cannon shell burst near the port wing root. I knew instinctively I had been jumped. I skidded to starboard. The 109 overshot me, and pulled up in front. He seemed to fill the whole of my view, blotting out everything else.

"I could see the pilot clearly as he sat in his cockpit, looking back. The range could not have been more than 20 yards. I fired. My shells struck first on his starboard wing, and, as he flew across my line of fire, travelled right across his cockpit and then crashed into his port wing. Pieces flew off him in all directions. He seemed to be cut in half. His machine literally collapsed and went down in bits of varying size. I blacked out momentarily. When I came to I was over the sea at about 2,000 feet, and my aircraft was in a vertical dive. I felt dazed and weak. I knew my aircraft had been hit badly, and from the cockpit could see a gaping hole in my port wing. I glanced in the mirror and could see a tear in my helmet. I nosed my Spit gently out of the dive and tested my controls. They responded, and I headed for Takali, landing without mishap."

Despite this graphic description, there were no witnesses and Hesselyn was credited only with a probable. However, it seems likely that his victim was Yellow 3 (7578) of II/JG53, from which Ltn Dr. Heiner Jörg baled out into the sea. *HSL128* set out from Malta to pick him up and he was rescued unhurt. The 35-year-old German pilot recalled:

"Seeing three Spitfires below, I dived to deliver a frontal attack while my No.2 manoeuvred into an up-sun position. After firing one burst I received a shot into my cooling system. I intended to fly as far away from Malta as possible, bale out and wait for the rescue Do24, but my cockpit rapidly became red hot. I baled out and was picked up by a launch."

He told his interrogators that he had shot down four aircraft during the brief Polish campaign in 1939 but was then invalided for a year and only returned to flying operations in the autumn of 1941. He was posted to Sicily in December of that year and had since claimed two Hurricanes shot down over Malta. Plt Off Mejor of 126 Squadron, flying his second sortie of the day in BP850/F, had a narrow escape:

"Ran into a squadron of Me109s when alone. Got badly shot-up. Short bursts of two-seconds at two 109s. Forced to break each time – Messerschmitts on my tail. 28 holes [in own aircraft]."

A Spitfire was claimed shot down by Ltn Ewald Schumacher of Stab II/JG53.

As evening approached, another raid began to build up on the radar screens and, at 1740, ten Spitfires from 601 Squadron were sent up in readiness. As the raiders approached – five Z1007bis with an escort of MC202s and RE2001s (the latter making their début over Malta) followed by Ju87s and Ju88s with a large escort of Bf109s – more Spitfires were scrambled (seven/185, eight/249, ten/603), and then seven from 126 Squadron some 15 minutes later. The original sections from 601 on patrol engaged the Italian formation, Sqn Ldr Bisdee leading an attack on Ten Domenico Robillotta's 211^Squadriglia bomber (MM23417), which blew up, the wreckage crashing into a field near Kalkara; three of the crew were killed and one injured, whilst a fifth was seen to bale out and fall into Grand Harbour when his parachute failed to open properly. Sgt Farfan claimed a second bomber as probably destroyed, and Sgt Jim Innes damaged a third; one of these, MM23400, was hit hard and landed at Gela airfield with two members of the crew wounded, one dying later in hospital. On board another of the Cants was Antonio Ferri:

"I'll never forget that mission. We were told at briefing to expect trouble; that the Germans had run into heavy opposition earlier in the day. There was anxiety as we put on our flying gear. None of the crew said much, but you could cut the tension with a knife. The squadron commander tried to relax us, pointing out we'd have dozens of fighters escorting us, but it did little good. I remember sitting on the grass under the wing of our plane, waiting for the signal to take off. It was so peaceful. The three engines had been tested, then turned off. The only sound was of the birds. You could see a donkey grazing nearby and you could smell the blossoms. It was about 5pm, so it wasn't terribly hot. The tranquillity of the scene, and the knowledge of what lay ahead, made me ache for life, if I can put it that way.

"We snapped on our parachutes and life jackets, the guns were checked, oxygen masks were hooked up and our pilot glanced over at Mount Etna to see which way the wind was blowing its smoke plume. At this point there was a nervous energy that was almost intoxicating. Then the engines roared into life and we taxied into position for take-off. You could see the grass being beaten down by the whirling propeller blades. Then we were off, with five other Cants coming just behind us. As we neared Malta we could see dust in the distance, where the British planes were taking off to intercept us. We looked around and could see our own fighters high above us in the sun. Flying over enemy territory always gave me a queer feeling. You knew they could see you, that people who hated you were running to their flak guns and planes, getting ready to try to kill you. Somebody suddenly shouted, 'There they are!' It never ceased to amaze me how quickly the Spitfires and Hurricanes would appear. One moment you were alone in the sky and the next second there they were, coming at you head-on, with guns blazing. When I first saw the guns winking on British fighters I thought they were turning their landing lights on. But by this time I was experienced enough to know better."[46]

Ferri saw Ten Robillotta's Cant about 100 metres ahead of him suddenly explode in an orange fireball:

"It went straight down; I didn't see anyone get out. That got your attention very quickly. Another Cant was hit and fell away, but the rest of us pressed on. By this time our fighters were mixing it up with the English so we were left alone for the moment. That's when the flak came up at us. You could see muzzle flashes all over Malta, or at least it seemed that way to me. Our plane was hit in the starboard wing and in the fuselage but none of the crew was hurt. We dropped our bombs and, as always, you could feel the old Cant rise up involuntarily as the extra weight of the bombs fell away. We turned for home, but half a dozen Spitfires were after us. I think there were so many that they got in each other's way, because they only put one cannon shell into our rudder. Our rear gunner was firing back for all he was worth. You could smell the gunpowder all over the plane. Somehow, we got the hell out of there. I was OK while we were airborne but after I got into my quarters I was shaking like a leaf and started to cry. I swore I wouldn't go to Malta again, but of course I did. None of us had any choice in the matter. If you refused to fly you could be shot."[47]

One of the Macchis was shot down by Plt Off Wally Caldwell (BR344/4-H), in which Cap Roberto Dagasso, CO of 97^Squadriglia, lost his life. Two RE2001s sustained combat damage but were able to return to Sicily. 601 suffered no losses despite claims by the Italian pilots for six Spitfires shot down[48].

The Spitfires (from 126, 185, 249 and 603) that scrambled as the raid approached all intercepted the German aircraft in the second wave. Flt Sgt Milner from 126 claimed a Bf109 probably destroyed in this action, as did Plt Off Tilley. Plt Off Mejor was attacking a Ju87, which he claimed probably destroyed, when he was shot down:

"Strikes on rear gunner and along port wing and fuselage. Range 50 yards. Me109 hit me from behind and below. Engine caught fire. Controls jammed. Kite turned upside down. Baled out at 2,000 feet. I had no time to send a 'Mayday' call and baled out into the sea. I saw two splashes close together, which I think were my Spitfire and the Ju87 I shot down – but I was credited with only a third of a kill because I couldn't be sure that my target was the one that hit the water. I was lucky to be picked up as the HSL crew were looking for another pilot who had sent a 'Mayday'. They didn't find him but found me instead."

He was rescued by *HSL107* about five miles off the coast. Sqn Ldr Douglas-Hamilton again missed out on the action:

"The barrage went up once more as about twenty 87s attacked the harbour. Down we dived. I picked an 87, but just as I was coming into range I saw another Spitfire already shooting at it. No future in poaching; I turned and saw a 109 some distance away. I could not catch it up, but in desperation fired a long-range burst which did not seem to do much good. The barrage was more terrific than ever this time, and I could see many parachutes coming down in it. 'Good show!' I thought. 'Half the Luftwaffe is baling out!' Suddenly one of the Huns blew up with a terrific explosion. When I got down I was told these were parachute mines sent up by the ground defences."

One of 603's new pilots, Flg Off Mitch Mitchell, who was flying No.2 to the CO, enjoyed a successful first engagement and later wrote:

"We climbed to 4,000 feet, and then the barrage was put up by the harbour defences and the cruiser. The CO dived down into it and I followed close on him. We flew three times to and fro in the barrage, trusting to luck to avoid the flak. Then I spotted a Ju87 climbing out at the fringe of the barrage and I turned and chased him. I gave him a one-second burst of cannon and he broke off sharply to the left. At that moment another Ju87 came up in front of my nose and I turned into him and I let him have it. His engine started to pour out black smoke and he started weaving. I kept the tit pushed hard, and after a further two to three-seconds burst with the one cannon I had left, the other having jammed, he keeled over at 1,500 feet and went into the drink. I then spotted a 109 firing at me from behind and pulled the kite round to port, and after one and a half turns got on his tail. Before I could fire, another 109 cut across my bows from the port side and I turned straight on his tail and fired till my cannon stopped through lack of ammo. He was hit and his engine poured black smoke, but I had to beat it as I was now defenceless and two more 109s were attacking me. I spiralled straight down to the sea at full throttle and then weaved violently towards land with the two 109s still firing at me. I went under the fringe of the smoke screen to try to throw them off, but when I came out from the other side I found them both sitting up top waiting for me. I therefore kept right down at nought feet and steep-turned towards them, noticing the smoke from their gun ports as I did so. After about five minutes of this I managed to throw them off. I landed back at Takali and made out my report, claiming one 87 destroyed and one 109 damaged."

The Stuka crashed in flames at Senglea and was almost certainly S7+FM of 7/StG3. Flt Lt Douglas (BP964) and Plt Off Forster jointly claimed a second, while Plt Off Neville King's aircraft returned with a damaged wing courtesy of a Bf109. One of the last to take off was 126 Squadron's Sgt Goldsmith (BP877):

"Was orbiting Luqa at approx 8,000 feet when two Me109s approached from the north at about the same height, going south. I engaged the second one attacking from the beam to quarter, giving three-seconds burst at range 200-150 yards; saw strikes on fuselage. He dived south towards the sea, smoking. I did not see him reappear. This engagement was watched from Luqa by Plt Off Bisley and Sgt Graysmark of 126 Squadron, who both saw a lot of black smoke from the e/a as it disappeared behind the cliffs. It was not seen to reappear. Later engaged one Me109 about eight miles north of St Paul's Bay, same height, head-on from underneath. Fired about six-seconds, closing to about 20 feet. Saw many strikes on bottom of fuselage. He dived straight into the sea. No parachute seen."

However, although it seems that Goldsmith's victim was almost certainly White 7 (7431) of II/JG53 flown by Uffz Erhard Ritterbusch, Luftwaffe records indicate that loss of this aircraft was caused by a collision with that flown by Ltn Hans Langer (10026). It seems likely that Ritterbusch's aircraft had been damaged by Goldsmith and had then collided with the other. In the event, both pilots survived, Ritterbusch being picked up from the sea at 1945 by *HSL128*, which had been sent out to locate a pilot reported down three miles south of Kalafrana. Meanwhile, Langer succeeded in flying his damaged machine back to Comiso where it crashed on landing and was totally destroyed. 185 Squadron's Plt Off Broad (BR294/GL-E) and Flt Sgt Dodd (BR291/GL-H) each claimed Bf109s damaged, the unit's Slim Yarra humorously noting:

"P/O Broad managed to get mixed up with a few of the little jobs and had a very enjoyable ten minutes being chased. However, Ernie committed one bad breach of form: no target, whether the aforementioned target be the drogue, ground triangle, aircraft, cow, or men on haystacks, shall return the fire of the practicing machine, or machines. P/O Broad flagrantly broke this important ruling and severely damaged one of the practicing Messerschmitts, much to the horror and disgust of the 109 pilot. P/O Broad sneaked back to the aerodrome amidst cries of 'shame' and 'bad' and muttered remarks of 'bodyline' from the 109 drivers. It has been reported from a reliable neutral source that the German chancellery is to make a very strong protest to the British government."

While other units thus engaged, the 249 flight was vectored on to the Messerschmitt escort, one of which was claimed shot down by Plt Off Watts (BP989/4-N). Plt Off Erik Hetherington opened his score when he claimed a probable and Flt Lt Ron West a damaged. Obfw Rollwage of 5/JG53 claimed his second Spitfire of the day at 1904, south of Valetta, while Ltn Wolfgang Schaller of 9 Staffel also claimed a Spitfire during the evening's battles, and Oblt Werner Langemann, Staffelkapitän of 10(Jabo)/JG53, was credited with a third.

A list of preliminary claims for the whole day was drawn up, with the following assessment: Spitfire pilots were credited ten Ju87s, five Ju88s, four Bf109s, one Z1007bis and one MC202, while AA guns were credited with five Ju87s, one Ju88 and one Messerschmitt. Actual losses appear to have been three Ju88s from 2/KG54 including B3+JH (one killed, three rescued) and B3+GH (Ltn Johannes Warkalla and crew missing); two Ju88s from I/KGr806 – M7+DL Ltn Helmut Kissling and crew missing; M7+KK Ltn Anton Schweinsteiger and crew missing; four Ju87s from III/StG3 including S7+GN (Uffz Gerhard Nicolai and Uffz Walter Kern killed), S7+FM (Uffz Walter Rastinnes and Uffz Walter Rauer POWs) and S7+EM (Uffz Christian Apmann and Uffz Heinrich Schäfer killed); the crew of the fourth was rescued by an Axis craft; and three Bf109s from II/JG53 – Ltn Dr. Heiner Jörg and Uffz Erhard Ritterbusch both POWs; Ltn Hans Langer wounded/injured and aircraft totally destroyed. The Italians lost one Z1007bis with a second badly damaged, and one MC202. Apart from the three Spitfires that were lost, six others returned with slight damage. This had been a serious and meaningful defence – no longer a token effort – and indeed 10 May can justifiably be claimed to have been a turning point in Malta's fortunes.

The reduction in aerial activity over Malta was noticeable next day (**11 May**). Italian fighters were out early, looking for survivors from the previous day's missing aircraft. The first Axis aircraft to appear over the island was a reconnaissance Ju88 with fighter escort. Four Spitfires of 249 scrambled at 0725, but Flt Sgt Brennan at once force-landed with a faulty engine as the remaining three pursued the intruder back towards Sicily. On approaching the coast, eight RE2001s of 20°Gruppo CT – incorrectly identified by the Spitfire pilots as MC202s – were encountered. Brennan later wrote:

"The other boys carried on. The new boy became separated from the formation and had to call for a homing in order to get back to base. Johnny [Plagis] and Willie the Kid [Flt Sgt Williams] located eight Macchi 202s. They became separated as they attacked. Johnny singled out one Macchi, and gave chase to it. The Italian was steep turning near the sea. Johnny, ignoring the Macchis on his own tail, got into position to draw a bead on the one in front of him. He was about to open fire when it crashed into the sea. The Italian pilot, possibly in fright at having a Spit on his tail, apparently had made his turn too tight. He stalled his aircraft and lost control. Johnny, turning into the Macchis behind him, had an odd poop at them, but without effect. Neither did Willie the Kid have any luck, and the Macchis made off homewards."

Plt Off Plagis (3-N) added:

> "I thought my last minute had come and decided to sell my life dearly. I flew straight at the nearest machine with the intention of ramming it. I did not fire a shot, but the Macchi pilot, suddenly realising his number might be up too, took violent evasive action, stalled and crashed into the sea."

One of the Italian pilots claimed hits on Plagis' Spitfire but, although his aircraft was not damaged, the Rhodesian was fortunate to get back safely due to lack of fuel, and landed with just three gallons in his tank. Brennan continued:

> "Johnny had a good opinion of the Macchis [sic]. He told me they were pretty good aircraft, and that their pilots, with the exception of the one who had crashed, had handled their machines well. He admitted he had found it more difficult than he had expected to get away from them, but had no doubt whatever that the Spitfire was far superior to the Italian fighters. This was the first time any pilots of our squadron had been engaged with them."

Up to 15 Ju88s and about 40 Bf109s approached just before 1030, and 23 Spitfires were scrambled including eight from 249 and six from 126, which were vectored onto a section of three bombers south-east of Kalafrana Bay. As Plt Off Plagis and Flt Sgt Williams dived on one of the bombers, eight Messerschmitts came down on them. Flt Sgt Brennan (3-N) called a warning and immediately engaged the attackers, becoming involved in an intense struggle during which he gained strikes on one but was almost shot down himself. He yelled over the R/T for help, Plt Offs Nash and MacLean arriving to chase away his assailants, but at this point Brennan heard that more Bf109s were off Grand Harbour, and gave chase:

> "It was not long before I saw two 109s about three miles out to sea, off the harbour. They were low down, and had just turned, leaving their tails to the sun. I dived on them, calling up other Spits that were milling about to come and lend a hand. The 109s were going faster than I had thought, and I had a long chase. It was not until we were 20 miles north of Gozo, roughly a third of the way to Sicily, that I caught up with them. I gave the rear one a short burst, but saw no result. He began to turn. I turned inside him, and gave him another very short burst. He could not have been more than ten feet from the water, and suddenly his right wing hit the sea. He cartwheeled on his wingtips and tail once or twice, then blew up."

Meanwhile, Nash (BR107) claimed one of the Messerschmitts with which Brennan had previously been engaged:

> "Got one of them two miles off Grand Harbour – went straight in from 5,000 feet. Only fired 20 rounds cannon all from one gun from 50 yards."

MacLean claimed another Bf109 damaged, and Williams believed he had probably destroyed a Ju88. Among the 126 section Sqn Ldr Barton claimed a Bf109 probably destroyed and Flt Lt Peck one damaged. At least one Messerschmitt (7278) fell in this action – possibly the joint victim of Brennan and Nash – no less a pilot than the Geschwaderkommodore of JG53, Maj Günther von Maltzahn, having been obliged to bale out into the sea off Valetta. Immediately his loss was known an intensive search was carried out, and he was safely picked up from his dinghy by a Do24. Flt Sgt Schade's confidence was shaken somewhat when he became engaged with the Bf109s:

> "Attacked six Me109s over Kalafrana Bay. Windscreen oiled up badly. Got shot-up by

a 109. Wounded by high-explosive incendiary bullets in the arm in three places."

Despite his injury, Schade was able to land safely and was taken off to sick quarters to have his wounds treated. While the Spitfires were thus engaged, bombers struck at Takali where a number of off-duty pilots were watching the blitz from the roof of Xara Palace, one of whom recalled:

"As the attack went in and the bombs were falling, the Bofors batteries blazing away and the Spitfires mixing it up above with the 109s and 88s, Bob Sergeant came running up the stairs on to the terrace. He had barely called out 'what's happening?' when he was hit by a stray bullet which fell from the sky. It clipped his lower lip and jaw before lodging dangerously in his chest. It was a chance in a million, but an object lesson in the sense of tin-hat wearing."

Plt Off Sergeant was evacuated that evening to Gibraltar aboard a Hudson transport, and from there was flown to England by Sunderland a few days later.

Three escorted Ju88s raided Hal Far and Luqa during the early evening, two Spitfires being badly damaged and one slightly so at the latter airfield. Twenty-one Spitfires were scrambled (two/126, seven/185, five/601 and seven/603). Flt Sgt Sim of 185 followed a Bf109 that had dived on some of the Spitfires, and claimed to have hit it with a deflection shot. He reported that it flicked over, pouring black smoke, when three 603 Squadron Spitfires came racing in from different directions to attack it. Flt Lt Douglas (BP964) opened fire and saw strikes, but then Plt Off Barny Barnfather (BP991/W) misjudged his approach and collided with Douglas's aircraft. Both pilots baled out, each having sustained slight injuries. Meanwhile, Plt Off Paul Forster also claimed strikes on the hapless Messerschmitt, which was reported to have crashed into the sea. Sqn Ldr Douglas-Hamilton commented:

"Bill was chasing a 109 with his section. He had already hit it, when another Spitfire collided with him, and the two aircraft broke up like a pack of cards thrown up in the air. 'Suddenly I found myself in the air with no aeroplane around me,' Bill said afterwards, 'so I just pulled the ripcord.' Both pilots were safe. Neither of them had any need to unstrap himself, and the other pilot came down with his Sutton harness still pinned together round him. However, they got the 109."

Flt Sgt Brennan, who watched the action from the ground, wrote:

"I witnessed the only collision between Spitfires which occurred over Malta while we were there. A 109 flew across at about 8,000 feet. He was pouring glycol, having been hit badly by Bob Sim. There were four Spitfires on his tail, and he was skidding violently to avoid them. Hardly had he passed over our heads than two Spits collided and disintegrated. Both pilots baled out and landed safely. The 109 boy had to follow suit, and was taken prisoner [sic]."

Barnfather later noted:

"I was just about to fire again at the Me109 when suddenly I found myself in the air with no aeroplane around me so I just pulled the ripcord. Both brollied down OK. Shared with Douglas and Forster."

Two more Messerschmitts were claimed probably destroyed by Sqn Ldr Bisdee of 601 and Plt Off Booth of 126, and one damaged by Plt Off McKay (BR306/3-D) of 185 while his colleague Plt Off Wigley (BR294/GL-E) damaged a Ju88. Plt Off Bill Johnson (BP973/2-J) experienced his first scramble from Malta and survived unscathed, but noted that 601 Squadron's Flt Sgt Shea had his Spitfire shot-up. Slim

Yarra commented:

> "The interception was carried out and everyone had a good time. Plt Off Wigley damaged a Ju88 and Plt Off McKay had a slight altercation with some spiteful 109s, damaging one. Owing to a rather strong crosswind, the boys had to land at Luqa."

12 May proved to be a day of more sustained fighter combat. After an initial abortive attempt by three patrolling Spitfires at intercepting an early morning reconnaissance aircraft, 30 Spitfires (eight/126, seven/185, eight/249, seven/603) and two Hurricanes were scrambled at 1055 to engage four Ju88s and a dozen Bf109s of III/JG53 raiding Hal Far. Immediately after take-off, Sgt Ray Hesselyn discovered that he had no oxygen supply and signalled Flt Sgt Brennan accordingly. Consequently, Brennan stayed on his wing and the pair remained at low altitude. Here they witnessed a 603 Squadron Spitfire, BR127 flown by Plt Off Bert Mitchell[49], crash into the sea, and immediately gave chase to its attacker, pursuing it out towards Sicily; Hesselyn reported:

> "I saw Mitch diving with the 109 on his tail at the same time as Paul. I broke away from Paul at once and dived after the 109. It was about 1,000 yards away and slightly below me. I closed on it rapidly, and when I had got within 500 yards he broke away from following Mitch and shot out seawards. I knew then he was my piece of cake. At 150 yards I gave him the first squirt. I was by this time wholly occupied with the 109, and had lost sight of Mitch and Paul. I saw my shells striking the water behind the fleeing 109. I realised I was firing too low. I pulled up the nose of my aircraft and gave him another quick squirt. This time my shells must have hit him, although I did not see them do so. His speed slackened perceptibly... I throttled back to avoid overshooting him. His speed continued to slacken as we skimmed the sea at about 50 feet. I fired another burst, checked for skid, and gave him another and longer burst. This time I hit him squarely. He flicked over on his back, hung poised for a second, and dropped straight into the drink. I circled around him to see if the pilot would get out. He didn't."

Meanwhile, as Hesselyn was so engaged, Brennan (BP953) was under attack by three others, all of which overshot without hitting him but the first then turned for a head-on attack. A cannon shell hit the portside of the Spitfire's armour-glass windscreen:

> "There was a sharp crack as though somebody had hit my cockpit with a sledge-hammer. Something hit my left arm and knocked it off the throttle quadrant. A tingling pain shot through it, but I found I was still able to use it. For a few seconds, expecting a row of bullets straight across my body, I did nothing. But the bullets did not come. The 109 had stopped firing and pulled away above my head, compelled to do so apparently in order to avoid a collision. I tested my controls. They were still working, but at that instant my aircraft flicked over and went into a spin. My aircraft had fallen 2,000 feet before I got it out of the spin. I cleared the cliffs, and made for home. Blood had seeped through my sleeve, and my arm ached. I landed at Takali, feeling dazed and shaken. An erk gave me a good stiff whisky, and I was taken to hospital."

As Hesselyn returned to Malta he engaged another Bf109 and "blew half its tail off" but it dived away, covered by two others. The bombers had not escaped unscathed, one being claimed probably destroyed by Flt Lt West, who shared in damaging a second with Plt Off Ossie Linton. 185 Squadron's Spitfires now joined the action, Sgt Yarra (GL-K) reporting: "Engaged 88 – no observed results. Jumped by four 109s; shot down leader, damaged others."

Plt Off Wigley (BR294/GL-E) claimed damage to a Ju88, but his own aircraft received a stray bullet through the cockpit hood from the rear gunner. Return fire was thought also to be the cause of Flt Sgt Pop Conway's 126 Squadron aircraft (BR137) being shot down. The New Zealander baled out and was soon rescued by *HSL107*. Plt Off Don Llewellyn was also shot down, in BP953. He also managed to bale out, slightly injured and of his assailant simply noted in his logbook: "Saw nothing". The pilots of III/JG53 somewhat overclaimed during the action, reporting five Spitfires shot down: Hptm Wolf-Dietrich Wilcke of Stab claimed his 38th victory, and others were credited to Ltn Siegmund Hosnedl of 7 Staffel (his 10th), Hptm Helmut Belser (26th), Ltn Karl-Heinz Quaritsch (3rd) and Obfw Werner Stumpf (33rd).

It was late afternoon before the next raid developed, reported to comprise four Ju88s and three Italian bombers identified as Z1007bis escorted by two dozen Bf109s and MC202s. The Italian bombers were, in fact, SM84s of 4°Gruppo Aut AS, covered by 15 RE2001s of 2°Gruppo Aut CT and 15 MC202s of 4°Stormo CT. Takali was attacked, where two Spitfires were damaged and two airmen wounded. A total of 36 Spitfires and six Hurricanes were ordered off, as recalled by Plt Off Sherlock:

> "Planes took off from different parts of the field in every direction, and what with the dust and the extreme hurry to get airborne, it was more dangerous at times of take-off than fighting the Jerries."

With 185 Squadron operating its Spitfires from Takali, the airfield was becoming congested. In the mad scramble to get off BR136/3-C collided with BR350, but neither Plt Offs Halford nor McNaughton of 185 was hurt, although the latter's aircraft was damaged beyond repair. Flg Off Hone (4-L) also experienced bad luck on his second operational sortie from the island when the oil leak burst, the subsequent film on his windscreen obscuring his vision to such an extent that he had to return and land blind. In the confusion, Flt Lt Barnham was ordered to land, but in doing so found that his 601 Squadron flight had been left leaderless, so took off again. On landing he was confronted by the two mangled Spitfires:

> "As I went down on the runway, sweeping past the wreckage, I remembered the take-off fiasco. I don't yet know who blundered the take-off. I have discovered that the Hal Far squadron [185] usually take off on four red lights on their own aerodrome, the same as us; so someone ought to have changed the respective signals; of course, they may have done, but I was not informed about it."

Of the confusion that often occurred on the airfields at this time due to congestion, Plt Off Pancho Le Bas of 601 Squadron recalled:

> "We remained at readiness from dawn to dusk waiting for the enemy to come to us; if they did not we stayed on the ground and it was the luck of the draw whether one did three scrambles a day or none at all. If one did receive the order to scramble, getting off the ground was always a bit of an adventure. Because of the general shortage of equipment, the scramble order had to be given by means of Very lights fired from the control tower. For example, two reds might mean that Red Section was to scramble and two greens after that might mean that Blue Section was to take off as well; if further sections had to scramble, things got complicated. At each blast pen someone had to be watching the control tower the whole time, because if a Very light was missed one could get in a muddle and either take off at the wrong time or not at all.
>
> "After the start up there was always a long run from one's dispersed blast pen, along the taxiway, to the end of the runway. This was made with an airman sitting on the wing, whose job it was to guide the pilot round any new bomb craters that had appeared. Immediately one reached the runway one took off; it was always much safer in the air. After take-off the fighters would orbit the airfield until the section or

squadron had formed up. Once we were airborne we could get our orders from the ground controller. He usually told us to go to the south and climb to a given altitude, then he would bring us in to engage the enemy."

Meanwhile, the two units in the air were heavily engaged. Plt Off Graves of 126 Squadron pursued a Ju88 out to sea and claimed to have probably destroyed it, but the engine of his BP877 was hit by return fire and he was obliged to turn for base. As he crossed the coast at 900 feet, his engine caught fire and he baled out. Another 126 Squadron pilot, Flt Sgt Joe Bush unintentionally belly-landed his damaged aircraft (BR346) at Luqa:

"I don't know what hit me – Me109 or ack-ack shell – but a hole was blown in my port wing three feet from the cockpit. This blew off my flap and caused a spray of shrapnel through the unprotected side of the Spit. The petrol feeds were cut, the instrument panel smashed and about 30 pieces hit my legs. I switched off the engine and did a steep diving turn from 20,000 feet. After deciding to try a landing, I put wheels down and came in fairly fast (about 120mph) because of no flaps, loss of lift from the wing and no air speed indicator. At the end of the runway was a pit where we kept crashed aircraft and, to avoid running into this, I put on a hard rudder and braked – wiping off the wheels! As I hit a small hill black smoke came out and I rapidly got out and tried to run but found that shrapnel had broken my right kneecap!"

Among the 601 Squadron pilots, Sgt McConnell claimed a MC202 probably destroyed, and Sgt Ken Lusty a fighter he thought was a Bf109 as damaged, but Sgt Ted Graysmark (BR196) was shot down into the sea – probably by Oblt Franz Götz (36th victory) of 9/JG53 – and was badly wounded. He managed to get into his dinghy, but had died by the time help arrived. Indeed, Flt Lt Barnham and Sgt Howard later took off to escort *HSL128* out to him, and became engaged in holding at bay four Messerschmitts that attempted to strafe the craft. In consequence, it was believed at the time that Graysmark had been machine-gunned in his dinghy.

Three of the 2°Gruppo Reggianes had been hit – it would appear by McConnell and Lusty – Serg Mario Marchio subsequently force-landing his burning aircraft near Noto (Syracuse) on the Sicilian coast; he had been seriously wounded, and died a month later from his injuries. A second Reggiane (MM7342) force-landed near Ispica, its undercarriage having been damaged by a 20mm cannon shell. The pilot, Serg Paolo Morcino, was unhurt and reported that he had shot down a Spitfire. TenCol Aldo Quarantotti's aircraft was also hit, and he belly-landed at Catania. Three Spitfires were claimed shot down by the Italians, two credited to the mortally wounded Marchio, and one to Cap Annibale Sterzi, the 358^Squadriglia commander; three others were claimed as probables and two as damaged.

Half an hour behind the initial wave of Spitfires had followed eight from 603 Squadron, just in time to catch the Italian bombers over the target area. Two were claimed shot down, one by Plt Off Dicks-Sherwood, the other jointly by Flt Lt Sanders and Flg Off Mitchell. The SM84 (MM23987) flown by Ten Vinicio Vego Scocco went down before it had released its bombs, and crashed into a garden near Dingli, where one of the crew was found dead near the wreckage; four others were seen to bale out over the sea. Flt Lt Barnham saw three of the parachutists floating down and waved as he flew past:

"As I was recrossing the coast at St Paul's Bay, my mouth went dry; three dots were rushing towards me. Three dots: 109s? Three dots with white smudges above them! Parachutes! I turned quickly to avoid those three white parachutes – three Italians, swinging to and fro and drifting southwards with the earth far below us. Circling round and round them was rather fun, for the three 'Ice-Cream Men', one slightly higher than the other two, appeared to go up and down like figures on a merry-go-round. As I watched them I became aware that they were staring back at me in terror; probably thought I was playing with them, that any second I would come in to attack them with blazing machine-guns or fly over the top of them to collapse their chutes. I gave them a wave. Immediate response – they all waved back."

The four Italian airmen were seen by watchers on Dingli cliffs to splash into the sea, while Barnham informed control of their situation and location:

"There they were; three white silk stains drifting in the swirling water; a lot of splashing too. I pulled up in a steep climbing turn over the cliff brink and back across a deserted landscape to dive again for another run past. A quick glimpse revealed the three of them trying to climb up on a ledge. On the third run I saw them all standing safe and sound. They were waving happily."

The second SM84 (Ten Panizzi's MM23955) had been very badly damaged and several members of the crew wounded, but it managed to struggle back to Sicily. One of the escorting Macchi pilots, Serg Mario Veronesi of 84^Squadriglia, attacked a Spitfire that was following the damaged Savoia and reported that it force-landed at Luqa (possibly Flt Sgt Bush of 126 Squadron). The third SM84 was also damaged, while Serg Teresio Martinoli's Macchi was hit in the tail by a Spitfire, although the pilot was able to claim another shot down. Finally, at 1745, eight 249 Squadron aircraft joined the fighting, Flt Sgt Williams claiming a Ju88 damaged and Flt Lt Lee a Bf109 damaged, while RAF ground defences at Takali reported strikes on another Messerschmitt. Oblt Ernst Kläger of 7/JG53 claimed two Spitfires, one at 1805 west of Malta, and the other ten minutes later. A third Spitfire was credited to Ltn Wolfgang Schaller of 9 Staffel at about the same time.

There was a sickening conclusion to this day, for when *HSL128* reached the location where the four Italian airmen from the downed SM84 had been seen to splash into the sea, only Serg Eugenio Rivolta, the second pilot, was to be found. It transpired that the other three had managed to reach the shore at Ta'Zuta (Dingli), as seen by Barnham. When a rescue unit arrived, however, it was to find that some person or persons unknown had deliberately rolled rocks over the cliff edge onto the helpless airmen, killing all three. This was not an isolated incident. Many Maltese understandably harboured a particularly deep hatred of the Italians, as recalled by Plt Off Sherlock of 185 Squadron:

"Another sad memory was when enemy aircrew, especially Italians, were coming down in chutes, the Maltese would position themselves accordingly, armed with pitchforks or any other weapon they could find. The enemy had little chance of surviving. It was difficult to blame the Maltese, who had lost homes, relatives, possessions. They had a real interest in the conflict, but to some of us it was still murder to kill an unarmed individual and who might have already been wounded. Several times, if the chutes were coming down close to the field, we would run out to try and save the enemy but usually it was too late. We all had big roundels painted on our Mae Wests, but even then there were several narrow escapes from the ever-ready pitchforks!"

Maltese AA gunner John Dedomenico added:

"I well remember an Italian pilot who came down in the sea just off the beach. People were preventing him from climbing ashore. It was a rocky beach and I don't know what happened to him. I don't know if he made it. And one German pilot was beaten to death with a shovel [by angry civilians]. There was a deep hatred for the enemy pilots, particularly in the countryside, where the people were less educated and tended to react violently. I never heard of any abuses of prisoners by the army or the police. But I know some villages treated the Germans quite roughly. The Germans seemed to bomb indiscriminately at times. Sometimes it seemed they were going after the civilian population, but that might not have been a fair assessment. It was such a small island that you couldn't help but hit civilian houses. But they did seem at times to go after things like schools and hospitals. That's the way it looked to some of us. And they dropped awful mines by parachute that had horns sticking out of them. They were very destructive. They also had sirens on their dive-bombers that scared the hell out of people."[50]

Fourteen-year-old George Scerri retained vivid memories of those torrid months:

"I was machine-gunned by a Messerschmitt 109. I was on a bicycle looking at the harbour when I saw a Messerschmitt coming down fast, strafing everybody who moved. And it dropped a bomb, too. I was scared. I could see soil and dust being kicked up by the bullets. I hid behind a wall. During another raid our school was blown up by the Germans. Fortunately, it was on a Saturday and no one was there. I remember another raid destroyed the village of Zabbar. I don't know why they did that. It was about two miles away from some anti-aircraft batteries but I think they were after the buildings. They hit our parish church on the side. If an enemy pilot came down, the people would kill him for sure. One day my cousin hit one in the face and he was sent to jail for 14 days."[51]

Another bizarre incident had allegedly been experienced by Wg Cdr Turner, when visiting a tiny café in Mdina one day. On enquiring as to what was contained in three large clay pots displayed behind the bar, he was horrified when the bartender opened one and pulled out a severed human head! Apparently it was the head of a German airman who had baled out safely over Malta, but who had then been butchered by a crowd of civilians. Whether there was any substance to this story remains debatable. Certainly, the following apocryphal tale circulated amongst service personnel – probably for the dubious benefit of new arrivals – ostensibly to encourage them to value their parachutes as parachute silk in wartime was worth – to quote – a maiden's ransom! It was rumoured that on one occasion a pilot had baled out and had pulled the ripcord, only to find that an old army blanket floated out! Jo Sherlock continued:

"This undoubtedly is a tall story although at the time I think all of us believed this to be true and we became very protective of our chutes as we realised that we might have to use them on any flight. To embellish the story further, it was rumoured that after this episode, there were quite a few Maltese girls wearing white silk panties, although, again, I did not check into this!"

To the low-flying Messerschmitt pilots any movement on the ground warranted a burst of machine-gunfire, and many civilians had been killed or wounded in this fashion; buses, ferry boats, fishing boats and rescue launches had all been strafed, so to many Maltese captured aircrew were considered fair game. Flt Lt Barnham found himself to be such a target on one occasion:

"Sudden engines, a rasp of machine-guns, dust flies up all around me, white scars appear on the stonework of the walls; I fling myself into the cover of the wall as two 109s, leaping towards me, tilt sideways over the tree-tops; they're banking round for a second attack. Am I the target? They're coming round, sweeping back towards me – a

Bofors gun has opened up, thank God; ascending red fireballs streak into the sky then kick backwards, in black puffs, close to the enemy planes. My God! shells bursting on the tree-tops, shrapnel tearing its way through the leaves, slithering into the earth beside me, thumping on the roadway behind, clanging on the wall against which I cringe in terror!"

The war in the air was not always fought in a chivalrous manner, either. More than one British pilot was believed shot on his parachute or in his dinghy and on one occasion two 185 Squadron pilots reported witnessing a Messerschmitt pilot strafe and apparently kill one of his own, under the obvious impression that the dinghy contained a British airman. Similarly, a Canadian pilot of 249 Squadron was seen to machine-gun survivors of a shot-down Ju88, and there were a number of other such incidents.

Stukas returned to Malta on **13 May**, 16 aircraft of III/StG3 escorted by 26 Bf109s raiding Hal Far at lunchtime. Eight Spitfires of 249 were among the dozen or so scrambled, but as Flt Lt West's section took off, Messerschmitts swept over and attempted to strafe them, albeit without result. Sgt Hesselyn, having escaped this attack, saw another Bf109 pass close by as he was climbing:

"We climbed up west of Gozo, reaching 12,000 feet without being molested. Eight of us were now together. I saw two 109s on my starboard beam and at about the same height. I told the rest of the formation, and turned towards them. The leader of the pair began climbing away, but his No.2 failed to follow, apparently not having seen me. I was able to get on his tail without trouble, and opened fire at about 100 yards. He was obviously a new hand, and kept going straight and level, enabling me to get a good bead on him. I gave him two-seconds. He dived straight down, with smoke and glycol pouring from him. I watched him crash into the drink."

R/T chatter then reported action over Kalafrana Bay, and on arrival there he spotted another Messerschmitt on a Spitfire's tail:

"I went in at once, attacking from the starboard quarter. I could see my shells striking its fuselage. He turned on his back. I turned on mine, firing all the time. He started to go down in a gentle dive, and I kept firing to make sure of him. He crashed into the bay and, as he hit the water, Ronnie West's voice came to me over the R/T: 'Spit that just shot down that 109, thanks a hell of a lot!'"

One of the Ju87s was damaged by Flt Sgt Bob Brown of 603 Squadron, while a Spitfire was slightly damaged – possibly by Obfw Rollwage of II/JG53, who claimed one just north of Luqa at 1302 for his 19th victory; a second was credited to Uffz Heinz Seggermann of 6 Staffel. As daylight rapidly faded, two Macchis were reported patrolling off the coast, and four Spitfires of 126 Squadron were scrambled to investigate. Sgt Goldsmith (BR244) claimed strikes on one of the fleeing fighters, as did Flt Lt Peck, and each was credited with one damaged. Three of 601 also scrambled, Plt Off Roy Johnson (BR161) reporting Macchis and Ju88s. As he closed in to intercept, a coolant seal burst and he was drenched in glycol. Despite smarting eyes he was able to land safely and was taken to hospital, where he was declared medically unfit and would remain so until near to the end of June.

The first main raid on **14 May** was plotted approaching at 0900, when 28 Spitfires (seven/126, three/185, eight/249, six/601, four/603) were ordered off to intercept three Ju88s of I/KGr806 and a number of Bf109 Jabo, all covered by a large fighter escort. The bombers raided Takali and Luqa, while the fighter-bombers also attacked Takali, where Sqn Ldr Douglas-Hamilton's aircraft had its fuel tank splintered. Flt Lt

West's 249 section of four saw the Ju88s some 30 miles out and about 1,000 feet below their level. West attacked the centre bomber of three, claiming to have shot it down before firing at the port aircraft, which was also attacked by Plt Off Linton; they reported seeing it make off with an engine on fire. West then became involved with the Messerschmitt escort and claimed strikes on one before it evaded and escaped. Sgt Hesselyn attacked the bomber on the right of the section:

> "I got on the tail of my 88, closed to about 50 yards, and opened fire. I could see three members of the 88's crew in the glasshouse, as well as the rear gunner, who had already opened fire. I gave it everything I had. I saw my shells strike along the 88's fuselage and smack into the glasshouse. It was carrying a bomb-load, and blew up. Pieces flew in all directions, being so widely scattered that I had to go into a violent turn to avoid the fragments. I could see Ronnie firing at his 88, and in a few seconds it went down in flames. As I went down I saw the remaining Hun bomber. He was heading towards Sicily, and smoke was pouring from his engines. Linny, apparently having used all his ammo, had given up chasing it, and was following us down."

It seems that Hesselyn and West may actually have fired at the same aircraft, for apparently only one Ju88 – M7+FH flown by the Staffelkapitän, Hptm Emil Braun – failed to return. Flt Sgt Williams, meanwhile, pursued a Bf109 for some distance but was obliged to break away after registering some strikes. On returning to Takali he belly-landed his Spitfire, having exhausted his fuel. The pilots of 126 and 185 were also engaged, but, as Sgt Goldsmith recorded: "Missed out on the bombers, got mixed up with 109s. Gave one a 12-seconds burst, set it on fire."

Apart from Goldsmith, Plt Off Tilley and Sgt Boyd (BR349/C) were also each credited with Bf109s shot down and Flt Lt Winfield with a probable, while Plt Off Bill Johnson (Spitfire/B) claimed one damaged. Of his combat, Boyd wrote:

> "We were attacked by four Messerschmitts from above. We climbed into them, circling with them and fired at various ones. I fired three seconds at one from port beam below to quarter astern. He streamed white smoke in puffs and then a steady stream. He headed east, slowing up and jerking slightly. I had to break off to avoid others. His glycol tank was obviously hit. In my opinion this e/a could not reach his base, with the loss of glycol, and the fact of a strong headwind against the trip to Sicily."

Nonetheless, the Messerschmitt did reach Sicily, Ltn Alfred Hammer crash-landing his 4/JG53 aircraft (7553) at Comiso airfield where it was badly damaged and subsequently written-off. One of 185 Squadron's long-serving pilots, Sgt Colin Finlay, was seen to be engaged by two Bf109s and his BR291/GL-H was set on fire, crashing into the sea 400 yards off Wied iz-Zurrieq. Finlay fell clear, but his parachute did not open; two Maltese soldiers – L/Corp Julian Sciberras and Gunner Spiro Zammit – at once launched a small boat, reaching the spot in ten minutes. The Messerschmitts were still circling overhead but, undaunted, they located Finlay and pulled him aboard; sadly, he was found to be dead when they reached the shore. The two soldiers were officially commended for their action. 185's Slim Yarra wrote:

> "Five aircraft led by Flt Lt Lawrence took off on the first scramble. It is unfortunate that we lost Sgt Finlay on this show. 'Ginger', who was due to leave the island at any moment, was attacked by six Messerschmitts and crashed [off] the coast."

Three of the defending fighters were claimed shot down, one each being credited to Uffz Erich Paczia of 6 Staffel, Fw Walter Kneur of 5 Staffel, and Ltn Karl-Heinz Quaritsch of 8 Staffel. The next alert sounded soon after midday as three more Ju88s of KGr806 headed in, escorted by Bf109s, MC202s of 9°Gruppo CT and RE2001s of 2°Gruppo Aut CT; their target was Takali. Seventeen Spitfires and four Hurricanes were sent off, Flt Lt Barnham leading a force from 126, 601 and 603 Squadrons to attack the bombers; four 185 Squadron aircraft engaged the Italian fighters, Flt Sgt Ferraby (BR294/GL-E) and Sgt Boyd attacking eight of these from below. Ferraby put a four or five-seconds burst into one Macchi, which spun away pouring black smoke and some pieces fell off; he claimed a probable. Boyd's BR349/C was seen to spin out of the fight, however, and it crashed near Takali. One Spitfire was claimed shot down by M.llo Rinaldo Damiani of 9°Gruppo, and two others by Ten Carlo Seganti and Ten Leo Venturini of 2°Gruppo. However, Boyd may equally have fallen victim to one of the Messerschmitts. Plt Off Tilley watched the fight while his Spitfire was being refuelled:

"A dogfight started overhead – some three Ju88s came in with 109 escort – ack-ack going like mad, bursts all over the sky – then I saw a 109 sit on a Spitfire's tail and I heard the brrr of cannon. The Spit rolled over and dived vertically in what appeared to be a controlled evasive manoeuvre, doing a series of aileron turns; there was no smoke trail and apparently he was OK but for some reason I felt he'd had it. Sure enough, he started to pull out too late, at 100 feet, then, when it looked as if he would make it, the pilot either died or lost consciousness and ploughed into the deck on the far side of the drome at 300mph. So at 1305 hours the career of Sgt Pilot Tony Boyd came to an abrupt and spectacular end – just a terrific explosion and a long sheet of flame."

Meanwhile, the main force of Spitfires attacked the bombers and claimed all three shot down. Barnham (BP975/1-K) and Plt Off Bruce Ingram (2-P) reported attacking one, which Barnham hit in the port engine and wing:

"With the 88s parading past in vic formation I'm diving fast on to the tail of the nearest, black against the blue sea, black against the white houses of Valetta – 109s alive to our attack? No – still flying steadily. Harbour barrage – shells burst red and black, friendly shells fired by our side. Bomber growing larger, backwards towards me – gun sight spot on his port wing – 200 yards – on his port engine – fire now; quick white flashes along the wing, one, two, three, four on the engine – a great burst of black smoke gushing back. Swerving right and tilting – enemy fighters? No. Over my left shoulder the sky filled with shell bursts; Spitfires behind other bombers; 109s breaking up too late from their tidy formation. Nearest Spit sliding up behind my burning bomber – strikes all down the bomber's fuselage, strikes along the wing, starboard engine splits into flame, bomber dropping below, tumbling downwards, pyre of blackness."

Flt Sgt Hurst of 603 Squadron also reported shooting down a Ju88 as it dived on Takali. This crashed on the edge of the runway, although AA gunners also claimed a share in this success. It seems probable that all involved had fired on Fw Günther Schwerdt's M7+CH, which did indeed crash at Takali. Although the pilot had attempted to crash-land the burning bomber, he and his crew perished in the wreck. One crewmember was seen to be seriously injured, but could not be reached. It was alleged that Wg Cdr Gracie drew his revolver and put the man out of his misery. Flt Lt Sanders and Flg Off Mitchell of 603 Squadron claimed a second Ju88 shot down into the sea, Sanders additionally reporting strikes on a Bf109; Plt Off Dicks-Sherwood of this unit also claimed a bomber, shared with Sgt Goldsmith of 126 Squadron, who reported:

"Scrambled with 601 by mistake. Fired everything at a Ju88 – 150 yards. Set both engines and fuselage on fire; knocked off some lumps."

It would seem that all four pilots attacked the same aircraft, a second Ju88 crash-landing at Catania on return in a badly damaged condition; it was also probably fired on by Flg Off Hone (3-R) of 601, who reported inflicting damage to the port engine of the bomber he attacked. Sqn Ldr Douglas-Hamilton, who was on the ground at Takali, witnessed the Ju88s heading for the airfield:

"They had not far to go, when I saw the rear one break away with smoke streaming from it. Then I saw Spitfires attacking, and another 88 broke away with smoke and flames pouring from it. The leader was now just starting his dive on my end of the aero-drome when I saw a Spitfire above it with its cannons puffing away. Almost immediately the wing of the 88 became a mass of flame; the petrol tank had been hit. The 88 jettisoned its bombs at the edge of the aerodrome, then did a drunken swoop across the aerodrome, and one of its engines fell out. It crashed just beside the landing ground and burned furiously with columns of black smoke. We got out of our slit trench and cheered. I went round to look at the wreckage. It was well smashed up. The pilot was reclining backwards in the front of the wreckage, quite dead, but still grasping the control column. He had evidently been trying to control the aeroplane until the end. Soon there was little left of him or the 88. I felt quite unmoved; he had just been trying to bomb me. Everybody else on the scene felt much the same. To my delight, I learnt that all the 88s were shot down by the Squadron, Johnny Hurst having got the last one."

The loss of the gallant Australian, Tony Boyd – doyen of the Hurricane pilots – was a sad blow. He and Colin Finlay – also killed that day – had earlier been advised that they were imminently due to leave the island, together with a handful of the Hurricane survivors.

Shortly after 1700, a third trio of KGr806 bombers approached, again under cover of a large fighter escort. Seven 249 Squadron Spitfires were first off, well in advance of the raiders' arrival, and these at once attacked a number of Jabo Bf109s that had just bombed and strafed Hal Far. Flg Off Buchanan claimed one probably shot down, while Flt Sgt Bud Fox, an American from New York, called over the R/T that he had also shot one down; moments later however, his Spitfire (BP878) crashed into the sea, victim of another Messerschmitt. Fifteen more Spitfires from 126 and 601 Squadrons followed at 1730, while six Hurricanes protected the airfields. Four Spitfires were led by Flt Lt Barnham, who, quite unofficially, had had the wings of his aircraft (1-U) painted:

"I look out at the wings of my Spitfire for they are covered with huge white spots; following up my ideas on air combat I wanted to be quickly recognised so that my companions can reform and deliver a second attack on any bombers we meet. I've also had my perspex hood removed. Chiefy disapproved of the spots, but the airmen have made a splendid job of covering the whole of my aircraft – he says all the enemy fighters will fasten on me: perhaps I'm stupid but it's worth a try."

The Spitfires were vectored onto the Ju88s at low level, and Barnham positioned his section for an astern attack and he managed to get on the tail of Uffz Johannes Prokesch's Ju88 (M7+BL):

"As I settled on the tail of the nearest bomber I was aware of a 109 creeping into position behind me – I fired a steady three-seconds burst, hitting the bomber all the time, watching cannon shells and bullets ripping into his black wing, a cascade of flashing white sparks just inboard of his port engine – then, breaking violently left, flashed past the attacking 109 astonishingly close; saw its bright red propeller spinner, oval shaped like an elongated egg with a rippling highlight, rotating in straggly slow motion. The German pilot jerked his head up to look at me – then open sky and sudden panic as other 109s fastened on my tail. Saw the bomber dropping from the dogfight above; its port wing, where my cannon shells had torn into it, had snapped off and was fluttering high above, while the rest of the machine, quite flat with flame gushing from its broken wing stump, was gyrating round and round, a gigantic catherine wheel. 109s on me again – we all had a hell of a fight to get home."

One Messerschmitt overshot, and Barnham opened fire at it before it disappeared from view:

"There's plenty of time to shoot him down. This should be easy. He's flying beautifully now, straight towards the red centre spot of my gunsight. Flashes on his wings and fuselage. Gigantic in size he disappears under my wing. I heave my Spitfire into a steep turn. On his tail now! Where is he? Damned if I can see it. A sudden call in my earphones: 'Something's gone in near Filfla.' It must be my 109 that has crashed – the splash must be right under me."

Pursued by five more, he headed low for Takali, there to be greeted by a burst of Bofors gunfire. On landing, he realised that the white spots on his wings had indeed attracted the attention of the German pilots, and at once arranged for them to be painted out again:

"I apologised to Chiefy for all the extra trouble I'd caused him. He smiled back at me with such a patient, kindly, understanding smile. I'm still shaken after that trip."

Later, when Sqn Ldr Bisdee arrived at dispersal, he ordered that the aircraft's cockpit hood be replaced – much to Barnham's chagrin. The demise of the bomber was witnessed by an AA crew, who also claimed to have shot it down. Returning German crews were of the opinion that this had indeed been their comrades' fate. However, although the pilot and two others of the crew were killed, the observer (Obgfr Herbert Burger) managed to bale out and subsequently confirmed that a Spitfire had shot down his aircraft. Watching the action from Kalafrana, Phil Chandler later recorded in his diary:

"One of them received a direct hit. Smoke poured forth immediately and he did a sharp turn, crossing the path of one of his comrades. This turn was perhaps too much for the stricken machine, for both engines fell out. Then the whole box of tricks fell to pieces. The whole mainplane came off and spun lazily down, leaving a spiral of blue smoke, amid a shower of smaller fragments which continued to flutter down for some minutes afterwards. One got away by parachute."

Two Bf109s were claimed shot down by Sqn Ldr Barton and his No.2, Plt Off Tilley, the former adding a second as probably destroyed, and the latter one more as damaged. The AA defences also claimed damage to a Bf109 and a Ju88, but no further German loss was recorded, although a second Messerschmitt crash-landed at Comiso during the day following combat. In addition to the loss of Flt Sgt Fox, one other Spitfire was damaged during this action, and a third on landing. JG53 reported victories over three Spitfires during the evening sortie, one apiece being credited to Obfw Werner Stumpf of 9 Staffel, who reported that his combat took place about ten miles south-west of Dingli. The other two were claimed by Hptm Helmut Belser (his 27th victory) of 8 Staffel, and Obfw Otto Schmidt of 5 Staffel, his first. German bombers were again over the island during the night, Hal Far being one of their targets, as 185 Squadron's Slim Yarra noted:

"Our three aircraft have now been reduced to two. Jerry came over and dropped a bomb near one. Some pieces of shrapnel entered the engine, rather spoiling the finish. However, we were on readiness again at dawn and spent the morning chasing reccos and things."

The Italians were back on the morning of **15 May**, three SM84s of 4°Gruppo BT, escorted by 30 MC202s of 4°Stormo CT, heading for St Paul's Bay at 0915, the crews briefed to bomb Fort Campbell barracks. A dozen Spitfires from 249 and 603 were scrambled and engaged the formation shortly after it had bombed, but only Flt Lt Lee was able to reach the bombers, claiming one damaged. The Spitfires were engaged by the escort and four claimed shot down, one apiece by Cap Franco Lucchini (his 16th victory), Ten Jacopo Frigerio, Ten Ferruccio Zarini and Serg Magg Mario Guerci; two others were claimed damaged, but in fact there were no losses and barely any damage suffered. 249's newly commissioned New Zealander Plt Off Lawrie Verrall was, however, able to get a telling burst into the Macchi flown by Cap Alberto Argenton, commander of 91^Squadriglia, who was killed. Two hours later, two flights from 126 and 249 were scrambled to engage a fighter sweep by an estimated 40-50 Bf109s covering an Italian ASR Z506B with close escort of MC202s. All returned safely although Plt Off Booth crash-landed BR229 at Takali, having been attacked by a Messerschmitt – almost certainly the 31st victim of Oblt Gerhard Michalski of 4/JG53 – and Sgt John Gray reported damage to two others he engaged.

In mid-afternoon a single reconnaissance Ju88 with a substantial fighter escort approached, two 185 Squadron Spitfires and four from 603 taking off, the first pair at 1537 and the quartet at 1610. Sgt Yarra (GL-K) recorded:

"Engaged seven 109s, damaged leader; was attacked by four 202s. Shot down one, who collided with his No.2. Fought the remaining two until out of ammo."

The Squadron diarist (Yarra himself) added:

"Flt Sgt Sim and Sgt Yarra became mixed up with seven Messerschmitts and four Macchis. Two Macchis were destroyed and one Me109 damaged before the boys ran out of popcorn and had to come down."

The 603 Squadron section meanwhile engaged a number of II/JG53 Bf109s near Hal Far, Sqn Ldr Douglas-Hamilton attacking one head-on. His fire appeared to cause the port wing of one aircraft to break off:

"I drew blood for the second time. We were stooging around at 25,000 feet for a considerable time; it was very cold and I even got frostbite in a finger. We were bounced once by a pair of 109s but avoided them successfully. Eventually we were told to go down. Suddenly I saw a 109 sweeping down on my No.2. It still came on, but this time at me, and we were approaching each other head-on at great speed. I resolved not to give way before he did, and he evidently made the same resolution. We were going straight at each other, and as soon as I got my sights on him I opened fire, and kept firing. He opened fire a second afterwards. It all happened in a flash, but when he seemed about 50 yards away I gave a violent yank on the stick and broke away to the right. As I did so, his port wing broke off in the middle, and he shot past under me. I turned and looked back; his aeroplane did about five flick rolls to the left and broke up. Then a parachute opened."

The Messerschmitt crashed behind Paola Hill. By a quirk of coincidence, the pilot was none other than Ltn Herbert Soukop of 6 Staffel, whom Douglas-Hamilton had unknowingly engaged on 1 May and was believed to have been shot down by him! Soukop baled out with his left arm broken by a cannon shell; unable properly to control his descent, his parachute caught on the roof of a house in a private garden at Zejtun, where he was left dangling in the air. This probably kept him safe from the crowd of angry Maltese who gathered before soldiers arrived to cut him down and take him to hospital. During this fight Australian Flt Sgt Bill Irwin claimed strikes on another Bf109, which was last seen going out to sea, emitting smoke; he was credited with a probable. Sqn Ldr Douglas-Hamilton paid Soukop a visit:

"He was a small, muscular, blond-haired, blue-eyed young man of twenty-one, with a squat Germanic face. We conversed in German, as he knew no English, and when I told him I had shot him down he surprised me somewhat by seizing my hand and congratulating me. He did not know what had caused his aeroplane to do flick rolls, and was under the impression that we had collided. He was rather disappointed that he had not hit my machine at all. Apparently it was he who had tried to bounce us earlier in the fight. He was a Sudeten German who had Czech relatives, and said he was not a Nazi, but just became a fighter pilot for the fun of it!"

In the same hospital 126 Squadron's Sgt Crist was still recovering from his wounds:

"When I was in hospital they put all the pilots in one ward. It didn't matter whether you were German, English, Italian or Canadian. The guy next to me was a Stuka pilot. We used to play checkers. I asked him what he was going to do after the war and he told me, 'I'm going to stay in the Luftwaffe.' I said, 'I don't think so.' At that time they were winning. He showed me pictures from his wallet of his girlfriend and his mom and dad back in Germany. He was just a kid. You were old if you were 24. I had no animosity for them. They were doing the same job as we were, just on different sides."

Again it was the Regia Aeronautica that opened the attacks on **16 May**, Z1007bis of 210^Squadriglia raiding Takali under cover of 30 Macchis and 15 Messerschmitts, including a number of Jabo. On the airfield one Spitfire was destroyed and another slightly damaged, while two airmen were killed. Nonetheless, 16 Spitfires succeeded in getting airborne to intercept. At their head once again was Flt Lt Barnham of 601 Squadron, although he was still suffering from Malta Dog and had been ordered not to fly; however, in the absence of others, he decided that he should lead. He ordered Blue Section to take on the bombers while he led his section up to great height to engage the fighter escort, but at 34,000 feet the cold was so intense that one pilot, the South African Bartleman, suffered frostbite to his fingers. Although given a clear run at the bombers, Blue Section failed to gain significant success. Flg Off Hone (Spitfire/P) and Plt Off Hagger jointly claimed one of the Cants probably destroyed, and Sgt McConnell a Macchi probable. Hone's aircraft suffered damage but he was able to land safely. Four 603 Squadron aircraft engaged Bf109s, Sqn Ldr Douglas-Hamilton and Plt Off Geoff Northcott (Spitfire/C) each claiming one damaged, but Flt Sgt Fred Johnson's aircraft was shot up by Ltn Ernst Kläger of 7/JG53, and the Australian crash-landed at Takali. 4°Stormo Macchi pilots claimed four Spitfires shot down, two by Serg Magg Massimo Salvatore – one reportedly as it was landing – and one each by Sottoten Mario Squarcina and M.llo Rinaldo Damiani; one more was claimed by gunners in the bombers.

Early in the afternoon a single Ju88, covered by an estimated 26 Bf109s (including five Jabo) and 15 RE2001s of 2°Gruppo Aut CT, attacked Kalafrana. Six 249 Spitfires were scrambled at 1440, followed 35 minutes later by five more from 126 Squadron. Flg Off Buchanan claimed an Italian fighter shot down, which he believed was a Macchi, and Sgt Gerry de Nancrède (BR117) reported gaining strikes on a Messerschmitt. Plt Offs Plagis (BR176/1-N) and Nash engaged another with greater success. Nash recorded:

> "Damn good party with Me109s off Kalafrana Bay. They attacked in pairs but Plagis and I fixed one from 300 yards. This is the 100th e/a destroyed on Malta by 249 Squadron."

It would seem they had shot down White 6 of JaboStaffel JG53, although the pilot, Uffz Dr. Felix Sauer, thought his aircraft had either been hit by AA fire or that the subsequent explosion in his engine had been caused by a technical problem:

> "Four Spitfires suddenly appeared. I moved to counter-attack but there was an explosion in the engine, which goes dead. I dived and escaped but there was nothing left to do, so I descend from 3,000 metres to 700 metres and take to my parachute. My comrades fly round me and make me understand that they have seen me, and that they will try to get some help. While baling out I hurt my chin and for a while was stunned. The cold water soon restored my senses. I detached myself from the parachute and inflated my small rubber boat."

When the 126 Squadron aircraft got into the air, Plt Off McHan also claimed damage to a 'Macchi', and Flt Sgt Milner's aircraft suffered slight damage. However, four Spitfires were claimed shot down by the Reggiane pilots, one each by Ten Giorgio Pocek, Ten Agostino Celentano, Sottoten Carlo Grillo, and Serg Magg Guerrino Prodi. In return, Grillo's aircraft (MM7210) was seriously damaged – probably by Buchanan – and force-landed at Comiso. About one and-a-half hours later 11 Spitfires were sent off to intercept a Do24 and its Bf109 escort, reported north of Malta and obviously searching for Sauer, who was now about eight miles from Marsaxlokk Bay; the German pilot later recalled:

> "While it [the Dornier] was trying to land, five Spitfires attacked it, though its markings were perfectly visible. This unfair attack was avenged at once; one of the Spitfires was shot down at the same moment. But the rescue aircraft had to turn back as well."

Sauer's observation was inaccurate, however, for none of the Spitfires – from 603 Squadron – that engaged were lost. In fact, Flt Lt Sanders and Flt Sgt Hurst each claimed a Bf109 probably destroyed, and Flg Off Mitchell damaged another, which he left trailing smoke after pursuing it for some 25 miles towards Sicily. The flyingboat was attacked by Plt Off Dicks-Sherwood, but he could not tell if he scored any strikes due to the glare of the sun. Either way, the Dornier returned to Sicily having not accomplished its mission. Flg Off Holland:

> "Johnny Hurst led Neville King, P/O Forster and me in an attack on the Do24 seaplane, heavily escorted by Me109s. We nearly got blown out of the sky by the escort, and were then chased back to Malta at sea level. We were all four lucky to get home intact and none of us could stay long enough to observe results. We had been ordered to attack, to prevent ditched enemy aircrew returning home to fight against us."

Felix Sauer's ordeal was only just beginning and it would be eight long days before he was rescued. 603 Squadron was now instructed to transfer three of its pilots to 126 Squadron to cover those currently down with Malta Dog. The three selected for the temporary posting were Plt Off Alan Boyle, Flt Sgt Mac Barbour (who was shortly to receive his commission) and Flt Sgt Hamish Haggas; on cessation of duty with 126 Squadron, Barbour returned to 603, but Boyle joined 601 and Haggas moved over to 185.

Two 249 Squadron Spitfires were scrambled after a lone reconnaissance Ju88D from 1(F)/122 at 0700 on **17 May**. They were expertly vectored onto the intruder, and Oblt Günther Steppmacher's F6+LH was intercepted over Valetta by Flg Off Buchanan and shot down into the sea; there were no survivors. Luftwaffe air-sea rescue aircraft were out early, obviously searching for both Sauer and the missing reconnaissance crew. At 0806, five 126 Squadron Spitfires were ordered to intercept these, as were a number of Spitfires from 249 Squadron. As the Spitfires began their take-off runs, Sgt Goldsmith's BP952 ran into a small hole caused by an unexploded bomb, one wheel being torn away and a wing damaged. The others intercepted an escorted Do24T CM+IN of 6 Seenotstaffel, which was shot down by Flt Sgt Parks. Obgfr Wilhelm Kühn (the air gunner) sustained wounds but was rescued along with other members of his crew. Flt Lt Winfield claimed one of the escorting Messerschmitts shot down, while at 0829 Obfw Rudolf Ehrenberger of 6/JG53 claimed a Spitfire, his 28th victory, some ten miles or so north-east of Valetta.

It had long been the RAF's policy to attack Axis air-sea rescue aircraft, even white-painted aircraft emblazoned with prominent red cross insignia. This was a decision with which not only Air Vice-Marshal Lloyd concurred, but one which had the approval of Prime Minister Churchill, who later wrote:

"We did not recognise this means of rescuing enemy pilots who had been shot down in action, in order that they might come and bomb our civilian population again. We rescued them ourselves whenever it was possible, and made them prisoners of war. But all German air ambulances were forced or shot down by our fighters on definite orders approved by the War Cabinet."

This decision had been reached during the early days of the Battle of Britain, when a number of such rescue aircraft had been observed flying in the vicinity of British convoys, and it was feared that they were reporting shipping movements; it was also noticed that they were generally armed and amongst the crews captured, there was a noticeable absence of medical orderlies. Air Vice-Marshal Lloyd's reasons for his approval have not been recorded but recent events around Malta would indicate that these included: (a) retaliation for German attacks on Malta's rescue launches; (b) it was believed that RAF pilots were not being picked up by Axis aircraft and, indeed, that some British pilots had been deliberately strafed in their dinghies; (c) that Axis survivors picked up by Malta's launches had proved very useful for interrogation purposes; (d) that since 1940 the destruction of such aircraft had been Fighter Command's policy in the United Kingdom.

A pair of 249 Spitfires was scrambled at 1155, joining six more from 603 Squadron, on the approach of a fighter-bomber raid. Plt Offs Nash and Verrall each reported shooting down a Messerschmitt, while the latter claimed another damaged. Only one was lost, however, Ltn Wolfgang Herrmann of 5/JG53 failing to return in Black 8. A second pilot of this unit baled out over Cap Scaramia, but allegedly as a consequence of technical problems. Another Messerschmitt then shot down Plt Off Pete Nash, who crashed to his death in BP951 near Dingli; the loss of the popular 20-year-old ace, with 11 victories to his credit, was a hard blow. He fell to either Uffz Erich Paczia or Ltn Hans Märkstetter, both of 6/JG53, who each claimed a Spitfire at more or less the same time; probably both fired on his aircraft. Meanwhile, the 603 Squadron pilots found another of 6 Seenotstaffel's flyingboats, which was shot down by Plt Off Les Barlow and Flt Sgt Hurst, while Plt Off King claimed damage to an escorting Bf109. Barlow's subsequent combat report revealed:

"One Do24. Evasive tactics – gentle turns. Tracer used in returning fire. Aircraft brought down with tail on fire – fell in sea two miles from Salina Bay."

An Italian air-sea rescue Z506B of 612^Squadriglia was out during the evening, protected by 19 RE2001s of 2°Gruppo. Plt Off Le Bas led off seven 601 Squadron Spitfires to intercept, the opposing fighters clashing over Takali. Cap Salvatore Teia and Serg Magg Rino Ricci each claimed Spitfires shot down, while one other was claimed as a probable and three more were believed to have been hit. In return, one Reggiane was damaged, as was the floatplane, struck by fire from both a Spitfire and shrapnel from a bursting AA shell. The Spitfire leader, Le Bas, and Plt Off Boyle each claimed Reggianes probably destroyed, and Wt Off Fred Belcher another as damaged, while Plt Off Caldwell (BR306/3-D) reported shooting down a Bf109. It is believed that Sgt Stan Howard (BR344/3-M) attacked the Z506B but he was then shot-up by the escort, his aircraft being hit in the glycol tank. He attempted to reach Luqa, but came in too low and hit a stone wall; the Spitfire cartwheeled across the airfield, shedding its wings and the Rhodesian suffered serious head injuries, from which he died three days later.

Seven more 249 Squadron Spitfires had by now got into the air and pursued the Italians out to sea, Plt Off Plagis (BR170/C-25) firing at one of the fighters, which he identified as an MC202: "Chased a Macchi which strafed Hal Far. Caught him up, fired every round at him 200 yards – and he got away – never forgive myself. Only damaged him." Similarly misidentifying the fleeing fighters, but as Messerschmitts, Flt Sgt Brennan reported: "Exchanged shots with some 109s, but without result either side. Shot at by Spit." Brennan's Canadian colleague, Sgt de Nancrède, had a frightening experience: "Scramble in BR117. Oxygen failure at 20,000 feet. Blackout. Bloody near died!"

185 Squadron's two remaining Spitfires were also scrambled:

"Flt Lt Lawrence and Sgt Yarra managed to become mixed up with about 14 Macchi 202s [sic]. The dogfight which ensued was quite good fun while it lasted. Although our boys managed to get a few good squirts in, no results were obtained."

That evening the four surviving former Hurricane pilots of the now defunct 605 Squadron still on the island – Plt Offs Ron Noble, Ian McKay, Phil Wigley and Joe Beckitt – plus a handful of inexperienced arrivals from the last reinforcement flight from *Wasp*, who had been so assiduously weeded out, boarded a Curtiss-Wright CW20[52] airliner-cum-transport (at that time the largest twin-engined land plane in the world) and departed for Gibraltar, from where they were eventually returned to the UK. From the comfort of his hotel room at Gibraltar, McKay later jotted in his diary:

"Our trip was postponed for two days on account of weather conditions, but we did get away on the 17th. Our trip to Gibraltar was uneventful and quite enjoyable. Now for the sad part of this story – Tony Boyd and Colin Finlay were to go, but fate took another hand and both were shot down and killed. We are all staying at the Rock Hotel and are living like kings but are hoping to get away to England soon. Still no news of when we leave for England, but we can't crab cause we are living like human beings again and have breakfast in bed every morning, a hot bath after getting up and no air raids (so far!). The nights are really beautiful and we usually spend the evenings before going to bed sitting on the balcony looking out over the Mediterranean and to Algeciras, a little Spanish town across the bay. Of course, they have no blackout and the sight of a city with its lights on is grand."

After two weeks of such luxurious living, the refreshed pilots were flown to England in a Hudson.

Early on the morning of **18 May**, 16 MC202s and eight RE2001s of 2°Gruppo Aut

CT set off towards Malta as cover for a number of Italian MTBs operating off the island. Four 249 aircraft were ordered to investigate, but at the last moment Sqn Ldr Grant's Spitfire became unserviceable. He rushed over to Flt Sgt Brennan's aircraft and ordered him to lead the remaining trio then taxiing for take-off; they were soon followed by Flt Lt Ron West, who scrambled to bring the flight up to strength, but when he caught up with the others he allowed Brennan to continue leading. About ten miles east of Zonqor, four fighters – believed to have been Macchis – were spotted 2,000 feet below and Brennan led an attack on these. He fired a short burst at one, seeing strikes on the port wing, but this pulled away and flew right across the nose of Sgt John Gilbert's aircraft. The latter also fired and the Italian fighter fell away, pouring coolant. Brennan, meanwhile, attacked another:

> "He promptly went into a vertical dive. I followed him, caught him as he was pulling out of his dive at 2,000 feet and, getting dead behind him, gave him a long burst. He hung there for a second, rolled on his back, and hit the sea. As he crashed I saw another aircraft spin into the sea half a mile away. As I thought it might be one of our boys, I called up the others, and Ronnie [West] told me he had just shot down one of the Eyeties. The one Johnny [Gilbert] had hit force-landed at Zonqor Point, and it was then we learned that the Eyeties had not been Macchis, but Reggiane 2001s."

The force-landed Reggiane had been flown by Ten Remo Cazzolli, the leader of the 152^Squadriglia flight, who recalled:

> "There were many Spitfires and few RE2001s, so when I ordered my pilots to break formation and engage, I found myself surrounded by Spitfires! As I opened fire, I saw before me in planform, like a cross, a Spitfire. I took aim and fired, seeing a long, black trail – possibly a sign that I had hit him ... suddenly there was a terrible noise like thunder and my engine stopped; it was the fire of 20mm cannon, which overwhelmed my senses. I realised at once the situation, and my face was covered with blood; by instinct I sought to open the cockpit canopy, but it was stuck, a shell having struck behind the seat armour and crushed the canopy forward against the windscreen. I thought it was the end. I was in an aircraft with no power, a radiator shot away, a shattered aileron fluttering, with the earth of Malta coming up inexorably to meet me! I tried to recover control. I do not know what condition the tail of the aircraft was in, but the aircraft seemed to have a life of its own; it would not kill me! I saw a rock flush in the sea, there was an indescribable crash, and I passed out."

By 0930 the presence of the Italian MTBs had been spotted and four Hurricanes were despatched to attack them. As they were searching, a big Axis fighter sweep began to form up and 18 Spitfires were scrambled to intercept this and to cover the Hurricanes. The latter had just come under attack by Bf109s when five Spitfires of 601 Squadron swept in to the rescue, Plt Off Scott claiming a Messerschmitt shot down. At almost the same time Plt Off Norm Fowlow was also shot down into the sea off Hal Far in BP993; he managed to climb into his dinghy despite slight wounds. A second Spitfire came under attack and Sgt McConnell's BR352/GL-W was badly hit, the New Zealander suffering wounds and burns. Nonetheless, he was able to avoid further action and safely returned to Takali, where his aircraft was written-off. *HSL128* was at once despatched to pick up Fowlow, four more Hurricanes providing close escort, with two 185 Squadron Spitfires at higher level. Many Messerschmitts were still about, at least 30 being reported, and several of these dived on to the Hurricane section, one of which was shot down with the loss of the pilot. Flt Lt Barnham noted:

> "The new boy [Fowlow] I initiated last week was shot down – he escaped by parachute.

In this same fight one of our sergeants had a lucky escape – his Spitfire was riddled with holes, his shoulders burnt by incendiary bullets and his legs peppered with shrapnel. Apparently Scotty, leading the formation, was surprised by 109s – but turning fiercely he got in a burst on a 109, which blew up, so they too paid the price."

Meanwhile, the top cover Spitfires had also become engaged, and Sgt Yarra (GL-K) shot down Uffz Johannes Lompa's 4/JG53 Messerschmitt (White 3) into the sea just off Hal Far. Lompa baled out and was seen to come down near Filfla, where he was promptly picked up by the crew of *HSL128*. They then continued to search for Fowlow, and about ten miles out from Benghaisa Point another figure was spotted in the sea. On board the launch, assisting the short-handed crew, was 185 Squadron's Plt Off Sherlock, a personal friend of the missing pilot:

"In view of the shoot-ups on the launch, the crew had no love for Jerries and sometimes were in no hurry to pick them up. In any event, as we approached a pilot bobbing around in his Mae West, the launch slowed down and one of the crew yelled out: 'English?' Upon receiving a negative reply, there were a couple of suggestions as to what he should do and where he should go. The launch started to move away while the downed pilot started to wave furiously. It was at this time I recognised Norm and informed the boat crew that he was Canadian and not English. Everyone thought this was a great joke except Norm."

Uffz Lompa helped haul the Canadian pilot aboard, warmly shaking his hand, before both rescued pilots fell into a deep sleep during the short journey back. Meanwhile Yarra's No.2, New Zealander Sgt Eric Shaw, had to return to Luqa when his Spitfire suffered considerable damage at the hands of the remaining Messerschmitts, but Yarra fought on alone, having claimed a second Bf109 as a probable before Shaw's departure. He later noted:

"Had 12 Messerschmitts to myself. Shot down two and ran out of ammo. Did dummy attacks on remainder until forced to return through lack of fuel. Landed at Takali deadstick."

By now two other sections of Spitfires had been scrambled to assist. Two from 126 Squadron took off at 1115, some 40 minutes after Yarra and Shaw had departed, followed by three more a further 20 minutes later. The first pair, Flt Lt Peck and Plt Off Rip Jones, encountered six Messerschmitts orbiting over the launch and carried out a bounce on these, each claiming one shot down, while Peck reported hitting another, which he considered would fail to make its base. Another Messerschmitt was claimed by Plt Off Bisley, a member of the second section to take off. Finally, at 1145, 249 Squadron sent off five more Spitfires to meet the launch as it returned. These engaged a number of Bf109s, Sgt Gilbert claiming one shot down, and Sgt Gray probably a second. Towards evening, 22 more Messerschmitts were reported approaching the coast and 14 Spitfires were scrambled. Six of these were from 126 Squadron. Flt Lt Peck and Plt Off Jones, again flying together, spotted a low-flying Bf109, which they chased and claimed shot down. The crew of an AA battery apparently reported seeing it crash into the sea; AA gunners also claimed the probable destruction of another Messerschmitt.

Malta fighters had thus claimed six Messerschmitts shot down during the day, plus four probables and one damaged. Only three losses were recorded by II and III/JG53. In addition to Uffz Lompa's White 3 (7596), Uffz Gerhard Beitz of 9 Staffel baled out of Yellow 2 (8670) into the sea near Filfla. 7 Staffel also lost an aircraft (10030) in this engagement off Hal Far, though the pilot was rescued during the afternoon by a

Do24 from 6 Seenotstaffel. In addition to Beitz's claim, Obfw Ehrenberger of 6 Staffel claimed a Spitfire at 1103 for his 29th victory, followed by 7 Staffel's Ltn Jürgen Harder shooting down another at 1255 for his 13th. Five MC202s of 4°Stormo flew a reconnaissance over Malta during the day, when Sottoten Vincenzo Fischer experienced engine trouble and had to return early. He crashed whilst attempting to force-land at Gela and was killed. The rest of the flight reported sighting a Beaufighter and two Spitfires, but did not engage.

Far to the west there had been further aerial action during the day, as a British naval force sailed eastwards to undertake Operation LB – the delivery of 17 more Spitfires to the island. These were the backlog of fighters which had remained behind at Gibraltar for one reason or another during recent ferrying operations, and which had all now been made serviceable. The force comprised the carrier *Eagle* on which were loaded the Spitfires, and also six Albacores as reinforcements for the RNAS at Hal Far. Four Sea Hurricanes of 813 Fighter Flight were embarked for protection duties, but could not be launched until after the departure of the Spitfires as the deck was so crowded. The old training carrier *Argus* was also present to provide some degree of air cover, carrying six Fulmars of 807 Squadron for this purpose. Escort was provided by a cruiser and seven destroyers. There occurred one encounter with hostile aircraft en route, albeit Vichy French D.520 fighters, a Catalina and a Fulmar being shot down off Algiers for the loss of one French fighter to another Fulmar.

The Spitfires[53] included BR126, the aircraft that Canadian Plt Off Jerry Smith had dramatically landed back aboard USS *Wasp* nine days earlier. Smith now joined the latest reinforcement, which comprised 13 pilots drawn from 131 Squadron under the command of newly promoted Sqn Ldr Bill New. The Spitfires were to be led in three flights by Flt Lts Lucas, McNair and Flg Off Daddo-Langlois, who had been flown to Gibraltar in a Lodestar for this purpose:

Flt Lt P.B. Lucas (flight leader) (BR115)	Plt Off E.H. Glazebrook RCAF
Flt Lt R.W. McNair RCAF (flight leader)	Plt Off J.A. Smith RCAF BR126
Flg Off R. Daddo-Langlois (flight leader) (BR175)	Plt Off N.J. Ogilvie RCAF (BR163)
	Flt Sgt K.W.S. Evans
Sqn Ldr W.G. New	Flt Sgt A.W. Varey
Plt Off F.D. Thomas	Sgt K.R. Mitchell
Plt Off J.H. Nicholls	Sgt H.R. Russel RCAF
Plt Off D.G. Newman	Sgt J. Braybrooke
Plt Off J.F. Lambert RCAF	Sgt J. Stamble

One of the pilots, Canadian Noel 'Buzz' Ogilvie, remembered the scene aboard *Eagle*:

> "We walked around our aircraft looking for imperfections, checked inside the cockpit and double checked the fuel gauges and the tanks themselves. I was to be number two off the carrier, immediately behind the CO. By evening, when we were assured all was ready, we went below for a briefing by a Royal Navy carrier pilot on the basics of flying aircraft off the deck of an aircraft carrier. Now the mood was a festive one; perhaps this was the only countermeasure the pilots could assemble before making their first take-off at sea the following morning. This joyfulness was reinforced by (a) an announcement that we might have to fight our way into the island, and (b) a note that was printed at the bottom of our instruction sheet. This read with typical British candour, and I quote: 'If you don't make it, don't flap or WORRY.'
>
> "As the *Eagle* was not a large carrier, we were promised a take-off wind over the deck of thirty knots. For a further take-off aid, as the Spitfire didn't have adjustable

flaps, a wedge of wood was inserted between the underside of the wing and the retracted flap. This was to be the icing on the confidence cake for a pilot who was about to make his first carrier take-off with an overloaded aircraft. This confidence build-up reached its climax when we were informed that no Spitfire would be allowed to return to the *Eagle* after take-off in the event of aircraft problems. If there was trouble, the unfortunate pilot would have a choice: (1) attempt a belly-landing on the sea, or (2) bale out near one of the escort ships in the hope of being picked up, or (3) if the above options lacked appeal, then fly south into North Africa, land, destroy the aircraft and then set out for home."

The first of the Spitfires were ready for take-off from *Eagle* by about 1430, but all was not well, as Ogilvie explained:

"Daybreak found the carrier off Algiers turning into, of all the things – a light wind. We were all strapped in our cockpits waiting for the word to start our engines. 'Twenty-two knots over the deck, sir!' The wing commander in charge of these operations gave the signal to start engines. Our CO, with the promise of thirty knots still ringing in his ears, and with his deep concern for the welfare of his pilots, immediately stood up in his cockpit and yelled back: 'Like bloody hell!' Well, things got a bit nervy amongst those in charge. Black smoke increased in volume from the stack, and I began to think that we were a beautiful target and were going to be torpedoed for sure in these hostile waters. Without waiting more than a minute longer, the loudspeaker announced that, by strange coincidence there were thirty knots over the deck. Then, one by one Spitfires coughed into life and were sent roaring down the deck. Our CO was a heavyset chap of about 230 pounds. At the time I weighed about 170 pounds and I quietly thought, as the CO was revving up his engine with the brakes on in preparation for take-off: 'If he gets off I should have no trouble.' When the CO got to the end of the carrier deck, he disappeared. 'He's bought it!' I whispered to myself, while easing my aircraft into starting position. I was wrong, for suddenly, off in the distance a little Spitfire appeared, struggling for height. 'He's made it! Alleluia!'

"With renewed confidence, I opened the throttle, raced down the deck of the carrier and found what it was like to drop like an elevator almost to the surface of the Mediterranean. When I was at a safe height, I dropped the flaps, out flew the little wooden wedges, retracted the flaps and settled in for the long haul to Malta. We levelled off at approximately 18,000 feet. There wasn't a cloud in the sky. Africa lay off to the right, Algeria floated behind and soon Tunisia appeared on the horizon, the air above it wavering in the torrid heat billowing off the land. Here, we banked south-east off Cap Bon for the run through the Strait of Sicily down to the island of Pantelleria, and then east to our destination. About twenty minutes after we passed Pantelleria, we caught sight of Malta dead ahead – like a big oak leaf lying in the emerald water of the Mediterranean. As we approached the landing fields, Malta-based Spitfires protected our arrival from any enemy fighters that might have come to intercept us. Flying under this protection, we whistled in from the sea and delivered the much-needed aircraft safely."

Flt Lt Lucas – who had spotted, but did not pursue, a Ju88 shortly after the flight commenced – recalled:

"Buck's formation was off first in the early morning, all his aircraft disappearing ominously, one after the other, beneath the bows of the carrier as they left the flight deck before appearing as the undercarriage of each Spitfire came up and its airscrew bit into the air. We, who were to follow, would have preferred not to have witnessed this disturbing scene!" He added: "Oh! Lord! Deliver us from such a task again!"

As with all the others of this flight, Plt Off Jerry Smith had no problems on his second attempt to reach Malta:

"Perfectly clear day. Could see far into Africa. Flew nearly 400 miles along the coast then cut across Pantelleria. At one point could see Tunis, Sicily, Malta, and far down the coast to Tripoli. Landed in Malta in the middle of a raid but all safe. Trip about 700 miles done in record time. Bags of petrol left."

The arrival of the latest Spitfire reinforcement coincided with a major withdrawal of Luftwaffe forces from Sicily for service in Libya and on the Russian front. One Bf109 Gruppe and two of Ju88s had already departed at the end of April, and were now followed by others, leaving only the Messerschmitts of II/JG53 and the Ju88s of KüFlGr606 and KGr806, plus the Regia Aeronautica units, which were soon reinforced from mainland Italy. The reduction of Axis strength on Sicily now caused a sudden and most noticeable falling-off in activity over Malta. During **19 May**, small numbers of Bf109s swept over the island until mid-afternoon, when three Z1007bis of 50°Gruppo BT approached, escorted by 13 Macchis of 10°Gruppo CT – on their last raid over Malta – and a corresponding number of Reggianes of 2°Gruppo Aut CT. Twenty Spitfires were scrambled, ten from 126 and 601 Squadrons intercepting after the bombers had carried out a high level raid on Luqa and Safi, without causing any damage. Plt Off Caldwell (3-M) of the latter unit succeeded in shooting down Sottoten Nicola Falcone's Z1007bis (MM23352), and claimed damage to a second bomber. All three Cants were in fact hit, Falcone carrying out a ditching in the sea; he and his crew were rescued suffering from only minor wounds and injuries. Flg Off Hone's Spitfire (3-N) was damaged by a RE2001, but the Rhodesian was able safely to return to Takali. Two 185 Squadron Spitfires also became engaged in the action, Flt Lt Lawrence (GL-B) claiming damage to a fighter, but both Spitfires sustained damage, as noted by the Squadron diarist, Slim Yarra:

"Flt Lt Lawrence and Flt Sgt Sim, our New Zealand combination, spotted three Cant 1007s. The Cants had their boy friends, the Macchi tribe, with them, and the Macchis took exception to Sim diving on their bombers and showed their displeasure in no uncertain manner, much to Sim's disgust. Flt Lt Lawrence sat behind a Messerschmitt's rudder and pumped cannon shells into him, but as only one cannon fired, the 109 escaped more or less in one piece."

Reggiane pilots claimed one Spitfire shot down by Ten Carlo Seganti, plus five damaged. Not yet operational, Plt Off Jerry Smith recorded:

"Went to drome at Luqa. Small raid by high-flying Eyeties. Located some kit at Naxxar. Meals here are awful. Watched wizard beat-up of Takali by Junkers 88s. Nothing hit by bombs. Ack-ack looked wonderful in different coloured streamers. Am now in 601 Squadron."

The Luftwaffe raid on Takali to which he referred occurred after dark, four Ju88s bombing the dispersal area. Here, in spite of Smith's comments, an unserviceable Spitfire (BR106) of 249 Squadron was burnt out.

20 May turned out to be even quieter for Malta's defences. The only raid that materialised during the day occurred just before 1600, when half a dozen Jabo Bf109s swept low over Takali, damaging a petrol bowser. An escorted Z506B floatplane of 612^Squadriglia was out early searching for survivors of a missing BR20M that had failed to return from a night sortie to Malta. One of the escort, Ten Giorgio Pocek of 2°Gruppo Aut CT, was obliged to return early with engine trouble but, near Gozo, he reported sighting a lone Spitfire which he claimed shot down. Despite the lack of action, 185 Squadron's diarist Slim Yarra was, however, full of himself:

"A Flight took readiness this morning with six aircraft [having received four replacements]. Flt Lt Lawrence led four aircraft on a scramble after a recco coming in. The boys saw some Messerschmitts stooging about but could not pick a fight. Flt Sgt Sim ran out of gas and had to make a deadstick landing at Takali. It is rumoured that Sim's dinghy had to go to stores to have a few holes patched up! Sgt Yarra and Flt Sgt Vineyard went up to look for some trouble. They saw two Messerschmitts but could not attack. Then they spotted two little jobs down on the 'measured mile'. Muttering abuse, they both went screaming down to the attack. Slim was not going fast enough and when trying to shut his hood, stuck his arm out in the slipstream, very nearly tearing the aforementioned member out by the roots. Due to this clottish manoeuvre, two Messerschmitts were allowed to go back to Sicily, laughing like hell."

Dawn at Malta on **21 May** brought with it a short, sharp fighter-bomber raid on Hal Far, five Bf109s sweeping in at low level, bombing and strafing. The defenders were caught unawares, but while two airmen were killed and another seriously wounded, little damage was caused. Shortly thereafter, a photo-reconnaissance Spitfire of 69 Squadron brought back photographs from Catania indicating the presence of an increased number of Ju88s – in fact, 83 compared with 28 aircraft spotted on the airfield four days previously. These must have been aircraft in transit, for no increase in attacks on Malta followed.

Soon after midday four Ju88s and ten Bf109s ventured over, ten Spitfires being scrambled, including four from 185 Squadron led by Sqn Ldr Lloyd. Sgt Yarra was again in action but as he engaged the bombers, his Spitfire (GL-K) was shot-up by Messerschmitts, although not badly damaged. Plt Off Jimmy Lambert (GL-C) claimed one of the attackers shot down. Yarra wrote:

"The boys were scrambled on to a plot of plus three. For once the boys found themselves in a perfect position to jump two Messerschmitts. They made good use of the advantage, and a spectator might have witnessed two 109s going like hell, with four avenging Spitfires on their respective tails. Sqn Ldr Lloyd fired all his rounds at one but could not quite get within range, which was very lucky for the 109. Plt Off Lambert pulled off a perfect deflection shot, which sent the second crashing into the sea in the approved fashion. Flt Sgt Ferraby also managed to get a squirt in."

Lambert had shot down Uffz Ernst-Hans Seidl of 8/JG53 (Black 2, 10060) who was killed. In the meantime, *HSL128* was sent out when a dinghy was spotted some three miles west of Benghaisa Point. It contained Uffz Gerhard Beitz, the 9/JG53 pilot who had been shot down three days earlier. He had been paddling desperately towards Malta when able to muster sufficient strength, and when rescued was stiff, weary and badly blistered by the sun. On reaching shore he was taken to hospital, where he later told his interrogator:

"When south of Kalafrana I saw three Hurricanes or Spitfires, and dived to attack. The Hurricane was executing a gentle turn and this offered me a perfect target. I shot it down for my second victory. Subsequently, my engine failed and I baled out into the sea. For two days I was in the dinghy expecting to be picked up. I then began paddling towards Malta, about five miles away. After 24 hours I reached the coast and was picked up by the Kalafrana launch."

Not until late on the morning of **22 May** did the first raid approach, when 20 Bf109s crossed the coast, four bombing Hal Far. Eight Spitfires scrambled and four from 249 intercepted two of the Messerschmitts off Kalafrana, Flt Lt McNair (BR170/C-25) claiming one shot down. A similar number of fighters, reportedly Bf109s and MC202s, patrolled off the coast between 1920-2012, when 14 Spitfires were scrambled including six from 603 Squadron. During the skirmish, Plt Off Barlow was attacked head-on by another Spitfire and received a cannon shell in the wing. Despite this, he was able to return and land safely. Flt Sgt Dodd (BR294/GL-E) of 185 Squadron claimed one Messerschmitt shot down (his seventh claim but only his second confirmed), and Plt Off Broad (BR126) a probable. Similarly, this was Broad's eighth claim but only two had been confirmed. Yarra the diarist added:

> "F/Sgt Dodd, madly gnashing his teeth, took after one Me109 and sent the pilot on a one way trip. F/Sgt Andrews also squirted at a 109 and severely frightened the Jerry therein, if nothing more."

On **23 May**, at 0715, a dozen Spitfires of 126 and 601 Squadrons were sent off to intercept five Z1007bis of 50°Gruppo BT, escorted by 16 RE2001s of 2°Gruppo Aut CT, approaching to bomb Takali. Four Bf109s from 4/JG53 accompanied the Italian formation. Plt Off Tilley claimed one fighter – identified as a MC202 – while Plt Off Rip Jones engaged one of the bombers, which he believed he probably destroyed. Flt Sgt Schade, recovered from his arm wound, also tangled with the escort and gained some revenge: "Jumped four Me109s about ten miles north of Grand Harbour. One destroyed, one probable." Plt Off Mejor (BR132) was also involved but was unable to make any claims:

> "Attacked five Cants. My Nos.2, 3 and 4 had lost me. Return fire from gunners. Three-seconds burst 200 yards dead astern on port one. Three Reggianes attacked from port bow above. Turned in head-on, firing at leader of vic. Saw no result."

The 601 Squadron pilots were led by Sqn Ldr Bisdee. As he closed on an Italian fighter and opened fire, his port cannon jammed and he found the Spitfire difficult to control. He was pursued by a RE2001, which he was unable to evade, but the Italian pilot flew up alongside him, waved and departed – possibly out of ammunition. Meanwhile, Sgt McConnell claimed a RE2001 probable, and Sgt Jim Innes reported shooting down a Reggiane, damaging a second, and also inflicting damage to a Cant. Plt Off Scott, when chatting to Barnham about the combat, commented:

> "These Italians are an odd lot – they either don't want to fight or they haven't got a clue. When you get behind them they do beautiful aerobatics, loops, roll off the top, anything but get out of the way and fight properly. Sergeant Innes' sitter was just like that."

No Italian fighters fell but two RE2001s were damaged, as was the leading Cant, in which M.llo Giovanni Durli[54] was mortally wounded and another crewmember less seriously hurt. The Reggiane pilots claimed three Spitfires shot down, one by Ten Giorgio Gasperoni, the other two by several pilots. A fourth was claimed by bomber gunners, and six others were believed to have been hit. Plt Off Jerry Smith of 601 Squadron watched the combat from the ground, and reported: "Watched a Macchi [*sic*] firing at a Spit. Spit pilot didn't even know it, but was unhurt. Learned later that Spit pilot was my CO!"

In his usual style, Yarra recorded in the diary:

> "A very quiet day today. The usual scrambles after Messerschmitts came along, but, although the boys chased all over the sky, nothing was encountered. It seems as though Jerry has really left Sicily – or is he just waiting for a convoy to come in? However,

whatever he is waiting for, it is giving us a rest and a respite from ring-twitch. It is rumoured that we are getting some replacements from the squadrons at Luqa and Takali. We need some new pilots. Quite a lot of chaps are down with that insidious malady Malta Dog. F/Sgt Sim is the latest victim – he even looks like a dog!"

24 May proved to be another quiet day for Malta's defenders, and it was not until shortly after noon that Plt Offs Halford (GL-B) and Ogilvie (GL-C) of 185 Squadron were scrambled and vectored south of Malta to investigate a suspected bandit; Ogilvie recalled:

"We climbed to about 4,000-5,000 feet and we were between the south coast and Filfla. We spotted a Ju88 flying very low over the water in south-easterly direction. Halford indicated to me he was going to make an attack. Of course we didn't have any trouble catching it because of the height we had on it. Halford made his attack; as he was firing he was hit by the rear gunner and pulled up. I then proceeded to make my attack but because of the speed involved I had to make a considerable allowance – couldn't see whether I was hitting the 88 or not. When I pulled up and looked around, the 88 had disappeared. Halford and I returned to base."

They were credited with shooting down this aircraft, although no loss was recorded by the Luftwaffe. Just over three hours later, three patrolling Spitfires of 603 Squadron met three Macchis about ten miles south of Kalafrana; two of these were claimed shot down by Plt Offs Barlow and Dicks-Sherwood, who also claimed a damaged. Although RE2001s of 2°Gruppo and MC202s of 54°Stormo patrolled off the island during the day, none apparently reported any engagements with Malta's Spitfires. The lull in air fighting allowed Sqn Ldr Douglas-Hamilton time to write another letter to his wife:

"When I first arrived, and for the first two weeks, the raids were really terrific. At least three times a day, waves of Hun bombers would come in and plaster the aerodromes and harbour. They did an insignificant amount of damage compared to the effort they spent, and the losses they suffered. The amazing thing was one could always get a grandstand view of it all from a nearby hill. It was an extraordinary sight. But once or twice, one had to be down in the thick of it all. Then the only thing to do was to seize a rifle and fire back, and one felt all right. We have also had them at night, and once I had the house next door to where I was sleeping hit twice. But one never minds or thinks twice about it – I just stayed in my bed! However, it certainly gives one the will to fight back, and, to start with, the fighting was certainly very intense and we were hopelessly outnumbered. But we hit back hard and with astonishingly small losses to ourselves. I have managed to destroy two Messerschmitts so far (sharing one of them with another chap) and have also damaged another fairly well. I have probably also hit several other Huns but couldn't see. I enclose a piece of the 109 I got all to myself – I shot the wing off in a head-on attack and the pilot baled out and is a prisoner (not a frightfully nice one at that, though he congratulated me warmly!) It's all so much a new experience, and I feel it's most interesting to go through it all."[55]

Eight Spitfires of 249 Squadron were ordered off at 1420 on **25 May**, followed 40 minutes later by 16 more from 126 and 601 Squadrons. Their opponents on this occasion were three SM84s of 4°Gruppo Aut BT (misidentified by the Spitfire pilots as Z1007bis), covered by 16 RE2001s as close escort with a dozen Bf109s as indirect cover. The 249 Squadron pilots intercepted first and became entangled with the escort, Flt Lt West claiming a Reggiane shot down and Flt Sgt Brennan reporting strikes on another, while Flt Lt McNair (BR109/C-30) claimed a Bf109 probably destroyed and

Sgt de Nancrède (BR111) one damaged. McNair reported:

> "As Green 3, when going to attack bombers, I saw an aircraft on my tail. I turned and found it to be a Messerschmitt. I gave fight and managed to get in two bursts on quarter astern attack; both seemed to be effective. The fight carried on until I lost him in cloud. Claim Messerschmitt damaged."

De Nancrède commented: "McNair stole one from me and came within inches of killing me!"

Flt Lt Lee managed to penetrate the fighter screen and fired at one of the bombers, claiming it badly damaged. Flt Sgt Goldsmith of 126 Squadron (Spitfire/H) engaged the same bomber and although his own aircraft was hit in the wing and engine, he was able to land safely. The Australian also claimed a RE2001 damaged, subsequently reporting: "Fired at a Cant 1007 [*sic*], left it burning. Also had a dogfight with a Reggiane 2001."

Sqn Ldr Bill New, who was flying with 126 Squadron while gaining experience over the island prior to taking command of 185 Squadron, also claimed damage to a bomber, and Plt Off Graves claimed a probable. The successes were marred by the loss of 19-year-old New Zealander Plt Off Wally Caldwell from Auckland who was shot down and killed in BR354, while another Spitfire sustained damage. 2°Gruppo pilots claimed four Spitfires shot down in this action, one each by Cap Annibale Sterzi, Ten Carlo Seganti, M.llo Dino Fabbri and M.llo Antonio Patriarca, while Cap Salvatore Teia, commander of 152^Squadriglia, claimed another shared with the crew of a bomber. Maj Günther von Maltzahn claimed a Spitfire at 1520, acknowledged in Italian records although apparently not confirmed. No Italian or German fighters were recorded lost or seriously damaged. However, all three SM84s were hit, two returning with wounded on board.

Flt Lt West's latest claim raised his personal tally to six and he was recommended for a DFC. His character is described by 185 Squadron's Plt Off Sherlock, a relative newcomer to the island, on the occasion of the latter's visit to 249's mess at Takali:

> "When I went into the mess there was a swarthy individual sitting in the hallway, naked except for his shorts and a towel wrapped around his head like a turban. He was sitting cross-legged and in front of him was a basket with a hunk of rope dangling over the side to represent a snake. This person was swaying back and forth and playing a clarinet, and rather well, too. I stopped and asked the pilot with me what the score was. He introduced me to the snake charmer, who was none other than Ronnie West, and who assured me, with a very straight face, that it was just a matter of time until all pilots went just as crazy as he was. After what we had gone through in the past weeks, this was easy to believe!"[56]

There were no further engagements until mid-afternoon of **26 May**, when eight 603 Squadron Spitfires scrambled, followed by four each from 185 and 249 Squadrons. A fighter sweep by 13 RE2001s of 2°Gruppo was engaged by the 603 Squadron flight. Flg Off Mitchell and Plt Off Barlow each claimed one shot down, and Flt Lt Sanders another as damaged. Cap Annibale Sterzi (commander of 358^Squadriglia) was shot down in a vertical dive to crash in a field near Ghaxaq. He managed to bale out but his parachute failed to open properly, and he fell to his death near Luqa; at least two other Reggianes returned seriously damaged, and one Spitfire was claimed in return by Ten Giorgio Gasperoni. It would appear that he may have attacked 185 Squadron's Sgt Yarra, whose aircraft (GL-B) developed a fire in its wing. He later recorded the incident thus:

"Flt Lt Lawrence led a section of four and went stooging off towards Sicily. Sgt Yarra was flying gaily along, making discordant noises to himself, when he noticed what he took to be slight vapour trails coming from his wings. Flt Lt Lawrence very nicely informed him he had sprung a glycol leak. Slim was trying to work out how the glycol leak could appear in his wings when he noticed sparks coming from the gun panels and realised his ammunition was on fire. After biting a large, circular piece out of his dinghy, Slim managed to arrive OK. Tex, who was flying No.2, was very brassed because he did not get some R/T procedure practice in, calling 'Mayday' for another.

"Later on, the boys were scrambled again and, after stooging round for some time, spotted two exquisite specimens of the genus Messerschmitt floating over the water. Muttering threats and imprecations, the boys went tearing down on the two suckers. However, the suckers happened to be rather more awake that usual and spotted them. The boys could not get in any effective squirts and the 109s disappeared over the horizon. F/Sgt MacNamara was rather astonished when he landed and found out the Jerry kites were 109s. He was under the impression they were Ju88s! It is rumoured that the two 109s overshot Sicily and landed in Venice. However, this is discredited by the official German News Service, who said that the two who did this were Italians! It is also rumoured that a certain pilot, while covering some minesweepers, saw a mine explode. He immediately called up his leader and with a marked Canadian accent, spouted forth: 'Say, Red One, did you see that bomb explode by that ship down there?' We are not mentioning names, but if F/Sgt MacNamara gives any more information away to the enemy, Joe Kesselring will probably award him an Iron Cross!

"During the afternoon the boys had two scrambles and were unfortunate to be jumped twice. F/Sgt Ferraby did some quick thinking when he discovered some Messerschmitts coming down, and found the rest of the formation unable to receive him on the R/T. He immediately turned into his No.2, who did a quick break to avoid collision, causing the sky to become littered with Spitfires doing amazing evolutions. However, the Hun was foxed completely and beetled off home, muttering threats."

Next day (**27 May**) proved to be even quieter for the defenders, only small formations of Bf109s being reported over the island, and no interceptions were achieved by those Spitfires that were scrambled. With sufficient Spitfires now to hand, the remaining pilots of 229 Squadron were ordered to return to the Middle East with their Hurricanes. A dozen departed at 0500, each fitted with long-range tanks, and were escorted part of the way by Spitfires of 185 Squadron. Yarra noted:

"229 Squadron went back to the Middle East today, taking with them the last of the Hurricanes. We are not sorry to see the Hurricanes go. Now that the boys are back flying Spitfires again, they don't want anything more to do with Hurricanes. A Flight had one scramble during the afternoon, and although the enemy fighters still outnumbered us slightly, they would not come down and fight, much to the chagrin of the boys in the air. Sgt Yarra chased a couple of Messerschmitts out to sea. He squirted but did not do any damage."

The next few days brought little activity over Malta. On **28 May**, during the late afternoon, four 126 Squadron Spitfires were scrambled on a warning that a number of hostile fighters were approaching. Two dozen Bf109s, including at least four Jabo, then crossed the coast and attacked Luqa where little damage was done. The 126 Squadron section intercepted and Flt Sgt Schade claimed a probable. Plt Off Mejor again found the Messerschmitts to be elusive:

"Me109s at 2,000 feet above us at 26,000 feet. They put their noses down and cleared off. We were attacked by about ten more. Got bursts at two. Saw no results."

A further alarm was sounded at 2050, when six raiders approached but did not cross the coast. Four Spitfires were scrambled and chased a number of Ju88s from KGr806 back towards Sicily, where Bf109s came to their aid. No claims were made, although one Ju88 (M7+MK) failed to return from an intended raid on Luqa; Fw Friedrich Brehm and his crew were posted missing. Despite the lack of activity, Yarra still found something to say:

"F/Lt Lawrence is now CO of 185 Squadron. However, the old boys who knew F/Lt Lawrence during the blitz would not recognise him now. That moustache, which was once the pride and joy of 185 Squadron, met with a fatal accident recently and is now being mourned by all and sundry."

29 May was even quieter than the previous day, with just two small fighter sweeps and a Jabo raid on Hal Far. There were no interceptions and negligible damage. Yarra commented:

"S/Ldr Lawrence led the only scramble we had today, but the Jerries again refused to co-operate with us. This is a damned poor show. Everyone is becoming browned off and if Jerry continues to refuse to mix it we will have to appeal to the referee for victory on a technical knockout. We are lucky in being able to obtain F/Lt West as one of our new flight commanders. F/Lt West had been pursuing the Hun with deadly intent and dark thoughts in his mind for quite a long time now. He has been with 249 at Takali since the blitz started, and it is indeed a privilege to obtain a man of his calibre for the Squadron."

Several small sweeps by German and Italian fighters occurred on the morning of **30 May**, eight Spitfires of 185 Squadron being scrambled on the third occasion but making no interceptions. As they returned to Hal Far to land, eight Bf109s followed them in but caused no damage. At 1800 four Spitfires of 185 Squadron, followed by four of 126 Squadron, were ordered off to intercept three SM84s of 4°Gruppo, escorted by 22 RE2001s and a dozen Bf109s. Luqa was the target, where one Spitfire was slightly damaged on the ground. Flt Sgt Ferraby (BP876) of 185 Squadron reported gaining strikes on a Messerschmitt, then attacked a bomber – identified variously as a Z1007 or a Breda 20 (BR20) – which was also attacked by Plt Off Bill Johnson (Spitfire/J), newly commissioned Plt Off Goldsmith (Spitfire/C), and Flt Sgt Milner of 126 Squadron; the tri-motor was claimed destroyed. Johnson wrote in his logbook:

"Three Breda 20s [*sic*] and fighter cover attacked by Red Section from below and abeam. One Breda probably destroyed. Had to attack while still being attacked by Macchis. Later confirmed destroyed – $^1/_4$ share."

The other three 185 pilots all reported cannon stoppages as they attempted to attack, but Flt Sgt Parks of 126 Squadron managed to gain strikes on a bomber – probably the same aircraft as that attacked by the others. Only the leading Savoia of the trio had been hit hard, the pilot landing his badly damaged aircraft at Catania with one crewman dead and another wounded. Goldsmith reported: "Had a squirt at a BR20 (or something), then attacked a Reggiane. Knocked off his radiator. Landed at Takali as Luqa was u/s."

185's erstwhile diarist Slim Yarra summarised the day's actions:

"The 'Three Twerps' [the regular flight of three Z1007bis or SM84s] came over again today, escorted by their tribe of Macchi 202s and RE2001s, but the boys were waiting for them. They went right in and soon the sky was filled with Italians doing violent aerobatics, trying to dodge the Spitfires. However, most of the boys had trouble with their cannons. Some very satisfying dogfights took place and, although we only claimed damaged Reggianes, we certainly shook the Italian war merchants and they'll think twice about peddling their wares on our island for some time. Today we have 70 Spitfires serviceable on the island. Quite a difference from the days when six Hurricanes and four Spitfires were considered amazing serviceability."

No Reggianes were lost but Cap Roberto Fassi's aircraft apparently suffered engine trouble, though despite this handicap, when pursued by two Spitfires he claimed to have shot one down. A second Spitfire was claimed by other 2°Gruppo pilots, who also considered they had damaged 15 more! A reconnaissance Bf109 (F6+YH) of 1(F)/122, flown by Ltn Herbert Toula, crash-landed at Catania on return from a sortie and the pilot was injured. It is not known if the aircraft had been damaged during the course of a sortie to Malta, but if so, it may have been Ferraby's victim.

The pilots of 601 Squadron were now given the facilities of a luxurious house in Sliema, as the new mess, by the owner who was about to leave the island. Flt Lt Barnham, sensitive artist and scribe, but depressed and deeply missing his wife5[57], noted his first impressions:

"Our new mess is on a high promontory; waves surging against the rocks; looks like Greece. I bless the Sliema lady for letting us have her beautiful house. I couldn't believe that a simple carpet on the floor could mean so much. Another seal was set on my life for it was my turn to have a hot bath – the first chance since leaving the aircraft carrier last April! I was apprehensive that the bombs that were falling might knock the wall down to leave me suspended and *exposé* in mid-air, but I sang for joy as I scrubbed and splashed in a foam of soap. Afterwards I settled in a deck chair on the flat roof at the back of the house; I watched a tender veil of grey being drawn over the sky, while lazy-looking clouds coming in from the north grew larger into great blocks of cumulus, taller and taller until their tips merged with the veil above them.

"Baron Scicluna invited us all to a cocktail party; his Dragonara Palace is built out to sea on a neighbouring headland. At the Baron's party, between the heads of his many guests, I noticed a girl in a white dress; I watched her proud little head that hardly moved as she talked; I watched her slim figure with her young breasts beneath the white material and her beautifully moulded arms and hands – she looked Greek. I got out my sketch book and, edging a little closer, started to draw. I suppose I'm a romantic idealist, a crazy dreamer, expecting her to be some kind of goddess – it was stupid of me but, so overwhelmed was I by sadness at her trite conversation that I left the party and walked back alone by the sea."

As a most welcome change, Sunday morning worshipers were not interrupted on 31 May, the only alarm sounding just before 1400 when 11 Spitfires were scrambled on the approach of a fighter sweep. The Spitfire pilots reported no contact. However, Ltn Franz Kunz of 5/JG53 claimed a Spitfire shot down about two miles north of Valetta at 1410, for his first victory. Later, Spitfires were sent to search for signs of the crew or wreckage of an overdue transit Wellington, the authorities on Malta unaware that the missing crew was already in captivity in Sicily. Plt Off Mejor of 126 Squadron carried out three sorties during the day, a sweep on which he saw nothing, a scramble that again proved negative, but on the final sortie he recorded: "Wizard scrap! Had fight with four Eyeties 20 miles off Sicily." Although no claims were made, nor damage sustained, the aggressive Anglo-Belgian pilot certainly appeared to enjoy an air fight. The lull in fighting caused Flt Sgt Brennan to record in his diary:

"The last few days of May were so quiet that we could afford to send off sections on practice flying, and many of the more recent arrivals went up with the old hands. For those of us who had been in Malta from the time the first Spits arrived, it presented a striking contrast to the conditions which had existed. Indeed, had anybody told us a few weeks earlier that we would be practice flying at the end of May, we would have told them they were crazy. But it happened, and it happened because the Spits had won a great victory."

More Spitfires would soon be on their way. Sqn Ldr Barton, accompanied by Flt Lt Peck and Flg Off Plagis, had been flown to Gibraltar in preparation to lead the next batch. That evening a Hudson lifted off from Luqa bound for Gibraltar. Among its passengers was Plt Off Tilley:

"I was ordered to be on board a Lockheed bound for Gibraltar that night, to lead some more Spits back from an aircraft carrier. I don't recall any other pilots on board, but an attractive Maltese woman and her young daughter were. Arrived at Gib the morning of 1 June. Called the Skipper [Sqn Ldr Barton] at the Rock Hotel. He was plenty surprised. That day we all had dinner – Skipper, Peck, Plagis and I. Then that afternoon they sailed with 32 Spits aboard the *Eagle*. I was to remain a week longer."

* * *

With the end of another critical month, it was time to take stock. During the first five months of the year, some 11,000 tons of bombs were estimated to have fallen on the island, more than three quarters of that total on Luqa, Takali and Hal Far. An estimated 520 tons had fallen during May, 75 per cent of that total being dropped during the first eight days of the month. There had been 177 daytime alerts, 59 of which had developed into raids when bombs fell; 65 more attacks had been made at night. The fighter pilots were credited with 122 destroyed, plus one shared with the AA defences, 41 probables and at least 100 damaged. The guns claimed $141^1/_2$ destroyed. Twenty-three Spitfires and two Hurricanes were lost in combat, including two shot down by the island's own AA guns, and two that had collided. 69 Squadron's PR Spitfire echelon received a third aircraft (BP908) during the month, 32 sorties being undertaken by Plt Off Harry Coldbeck and Sgt Les Colquhoun, totalling 148 hours flying time.

By the end of the month several of Malta's Spitfire pilots had been advised of awards for their recent performances. Within 126 Squadron DFCs were announced for Flt Lt Tim Johnston, and Americans Flt Lt Jimmie Peck and Plt Off Reade Tilley. Plt Off Tim Goldsmith was awarded the DFM while 249 was honoured with DFCs for Sqn Ldr Stan Grant, Flg Off Buck Buchanan and Plt Off Pete Nash (deceased). Sgt Ray Hesselyn received a Bar to his DFM; both he his best friend Flt Sgt Paul Brennan received their commissions shortly thereafter.

The decision had been taken to evacuate more of the tour-expired and/or battle-fatigued, wounded and sick pilots, since sufficient numbers of acceptable replacements were now available and more were on the way. Amongst the first to depart were two of 601 Squadron's pilots, including the Australian Plt Off Tommy Scott[58] who had remained in a very distraught state since the loss of his close friend and fellow countryman, Max Briggs. Flt Lt Barnham noted:

"With mixed feelings I learn that two of our pilots are leaving. One is Scotty. After

Max's death Scotty has no doubt been living in an agony of solitude; what inward tortures he has been enduring no one can tell. I am glad Scotty has survived. The other man is a flight sergeant from B Flight. He is being sent home in disgrace for cowardice. I feel for him in a strange inner way; he must have suffered horribly because of his fear of flying, yet some day he must turn round and face it squarely or his life will be ruined for ever. May God be with them both."

Others to leave round about this time included Sqn Ldr Lloyd of 185 Squadron (tour-expired), 603's Flt Sgt Alan Otto, who had suffered concussion following his accident earlier in the month, and fellow Canadian Sgt Dick Buckley. The American Flt Sgt Artie Cleaveland[59], a 24-year-old from Springfield, Ohio, also departed the island, as did new arrival Sgt Braybrooke.

Since the middle of the month, as noted, many Luftwaffe units had begun pulling out of Sicily in preparation for the new summer offensive on the Eastern Front, while others were transferred to bases in Cyrenaica to aid Rommel's planned push in the Western Desert. The Bf109s of II/JG3 and the Ju88s of II and III/KG77 had in fact departed for Germany and France by the end of April, though II/JG3 did not remain in Germany for long but was soon redeployed to the Eastern Front, where it was joined by I/JG53. Meanwhile, III/JG53, the Ju88 night fighters of I/NJG2, the Bf110s of III/ZG26, and the Ju87s of III/StG3 – or such elements of these that were still in Sicily – were moved across the Mediterranean, and I/KG54 (Ju88s) was sent to Crete. Hence, there remained in Sicily only Stab and II/JG53 under the command of Hptm Walter Spies with 54 Bf109s, of which 39 were serviceable at the end of the month, approximately 90 Ju88s of KüFlGr606 and KGr806, plus the air-sea rescue and reconnaissance units.

The Regia Aeronautica was also anxious to strengthen its air force in North Africa, and 4°Stormo CT was ordered to Libya, but 33 new MC202s of 155°Gruppo CT under the command of Magg Duilio Fanali, moved to Gela airfield from mainland Italy. The Gruppo comprised 351^Squadriglia (Cap Riccardo Spagnolini), 360^Squadriglia (Cap Carlo Miani), and 378^Squadriglia (Cap Bruno Tattanelli). To replace the Stukas of III/StG3, two squadriglie of Ju87Bs of 102°Gruppo Tuffatori also arrived at Gela, and two squadriglie of Z1007bis of 33°Gruppo BT arrived at Chinisia to strengthen the offensive potential. Malta could now field up to 70 Spitfires and the pilots were confident that they could match anything their neighbours could throw their way.

CHAPTER V

ON THE BRINK OF VICTORY

June 1942

June began as quietly as May had ended. At 0935 on the first day, four Spitfires of 185 Squadron scrambled as part of a force of eight intercepting six Bf109s making a Jabo attack in the Tas-Silc area. Four Messerschmitts were attacked 20 miles east of Zonqor Point, Flt Sgt Yarra (GL-K) claiming one shot down, and Plt Off Broad (BR294/GL-E) one damaged; two more then bounced the Spitfires and Ltn Hans-Volkmar Müller of 5/JG53 shot down 20-year-old, Toronto-born Plt Off Andy McNaughton (BP950), his ninth victory. The Canadian pilot's body was later recovered from the sea by *HSL128*. Slim Yarra, 185's diarist, wrote: "Andy, who had joined the squadron only recently, was very popular with everyone. We cannot afford to lose men like Andy – they are too hard to replace."

Flt Lt Barnham of 601 Squadron noted in his journal:

"The usual successes and occasional losses – it's always the new boys that go – two of them recently [probably referring to Plt Offs Andy McNaughton and Wally Caldwell, lost the previous week]; one through inexperience, but the other [Caldwell], who held great promise as a fighter pilot, was stupid – he wanted to be a great individualist – he would break away from the formation to go hunting alone – although warned – that was the end of him."

In the afternoon Magg Fanali led MC202s of 155°Gruppo CT on their first sweep over Malta, but no fighters were seen.

During the early morning of **2 June**, a raid was reported forming up over Sicily and, at 0910, Sqn Ldr Lawrence led off six 185 Squadron aircraft, followed by 14 more – drawn equally from 249 and 601 Squadrons – these all climbing out to sea and encountering the incoming force 15 miles east off Kalafrana. The raiders were three SM84s escorted by almost two dozen RE2001s, with 32 MC202s as indirect escort. Their target was Safi. Flt Sgt Don 'Shorty' Reid, a newly arrived Canadian in 185 Squadron, claimed damage to one of the bombers, which he identified as a Z1007, and then claimed a Reggiane probably shot down. Meanwhile, 2/Lt Bartleman (BR125/1-P) of 601 Squadron engaged a Macchi; he reported:

"Macchis flying top cover for bombing raid – scrambled in time and at 25,000 feet up sun, saw bombers about 5,000 feet below, with top cover above and behind; attacked from quarter line astern out of sun – Macchis flying straight and level (at least 12 in formation). Selected victim performed rolls as I closed in – saw shells strike; fell out of control and believed burst into flames and disintegrated; no chute seen."

Bartleman's opponent was undoubtedly a 2°Gruppo Reggiane and he had probably hit Serg Giovanni Dringoli's aircraft (150-7/MM7216), which was severely damaged in the port wing and subsequently belly-landed at Comiso. Ten Giulio Bartolozzi's 150^Squadriglia Reggiane was also damaged – possibly by Reid – although two more were claimed damaged by Plt Off Hagger of 601 Squadron and Sgt Edwin Moye of 185 Squadron, an American volunteer from Alabama, known as 'Alabama' or 'Cactus'. Another RE2001 was badly damaged when M.llo Patriarca, who had suffered a severe bout of air sickness, force-landed MM7252 on return; however, there is no evidence to suggest that his aircraft had been hit in combat. The Italians reported being attacked by ten Spitfires, 2°Gruppo claiming two shot down (one each by M.llo Luigi Jellici and Serg Dringoli) and three more damaged; Cap Miani of 360^Squadriglia made the first claim for the new Macchis of 155°Gruppo. 185's diarist Slim Yarra recorded the raid in his usual light-hearted way:

"B Flight were on at dawn and took the dawn patrol. However, it was just the usual stooge patrol – nothing sighted. But later on in the morning this began to happen. The 'Ice Cream Vendors' came over peddling their wares, at their usual height. The parade was composed of three Cants [*sic*] and about 20 RE2001s, two boys blowing bugles marching out in the front, and a couple of dogs bringing up the rear! Four Spitfires went up to watch the proceedings, and, in their usual style, waited until the Italians were not looking before commencing to make a series of darts at the enemy aircraft. F/Sgt Shorty Reid damaged one Cant and one RE2001 in the ensuing mix-up. The boys are getting rather annoyed at the Italians for poaching on our preserve. We don't mind them coming over if they ask permission first, but when they just sneak over and use up a lot of our air to fly their aeroplanes in, it is becoming a bit too thick. We had to teach the Jerry bombers a sharp lesson when they were doing it, and we cannot see our way clear to let the Italians get away with it. We don't poach on their preserve much, so why don't they keep on their own side of the fence. They've got lots more room to fly over there – Sicily is much bigger than Malta."

One Spitfire actually fell in this action, 185's Plt Off Halford ditching BR285 in Kalafrana Bay beside the sunken supply ship *Breconshire*, from which supplies were still being salvaged. He was swiftly rescued by seaplane tender *ST338*, as Flt Lt George Crockett, OC Marine Rescue Unit, recorded:

"After the number of unsuccessful searches we had made for the pilots of single-seater fighter planes who had been forced to ditch their aircraft in the sea instead of baling out by parachute, I was beginning to think it was impossible to ditch a single-seater modern fighter with any chance of the pilot getting out before it sank. I was looking out towards the work going on at the *Breconshire* when an aircraft caught my eye coming in very low from the south-east. It was a Spitfire and, as I watched, it passed at sea level towards the far side of the wreck. The propeller stopped and a moment later it slithered along the surface of the water and came to a stop in a smother of spray with its nose down and its tail in the air. Running down to the camber-side I jumped aboard the first craft available, the old pinnace, and we chuffed over to the scene of the crash. But Corporal Surry, the coxswain of the seaplane tender standing-by *Breconshire*, had already seen the Spitfire and picked up the pilot by the time I got there.

"The pilot of the aircraft was unhurt and cheerful, so I sent him ashore with Corporal Surry for a routine check-up at sick quarters, while I had a try at towing the Spitfire to shallow water. The aircraft was on the bottom by now but Corporal Surry had thought to slip a towrope round its tail wheel before it sank. I only managed to move it about a hundred yards before it got completely wedged in between some of the ledges of rock, which form the bottom of the bay. As we couldn't move it any more, we buoyed and left it – the Spitfire's final resting place being close to that of a Stuka dive-bomber shot down almost a month before and whose pilot could still be seen down through five fathoms of crystal-clear water, sitting at the controls wearing a flying helmet and goggles."

As a sequel to this incident, Plt Off Sherlock added:

"We used to paddle over these two planes – we had dinghies from Ju88s and Me109s

– to reach the wreck of *Breconshire*, where we used to try and salvage tinned food. We joked about it being a sad day to see a Spit and a Stuka in formation in 30 feet of water."

Sherlock's friend Buzz Ogilvie recalled:

"When the air raids were on it was hard to sleep. Our beds were upstairs and we would run downstairs with our tin hats on and crouch under a big oak table. After a while we realised if we had a glass of Scotch before going to bed we'd sleep right through it, rather than getting up and hiding under that table. I can recall there was a ship sunk in the bay and navy divers went down and retrieved Black & White Scotch from it. They sold it to us for three dollars a bottle. On Gozo they made red wine, which they sold to us for one dollar per bottle. It was pretty ropey wine, but we were apt to drink anything so we could sleep."

There were no actions of note over Malta on **3 June**, but far to the west a cruiser and five destroyers escorted *Eagle* as she headed towards the launch point carrying a further 32 Spitfires. This was Operation Style. The Spitfires were to be led to Malta by Sqn Ldr Barton, Flt Lt Peck and Flg Off Plagis. The pilots are believed to have included:

Sqn Ldr A.R.H. Barton DFC (flight leader)	Wt Off C.B. Ramsay RCAF
Flt Lt J.E.Peck DFC (flight leader)	Flt Sgt T.F. Beaumont (BR313)
Flg Off J.A. Plagis DFC (flight leader)	Flt Sgt P.C. Terry
(BR295)	Flt Sgt J.H. Ballantyne RCAF
Flg Off E.A.C.G. Bruce	Flt Sgt R.G. Middlemiss RCAF
Flg Off J.H. Menary (BR322)	Flt Sgt H.D.K. Macpherson RCAF
Flg Off D.H. Smith RAAF	(BR308)
Plt Off A.A. Glen DFC	Sgt D.K. Parker
Plt Off J.L. Hicks	Sgt A. Drew
Plt Off C.R. Scollan RCAF	Sgt D.P. Motion
Plt Off H.C. Charlesworth RCAF	Sgt J.D. Tuttle
Plt Off G. Carlet RCAF (French)	Sgt W. Young (Rhod)
Plt Off D.F. Rouleau RCAF (BR358)	Sgt H.J. Smith (Rhod)
Plt Off E.W. Wallace RCAF	Sgt C.P.J. Taylor RCAF
Plt Off J.H. Curry RCAF (US) (BR232)	Sgt Q. di Persio RCAF
Plt Off F.E. Jones RCAF	Sgt S.E. Messum RCAF
Plt Off H.W. McLeod RCAF	Sgt L.S. Reid RAAF (BR230)

All went well with the launch of the Spitfires but on this occasion – for the first and only time – the Luftwaffe managed to intercept, a dozen Bf109s of II/JG53 taking off from Pantelleria to claim five Spitfires shot down; four were actually lost, two near Pantelleria and two more near Gozo. Piloting one of the Spitfires in Plagis' flight was Australian Len Reid, who recalled:

"Near Pantelleria we saw some Messerschmitts sitting out there watching us for five minutes. I could see them getting in position, saw them closing. I recall 'T' [presumably Tom Beaumont] shouting the 109s were attacking. I saw them coming. Plagis suddenly rolled over and dived for the sea. He left the rest of us up there like sitting ducks. Those 109s just flew in behind us and shot 'T' out of the sky. 'T' was alongside me; he was shot, obviously, as the stick came back into his stomach, and I saw him go up, smoke coming out. He was probably dead, and it was a matter of rolling over and diving for the sea. Everybody had to look after himself. I had one or two on my tail – tracer bullets flying past but fortunately they didn't hit me – and followed right down to the sea. I remember zig-zagging madly across the water, and in the finish I was on my own. I didn't know where I was, but knew I had to steer a certain course which might bring me to Malta. It did. I was supposed to land at Takali, but landed at Hal Far, as I came in from that direction."

Another of the new arrivals, 26-year-old Canadian Plt Off Wally McLeod, also narrowly escaped being shot down:

"Twelve 109s attacked out of the sun when we were about halfway to Malta. It was a perfect bounce. I didn't even know they were there until tracers started streaking over my starboard wing. One got on my tail, but thank God he was a poor marksman and I was able to get away before he could nail me."[60]

The four pilots who were lost were Flg Off Jim Menary, a young Irishman; Plt Off David Rouleau, a 24-year-old Canadian from Ottawa; 27-year-old Flt Sgt Tom Beaumont from Soham in Cambridgeshire – a former air-sea rescue pilot; and Flt Sgt Hugh Macpherson, another Canadian, from Vancouver. It seems likely that some of the Messerschmitts were already airborne, escorting a FW58B of Stab II/JG53, when the Spitfires approached, two of which – probably those flown by Menary and Rouleau – were seen to dive on the twin-engined communications aircraft (RC+NQ/58072) and shoot it down into the sea before the escort could intervene. All those on board the ditched aircraft were rescued apart from Ltn Hollmann, the W/Op. None of the four downed Spitfire pilots survived. Their assailants were led by Oblt Gerhard Michalski of 4/JG53, who claimed one as his 32nd victory; Uffz Heinrich Sedlmaier of 5 Staffel claimed two, while his colleague Ltn Wilhelm Ruge was credited with one, his ninth victory. A fifth was claimed by Ltn Ewald Schumacher of Stab II/JG53.

Upon reaching Malta one of the remaining Spitfires crashed on landing at Takali, though the pilot escaped unhurt. Aircraft from 249 and 601 Squadrons were scrambled to cover the new arrivals and to search for the missing pilots. Flg Off Daddo-Langlois spotted one of the NCO pilots in the sea off Gozo, orbiting for an hour overhead, but sadly no help was forthcoming and the pilot drowned. Flt Lt Barnham and his section from 601 Squadron found only an empty dinghy. Amongst the new arrivals was Plt Off Arthur Glen DFC (known as 'Pinkie' to his friends) who had three victories to his credit. Among them also was Plt Off Guy Levy-Despas, a 20-year-old Paris-born former student who was studying in the USA when war broke out. Unable to return to France, he joined the RCAF using the *nom de guerre* Guy Carlet to protect his family at home, and was eventually posted to the UK[61]. On his return to Malta, Flg Off Plagis learned that he had been promoted to Acting Flight Lieutenant and was posted to lead a flight of 185 Squadron.

Twice during the early afternoon, single photo-reconnaissance Bf109s of 1(F)/122 were despatched to Malta, one pilot briefed to observe and photograph the airfields, the other to check upon shipping at Valetta and Marsaxlokk. Neither was intercepted. Of the new arrivals, 185's Slim Yarra wrote:

"The boys were busy getting a new delivery of Spitfires ready for combat. We obtained four of these new jobs as our quota, bringing our strength up to 16 aircraft. We will be able to put 12 aircraft on the lines from dawn to dusk everyday now and still have some spare. We are a little short of pilots, but received some new ones today, which will help a lot."

With daylight on **4 June**, a flight of Spitfires was despatched to search for a missing aircraft. Flt Lt Barnham and his section from 601 Squadron was again involved:

"At dawn search for the crew of a lost Wellington bomber; banks of mist over the cliffs;

the sun rose from the sea – all the moving water shone into green; we searched for an hour and-a-half. No trace of them."

Two small-scale Luftwaffe fighter sweeps came over, four 185 Squadron aircraft encountering Messerschmitts head-on before being jumped by others from behind. Flt Sgt Yarra (BR353/GL-D) was chased back to base but his aircraft was not hit. 603 Squadron was called upon to scramble a section when a hostile plot appeared on radar, Plt Offs Slade and Barnfather (Spitfire X-Z) meeting two Bf109s, as the latter noted in his logbook: "Scramble – Jack Slade and I bounced by 109s. Spun off turn and lost Jack and the Huns and bags of height!"

5 June was marked only by four small-scale fighter reconnaissances, each by a pair of Bf109s. 249 Squadron sent up two sections of Spitfires, one piloted by Wt Off Jack Rae flying his first sortie since being shot down four weeks earlier. He was now with 249. There was no contact. Next day (**6 June**), heralded the busiest day for two weeks, and was to be the blackest of the war for 2°Gruppo Aut CT. At 0445 two Spitfires of 185 Squadron took off on a dawn patrol, but shortly after they had got into the air, radar indicated the presence of at least two hostiles, and at 0525 four 249 Squadron aircraft were scrambled. As the latter climbed to gain altitude, the 185 Squadron pair spotted a Ju88 at sea level, 30 miles south-east of Kalafrana, which Flt Sgt Haggas attacked at once from astern, seeing strikes on the fuselage and a stream of glycol. Flt Sgt Jim MacNamara also attacked, reporting strikes.

However, 249 Squadron was also in on the act. Flt Lt Lucas, who was leading in BR109/C-30, later reported that he believed he had seen 185's victim fall into the sea. Two more Ju88s were then observed and attacked by the 249 quartet, Lucas and Plt Off Frank Jones (BR246/C-40) shooting down one and Plt Off Linton (BR111/C-18) and Flt Sgt Micky Butler (BR377/C-41) jointly claiming the second. Of the action, Lucas wrote:

"We got our attacks spot on. With all the advantage of height, each pair made a nicely judged, beam-to-quarter attack from opposite sides, pressed right home to near point-blank range... The shooting was good, so one attack from each side was enough to do it. As, first, Jonesie and then Micky pulled away, I saw the port Ju88 start terraplaning over the water before rearing up and sinking in a cloud of spray."

The second quickly followed suit; Lucas continued:

"We circled the spot for a full five minutes, climbing up to give fixes for the ground station (and, no doubt, the enemy) to pinpoint the area. There was no sign of survivors, only two patches of spreading oil and debris. I was sorry, for each crew and, in particular, each rear gunner had fought the attack in the best tradition of the Luftwaffe. But such is war."

The rear gunner of the aircraft attacked by Lucas had gained a hit on the engine of his Spitfire before his own demise:

"A glance at my radiator temperature gauge shot a current through my body. It was already off the clock and the engine was beginning to run rough. My aircraft had obviously been hit in the coolant tank by return fire from an 88 without my noticing it. As we were about to cross the south-west coast by Dingli cliffs at some 3,000 feet, and still struggling for height, my motor seized completely. Smoke began to issue ominously from under the engine cowlings. Cutting all the switches, I realised I wasn't going to have enough height to stretch a glide with a dead stick and reach anyone of the island's three airfields for an emergency landing. I had always had a fear of baling out.

Ever since I had first learnt to fly I had made up my mind that only in the ultimate resort would I take to a parachute. My problem now was that a forced-landing in Malta was roundly accepted to be an exceptionally dodgy affair and to be avoided if reasonably possible. Hundreds and hundreds of stone walls marking myriad small plots of rock-strewn land covered the island's white and arid surface. The consensus was that eight times out of ten it was better to bale out. The temperature in the cockpit was getting hotter and the smoke from the engine thicker. A tiny, but apparently cultivated piece of land, marked out by stone walls, caught my eye below. It was on the outskirts of a village, which turned out to be Siggiewi. I now had about 1,000 feet to work with. A tight slipping turn into the field, with wheels up and flaps down and the speed kept just above the point of stall, brought the aircraft heading into such breeze as there was with, I guessed, only a few feet to spare above the 'downwind' wall. With only 80 to 100 yards to go to the stone wall ahead, the Spitfire – aerodynamically sympathetic, the easiest operational aeroplane in the world to 'feel' on to the ground – settled unbelievably gently on to the soft earth. A shot in a thousand. I would never have made the same job of it again.

"Without so much as a scratch, a bruise or a burn, I undid my straps and jumped down quickly from the cockpit, distancing myself from the hot, smoking aircraft. I then noticed three old Maltese women in long black dresses, almost touching the ground, and black scarves covering their heads, coming stumbling over the rough ground, as fast as they could, towards me. Each was carrying some scooping implement and a hessian sack in her hand. As they came near, they stopped and, breathlessly, started shovelling earth into the sacks, intent upon getting up on to the wing and emptying the contents on top of the smouldering engine. They could not understand English, but I explained by gestures that this wasn't sensible as there was the danger of explosion. Palpably dispirited by my caution, they turned away. The oldest and obviously the senior of the three then walked slowly back to the Spitfire and touched the wing lightly with her hand. Returning to me, she rested her hand gently on my forearm. As she did so she looked up into my eyes. A smile of benign serenity spread across that heavily lined, endearing face. Making the sign of the cross deliberately across her chest, she touched my arm again. With that, she turned with the others and went back to tending the land."

Records show that two Ju88s of KüFlGr606 were lost during this action, 7T+HK flown by Uffz Heinz-Wolf Bartels and 7T+BL commanded by Ltn Werner Dielas.

A second scramble was called an hour later, four more 249 aircraft and 11 from 603 Squadron going off to intercept five 50°Gruppo Z1007bis bombers (two from 210^Squadriglia and three from 211^Squadriglia) which attacked Safi, escorted by 24 MC202s of 155°Gruppo and a dozen RE2001s of 2°Gruppo. Wt Off Ramsay (BR387/GL-W) and Sgt Gilbert (BR119/1-C) each claimed a Reggiane shot down; one, or both, had attacked Ten Leonardo Venturini of 358^Squadriglia who radioed that he was about to ditch in the sea just off Malta, but was lost. Sgt Gray (BR175/C-31) claimed damage to a fighter he identified as a Bf109, while Gilbert and Plt Off Watts (BR170/C-25) reported damaging one of the bombers. This aircraft was also attacked by 603 Squadron's CO, Sqn Ldr Douglas-Hamilton and Plt Off McLeod; the latter's aircraft (2-C) was hit by return fire in the tail and wing however and the engine cut, but he landed safely. Other Reggianes were claimed probably destroyed by Plt Off Neville King and Flg Off Mitchell of 603 Squadron, whereas another of the bombers was claimed damaged by Plt Off Eddie Glazebrook (who identified it as an SM84). One Cant sustained damage to the fuel tanks and engines, but managed to return to Sicily. Bomber crews claimed two Spitfires shot down in return, and another was claimed by M.llo Olindo Simionato of 2°Gruppo, who reported that it fell in flames; other Reggiane pilots added a probable and reported strikes on many others to increase the tally. A fourth Spitfire was credited to Ten Giuseppe Bonfiglio of 155°Gruppo, who believed that it crashed into the sea and he also claimed another as damaged. One of the Macchi pilots involved in this action was Ten Giovanni Ambrosio of 378^Squadriglia, who had initially experienced engine problems but was then able to rejoin his flight:

"In the instant I retook my position, all the Macchis scattered in the sky. The aircraft were darting through the air. Were there enemy fighters? I had a moment of hesitation and once more found myself alone. Overhead I saw five to six fighters diving. I thought they were our RE2001s so I pulled up to join that flight. I realised when one was near me that it was a Spitfire, with coloured cockade and number on fuselage – I was his target. It tried to get on my tail but I took the advantage and fired a burst at one who seemed to be the leader. My tracers bent behind the tail of the enemy. I fired once more. This time I saw rounds enter the fuselage and 'crackle' over the engine of the Spitfire; black smoke emitted around the fuselage. After a swift reversal and in a dive, I swivelled my neck to see if I was under the fire of other Spitfires."

By diving to sea level Ambrosio evaded further attention and reached Gela safely. He had survived his first combat.

The day was still young, however, and at 0920 an estimated 20 Axis aircraft were reported searching to the east of Malta; in fact, 11 RE2001s led by TenCol Aldo Quarantotti were out looking for the missing Venturini. They spotted some possible wreckage and oil where his aircraft was believed to have ditched but of the pilot there was no sign. While so engaged and flying low, they were attacked by four 249 Spitfires that had been scrambled, Flg Off Daddo-Langlois (C-22) and Plt Off Frank Jones (BR246/C-40) each claiming a Reggiane shot down, with Plt Off Linton (BR111/C-18) and Flt Sgt Butler (BR377/C-41) each claiming one damaged. Four more 249 Spitfires, which had scrambled at 1020, then arrived and Sgt Gray (BR175/C-31) claimed damage to a RE2001 while Flt Lt Lucas (BR109/C-30) reported strikes on a Bf109. Of the skirmish, Daddo-Langlois recorded:

"Section met four RE2001s east of Zonqor. Jones destroyed one. I got one destroyed. Linton and I were jumped by four 109s. Running fight to Kalafrana from 15 miles out. These yellow-nose boys know their stuff."

One Reggiane (MM7235) flown by Ten Arnaldo de Merich had gone down at once and crashed into the sea, with a second – MM7214 flown by Cap Salvatore Teia – being seriously damaged and belly-landing on return to Caltagirone. There was danger on the ground as well as in the air, as Flt Lt Barnham discovered when he and B Flight/601 Squadron were also scrambled:

"I had to taxi fast to reach the runway and take off before the coolant temperature of my engine went beyond the danger mark. Taxiing fast was not easy, with my wingtips perilously close to the cliff face on one side of the narrow track, and a stone wall on the other – the long nose blocking my vision did not help. Suddenly a bus came round the corner at me – I risked tipping the Spitfire on to its nose by applying fierce brake – but the bus, without making any attempt to stop, swerved towards the gap between my wing and the wall: there wasn't room; the driver's cab struck my wingtip with a crash of metal; the nose of my aircraft, with its turning propeller swung towards the passengers crowding the bus windows – an anxious moment – but managing to stop the propeller I enjoyed the inevitable impact. The cannon protruding forward from my starboard wing ended up inside the passenger's compartment; the expressions on the quickly withdrawn faces were magnificent. The Maltese streaming out of the bus ran off down the road – with the driver running after them. Time was short, the raid was approaching; Chiefy was quite right in not wanting me to fly the damaged plane: the crumpled wingtip did have an adverse effect on the controls as I climbed steeply into the sky."

The Italians were back in the afternoon, this time 13 RE2001s and six MC202s escorting a Z506B of 612^Squadriglia on a search for the missing pilots to the east of Malta. Four 185 Squadron Spitfires were scrambled to intercept at 1605, followed by four more (Blue Section) ten minutes later. The initial section, led by Flt Lt Plagis (BR321/GL-J), chased the Reggianes 40 miles out to sea; he recorded:

"Intercepted about 10-12 enemy aircraft 30-40 miles east of Malta – joined by another 36 e/a. Reid got one RE2001. Blue Section got blood wagon. I got two RE2001 destroyed. Both pilots baled out!! RIP."

Flt Sgt Shorty Reid actually claimed one destroyed and another damaged. Against the three 'confirmed' claims submitted, two Reggiane pilots were lost, Ten Giuseppe Baraldi's MM7228 last seen trailing black smoke, while Serg Magg Aldo Geminiani's MM7223 crashed into the sea; like de Merich, both were members of 152^Squadriglia. Two weeks later a dinghy containing Geminiani's body was found by the Italian hospital ship *Arno*. On this occasion the 2°Gruppo pilots had only been able to claim a single joint victory against a Spitfire, and a second was claimed by Serg Magg Giovanni del Fabbro, a Macchi pilot of 378^Squadriglia. One Spitfire was damaged in the fight, Plt Off Sherlock being forced to crash-land BR109/C-30 at Hal Far on return; he was unhurt. Meanwhile, Plt Off Ogilvie had encountered the white-painted, red cross-emblazoned Z506B:

"I didn't know what the hell to do with this thing. Jerry had been shooting up our rescue launches, and I thought this was fair game. However, I pulled up alongside of it – formating on it almost to within a 100 yards of its right-hand side – indicating to the pilot that I wanted him to turn around and land at Malta. While all this negotiating was going on, someone came up behind and blew it out of the sky. It must have been carrying a tremendous amount of petrol on board. The explosion was tremendous."

The destruction of Sottoten Arduino Marega's floatplane (MM45272) was credited jointly to the other three Canadians of Blue Section, Plt Off Jimmy Lambert, Flt Sgt Dodd and Sgt Hugh Russel; there were no survivors. Slim Yarra had a field day:

"We were kept busy all the morning, scrambling after Messerschmitts, blood wagons, seagulls and plots of 'SFA' [Sweet Fanny Adams]. However, an enjoyable time was had by all and the party finally broke up when B Flight arrived to take over. They had their share of fun during the afternoon. F/Lt Plagis and his boys went up and caught the blood wagon. Johnny [Plagis] picked on a bunch of RE2001s and induced one pilot to bale out. The second guy was not so lucky – he was last seen going into the drink doing about 500mph. It is considered unlikely that he survived. Shorty Reid also did a little beating up and destroyed an RE2001 and damaged another. P/O Lambert, F/Sgt Dodd and Sgt Russel found the blood wagon stooging along and did some OTU-style practice attacks on it. However, they used live ammunition and made quite a mess of the floatplane. We did not lose one aircraft, but according to the Italian radio the boys in the RE2001s destroyed six Spitfires!"

After dark an estimated 20 bombers crossed the coast, Ju88s included, and bombs fell on Luqa, Takali – where a decoy Hurricane was burnt out and an ambulance slightly damaged – and Dingli. On this occasion four or five flare-dropping aircraft arrived first, releasing several dozen green, white and red flares, which descended quite slowly from 5,000 feet over Luqa, the bombers then concentrating their attack. Two Spitfires were sent off but were not able to make any interceptions; AA gunners claimed one Ju88 shot down, although no loss was recorded.

Four Spitfires of 185 Squadron were scrambled shortly after midday on **7 June**, as part of a force of 11 sent up to intercept 15 Bf109s on a sweep; of his 12th and last Malta victory claim, Flt Lt Plagis (BR321/GL-J) noted in his logbook: "One Me109F destroyed five-seven miles east of Delimara Point – confirmed." A second Messerschmitt was claimed probably destroyed by Flt Sgt Shorty Reid, although no Luftwaffe losses are recorded on this date. 185 Squadron was again involved in the afternoon's action, when eight aircraft were ordered to investigate a further force of fighters approaching the coast. Although the main body of Spitfires failed to make contact, Flt Sgt Yarra (GL-N) was obliged to return to base early due to engine trouble and en route was attacked by three RE2001s; turning into these, he claimed to have inflicted damage on two. 185's redoubtable diarist Yarra later recorded the action in detail:

"B Flight were on dawn readiness today. F/Lt Plagis and a section of four went off to intercept a plot of 12-plus. They found four Messerschmitts stooging about and proceeded to bounce them properly. Plagis destroyed a Me109 and F/Sgt Shorty Reid probably destroyed another. This combat made the second engagement in two days in which F/Lt Plagis figured, during which period he destroyed three enemy aircraft. In the afternoon another section of four were scrambled and chased some Messerschmitts. However, contact was not established. F/Sgt Yarra was returning to base with a dud motor when he was jumped by four RE2001s. During the ensuing mix-up two of the RE2001s flew across Slim's sights and stopped some lead. At the same time as this mix-up was taking place, F/Sgt Sim was chasing two Messerschmitts who had their noses down going for home. However, the 109s had their 'tits' pressed as usual and disappeared over the horizon to the tune of muttered curses from F/Sgt Sim."

The Messerschmitts of II/JG53 accounted for two of Malta's Spitfires during brief skirmishes over the island during **8 June**, Plt Off Barlow (BR231) of 603 Squadron being shot down as nine aircraft of his unit scrambled to intercept a sweep shortly before noon; his aircraft fell into the sea and the 27-year-old South African was killed. Only Flt Sgt Bob Brown managed a passing shot as the Bf109s sped out to sea again, claiming one damaged. During the afternoon, a dozen Spitfires of 249 Squadron were scrambled to intercept a dozen Messerschmitts. Four were encountered, resulting in Flt Sgt Butler's aircraft (BR312) sustaining damage; the Canadian crash-landed in a field near Takali and was slightly injured. One of these Spitfires fell to Maj von Maltzahn as his 63rd victory, the other to Oblt Gerhard Michalski of 4/JG53 (his 33rd).

Far to the west, a further reinforcement operation was underway – the third in less than a month – as 30 Spitfires were ferried towards Malta aboard *Eagle*. Anti-submarine aircraft from Gibraltar preceded the carrier and escort – two cruisers and six destroyers – to clear the way. Among the pilots was Plt Off Tilley, who had been sent to Gibraltar to lead a flight. The new pilots are believed to have included:

Plt Off R.F. Tilley RCAF (flight leader)	Flt Sgt C.H. Parkinson RAAF
Flt Lt A.C. Rowe RNZAF (flight leader)	(BR376)
Flt Lt P.W. Lovell	Sgt A.E. Budd
Flg Off J. Smith	Sgt D.F. Hubbard

Flg Off K.L. Charney
Plt Off R.G. Smith (BR382)
Plt Off G.P.B. Davies
Plt Off H. Kelly (US)
Plt Off E.W. Spradley RCAF (US)
Plt Off J.F. McElroy RCAF (BR388)
Plt Off J.H.R. Paradis RCAF
Plt Off G. Stenborg RNZAF
Plt Off C.H. Lattimer RNZAF
Flt Sgt R.A. Stevenson
Flt Sgt B.W. Reynolds RCAF
Flt Sgt J.A.H. Pinney RCAF

Sgt M.E. Tomkins
Sgt L.G.C. de l'Ara
Sgt M. Irving Gass
Sgt G.F. Beurling (Canadian) (BR380)
Sgt N. Marshall RCAF
Sgt R.H. Davey RCAF
Sgt C.E. Mutch RCAF
Sgt A. Richardson RAAF
Sgt C.J. Baxter RAAF
Sgt E.T. Brough RNZAF
Sgt C.L. Wood RNZAF

Early on the morning of **9 June**, the Spitfires were launched, the first flight being led by Tilley. Australian Colin Parkinson recorded:

> "Took off from *Eagle* about 7am. Eight of us with an inexperienced flight lieutenant to lead us. His speeds varied from 100mph to 200mph. On the way we saw a sub being refuelled by a depot ship just off the coast of Africa. The flight leader was doing one of his usual little tricks of 100mph when my long-range tank ran out. My kite dropped like a stone; however, I managed to get it going again OK. Jettisoned the tank over Tunis. It took approx four hours to get to Malta where we all landed safely without too much damage to the aircraft; two were pranged."

20-year-old Canadian George Beurling, of Swedish father and English mother – soon to become Malta's top fighter ace – experienced an uneventful flight, as he later recalled:

> "The weather was cloudy but we were told to expect excellent visibility at Malta. The wing commander had said: 'Keep your eyes peeled for Jerries as you come near home. The last time we came down this way the blighters lay in wait between Tunis and Pantelleria and shot down three or four of them. Knocked every one of them into the sea and every pilot killed – just because he didn't keep his eyes peeled!' By 0605 the first eight were on the way, leaving the flight deck about two minutes apart. As each plane became airborne it climbed and made left-hand circuits of the carrier until joined by its mates. At 2,000 feet they formed up over the ship, then legged for Malta, climbing hard. I went away with the third flight at 0630. Malta came into view at 0950 from 20,000 feet. My gang made Takali, all right side up, at 1030. Right then the war began in earnest for Sergeant Beurling!"

The flight was made safely and landings began at Takali from 1000 onwards. One aircraft – BR388 flown by Plt Off John McElroy – Mac to his friends – had damaged its tail on take-off and subsequently crashed on landing. An irate Wg Cdr Gracie, not fully aware of the facts, immediately grounded the luckless Canadian and threatened to have him posted to the Middle East.

No sooner were the new Spitfires down when, at 1050, 36 of those already there were ordered off as 16 Bf109s approached. Four 603 Squadron pilots gave chase and Sgt Len Webster claimed damage to one. All then remained relatively quiet until early evening, when three SM84s with a large escort of Macchis and Reggianes raided Takali where an already damaged Spitfire was destroyed on the ground. A total of 22 Spitfires of 126, 601 and 603 Squadron were scrambled, and newly commissioned Plt Off Hurst of the latter unit claimed a bomber damaged, and Plt Off Graves (MK-E) of 126 Squadron claimed a Bf109 shot down – apparently an aircraft (10047) from

5/JG53 that crashed at Pantelleria following combat and was totally destroyed; the pilot baled out and survived unhurt. He also damaged a second. Plt Off Jerry Smith was up:

"What a time! I chased a couple of 109s about one third of the way to Sicily. Had a dogfight. Had a couple of squirts but didn't observe hits. Shot up St Julian's on the way back."

Flt Sgt Ken Evans (BP992) of 126 Squadron claimed a Reggiane probable, while Plt Off Don Llewellyn (BR465), flying his first sortie since being shot down the previous month, reported being pursued by an Italian fighter but managed to evade without damage. The Macchi pilots of 155°Gruppo in turn claimed three Spitfires shot down, one apiece being credited to M.llo Pasquale Bartolucci and Serg Magg Angelo Cerri, the third being credited jointly to M.llo Lorenzo Serafino and M.llo Aldo Romagnoli; others were believed damaged. Only one Spitfire suffered any damage, 126 Squadron's Flt Sgt Bernie Reynolds crash-landing BP869/T-K at Takali. 185 Squadron had another fairly quiet day, although there was some excitement as the diarist noted:

"The day was spent doing patrols and scrambles over the island but nothing was encountered. P/O Halford was stooging along with his section and made a pass at four 'aircraft'. However, these 'aircraft' turned out to be four seagulls who were doing a practice formation. The seagulls were very annoyed and threatened to dive-bomb our dispersal if the incident is repeated. Today we received four more Spitfires to add to our collection. This brings our strength up to 20 aircraft."

185 also received two reinforcement pilots from the latest delivery, New Zealander Plt Off Gray Stenborg who had four victories to his credit, and Flg Off Ken Charney, who was shortly promoted to take command of B Flight. Most of the new pilots were promptly attached to the other fighter squadrons. Flt Lt Peter Lovell, Plt Off Dudley Newman, Plt Off Ray Smith and Flt Sgt John Pinney went to 603 Squadron, as did Sgts Ernie Budd, Tim Brough, and Colin Baxter RAAF, although the latter moved over to 249 a couple of days later. Flt Sgt Colin Parkinson also joined 603, and was not enamoured by first impressions:

"I have been posted to 603 Squadron. Sqn Ldr Lord Douglas-Hamilton is the CO. I'm in B Flight so won't see much of him, thank goodness. 603 is very much an officers' squadron, sergeants don't get a fair deal. Officers and NCOs have very poor food, though it's quite possible to buy meals consisting of eggs, pork chops, tomatoes, fresh beans, lettuce and potatoes at various Maltese shops, which on the whole look filthy (the shops I mean), so while I have some money I won't starve."

Plt Off Bruce Downs, an American attached to 603 now joined the American Flight being formed within 126 Squadron, while Plt Off Mac Barbour moved over to 603 from that unit in exchange. Posted to 249 from the latest batch of new arrivals were Flg Off John Smith; Plt Offs Jean Paradis RCAF, a French-Canadian from Quebec; Harry 'Tex' Kelly, an American in the RAF; Charlie Lattimer RNZAF, and Ernie 'Tex' Spradley RCAF, another Texan; Flt Sgts Louis de l'Ara (of Anglo-Spanish ancestry) a former Spitfire test pilot, and Maurice Tomkins; Sgts Rip Mutch RCAF and George Beurling, another native of Quebec – soon to be nicknamed 'Screwball' by his contemporaries. Also posted to 249 was the New Zealander Wt Off Jack Rae, who had recently been discharged from hospital following an argument with a Messerschmitt when flying with 603 Squadron. Beurling wrote:

"I was assigned to 249 Squadron, proud of its record as the fightingest outfit in the RAF, with 180 German and Italian aircraft in its bag when I joined. The Squadron Leader was Grant, a swell Englishman and a swell pilot. The flight commanders were Laddie Lucas and Buck McNair, both top-drawer guys."

Beurling, despite two recent victories to his credit while fighting over Northern France, had however gained a bad reputation for his lack of discipline, and this followed him to Malta, as Flt Lt Lucas recalled:

"One of the squadron had served with George Beurling in England. Seeing his name on the list, he had given me a run-down. 'I was with him in 41 [Squadron]. He was a loner who was always getting separated from the squadron on the sweeps and going off on his own. A dim view was taken of it and he didn't seem prepared to learn. But, make no mistake, he can fly aeroplanes, has got flair and can shoot. He'll either buy it very quickly here or shoot some down.' Buck clearly didn't want him for his flight. OK, I said, it's 249's pick first, so I'll have Sergeant Beurling for A Flight. I had a talk with him the day after he joined us. I told him straightly that I knew of his reputation he had made for himself and the problems this had brought. At the same time, I had been told that he had flair, could fly well and could shoot, all of which appealed to me. I added that he would start with a clean slate here and provided that he toed the line, stuck as a pair with whoever he was flying with and didn't go chasing off on his own, he would get every chance."

Four Spitfires were in the air on the morning of **10 June**, to cover the arrival of Beaufighters from Gibraltar, one having been lost en route. Two Bf109s were seen but no contact was made. There was again no contact when 11 Spitfires were scrambled after nine Messerschmitts on a sweep at 0930 but a patrolling minesweeper was attacked, the crew claiming to have shot down one of the German fighters and to have damaged a second. Ten 249 Squadron Spitfires were sent off at 1100 as more Axis fighters appeared, ten Bf109s and MC202s being reported, Flt Sgt Gray (T-W) claiming one of the latter shot down. On returning to Takali, Gray undershot as he came in to land and crashed, but suffered only minor injuries. A little while later an escorted Do24 approached the island and a dozen Spitfires were ordered off to investigate, three of 249 Squadron making an interception. Wt Off Ramsay (BR170/C-25) claimed a Bf109 probable out of a dozen met, while Flt Lt Lucas (BR108/C-20) and Plt Off Linton reported damaging the flyingboat. During this engagement Obfw Rudolf Ehrenberger of 6/JG53 claimed a Spitfire shot down.

At 1810, eight 249 Squadron Spitfires took off, led by Sqn Ldr Grant, to cover the arrival of a formation of nine Beaufort torpedo-bombers flying in from Gibraltar, which had radioed that they were under attack by a fighter. Their attacker was identified as a Bf109 but was probably a MC202 of 54°Stormo CT, operating from Pantelleria. One bomber was damaged and obliged to force-land on arrival at Luqa. Before the 249 Squadron flight could reach them however, they were vectored onto an incoming raid, and a dozen more Spitfires (eight/601 and four/185) were scrambled at 1845. The raiders, which reached the island half an hour later, were five Z1007bis escorted by 27 MC202s and 19 RE2001s; their target was Safi. It appears that Messerschmitts of II/JG53 were also present. All three Spitfire formations engaged; for 249 Squadron Sqn Ldr Grant (BR170/C-25) claimed a RE2001 shot down (bringing his victory tally to at least five). This was undoubtedly the machine flown by Serg Giovanni Dringoli of 150^Squadriglia; the pilot was believed to have been mortally wounded and his aircraft was seen to crash into the sea. Flt Sgt

Williams (BR163) claimed a second as damaged – probably Ten Agostino Celentano's aircraft which was badly damaged, but managed to reach base – and Flt Lt McNair (BR107/C-22) claimed a Bf109 for his seventh victory; his victim may have been Uffz Heinrich Sedlmaier of 5/JG53, who was reported by the Luftwaffe to have been shot down north of Valetta, allegedly by AA; he baled out, wounded, and was subsequently rescued. Oblt Günther Hess, Staffelkapitän of 6 Staffel, claimed a Spitfire shot down (his fifth victory) during this engagement. Of this action, McNair recalled:

> "I got up-sun and saw a gaggle of 20 Me109s escorting bombers. The 109s weren't acting like the German flyers we were accustomed to seeing. They had no formation of any kind, but bunched together in a way that made me think of a bunch of cattle all trying to get through a gate at the same time. By now they were right under us. One of them turned and I turned with it, giving it a squirt as I dived. He dived too, with me after him. I pranged him again and he baled out. My section had followed but they didn't get any but Stan Grant did. As I saw the fighter going down, I saw a Spitfire going down too, both in the same area. I called up control and said two were going into the drink, one of them ours, one theirs. Then I went to escort the launch because, sometimes, enemy fighters machine-gunned them and sometimes the launch crews refused to go out without an escort. I directed the boat to the green colour, which marked where the Spitfire pilot had hit the water. We couldn't find the German pilot."

Meanwhile, Plt Off Percy Sewell of 601 Squadron shot down a 155°Gruppo Macchi flown by M.llo Lorenzo Serafino of 378^Squadriglia, witnesses on Gozo reporting seeing two fighters – obviously those flown by Serafino and Dringoli – crash into the sea about two and-a-half miles south of Mgarr. In return, 155°Gruppo reported four Spitfires shot down, claimed by Ten Giobatta Caracciolo Carafa, Ten Giuseppe Bonfiglio, Ten Vittorio Bastogi and Serg Magg Angelo Cerri. In fact, only one Spitfire (BP875) was lost – that flown by Plt Off Jim Innes of 601 Squadron. He later reported that a cannon shell exploded under his seat, which fell forward and pinned him against the instrument panel. The Spitfire plunged vertically from 25,000 feet, the speed causing the aircraft to break up, and Innes was thrown out. His parachute opened and he landed safely in the sea, from where he was soon picked up by *HSL107*. A second Spitfire (GL-N) of 185 Squadron was struck in the windscreen by return fire from one of the bombers, Flt Sgt Yarra sustaining slight injuries to his face caused by splinters of glass. However, he returned to base without further damage. The rescue of Innes by *HSL107* could well have ended in disaster, as recalled by one of the crew, W/Op LAC Bill Jackson:

> "Called out early in the morning to search for a lost Spitfire pilot down in the sea about 25 miles from base. We soon found the patch of oil and wreckage that marked the place his aircraft had entered the water but significantly there was no sign of a spreading patch of the orange dye coming up from below the surface. This in itself was a good sign because it told us that he had not gone down with it but had probably baled out and had drifted away on his way down. The trouble was that there was a fairly stiff breeze blowing which we knew from past experience could carry him for miles before he alighted. With this in mind we made a fairly perfunctory search of the immediate area without success and started a square search that concentrated downwind of the oil patch.
>
> "The search took us well into the afternoon, each leg getting longer and longer with every spare hand on deck to look out for either a K-type dinghy or the tell-tale yellow of a Mae West, neither of them very big to see. Suddenly, there it was, wallowing in the

waves. An obscene black object bobbing up and down about 200 yards off our port side. Joe Maitland [the launch's gunner] had never fired his guns in anger against any target but this one seemed ideal for attention from his twin Vickers 'K'. For safety's sake we retired a little further away from the menace as Joe lined up his sights and let fly. We could see where his rounds were splashing the water all round the thing and from this we knew that some of them were hits on the metal casing but we waited in vain for the familiar eruption of water we saw at the cinema when our intrepid hero managed to explode his mine with a couple of rounds. When Joe's machine-guns still proved unsuccessful most of us armed ourselves with .303 rifles and added to the amount of steel that was fired at the mine and we had plenty of ammunition to carry on firing for some time. One of our many jobs was the dumping of ammunition that the armourers decided was faulty and at first we dumped it over the side in deep water. Then one day some of it looked fairly good so from then on we spent many of our spare hours waiting to put to sea sorting out the good from the bad. This way we would always have plenty of ammo for the machine-guns and for the rifles we carried should it be needed.

"Exploding the mine was far more difficult than we had believed and decided we would carry out the procedure we were supposed to carry out and report its position instead of trying to sink it. It seemed that the only way it would detonate was if one of our shots was lucky enough to hit one of the main spikes or horns that protruded from its circumference. It was as well that we stopped firing because, as we did, one of the deckhands saw a tiny speck floating in the sea about 100 yards away from the mine. It was the head and shoulders of the pilot we had been seeking. He was sufficiently far from the mine to be safe from our fire but had the mine gone up, the blast through the water would probably have pulverised him, certainly it would have done him no good.

"He was still white-faced as we lifted him over the side and he realised how near he had been to death but we all thought that it was yet another occasion when a man's name not been called by the heavenly host. On our way back to Kalafrana and, with a tot of rum inside him, the pilot we rescued told us of his escapade that morning. In the ensuing fight his aircraft had taken a burst that caused the engine to seize. He had time to make only one 'Mayday' call before baling out. At first he couldn't get the canopy to open. But after struggling with it for what seemed like hours, the thing finally flew off into space. But as he scrambled out of the cockpit and released his chute he was horrified to feel a tremendous tug as the parachute caught-up in the tail of his aircraft. He told us that he had visions of being dragged down into the water below, by the falling Spitfire, when the chute dragged itself clear. He was able to watch the kite splash into the sea below him and then realised he was drifting along and would finally drop into the waves quite a long way from where his aircraft disappeared. Floating in the water he watched us come nearer and nearer and then stop. He admitted he was puzzled as to why we stopped, then he saw the splashes of Joe's bullets. It was then he spotted the mine floating uncomfortably close to where he floated and began to pray that we wouldn't hit it. His prayer was answered and we stopped firing. When we did, he waved his arm frantically hoping that we would spot it. We did and as a result pulled him inboard.

"An ambulance waited for him on the jetty as we tied up and, after he walked across to it and climbed aboard, he turned before he disappeared inside to give us a wave and a cheery grin. That small thing made us realise that fate and fortune still played a big part in many people's lives both in peace and in war, but especially in war."

11 June was to be a day of limited action, a dozen 126 Squadron Spitfires being ordered off at 0940 to intercept six Bf109s on an offensive reconnaissance sortie. Plt Off Bill Johnson noted:

"White Section patrolled minesweepers. Four 109s jumped 20 miles out to sea and chased 15 miles. P/O Bisley got one. The others ran faster than we could."

249 Squadron had four aircraft airborne, including one flown by Wt Off Rae, who recalled:

"Raoul Daddo-Langlois was flight leader that day. His No.2 was one of our new arrivals from the last delivery of Spits. I was flying No.3 and my No.2 was also a new boy. There were quite a number of Me109s flying over the island. The idea of this flight was to familiarise newcomers with the formations and possibly give them some combat experience. We four were flying along straight and level, tensely watching the skies and ready for action. Suddenly Raoul's No.2 winged hard over. In the flying atmosphere in which we lived that sudden action meant 'break hard, being attacked'. Raoul and myself were halfway round before we noticed that this oaf was just playing around doing a full roll. 'Gosh, it was getting boring. I could see the enemy fighters but they were a long way from us, so I thought it would be fun to do some aerobatics,' he said later. Raoul was absolutely furious and gave the pilot a severe dressing down after we landed. 'I never want to fly with that fool again,' he told us.

"The pilot was Sergeant Beurling. Later, because he was always referring to just about everyone and everything as a 'screwball', we nicknamed him Screwball. He was a strange, intense young man who loved his flying. But he worried those of us whom he regarded as old hands by asking question after question. He had far above average long distance sight. Sometimes when air raids were sounded and we were not flying we used to stand on the bastion of Mdina, straining to see the enemy formations approaching and count the number in the attack. We were always amazed at the far-sightedness of some of the Maltese who would start getting excited and counting aircraft while we were still gazing at an apparently empty sky, unable to see a thing. We soon discovered that Screwball had even better sight, beginning to count long before the Maltese had made their first spotting and giving the direction in which the enemy aircraft were heading."

Following Daddo-Langlois' adverse report on Beurling's behaviour, Flt Lt Lucas called the errant Canadian into his office:

"I told him that by behaving like this in the air, no matter how confident he might be himself, he was letting the Squadron down and increasing the risks for others, which were high enough already. I added a rider. I said from what I had heard from his flight commander and the little I had seen myself, he had the ability to make a success of his time on the island if he played things 249's way rather than selfishly for what he thought were his own ends. I said, if you don't toe the 249 line then let's be quite clear about this. You'll be on the next aeroplane into the Middle East. Those blue eyes were still fixed on mine. 'Boss,' he said (he never called me 'Sir'), that's OK by me. I'll play it your way.' What's more, I felt sure he would. Screwball never let me down nor, so far as I am aware, did Daddo-Langlois ever have another cross word with him."

An early morning raid by two Ju88s next day (**12 June**) was directed against Safi, 15 Bf109s providing cover and also strafing but very little damage occurred. Three of the Messerschmitts were claimed damaged by Flt Sgt Peter Terry of 185 Squadron, and Plt Off Percy Sewell and Sgt Ken Lusty of 601 Squadron. Plt Off Jerry Smith (BR175/UF-Z) was flying with Sewell as a section:

"Chased two RE2001s [*sic*] towards Sicily. Gave one a quick shot on a beam quarter attack, and another beam attack. Did not observe any hits. Percy damaged the other."

185 Squadron noted:

> "Two Ju88s dashed in and dropped some bombs on Safi about 7am. They took us by surprise, but one section was scrambled and chased the 88s. However, Messerschmitts interfered and the boys had to deal with them. Sgt Terry damaged one of the little jobs, but by the time the 109s beetled off home, the 88s were out of sight."

Fighters only comprised the next intrusion, eight Bf109s crossing the coast during mid-morning. 249 scrambled four Spitfires and a number of dogfights developed, with Sgt Beurling (BR170/C-25) opening his Malta account when he engaged a Messerschmitt:

> "I was in Red Section and Red is always first off, just an old air force custom, I guess. We had been aroused at four o'clock and at half past the bus was outside our sleeping quarters waiting to take us to the field. From then until about seven we sat around the dispersal hut, drinking hot chocolate and talking. Then the phone rang and Ops sang out, 'Scramble four aircraft!' and we were away, Daddy Longlegs [Daddo-Langlois], Berkeley-Hill, Jack Rae, and I – off the ground in a few seconds over the minute. Almost as soon as we were airborne the orders came over the R/T: 'Gain angels as quickly as possible!' We did. Those four Spitfires went up the big hill together like dingbats and were at 18,000 feet in something better than ten minutes. There, Ops came in again: 'Party of 15 enemy aircraft coming in from Zonqor Point at 21,000 to 22,000 feet. No big jobs.'
>
> "We flew line abreast, the better to watch each other's tails. The Jerries came down to the attack, peeling off in pairs and diving, after sending down one lone Messerschmitt as decoy. Then the mêlée started. The Messerschmitts split us and Berkeley-Hill and I found ourselves alone. About four Jerries jumped B-H and as they did I pulled up sharply under one and blew his tail off. He went down vertically and that was the last I saw of him. Nobody saw him hit the deck, but B-H had seen my burst hit, so I was credited with a damaged. Meanwhile, Jack Rae had tangled with another Hun and pumped lead into him. Daddy Longlegs had tried a head-on attack on a Messerschmitt and picked up a few bullet holes in his own wings for his trouble. We were all milling around like madmen, the four of us trying to keep our own and each other's tail clean and at the same time manoeuvre Jerries into our sights. After about ten minutes the visitors decided to call the whole thing off, put their noses down and high-tailed towards Sicily. In those brief moments of combat I had proved, to myself, that I had the stuff to match flying and shooting with the gentlemen from Sicily. That is what I wanted to find out in a hurry. As we walked away from our Spits, Daddy Longlegs grinned at me and said: 'Good show, Beurling!' I felt swell."

Wt Off Rae (BR254/X-G) was also credited with a damaged, whereas Flg Off Daddo-Langlois (BR107/C-22) had met three Messerschmitts alone and his aircraft was hit in the tail, wings and fuselage, although he was able to fly it back to base.

There was barely any enemy activity over Malta during the next two days – the Axis air forces being engaged in operations against a convoy (WS19Z) which had left the UK with the intention of resupplying the besieged garrison. It passed through the Straits of Gibraltar in the early hours of 12 June, where it picked up a strong naval escort which included *Eagle* and *Argus*; on this occasion the carriers were not ferrying Spitfires but had embarked Sea Hurricanes and Fulmars for the defence of the convoy, now codenamed GM4. As the convoy steadily progressed towards Malta, its fighter escort was involved in many aerial encounters with Axis reconnaissance aircraft, Sicily-based bombers and Italian warships though not without heavy cost in fighters and ships: three merchantmen were sunk before Malta-based Spitfires were able to provide cover. Simultaneous with this desperate effort to supply the island from the west, another convoy (MW11) comprising 11 merchantmen had set sail from Alexandria, Port Said and Haifa, escorted by warships of the Royal Navy's Mediterranean Fleet, but the heavy losses suffered en route resulted in the survivors turning back[62]. However, with the imminent arrival at Malta of the three surviving freighters from WS19Z, 69 Squadron's Sgt Colquhoun was ordered to fly (in BP908) to Taranto to check on the state of the Italian fleet. He brought back photographic evidence of the presence of three battleships, four cruisers, the seaplane carrier *Giuseppe Miraglia*, 20 destroyers, the liner *Gradisca* and 14 smaller vessels. At the seaplane base were identified 13 Z501s, 20 Z506Bs and four Ro43 floatplanes, while on the slipway ashore were nine more Ro43s, one Z506B, two Z501s and a large flyingboat identified as one of the new Luftwaffe six-engined Blohm & Voss Bv222s. 185's diarist reported on the prevailing situation and mood:

"Today [**14 June**] was a quiet day. We only had two scrambles. One plot was an Italian effort, which turned back. The other was a Baltimore on delivery from the Middle East. There have been a lot of various aircraft coming to the island during the last few days. Baltimores, Marylands, Wimpys and Beaufighters have been arriving at Luqa to do escort work for the convoy, which is expected in at any time now. The Luqa boys are all fitting long-range tanks on to their Spitfires to do long-range protective cover over the convoy. In fact, everyone is looking forward to the promise of some large scale trouble with the Jerries and Italians."

To enable the Spitfires to have sufficient endurance to provide adequate cover for the incoming ships, they were fitted with locally modified Hurricane overload fuel tanks, two of these jettisonable tanks being slung beneath the central fuselage, which allowed for a maximum 60 minutes patrolling over the convoy at this range. At 1040 on **15 June**, the first four long-range Spitfires – flown by Flt Lt Winfield, Plt Off Goldsmith (MK-J), and Flt Sgts Ken Evans (BR496) and Gord Farquharson of 126 Squadron – arrived over the convoy. In the event, these arrived too late to catch Ju88s reported in the area, but an assortment of other machines came their way. Goldsmith had an exciting time:

"Long-range job. Arrived on convoy 160 miles west of Malta. Found ship burning and sinking. Passed two Italian cruisers on way. Found a three-engined Dago floatplane on deck, heading for Pantelleria. Gave him a three-seconds burst and he went into the sea. Then attacked a BR20 at 6,000 feet and set him on fire with a three-seconds burst from port cannon, and he went in, a flamer. Two chutes. On the way home met a MC200 and had a good scrap with him. Left him streaming oil."

The 'three-engined' floatplane was undoubtedly a twin-engined RS14 (144-5/MM35391) of 144^Squadriglia from Stagnone di Marsla, flown by Ten Antonio Carnielli, which had taken off at 0825 to relieve another RS14 shadower; all aboard perished. The bombers encountered were, in fact, part of a formation of nine SM84s from 4°Gruppo, which were engaged in a high level attack on the convoy, hits being claimed on two steamers. Although Goldsmith appears to have claimed one as his success alone, he was apparently credited with a shared victory with Evans, while Winfield also submitted a claim for a BR20 and Farquharson for one damaged. Two of the Savoias indeed fell to the Spitfires, M.llo Aldo Pinna and his crew in MM22504 perishing, whilst three of the crew of MM23986 (flown by the Gruppo commander Magg Gastone Valentini) baled out into the sea, from where they were later rescued. On board the latter aircraft a stowaway had been discovered – a technical officer,

Sottoten Achille Zezon, who had a passion for flying. When the Spitfires attacked, Zezon had manned one of the guns but was killed before the bomber crashed into the sea. Valentini and the two other survivors subsequently claimed that Zezon had shot down two of the attackers before his death, one of which allegedly crashed into the sea in flames. In the heat of battle it seems likely the crew had confused Pinna's falling aircraft with that of a Spitfire; Zezon was posthumously awarded a *Medaglia d'Oro*. During the return flight to Malta, Goldsmith encountered a fighter, which he identified as an MC200 – probably an aircraft of 54°Stormo from Pantelleria – and engaged in a brief fight; he left it streaming oil and apparently claimed its destruction, but there is no evidence of such a loss.

With the departure of the Spitfires, and before their reliefs had arrived, 11 Ju88s of I/KG54 swept in at 1120, attacking in three waves. Their target was the freighter that had been disabled by a near miss. She was abandoned and her crew rescued by two destroyers. Activity over the convoy increased in the late morning, when a strike force from Malta at last arrived to engage the Italian cruisers. Only two serviceable Beaufort torpedo-bombers with very inexperienced crews were available, together with four vulnerable torpedo-armed Royal Navy Albacore biplanes. The small formation set out with the benefit of an escort of two Beaufighters and 16 Spitfires provided by 249 Squadron *sans* long-range tanks, and therefore had insufficient range and endurance to escort them the whole way. Despite an attack by two Macchis, the small strike force survived and all returned safely to Malta.

Two more Beaufighters headed for the convoy at 1105, although they were driven off by hostile twin-engined aircraft. They were immediately followed by four Spitfires from 601 Squadron. As these were approaching the end of their stint, the next raid developed. Under the leadership of Cap Giuseppe Cenni, ten Ju87s of 102°Gruppo B'aT appeared on the scene, covered by 25 MC202s from 155°Gruppo CT. On sighting the convoy, the Italian Stuka crews dived to 1,200 feet to release their bombs as the defending Spitfires attacked. Plt Off Bruce Ingram (UF-M) and Sgt Allen-Rowlandson jointly claimed one shot down, while Wt Off Fred Belcher claimed damage to one of the escorts, which he identified as a Bf109. The extra fuel expended during these actions proved too much for Allen-Rowlandson's aircraft and during the return flight to Malta he was forced to bale out of BR360 as the engine spluttered; he floated down into the sea some 20 miles short of the island. Help was soon on its way, however, and within the hour he was picked up by *HSL128*, while a section from 603 Squadron provided cover. A second flight of four Spitfires from 601 Squadron, led by 2/Lt Bartleman, arrived half an hour after the first and these too became involved with the Stukas. When the Ju87s were spotted below, Bartleman ordered his pilots to jettison their long-range tanks and led them down to attack in line astern:

> "I closed in to 100 yards on the rear aircraft and saw strikes – it burst into flames and spun down. No chutes were seen. Saw second Ju87 ahead and opened fire, seeing pieces fly off, when I was jolted by a fearful noise – instinctively broke away from contact, and saw several 109s. Headed back for Malta."

The damage to his Spitfire (UF-G) was minor, just one bullet through the tailplane. The South African's first victim was almost certainly the aircraft flown by Serg Magg Gastone Converso and 1°AvMot Enrico Boerci, which was shot down into the sea after the gunner had claimed damage to one attacking Spitfire; the crew were rescued. Plt Off Jerry Smith (BR175/UF-Z) went through the heavy AA barrage to fire at one Ju87:

> "What a day! Patrolled for 15 minutes, then Ju87s and Messerschmitts arrived. I went

through flak after a Ju87 and saw huge pieces breaking off. Had a dogfight with a 109 and it left trailing smoke, heading for Pantelleria. Was hit by flak but got back a few minutes before engine would have packed in."

Of the other pilots, Flg Off Hone (UF-P) was unable to jettison his supplementary fuel tanks and was chased away by the fighters before he had a chance to come to grips with the dive-bombers. Towards the end of this action a third flight of 601 Squadron arrived, Plt Off Clyde Scollan claiming one Stuka probably destroyed, but 21-year-old New Zealander Sgt Jack McConnell from Auckland was shot down and killed by the escorting Macchis; his aircraft (BR306) was seen gliding down, followed by a big splash as it crashed into the sea, taking its pilot down with it. In addition to the Stuka shot down, three others were badly hit by the fighters during this action, and one was forced to ditch about three miles south-east of Pantelleria, the crew of which were seen clinging to the tail section of the sinking aircraft by M.llo Gino Gamberini. Although he dropped his dinghy to the struggling men, neither M.llo Antonio Marchetti (the pilot) nor AvScMot Luigi Grosso, were subsequently found by rescue craft. The aircraft flown by Cap Aldo Stringa and M.llo Zaccaria Perozzi were both very badly damaged but managed to regain their base at Chinisia; two further Ju87s were damaged by AA fire. Somewhat optimistically, the returning crews claimed one auxiliary cruiser and two merchant vessels sunk, but they had not in reality hit anything. Meanwhile, the escorting Macchi pilots claimed four of the Spitfires shot down and another as probably destroyed, without loss. Cap Carlo Miani was credited with one and one probable; Magg Fanali (the Gruppo commander) and Sottoten Tullio Martinelli, one each, while M.llo Remo Zedda and M.llo Roberto Gaucci jointly claimed another.

At 1410, another four Spitfires from 126 Squadron had arrived over the convoy and during their patrol encountered a number of fighters, which they identified as Bf109s. One was claimed shot down by Flt Sgt Schade (Spitfire/F):

"Patrolled convoy 140 miles out to sea. Was attacked by three Me109s. Did head-on attack. Messerschmitt spun down. There was a big splash in the sea. Confident Messerschmitt went in."

Schade now had five victories plus three probables to his credit in quick time. Shortly thereafter, another quartet from the same unit – Flt Lts Bailey and Rowe, Plt Offs Freddie Thomas and Wally Wallace – also saw action when they encountered a Z506B (1-288) of 288^Squadriglia. This floatplane had taken off at 1505 on a reconnaissance but reported being attacked by "ten Hurricanes"; Sottoten Ugo Cusmano's crew claimed one of the attacking fighters shot down with a second probably so, but the burning Cant was obliged to crash-land on the sea ten miles from Linosa, turning on its side. Despite the Spitfire pilots strafing the machine until it sank, Cusmano and his crew survived their ordeal and were subsequently rescued by a motor fishing boat from Lampedusa.

The early evening attacks were undertaken by the Luftwaffe. Nine Ju88s of KüFlGr606 and escorting Bf109s were met by a 601 Squadron section at 1800. Plt Off Jerry Smith (BR381), on his second sortie of the day, again found himself in the thick of the action:

"Over convoy for an hour when Ju88s and Me109s bombed it. Damaged an 88, shot at a 109 and shot down another 88. Its rear gunner shot me up and as I headed back for convoy, it caught fire. I baled out and was picked up in 15 minutes by the destroyer *Blankney*."

Meanwhile, Flg Off Hone also attacked the Ju88s and succeeded in shooting-up one bomber, causing the starboard engine to catch fire. He then fired at three others before being intercepted by one of the escort. By now short of fuel, he put BR122/2-O into a dive only to have the windscreen covered in oil when a seal burst. So steep was the dive that he blacked-out, recovering at 3,000 feet to find himself going up! Although he had great difficulty in seeing through the windscreen, he successfully landed at Takali to discover that both wings of the aircraft were wrinkled from the force of the pullout.

At 1800, four 249 Squadron Spitfires were scrambled, followed by four more from 185 Squadron ten minutes later, and another four from this latter unit at 1840. The first quartet intercepted three Z1007bis and Bf109s over the convoy – still 30 miles out – south-west of Gozo. Flt Sgt Williams (BR107/C-22) claimed a Messerschmitt damaged and Flg Off John Smith (C-26) a Cant damaged. Plt Off Linton (BR364) experienced an oil leak, which obscured his forward vision:

"As I was returning to base, wondering what had happened to my No.2, I suddenly saw Ju87s on either side of me, and only a few yards away, going in the opposite direction! I then realised I was in the final moments of flying straight through the flight path of returning bombers, with their gunners loosing off at me for all they were worth."[63]

Fortunately for Linton the German gunners were almost as startled as he was, and their aim was not accurate. Once on the ground, he examined his Spitfire for damage:

"Several shells had entered the fuselage behind me, and one had passed through the small space between the upper and lower petrol tanks, immediately in front of the cockpit. I wondered what must have been the thoughts of the German crews as they saw a Spitfire closing on their flight path, flying straight through it, and neither firing nor turning to engage."[64]

Slim Yarra detailed 185's adventures:

"F/Lt West [GL-J] led a section of four out to the convoy, which had magically appeared on the horizon. During the patrol some Ju88s appeared and prepared to lay a few eggs. However, the boys got right amongst the Jerries, much to the consternation of the Ju88 pilots, most of whom ditched their bombs in the sea. F/Lt West destroyed a Me109 who was trying to spoil our boys' fun, and then dashed into the 88s and probably destroyed one of the big jobs. F/Sgt Sim was beetling along after an 88 who was making rapidly for home. He was having some difficulty in catching the 88 when he noticed another one flying in formation with him. The pilot in the 88, noticing the evil look on F/Sgt Sim's face, immediately buzzed off, hotly pursued by Simmie, who proceeded to shoot great pieces off the enemy bomber. However, the aforementioned pieces kept bouncing off Sim's Spitfire and tore some holes in various places, but did not prevent the destruction of the 88 or the return of Sim. P/O Stenborg also got mixed up in the fun and damaged two 88s."

Plt Off Stenborg (BR375/GL-A) also claimed a Bf109 shot down in addition to the two Ju88s damaged, while Plt Off Jimmy James (GL-K), now recovered from his wounds, fired at two bombers but made no claims. Flt Sgt Sim had to belly-land BR126/GL-O at Luqa following a glycol leak, damaging the aircraft beyond repair. Yarra continued:

"P/O Broad [GL-R] took four out to relieve F/Lt West's boys and ran into the end of the scrap. Broad destroyed a Me109 after a hectic few minutes. P/O Baril [BR353/GL-D] was shot down by another 109, but he baled out and was picked up by one of the escorting destroyers. The excitement was continued for the rest of the day and finished off with a very nice forced-landing on the aerodrome by Sgt Tony Drew, whose motor failed in the circuit."

Plt Off Paul Baril, who was shot down by Ltn Fritz Dinger of 4/JG53 (his 15th victory), was rescued by *Blankney*, the same destroyer that had picked up Plt Off Jerry Smith earlier in the day. 603 Squadron, which had been putting up patrols all day, failed to make contact with the enemy during any of its sorties. Sqn Ldr Douglas-Hamilton, flying one of the final sorties of the day, noted:

"I looked down and saw many little ships rippling their way through the water. There were no Huns about, and everything looked so peaceful, it was hard to believe that those ships had been through such hell earlier that day and during the whole of the previous day. Only telltale streaks of oil on the water behind some ships indicated that all of their journey might not have been so uneventful as it then appeared. In fact, there was not a ship that had not had several near-misses, and many had been damaged."

KüFlGr606's Ju88s again appeared over the convoy with the last light of this hectic and traumatic day, a dozen attacking from out of the setting sun; three or four bombs fell within 30 feet of one of the freighters but caused no serious damage. A pair of 601 Squadron Spitfires from the earlier patrol were still over the convoy, Plt Off Ingram (UF-G) catching one of the bombers and claiming it shot down. The final interception of the day occurred in the late evening when four Spitfires took off at 2105 – Plt Offs Linton (BR111/C-19), Frank Jones (BR119/1-C) and Watts (BR254/X-G) led by Flt Lt Lucas (BR377/C-41) – to intercept about a dozen KGr806 Ju88s heading for the ships, apparently relying on the darkening sky to protect them. Control ordered the Spitfires to orbit the convoy at 17,000 feet until the bombers came within range, but with dusk rapidly approaching Lucas realised the raiders would not be seen against the sea and took his section down to lower levels. The bombers were consequently sighted against the light western sky, as he later recalled:

"The Ju88s were flying straight and level in quite tight boxes of four aircraft each. They hadn't seen us coming out of the darkening eastern sky. I gave the instruction. Lint and Watty would take the starboard box, and Jonesie and I the one to port. Then both pairs would have a go at the centre formation if we could. Our assault came off to a 'T'. The rear gunners never saw us as we attacked upwards from underneath, against the dark waters below. It was difficult to see the results, but Watty and I reckoned that we had shared an 88 between us, Jonesie got another – a flamer – while Lint and I felt we had severely damaged an additional 88 apiece."

There seems little doubt that two of the bombers, M7+HL and M7+FK, commanded by Uffz Heinz Kaufmann and Oblt Kurt Kehrer (the Staffelkapitän) respectively, were shot down in this action. From a third aircraft, the air gunner (Uffz Heinrich Kalbfeld) baled out into the sea and was lost. Apparently he had panicked and abandoned his aircraft when it came under attack.

Malta had lost three Spitfires and one pilot defending the convoy. Although the Spitfire pilots included five Bf109s in their mixed bag of 16 claims during the day's actions, it seems that only one Messerschmitt was lost, Fw Otto Schmidt of 5/JG53 ditching his aircraft (7284) in to the sea off the Sicilian coast, apparently the result of engine failure possibly due to combat damage; he was later rescued unharmed. Nonetheless, the Spitfires had done their job well – not one merchant ship or escorting warship had been hit while they were providing cover, and a total of 170 sorties had been flown. Although 601 Squadron bore most of the brunt of the action, other units were in the air as much; 603 Squadron, for example, undertook over 40 sorties yet spotted only one enemy aircraft all day – a lone Ju88 in the distance, and that too far away for an interception. 126 Squadron, on the other hand, flew 42 sorties, its pilots claiming six aircraft shot down.

As the two surviving merchant vessels made for Grand Harbour, disaster overtook the ill-fated convoy. With salvation so close, the escort now blundered into a newly laid minefield. Three destroyers were damaged, one sinking. One of the freighters also sustained damage but was able to gain the dubious sanctuary offered by Grand Harbour, where both at once began unloading under cover of a smoke screen. The cargo was handled by a combined force of civilians and service personnel, including 2,500 soldiers. Whilst the supplies delivered were inadequate to replenish the island's larders – with fuel and food so desperately short – every ounce of the 15,000 tons (which included ammunition and flour) was more than welcome. The following morning, when the destroyer *Blankney* disgorged its human cargo plucked from the sea, the two rescued pilots, Plt Offs Baril and Smith, made their way back to their respective units. Their return caused welcome surprise, for both were feared lost. Of Jerry Smith's return, Flt Lt Barnham noted:

"A few minutes ago Smith, whom we thought was dead, walked in the lounge here. He's been telling us that, over the convoy, he shot down an 88 but his own engine was set on fire. After baling out he was picked up by a destroyer. He's been describing how the deck of his destroyer was already crowded with merchant ship survivors, how they stood as Ju87s and 88s dived on them."

Barnham, his depression deepening, continued:

"All this makes me realise how much a fighter pilot's life is abstracted from the horrors of war: courageous McConnell, for instance, no horror in his passing – someone saw what they thought was a bird, but no – it had Spitfire's wings as it glided towards the water – then a splash far below. When I consider what the Navy and the Merchant Navy have faced I am utterly ashamed of feeling so utterly tired and burnt out. Would it be different if I'd had any successes in the last two days? If I had met enemy planes over the convoy and shot some down I might have felt entitled to lead all these keen men so full of energy. I am flight commander in name only. I have never possessed the offensive spirit; in combat I have always erred on the side of caution. I have only one thing to be happy about – I have never lost a single pilot whom I have actually been leading in the air – but nobody cares about that. I've destroyed seven enemy planes, one of them shared, but inevitably it's an unofficial score, so it's not much good. And now I'm burnt out."

As a consequence of the disappointing results of the convoy operations the Governor, Lord Gort, advised the people of Malta:

"Some days ago, two convoys set out, one from the west and one from the east to bring supplies which we need to restore our situation. The western convoy had to endure severe and prolonged attacks, and only two merchant ships survived the ordeal. They are now in the Grand Harbour. These cargoes are essential for our future and well being. The eastern convoy, after suffering from prolonged and intense attacks by the Luftwaffe, was ordered to turn back. I must break to you what the arrival of only two ships means to us. For some time past we have been short of supplies and further privations lie ahead of us. We must stand on our own resources and every one of us must do everything in his or her power to conserve our stocks and to ensure that best use is made of all the available resources that remain to us. We must make all possible savings in every commodity and stock."

Four Ju88s and a dozen Bf109s crossed the coast at 0645 on **16 June**, but were engaged by some of the 20 Spitfires, which had been scrambled on their approach. One Messerschmitt was claimed shot down by 126 Squadron's Plt Off Goldsmith (1-D), whose run of success continued:

> "Had a dogfight with four 109s about 30 miles north; squirted at one and he dived into the sea. Was attacked head-on and hit in the port wing by cannon shell. Little damage. Then attacked another 109, but cannons contributed one round between them, so I came home smartly."

A further fighter sweep by a dozen Bf109s during mid-morning was also met by patrolling Spitfires, 20 of which had been ordered up, including eight of 185 Squadron. Flt Sgt Yarra (GL-J) also reported shooting down a Messerschmitt, but received a bullet through his engine in return; not so fortunate were two of his squadron colleagues, Flt Sgts Tex Vineyard and Jim MacNamara, both of whom were shot down in BR163 and BR230 respectively. Three Spitfires were claimed shot down by 6/JG53, two being credited to Fw Erich Paczia (his fifth and sixth victories) and the other to Ltn Hans-Jürgen von Möller (his ninth). Slim Yarra provided a report on the day's proceedings, including his own:

> "F/Sgt Yarra was scrambled with his section. The boys went up looking for Messerschmitts. They found what they were looking for – 12 of the genus Me109 coming down out of the sun. Four Spitfires broke in all directions, but as F/Sgt MacNamara turned into the 109s, a very spiteful one shot his controls away and Mac was forced to take to the silk, landing in the sea with a juicy splash, much to his disgust. F/Sgt Vineyard pulled out of a spiral dive and his seat promptly came loose and pinned him against the dashboard. Tex also had to bale out and had some trouble getting loose from his machine. One of the gremlins in the cockpit grabbed him by the foot and refused to let go for some time. However, Tex managed to trade his flying boot for his life and got away. He came floating down about three miles away from Mac, mouthing uncouth Texan oaths. All the boys then went up and did some air-sea rescue patrols until the boys were safely in. Tex was none the worse for the enforced swim, whereas Mac got off with minor bruises."

Six Bf109s approached Malta at 1600 next day (**17 June**), but two only crossed the coast and 11 patrolling Spitfires of 126 Squadron were ordered to engage; Plt Offs Goldsmith (1-I) and Dusty Miller jointly claimed one damaged, as noted by the former:

> "Wizard interception of 109s but a little low. Later, Dusty and I got in a good squirt at one, hitting him twice. We then chased another back to Sicily."

The lull in activity occasioned 185's Slim Yarra to comment:

> "Very quiet today. The 'yellow-noses' seem content to sit back and shoot a line to each other about their victory yesterday. Only one plot came on the board all day and that was too hard to catch, so we did not get a chance for revenge."

The Axis air forces across the water were conspicuous by their absence over the ensuing few days, most of the action during this period taking place far out to sea, with Malta's strike force of Beaufighters, Beauforts and the FAA biplanes engaging two convoys that had been sighted by Malta's reconnaissance aircraft; one plying off the Tunisian coast, the other steaming from the Gulf of Taranto. One German freighter from the Tunisian convoy was sunk by the Beauforts and two reconnaissance Ju88s were shot down by the protecting Beaufighters, but four Beauforts were lost. The actions were too distant for the Spitfires to provide assistance. Yarra continued:

> "The boys are still determined to give the Messerschmitts some sorrow for the way they beat us up on the 16th, but the Jerries seem determined not to give us the chance. They absolutely refuse to play with us these days. Today was a succession of scrambles without interception."

Round about this time – following the reduction of air raids and with sufficient stocks of Spitfires available – the squadrons were instructed to paint official identification markings on their aircraft. Hence, 185 Squadron now reverted to its original GL code letters and 601 to UF, but 126 Squadron was allocated MK (having previously been HA), and 249 Squadron the single letter T (whereas it had previously carried GN). 603 Squadron's marking became X rather than its original XT. It was generally assumed that someone in authority at Air HQ, with time on his hands, had made these momentous decisions.

Trade at last resumed for the Spitfires during the early evening of **21 June**, when a reconnaissance Ju88 with Bf109 escort approached the island at 1950. Four Spitfires from 185 Squadron were scrambled, Flt Sgt Yarra (BR387/GL-W) claiming two of the Messerschmitts shot down in addition to inflicting damage on the Ju88:

> "Engaged four Me109s – shot tail off one. Terry shot up. Chased 88 and damaged it – was attacked by three 109s and shot one down; beat it for home. Met Baltimore and escorted it back to the island."

Flt Sgt Terry's Spitfire (BR112/GL-X) was indeed shot-up and he crash-landed, fortunately without injury. Ten minutes later four more Spitfires went off, Flt Sgt Sim (GL-D) also claiming a Bf109 and a second damaged, but Flt Sgt Pop Conway's aircraft was hit; the New Zealander, who had apparently baled out on three previous occasions, decided to try to get his damaged aircraft (BR315/GL-T) back to Takali but was badly hurt in the crash-landing. Fellow New Zealander Wt Off Rae remembered the incident:

> "Suddenly we heard gunfire. It was the recognisable sound of 109 cannon fire, not ours, and then out of the blue haze above came a Spitfire obviously in very bad shape. We could see that a large piece of his tail unit was in tatters and would be extremely difficult to control. We watched anxiously, expecting the pilot to jump at any minute. In fact we were all trying to will him to jump. It was plain to see he would never be able to land and could lose control at any minute. 'Jump damn you, jump while you have enough height,' was the unspoken thought of all of us. But no, on he came, making a slow skidding highly unstable turn. Then unbelievably he put his wheels down and headed for our aerodrome, losing height rapidly. He tried to turn into wind but had no control, went sideways over our flight-path and crashed into the rocky bank on the other side. A large plume of smoke and dust billowed up as we watched in horror, convinced the pilot had been killed. There was a rush to the crash site. To the utter amazement of everyone, from underneath the smouldering wreckage came a voice: 'Get me out of here.' Incredibly he was in remarkably good shape although his back was injured and he subsequently returned to New Zealand. When asked why he didn't bale out instead of taking such a dreadful risk his reply was that he was sick of baling out. Someone must have been looking after him, for when his parachute was examined it was found to be full of shrapnel and pieces of cannon shells and would never have opened."

Despite claims for three Messerschmitts shot down in this action, just one aircraft (7351) of 5/JG53 crash-landed at Comiso in a damaged state. Yarra was upbeat in his report:

"A Flight did not scramble until 7pm, when two sections took off to intercept a 12-plus plot, which turned into a lone Ju88, protected by fighters, doing a recco. F/Sgt Yarra and his section managed to trick four Messerschmitts into coming down. The boys engaged and Yarra sat on one 109 and shot his tail off with a juicy crunch. F/Sgt Terry had a cannon shell explode over his cockpit and had to crash-land on the aerodrome. Yarra then spotted the poor old recco Ju88 and, madly gnashing his teeth, went down to attack. He managed to damage the Ju88, but was in turn attacked by Messerschmitts. A merry mix-up ensued in which one Me109 was shot down. Yarra returned with large pieces bitten out of his dinghy, but otherwise was quite OK. Thereby, the ignominious defeat of the 16th avenged. Not content, F/Sgt Bob Sim picked on a Me109 who was endeavouring to beat up a Spitfire. Sitting behind the Jerry, he poured a 12-seconds burst into the surprised 'Yellow-nose', causing it much trouble. The 109 could not do much about this unprecedented attack and now the pilot is probably learning to play 'Tuxedo Junction' on a harp, under the tutelage of a venerable old fellow with a long white beard and halo."

The only Axis aircraft to appear in Maltese skies on **22 June** were mainly on reconnaissance, the last being six Bf109s that swept across the coast just before 1930, although these did include a number of Jabo. Bombs fell on Hal Far, where the sole surviving Sea Gladiator (N5520) from the early days of the war was damaged by blast. Flt Lt Halford led four Spitfires of 185 Squadron to intercept, Flt Sgt Shorty Reid (BR126/GL-O) claiming one Messerschmitt shot down, with Flt Sgt Ferraby (BR293) pursuing another:

"I was diving very steeply down after a 109; didn't look at the speed, but the controls became very hard and it took all my strength to pull out without breaking something! I'd seen tracer going past me and that's what caused me to pull out. Probably just as well or I might have dived in. It was another Spit firing at me. Found out it was Halford."

Following the recent relatively quiet period, there was considerable action over and around the island on **23 June**, starting at first light when a transit aircraft arrived having been intercepted by two Macchis off Pantelleria; its air gunners claimed strikes on both attackers. Soon after, at 0820, a dozen Spitfires of 603 Squadron scrambled to engage six Bf109s, two of which were claimed damaged by Plt Offs Slade and Glen; one German fighter was reported to have been seen in the sea.

At 1750, a dozen more Spitfires (this time from 249 Squadron) with another eight from 603 Squadron, took off from Takali – BP980 crashing in the process, though without injury to the pilot – to intercept an incoming Italian raid of some size. This comprised three SM84s from the 4°Gruppo BT, escorted by 27 MC202s of 155°Gruppo CT, with indirect support provided by 18 RE2001s of 2°Gruppo Aut CT. The 249 Squadron aircraft went for the bombers – misidentified, as usual, as Z1007s – and Plt Off Charlie Lattimer fired at the one in the centre, reporting strikes, while Sgt Colin Baxter shot at two of the Reggianes, claiming that one appeared to shake, but 2°Gruppo surprisingly reported no notable action. Plt Off Brennan's Spitfire (C-38) was damaged by AA shrapnel as he approached the bombers but he was able to land safely. Despite these attacks, the Savoias released their bombs over the Takali area – although the airfield suffered little damage. Some of the wayward bombs fell on Mosta, where three persons were killed and six injured.

It was the 603 Squadron pilots who enjoyed greater success on this occasion, Plt Off Dicks-Sherwood and Flg Off McLeod (X-B) seeing a dozen Macchis west of Gozo, which they attacked in a dive from 29,000 feet. Dicks-Sherwood saw strikes on the fuselage and starboard wing of one, and McLeod reported strikes on the fuselage of another when he fired a burst at 100 yards. He gave chase to others and finally closed on one from 250 yards astern. After a long dogfight he put in a burst, closing to 25 yards, and claimed and the Macchi dived into the sea from 5,000 feet – reportedly "out of panic". Meanwhile, Plt Offs Newman and Ray Smith (BR128/3-W) alternately attacked one of the bombers, seeing strikes on the fuselage, pieces of debris fly off and the crew baling out. They were apparently credited with its destruction. Flt Sgt Parkinson (X-N), having been driven away from the bombers by the Macchis, spotted Newman apparently getting the worst of the exchange with the Macchi:

> "I sailed in and the other Spit sailed out. Made one three-quarter head-on attack. The Eyetie flicked and turned away, presenting his tail to me. I was about 200 feet behind with the bead dead on and firing. I saw something break off the fuselage and then the pilot baled out. His kite went into the sea. I circled the pilot whose chute had opened. He looked dead to me so I eventually flew straight at him and then decided he wasn't dead because he started to wave his arms frantically."

This was M.llo Aldo Buvoli of 360^Squadriglia, who baled out into the sea. It would seem that all three 603 Squadron pilots had attacked the same aircraft for it was the only loss reported by the Italians. Apart from the claims for the Macchis, Plt Offs Slade and Glen again each claimed Bf109s damaged. One Spitfire (BR385) was shot down, Flg Off Mitchell baling out into the sea from where he was picked up by *HSL128* within an hour, thereby becoming the ASR unit's 100th recovery. Five minutes behind the Takali Spitfires came the Hal Far-based aircraft of 185 Squadron. These also engaged fighters, Flt Sgt Vineyard (GL-Z) claiming damage to a Bf109. Two more of 185 Squadron's aircraft were scrambled at 1840 but failed to make contact. Flt Sgt MacNamara crashed on landing although his BR362 was not badly damaged. Yarra, the diarist, noted:

> "The boys had some fun with the Italians today. It was unfortunate that through bad controlling they missed the bombing force until it was on the way home. However, P/O King and F/Sgt Vineyard chased the 'Ice Cream Boys' halfway back to Sicily, and Tex got very nasty with a Messerschmitt who tried to interfere. These Italians are in for a rude shock one of these fine days. They have been getting away with too much lately. There was quite a little activity today. The squadron was scrambled twice and different sections kept going and coming all day. The boys got quite a few operational hours in but, apart from the episode of the Italians, nothing was encountered."

The Italian pilots claimed four Spitfires shot down and one more damaged. Sottoten Giuseppe Riccardi claimed one and two damaged, while the others were credited to Serg Magg Giovanni Del Fabbro, M.llo Gino Runci, and the missing Buvoli – his sixth victory – who survived his encounter with the Spitfires:

> "While I was flying in a tight turn, I heard the terrific noise of a burst fired from behind at close range; at that moment I saw the dark shape of an aircraft overtaking me very fast! I was sure my Macchi was hit! In fact, everything began to vibrate. All efforts to control the aircraft were in vain, and then sudden warmth came from under the cockpit. Fire! I unhooked the canopy and baled out! The smell of smoke, the noise of the engine

and the rush of air stopped, and there I was suspended from my parachute; below me the sea, above the confusion of the battle between the Macchis and the Spitfires. Coming down in the sea, I realised I was north of Gozo, the little Maltese island appearing through the sea mist. The sea was not very calm. From high above it had seemed perfect, but in the water the waves were running. I got out of my parachute, inflated my life jacket, but at every jolt I drank seawater! Gozo appeared very distant and the waves seemed to push me away. Ninety minutes passed and I was cold, tired and discouraged. Gozo seemed to be getting further and further away. Despite trying to remain still, lying supine on my back, I still continued to swallow seawater.

"Sunset was now near; I was cold and began to think it impossible that I could survive the night in the sea: I had a presentiment that these were my last hours of life! I tried to resign myself, but the instinct for life is strong, despite my inability to help myself. I thought of being devoured by sharks! While I was being assailed by these dark thoughts, I saw in the distance a sailing boat; it was steering towards me. Driven by a strong wind, it was by me in a few minutes. I could see a woman at the tiller and a man in a strange uniform in the prow waiting to pick me up. In a second I was hauled aboard and laid in the bottom of the boat. Almost exhausted, feelings of unease came over me. I was very cold and I vomited. The man and woman were silent; no word, no sign, only some piercing glances. Probably they had hoped to rescue an English pilot! They remained cold and impassive. Before we reached Gozo, to which the sailing boat was heading, I saw another boat, this time a naval motor launch. This came alongside and 'claimed' the survivor. It then headed direct to Gozo."

Flt Lt Laddie Lucas was promoted to command 249 Squadron on **24 June**, vice Sqn Ldr Grant, who was promoted to Wing Commander Flying at Takali. Daddo-Langlois was also promoted to take over Lucas's flight. Of this period, Lucas wrote:

"One June dawn, soon after I had taken over command of 249 Squadron, I was sitting in my Spitfire at Takali at advance readiness. It was barely light, but already our radars were picking up the enemy moving south from Sicily. I heard a heavy thump on the fuselage of my aircraft. Looking down I was astonished to see the Governor and C-in-C [newly arrived Lord Gort VC], by himself, red tabs and all. Whipping my flying helmet off, I made as if to get down from the cockpit only to be met with a brusque, 'Stay there, Squadron Leader, stay there, please.' Gort nipped up on the port wing of the Spitfire and held out his hand: 'Good morning, Squadron Leader, my name's Gort. I'm the Governor. I just called in to see the Squadron. I know how well 249 has been doing and I wanted to say so to you personally. Keep it up and good luck with the Squadron.' With that, he jumped down off the wing and started to talk to my groundcrew clustered around the blast pen. He knew their worth and, I gathered afterwards, saw to it that they understood it. Gort knew there was only one place from which to lead – from the front."

185 Squadron had only two scrambles, the first in the morning when two Bf109s were seen and not engaged. On the second scramble, again after marauding Messerschmitts, nothing was sighted. PRU pilot Sgt Colquhoun had a frightening experience when over Trapani, in BP915, while searching for a reported convoy. His engine started spluttering but he managed to nurse his ailing machine back to Luqa and landed virtually out of fuel. Due to a fault in the carburetor, the air intake was full of petrol.

Nothing much happened over Malta on **25 June** until the late evening, when nine Bf109s on a fighter sweep approached the coast at 2010. 249 Squadron was ordered to scramble a dozen Spitfires and these intercepted the Messerschmitts over Gozo. Plt

Off Owen Berkeley-Hill attacked a section of five, and grey smoke poured from the fuselage of one which turned over and dived away; it was seen by Sgt Gerry de Nancrède to stream coolant and Berkeley-Hill was credited with its probable destruction. Plt Off Lattimer (BR108) attacked another from 100 yards astern, which poured black smoke and apparently went down out of control, then fired on a second from quarter astern and slightly below. He reported that "it blew up in the air". This was undoubtedly an aircraft (7259) from 4/JG53 that crashed in the sea near Gozo, from which the unidentified pilot was later rescued by an ASR craft from Sicily. Flt Sgt Maurice Tomkins was not so fortunate; he endeavoured to nurse his damaged Spitfire (BR382) back to Takali, as recalled by Sgt Beurling:

"Tommy Tomkins' Spit was pretty badly shot-up and he was hit in the engine and radiator. He pulled out of the mix-up and tried to make Takali, instead of going over on his back and baling. At that he nearly made it. He came in over the island streaming glycol and trying his damnedest to stretch his glide. He cut it too fine and suddenly flicked into a spin at 150 feet, bursting into flames as he hit the ground."

Army and RAF personnel rushed to the scene. The soldiers were first to arrive but were unable to undo the pilot's straps. By the time some pilots arrived, Tomkins – a 22-year-old from Weston-super-Mare in Somerset – had been terribly burned and blood was pouring from his ears. They got him out. He tried to talk, but seconds later died. His body was wrapped in the shrouds of his parachute to await collection. Another to witness the crash was Flt Sgt Parkinson:

"This afternoon I was sitting in my kite ready to take off when I heard a Spit in a power dive. Looked up and saw it coming down with glycol pouring out. The pilot made for the drome, did a circuit and started to fly across the drome at low speed. About halfway across, his motor cut dead. His wings started to wobble as he lost speed, heading straight for my kite. When almost directly overhead he tried to turn; he stalled at about 60 feet and spun. The aircraft immediately burst into flames. The fire tender was about to approach but the ammo started to go off so they stopped. The kite had nearly burnt itself out before they went near it. I went over to have a look and saw the pilot caught in amongst the wreckage. I could smell his clothes burning. It was Flt Sgt Tomkins, who sleeps next to me."

Not until 1800 next day (**26 June**) were six Spitfires of 126 and 601 Squadrons scrambled, followed shortly thereafter by ten of 603 Squadron and then by eight more from 185 Squadron some 20 minutes later. They were up to intercept a raid comprising five Z1007bis of 33°Gruppo, escorted by 29 MC202s of 155°Gruppo, and 18 RE2001s of 2°Gruppo Aut CT; the Reggianes were apparently misidentified by the RAF pilots as Bf109s. Two Macchis were claimed shot down, one by American Plt Off John Curry (BR301/UF-S) of 601 Squadron and the other by Flt Sgt Schade (MK-B) of 126 Squadron: "Attacked two Macchi 202s. Fired three-seconds burst at one, which went straight down, from 20 yards. Dogfought with the other for a bit, then came home." Sgt Calvin Taylor's aircraft was badly shot-up in return, the Canadian pilot being wounded in the leg by splinters. He managed to land with a dead engine. Plt Off Jerry Smith was on this scramble: "Scrambled to 24,000 feet. Had no oxygen and came down. Blacked out to 1,000 feet after staying up for better part of an hour."

The 603 Squadron pilots reported meeting Bf109s, Plt Off Glen claiming one of these shot down and then damaged a second before gaining strikes on one of the Cants. Another bomber was damaged by the combined fire of Plt Off Geoff Northcott and Flt Sgt John Pinney, while Flt Sgt Bill Irwin claimed strikes on one of the escorts, also identified as a Bf109. One Spitfire was slightly damaged in return when Sgt John

Stamble, having fired at a bomber, pranged on landing. He was unhurt. By the time 185 Squadron entered the fray the raiders had turned for home and only the escort were engaged; one of these – a Reggiane – was claimed shot down by Flt Lt Ronnie West (GL-J) for his eighth and last victory. Slim Yarra had much to say:

"Today was very quiet up till six o'clock when the Regia Aeronautica came over giving another practical example in the series 'The Bombing of Malta – High Level'. The squadron was scrambled and vainly chased the returning bombers halfway back to Sicily. F/Lt West managed to catch up with an RE2001 and severely battered him. The RE2001 finally gave up the ghost, and one more Italian pilot went off the list. Mussolini claimed six Spitfires shot down in this engagement and his official gen sheet stated 'none of our aircraft are missing'. So someone is lying and in the words of the prophet, 'it sure ain't us, boy.' The boys had one more scramble during the afternoon but just stooged about the sky getting some operational time up."

None of the RE2001s was lost, but M.llo Gino Runci's 378^Squadriglia Macchi was shot down, the pilot being seen to bale out; but not subsequently found. Two Spitfires were claimed by this unit, one each by Cap Carlo Miani and M.llo Remo Zedda, while two of the Reggiane pilots, Cap Salvatore Teia and Serg Magg Rino Ricci jointly claimed one more. Other pilots believed they had probably shot down one more and damaged two others. Although Luqa was the target, where an airman was killed when handling an unexploded bomb, nearby Pieta was also badly hit; here, ten civilians were killed and at least another nine seriously injured.

Four 249 Squadron Spitfires scrambled during the morning of **27 June**, led by Flt Lt Daddo-Langlois, and encountered a seaplane which he identified as a Do24 (which was in fact a red cross-marked Z506B) with an escort of a dozen MC202s provided by 51°Stormo. They were searching for Macchi pilot Runci shot down the previous day. The Spitfire pilots reported bouncing eight RE2001s some 15 miles south-east of Sicily, Wt Off Rae (BR377/T-K) claiming one shot down and a second probable, Flt Sgt Bob Middlemiss (BR184/C) one and a damaged, and Plt Off Verrall (BR295/T-H) yet another. Apparently the wreckage of three of the Italian fighters was seen in the water within 200 yards of each other. In return, a Spitfire was claimed by one of the Italian pilots. 185 Squadron provided a number of patrols:

"Most of the day's work consisted of protective patrols over minesweepers operating out from Grand Harbour. However, Johnny Sherlock, in his inimitable style, managed to get mixed up with four Messerschmitts. Johnny squirted, the Messerschmitts squirted, the ack-ack squirted, and nothing whatsoever was hit. Must have been good shooting on everyone's part!"

There was not much activity over Malta next day (**28 June**), only occasional reconnaissance aircraft crossing the coast, none of which were intercepted. 185 Squadron scrambled a section when a hostile plot materialised. Yarra reported:

"Lots of negative scrambles today. F/O Stoop and his section careered madly out to sea in search of some enemy bombers, which were rumoured to be stooging about with evil designs on this beautiful island. However, much to the disgust of the section, the 'enemy bombers' developed into a tribe of Beauforts who were coming back after doing a lot of no good to the Italian navy."

After dark, however, the assault on the island's airfield continued. Just after midnight two Ju87s were observed near Mellieha Bay, one of them falling to a patrolling Beaufighter night fighter. Two black-painted Spitfires flown by Sqn Ldr Douglas-

Hamilton (believed to have been X-F) and Flt Lt Douglas (BR128/3-W) of 603 Squadron, and two Beaufighters, took off at 0455 on 29 June to intercept more raiders approaching the coast. Although they themselves were unsuccessful, the Spitfire pilots witnessed a Ju88 fall into the sea in flames, another victim of the Beaufighters. At 0855, four Spitfires, again from 603 Squadron, were sent off after eight Bf109s. Plt Off Barbour (BR320/X-K) was jumped by two and shot down by Oblt Gerhard Michalski of 4/JG53, his 35th victory. Barbour baled out into the sea, about five miles off the coast. *HSL128* sped to his rescue and within the hour he was back on dry land.

That evening a Hudson departed for Malta carrying five pilots to Gibraltar, four of whom – Flt Lt Peter Lovell, Flg Offs Bill Johnson, Les Watts and Jimmy Lambert – were to lead more Spitfires back to Malta. Also aboard the aircraft was Sqn Ldr Tony Lovell DFC[65] (no relation to 603 Squadron's Peter), a Battle of Britain veteran who had recently arrived at Malta from the Middle East. He had been advised that he was to take command of a new Spitfire squadron soon to be formed on the island, and had been summoned to Gibraltar for briefing. While at Gibraltar, Johnson, Watts and Lambert were advised of their immediate promotions to flight lieutenancy.

The only daylight action on **30 June** occurred when eight Spitfires of 249 Squadron were sent off to intercept a fighter sweep. After 40 minutes milling around without making contact, they were ordered to return. It was then that two aircraft identified as Bf109s bounced Plt Offs Berkeley-Hill and Lattimer, both of whom had their aircraft damaged in combat. Both force-landed at Takali, shaken but otherwise unhurt. Their opponents may, however, have been Macchis or Reggianes. After dark two Spitfires were scrambled, again flown by Sqn Ldr Douglas-Hamilton (X-F) and Flt Lt Douglas (BR128/3-W) of 603 Squadron, to join patrolling night fighter Beaufighters, when a reported 15-plus raid was plotted. Although Douglas sighted a pair of Ju87s, he was unable to engage. The Beaufighters similarly failed to make contact. Following this disappointing result, it was decided that night flying of Spitfires should cease.

At the end of the month the pilots and aircraft of 601 Squadron left Malta for the Middle East, most pilots flying Spitfires[66] fitted with long-range tanks, the remainder following by whatever air transport was available, including Wellingtons in transit. The island's defences had become sufficiently strong due to recent deliveries of Spitfires, coupled with a reduction in air raids, that it was decided that one squadron could be spared to strengthen the forces of the Desert Air Force, which was struggling to stem Rommel's advance towards Egypt. There were a few changes in personnel involved. Flt Lt Denis Barnham, despite being constantly ill, had emerged as the squadron's top scorer with four and one shared victories. Much to his elation he left the island for the UK, tour-expired[67]. Another to return to the UK was fellow flight commander Flt Lt Hugh Parry, who similarly had been ill for most of his stay at Malta[68]. There was some shuffling of pilots at this time, Plt Off Llewellyn joining 601 from 126, while Plt Off Jerry Smith was posted from 601 to 126 in exchange. Smith recorded his satisfaction with the change: "126 are a damned good squadron and I'm not sorry to stay, although the old 601 gang were a bloody good lot!"

Among those advised that they would be leaving as soon as air transport was available, was 603 Squadron's Plt Off Barnfather, who was apparently still suffering the after effects of his air collision the previous month. His last flight was made on 23 June, as noted in his logbook: "Spitfire Code S: Practice Flying. Stood down owing to twitch sickness still persisting."

According to figures issued by Air HQ, Malta's fighter pilots had been credited with 64 victories during the month (including those by the night fighter Beaufighters), with 15 probables and at least 57 damaged. Losses included a dozen Spitfires, but only two pilots. The four photo-reconnaissance Spitfires of 69 Squadron (BP915 having joined the unit during the month, its pilot Flt Sgt Jo Dalley being retained by the unit) had clocked 56 far-ranging sorties (183 flying hours), all without loss. A number of decorations and promotions had been announced for the fighter pilots during the month, including: a Bar to DFC for Sqn Ldr Sailor Barton, who now handed over command of 126 Squadron to promoted Sqn Ldr Phil Winfield; and DFCs to Plt Offs Tim Goldsmith DFM, John Bisley and Mike Graves, all of the same unit. Within 249 Squadron the new CO, Sqn Ldr Laddie Lucas, was awarded a DFC. He was naturally delighted and promptly wrote to his mother[69]:

> "The big news since I last wrote is that the AOC Malta recommended me for the DFC, and that his recommendation was granted. I question really whether I was ever so pleased in all my life. Colours at Stowe, a 'Blue' at Cambridge, a job on the *Express*, winning the Boys Golf Championship at Carnoustie – all these things gave inexpressible satisfaction. But I believe this DFC has pleased me more than any of these achievements. For I can say with truth that I've longed to get it and worked and tried like the devil to win it."

603 Squadron's Flt Sgt Johnny Hurst was commissioned and awarded the DFC. Meanwhile, Flt Lt Buck McNair DFC, who left 249 Squadron on completion of his tour, handed over his flight to Flt Lt Raoul Daddo-Langlois. 185 Squadron also received a new commander when Sqn Ldr Bill New took over from Sqn Ldr Keith Lawrence, while Flt Lt Johnny Plagis received a Bar to his DFC. With the imminent departure of Flt Lt Ronnie West, who was also tour-expired, John Halford was promoted to lead his flight.

The Regia Aeronautica was at this time reinforcing its Sicilian contingent and the HQ flight of 51°Stormo CT (the parent unit of the 155°Gruppo CT) arrived at Gela, led by TenCol Aldo Remondino, with the unit's second Gruppo, the 20° under Magg Gino Callieri. This latter unit's three squadriglie were: 151^Squadriglia (Cap Furio Doglio Niclot); 352^Squadriglia (Cap Luigi Borgogno); and 353^Squadriglia (Cap Riccardo Roveda). The pilots brought with them 36 brand new MC202s, with which they were extremely keen to enter the fray. Cap Doglio Niclot, at 34-years of age, was rather old for a fighter pilot, but was a highly skilful and talented former test pilot. One of his pilots, Ronaldo Scaroni, recalled:

> "We were certain that he could outfly anyone in the RAF. It was clear not only from the number of new planes flying in, but also from the calibre of the air crews, that the High Command was serious about winning, and that was a big boost to everyone's morale. We knew we had the English badly outnumbered and we didn't see how we could possibly lose. There was a feeling that the whole thing would be over by the end of the summer at the latest. Our morale could not have been any better. We were certain we were going to crush Malta and win the war. I can remember listening to Rome radio every night, hearing about yet another Axis victory. Whether it was us, the Germans or the Japanese, we were winning everywhere. It was uncanny. Maybe even sooner. I'm afraid we badly underestimated the determination of the RAF pilots to hold out, no matter what."[70]

Soon after their arrival at Gela, however, 51°Stormo pilots encountered the vibration phenomenon caused by compressibility when diving away from, or after, Spitfires. This was to plague them in coming weeks, and was first manifested when Cap Carlo Miani suffered such violent vibration that he believed his Macchi had been critically hit in the tail. He baled out over the Sicilian coast, ending up in Scicli hospital as a result.

At this time, Z1007bis bombers also began arriving to replace the BR20Ms of 88°Gruppo BT. The relatively quiet spell that followed the arrival of the June convoy did not last long. The Regia Aeronautica was now planning a resumption of activities to be launched as the second major Italian assault against Malta, and due to commence on the first day of the new month. Even more daunting for the defenders of Malta was the arrival of more Luftwaffe units. To support their allies, the Germans had also taken steps to reinforce Fliegerkorps II in Sicily, two bomber Gruppen (II and III/KG77) arriving from France, together with a fighter Gruppe, I/JG77, from the Eastern Front. Commanded by Hptm Heinz Bär, credited with 113 victories, the three Staffeln of I/JG77 boasted a sprinkling of top aces including 3 Staffelkapitän Oblt Fritz Geisshardt (82 victories), 1 Staffelkapitän Oblt Siegfried Freytag (49) and Ltn Günther Hannak (41). One of the NCO pilots, Uffz Horst Schlick of 1 Staffel, wrote:

> "Our comrades from JG53 welcomed us in a particularly warm manner, because the battle over Malta had already torn considerable holes among the pilots – Spitfires and flak were responsible for this. But the ones who were especially delighted to see us were the fighting men of KG77, who carted their bombs every day to Valetta, Marsa Scirocco [Marsaxlokk] and Venezia [Takali], and many times came back shot to pieces – we were all able to sing a little song together. With a few words, Maltzahn introduced us personally to the battle scene. The technical staff sleep in the main building and we pilots were in the second officers' quarters in the town of Comiso, which was five kilometres away and numbered about 10,000 inhabitants. I sleep in a room with Sauer and Engels. I have my own plane, with the number '3'."

This confident, experienced unit – with in excess of 630 accredited air victories – would soon prove to be a most dangerous adversary for Malta's Spitfires.

CHAPTER VI

BLOODY JULY

July 1942

The afternoon of **1 July** saw the new offensive open when ten of 20°Gruppo's MC202s, led by Cap Luigi Borgogno, escorted a Ju88 over the Maltese airfields at 1450, apparently on a reconnaissance. 5/JG53 also participated in the escort, for at 1504 Obfw Herbert Rollwage claimed a Spitfire shot down (his 20th victory) over St Paul's Bay, the Luftwaffe's only claim of the day. The Italians also reported engaging Spitfires, Borgogno claiming one shot down, while other pilots claimed four damaged. Their opponents were a half a dozen Spitfires of 185 Squadron's B Flight led by Flt Lt Halford (BR387), which soon became engaged with the escort. Slim Yarra wrote:

"B Flight found lots of fun waiting for them. The Italians came in again and the whole flight was waiting for them. F/Sgt Reid [BR294/GL-E] destroyed a Me109 and damaged another. This brings Shorty's score to four destroyed, which is a very good performance on the part of the 'Kid'. Johnny Sherlock [BP876] beat up a Me109 and came back curling his moustache with a look of triumph on his handsome face. Hal Halford also damaged a Me109, very severely, which rather discouraged the Jerry pilot therein, while F/O Charney damaged a Me109 and a Macchi 202. F/Sgt Tubby Mahar [BR292] also managed to get amongst the enemy and also damaged a Macchi 202. The combined efforts of these boys must have produced a few grey hairs in our old pal Joe Kesselring's hair."

Flg Off Charney's aircraft (BR380/GL-R) was hit, causing him to crash-land at Hal Far. Plt Off David Kent's Spitfire also sustained damage during this action and he, too, had to force-land at Hal Far on return. Jo Sherlock considered the IO's assessment of his initial claim as somewhat unjust:

"I recollect turning into a couple of Messerschmitts as they turned in to attack my section. For some reason the leader broke too soon and I got in a lucky deflection shot on his port wing and big chunks flew off. The plane turned over and went straight down, partly on its back. I was involved in further chasing around with his No.2 and other 109s and could not see what happened to the one I hit. There was no doubt, in my mind, that not only was he badly hit but also the pilot had been hit. After I landed I reported that I had shot down a 109 but admitted I had not seen it go in. When questioned by our IO about the plane being classed as damaged I became a little sarcastic and suggested that it could not fly back to Sicily with half a wing and a dead pilot. I started to walk away when Ken Charney came in, having landed after I did, his plane being badly shot up. At this time he asked who had shot the port wing off a 109. I told him I had and asked him if he had seen it go in. He stated he was about 300 feet behind a Messerschmitt, firing when another came straight down, passing between him and the plane he was shooting at. This plane was making no recovery efforts, the left wing was mostly missing and the pilot was slumped forward. It was around 5,000 feet or less, but Ken did not see it go in as he continued firing at the 109 ahead of him. The IO mentioned he might raise my claim to probable, and I told him to hell with the claim."

However, it would seem that Flt Lt Halford's claim was upheld and he was credited with one destroyed. The next engagement occurred just after 1845 when radar showed approximately 30 aircraft approaching the island, at least two of which were reported as BR20s; they were in fact two SM84bis of 4°Gruppo BT, their crews briefed to bomb Takali. Escort was provided by 22 Macchis led by TenCol Remondino, who reported being intercepted by 16 Spitfires before the island was reached. Remondino personally claimed one shot down, while other 51°Stormo pilots reported hits on six more. Behind this force came three more SM84bis with an even larger escort comprising 48 more Macchis from 51°Stormo, plus 15 RE2001s of 2°Gruppo Aut CT. During the ensuing engagement seven Spitfires were claimed shot down by the Italians, MC202 pilots claiming four of these, one each by M.llo Ennio Tarantola (20°Gruppo CT), Sottoten Nicola Longano, M.llo Cesare Ferrazza and Serg Willy Malagola of 155°Gruppo CT; two more were credited to Reggiane pilots Sottoten Francesco Vichi and M.llo Luigi Jellici, and one to gunners aboard the bombers. Two Macchis were damaged – those flown by Ten Giobatta Caracciolo Carafa and Sottoten Longano – although both pilots regained Gela without further mishap. A dozen Spitfires of 603 Squadron, the pilots believing their opponents to have included Bf109s, had initially encountered this formation. One of these was claimed shot down by Flt Sgt Jim Ballantyne, who also reported strikes on a second before his aircraft (BR367/X-O) was shot down into the sea. Slightly wounded in the neck, the Canadian baled out and was picked up by *HSL107* after being sighted by his friend and fellow Canadian Plt Off McElroy:

"I found Jimmy Ballantyne floating in his dinghy 20 miles from home. I stayed with him for nearly an hour giving him cover, and knocked down [*sic* – chased away] a Me109 that came too close. Meanwhile, Jimmy was practicing back dives off his dinghy into the Mediterranean and thumbing his nose at me every time I went by."

Flg Off Mitchell also claimed a Messerschmitt probably destroyed, while Plt Off Hurst believed he had probably shot down one of the bombers; his own aircraft was hit by return fire and by the time he landed the engine had lost all its coolant. Plt Off Eddie Glazebrook damaged a Macchi, and a Reggiane was claimed by Flt Sgt Parkinson (BR184/X-C), as he later recalled:

"I found an RE2001 with finger trouble. Flew out to one side, recognised it as an RE2001, flew in behind, gave a long burst – saw strikes. The kite faltered, glycol pouring out and went into a vertical dive. A shower of enemy fighters attacked me so I did a wild dive and escaped them. Last I saw of the RE2001 it was still heading for the drink at about 5,000 or 6,000 feet."

As soon as the Spitfires landed following the departure of the Italian force, five more from 126 Squadron were scrambled, and engaged a reported six Bf109s, one of which was claimed destroyed by Plt Off Mike Graves (MK-P). So, on this first day of the new offensive, Axis claims for ten Spitfires destroyed, one probable and ten damaged had actually netted one Spitfire shot down and three damaged, whereas RAF claims for three fighters shot down, four probables and eight damaged had, in fact, resulted in damage to just two Macchis. However, the following day would prove a substantially more costly day to both sides as the fighting escalated.

Eight Spitfires of 185 Squadron scrambled at 0815 on **2 July**, followed by eight from 603 Squadron, on the approach of 18 Bf109s, four of which crossed the coast and were intercepted. Again Flt Sgt Shorty Reid (BR294/GL-E) was successful and claimed one shot down for his 5th victory, while Flg Off Mitchell reported strikes on a second, but Plt Off Hurst (BR184/X-C) failed to return. No one saw him go down except, perhaps, his victor – probably Ltn Fritz Dinger of 4/JG53 (his 16th victory), who claimed a Spitfire about ten miles north-east of Valetta. 24-year-old Johnny Hurst, a married man from Kent, was 603 Squadron's first pilot to be decorated on the island; with six confirmed and six probable victories, plus four damaged, his was an irreplaceable and sad loss. His CO, Sqn Ldr Douglas-Hamilton, later wrote:

> "Nobody saw what happened to him, but it was almost certain he was killed outright. He was a fine fighter pilot and used to take enormous odds all on his own. After several combats, he had come down with his machine riddled with holes, but he had generally done much more damage to the enemy."

Two pilots of 185 Squadron also had their aircraft shot-up by Bf109s during this engagement, Plt Off Ogilvie force-landing BR387/GL-W at Takali:

> "The radio in my Spitfire had given up, so I didn't hear the call to break formation. And as a result I found myself alone, engaged with six enemy fighters, each trying to do me in. But my intrepidness was of no avail, for my aircraft was suddenly hit with cannon and machine-gun fire, the shells blowing a large hole in the fuselage directly behind the cockpit, and the machine-gun bullets penetrating the engine, spewing oil and glycol all over myself and my aircraft. The Spitfire shuddered and stalled, then plunged into a dive streaming black smoke and white vapourised glycol."

Ogilvie's assailant was probably Oblt Gerhard Michalski, Staffelkapitän of 4 Staffel, who claimed a Spitfire near Takali (36th victory). Meanwhile Flt Sgt Dodd, despite minor shrapnel wounds, also managed to return safely to Hal Far. However, on landing back at Takali, Flt Sgt Reid's port tyre burst and his Spitfire tipped over onto its back; fellow Canadian Jo Sherlock was amongst those who went to his aid: "I remember helping Shorty from under the Spit and thought that had he been any taller, he would have had more than a scratched head and a headache!"

Slim Yarra summed up the morning's action:

> "B Flight was on early readiness and the boys went up and got right amongst the Jerries. Shorty Reid destroyed one Me109. Buzz pulled off a very nice forced-landing at Takali after being badly shot-up by some particularly nasty 109s. He got in wheels down, rather a difficult thing to accomplish on this island. F/Sgt Moye also landed at Luqa, but was able to fly his aircraft back to Hal Far."

With the return of B Flight's Spitfires, 603 Squadron scrambled A Flight's eight aircraft at 0915, followed five minutes later by a dozen of 249 Squadron led by Sqn Ldr Lucas. About 40 minutes later five Z1007bis of 33°Gruppo BT were seen on their way to bomb Safi and Kalafrana, while their escort of 24 MC202s of 51°Stormo and 15 RE2001s of 2°Gruppo Aut CT tangled with the Spitfires. The Macchi pilots claimed three shot down, one each by Magg Duilio Fanali and Ten Giovanni Franchini, the third jointly by several pilots, and seven more were credited to the Reggiane pilots: Serg Magg Rino Ricci and Serg Cesare Di Bert claimed two apiece, and Cap Salvatore Teia, Ten Giacomo Mettellini and Sottoten Romano Pagliani each claimed one, the latter sharing a second with 51°Stormo. Again the Spitfire pilots thought Messerschmitts were present, Flt Sgt Parks (BR379/T-V) of 249 Squadron claiming one shot down, while Sqn Ldr Lucas (BR324/T-R) probably destroyed one more and Plt Off McElroy (BR254/T-S) damaged a third. A Macchi was probably destroyed by the combined fire from 603 Squadron's Flg Off Neville King and Plt Off Glazebrook, although both were hit in head-on attacks, crash-landing BR345 and BR365 respectively on returning to Takali. Two more of the unit's pilots, newly commissioned Plt Off Fred Johnson and Flt Sgt Colin Parkinson (X-S) each damaged a RE2001, the latter recording:

> "Had another scramble, saw some Eyetie bombers but we were jumped before we could attack. I saw a Spit being attacked by a RE2001, so attacked the RE2001. Saw strikes under the wing and fuselage, but having no height or speed, I spun off before I had a chance to see if there was any serious result. I came home like a bat out of hell and claimed one RE2001 damaged."

Sottoten Giuseppe Riccardi's Macchi of 351^Squadriglia was shot down into the sea about 18 miles south-east of Valetta, while Serg Magg Willy Malagola's aircraft was badly damaged; a number of Reggianes were damaged but all managed to return to Gela. Several of the Spitfires evaded the close escort and attacked the bombers, but could only claim damage before being forced away. Three pilots of 603 Squadron – Plt Offs Ray Smith and Dudley Newman, and Sgt Ken Mitchell – together with Sgt Gerry de Nancrède (BR246/T-J) of 249 – jointly claimed severe damage to one of the Cants. De Nancrède then gained strikes on another bomber as Wt Off Chuck Ramsay (BR251/T-E) also attacked a bomber, both he and de Nancrède afterwards mixing with the escort – thought to be Messerschmitts – each claiming strikes on their opponents before being chased away.

The next raid – by three Ju88s of III/KG77 escorted by four fighters – was picked up on the radars at 1415; Luqa was the target where two civilians and two soldiers were killed, two others being wounded. Eight Spitfires of 185 and seven more from 249 Squadron were airborne to meet this threat. Two pilots of the latter unit, Plt Offs Linton (BR347/T-Z) and Tex Spradley, were joined by Flt Sgt Sim (BR321/GL-J) of 185 Squadron in engaging two of the bombers; Flt Lt Daddo-Langlois (BR170/T-B) pursued another for 40 miles before shooting it down into the sea; two members of Fw Herbert Leiwelt's crew of 3Z+JT were seen to bale out, this subsequently being recorded as 249 Squadron's 100th victory whilst flying Spitfires. Again, 185's diarist Slim Yarra provided a graphic account:

> "A Flight took over. Eight aircraft were scrambled with F/Sgt Yarra leading and they intercepted the bombers over the island. F/Sgt Sim sat behind a Ju88 and squirted all his ammo into the black bastard, but the 88 failed to come down – against all the laws of nature – and Bob had to be content with a damaged. P/O Stenborg also got into a good position behind a Me109 but his cannons jammed, much to the relief of the 109 pilot."

However, 249 Squadron's Texan pilot, Plt Off Harry Kelly (BR356) failed to return, shot down by the formidable Oblt Gerhard Michalski for his second victory of the day and his 37th in total. One of the Messerschmitts was claimed shot down in return by Flt Sgt Bob Middlemiss (BR295/T-H), but it would seem that what he saw was Kelly's aircraft crashing into the sea, not his victim. 185's Flg Off Charney returned in a slightly wounded condition, his aircraft (BR376) badly shot-up. Of Kelly's loss, Beurling commented later:

> "He'd been feeling like hell for days – a touch of the Dog, I guess – but wouldn't go sick. Getting into the action, he had lagged out of formation for a moment and some watchful Hun had spotted him and dived. Over the R/T I heard somebody yell Harry's identification call. But the call came too late and one short burst got him."

The final attack of the day occurred between 1945 and 2020 when three SM84bis of 4°Gruppo BT, with a close escort of ten MC202s of Cap Doglio Niclot's

151^Squadriglia, approached; 18 more Macchis provided indirect escort but three had to return early. Seven Spitfires of 249 Squadron had already been scrambled and these were joined by four more from 185, the latter pilots enjoying a successful encounter. Flg Off Jim Stoop (BP979) shot down one fighter, which crashed in a field near Mellieha, Serg Magg Alberto Porcarelli of 151^Squadriglia being killed. Meanwhile, Sgt Haggas (BR387) carried out a head-on attack on another Macchi, which half-rolled towards the sea; Haggas followed and fired two more bursts, leaving it still diving at 5,000 feet. Other pilots confirmed that it went straight into the sea about two miles off Sliema Point and was undoubtedly Ten Ennio Chierici's machine, the pilot baling out to be rescued by *HSL107*. Sqn Ldr Lucas (BR324/T-R) claimed another fighter damaged, as did Flt Sgt Parks and Sgt Len Reid (185 Squadron, flying BR166), all three believing their opponents to have been Messerschmitts. Sgt de Nancrède's BR377/T-K was hit during a head-on attack and crash-landed at Takali. He was probably the victim of Cap Doglio Niclot, who claimed one Spitfire shot down, while other Macchi pilots claimed a further six damaged. 185's diarist continued:

> "A second show developed later in the day. F/Sgt Haggas beat the hell out of a Macchi 202 and it went down in the sea a little too fast for comfort. F/O Stoop also performed a very neat operation on a MC202 who was flying around the sky, and caused the sudden demise of one more Dago. Sgt Len Reid damaged a Me109 who was trying to shoot a Spitfire down. On the whole we had a very good day and everyone went home satisfied with the day's work, except of course the Jerries and Dagos."

Thirty-six MC202s of 51°Stormo escorted three Z1007bis over Takali on the morning of **3 July**, but while many fighters were encountered no casualties were actually suffered by either side and no claims were submitted. Jammed cannons continued to cause a problem, as 126 Squadron's Plt Off Mejor noted:

> "Three Cants and a squadron of Macchi 202s. My cannons jammed, so did Jimmie Peck's. Too bad. Had nice fight with the Macchi 202s. Dimwits!"

A Spitfire was lost when eight of 126 Squadron scrambled at 0830 to meet this raid, Plt Off Freddie Thomas' BR564 crashing into the sea following propeller malfunction; the 20-year-old pilot from Coventry was safely picked up by *HSL107*. Shortly after, four more 126 Spitfires were scrambled on approach of further hostiles, Plt Off Sandy McHan leading. The quartet was ordered to climb to 28,000 feet and to await further instructions, but four Bf109s then appeared; the American McHan later recalled:

> "Something hit my Spitfire (BR465/MK-X) – the engine seemed to explode in front of me. The ship was on fire and the gas from the cooling unit was streaming into the cockpit. Throwing the hood back would suck the flames outside into the cockpit, and if I turned the ship over, as so many pilots do, the petrol might have spilled to send more flames through the ship. I told an officer on the ground, 'I'm going to crash-land', but he said: 'Bale out'. I came down to 15,000 feet straight down, and levelled off. At 10,000 feet I knew the petrol tank might go any second, so I got out, wounded and on fire. I passed out. I remember pulling the ripcord at about 4,000 feet, then passing out again. I came to in a hospital."

The semi-conscious pilot had landed on the roof of a house from which he fell off and hit a wall, then fell to the ground, knocking out two teeth, badly cutting his lip and fracturing his already wounded ankle. In hospital he found the occupant of the next bed to be a wounded German airman; McHan continued:

"They (the hospital authorities) didn't worry about German prisoners escaping – the Huns were afraid of the Maltese who would have been very happy to get hold of them."

A section from 185 Squadron was also scrambled, led by Flt Lt Halford, but failed to intercept the Italian bombers, although it did achieve some success:

"The interception was not successful but Sgt Ginger Parker [BP979] found a nest of Me109s near Gozo and beetled off and shot one down in the approved fashion. Tony Drew also managed to get mixed up in a spot of bother, and, although he squirted at some 109s, he did not claim."

Ten 249 Spitfires were up to meet the early morning raid on **4 July** when three Z1007bis and 14 fighters were reported approaching the coast just before 0900. The attacking force actually comprised three SM84bis of 4°Gruppo BT, escorted by 22 MC202s of 51°Stormo, with a further 17 Macchis accompanying them as indirect escort. Before take-off, Sqn Ldr Lucas had briefed his pilots to go for the bombers, each section being instructed to tackle a given target:

"Red Section – my section – would take the bomber on the port side; Blue Section, led by Raoul Daddo-Langlois, the one to starboard. Yellow Section, with Jack Rae in the lead, would split into two pairs to cover Red and Blue Sections from the fighters as they went in, and then if they were still disengaged, go for the leading bomber."

Plt Off Rae (BR233/T-Q) remembered:

"We were scrambled relatively early, as the raid had not yet reached the island. Our flight was flying as three separate sections of two, climbing rapidly to gain maximum height. Woody was advising a very big party coming in with major formations of fighters and that there were also some 'large jobs' there for us. Woody's vectors proved to be immaculate. Alan Yates was again with me. As we levelled off at about 28,000 feet, there below were swarms of enemy fighters. The 109s were sweeping over the huge gaggle and below them was formation after formation of RE2001s. Underneath all this mass were three large Cant 1007s flying towards Grand Harbour. The three pairs of Spits reformed at our agreed ceiling height. What we were seeing was obvious bait with all those fighters just waiting to carve us up. It looked like sheer suicide to dive in there, and yet . . . ? It was so unusual not to be hassled by fighters at this moment, to be able to observe and have time to formulate strategy. Those heavily protected bombers looked so tempting."

Lucas continued:

"The Squadron went straight through the fighter screen, unseen and unmolested, and closed fast with the bombers. In a few seconds all of us were diving straight for the ground with the fighter cover spread-eagled all over the sky above us. As we pulled out at deck level... three streaming balls of smoke and flames falling slowly from the sky to the south of the island told the story. All three Cants [sic] had been destroyed."

One was credited to Lucas (BR324/T-R), another to Plt Off Rae, the third falling jointly to Daddo-Langlois (BR170/T-B) and Flt Sgt Middlemiss (BR295/T-H); Rae recalled:

"As the last to dive I expected to have a great mass of fighters who would be attacking the first two pairs, but the speed of the attack caught them completely unprepared. Instead of having to defend the others there was my huge Cant looming up to be destroyed. The result of this attack was a morale boosting for the island. The Maltese were delighted to see those arrogant bombers eliminated. There were never any repeats."

An aircraft of 14^Squadriglia flown by Serg Magg Romolo Cristiani fell in flames near Takali, crashing into a field. The bodies of three crewmembers were found in the wreckage. A second bomber, flown by Ten Raffaele Notari of 15^Squadriglia, crashed into the sea some miles from Marsaxlokk, but the third (also of 15^Squadriglia), although badly damaged by fighter attack and AA fire, limped back to Sicily, its gunners claiming to have shot down a Spitfire. Three more Spitfires were claimed by the Macchis, one apiece being credited to TenCol Aldo Remondino, Cap Riccardo Roveda and M.llo Ennio Tarantola. Although the Spitfires flown by Daddo-Langlois and Middlemiss were shot-up, both made safe landings at Takali. There were two survivors from the shot down bombers including a gunner, AvScMarc Arduino Perneschi from Cristiani's aircraft, who was rescued from the sea by *HSL128*; the coxswain, Flt Sgt George Head, recorded:

"This man, when found floating in his Mae West, appeared to be holding in his hand a white handkerchief. When rescued it was found that the 'white material' was the remains of his shattered hand, which had been washed clean of blood by the sea water. He had a resigned and pitiful look on his face which simply mirrored the horrors of war."

Perneschi told his captors:

"[My aircraft] was one of three SM84s which came over on a bombing/photo-recce raid. After releasing our bombs we ran into an AA barrage and the aircraft was hit several times and damaged. I was severely wounded by one of the bursts and jumped before the fighter attack which set the aircraft on fire."

No sooner had this raid disappeared from the radar screens than another was plotted. Four Spitfires of 603 Squadron escorting the rescue launch were warned to watch out for fighters, but three Macchis caught Flg Off Neville King unawares, inflicting some damage to his aircraft. The Macchis were probably part of the sweep being carried out by 20°Gruppo CT in advance of a raid by five Z1007bis of 33°Gruppo BT, which serenely sailed over Malta at 20,000 feet. Escort was provided by 20 Macchis and ten RE2001s, but Plt Off Ray Smith (BP990/4-O) claimed a Messerschmitt shot down:

"After an inconclusive dogfight when I did not get near enough to the enemy to fire my guns, I caught a 109 cruising back to Sicily, straight and level, and shot it down."

Eight 249 Squadron Spitfires were already up to meet this armada, Sqn Ldr Lucas again at their head, and were soon joined by a dozen more from 126 Squadron. These made for the bombers, two of which were hit and damaged by Sqn Ldr Winfield and Plt Off Graves (MK-P); the latter believed his victim probably failed to get back. He also damaged one of the escorting Macchis. Plt Off Jerry Smith wrote:

"I had a squirt at three Macchis, one of which was firing at a Spit. Was fired at several times, once by bombers when I raked across them with only one cannon firing. All our chaps got down safely, but only one bomber was probably shot down and one damaged. Pretty poor show, but fun while it lasted."

Meanwhile, the 249 Squadron Spitfires had become engaged with the escort, Plt Off McElroy (BR111/T-M) claiming a Reggiane probably destroyed and Flt Sgt Louis de l'Ara (BR254/T-S) another damaged. Sqn Ldr Lucas (BR324/T-R) had a narrow escape, noting in his logbook: "Shot-up by a 109 and bounced by Reggianes while attacking five Cants!"

The two Cants attacked by 126 Squadron were badly damaged but succeeded in returning to their base; the bomber gunners claimed one Spitfire shot down and one damaged, with the Macchi pilots claiming two more – Serg Spiridione Giudici and M.llo Pietro Bianchi sharing one and Serg Magg Francesco Pecchiari being credited with another – others claiming three probables and two damaged. Three more were credited to the Reggiane pilots – Ten Carlo Seganti, M.llo Luigi Jellici and Serg Magg Cesare Di Bert with one apiece. Probably Flg Off King's aircraft of 603 Squadron was one of their victims. The Spitfires failed to keep the bombers from crossing the coast and bombs fell at Mosta and Takali.

The three raids on Malta on **5 July** were carried out by small but heavily escorted formations of Ju88s, the first arriving just after 0715. The bombers headed for Takali where a Spitfire was destroyed on the ground; a number of delayed-action bombs were distributed around the airfield, subsequently obliging the pilots of the 20 Spitfires – which were in the air to meet the raid – to land at Luqa on return. On the ground frenzied efforts were made to remove all possible equipment from the aircraft before the bombs exploded. Eight Spitfires of 185 Squadron led by Flt Lt Halford scrambled to counter this raid but five aircraft promptly returned with various problems, mainly R/T failure. Halford and the other two continued with Halford (BP887) engaging one of the bombers, claiming it damaged. The escort of a dozen Bf109s and 29 Macchis kept the others at bay. Four Spitfires were claimed damaged by the Italian pilots.

It was late afternoon before the next raid came in, a further trio of Ju88s and 15-20 Messerschmitts being reported. The Ju88s were escorted by Bf109s from both II/JG53 and I/JG77, the latter unit flying its first sorties over Malta. Ltn Armin Köhler of 3 Staffel, with 11 victories to his credit, wrote in his diary:

> "1500 hours: first mission against Malta. Lifejackets, dinghies and waterproof leggings are handed out. The assignment: escort for Ju88s, to be taken up 5,200 metres over the ground. Target: Luqa/Mqabba airfield. A huge group of Me109s struggle through the air at between 5,000 and 6,000 metres. There – land! The island of Gozo and then, south of it – Malta! 20 'Indians' [enemy fighters] are reported at 8,000 metres. The Ju88s plunge to the ground – the flak is firing well. I continually take bearings above me and in the vicinity of the sun, because every moment I am expecting Spitfires. And then, right away, they come diving down on us. For a brief moment, I come to be sitting right behind one, but it notices me and, as I press the button, makes a downward turn. All planes come back."

Twenty-two Spitfires of 185 and 603 Squadrons intercepted, Flt Sgt Yarra (BR387/GL-W) leading four of the former. The seemingly tireless and fearless Australian claimed a bomber shot down and two of the fighters damaged, one of which he believed probably failed to get back:

> "Intercepted four Me109s. Crawled up on them and fired like hell. Broke off and spotted nine [*sic*] Ju88s with Messerschmitt escort. Attacked rear Ju88 and shot it down. Was chased back by 109s; shot-up badly – crash-landed."

Yarra was possibly the victim of Fw Otto Pohl of 2/JG77. Plt Off Stenborg (BR380/GL-R), reported that he had shot down two Messerschmitts but a third member of the flight, Flt Sgt Haggas, had his own aircraft slightly damaged in the encounter. One further Bf109 was claimed damaged by Flg Off Wally McLeod of 603

Squadron. 185's diarist reported the battle thus:

"A section of eight led by F/Sgt Yarra met a very nice party of Ju88s and Me109s. The boys engaged over the island and treated the Maltese to the spectacle of enemy aircraft being severely beaten up. Slim became mixed up with the gaggle and destroyed a Ju88, probably destroyed a Me109 and damaged another. P/O Stenborg sailed into a flock of 109s and shot two down, much to the disgust of the Me109 pilots, who beetled off home at high speed to complain about the episode. Once again everyone returned to the billets happy."

Uffz Horst Schlick of 1/JG77, experiencing combat with Spitfires for the first time, was reasonably impressed although somewhat confused by numbers of aircraft encountered:

"Straightaway, with the first flight, we – about 70 Me109F-4s with 30 Ju88s – made contact with 50 [sic] Spitfires over the island at 9,500 metres. Now I began to grasp for the first time what it meant to come through an air battle – the Spitfire V was, admittedly, somewhat inferior in terms of speed, but climbed just as well as, and turned far better than, the Me109. And there were thorough experts among the Tommies. For the first time one could fight so as to register a shooting-down as a prize. The fighting men of KG77 were very satisfied with our protective escort and hoped this would continue."

The third raid of the day comprised just two Ju88s and an escort of ten Bf109s, Takali being attacked on this occasion. 603 and 126 Squadrons had aircraft up, these becoming so heavily embroiled with the escort that the bombers escaped interception. Flt Sgts Schade (MK-H) and Evans (BR122/MK-O) each claimed fighters shot down, the latter adding one more as probably destroyed. Of his seventh victory, Paddy Schade noted:

"Attacked two Me109s north of St Paul's Bay. Fired two two-seconds bursts. White smoke poured out. Strikes all along the fuselage and port wing root. One Me109 destroyed."

A probable was credited to Flt Lt Jimmie Peck, and another to Plt Off Mejor (BR244), who wrote:

"Me109 yellow-nose probable. We attacked from very close. Saw strikes on cockpit. Piece dropped off starboard wing. He poured oily smoke and went down on his back. His No.2 attacked from line astern but we broke with lots of skid. He went nose-down for home. We found Ken Evans scrapping with four 109s. They cleared off."

Three more fighters were damaged by Sgt Wally Shepherd, Flg Off Wallace – who thought his opponent was a radial-engined MC200 – and 603 Squadron's Plt Off Dicks-Sherwood. None of the Spitfires were hit. Ltn Köhler of 3/JG77 again participated:

"1830 hours: next mission. Ju88s attack the Ta Venezia [Takali] airfield. Some planes come back with hits. The British pilots fly cleverly. The altitude, which we aren't accustomed to, makes itself felt on the planes, too. The engines suffer in the heat."

During the day, Sqn Ldr Lucas, Flt Lt Daddo-Langlois and two others drove to the Military Hospital at St Patrick's Barracks to visit the survivors of the SM84s shot down the previous day, as Lucas recalled:

"As I walked over to the bed occupied by one of the two survivors [Perneschi], a good-looking Italian in his middle to late twenties looked up at me with sad, plaintive, dark eyes which seemed to be appealing for sympathy. As he gazed at me, he slowly and painfully lifted a heavily bandaged arm. The hand and a part of it had been blown off by a cannon shell during the attack. Sickened, I bent down and held the Italian's other hand in mine, shaking my head in sympathetic belief as I did so. I then turned away and at once withdrew to wait at the door of the ward while my other squadron colleagues finished their conversations with the Italian through an interpreter. The same evening, I told my two flight commanders that the squadron's practice of visiting badly wounded prisoners – German or Italian – in hospital must cease forthwith. Those with commonplace and non-evocative wounds were a different matter. I explained that a repetition of my emotive experience that afternoon could only harm morale."

Spitfires of 603 Squadron engaged the early morning raid on **6 July**. Escorting half-a-dozen Ju88s were an estimated 15-20 Bf109s from II/JG53. There was little contact, although Obfw Herbert Rollwage of 5 Staffel engaged a Spitfire south-east of Gozo and claimed this shot down at 0837 (his 21st victory), while in return only Flt Sgt Colin Parkinson (UF-N) was able to make a claim:

"Our section didn't see the bombers but saw some fighters. A 109 swung in to attack a Spit but the Spit turned towards it. They then both went in opposite directions. I put my nose down and went after the 109 with everything pushed. Got to within 150 yards and gave a long squirt… saw strikes and black smoke pour out of the 109. He pulled up slightly and dived steeply. I kept on squirting till my cannon ran out of ammo. Another 109 bounced me but I turned up sun and he lost me. Another kite dived at me and I swung up sun again and did a steep turn on to his tail. It was a Spit!"

Bombs fell on Takali and a Spitfire was badly damaged in its pen. No sooner had the Spitfires landed than 11 more from 249 Squadron were off to meet the raid – which comprised three Z1007bis of 9°Stormo with 14 RE2001s of 2°Gruppo as close support, and 24 MC202s of 20°Gruppo as indirect support although three of these had to return early. Yet more Macchis of 151^Squadriglia, led by Cap Doglio Niclot, flew a sweep in advance to clear the way for the bombers. Flt Lt Lee (BR379/T-V) led the Spitfires in a head-on attack on the Cants, causing them to jettison their bombs into the sea; four pilots – Lee, Flg Off John Smith (BR295/T-H), Plt Off MacLean (BR111/T-M) and Sgt Beurling (BR323/T-S) – claimed strikes as they swept past, although none of the bombers was seriously damaged. Beurling wrote:

"Smith knocked one full of holes and it was last seen limping away toward Sicily. I got a two-seconds angle shot in on another and could see cannon shells and machine-gun bullets pepper his fuselage. Later we heard through Intelligence [presumably via Y Service] that the pilot had been killed and that the observer had flown the wounded crew home to a crash-landing. Two out of three Cants damaged."

20°Gruppo then engaged the Spitfires, Ten Francesco Montagnani claiming one but Serg Francesco Pecchiari of 352^Squadriglia was shot down, almost certainly by Beurling:

"As the bombers turned to run I saw a Macchi 202 boring up on Smitty's tail. I did a quick climbing turn and bored in on the Eyetie, catching him unawares. A one-second burst smacked him in the engine and glycol tank. He burst into flames and went down like a plummet. The same performance followed with another Macchi. Like the first one this baby picked on Smitty, and I on Smitty's friend. He saw me coming, however, and broke away diving. We were down vertically together from 20,000 feet to about

5,000 feet and I let him have it just as he pulled out, from about 300 yards and slightly to starboard. God knows where I hit him but he exploded into a million pieces. Number Two.

"As I pulled out and started to climb back up to the main dogfight I saw a lad go into the sea in flames about two miles south of my own position and was able to confirm him for Norm Lee. Al Yates, who had followed me down, thinking I was hit, was able to confirm my second Macchi, and Lee had seen both of them. So there was my confirmation for two destroyed. Yates's own ship [BR246/T-J] was bullet-riddled and Al had to make a dead-stick landing, but escaped unscathed. By then the enemy was ready to call it a sweep and go home.

"When I hopped out of the cockpit I discovered my own Spitter pretty well perforated in the wings and fuselage and couldn't for the life of me remember where I'd picked the stuff up. Sloppy work, somewhere! Anyway it had been a pretty good show – we were only away thirty-five minutes. We had knocked off three Macchis and damaged two."

It would seem that one of these claims actually related to a RE2001 rather than a Macchi since Sottoten Romano Pagliani of 152^Squadriglia was also shot down. He was seen to bale out although his No.2 reported that he believed that his parachute failed to open. The stricken Reggiane crashed near Zejtun. Five other 2°Gruppo aircraft returned with varying degrees of damage including that flown by TenCol Quarantotti. Meanwhile, the Macchi pilots of 151^Squadriglia reported meeting five Spitfires apparently trying to cut off the escape route of the retreating bombers. Cap Doglio Niclot claimed one shot down, which his No.2 reported crashed north of Valetta, but this would have been Pagliani's Reggiane he had seen crashing rather than a Spitfire; a second Spitfire was claimed by Ten Michele Gallo, but 249 suffered no losses.

In the early afternoon, Beurling was called to fly escort for *HSL128* searching for survivors and he reported that the two pilots he had shot down earlier were both recovered, but:

"One died that night in hospital, badly burned. The other had been hit in the leg by a cannon shell and in the shoulders and arms with machine-gun bullets. The doc had to amputate the leg. The pilot survived."

However, available records suggest that only one of the Italian pilots was picked up by *HSL128* from the sea, about three miles out from Kalafrana; possibly another craft picked up the other or the pilot actually came down on land, as seems more likely in Pagliani's case.

Later during the morning a raid by five Ju88s and escort, directed at Hal Far and Safi, was challenged by no less than 27 Spitfires from 185 and 603 Squadrons. Aircraft from the latter unit dived onto the bombers, only to be bounced by the escort, but were able to claim two Ju88s shot down by Plt Offs Glen and Guy Carlet. One of these was almost certainly M7+ML of KGr806, flown by Obfw Peter Wilbertz, who was killed. On interrogation, one member of his crew (Gfr Hans Albrecht) declared that the aircraft had been hit in the port side and engine by a Spitfire when at 15,000 feet, and had burst into flames; he and two others (Gfr Heinz Stiller and Fw Sebastian Krumbachner) had managed to bale out. The other aircraft, Oblt Walter Pruger's 7T+KK of KüFlGr606, came down in the sea off the Sicilian coast, but only the injured W/T operator, Uffz Walter Pfeifer, was rescued. Flt Sgt Irwin and Flt Lt Douglas (BR345/X-A) each claimed one of the escorting fighters damaged. The Squadron diarist wrote:

"Attacked by 109s at about 5,000 feet, but Glen and Carlet managed to go on and destroy two 88s on the way home. Pinkie got hit by return fire. Rest had dogfight with 109s and Douglas was shot-up and had to crash-land without flaps, unhurt. Irwin shot-up that 109 and probably destroyed it. He too had a couple of bullet holes in his aircraft. Slade too was shot-up and had to land at Luqa, wheels down, but unhurt."

Sqn Ldr Douglas-Hamilton added:

"We dived down on them, but just as we were drawing near them a number of 109s dived down on us. A terrific dogfight ensued, in which the 109s for once stayed and fought. They were good, those yellow-nosed 109s. We twisted and turned around each other, blazing away every now and then; but most of us could not get away to chase the 88s."

185 Squadron pilots enjoyed greater success, as Slim Yarra recorded in the diary:

"The activity on the part of the Jerries has been continued now for the past week and today he really started to go to town. Although this phase cannot be compared with the period of the 'blitz', there certainly is plenty of action going on for all and sundry. B Flight was scrambled and really became mixed up with the hostiles. F/Sgt Moye was the only one who failed to return, being shot down by Me109s. 'Cactus' had not been in the Squadron long, but it was a blow to lose him so soon. The rest of the flight put up quite a score amongst themselves.

"Sqn Ldr New [BR321/GL-J] probably destroyed a Ju88 and damaged another, Johnny Sherlock [BR166] damaged a 109. Buzz Ogilvie got into quite a mix up, but did not claim anything. F/O Charney [BR380] destroyed a 109. F/Sgt Dodd destroyed a 109. F/Lt Halford [BR387] was leading one section and every member of that section scored. Hal damaged one Ju88 and two 109s. Tony Drew [BR119] destroyed a Ju88, Shorty Reid [BR317] probably destroyed a 109 and damaged an 88, while F/Sgt Andrews [AB500] squirted at numerous things but did not observe any results."

Of his engagement, Dodd (BR303) reported:

"Two-seconds burst at 2,000 feet over Delimara – saw two flashes on port wing; second attack and flashes on tail – big flash and lots of smoke, aircraft went down."

The American Flt Sgt Ed Moye apparently drowned after his Spitfire (BP979) was shot down into the sea, the victim of Oblt Siegfried Freytag of 1/JG77. Recalled Jo Sherlock:

"He was my No.2 when we intercepted 30-plus 109s and six Ju88s. I fired at three yellow-nosed 109s at which time I found my No.2 was missing. I did not see him shot down."

At 1840 a further raid was shown to be approaching, a mass of fighters – 39 MC202s from 155° and 20°Gruppi – escorting four Z1007bis of 9°Stormo BT. These were engaged by 11 Spitfires of 126 Squadron and six from 603, led by Sqn Ldrs Phil Winfield and Douglas-Hamilton respectively. Two Australians of the former unit, Plt Off John Bisley and Flg Off Don Smith (BP873), attacked the same bomber as Flt Sgt Gord Farquharson, and were joined by 2/Lt Zulu Swales of 603; Smith, flying BP873, noted:

"Flying No.2 to Bisley. Attacked five Cants through fighter screen. We both fired at same machine. Confirmed by Y Service."

A second bomber was credited to Sqn Ldr Winfield as probably destroyed, while Flt

Sgt Farquharson damaged another, as did Flt Sgt John Pinney. Sqn Ldr Douglas-Hamilton and Plt Off Glen also jointly damaged a bomber. Two of the Z1007bis were badly hit and on return to Sicily one ditched in the sea off Cape Passero, and the other landed on fire between Cape Religione and San Pietro, near Pozzallo.

Meanwhile, the fighters had clashed, Plt Off Carlet shooting down Sottoten Adolfo Giovannini's 353^Squadriglia Macchi into the sea and claiming hits on a second, while Cap Riccardo Spagnolini was wounded in the leg. This was probably as a result of an attack by Sqn Ldr Douglas-Hamilton and Flt Lt Bailey, who each claimed a probable; another was believed damaged by Flt Lt Douglas, whilst Flg Off Wally McLeod's Spitfire (BR345/X-A) was hit in return and was further damaged when landing. Ten Ettore Malosso claimed one Spitfire shot down and others claimed four probables and hits on 15 more!

The final raid of this hectic day occurred at 2030 when three Ju88s of II/KG77 swept in at low level to bomb Takali, escorted by Bf109s of II/JG53 and I/JG77. Five of 603 Squadron were involved, as were others from 249 and 185 Squadrons, a total of 20 Spitfires taking off. Sqn Ldr Douglas-Hamilton led the 603 Squadron flight after the bombers, his guns jamming after a few rounds had been fired; nonetheless, all three bombers were claimed shot down, one by Plt Off Glen, who reported that his victim's wing broke away as the aircraft caught fire, another by 2/Lt Swales and the third shared by Plt Off Carlet and Flt Sgt Irwin. Flt Lt Douglas almost collided with the bomber he attacked but made no claim. Two bombers actually failed to return. Ltn Reinhold Boger's 3Z+JN of 5 Staffel fell into the sea just off Grand Harbour – three survivors later being rescued from their dinghy by *HSL128*, two of whom had suffered burns. The other aircraft, from 4 Staffel, ditched in the sea just off the Sicilian coast. None of the crew was hurt.

As if losing two-thirds of its attacking force was not bad enough, this costly raid was rendered even worse when a Messerschmitt from I/JG77 was also shot down into the sea. Claims were submitted for three Messerschmitts, one each by Sgt Beurling, Plt Off Glen (his third claim of the day) and Flt Sgt Dodd (BR303) – his second of the day. Strikes were claimed on two more Bf109s by Flt Sgt Tubby Mahar (BR292) and Sgt Tony Drew (BR119), while two Spitfires were damaged in the clash; Obfw Rollwage of 5/JG53 claimed one shot down north-east of Valetta for his second victory of the day, and Oblt Ernst-Albrecht Schultz, also of 5 Staffel, claimed another (his 18th). One of these probably attacked Plt Off Dick Turlington's aircraft, which suffered a cannon shell strike in the engine. Despite the damage Turlington made a good belly-landing at Hal Far and escaped unhurt. Of his combat, Beurling wrote:

> "... two Messerschmitts dropped on me, but I did a quick wing-over and got onto one's tail. He saw me coming and tried to climb away. I figured he must be about 800 yards away from me when I got him in the sights and let go at him. It was a full deflection shot, and I had to make plenty of allowance for cannon-drop. I gave him a three-seconds burst, smack on his starboard flank, and got him in the glycol tank. He started to stream the stuff, leaving a long white trail of smoke... I followed my man down to sea level, where he burst into flames and went in the drink."

Beurling's victim was almost certainly Fw Anton Engels of 1 Staffel whose White 4 (13386) crashed into the sea with the loss of the pilot – possibly the same aircraft as that attacked by Glen and Dodd – although according to Ltn Köhler of 3/JG77, it was believed to have been shot down by AA fire:

> "We suffered a total loss today. Fw Engels was shot down by flak and crashed in his

burning aircraft into the sea. One aircraft is missing from the II/JG53, the bombers have three losses, one at night and two in the day, shot down by Spitfires."

Fw Horst Schlick was of the same opinion that Engels had fallen to the AA defences rather than a Spitfire:

"Unfortunately, the really good flak from Malta claimed the first victim of our formation in the afternoon; on a mission as direct protective escort for Ju88s, in which we had to force our way together with the men through the 'hail of iron', a piece of flak hit Fw Engels' plane. It burst good and proper under our very eyes, and did real credit to the phrase 'cloud of flak'".

Perhaps Beurling's victim was the missing II/JG53 machine. Either way, he had notched up three victories in his first proper air battle at Malta. A sign of things to come. By way of contrast, 126 Squadron's Plt Off Jerry Smith had not experienced a very happy day:

"Scrambled but had to return – undercart wouldn't retract. Three 88s bombed the drome, very low and the bombs dropped very close. Two were hit and went into the sea off Grand Harbour. Felt very sick again and ate very little supper."

7 July turned out to be another very violent day, which began with a raid by a dozen Ju88s on Luqa, escorted by 24 Bf109s from II/JG53 and 30 MC202s (20 from 20°Gruppo and ten from 155°Gruppo CT). A dozen Spitfires of 249 Squadron led by Sqn Ldr Lucas and six from 185 Squadron were scrambled to intercept at 0730 and a swirling dogfight commenced, the Messerschmitts and Macchis reacting strongly. Flying AB526, it was to be Plt Off Brennan's last operational flight of his tour; he later wrote:

"I had nine confirmed victories and was most anxious to reach double figures in Malta. We had 12 aircraft at readiness. Raoul was leading four aircraft in Blue Section, and I four in Green Section. We planned to operate as a squadron, so we could tackle the Hun no matter what height he came in.

"At 15,000 feet we left Raoul and his section to deal with the bombers if they dived, and Laddie and I took our sections up to 20,000 feet. I could see six Ju88s but at first could not pick out their fighter escorts. However, as we got closer I could see that the bombers had fighters swarming all round them. They tried to head up sun. Telling Laddie I would head them off, I manoeuvred into position, and then led my section in, head-on. The 88s were flying line abreast, and as we got into range all six of them opened fire with their two forward guns. I pressed my own gun button when the range was about 450 yards, aiming at the extreme starboard 88. I gave him a couple of seconds. As I grew rapidly closer to him his tracer whipped by me, but without hitting my aircraft. I went in until I was only 50 yards from him, and then I had to break down to avoid a collision. At the same instant he pulled up away from me.

"I had no time to observe results. The 109s started coming down on me and, having learnt my lesson the day I had been shot-up, I dived down immediately and gathered speed. Three 109s followed me. As soon as I had gained sufficient speed, I whipped my aircraft out of their line of fire, turned slightly and skidded away to the left. Their leader shot past under my starboard wing. I slipped back on his tail, 50 yards behind him, and gave him three-seconds. I saw my shells travel up his fuselage and hit the motor and cockpit. A streak of oil appeared on his port fuselage and he went into a vicious spiral towards the sea. He was out of control, and crashed into the drink."

Brennan's victim, his 10th, was seen to go down into the sea; a second was claimed by Plt Off Linton (BR324/T-R), a third by Flt Sgt Mahar (BR292) of 185 Squadron, while Flt Sgt Dodd (AB469) damaged another. Plt Off McElroy (BR301/UF-S) claimed a Macchi and Flt Sgt Parks (BR165/T-Y) damaged a Ju88 but his aircraft was hit by AA fire directed at the bombers, which blew off its tail and he baled out, coming down on land near Zebbug with nothing worse than a bruised eye. Flt Sgt Middlemiss (BR251/T-E) was shot down by the Messerschmitts, wounded and baled out into the sea:

"Suddenly my right hand left the stick with the impact of being shot in the right arm and back. Had I not been sitting back and looking over my left shoulder, I would have been a goner. The Spitfire was in a spin and smoking. I was unable to eject because of the centrifugal force but I managed to roll the aircraft over and fall out. I opened the parachute and drifted down, eventually landing in the water. I shed the parachute and pulled out my dinghy. The words went through my mind: 'Slowly turn the tap of the CO_2 bottle'. To my dismay, as I frantically continued turning, I discovered that the bottle was empty. With my right arm useless, I had problems trying to attach the bellows pump to the dinghy; the cord attached to the dinghy kept getting in the way but I finally took out my knife and cut the cord, held the dinghy with my bad arm while I screwed in the pump and began the inflation. After a while there was enough air in the dinghy to allow me to climb in and begin paddling towards the island.

"I had been shot down on the eastern side of Malta but, unfortunately, the Squadron was searching for me on the western side. Only when Paul Brennan and Sgt de l'Ara flew out on patrol to protect some minesweepers was I spotted in the drink. They made one pass over me and then approached again. I thought of jumping into the sea in case they attacked the dinghy. However, they waggled their wings and I breathed again. Shortly afterwards, HSL128 reached me and I was hauled aboard, wrapped in blankets and given a shot of navy rum, which nearly made my eyes pop out. Later I saw the holes in my arm. The surgeon who operated on my back said I had missed death by about a quarter of an inch."

185 Squadron also lost a Spitfire in this action, as related by Flt Sgt Dave Ferraby (AB500) who baled out to come down near Zebbug also, his Spitfire crashing near Qormi:

"The first two Spits to take off left a dust cloud right down the track. I took off by myself as close to the dust cloud as I could. My No.2 failed to take off due to dust and I hoped I would be able to join up with some other Spits but, as was often the case, I didn't see a plane in the sky and climbed to 10,000 feet by myself. I can't have kept a good enough look out, because soon there was a loud bang and flames belted into the right side of the cockpit. The hood was open and I pulled the harness release handle and shot half out of the cockpit. I have very long thighs and my knees jammed on the rim of the windscreen. So I had to pull myself back in and straighten my legs. The parachute had caught on the head pad, which stuck out a few inches behind one's head. The plane was going down at about 450mph with engine still on – forgot to shut throttle – and there was no control from stick. Anyway, got out in the end and pulled ripcord. I much enjoyed floating down and saw a Spit circling me. Turned out it was Dodd, a good pal. Just missed a ten-feet high wall in a village; chute went in over the wall and I landed in a lane. I suppose all the women who gathered round didn't know if I was English or Jerry, but they kept touching my bleeding knees for some reason; burns were just down my right leg from knee down. I'd been flying in shorts and gym shoes."

Luftwaffe claims included one Spitfire by Obfw Rollwage of 5/JG53 (his 22nd) north-east of Zonqor Point at 0747, another one minute later by Ltn Karl-Heinz Preu (seventh) of Stab, and two more a few minutes later by 4 Staffel's Uffz Heinrich Frankenberger (his first) and Ltn Franz Dinger (his 17th), while Cap Doglio Niclot and M.llo Ennio Tarantola of 51°Stormo CT claimed another jointly, seeing the pilot bale out as the Spitfire went down to crash east of Valetta. Other Italian pilots claimed two probables and two damaged. Two Macchis were badly damaged in this action although the pilots were able to reach Sicily safely.

The next raid proved just as costly for the defenders, when Spitfires from 126 and 249 Squadrons clashed with 18 Messerschmitts. Sgt de Nancrède (BP990/4-O) of the latter unit and fellow Canadian Sgt Rupert Davey (BR566) were both shot down into the sea, from where they were picked up by the hard-working crew of *HSL128*. De Nancrède had been attacking a Ju88:

"Attacked three 88s from beneath, seriously damaging starboard one. Stuck in cockpit by return fire – wounded. Parachute descent from approximately 10,000 feet. Landed in sea ten miles south-west of Kalafrana Bay at 1210. Rescue launch picked me up at approximately 1300."

Two other Spitfires were hit and both pilots obliged to crash-land on return, Flg Off Wallace (BR115) sustaining slight wounds while Flg Off Erik Hetherington (BR347/T-Z) escaped unscathed, his aircraft also having been hit by return fire from the Ju88 he was attacking, which he claimed badly damaged. Spitfires were claimed by Ltn Hans-Jürgen Frodien of Stab/JG53 (his fourth), and Oblt Ernst-Albrecht Schultz (19th) of 5 Staffel. On this occasion no less than five Messerschmitts were believed to have fallen to the Spitfires but available records indicate only one aircraft, White 5 (7412) of 4/JG53, sustained any serious damage, the pilot of which returned safely to base. Flt Sgt Schade (MK-G) claimed two:

"Attacked two 109s off Kalafrana. Fired six-seconds burst. E/a went into sea. Was then jumped by two more. Skidded out to port, they went past and I came back into position. Fired six-seconds burst. E/a rolled over and also went into the sea. Two Me109s destroyed."

Plt Offs John Hicks and John Mejor (MK-R), who also damaged a Ju88, were each credited with shooting down Messerschmitts, the latter noting:

"Me109 yellow-nose destroyed. Ju88 damaged. Jimmie Peck attacked first but cannons would not work – 109 flying 1,000 feet and to port of three Ju88s. I took Jimmie's place and fired from 100 yards. He poured black, oily smoke and spun down leaving a very long trail. We peeled off and went into the 88s from astern. I took port one and saw strikes on side of fuselage by wing roots. He turned away from formation. The rear gunners poured tracers at us and we were forced to break."

Another was claimed by Plt Off Jack Rae (BR323/T-S), who reported that his victim fell in a head-on attack, the pilot baling out. The American Plt Off Rip Jones claimed strikes on one more, and a bomber was damaged by Australian Sgt Baron Richardson.

Another two Spitfires fell in the last raid of the day, this time both pilots losing their lives, victims of 6/JG53's Fw Hans Feyerlein (his first victories). Twenty-two Spitfires were ordered off to meet five Z1007bis of 9°Stormo as they headed for Luqa, many escorting fighters being reported. In fact, there were 35 Macchis, of which 23 were from 155°Gruppo and 12 from 20°Gruppo, and a dozen RE2001s. Possibly Messerschmitts were also involved as indirect support. Some of the Spitfires were able to penetrate the fighter screen to reach the bombers, Flt Sgt MacNamara of 185

Top left: Sqn Ldr Stan Grant CO of 249 Squadron.

Top right: Wg Cdr Jumbo Gracie CO of 126 Squadron and OC Takali Wing.

Bottom left: Plt Off Pete Nash 249 Squadron, killed in action 18 May 1942.

Bottom right: Flt Lts Johnny Plagis (left) and Ron West served with both 249 and 185 Squadrons.

A few of the American pilots

Top left: Plt Off Don McLeod 126 Squadron.

Top centre: Flt Lt Jimmie Peck 126 Squadron.

Top right: Plt Off Reade Tilley 126 Squadron.

Bottom left: Flt Lt Andy Andrews 185 Squadron.

Bottom right: Plt Off Doug Booth 126 Squadron.

Top left: Sqn Ldr Sailor Barton of 126 Squadron.

Top right: Sgts Paul Brennan (left) and Ray Hesselyn of 249 Squadron with Wg Cdr Jumbo Gracie in the background.

Bottom: Sqn Ldr Lord David Douglas-Hamilton (left) CO of 603 Squadron with Flt Lt Bill Douglas.

Top left: Plt Off Ray Smith 603 Squadron.

Top centre: Plt Off Barny Barnfather 603 Squadron survived a mid-air collision with the Spitfire flown by Flt Lt Bill Douglas.

Top right: Sqn Ldr Laddie Lucas CO 249 Squadron.

Bottom: Flt Lt Denis Barnham (in cockpit) and Plt Off Pancho Le Bas of 601 Squadron.

Top left: Flt Lt Tim Johnston 126 Squadron.
Top centre: Flt Lt Buck McNair 249 Squadron.
Top right: Sgt Junior Tayleur 249 Squadron.

Bottom: 185 Squadron sergeant pilots: Jim MacNamara (Canadian), Tex Vineyard (American), Shorty Reid (Canadian), Len Reid (Australian), and Ken Mitchell (Australian).

Top left: Plt Off Jerry Smith, the Canadian who landed back on USS *Wasp*, only to be killed flying from the island.

Top right: Plt Off Rod Smith, younger brother of Jerry; both served with 126 Squadron.

Middle left: Plt Off Tim Goldsmith, Australian ace served with both 185 and 126 Squadrons.

Middle centre: New Zealander Plt Off Jack Rae served with both 603 and 249 Squadrons.

Middle right: Sgt Red Parker 185 Squadron scored two victories.

Bottom: Canadian friends Sgts Junior Crist and Jack Ryckman with 126 Squadron; the latter was killed at Malta shortly after arrival.

Top left: Plt Off Jack (Willie the Kid) Williams 249 Squadron survived the battle only to be killed in the Liberator crash at Gibraltar.

Top right: Flt Lt Ken Charney 185 Squadron.

Middle: Flt Lt John Halford 185 Squadron with Slim Yarra's Spitfire.

Bottom right: Sgt Slim Yarra, Australian ace and 185 Squadron's one-time diarist.

Top left: Plt Offs Bob Middlemiss (left) and Screwball Beurling of 249 Squadron, the latter the island's illustrious top-scorer.

Top right: Flt Sgt Ken Evans 126 Squadron, another ace.

Bottom left: Flt Sgt Paddy Schade 126 Squadron, second only to Beurling.

Bottom right: Sgt Claude Weaver III, the American top-scorer, who flew with 185 Squadron.

me + my "Spit."

Top left: Flt Lt Wally McLeod 1435 Squadron's top-scorer.

Top centre: Anglo-Belgian Plt Off John Mejor 603 Squadron.

Top right: Irish-American Flg Off Leo Nomis 229 Squadron flew an unauthorised solo mission to attack a Sicilian target at night.

Middle: 229 Squadron's American Flt Lt Art Roscoe performed a feat that might have warranted a VC in another theatre of operations.

Bottom left: From NCO to Flt Lt in a few weeks, 229 Squadron's Flt Lt Colin Parkinson, a top-scoring Australian.

Top left:
Sqn Ldr Tony Lovell
CO 1435 Squadron
(left) and Wg Cdr
Prosser Hanks OC
Luqa Wing.

Top right:
Plt Off John
McElroy, another
Canadian ace with
249 Squadron.

Middle:
New Zealand ace
Sgt Nigel Park,
known as Tiger, with
Flg Off Wally
Wallace (Canadian);
both flew with
126 Squadron.

Bottom left:
Flt Lt Bill Rolls,
a Battle of Britain
veteran.

Bottom right:
Wg Cdr Tommy
Thompson OC Hal
Far Wing.

Top left: Wg Cdr Mike Stephens CO 249 Squadron and OC Takali Wing.

Top right: Sqn Ldr Bryan Wicks CO 126 Squadron killed in action 12 October 1942.

Bottom left: Wg Cdr Arthur Donaldson OC Takali Wing until wounded.

Bottom right: Wg Cdr Adrian Warburton, the intrepid reconnaissance pilot and CO of 69 Squadron.

Top left: Hptm Gerhard Michalski (II/JG53), the Luftwaffe's top-scorer over Malta with 26 victories.

Top right: Major Günther von Maltzahn, Kommodore of JG53 (right) with Oblt Friedrich Geisshardt (I/JG77).

Middle left: Oblt Siegfried Freytag (I/JG77) was a close second with 24 victories.

Middle right: Obfw Herbert Rollwage (II/JG53) claimed 20 Spitfires over Malta.

Bottom right: The celebrated Cap Furio Doglio Niclot, commander of 151^Squadriglia and top Regia Aeronautica pilot, was killed in action on 27 July 1942.

A selection of Malta Spitfires

Top: Low pass by BP845 following take-off from HMS *Eagle* March 1942.

Middle left: USS *Wasp* 18 May 1942 – Plt Off Jerry Smith making his first low pass prior to landing on the carrier.

Middle right: USS *Wasp* – Plt Off Jerry Smith about to take off for a second time; Lt Cdr David McCampbell USN, the DLO, in helmet.

Bottom: Spitfire fitted with Hurricane long-range fuel tanks for convoy protection duties.

Top:
X-A of 229 Squadron takes to the air.

Middle left:
Refuelling by hand.

Middle right:
Spitfire being pushed into its blast pen.

Bottom:
Ready for action.

Top left: Fitting a bomb to one of the first Spitbombers.

Top right: Bomb being readied for action.

Middle: Battle-scarred bowser with fuel for a protected Spitfire.

Bottom: V-S of 1435 Squadron undergoing maintenance in the field.

Top and middle left:
Scenes of intense
activity.

Middle right:
Awaiting the call.

Bottom:
Graceful duo.

Squadron claiming two damaged and Plt Off Miller of 126 Squadron another, while other sections had been ordered to engage the fighters, as did Flt Sgt Yarra (BR387/GL-W):

"Intercepted five SM84s [*sic*] with fighter escort. I took my section down and engaged the fighters – odds six to one. Destroyed two RE2001s. Haggas and Terry both shot down. I was shot-up by 109s and had my wing panels shot away. Crash-landed on aerodrome."

Flt Sgt Peter Terry's Spitfire (BR317) crashed on land killing the pilot, and Flt Sgt Haydn Haggas (aka Hamish) died when BR283 fell into the sea. *HSL128* was sent once again to look for the missing pilot but all that was found were the remains of an airman – presumably Haggas – about three miles out from Dingli; some personal belongings were retrieved for identification purposes, then the remains were buried at sea. The Macchi flown by Ten Fabrizio Cherubini of 353^Squadriglia also crashed into the sea, obviously one of Yarra's victims, and his colleagues claimed five Spitfires badly damaged; one was claimed shot down by Reggiane pilot M.llo Olindo Simionato and a Messerschmitt pilot may also have claimed. One of the Cants – MM23243 flown by Ten Francesco Antonelli – was hit by AA fire and started to stream smoke before falling out of formation, as recounted by 603 Squadron's Colin Parkinson:

"The 'Big Five' came over this afternoon. Ack-ack got one down; two of the crew baled out but shrapnel from the flak blew their chutes to pieces. They had to be dug out of a churchyard. Halfway down the bomber blew up. Two more of the crew came out and their chutes didn't open."

The main wreckage crashed onto a house at Siggiewi where an occupant was injured. There were no survivors from the bomber. Of the afternoon's actions, Slim Yarra wrote in the diary:

"A Flight [185] took over in the afternoon. On the first scramble the Italians brought in a flock of SM84s and indulged in a spot of their usual high level bombing. Our boys were right with them, doing their little bit to hinder proceedings as much as possible. During the engagement both Sgt Haggas and Sgt Terry were shot down. These two boys had been with the Squadron for some time and both had flown very well and done their job. They both died fighting against far superior odds and will be remembered as long as 185 Squadron remains on operations. The rest of the Flight did a very good job. The bombers were forced to ditch their bombs and not one fell in the target area."

Despite the losses, there was a celebration in the Takali mess that evening when 185 Squadron's successful and popular former flight commander Flt Lt Ron West was advised of the award of the DFC, a Bar to the decoration rapidly following, as recalled by Plt Off Sherlock:

"Ron had been recommended for the DFC, this recommendation going through the Middle East Command, which seemed very slow with all matters dealing with Malta. While waiting for the award to be gazetted, Ron received an immediate award of the Bar. Ron's sense of humour took over and he sewed the small rosette under his wings. He was checked one day by the AOC, who icily demanded what that 'object' was under his wings. Ron, who could keep a very straight face and at the same time look very innocent, stood to attention and advised him that it was a Bar to a DFC. Asked why he was not wearing the ribbon to the DFC, Ron advised him, and quite truthfully, that he had not yet received the DFC but he already had the citation for the Bar. The DFC citation arrived very shortly after what undoubtedly was a very hostile phone call from the AOC!"

The morning of **8 July** began with a raid on Luqa at 0730 by seven Ju88s, the bombers escorted by Bf109s of I/JG77, II/JG53 and 21 MC202s of 20°Gruppo. This formation was intercepted by 24 Spitfires, eight from 126 Squadron being scrambled on the approach of the raiders at 0710 to assist the standing patrol of eight from 603 Squadron, while eight more from 249 Squadron were sent off after the attack had commenced.

Flt Lt Sanders led his 603 Squadron flight after the bombers but they had to penetrate the fighter screen first. As they dived on to the formation, Sanders and his No.2, Flg Off Neville King, encountered a Messerschmitt, at which both pilots fired, reporting strikes before it dived away. Then, as the bombers turned northwards over Gozo, a lone Ju88 was attacked by Sanders who saw strikes on its fuselage; however, as he closed in, the German rear gunner achieved a direct hit on the Spitfire's armoured windscreen, forcing him to break away. By now the Spitfires were at sea level and as they turned sharply away from the fleeing bomber, King's wingtip, according to Sanders, dipped into the sea and BR198 crashed; the 29-year-old Irishman, a former London policeman and married man, went down with his aircraft. However, it would seem that he fell victim to one of the Messerschmitts.

Two Bf109s of 1/JG77 flown by Ltn Heinz-Edgar Berres and Uffz Horst Schlick (White 3) now latched onto Sanders' Spitfire and chased it all around Gozo, Berres gaining a number of telling strikes. With his aircraft streaming glycol, and finding himself too low to bale out, Sanders decided that rather than put the Spitfire down in one of the small stone-walled fields and risk serious injury, it would be wiser to ditch it in picturesque Marsalforn Bay, coming down about 100 yards offshore. As his aircraft (BR108) touched the sea, Sanders hit his face on the gunsight and collected a black eye but this was the only injury he sustained, and he was able to scramble out before the aircraft sank. The victorious Messerschmitt circled overhead but did not shoot at him. Of the action, Horst Schlick wrote:

"The third flight brought me my first success over Malta. We flew in formation, me as No.2 to Ltn Edgar Berres. At 9,000 metres we met twelve Spitfires; a British plane tried to get me in front of his guns, which, thanks to his good capacity in curving, he actually managed to do. No course of action was open to me but to disappear downwards or to curve inwards. I did the latter. We came at each other nose to nose, both shooting, and I scored. The Spitfire's engine shattered, from which a tongue of flame then flowed. The Briton crashed in bright flames and hit the water very close to the north coast of Comino, one of the small islands north of Malta. Berres, who was in my vicinity fighting a running battle with three Spitfires and was under great pressure, saw the shooting-down and, as an acknowledgement, shouted briefly over the R/T. He, too, sent a Briton into the water, which I was able to witness, but his didn't burn as brightly as mine did. When an enemy plane is shot down in flames, this means, on both sides, a special source of pride for the marksman."

Help for Sanders was soon to hand. Four members of the Debono family – Frank, Manuel, Anton and William – had just returned from an early morning fishing trip in their small boat S132, and were by the quay on the side of the bay when they spotted the Spitfire coming towards them, flying low down in the valley. Within minutes of the ditching, Frank and Anton rowed out and picked up the severely shaken pilot. When LAC Metcalf heard the news, he wrote in his diary:

"In today's first raid F/O King and F/L Sanders were shot down. King failed to bale out. I nearly cried when I knew because he's the greatest guy I've met yet and that's saying a lot."

Meanwhile, other pilots of the flight had also closed with the bombers, two being claimed damaged by Plt Off Glazebrook, another by Plt Off Newman, while one of the escort was similarly claimed damaged by Flt Lt Mitchell; Flt Sgt Ballantyne gained strikes on another Messerschmitt and also admitted firing at a Spitfire, fortunately without hitting it. One of the unit's Australians, Plt Off Fred Johnson, was shot-up and wounded in the left arm and leg – possibly by Oblt Gerhard Michalski of 4/JG53, who claimed his 38th victory during this early morning sortie – but succeeded in force-landing BR183 back at Takali. His fellow countryman, Colin Parkinson, who was not flying on this occasion, witnessed some of the fight, and noted:

"Was awakened by the sound of gunfire and planes dive-bombing. Went up on the roof and saw Me109s all over the place, as low as 2,000 feet in some cases. Saw four 109s pass overhead down sun and dive on four Spits who were flying up sun. The Spits did nothing until the 109s opened fire and one Spit was hit and dived straight for the deck. The other Spits mixed it. Johnson, an Australian, was the pilot shot down. He's OK. The gun panels were shot off, tyres flat, one aileron u/s, flaps u/s, glycol leak. He was wounded in the arm and leg but made a perfect forced-landing with wheels down."

Among the 126 Squadron pilots, Flg Off Don Smith (BR122/MK-O) led a section of three to engage four Bf109s, which had been spotted above at 24,000 feet. Smith claimed one probably shot down and this was later confirmed as destroyed, while Flt Sgt Joe Bush also claimed one shot down. Plt Off Jerry Smith saw seven Ju88s but his propeller was giving trouble, and he glided through these and a number of escorting Messerschmitts to force-land at Luqa. 249 Squadron enjoyed more success during this engagement as they, too, attempted to engage the bombers, only to become entangled with the escort. Plt Off Hesselyn (AB526) recalled:

"We were then south-east of the island, and we turned to come in towards Filfla. Woody advised that 88s were dive-bombing Luqa. We were a fair distance out, and I put down my nose to pick up speed in the hope of reaching Luqa before the bombers left. We arrived too late, the bombers having already turned for home over Hal Far. Willie the Kid [Plt Off Williams] and I stooged back to Filfla, and there we mixed it with a number of 109s at 2,000 feet. I saw Willie get on the tail of one. It went into a spin after a few seconds, and crashed into the drink. Four 109s passed right across in front of me, and I attacked the rear one from starboard. I gave him about four seconds before my cannons packed up. I could not see my shells strike and as he kept on flying I thought I had missed him, but a few seconds later he flicked on to his back and dived straight into the drink. More Spits arrived and while they were engaging the 109s Willie and I went home. This was the first aircraft I had shot down since 14 May, and I felt so pleased about it that I punished everybody's ears with my story of how I had got it."

Sgt Beurling (BR128/3-W) got his sights on another and fired a two-seconds burst; black smoke poured out and he too reported that it went into the sea off Gozo:

"The scramble call had come a bit late, with the result that the Huns were over the island at 18,000 feet while we were still at 12,000 feet on the way up to meet them. The Messerschmitts came down on us in a cloud, so we never got near the Junkers, which dive-bombed the Takali field, but missed, letting most of their stuff go into the nearby village of Attard. The Messerschmitts chased us all over Malta, the yellow-nosed bastards! You were flying in tracer smoke all the time and it seemed you would never get a chance to pick yourself an opponent. There were so many of them they kept you too damned busy watching your own tail. Finally I got one guy into my sights, from the tail, just for an instant. I let him have a two-seconds burst. He began to pour black smoke and hit the sea about three miles south of Gozo. Two of the Hal Far lads saw him go in and he was confirmed as destroyed.

"The scrap was short but sweet. Smitty had tried to bore in on the bombers, all on his lonesome and about twenty Messerschmitts leaped after him. Smitty must have decided it was too hot, for he whipped around in a hell of a hurry and surprised the whole pack by dashing in under them and streaking for home and mother. The Jerries gave chase, and that broke up the main mix-up. Meanwhile Gilbert and Willie the Kid were milling around in the mess of Huns, each trying to pick one for himself. Neither had any luck, but each came home with his ship riddled like a sieve. 'Jesus! That was hot while it lasted,' said Willie, as we ambled back to dispersal. Hot is right. Yet we were off the ground only twenty-five minutes, not a second more!"

Meanwhile, Sgt Colin Baxter belly-landed BR295/T-H at Takali, although on this occasion not due to combat damage but to lack of fuel. The two successful 1/JG77 pilots, Ltn Berres and Uffz Schlick were late in returning to Comiso, as the latter recalled:

"There was a whole lot of concern on the ground; we had already been given up for lost and, during the air battle, hadn't looked at the petrol gauge at all – the planes were completely flown to their limit, something that happened ever more often during the time that followed. The reception from the mechanics was fantastic, we'd got both our first shootings-down over Malta, me my third. To celebrate the day, we inaugurated a real bar in the canteen, and there was still an additional reason for celebration: Maltzahn decorated me with the EK [Iron Cross 2nd Class] and Berres the well-deserved EK I [Iron Cross 1st Class]."

Although the Spitfire pilots did not report engagements with Macchis, clearly they were involved. M.llo Maurizio Iannucci of 352^Squadriglia claimed one Spitfire shot down during this combat, others claiming one probable and six damaged. Ten Manlio Biccolini of 378^Squadriglia was hit and wounded in the neck and leg, his Macchi damaged by a 20mm shell and several machine-gun bullets in the tail and wings.

The Luftwaffe was back just after midday, a total of 23 Spitfires intercepting seven Ju88s of II/KG77 and a dozen escorting II/JG53 Messerschmitts; the bombers again attacked Luqa. 249 was in the forefront and broke through the fighter screen to reach the bombers, Plt Off Hesselyn (AB526) gaining strikes on one, causing an engine to catch fire, which he claimed shot down for his 12th and last victory whilst flying over Malta; he went on to damage a second.

"We intercepted seven 88s just before they began to dive. The bombers had a heavy fighter escort on either side, but I called up Woody and told him it was a piece of cake, and that I would cut him off a slice. Instead of going in one after the other we went down in pairs and got on the tails of the bombers as they were diving. We flew right through the flak and, at the speed which we were travelling, rapidly overhauled the 88s. I singled out one, and opened fire at about 50 yards. After about three seconds, my cannons packed up, but I had set the 88's starboard engine on fire. He started to dive towards the drink, and I thought I had got him. He pulled out, however, and the last I saw of him he was heading out to sea, low down. I saw Willie [Plt Off Williams in BR111/T-M] on the tail of another. He set its port engine on fire. It turned seawards, with Willie still on its tail, and then, apparently badly damaged, doubled back towards Malta. Willie stayed on its tail and gave it another long burst. It went down in flames off Filfla."

One of these was undoubtedly 3Z+GR flown by Oblt Erich Behr, the Staffelkapitän of 7 Staffel, who was lost with his crew. Another bomber was damaged by Plt Off Berkeley-Hill (BR324/T-R), while one more was fired at by Sgt Beurling (BR128/3-W) who reported seeing flames appear from its starboard engine, before he was himself attacked by five Messerschmitts. He claimed strikes on one, which dived for Filfla with its engine apparently on fire, and was credited with its probable destruction:

"The second scramble of the day seemed to open in highly favourable circumstances, yet it ended tragically, costing 249 two of its best pilots. Again the visitors consisted of seven Ju88s, heavily escorted by fighters. We had much more warning than for the earlier mix-up and there were more of us to handle the job. But somehow it didn't come off. Eight of us scrambled together. We were ready and waiting for the Junkers at 25,000 feet as they came in over Malta at 14,000 feet. The lot of us dived vertically, hitting between 550 and 600mph down the hill. I wanted to get a bomber, so I picked the one on the starboard flank and went down on him through the screen of fighters. As I came in on him, levelling off, I gave him the works on a deflection angle right in the starboard engine, which burst into flames. What happened to him after that I don't know, because right then five Messerschmitts came at me from as many corners of the compass. I dogfought the whole bunch, trying my damnedest to line one up in the sights without exposing myself to the others, and finally got one where I wanted him. I gave him a quick burst while I had him there and his engine took fire. He was last seen diving vertically towards Filfla, three miles south of Malta. The other Messerschmitts cleared out.

"Willie the Kid came close to hearing harps that morning. For Willie had broken through the fighters with the rest of us to pick out a Ju88, which caught fire from the port gas tank as soon as Willie put a burst into him. Willie was always a lad to get a great bang out of everything and he stuck around to watch his flamer go down, about as foolish, if human, a thing a guy can do, because a flaming aircraft attracts attention all over the sky and brings all sorts of unwanted people around. When I spotted the Kid he was flying around his burning bomber, seeing the sights and completely oblivious to three Messerschmitts hovering over him, waiting to pounce. I went in fast on those Messerschmitts, head-on, the only way I could take their attention away from Willie. As I came whipping in they broke upwards. I didn't get a chance to put a burst into any of them, they beat it so fast."

Flg Off John Smith and Flt Sgt Johnny Gilbert were also attacking the bombers when a number of Bf109s dived on them. Smith's Spitfire (BR233/T-Q) caught fire and was then hit by two more Messerschmitts before he could bale out; his aircraft blew up. The same fighters then attacked Gilbert's aircraft (BR227/T-T), which turned on its back and went into the sea off Wied iz-Zurrieq. Both pilots were killed. Beurling wrote later:

"Smitty took fire on the first burst. Two more Messerschmitts bored in and pasted him again, blowing his Spit to bits and giving Smitty no chance to bale out, if he was still alive. The same gang got Gil in the same second of sudden death. He simply went over on his back and fell headlong into the sea."

Plt Off MacLean (BR323/T-S) claimed one of the Messerschmitts damaged, but others badly damaged the aircraft flown by Flt Sgt Butler although he was able to land safely. It seems likely that they had been engaged by Messerschmitts flown by Oblt Michalski (his second victory of the day), Obfw Rollwage (his 24th victory), Fw Paczia (seventh) and Uffz Egbert Willenbrink (sixth), all of II/JG53, who each claimed Spitfires shot down, as did Obfw Walter Brandt (his 21st) of 2/JG77.

The last raid of the day was a smaller affair, three Ju88s and 15 Bf109s attacking Luqa and Hal Far at 1940. Sixteen Spitfires were sent up including six from 185 Squadron. Flt Sgt Dodd (AB469) reported meeting a Bf109 at 20,000 feet near Dingli. Opening fire, he closed to 50 yards then lost sight of it in the sun; two airmen on the ground reported seeing a Messerschmitt at about this time streaming glycol and heading for St Paul's Bay, and on the strength of this he was awarded a 'confirmed' victory. Another of the unit's pilots, Flt Sgt Yarra attacked a Ju88 but received two bullets through a propeller blade of his aircraft (BR387/GL-W). AA gunners made one of their now rare claims during this reporting that a Bf109 fell into the sea as a result of their shooting. Despite the many claims for Messerschmitts shot down or damaged, only one (7170) appears to have been damaged and this force-landed at Comiso when its undercarriage collapsed.

The previous two days had seen much over-claiming on the part of the Spitfire pilots, when a total of 15 Messerschmitts and three Italian fighters were believed to have fallen to their guns, whereas just one Macchi had failed to return and three others were seriously damaged, together with two Messerschmitts. Many of the aircraft seen to crash were, in fact, Spitfires. Despite this, the skies over Malta had now become unsafe for intrusion by Axis aircraft.

Shortly before 0900 on **9 July**, six Ju88s swept in at low level and carried out a raid on Takali, while the strong escort kept the defenders at bay. Of the 24 Spitfires up only two pilots managed to engage the bombers. Flt Sgt Webster (603) and Sgt Richardson (126) each claimed damage, although AA gunners did succeed in shooting down Uffz Herbert Schlitt's 3Z+ET of 9/KG77, which crashed in flames in Callus Street, Mosta with the loss of all the crew; although houses were demolished in the crash, there were no civilian casualties. On the first of his three ops this day, Plt Off Mejor (MK-R) noted: "Got jumped by 109s. Section split up. Got jumped again whilst above at 28,000 feet. Saw them just in time."

The pattern of raids differed little to that of previous days – an early morning raid, followed by another around midday and a third during the evening. In fact, the 'midday' raid arrived nearer 1300 when seven Ju88s bombed Luqa and the Safi dispersal area, where a Wellington and a Beaufort were destroyed, two more of the latter sustaining damage. Escorting Macchis from 20°Gruppo and Bf109s of I/JG77 and II/JG53 clashed with Spitfires of 126, 249 and 603 Squadrons. For 126 Squadron Plt Off Tilley claimed a Messerschmitt shot down, and Flt Sgt Evans (BR244) a Macchi. This was probably the aircraft of Ten Francesco Montagnani of 352^Squadriglia, who radioed his companions that his aircraft had been hit, and he was attempting to fly back to Sicily when his engine seized. Although he was seen to bale out into the sea he was not found. Slim Yarra noted in 185's diary:

> "The boys did one search for a pilot who was reported in the sea. He was not found, but as it was a Jerry or Italian pilot nobody cared very much. The water would do him good, and it is said that drowning is a pleasant death, which is much too good for a German."

Plt Off John Hicks (BR355) of 126 Squadron was shot down and posted as missing. On return from this sortie, Plt Offs Tilley and Mejor went out to search for their missing companion, a 27-year-old from Liverpool: "Looking for P/O Hicks with

Reade Tilley. No sign of him. I found an abandoned dinghy. Hicky's bought it."

603 Squadron also suffered a loss when their successful 20-year-old French pilot, Plt Off Guy Carlet (the alias of Levy-Despas) was last seen diving after a Ju88, and was killed when BP957 was shot down; he would be awarded the *Legion d'Honneur* and the *Croix de Guerre* posthumously. In return, Flg Off Northcott (X-N) claimed a Bf109 probably destroyed, and one of the bombers was claimed shot down by two of the 249 Squadron pilots, Plt Off McElroy (BR301/UF-S) and Plt Off Rae (BR323/T-S), the New Zealander also claiming a Macchi as probably destroyed. Another Ju88 was reported damaged by Plt Off Jean Paradis (BR128/3-W) whose own aircraft was then attacked and damaged by a Bf109. Ltn Köhler of 3/JG77 claimed one Spitfire south-east of Marsaxlokk for his 12th victory. Two more were claimed by Ltn Franz Schiess of Stab/JG53 (his 18th and 19th), and Uffz Otto Russ of 4/JG53, his first, while the Macchi pilots claimed three more badly damaged.

Takali was the target for six Ju88s during the evening raid, which approached the coast shortly before 2000, escorted by Bf109s of both II/JG53 and I/JG77. Seven Spitfires of 126 Squadron were first off at 1935, followed five minutes later by eight from 185 Squadron and at 1940 by eight of 249 Squadron; finally, at 2000, eight of 603 Squadron were ordered off, making a total of 35 Spitfires to engage the raiders. Four of the bombers were claimed shot down: 126 Squadron's Plt Offs Reade Tilley and John Mejor (MK-F) were credited with one apiece: "Ju88 destroyed. Fired from beam, passing quarter astern. It blew up and tail came off. Two burning chutes."

Flt Lt Mitchell of 603 Squadron also claimed a Ju88 destroyed, while the fourth was awarded to AA gunners. Flg Off McLeod of 603 claimed the probable destruction of another despite having only one cannon operating, and having been engaged by a fighter, which shot away his flaps, resulting in a crash-landing. Yet another bomber was damaged by the combined fire of four pilots of 126 Squadron – Flt Lt Rowe, Plt Offs Graves and Miller and Sgt Norm Marshall. Two bombers were reported to have crashed into the sea about two miles off Ghar Lapsi, and at least one aircraft from 4/KG77, 3Z+AM flown by Ltn Friedrich Kleimeier, failed to return with a second from the same unit crash-landing at Comiso. Although available German records suggest that no Messerschmitts were actually shot down, no fewer than five were claimed – two by Flt Sgt Schade (MK-N):

"Attacked two Me109s off Filfla. Fired three-seconds burst at port Messerschmitt. Strikes along fuselage. White smoke issued and it hit the sea. Attacked two more Messerschmitts north-west of Gozo. Strikes were seen along starboard wing. White smoke poured out from the e/a. Two Me109s destroyed."

Two more were claimed by 185 Squadron's Plt Off Stenborg (BR109), the fifth by Flt Sgt Parkinson (BR464/X-S), who recorded:

"Took off and climbed into the sun over Gozo. Reached about 11,000 feet, turned south-east down sun and reached Malta coast in time to see ack-ack bursts over the centre of the island. Dicks-Sherwood leading. It was our job to prang the bombers. As we drew level with the coastline in a steep dive, I saw a Ju88 underneath with black smoke pouring out of the centre of the fuselage. I rolled on my back and dived after it. At a range of about ten yards I opened fire. The 88 tried to gain height but burst into flames and finally disintegrated. My machine flew right through the falling wreckage. The 88 was a definite goner before I attacked it.

"I broke away up sun and saw a 109 weaving in and out among a number of Spits. It was about to give one of them a burst but I got a burst in instead. The 109 continued weaving on its way westward unmolested. I was close behind. It evidently saw me and started to dive. I gave a long squirt and followed it down through light cloud to about 700 feet above the water. The Messerschmitt continued diving and crashed straight in. I stooged about for another quarter of an hour and then came down to pancake."

Two more Bf109s were claimed damaged by Flt Sgt Evans (BR244, 126 Squadron) and Plt Off Frank Jones (249 Squadron), but 603 Squadron's Flt Sgt Ballantyne was shot down for the second time in just over a week, his aircraft (BR364) falling into the sea. The Canadian again successfully baled out and was picked up, this time by *HSL128*. During the evening raid two Spitfires were claimed by II/JG53 pilots, one apiece being credited to Obfw Rollwage of 5 Staffel (his 25th), and Ltn Hans-Jürgen von Möller of 6 Staffel (his 10th), while another was claimed by Ltn Berres of 1/JG77 (his ninth). Although Oblt Siegfried Freytag of 1/JG77 believed that he also shot down a Spitfire, it was not confirmed.

Nineteen MC202s of 20°Gruppo and six of 155°Gruppo CT, together with Bf109s from II/JG53 and I/JG77, provided cover for four Ju88s raiding Takali on **10 July**. Spitfires first engaged when the raiders were still some 20 miles off Malta, then the fighters clashed south of Rabat. Cap Doglio Niclot and his No.2, M.llo Ennio Tarantola, jointly claimed one and Sottoten Pietro Menaldi another. It would seem their initial opponents were seven Spitfires of 249 Squadron. Plt Off Lattimer (BR128/T-W) reported damaging a Messerschmitt and shooting down a Macchi, probably Tarantola's aircraft (2-151/MM9066), which was badly damaged in the fuselage and fuel tank; the Italian pilot was, however, able to reach base safely. Meanwhile, Sgt Beurling (BR323/T-S) was in action:

"Our opponents were four Ju88s escorted by thirty Messerschmitts. The Luqa and Hal Far lads knocked off three bombers. We drew the job of attending to the top escort fighters. It was the old story of few against many, which means you split up and go hunting around until you can pick yourself a spot to get a Jerry, at the same time trying to keep out of harm's way. Most of the forty minutes we were up were spent in milling around, trying to come to grips. Lattimer added a Macchi to his tally and I had the good fortune to bump into a Hun who forgot to keep his eyes peeled while he was getting ready to dive on one of our guys. All I had to do was to dive on him quickly, pull up sharply and to starboard as I got under him, and put a burst into his belly. The squirt must have killed the pilot. The ship didn't catch fire. No bits and pieces flew off. I saw no oil or glycol smoke. One second he was in my sights. The next he was diving headlong for the Mediterranean!"

This was possibly Ltn Hans-Jürgen Frodien of Stab/JG53 who was shot down near Rabat in Black <2 (7366). The German pilot, with four victories to his credit, did not survive. Seven more Spitfires from 603 Squadron had by now arrived to support those of 249 Squadron, Flt Sgt Parkinson (BR464/X-S) reporting:

"Was scrambled nearly too late. Climbed to about 7,000 feet and came round south of Gozo to the Malta coast and met the Ju88s coming out, about 12 of them. Attacked an 88 from beam and astern and strikes on the fuselage, wings and wing roots. Cannons packed up so came home and claimed a damaged."

One of the Junkers was claimed by Plt Off Dicks-Sherwood. The attacks on the bombers were then taken up by eight pilots of 126 Squadron as the raiders fled northwards, another being claimed by Flg Off Don Smith (BR366):

"Made head-on attacks on Ju88 at 1,000 feet north-east of Gozo. Hit starboard engine and cockpit. Enemy aircraft turned back with bombs on. Four Messerschmitts escorting broken up. One stayed with the bomber. Chased e/a 35 miles before he packed-up. Claim Ju88 destroyed, 109 damaged. Reflector sight u/s."

Cap Doglio Niclot, leading the 20°Gruppo Macchis, reported meeting four more Spitfires near Gozo. He claimed one shot down, another being shared by Ten Paolo di Porcia Guacella Brugnera, M.llo Maurizio Iannucci and Sottoten Dante Dose, the latter then being shot down, possibly by Smith's flight leader, Flt Lt Slade, who claimed a 'Messerschmitt'. Although four Spitfires were claimed by the Macchi pilots, and four more by I/JG77 – two by Oblt Siegfried Freytag for his 58th and 59th victories, one by Obfw Georg Ludwig (25th) and Obfw Walter Brandt (22nd) – only one was lost, BR244 flown by 126 Squadron's Flt Sgt Bernie Reynolds, a 23-year-old Canadian from Vancouver, who failed to return.

At 1115, 18 Spitfires (eight/126, six/249, four/603) were scrambled to meet the next raid, comprising six Ju88s with an escort of Messerschmitts from I/JG77 and a small number of MC202s from 20°Gruppo. Three pilots of 378^Squadriglia – Ten Giovanni Ambrosio, Serg Magg Francesco Visentini and Serg Magg Giovanni Del Fabbro – were jointly credited with two Spitfires shot down in flames but then the latter was shot down and killed, while Visentini baled out, wounded in an arm and leg and was rescued from the sea three hours later by a Z506B floatplane from Sicily. Serg Magg Mario Varacca's Macchi was very badly damaged, the pilot sustaining minor splinter wounds to his left eye. It seems likely that Sgt Beurling (BR323/T-S) shot down Visentini:

"The Eyetie went into a steep dive, pulled out and twisted away, rolled and pulled into a climb. Finally he went into a loop at the end of this climb and I nabbed him just at its top. A two-seconds burst blew his cockpit apart. The pilot baled out in a hell of a hurry. I circled over him as his parachute opened. He seemed to be healthy, so I gave 'May Day' on the R/T, specifying that the gent was Italian, not one of our boys."

This latest victory raised Beurling's Malta tally to five in just four days. Plt Off Williams (BR324/T-R) was credited with a Messerschmitt and Flt Sgt Butler (BR301/UF-S) gained strikes on another. A Bf109 (13188) of I/JG77 crash-landed at Comiso on return and may have been involved in this action. Meanwhile, Flt Lt Mitchell of 603 Squadron also claimed a Macchi shot down, while 126 Squadron's Flt Sgt Milner claimed a Messerschmitt, as did Flt Sgt Bush. It would seem that some of the RAF pilots had misidentified the Macchis as Messerschmitts in the heat of the battle. Two Ju88s were also claimed shot down, as Plt Off Jerry Smith (AB465) recorded:

"Rip Jones and I jumped seven [sic] Ju88s and shot down one each. Rip was being fired at by a 109 while firing at the bomber – I wonder he didn't 'buy it'. Larger raids coming in these days and far too many fighters. Had bloody great dogfight with 109s and Macchis off Gozo. Was shot up thrice. One in head-on attack at fighter, once by bombers, and was hit in oil tank by 88 I got; force-landed at Hal Far while Luqa was being bombed."

Of the four Ju88s claimed during the two raids, it would appear that only two were actually lost, both from 5/KG77. Possibly Don Smith and Dicks-Sherwood had fired at the same aircraft during the earlier raid, whereas Jerry Smith and Rip Jones had similarly attacked the same aircraft during the second raid. In the event, three crew of 3Z+LN survived although the pilot, Uffz Günther Merz, was killed, while Uffz Joachim Schierz and his crew of the other downed bomber were more fortunate;

although all were injured or wounded, they were rescued from the sea off the Sicilian coast.

The intense heat of the summer added to the pressure of the fighting, both of which had a demanding effect on the pilots. Sqn Ldr Douglas-Hamilton wrote:

"We did not always get sent up even when a raid did come over, but whatever happened, most pilots were tired and generally felt like going to sleep after a spell of readiness. In the quieter days of June it had been the rule that most pilots on readiness read books. Now it seemed harder to concentrate on reading; we just sat round in the dispersal hut and waited. Some would chat with others and argue, but conversation was generally very mundane. Everybody concentrated on doing the job in hand – none knew what the morrow would bring. Some days a hot sirocco blew up from the south and nearly boiled us all. It made readiness periods very exhausting, and on our 'off' periods we would lie down naked on our beds and swelter."

At the end of the day Slim Yarra updated 185's diary, echoing the feelings of all the fighter pilots at Malta:

"Rumour has it that the new batch of Spitfires we are expecting will arrive tomorrow. It is about time as we are getting rather short of aircraft. F/Lt Jimmy Lambert went to Gibraltar some weeks ago to lead the new boys here. He is probably enjoying himself in Gib, getting very drunk."

There was a short, sharp raid on Takali by 13 Ju88s between 0925 and 0955 on **11 July**, when a petrol bowser was destroyed and a steamroller damaged. Only a few of the dozen 249 pilots vectored to intercept them were able to make claims, the large fighter escort – 23 MC202s and two dozen Bf109s – successfully warding off attacks. Sqn Ldr Lucas gained strikes on one bomber while Plt Off Yates (BR301/UF-S) and Wt Off Chuck Ramsay (BR111/T-M) shared in the claimed destruction of a Messerschmitt. Flt Lt Daddo-Langlois (BR565/T-T) also shot down one, an aircraft (13148) of Stab II/JG53, which crashed near St Julian's after the pilot had baled out. The final act was witnessed by 126's Plt Off Jerry Smith:

"Stood on porch watching raid and we saw a long spiral at about 2,000 feet – a Me109 had been shot-up. Pilot baled out. The aircraft came streaking down and crashed straight into rock about 300 yards from us. We could see the markings clearly. Got tail wheel as souvenir."

The uninjured 22-year-old pilot, Ltn Heinz-Otto Riedel, was taken prisoner by soldiers from the nearby Ta'Giorni AA battery. He later told his captors:

"I was in a section of two and was about to engage Spitfires flying below when I was hit [he believed his aircraft had been hit by AA fire]. I told my section leader I was returning to base but then received another hit. My aircraft went out of control and I baled out."

Ten Ju88s, Bf109s from I/JG77 and eight RE2001s of 2°Gruppo made up the afternoon raid that arrived just after 1430, meeting eight Spitfires of 126 Squadron, which had scrambled with elements of two other units. Sqn Ldr Winfield and Plt Off Mejor (MK-P) claimed to have jointly shot down one of the bombers:

"Ju88 destroyed shared with CO, S/Ldr Winfield. We attacked formation of 88s and 109s. Heavy black oil smoke from both engines. Confirmed by Y Service. Blood wagon looked for them."

Plt Off Junior Crist damaged another bomber, as other pilots engaged the Reggianes; one was claimed (as a Macchi) by Flt Sgt Farquharson and another damaged by Sgt Arthur Varey, while Plt Off Miller and Flt Sgt Evans each had their Spitfires shot-up. Flt Sgt Schade (MK-E) frustratingly noted: "Had Ju88 in sights. Guns jammed." In return, the Reggiane leader, TenCol Quarantotti claimed a Spitfire shot down, as did Serg Magg Elio Cesaro, and others recorded hits on three more. Oblt Fritz Geisshardt, Staffelkapitän of 3/JG77 claimed two Spitfires but was credited with only one, his 83rd victory.

249 Squadron was not involved in the afternoon raid but was called into action at 1810 on the approach of ten Ju88s, 16 Macchis and two dozen Bf109s from I/JG77 and Stab II/JG53, the bombers heading for Takali. The attack on the airfield was fairly successful and one Spitfire (BR464/X-S of 603 Squadron) was destroyed in its pen, another two sustaining damage. The eight aircraft of 249 were joined by eight more from 126 Squadron and a further eight from 185. There ensued a series of engagements with the escort, Plt Off Frank Jones of 249 claiming one Messerschmitt shot down and another as damaged. Two more were damaged by Plt Off Paradis and Flt Sgt Parks, but Wt Off Chuck Ramsay (BR111/T-M) was shot down and lost. Beurling commented: "Nobody saw what happened. When we all came home Chuck just wasn't there... old Mother Mediterranean had claimed another good Canuck."

Meanwhile, 126 Squadron's Flt Sgt Paddy Schade (MK-K), on his second scramble of the day, claimed another Messerschmitt, his sixth in a week, raising his total to $13^1/_2$. He was rather fortunate on this occasion:

> "Missed bombers. Was attacked off Gozo by two 109s. One jumped me, but it went past, straight into the drink. I didn't fire my guns at all! Landed at Takali without a drop of gas. One Me109 destroyed."

Although it was the height of summer, flying at high altitudes could still be extremely cold, as Plt Off Mejor (MK-P) found out on his second sortie of the day:

> "Attacked formation of about 30-40 88s and 109s together with S/Ldr Winfield. Gave 88 two-seconds burst but had to break as 109s were playing behind us. We nearly bought it. Lost fight. Ring twitch. Got frostbite."

Newly commissioned Plt Off Yarra (BR305/GL-N) of 185 Squadron increased his tally to 12 when he claimed another Messerschmitt:

> "Scrambled after 40-plus plot. Joined up with another Spit. Saw two 109s and attacked one and shot it down (yellow-nosed). The other boys could not get amongst the Jerries so we had to be content with one victory for the day. Escorted shot-up Spit back to base."

The badly damaged Spitfire flown by Flt Sgt Louis de l'Ara (BR347) was escorted back to Takali, where it crash-landed, slightly injuring the pilot. Macchi pilots claimed two Spitfires shot down including one by Cap Doglio Niclot, who shared a second in collaboration with several of his pilots. Messerschmitt pilots claimed two more, one by Uffz Simon Pohlein of 3/JG77 over Gozo, his first; the other was credited to Ltn Karl-Heinz Preu (his eighth) of Stab/JG53. Once the raiders had departed, 249 Squadron despatched two Spitfires to search for the missing Ramsay, but nothing was sighted. That evening, at about 2130, the corpse of a German airman was washed ashore at Marsalforn Bay, Gozo, probably that of a crewman from one of the downed Ju88s.

A dozen Ju88s attacked Takali on the morning of **12 July**, but Spitfires of 603

Squadron on early morning patrol failed to find the bombers and were eventually ordered back to Takali, as Flt Sgt Parkinson recalled:

"Taxied into the bay in time to see the crews running like hell for the so-called shelters and a flock of Ju88s overhead. Nipped smartly out of my kite and made the world's record for a 200 yard sprint to the surface shelter. One bomb lobbed just at the back of the shelter and shook us all to our underpants. A stick of bombs had fallen along the dispersal pens and punctured my new kite [BP966/2-L] in the wings. After inspecting the kite I walked back to dispersal. With a terrific roar a D/A (delayed-action bomb) went off 20 yards from my kite. More holes and a rock bashed the spinner. We, B Flight, are left with six aircraft instead of twelve."

Of the attacks, 603's diarist wrote:

"Raid at 1000 hours by eight 88s on Takali. Eight of 603 airborne. Some bombs pretty wild again, and none on the aerodrome this time. High level bombing. More sheltering under billiard table at mess. 603 climbed up to 23,000 feet but failed to intercept owing to haze although they chased 30 miles out to sea. As they were returning, they saw gaggle of enemy aircraft coming in and thought they were fighters, but there were six 88s amongst them and they again bombed Takali, but did no damage, just after our aircraft had landed. Actually one aircraft was slightly damaged by an eight-minute DA dropped just in front of a pen."

The raid coincided with the arrival of a Sunderland flyingboat, which alighted safely in Kalafrana Bay. Two Spitfires of 185 Squadron had been sent out to escort this, encountering a number of Bf109s en route, one of which was claimed shot down by Flt Sgt Sim (BR321/GL-J). Meanwhile, Spitfires from 249 Squadron attempted to engage as the raiders raced out to sea again, but were frustrated by the strong fighter escort of 18 Macchis, 16 Reggianes and a dozen Messerschmitts, which prevented them from reaching the bombers. One section spotted Ten Francesco Vichi's 358^Squadriglia RE2001 about 25 miles north of Gozo, Sgt Beurling (BR565/T-T) firing a one-second burst at this, following which the pilot baled out:

"The bombers got away clear, without a shot being fired. Half a dozen Macchis and a couple of the Reggianes dove through us as we climbed and sprayed us with lead as they passed and Jonesy picked up some bullet holes in his wings. Meanwhile, Ops called through on the R/T to tell us to keep on climbing, another raid was on the way. This time we were in better shape to meet them. Nine Ju88s and an escort of more than forty fighters made up this show and the bombers actually got through over Takali, dropped their bombs – but missed the drome. We chased them 35 miles out to sea. There I got a chance to pick a Macchi from above. I went down vertically, about three hundred yards to his starboard side. He never saw me coming. At his own height, from an angle, I gave him a sharp one-second burst. The pilot baled out and one of the lads from a neighbouring squadron saw him drifting down in his chute, confirming him as destroyed."

Apparently this aircraft was also attacked by Flg Off Erik Hetherington, as witnessed by Plt Off Owen Berkeley-Hill who called over the radio, "I saw it, Hether old boy!" But Berkeley-Hill's aircraft (BR324/T-R) was then attacked by two fighters, reported to be Messerschmitts, and was shot down; the handsome 20-year-old Anglo-Indian was killed. He was probably the victim of Ltn Wilhelm Scheib of 1/JG77 (his seventh victory), although Uffz Simon Pohlein of 3 Staffel also claimed a Spitfire but it was not confirmed.

Despite bad weather, TenCol Aldo Quarantotti, commander of 2°Gruppo, at once led three others to search for the missing Ten Vichi, but as they flew low over the sea one Reggiane was forced to return early with engine trouble. Some 15 minutes later, M.llo Antonio Patriarca went back to Gela on his own. Neither Quarantotti nor Ten Carlo Seganti came back, and it was believed by the Italians that they might have collided; in fact, both had been shot down by Beurling. The Canadian and his section leader, Flg Off Hetherington, on returning from the earlier sortie, had volunteered to search for their missing colleague, Berkeley-Hill, when the two low-flying Italian fighters were seen in low cloud. Although misidentifying these as Macchis, they correctly assumed that they were also searching for their own missing pilot. Hetherington climbed to give cover while Beurling pursued one, which was lagging:

> "The boys must have been intent on the search for their missing sidekick, for I swear neither had seen me yet. I simply sneaked up behind the tail-ender [probably Seganti] and gave him a one-second squirt. He burst into flames and went down. Without further ado I whipped around on the other lad ... I came right underneath his tail. I was going faster than he was; about 50 yards behind. I was tending to overshoot ... I closed up to 30 yards and I was on his port side coming in at about 15° angle. I could see all the details in his face because he turned and looked at me just as I had a bead on him."

Beurling fired a short burst, which apparently killed the pilot, TenCol Quarantotti: "He dived in beside his mate. From the firing of the first shot until both Macchis [*sic*] went down no more than six or seven seconds had elapsed. Things happen fast in this racket."

At 1512 a further strike was carried out on Takali by a dozen Ju88s, and Spitfires from 126 and 185 Squadrons engaged the escort, identified as MC202s and Bf109s. Flt Lt Charney (BR368) was credited with a Macchi destroyed, Sqn Ldr New (BR321/GL-J) and Plt Off Tilley with a damaged apiece, and Plt Off Jerry Smith (MK-A) with a Messerschmitt damaged; Smith later noted in his diary: "Had a smack at a 109 today; damaged him. Later learned that two went into the sea, so he may be confirmed destroyed." It was not. One Macchi was damaged, allegedly by AA shrapnel, whereas other Italian pilots claimed hits on two Spitfires. Again Spitfires were damaged on the ground, as 603's diarist related:

> "Another raid by 88s about 1600 hours. 603 not scrambled in spite of repeated requests. Results: three of our aircraft damaged, and two damaged of 249. One bomb landed slap on western dispersal hut, completely destroying it and burying all flying kit etc. Some airmen in slit trench five yards away had a narrow shave. A DA landed by No.1 pen. Damn poor show by Ops, and everybody feels browned off that in two days 603 has four times been bombed on the ground."

An even larger force of bombers – two Staffeln from II/KG77 comprising 18 Ju88s – were tasked to carry out the early morning raid on Luqa on **13 July**, arriving over the airfield at about 0800. Two dozen Spitfires from 126, 185 and 603 Squadrons rose to the challenge, claiming at least two bombers before the escorting Bf109s, MC202s and RE2001s intervened. Despite a substantial escort of Bf109s from I/JG77 plus ten MC202s of 20°Gruppo and six RE2001s of 2°Gruppo, the bombers were engaged. Sgt Tony Drew of 185 Squadron claimed damage to one Ju88, then 16 more Spitfires – equally drawn from 126 and 603 Squadrons – attacked, Flt Sgt Varey (126) and Flt Lt Northcott (603) each claiming a bomber shot down, while others were claimed damaged by Flt Sgt Farquharson, Sqn Ldr Douglas-Hamilton (two) and Flt Lt Douglas (BP871/UF-R). For Flt Sgt Arthur Varey it was his first victory after two months on the island, for no matter how hard he had tried previously he had been unable to shoot anything down:

"Very soon we sighted the bombers flying in a tight formation below us, and hardly had our leader given the word before I was pointing my nose towards them. Down came the Hun fighters, and their tracer bullets came whistling past my wing tips. I twisted and turned, still heading for the bombers. As the last bomber grew larger in my sights, I pressed my gun button and just gritted my teeth as I kept it pressed for six seconds. I could see my bullets hitting him, and almost before I had finished firing both his engines caught fire. I was so excited that I forgot about the two fighters who were still intent on knocking me down, until the sight of their tracers made me instinctively get a move on, and when I did eventually shake them off it was to see my bomber going down in flames. It was my first victory, yet I felt no personal animosity."

Cap Doglio Niclot's flight of Macchis clashed with a dozen of the Spitfires, the Italian leader claiming two shot down and another damaged, and Ten Italo D'Amico one more, but two Macchis were lost: Sottoten Rosario Longo and Sottoten Pietro Menaldi, both of 151^Squadriglia, were shot down and killed. One of the RE2001 pilots, Ten Giorgio Pocek, also claimed a Spitfire. For 126 Squadron, Flt Sgt Evans (BP992) claimed one Macchi and Sqn Ldr Winfield a probable. They were joined by eight Spitfires from 249 Squadron that had been scrambled late. These also engaged the Macchis of 20°Gruppo, although Plt Off Rae (BR323/T-S) identified his victims as Reggianes, one of which he claimed shot down before gaining strikes on two others:

"After attacking numerous formations of RE2001s involving multiple combats, the sky, as so often happened, was suddenly empty. Well, almost empty. Still with me was one of the best No.2s I ever had the pleasure of flying with – Alan Yates. Alan was a great person to have with me in the chaotic flying that confronted us every time we entered combat and we shared many battles together. There was one other aircraft with us in that piece of sky, a lonely RE2001 completely at our mercy. I attacked him immediately and found myself involved in some incredibly complex combat manoeuvres that gave me extreme difficulty in obtaining anything like a direct shot. I could only see minor damage inflicted. To add to my problem I ran out of cannon shells. Finally it was a case of calling Alan in as he still had some ammunition. Alan then tried, again and again, nearly getting himself into trouble with this difficult customer. We were getting nearer and nearer to Sicily and fuel levels were running low. I called Alan to break off the attack, as we had to return to base. The Italian was smoking badly and probably would not be able to get back so we turned and left him, setting off back to Malta. To our surprise (and admiration) he turned back and chased us as a gesture of his defiance. If he ever did get back to his base, and both of us secretly hoped he would, I'll bet he had a wonderful story to tell."

Plt Off McElroy (BR301/UF-S) identified both his opponents as Messerschmitts, claiming one destroyed and one damaged. 126 Squadron lost a Spitfire (BR242) from which Sgt Vernon Willie successfully baled out, burned and slightly wounded, some 20 miles out to sea. Help was soon on hand in the guise of *HSL128* and the Canadian was on his way back to Malta in little over an hour. Plt Off Mejor (MK-H) was also involved: "Attacked 88s but only had short burst – 109s on my tail. Had three short squirts at 109s during the fight but saw no result." Three other Spitfires were damaged, including BR565/T-T of 249 Squadron flown by Sqn Ldr Lucas:

"It always used to be said that if you could actually recognise a 109 in the mirror, it was too late. Now, I could identify not one but four of them in line astern, coming in from five o'clock and a little above in a fast curving arc. As I whipped my aircraft over into a tight diving turn towards the attack, a salvo of 20mm cannon shells hammered into the starboard wing of the Spitfire with strikes from 7.9mm machine-gun incendiaries along the side of the engine. As the smoke and heat increased in the cockpit, tiny flames started to lick the engine cowlings along the top of the nose in front of me. I was still at 18,000 to 20,000 feet over the sea, five or six miles south-east of the island, losing height in tight diving turns. I tugged at the black rubber toggle at the top of the cockpit to release the canopy. The bobble came away in my hand. The hood was stuck fast. I was now at 15,000 feet, still over the sea, two or three miles out from Kalafrana Bay; the heat and smoke were intensifying. Then, astonishingly, as I went on diving, the smoke in the cockpit began to thin and the heat perceptibly to lessen. The flickering flames at the side of the nose seemed to have gone out."

249's CO headed for the nearest airfield, Hal Far, where he successfully landed downwind without flaps and amid a shower of red Very lights, in the path of two Swordfish that were just taking off:

"The aeroplane came to a stop 20 yards from what had once been a hangar or a store. I must then have blacked out, with the noonday sun blazing down on the cockpit and the effect of the delayed shock, for the next thing I was conscious of was an airframe fitter on either side of me, with tools, trying to lever the canopy backwards along its runners…"

On returning to Sicily alone, with no ammunition, Cap Doglio Niclot came across a Ju88 being attacked by two Spitfires, and managed to drive them away. He then escorted the damaged bomber, the German pilot landing at Gela, 20°Gruppo's base, personally to thank Doglio Niclot for saving them from being shot down. In this encounter Spitfires were claimed by Obfw Walter Brandt of 2/JG77, as his 23rd victory, and Uffz Simon Pohlein of 3 Staffel, although the latter's was not confirmed.

During the lull between raids, a PR Spitfire (BP908) flown by Flt Sgt Dalley made its safe return to Luqa from an eventful sortie over Sicily: "Over Palermo I was greeted by accurate AA fire and two inaccurate fighters, probably MC202s, which were out-turned and out-distanced."

The late morning raid was an all-German affair, seven Ju88s with Messerschmitt escort raiding Luqa. The attack was effective – a Hurricane and a Beaufort were totally destroyed and three Beaufighters, two Beauforts and a Wellington were damaged. Eight 603 Squadron Spitfires were too late to prevent the attack but two pilots caught the bombers as they raced northwards, Flt Sgt Irwin claiming to have shot one down; the Australian's aircraft was hit by return fire but he got back safely. A second bomber was claimed damaged by Flt Lt Northcott.

603 Squadron gained greater success during the late afternoon raid when 15 Ju88s and 15-20 Messerschmitts raided Takali, where a Spitfire was destroyed on the ground and another damaged. Of the 32 Spitfires airborne, only the ten of 603 were able to engage the raiders over Sliema and off Filfla. These claimed four Ju88s damaged – two by Flt Lt Mitchell, one each by Plt Off Dicks-Sherwood and Flt Sgt Ballantyne, while a Messerschmitt was hit and claimed probably destroyed by Flt Sgt Parkinson (GL-T). Flt Sgt Bob Brown also claimed a probable, and a Macchi was claimed damaged by Flg Off McLeod before another fighter scored hits on his aircraft, which pierced the oil tank and necessitated a forced-landing on returning to Takali. Plt Off Mejor (MK-H) of 126 Squadron, up on his second sortie of the day, again found himself isolated:

"Few 88s, bags of 109s and Macchis. Attacked 109s, had separate dogfights with two. Was separated from others and attacked two 109s about ten miles north of the island. Very foxy blighters. Another Spit came to help and they beat it."

Seven Spitfires of 249 Squadron were also up and searched for the raiders. Plt Off Frank Jones was jumped by an unobserved fighter and had his elevator controls shot away. Despite the damage, he got down safely. But there was more to this incident than meets the eye:

"My section of four had climbed to about 25,000 feet south of the island, beautifully positioned up sun by Woody, our wonderful ground controller, to meet the advancing force of Ju88s with their high cover of Me109s. Quickly checking my rear to ensure that no 109s would overtake us in the dive, and seeing my other three Spitfires close behind, I moved in fast from the port quarter against the enemy bombers, opening fire as I closed. My aircraft was hit several times as I passed beneath the attacking force. I flipped over onto my back and headed straight down from 18,000 feet. The stick became sloppy in my hands. I eased back on it to curb the dive, without any response. I tried again and again; I realised then that I had lost control and would have to bale out. I reached up and grabbed the cable-suspended knob, which released the cockpit canopy. One sharp pull and the rubber bobble came away in my hand, leaving the canopy still firmly in place. I was now hurtling earthwards at some 500mph, unable to get out and with the aircraft out of control. I called up Woody on the R/T and told him I was going in!

"In this moment of extreme, terminal danger, I saw an extraordinary vision before me. Whether it came from the assiduous study I had earlier made on the aircraft, or the lessons I had learnt in ground school, I don't know. But, suddenly, I saw in front of me the image of an open-plan diagram of a Spitfire showing the separate system of bias-trim cable, which was apart from the regular elevator controls. My hand moved automatically to the trimming control, which I moved back anti-clockwise. The aircraft started gradually to respond and recover from its dive as the nose was slowly raised. I pulled out at less than 100 feet over the water only to see just above six 109s which had obviously followed me down to finish me off. I called up Woody again and told him of my predicament and position. He came back to say that Laddie Lucas and Raoul Daddo-Langlois were above me with their No.2s and would be coming down. The 109s were scattered, and all at once, as so often happened in the air, I was alone. There wasn't an aircraft to be seen. With careful use of the throttle, and manipulating my elevator trimmers and the aileron (lateral) control I still had, I put the aircraft down between three great bomb craters in the middle of Takali. At that moment the airfield was strafed by more 109s. I leapt out of the cockpit and took cover in one of the bomb craters. I must then have passed out, for the next thing I knew was that the groundcrew who had raced over to me were picking me up and talking. That miraculous vision I had seen in the cockpit of the separate elevator cable layout had saved my life. The human brain reacts extraordinarily in extreme danger."

The second Italian offensive against Malta, though not officially over, was now almost at a standstill. Italian bombers had practically ceased operating and the steam was certainly going out of their fighter force. The first raid on the morning of **14 July** was by seven Ju88s of KüFlGr606, which bombed Luqa shortly after 1000. A large force of Spitfires from all four squadrons – 30 aircraft – were waiting to ward off the raiders, two of which were claimed shot down by 126 Squadron's Flg Off Don Smith and Plt Off Rip Jones, having been intercepted over the sea at 15,000 feet. Smith reported diving past the rear of four Messerschmitts of the escort to attack his victim, which spiralled down into the sea after he had shot off its port aileron and had seen the port engine blow up. He recorded that the escort became "extremely savage after the 88 went in" and his Spitfire (BP992) was hit eight times, one bullet hitting his ankle and severing the artery. While two of the Messerschmitts circled the downed bomber, the other two kept after him. He performed a tight turn onto their tails and at 100 yards tried to fire, but the Spitfire's hydraulic system had been damaged and the guns would not work. He finally reached the island – still under attack – and landed without flaps or brakes. Climbing out, he then collapsed unconscious through loss of blood and was rushed to hospital.

Another Junkers was claimed probably destroyed by Flt Sgt MacNamara (BR460) of 185 Squadron, while two other pilots from this unit – Plt Off Cy King (BR321/GL-J) and Sgt Ken Mitchell (BR109) – jointly damaged another, and Sgt Len Reid (BR376) claimed strikes on a third. Plt Off Yarra, on his last operational sortie from Malta, also engaged the bombers but his cannons failed to operate. It would seem likely that either Smith or Jones had attacked Fw Heinz Geschlössel's bomber – 7T+GK – that failed to return, while a second aircraft from this unit crash-landed at Catania.

Meanwhile, the fighters clashed. The Messerschmitts were particularly aggressive, shooting down Flg Off Jim Stoop's Spitfire (AB469) into the sea, some 20 miles from the coast. The pilot sustained burns to his face before baling out and *HSL128* rushed to his aid. Plt Off Williams (BR301/UF-S) damaged one of the Messerschmitts, but two of the seven 249 Spitfires were hit in return, Flg Off Hetherington being obliged to force-land his aircraft (BR379/T-V) at Hal Far, while Sgt Beurling (BR130/2-H) was wounded in the heel by shrapnel from an explosive bullet; he recalled:

> "I spotted a batch of Macchis, travelling in a tight V about 500 feet below me and a mile away. I went in to break them up. As I did, three Messerschmitts and two Reggianes came out of the sun at me from opposite angles, putting the scissors on me. I had to break one way or the other in a hurry, so I decided to let the Reggianes shoot at me, as they have less firepower than Messerschmitts. The bastards riddled the old Spit! They put better than 20 bullets through the fuselage and wings. An explosive bullet nicked my right heel. I did a half-roll and went away in a hurry as another bunch of Reggianes ganged me. From that moment the Spit was in no shape to fight, but I messed around and kept our friends as busy as I could, keeping clear of any close-in action. I limped home to be kidded to death by the rest of the guys for getting myself shot-up."

Another Messerschmitt was claimed probably destroyed by Plt Off Tilley of 126 Squadron, and Flt Sgt Parkinson (GL-T) reported one shot down:

> "Everything quiet until about 0830. Scrambled up to about 24,000 feet and were bounced by 109s out of the sun. We all became separated so I joined up with another bloke at about 7,000 feet. He broke away so I joined up with a nest of two who flew out to sea. We saw two 109s below so we bounced them. I gave one a good squirt and saw burst of cannon shell all over the fuselage and wings. The Messerschmitt flew level for a few seconds and then did a slow dive down to the sea and right in."

603 Squadron suffered damage to two of its Spitfires in this action, those flown by Flt Sgt Ballantyne and Plt Off Ray Smith, but both landed safely. Four Spitfires were claimed, three by pilots of II/JG53, one apiece being credited to Ltn Franz Schiess of Stab/JG53 (his 20th), Obfw Rollwage of 5 Staffel (26th), and Obfw Ehrenberger of 6 Staffel (32nd); Fw Otto Pohl of 1/JG77 claimed the fourth as his seventh victory.

The day saw the arrival by Sunderland flyingboat from Egypt of Air Vice-Marshal

Keith Park MC DFC to take over command of Malta vice Air Vice-Marshal Lloyd, whose tour of duty had expired. Previously commander of 11 Group Fighter Command in the Battle of Britain, Park was seen very much as a fighter pilots' man, whereas Lloyd, a former bomber commander left many of his subordinates feeling that he did not fully understand or appreciate their operating problems. With the new AOC there would be no such reservations, for no one knew better how to handle an air defence against the odds. AVM Park soon issued his 'Fighter Interception Plan', which called for interceptions to be made north of the island, well out to sea, before the bombers could reach their targets. This strategy was now possible with the numbers of Spitfires being made available by the carrier deliveries. The plan necessitated three squadrons working together; one to intercept the high cover, the second to engage the bombers' close escort, while the third would make a head-on attack on the bombers about ten miles from Malta's coast. If a fourth squadron was available, it would be responsible for the interception of any bombers that broke through the fighter screen.

Arriving with Park in the Sunderland was Wg Cdr John Thompson DFC[71], a former Battle of Britain squadron commander, who had been invited by Park to accompany him to Malta with the promise of command of a fighter wing. Park was as good as his word and within days Thompson was posted to take over the Takali Wing. Thompson had been one of the instigators of head-on attacks against bomber formations during the 1940 fighting, and was therefore an ideal choice to implement Park's ideas for the defence of Malta.

As the assault on Malta cooled off, stock could be taken. Since the beginning of the month – in just two weeks of concentrated fighting – the defenders had lost some 36 Spitfires destroyed or badly damaged in action, with three more written off in accidents. This represented about 40% of all available fighters with half as many again having suffered damage of a lesser degree. Although losses of pilots – still much more plentiful than were the mounts for them – had been at a much lower level, the rate of attrition of Spitfires was indeed severe. Help was again on the way, however, for *Eagle* had sailed again from Gibraltar with a deck cargo of 32 new Spitfire Vcs, to be flown off at dawn on **15 July**, as Operation Pinpoint. Les Watts, Jimmy Lambert and Bill Johnson had been flown to Gibraltar to lead the Spitfires to Malta. The pilots were believed to have been:

Flt Lt L.W. Watts (flight leader) (EP196)	Sgt D.F. Ritchie RCAF
Flt Lt J.F. Lambert (flight leader)	Sgt J.G. Livingston RCAF
Flt Lt W.J. Johnson (flight leader) (EN968)	Sgt N.G. Brydon RCAF
Flt Lt P.W. Lovell (flight leader)	Sgt C. Weaver III RCAF (US)
Flt Lt A.H.B. Friendship DFM	Sgt D.J. Hartney RCAF (US)
Flt Lt G.W. Swannick	Sgt J.E. Otis RCAF (US)
Plt Off J.W. Guthrie[72]	Sgt V.H. Wynn RCAF (US)
Plt Off V.K. Moody RCAF (US)	Sgt W.B. Knox-Williams
Plt Off R.I.A. Smith RCAF (EP140)	RAAF(EP117)
Plt Off J.L. Lowery RCAF (US)	Sgt H. Roberts RNZAF
Plt Off R.P. Round RNZAF	Sgt J.H. Tanner RNZAF
Flt Sgt G.A. Hogarth RCAF	Sgt N.M. Park RNZAF
Flt Sgt H.G. Reynolds RCAF	Sgt C.L. Kelly RNZAF
Flt Sgt I.R. Maclennan RCAF	Sgt G. Philp RNZAF
Sgt J.L. Sidey	Sgt M.L. McLeod RNZAF
Sgt T.J. Gunstone	Sgt N.L. Pashen RAAF (EN972)
Sgt W.S. Shewell RCAF	

The first flight departed without incident but then one aircraft, EP117 flown by Australian Bill Knox-Williams, who had been flying Spitfires with 278 ASR Squadron, crashed into the bridge on take-off. Fellow Australian Noel Pashen mentioned this incident in his diary:

"Crawled out at 0430 and went up to the flight deck ready for action at 0530. Everyone in the first section got off quite well, although two of them gave us a sinking feeling. Then old Knox-Williams tried to take off without petrol and ran into the bridge, the kite being pushed over the side after he pranged. Another lad took off his wingtip on a 6-inch gun. Apart from that everything was fine. As last man I had a bird's-eye view of the proceedings. The trip to Malta was quite uneventful and we landed about three hours after leaving the carrier."

The remaining Spitfires arrived safely, flown in by a predominantly Commonwealth group of pilots including a high proportion of Canadians, including Ian Maclennan, a 23-year-old from Saskatchewan:

"The *Eagle* had to show eight or ten knots on the wind indicator before they let us take off with our big overload tanks. It was nerve-wracking, but very easy to do once you've done it. Yet until you've done it, you're not sure; it looked agonizing. I was about the fifth off. The whole thing was improvised. We had to fly as near to land as we dared; in North Africa there were French Morane fighters ready to intercept us. We had orders not to engage them, just avoid them, and if you climbed up you could avoid them, though you could see them coming up trying to catch you."

Amongst the new arrivals was Plt Off Rod Smith, one of the first to land; Rod was the younger brother of 126 Squadron's Jerry Smith and recorded:

"Took off from *Eagle*, 500 foot run, at dawn; second off. Flew in first batch of eight to Luqa. We saw Algeria, made landfall at Tunisia, passed over Tunis; changed tanks in sight of Pantelleria, and landed still in a group – Jerry was at Luqa! Small world!"

His brother added:

"Very dull day, windy and dusty. New Spits arrived in the morning and was amazed to find that Rod landed here. He was in AOC's car when I saw him and we had a chat before he left for the mess."

Rod Smith would be posted to join his brother in 126 Squadron, together with other new arrivals including Flt Lt Basil Friendship DFM[73], a Battle of France veteran who was not, however, destined to stay very long. Five more Americans were included in this party – Plt Off Joe Lowery and Sgts Danny Hartney, Joe Otis, Vasseure Wynn, and 19-year-old Claude Weaver III from Detroit, the latter of German parentage.

Malta, however, saw little action on this date, although 23 Spitfires were scrambled in mid-afternoon when a fighter sweep by 16 Bf109s from I/JG77 approached the coast, probably to reconnoitre the airfields for signs of the new arrivals. Only one engagement resulted when Sgt Richardson of 126 Squadron skirmished with a Messerschmitt, which he initially claimed damaged, although this was later upgraded to 'confirmed'. Ltn Köhler of 3 Staffel noted:

"Free hunting with 16 aircraft over Malta and Gozo. Fifteen-minute battle with 20 Spitfires. I managed to shoot twice, but my *Kaczmarek* [No.2] came into my firing zone and we hit one and the other[74]. Not bad. We went home on our own."

Next morning (**16 July**) at dawn, Spitfires of 603 Squadron were sent off to protect

214 SPITFIRES OVER MALTA

the incoming supply ship *Welshman*, on yet another high speed run to Malta, from further attack. Flt Sgt Parkinson:

> "The *Welshman*, a supply ship, was being pranged by Ju87s off Pantelleria island. We were supposed to patrol and help protect her. She must have made good time during the night because at 6 o'clock she was only 20 miles off!"

All was relatively quiet over Malta during the day, only occasional reconnaissance aircraft and small fighter sweeps causing patrolling Spitfires any concern. There were no conclusive results from the skirmishing, as Ltn Köhler of 3/JG77 again reported:

> "Free hunt over Malta and Gozo with six aircraft. Suddenly six Spitfires came up from behind. I managed to get behind two and opened fire, but the Tommies were called back to base."

185 Squadron's new diarist, Plt Off Jo Sherlock, maintained the light-hearted banter established by his predecessor:

> "A Flight took over at dawn and had an early scramble to shake off the cobwebs, but failed to contact the wily Hun. B Flight took over at 1pm and spent a very enjoyable afternoon sitting in dispersal thinking of Jerry, who spent all the afternoon sunbathing in Sicily with bags of female company."

The Axis forces were back during the mid-afternoon of **17 July**, when five Ju88s raided Luqa and Safi, where two Beauforts were damaged. Two dozen Spitfires were up – eight each from 126, 185 and 603 Squadrons – and these claimed four of the 20 escorting I/JG77 Messerschmitts shot down, with three others damaged; but there were no reports of engagements with any of the 18 MC202s also taking part in this raid. An account of this action is revealed in Ltn Köhler's diary:

> "Guided by three Ju88s towards Malta. The bomber group was heading for the south part of Malta, before we turned and headed for home. When we passed bay of Scirroco [Marsaxlokk], 20 'Indians' [enemy fighters] were reported, and Geisshardt, Witschke and Häcker, went off in a line to the left. I and Pohlein and the rest of the group followed, but lost sight of them. We were right over the bay of Marsa Scirroco, and tried to keep our minds on the Spitfires. They were 1,000 metres higher than us, and were up sun. For them, we were perfect targets! They attacked, and we just had to get moving. Our leader went to the left with his pilots, and I and the rest of the group went right.
>
> "This time we really made bad calculations, because suddenly we had three Spits behind us in good position. Five of us managed to fight our way through, and we met up with Pohlein and Kletten. Pohlein must have been hit badly, because a long white trail came out of his plane. We waited together higher up to see what would happen. Suddenly his plane started to burn, and we could see that he had jumped. His parachute opened. His aircraft turned upside down, and with a long tail of fire and smoke, it went straight in to the sea. I turned around and went back to where he went down but could not see anything, not even his parachute. There was only a big spot of burning oil on the water. Again we spotted Spitfires 20km from Valetta, and they saw us. We knew it was best to get back to base, but four Spits attacked us, and Fw Sauer was shot down."

Flt Lt Halford (BR321/GL-J) of 185 Squadron attacked a straggler seen ten miles north-west of Gozo, and following two three-seconds bursts there was an explosion and pieces fell off the fuselage. It was last seen pouring black and white smoke. A member of his flight, Flt Sgt Shorty Reid (BR380) claimed a second plus another damaged, while Sgt Weaver (BR292) was credited with one more. Flg Off McLeod (of 603, flying 249's T-D) also submitted a claim for a Messerschmitt destroyed, two others being claimed damaged by 126 Squadron's Flt Sgt Evans (BR311) and Sgt Baron Richardson. Wally McLeod later reported of his victim:

> "The pilot was thrown clear and his chute opened. After he had hit the water I circled him and he waved to me, apparently quite cheerfully. So I dropped my dinghy to him to show I had no hard feelings either. He did not make any attempt to climb into the rubber dinghy and the reason became apparent when one of our rescue launches came out to pick him up. He had a cannon shell through his chest."

This was Fw Heinz Sauer, who had baled out of White 6 (7555) about eight miles from Kalafrana. Uffz Simon Pohlein's Yellow 9 (13191) had fallen into the sea off Valetta with the loss of the pilot. Within the hour, however, Sauer was picked up by *HSL128* as recalled by her skipper Flt Sgt George Head:

> "This man was badly injured and holding on to a dinghy, just supported by his Mae West. One of the Spitfire pilots (McLeod) who had taken part in the engagement came down to sea level and noticed the man's plight. The Spitfire pilot managed to throw his own survival dinghy out of his over-flying plane to Sauer in the water below. Certainly an act of mercy and self-sacrifice on the part of the Allied pilot."

Sadly, despite the efforts to save him, Fw Sauer had been severely wounded and died soon afterwards in the launch. In this skirmish Obfw Walter Brandt of 2/JG77 claimed a Spitfire for his 24th victory.

Shortly before this raid developed Flt Sgt Maclennan had been ordered to fly one of four new Spitfires over to Luqa from Takali, as there were insufficient blast pens available. He arrived as the attack was underway and found that only one flap was working, as a result of which he landed very hard and almost crashed:

> "I was soon made aware how valuable such aircraft were in Malta. The airfield was still being shot-up, but I ran across the tarmac and climbed the control tower where the Wing Commander [Gracie] was observing all this. I saluted and said I wanted to report a damaged Spitfire. His reply was, roughly, 'Get into a slit-trench, you son-of-a-bitch; I'll deal with you later!' I felt pretty mortified and was told I would have to report to the Air Officer Commanding... It was a long time before I had to go before him. I saved my Canadian issue shirt and shorts for the occasion, but when it finally happened, on short notice, I was wearing RAF shorts and shirt – all battle-worn – and I looked terrible. I was marched into his presence between [Flt Lt] McLeod and [Sqn Ldr] Lovell, and he was advised that I had damaged an aircraft. Lovell then said that I was now an experienced Malta pilot, doing good work. The AOC looked me over, lectured me sternly about how I should be honoured to be in Malta and how terrible my action had been. However, he said that clearly I was doing good work. All seemed forgiven. I thought I might improve on this situation by explaining how the accident had happened. Before I could really get started, Lovell snapped off a salute, and I had to do the same, and then my friends escorted me out of the room. The message conveyed was quite clear – don't bother a busy man with excuses."

Only one raid was intercepted on **18 July**. The early morning raiders turned back when halfway across the Strait, although four Messerschmitts sped across the island. Eight Spitfires of 603 Squadron were airborne and as they broke formation to attempt an interception, Flt Sgt Parkinson became separated:

> "I dived down at about 380mph. I tried to pull out of the dive but the stick was loose in my hands. Boy, did I get the twitch. However, by throttling back she lost speed and I

gradually regained control. My leader, White 3, is not fit to fly on ops. I will refuse to fly with him again."

To meet the afternoon raid eight of 249 Squadron scrambled at 1405, followed by eight more from 126 Squadron 15 minutes later. The former chased a single Ju88 – obviously a reconnaissance machine – and 15 escorting Bf109s at sea level, but Plt Off Chuck MacLean's aircraft (BR323/T-S) was hit and caught fire. It took the Canadian a full minute to escape from the inferno, by which time he was badly burned about his arms, thighs, groin, chest and face, and was barely able to pull the ripcord of his parachute. He later wrote[75]:

> "I heard that all too familiar bop-bop-bop sound behind me; my right eye caught the flash of the cannon shell as it passed over my right shoulder near my head, and at the same instant my left arm was jerked off the throttle lever as though some hidden force had flung it away from my body. There was a faint tinkle of glass; the petrol tanks exploded in my face. For a fleeting second I felt the searing pain shoot through my right bicep, down my left arm. Then it was killed by the wave of flames that roared up and enveloped me. I tried to reach for the key of my Sutton harness, but my arms were nowhere. Pain darted through my fists, my left foot – then it shot through my belly. If only I could get outside, away from this heat. If only I could get my head outside the slipstream might pull me and the seat out. The slipstream picked up my head and smashed it against the rear edge of the cockpit. With all the strength in my frame I both shoved and pulled. The harness key came out. At the same moment I pushed forward with my chest and the safety straps fell away.
>
> "I heaved, propelling my body over the right side of the cockpit. I was floating out in the cool air without any sensation of falling. The smouldering rags, protected by the fire-resistant crotch straps of the parachute harness, fanned by the fresh wind, burst into renewed flame. As quickly as my dulled brain would respond, I began beating furiously at my burning crotch. I tried to pull off my left glove, but it was stuck to my hand. I tried the right one, got the fingers loose and, it too, stuck to my skin. In a savage angry burst, I tore the glove off. With it came the skin of all five fingers. I found the ripcord, and with all my force pulled it. There was a sudden swish of air, a plop followed by a wave like a curtain slapping in the wind, and the chute opened. I smacked the water with a splash."

MacLean had come down about four miles off Gozo. He was too weak to inflate his dinghy and floated instead in his Mae West – fortunately for only 15 minutes – until *HSL107* came speeding to his aid. The launch had been alerted by Sgt Red Brydon, who had circled him on his way down. A second 249 Squadron aircraft (BR170/T-B) was also hit in this encounter and Plt Off Lattimer slightly wounded, but he managed to crash-land at Takali without further injury. When the 126 Squadron pilots caught up with the action some ten miles west of the island, the Smith brothers – Jerry in BRI76/MK-Q and Rod in BP952/MK-F – came across the recce Ju88, as the former noted:

> "Rod and I found an unescorted Ju88 about ten miles west and left it with engine pouring white smoke, going very slowly, with tail down at sea level. Very bad shooting on my part."

Flt Lt Bill Johnson (BR311/MK-L), leading the flight, claimed one of the escorting Messerschmitts probably destroyed. The Luftwaffe fighter pilots, from both II/JG53 and I/JG77, were credited with three victories, one of which was claimed north of Valetta by Ltn Berres of 1/JG77 (his 10th), a second by Oblt Freytag, the

Staffelkapitän's 60th victory, with the third being claimed by Ltn Schiess of Stab/JG53 (his 21st). Ltn Köhler of 3/JG77 was also involved:

"Escorting Ju88s, we went on another flight. I had to be sure what the Tommies had in mind. At that time we felt no fear, but they met us, and I was sure they knew we were coming. We had nothing to fight back with, then suddenly a Ju88 and a Me109 from our group fell out of the sky. With faster planes, even in bad condition, we made home. I really wondered how we could strike back, if we had no new planes coming. We called up the base and said we were coming into land, and when they spotted us, they really had a good laugh when they saw us try to land with a 'junkyard' of a Ju88."

The day saw a complete change of command for 249 Squadron, Sqn Ldr Laddie Lucas and his flight commanders, Flt Lts Daddo-Langlois and Lee, preparing to leave for the UK. The news had been broken to them in the bar, as Lucas noted:

"Leaving 249 which, for months, had been my life, and where I found friendship, kindness and loyalty, was just like going away to school. I longed suddenly to be picked up from the bar, parcelled up and, without anyone else noticing, deposited by some magic spirit in London, without having to say any goodbyes. I didn't know how I was going to face them. I was close to tears when I put my head on the pillow of my bed that night. Exhaustion leaves you with no resistance once you let go."[76]

Flt Lt Mitchell was posted in from 603 Squadron to take over command, Flt Lts Hetherington and Watts taking over the flights. 603 Squadron was also about to receive a new commander, Flt Lt Douglas taking over from Sqn Ldr Lord Douglas-Hamilton, who was promoted to Acting Wing Commander, and became assistant station commander at Takali:

"It was very sad to leave the Squadron after so many stirring days together, but at least I could feel it was in good hands. On leaving Takali I had a few days' leave at a rest camp for the RAF in St Paul's Bay. It was the first leave I had had since arriving, and it was a pleasant change of surroundings. I spent every day lying in the sun and bathing off the rocks. There was also sailing to be had in small boats."[77]

Flt Lt Sanders[78] also departed at this time, leaving for the UK. Also leaving were two more of 249 Squadron's successful pilots, the inseparable Plt Offs Ray Hesselyn DFM (12 victories) and Paul Brennan DFM (10 victories)[79]. The New Zealander Plt Off Dusty Miller had also finished his stint on the island. Although he had been unable to claim any confirmed victories, he believed he had damaged at least seven of his opponents[80]. Among the sick and wounded being evacuated were 126 Squadron's Flt Lt Rowe and 603's Plt Off Barnfather, who commented: "Spent most of the time in a drunken stupour brought on by accompanying Group Captain Woodhall on a terrific round of farewell drinks."[81]

There was but one brief appearance of Axis aircraft on **19 July**, when at least a dozen fighters – reported as RE2001s, although they were Messerschmitts from I/JG77 – were encountered by eight Spitfires of 126 Squadron during the afternoon. The aircraft (BP861) flown by Sgt Joe Otis, one of the newly arrived American pilots, sustained damage, and as he approached Luqa to land, the Spitfire suddenly lurched, crashed into a field near Gudja and was totally wrecked. Otis was killed. It seems likely that he was shot down by Ltn Hans-Joachim Gläss of 3/JG77 (his sixth victory). Ltn Köhler commented: "With Ju88s I went to Malta again. Big fight with eight Spitfires."

A further Spitfire was severely damaged during the day when another recent arrival, American Sgt Danny Hartney, took up BR305/GL-N of 185 Squadron on an air test:

> "He landed down wind and crashed into 'E' Pen, knocking himself out and fracturing his skull. The doctor, however, is quite reassuring in that Hartney would soon be up and around again."[82]

With dawn on **20 July**, radar plotted at least two aircraft approaching the island, the crews of which were presumably searching for signs of a Ju88 shot down during the night. *HSL107* was performing a similar task, accompanied by six Spitfires as escort. Six miles to the north and 20 miles to the east of Gozo, the rescue craft picked up two Luftwaffe airmen from a raft. In the late morning a lone bogey showed up on the radar screens, eight patrolling Spitfires of 185 Squadron being ordered to investigate, with a further four of 603 Squadron being scrambled. When intercepted, the bogey turned out to be a returning PR Spitfire.

Two hours later, however, three Ju88s and about 20 Bf109s swept in to attack Luqa, one bomb killing the entire crew of a Bofors gunsite. Eight Spitfires of 185 Squadron were already on patrol to the south-east of the island as the formation approached, and four of these promptly engaged. Although Flt Sgt Ginger Parker (BR387/GL-W) reported shooting down one Messerschmitt into the sea 15 miles east of Malta, the Bf109s got the upper hand and shot down Sgt Hugh Russel, a Canadian from Toronto, who was killed in BR117; his flight commander and fellow Canadian Flt Lt Lambert (BR460) also fell to their attacks, as Plt Off Sherlock recalled:

> "JF (Lambert) was blown out of his cockpit and his chute was, fortunately, ripped open which saved his life as he was still unconscious when pulled out of the drink, and his parachute D ring was still unpulled. I fired at a Ju88, which flew away smoking. I did not see it go down but later someone said they thought they saw a Ju88 go in off Zonqor Point, but it may have been hit by flak, which was fairly heavy."

Lambert came down in the sea not far from the coast, suffering slight wounds. Two soldiers from the Dorsets rowed out and picked him up, transferring him to the tug *Swona* that had arrived on the scene. 126 Squadron also scrambled sections of Spitfires, two flown by brothers Jerry and Rod Smith:

> "Scrambled too late on bomber raids – maddening. Nearly made it second time but they pulled slowly away from us before we could open fire. We were shadowed by six 109s, two of which attacked Rod and me about ten miles west of Grand Harbour. Did head-on attack at one. Played about but they had advantage of height, so we finally broke off."

By now eight Spitfires of 249 Squadron had been sent to help, engaging both the bombers and their escort but without tangible result, except that Sgt Georgia Wynn's aircraft (BP867/T-E) was shot-up by a Messerschmitt, the American pilot being slightly wounded in the leg. There was an attempted repeat raid on Luqa and Safi at 1645 by three Ju88s escorted by at least 18 Bf109s. These were engaged over Dingli by eight Spitfires of 603 Squadron but only Flt Sgt Irwin was able to claim. He reported seeing 16 Messerschmitts in line abreast, which he attacked, hitting two, one of which was claimed probably destroyed and the other damaged. The Spitfires had tangled with aces of I/JG77, who claimed three victories; Oblt Friedrich Geisshardt one for his 84th victory, Obfw Walter Brandt of 2 Staffel one for his 25th victory, and the other by 1 Staffel's Lt Wilhelm Scheib (his eighth), while StFw Helmut Gödert and Fw Horst Schlick (both of 1 Staffel) were each awarded a probable, but Ltn Köhler was not successful. His diary simply noted: "Same as yesterday, but this time

I had to run. Too many Tommies."

Next day (**21 July**) saw the successful arrival at Malta of a further 31 Spitfires that had been ferried from Gibraltar by *Eagle* (Operation Insect). The flights were led by Frank Jones, Rip Jones, Dudley Newman and Buzz Ogilvie, all of whom had been flown to Gibraltar for the task. The pilots included:

Flg Off F.E. Jones RCAF (flight leader)	Sgt A.H. Scott
Flg Off R.O. Jones (US) (flight leader)	Sgt L. Evans
Flg Off D.G. Newman (flight leader)	Sgt J.B. Crawford
Plt Off N.J. Ogilvie RCAF (flight leader)	Sgt M.A. Lundy
(EP187)	Sgt J.S. Hamilton
Plt Off K.C.M. Giddings	Sgt R. Hawkins
Plt Off W.L. Thompson	Sgt W.R. Wilson
Plt Off A.R. Stewart	Sgt G.W. Turner
Plt Off W.C. Walton	Sgt W.H. Walker RCAF
Plt Off A.D. Owen	Sgt J.R. Harmer RCAF
Plt Off L.G. Bazelgette	Sgt R.W. Lamont RCAF
Plt Off J.G.W. Farmer	Sgt H.P. Milligan RCAF (US)
Wt Off P. Carter RCAF (US)	(EP209)
Flt Sgt C.A. Long	Sgt S.S. Williams RNZAF
Sgt A.J. Tiddy (SA)	Sgt W. Parks RAAF
Sgt I.H. Forrester (SA)[83]	Sgt R.A. Buntine RAAF
Sgt G. Debenham	

A number of the Spitfires had already successfully taken off but another (possibly EP703) piloted by 23-year-old Lewis Evans from Merionethshire, started to weave, failed to gain sufficient speed, and crashed into the sea; the Welsh pilot was lost. The remaining Spitfires reached Malta safely, although, puzzlingly, American Bud Milligan noted in his logbook: "Eddy's overload tank wouldn't work – baled out and had a streamer." This entry may have been as a result of hearsay as there is no record of a second Spitfire being lost or of any casualty apart from Evans. Of his second trip, this time as a leader, Ogilvie recalled:

"This time we were launched with greater authority and for two reasons. These new Spitfires had laminated wood hydromatic propellers, giving us much greater acceleration, and also because the desperate Malta diet had reduced our weight considerably! In preparing the course from the *Eagle* to Malta, and not looking ahead to the long haul around Tunisia, off Cap Bon, I decided to shorten the flight by cutting across the so-called neutral land, from its western border at the Mediterranean to its eastern coast at the same latitude as Malta. The gamble here was no greater in my mind, than the risk of a dogfight with enemy fighters rounding Cap Bon, especially with us carrying 90-gallon belly tanks. As we left the east coast of Tunisia on our last leg, I checked my reference point and set course for Malta, being a little south of due east. Here we encountered a dark haze, where we could see straight down, but not ahead. About 20 minutes off the east coast of Tunisia, with only the sight of water below, I began to hunger for a little reassurance that I was on the right course. I had visions that I might miss that tiny island of Malta and lead all my followers off into the wild blue yonder.

"So I called fighter control at Malta for a homing vector. At once a socialist democratic Cambridge accent came over the radio, which I didn't recognise: 'Oh! Hello, Bullet Blue One, old chap, steer 40°, over and out.' At that moment all hell broke loose in my cockpit. I was steering 105°. And with this new course being heard by the members of my following, the tail of every Spitfire twitched nervously, with the pilots no doubt thinking they had a clot for a leader. My God, the winds must have changed drastically, I thought! I must be near the coast of Libya! At that moment I got religion again, mentally indicating to the Lord that I would become a monk if He got me out of this one, when fighter control at Malta nearly blew the earphones out of my helmet with: 'No, no, no, Bullet Blue One, steer 105°, 105°, over.' There was no mistaking that voice. It was Group Captain Woodhall all right. A German fighter controller in Sicily had been up to his old tricks again, trying to home me into Sicily. With Woody's reassurance, I held my course of 105°, gradually losing height, till we roared over the coast of Malta at 500 feet. We still had plenty of fuel in reserve and had knocked off considerable time taken by other flights."

The Germans made a seemingly half-hearted attempt at planning an interception of the incoming Spitfires, as Ltn Köhler's diary suggests:

"The aircraft carrier *Eagle* is still off Sardinia and sends off plane after plane. I know the ship carries about 200 planes [*sic*]. We fly towards the isle of Pantelleria and will try to close the bay where the road to Malta is. We started at 0945, and landed 30 minutes later. We were told that the Tommies were coming. We flew over Lampedusa, but did not see one Spitfire. Later we were told that they flew over the African coast. We flew towards Gozo and then back to Comiso."

The new aircraft more than restored the strength of the defences and allowed some changes to be made. At Luqa the former 1435 Night Fighter Flight was reformed, this time as a day fighter unit and became 1435 Flight (later raised to Squadron status), equipped with some of the surplus Spitfires. Initially it was to share messing facilities with 126 Squadron, and was placed under the command of Sqn Ldr Tony Lovell, who had returned to Malta from his trip to Gibraltar. Among those posted to this new unit were Flt Lts Halford and McLeod, who were to be his flight commanders; also posted to the new unit were Malta veterans Plt Off Mejor (ex-126 Squadron), Flt Sgts Vineyard and MacNamara from 185 Squadron, Plt Off Lattimer and Sgt Baxter from 249 Squadron, Flt Sgts Ron Stevenson and John Pinney, Sgts Colin Wood, Wally Shepherd and Don Hubbard.

With all these new pilots arriving, more old hands were released to return to the UK. 185 Squadron said goodbye to half-a-dozen of its seasoned pilots: Plt Off Ernie Broad (five including two probables), Flt Sgt Bob Sim (three), Flt Sgt Ginger Parker (two), Sgt Wilbert Dodd (seven including two probables), Flt Sgt Dave Ferraby (two shares and one probable) and Plt Off Slim Yarra DFM (14 including two probables), all of whom had added to the Squadron's laurels.[84]

Over Malta little was seen of the Axis air forces, the only engagement being noted at about 1600 when eight 126 Spitfires made contact with a similar number of Bf109s off Gozo. Flt Sgt Varey claimed one probably shot down, while two Spitfires suffered damage, including Varey's, who recalled:

"I was very lucky in a dogfight right over the island at 25,000 feet. Shells hit my aircraft and stopped my engine. Fortunately, I was able to glide down and land all right, only to find two cannon shells imbedded in the armour plating behind my head!"

The other Spitfire, BR366, was flown by Flt Lt Friendship, making one of his first flights from the island. His aircraft sustained three bullet strikes but he was also able to land safely. Fourteen Spitfires from 185 and 249 Squadrons intercepted the late morning raid on **22 July**, when still some 20 miles off Zonqor Point, but two promptly fell to I/JG77's escorting Messerschmitts. 249 Squadron's French-Canadian Plt Off Jean Paradis (BR128/3-W) – a particular friend of Beurling – was shot down into the sea; Paradis had just spotted the three Ju88s, which formed the nucleus of the raid, when he was bounced. 185 Squadron's Flt Sgt Shorty Reid witnessed Paradis' Spitfire crash into the sea and orbited the point of entry; he was seen to engage a Messerschmitt which was believed shot down, before another got onto his tail and shot down his aircraft, BR203/T-X also; neither Paradis nor Reid survived. The American Sgt Weaver (EP122) of 185 Squadron claimed two of the German fighters shot down in return, but no losses were recorded. Of the loss of one of his few genuine friends, Beurling reflected:

> "Jean and I had always been good friends. Only a couple of days before his last scramble we had gone swimming together at Sliema – we were just a couple of kids who lived within 100 miles of each other back home."

Of the loss of Shorty Reid, his friend Plt Off Sherlock added:

> "We announce, and I speak for every pilot of 185, with deepest regret that one of the ablest, keenest and most popular pilots on the island, Shorty Reid, is missing from this scramble. B Flight took over at noon and continued to search in the hope of finding Shorty, but with no success."

I/JG77's pilots claimed a total of five Spitfires in this action, Oblt Siegfried Freytag being credited with two and was almost certainly responsible for shooting down Shorty Reid; others were credited to Fw Otto Pohl (his eighth), Uffz Schlick (his fourth), and Ltn Berres (11th). Lt Köhler wrote:

> "Flight with a whole squadron of planes when suddenly eight Spitfires crossed our course. We dived down but the Tommies saw us and attacked. We turned and went straight in to the fight. We shot down four [sic]. To see four burning planes, each with a white tail, was a fantastic sight. The other Tommies went crazy and went straight in to us in blindness over their lost mates. Suddenly I had a Spitfire behind me and I had to dive when he came from behind very fast. My friend Freytag cried out on the intercom: 'Dive on, dive on and I will try to cut him off from behind.' Freytag took care of my problem and we had to admit that we were proud with five planes shot down for no losses. But JG53 had to admit to losses."

JG53's losses in this action are uncertain, however. Records show that an aircraft of 6 Staffel (Yellow 4/7567) flown by Uffz Friedrich Meier went missing on a 'ferry flight' but may have been diverted to take part in the sweep. Another raid approached at 1445 when three Ju88s with an estimated 14 Bf109s as escort headed for Hal Far and Kalafrana. Of the 16 Spitfires sent off to intercept, four had to return early, and another four from 185 Squadron were bounced three miles north-east of Zonqor with Flt Sgt Mahar's BR109 shot-up and damaged; as they returned to the island a second Spitfire was slightly damaged by shrapnel from an exploding AA shell.

Eight 249 Squadron Spitfires led by Sqn Ldr Mitchell were scrambled mid-morning on 23 July, as graphically recounted by Sgt Beurling (EP135/T-Z):

> "The scene in dispersal when the call to scramble came through was something for the movies. In the centre of the hut a hot stud game was in progress. Tables, cards and everybody's bankroll hit the floor as Hether, Shewell, the Kid, Giddy, Georgia and Hogy swarmed for the door. Rae baled out the window behind me. Squadron Leader Mitchell was somewhere in the mêlée. Hether, Georgia, Willie, and I were the first four off. As we pulled up our undercarts and began to climb, Ops called: 'Gain Angels quickly!' and we hit 22,000 feet before you could say 'wink.' As we did, three Ju88s and about 40 fighters hove in sight at about 15,000 feet and we went to work. From the

sun a cloud of Spits went down through the top-cover fighters to get at the bombers. Mitchell knocked one off as we went through, his Jerry hitting the sea in a cloud of smoke from its engines. I damaged another, catching him in the 88's weak spot, the starboard engine, without which he can't maintain height and to which the whole hydraulic system, controlling his undercarriage, is hitched. Hit an 88 in the starboard engine and you have a Jerry as good as destroyed, even though he may manage to limp home. Hether damaged the third bomber and had his starboard engine smoking as he broke for Sicily. I'll take a bet those Junkers' crews were grey-headed by the time they crash-landed at home. We sure had put on a party for them!

"The fighters came diving down after us as we went for the bombers. A Reggiane and I chased each other around for a hell of a time, looping, rolling, doing tight turns, diving on and away from each other and generally helling around the sky. At last I managed to get in a quarter-attack from below, behind, and to port. It was a pure deflection shot and it blew his left wing off. He fell over, streaming smoke, and ploughed into the sea. None of his pals came to his aid, but left us to dogfight it out."

Sqn Ldr Mitchell (BR301/UF-S) was credited with shooting down one bomber. 151^Squadriglia reported the loss of Serg Magg Bruno Di Pauli who failed to return. It would seem, however, that the Macchi pilot may not have fallen victim to the Spitfires, for he reported:

"As we approached the target, we received a heavy AA barrage. Suddenly, I was hit by an AA shell, which damaged both wings, but at first without preventing me from carrying out my job. After we had accomplished our mission, we swiftly headed home, but while the formation went on, my aircraft started loosing speed. I looked back and saw six Spitfires in line astern, following me without firing. I understood that I was in a hopeless state, so broadcast my position but in the confusion of that moment, I said, 'It's Gatto speaking', and parachuted down. I shot a signal rocket; they [the Spitfires] saw me. After one hour, I saw them looking for me again; I shot the two rockets left but they did not make for me, although the rockets made a lot of smoke. The hours went by. However, when the sun was going down, I saw the British aircraft again, at very low level. As I had nothing to let them see me, I started beating the water with my hands, making a lot of foam. I was very lucky; one of them saw me and dived low over my head and the other followed. Finally I saw a launch which came by and took me on board."

The Italian pilot was picked up from the sea by *HSL128*, about five miles east of Kalafrana, and was relieved of his valuables – a gold bracelet, watch and neck chain; these were later returned following a complaint to an interrogating officer, who apparently initially believed that Di Pauli was actually Maggiore Gino Callieri, commander of 20°Gruppo. The confusion had arisen following Di Pauli's emergency radio broadcast when he had used the name 'Gatto'; the message was also intercepted by operators of Y Service, to whom the codename 'Gatto' (Cat)[85] was known to refer to Callieri.

Two Spitfires of 1435 Flight were flying a protection patrol over a minesweeper off Grand Harbour as the raid swept in. Flt Lt Halford attacked a Messerschmitt and saw strikes on its starboard wing; smoke issued and pieces fell off before the Bf109 dived into cloud at 800 feet and Halford was credited with its probable destruction, although this was apparently later upgraded to 'confirmed.' The bombers blitzed Luqa as they passed overhead, five aircraft sustaining damage on the ground from blast and debris. Flt Sgt Maclennan, flying his first combat sortie from Malta, noted: "Scramble – 45 minutes. Bounce four 109s, bounced by two Reggianes. No score."

249 Squadron was again involved in the afternoon raid when five Ju88s bombed Luqa. Flt Lt Watts led his flight after the bombers but the I/JG77 Messerschmitt escort kept them busy, one of which Watts (BR373/T-N) and Plt Off McElroy (EN976/T-C) jointly claimed probably destroyed; McElroy claimed a second damaged and another was damaged by Plt Off Reg Round (EP135/T-Z). 126 Squadron and 1435 Flight each scrambled eight Spitfires while 185 Squadron put up another seven, all three units engaging. The 126 Squadron flight encountered the escorting fighters five miles north-east of Kalafrana. Sgt Len Reid noted:

> "Intercepted a party of 109s and Macchis. Engine cut dead and came gliding down past enemy fighters. Almost baled out but eventually made base and landed safely."

Plt Off Bruce Downs claimed a Messerschmitt probably destroyed. He later requested this to be upgraded to 'confirmed' on the strength of a remark by his CO, Sqn Ldr Winfield, who reported seeing fluorescent dye in the sea near to where the combat took place. Flt Sgt Varey damaged another and Plt Off Reade Tilley damaged a Macchi. A pair from 185 Squadron also engaged the fighters 15 miles east of Zonqor Point, Sgt Ken Mitchell claiming a Macchi damaged; meanwhile Sgt Claude Weaver (EP122) for the second day in succession reported he had shot down a brace of Messerschmitts. Three pilots from 1435 Flight succeeded in reaching the bombers, two being claimed damaged by Sqn Ldr Lovell, Flt Lt Halford and Flt Sgt Ron Stevenson. In return, Spitfires were claimed by Ltn Berres of 1 Staffel (his 12th) and Ltn Köhler of 3 Staffel (his 13th):

> "I led a *Schwarm* of Ju88s towards Malta. We flew over Salina Bay at about 5,500 metres. We dived through the holes in the clouds and straight in to the war zone. I stayed 50 metres higher just to watch what to do. The Ju88s took a left turn over Valetta and came back. Four Spitfires came from above with the sun behind. They came closer and closer. I made a sharp left turn that surprised them, and attacked. A thick fog was lying over the sea from 50-300 metres. That would be a nice place for the Ju88s to hide, but the Tommies had already gone through it. I saw the Ju88s go into the fog, but I had my own problems. A Spitfire, just 200 metres away kept shooting at me, but I was a little higher up than him, so I rolled round and got him in my sight. I pumped bullets into him, and then, thank God, a big flame showed up and a white trail told me I had hit him hard. He went down with a white banner hanging after him. The Ju88s stayed in the fog for a while. They were all badly hit."

During the day, one of the island's remaining Hurricane IIBs was lost when the engine of Z2825 failed on a test flight, killing 185 Squadron's 20-year-old Plt Off David Kent from Hertfordshire when the aircraft crashed. A number of the redundant Hurricanes were being test flown prior to their experimental use as fighter-bombers. The unit's diarist commented:

> "Dave Kent, while practicing in a Hurricane for bombing Sicily, had the engine pack up on him on take-off and crashed into the wrecked hangar and was killed. Dave was a very keen type and we cannot afford to lose men like him."

It was not until 1015 on **24 July** that the first scramble was ordered, eight 1435 Flight Spitfires intercepting up to 20 Messerschmitts escorting five Ju88s of KGr806, some 30 minutes later. Plt Off Lattimer made the unit's first confirmed claim when he reported a fighter shot down. Flt Lt McLeod and Sgt Baxter both claimed probable victories, the latter also claiming one damaged, as did Sgt Wally Shepherd. I/JG77 was involved, both Obfw Brandt (his 26th victory) of 2 Staffel and Fw Pohl of 1

Staffel claiming Spitfires shot down. Ten minutes behind them came 16 more Spitfires from 126 and 185 Squadrons, which got through to the bombers. When over Takali at 18,000 feet, Plt Off Rod Smith (BR122/MK-O) of 126 made a port quarter attack on a Junkers on the left of the formation:

"We were vectored onto five Ju88s coming south at 18,000 feet. We met them at their height virtually over the centre of the island. Their fighter escort was lagging badly behind them. They were several hundred yards to our left. I was on the front left corner of our formation of eight, and therefore nearest to them. I began my 180° turn to port, to get in behind them, slightly ahead of the rest of our pilots. I came in behind and made a port quarter attack on the one on the extreme left of their formation, which was the nearest one of course. I chose the port engine of the 88 to start with and fired a six-seconds burst, from 250 yards closing to 150, emptying both drums. The port engine immediately streamed black and white smoke and caught fire, and I shifted my aim to the wing root and then the fuselage, both of which became enveloped in flames.

"The whiteness of fuel-fed flames surprised me, as I had thought they would be orange. Many pieces came off the aircraft. When I finished firing I broke violently down into a diving aileron turn to the left, and kept in it until my ailerons hardened up, my speed being well over 400mph by then. When I came out of the dive I was all alone and saw the 88 coming down streaming fire and smoke in a great downward arc to the south. I then noticed a parachute high up over the centre of the island, and I could see the figure of a man in it. I hadn't noticed anyone bale out but some of the pieces coming off the aircraft were quite large, and it was hard to distinguish between them and a man while concentrating on firing. I was back on the ground in a mere two or three minutes, my entire sortie being logged as 20 minutes."

The bomber crashed to the south of Luqa, near Qrendi; two of the crew were found dead in the wreckage while the one who baled out landed nearby, slightly injured. This was possibly the occasion recalled by another pilot. He saw a German airman land about 200 yards away from where his aircraft was dispersed and as he walked towards him, about a dozen Maltese women armed with spades and pitchforks rushed to the scene. The terrified German airman threateningly produced a small pistol from his flying boot, but on seeing the British pilot wisely surrendered. He was taken into custody and handed over to soldiers when they arrived. Rod's brother Jerry was also involved in the action, flying MK-A, as he recorded:

"Got off late on a scramble. Joined the others just as they attacked the bombers. Started to aim at port Ju88, when Rod opened fire – it went down in flames. Moved over to the next one and opened fire, putting port engine aflame. Was hit in glycol [tank] and force-landed at Luqa (third time this month). Sgt Tiddy saw my Ju88 go into the sea."

Flt Sgt Evans (BR122/MK-O) claimed a bomber damaged. For 185 Squadron Plt Off Jimmy Guthrie (EP200/GL-T) and Sgt Len Reid (AB526) each claimed one of the bombers, the latter recording:

"Intercepted four Ju88s together with large fighter escort. Dived straight down on one at a 45° angle, opening up with cannon at 500 yards closing in to 100 yards, giving one long burst. Hit top of cockpit and starboard engine which immediately gave off black smoke and went into a spin. One Ju88 destroyed."

A third bomber was credited jointly to Sgts Weaver (EP122) and Tony Drew (EP139), while Plt Off Cy King (BR374) and Sgt Mitchell (BR292) damaged another, King noting:

"I was Blue Leader. We climbed to 22,000 feet south-east of Kalafrana. Saw the Ju88s going out towards Filfla and went in. I got abeam and astern, fired all my ammo and saw a flash on cabin. One Ju88 damaged and down!"

With the two units attacking jointly, it is apparent that some double claiming occurred on this occasion. At least one bomber failed to return, Ltn Sepp Hörmann's M7+KH crashing close to Hagar Qim on the south coast. Apart from the damage to Jerry Smith's aircraft, one other Spitfire sustained slight damage during this action. Rod Smith continued:

"126 Squadron's dispersal was along the west-south-west quadrant of Luqa. We could see almost the whole of Malta from there. The arc of black smoke the 88 had trailed behind it remained in the air for quite a long time. The wreckage burned for a very long time, giving off a pillar of black smoke all the while. The groundcrew brought me a burnt piece of aluminium sheeting they said had fluttered down to the aerodrome from the 88. The parachute seemed to take ages to come down, and it drifted slowly to the north. As it got close to the ground it disappeared behind a low ridge to the north-west."

The parachutist was 20-year-old Ltn Heinz Heuser, the W/Op, who confirmed that his aircraft was at 15,000 feet in formation when it was attacked fom the port side and below by a Spitfire with the result that an engine was hit, the machine caught fire and only he was able to bale out. Two bodies were found in the wreckage and the third apparently some distance away.

The Luftwaffe was back during the late afternoon, five Ju88s raiding Luqa at 1800, where an unserviceable Beaufort was destroyed and two others damaged, as were two Spitfires. Although 32 Spitfires were up only a small number made contact, three 126 pilots making claims. Flt Lt Slade and Plt Off Wallace jointly damaged one of the bombers, with Sgt John Tanner reporting strikes on one of the escorting Messerschmitts.

'Blips' that appeared on Malta's radars just after 0100 represented three Ju87s of 102°Gruppo B'aT as they approached the coast in bright moonlight. The two black-painted Spitfires were scrambled in the hands of Wg Cdr Stan Turner and Flg Off Rip Jones to join a patrolling Beaufighter. The Spitfire pilots enjoyed no luck but the Beaufighter engaged one of the Stukas, which suffered damage to its tail.

The main event of **25 July** was the return of the Italians to the skies over Malta, when a dozen MC202s of 20°Gruppo and seven of 155°Gruppo joined Bf109s to cover five Ju88s to Luqa and Hal Far during the afternoon. On the latter airfield two Hurricanes were damaged by shrapnel and debris, whereas over the target area the Italians reported that six Spitfires were encountered. Two of these were claimed shot down, one by M.llo Ennio Tarantola which he reported crashed near Delimara Point and one east of St Thomas Bay by Ten Italo D'Amico, and Cap Doglio Niclot claimed a probable. Four more were claimed damaged, but D'Amico's Macchi was hit five times in the starboard wing. Plt Off Glazebrook, one of eight 603 Squadron pilots scrambled to intercept, claimed a Macchi shot down. His opponent may have been D'Amico or possibly a Bf109 of 2/JG77, as Obfw Kurt Görbing was reported missing from a combat in Black 4 (13179). The German pilot was located in the sea and was soon rescued by an ASR Dornier from Sicily. Two pilots of 1435 Flight managed to reach the bombers, two of which were damaged by Canadian Flt Sgts Maclennan and Pinney. One Spitfire was slightly damaged.

It was on this day that Air Vice-Marshal Park issued his 'Fighter Interception Plan', as mentioned earlier. Until now, usually out of necessity due to the small numbers of defending fighters available but latterly also out of habit, flight leaders would fly south of the island to gain height and then attack any enemy seen, usually following bombing attacks; hence, during the first two weeks of July, 34 aircraft had been damaged on Malta's airfields. Sufficient numbers were now available – if not to actually take the fight to the enemy – at least to meet him halfway, and that meant over the sea. Park issued instructions that raids would be intercepted north of the island, well out to sea and before the bombers could reach their targets.

The intensity of the raids increased on **26 July**, those that approached at 1038 interrupting Sunday morning church services around the island. Seven Ju88s planted their bombs on Takali, where a Spitfire was burnt out. Other Spitfires intercepted, Flt Lt Bill Johnson (MK-W) leading his flight of eight from 126 Squadron after the fleeing bombers, personally claiming one probably destroyed:

"Weaved into bombers over Takali just after dropped bombs. Got one engine on one, which started losing height but couldn't see it go in. Boys damaged nearly all rest."

Other bombers were attacked and damaged by Flt Sgt Varey (two) and Plt Off Downs. Another eight pilots from 1435 Flight tangled with the escort, Sqn Ldr Lovell identifying the fighter he damaged as a Macchi. Oblt Geisshardt of 3/JG77 claimed his 85th victory in this action when he reported shooting down a Spitfire. Ltn Köhler reported:

"Three more flights to Ta Venezia [Takali], Hal Far and Ta Venezia again. On the third, we saw Spitfires and they saw us, but neither was in the mood for a fight. Suddenly, three big spots of oil showed on my windscreen. I was only doing 300kmph. Then I realised the pumps for the landing gear had broken. I thought: 'If the Tommies saw me now?' And, of course, they did! I increased speed as much as I could, and outflew them. It seemed to have lasted for ever, but I got home safely. I had problems with my landing, but I came down safely."

Although B Flight of 185 Squadron was airborne, the pilots gained no success:

"The Black Knight (F/Lt Ken Charney) led B Flight into the azure blue after some dirty Ju88s and their little brothers – Me109s. The Red Knight (Buzz Ogilvie), however, was the first to attack, he and Jo Sherlock squirting at Ju88s while F/Sgt Andy Andrews went into the fighters alone, splitting them enough for the other two to get out again. However, the shooting was bloody awful on both sides and nobody got hurt."

Shortly after 1400 the bombers were back, five Ju88s targeting Hal Far, where two more Hurricanes were damaged. Although eight 603 Squadron Spitfires and four of 1435 Flight were sent after them and their escort, no contact was made. Two hours later more returned – seven Ju88s blitzing Luqa and Safi, where a Spitfire was destroyed and three Beauforts and an ASV Wellington were damaged. Eight Spitfires of 126 Squadron pursued the bombers as they fled northwards over the sea, Plt Off Jerry Smith (BP952/MK-F) catching up with one four miles out from Grand Harbour:

"Attacked from above but got only one hit. Passed 109 on way down, which Rod squirted at. As I broke over the bombers, was hit in glycol and force-landed at Hal Far while Luqa was being bombed. Rod escorted me down."

The American Flg Off Rip Jones fared better and claimed one of the bombers shot down about 30 miles out to sea, but as Sqn Ldr Phil Winfield[86] closed in on another his aircraft was hit and he was badly wounded. Despite a massive loss of blood he managed to land safely at Takali, where he was tenderly lifted from the cockpit and rushed by ambulance to hospital. He believed he had been struck by return fire from the Junkers he was attacking, although he may have been hit by a Messerschmitt, as Obfw Walter Brandt of 2/JG77 claimed a Spitfire that was not confirmed. Again 1435 Flight was involved, Sqn Ldr Lovell gaining hits on one of the escort over Luqa, but it escaped serious damage.

The AOC's intention for a more offensive attitude was immediately acted upon that night, when three Hurricanes, each with two 250lb bombs slung underwing, set off to bomb Gela airfield. Flown by Wg Cdr Tiny Dawson (station commander at Hal Far) and two of 185 Squadron's Spitfire pilots, Sgts Weaver and Len Reid, the sortie was not a success, however. Although taking advantage of the bright moonlight, Weaver was unable to locate Gela and returned with his bombs intact, while Reid was unable to reach the designated target owing to heavy fuel consumption and released his bombs in the vicinity of Scicli instead. Consequently, only Dawson actually arrived over Gela and although the two bombs were dropped on the airfield from about 3,000 feet, no results were seen. Buildings and M/T were then strafed by Dawson, who reported a lack of opposition from the defences. Although not deemed a success, it was the forerunner of events to come.

At 0835 on **27 July**, eight Spitfires of 185 Squadron were ordered off, followed 20 minutes later by six of 249 and eight of 126. All were vectored on to nine Ju88s heading for Takali, but arrived too late to intercept before the Germans completed their bombing. On the airfield two Spitfires including BR316 were damaged. Later, when a delayed-action bomb exploded, a further two Spitfires and two Hurricanes were also damaged. Meanwhile Spitfires, including those of 126 Squadron, engaged as the bombers headed out to sea on their way home, apparently having lost their Messerschmitt escort. Thirteen Macchis (11 of 20°Gruppo and two of 155°Gruppo), flying as indirect support, moved in to help the bombers. Ten Mario Mazzoleni pursued one Spitfire down to 1,500 feet above the sea and claimed its probable destruction, while other pilots claimed strikes on a further six. At this moment the 249 Squadron pilots spotted the Macchis and closed in with deadly effect; as the indefatigable Sgt Beurling (in BR301/UF-S) later recalled:

"I spotted four Macchis running in line astern and took No.4. They saw me coming and pulled into a climbing turn to the right. As they did I came up on my man's starboard quarter and let him have a burst. It was a straight deflection shot which went into his engine and radiator. He flicked into a spin, but managed to pull out and crash-landed on Gozo, able to walk away from the mess."

The Italian pilot, Serg Magg Falerio Gelli of 378^Squadriglia, who had claimed three Malta Spitfires during his tour, later told his captors:

"I saw one Spitfire firing at me but felt no hits. I took violent evasive action and when disengaged noticed that the engine temperature was mounting rapidly. I turned north in an effort to reach my base but soon realised I could not do this as my oil tank was hit, as well as my radiator. I turned back and force-landed on Gozo, getting away with a few bruises."

Having disposed of the Macchi, Beurling immediately latched onto another, which was seen to waggle its wings as he closed in and opened fire: "The poor devil simply blew to pieces in the air."

So died Cap Furio Doglio Niclot, commander of 151^Squadriglia and one of Italy's leading fighter pilots, having claimed six victories plus three more shared. He was killed instantly. Adrenalin must have been pumping into Beurling's veins as he moved towards the next Macchi, only to be distracted by a couple of Messerschmitts he spotted below:

> "I half-rolled and shot past the Messerschmitts, pulling up sharply under their bellies. I let the first guy have it full-out and caught him in the gas tank. Down he went. I still had time for a shot at his team-mate and blew pieces off his wings and tail. He flew off in a hurry, skidding all over the sky. What happened to him God knows."

Other pilots of the flight were also engaged with the Messerschmitts. Sgt Red Brydon (EP196) believed his attack killed the pilot of the one he engaged as it was reported to have dived straight into the sea from 20,000 feet, and Plt Off Williams (EN976/T-C) claimed another. Fw Kneur of 5/JG53 claimed a Spitfire shot down for his third victory. Of the loss of Doglio Niclot, one of his pilots, Ronaldo Scaroni, recalled:

> "When he died, some of the fighting spirit of the Regia Aeronautica died with him. There was a feeling that if Doglio Niclot couldn't survive, none of us could. For the first time we began to doubt that Malta could be taken."[87]

Spitfires of 185 Squadron had by now joined the action, and Plt Off Guthrie (AB526) reported seeing some 20 Bf109s five miles off Gozo, one of which he attacked. He gave it an eight-seconds burst following which smoke was seen gushing from it. Two pilots of his flight, Sgts Drew and Mitchell, later confirmed having seen an aircraft dive into the sea in the vicinity of the combat. It seems that at least some of the reported Messerschmitts were in fact Macchis, for two more aircraft of 20°Gruppo were damaged in this fight, M.llo Ennio Tarantola being wounded in one arm. Despite his wound he, and the pilot of the other damaged machine, M.llo Alessandro Sicco of 353^Squadriglia, both regained their base safely. Owing to further damage to Takali airfield, the returning Spitfires were ordered to land at Luqa.

Lunch was interrupted at Takali by the approach of five Ju88s of III/KG77, but the defending fighters prevented them from reaching their objectives. All four squadrons had aircraft up – a total of 25 Spitfires (seven/126, seven/185, six/249 and five/603) – in an attempt to comply with the AOC's latest instructions. It fell to Flt Lt Bill Johnson's flight from 126 Squadron to make the suggested head-on attacks on the bombers. Johnson (MK-W) noted in his logbook:

> "Met four Ju88s line abreast with escort above and behind. Got two myself, F/Sgt Varey got another. All jettisoned bombs and tried to run. $2^{1}/_{2}$ Ju88 destroyed."

Apparently all four Ju88s were claimed destroyed, Johnson sharing a third with Flt Sgt Ken Evans (AB531) and Flt Sgt Joe Bush, but claiming the lion's share; damage to others was claimed by Varey (two) and Sgt Norm Marshall. These potentially deadly head-on tactics worked ideally on this occasion, three bombers from 7 Staffel falling into the sea, including 3Z+JR flown by the Staffelkapitän Oblt Josef Zimmer, who was lost with his crew. There was one survivor, the gunner, from Fw Helmut Heurer's 3Z+BR, but the observer was killed aboard Ltn Günther Bohnet's 3Z+DR, the other three members of the crew being rescued. An aircraft from 6 Staffel was also hit and the pilot, Obfw Rudolf Panz, wounded. Flt Sgt Evans also claimed an escorting Messerschmitt shot down, with a second as probably destroyed. Another was claimed by Plt Off Downs, who reported:

> "I was attacked by three 109s from above and behind – two were firing at long range. I made a quick 180° turn and then the 109s started to break away (two one way, one the other). I got a two-seconds burst at the last of the two 109s. I saw strikes and the 109 plunged into the sea from a height of 75 feet – one wing hit first and the plane seemed to do a complete cartwheel before it disappeared. No. 3 of Red Section observed the

crash from several thousand feet above."

As 126 Squadron efficiently and speedily dealt with the bombers, the 249 Squadron flight battled with the escort, a number of which were spotted circling around the descending parachutes of crew members of the shot down Ju88s. Plt Off Williams (EN976/T-C) and Sgt Brydon dived on these but the latter's aircraft (EP297) was attacked by another and shot-up quite badly. As Williams headed back to Luqa he spotted a lone Messerschmitt below him, which he attacked in a dive. A quick burst and he reported that the German fighter burst into flames and went into the sea. Sgt Beurling (BR301/UF-S) joined the fight and saw two Messerschmitts:

> "I started chasing one of them around in tight turns and we split-arsed uphill and down dale until he went into a dive to get away. I went along, picked him up in the sights and put a one-second squirt into his glycol tank. He rolled over and went into the sea from 1,000 feet. During the mix-up I had been on the second Messerschmitt's tail for a split second, just long enough to give him a quick one. He streamed black, oily smoke from his engine."

With his fourth victory of the day, Beurling had raised his Malta claims to 14 – all achieved during July – and thereby had become the island's top-scorer, a position he was never to relinquish. II/JG53 was involved in this action, Ltn Hans-Jürgen von Möller of 6 Staffel submitting a claim for a Spitfire south of Salina Bay, but it was not confirmed.

Hardly had the various flights of Spitfires landed to refuel and re-arm, when eight from 126 Squadron were scrambled as more enemy aircraft approached the island. It would seem, however, that these were on a mercy mission searching for survivors of the missing aircraft. Two Messerschmitts were sighted, one of which was damaged by Flt Lt Bill Johnson (MK-W):

> "Found two Me109s on sea [meaning at sea level] 20 miles north of Grand Harbour. F/Sgt Evans got probable and I saw strikes but no result."

The final raid of the day occurred just before 2000, three Ju88s being escorted towards Luqa by Bf109s and MC202s of 51°Stormo. Again 249 Squadron was involved in the interception, seven Spitfires joining eight others from 603 Squadron, but only Plt Off Rae (BR323/T-S) was able to make any definite claims. He reported the probable destruction of a Messerschmitt before he went on to damage a Macchi, which he misidentified as a Reggiane. Of the eight Messerschmitts claimed during the day, at least two had undoubtedly been misidentified as records show the combats to have been with Macchis. However, three Messerschmitts were lost: Ltn Karl-Heinz Preu, eight-victory ace of Stab/JG53 (Black<3/7525) and Uffz Heinrich Freckmann of 6/JG53 (Yellow 11/7447), were both reported missing, and an aircraft of 3/JG77 crash-landed on return and was totally destroyed, although the pilot survived.

Two hours after this latest raid on the island, three Hurricanes departed for a further intruder sortie to Sicily, their target being Comiso. Wg Cdr Turner led this time, again with Sgts Weaver and Len Reid. Two of the Hurricanes dropped their bombs over the south-west corner of the airfield from 4,000 feet, experiencing light but accurate AA fire. The other Hurricane pilot was unable to release his bombs. While the Hurricanes were away, the two black Spitfires flown by Wg Cdr Douglas-Hamilton and Plt Off Glazebrook carried out two patrols, but sighted nothing.

28 July proved to be another good day for the defenders, but it began badly when eight 1435 Flight Spitfires went off at 0850. They were bounced by Bf109s from both II/JG53 and I/JG77, part of a fighter sweep comprising a reported 27 aircraft which led a reconnaissance Bf109 of 1(F)/122; this aircraft later force-landed on return to Comiso, possibly as the result of combat damage. Meanwhile, Obfw Rollwage of 5/JG53 claimed one Spitfire shot down west of Zonqor Point, while Oblt Freytag (63rd) Staffelkapitän of 1/JG77, Obfw Brandt of 2/JG77 (27th) and Uffz Karl-Heinz Witschke of 3 Staffel (his third), also each claimed one. Flt Sgt Bob Brown baled out of BR303 into the sea from where he was subsequently rescued. Sgt Don Hubbard's aircraft (EP189) was also shot-up and it crashed in a field near Kirkop when attempting to approach Luqa; it smashed into a stone wall, ripping off a wing and narrowly missed careering into some parked Beauforts; the 20-year-old Leicestershire pilot was killed.

At 1130, five Ju88s with an escort of 16 Messerschmitts and four MC202s of 51°Stormo were intercepted well north of the island by 23 Spitfires of 185 and 249 Squadrons, only two of the raiders eventually crossing the coast to attack Hal Far. Pilots of the latter unit reported intercepting three bombers, eight Bf109s and two RE2001s, obviously misidentifying the Italian fighters. There were no conclusive results of the ensuing action in which Sqn Ldr Mitchell (BR373/T-N) claimed one bomber probably destroyed:

> "I sighted three Ju88s 5,000-6,000 feet below us and dived sharply on them. I attacked first, full beam, closing to astern and observed strikes on both mainplanes and fuselage. As I broke away I observed both engines pouring black smoke and the aircraft diving steeply. This was observed by Plt Off McElroy, No.3 of my section."

Plt Off Rae (BR323/T-S) and Sgt Irving Gass (EP196/T-M) shared the probable destruction of a second of the bombers, as Rae reported:

> "I carried straight in on the bombers opening fire on the rear one from about 300 yards on the beam, closing to almost astern; strikes were observed on the fuselage. I broke down and underneath this e/a. The fire from the rear gunner ceased before breaking away. I then came up underneath the leading bomber, opening fire for about three seconds from almost dead astern. E/a commenced smoking from starboard engine and wing root. Sgt [Irving] Gass also attacked this e/a observing it smoking before attacking."

Plt Off Yates (BP975/T-T) damaged one more. Others tangled with the escorting fighters, Flt Sgt Tommy Parks (EP131/T-O) being credited with a Messerschmitt probably destroyed, while Sgt Wynn (BP869/T-K) and Plt Off McElroy (EP135/T-Z) damaged two more. The latter also claimed damage to an Italian fighter. Following behind, 185 Squadron also became involved but only Flt Sgt Andy Andrews (EP316) was able to make any claims when he damaged two more Messerschmitts. Having gained strikes on the first one:

> "I was forced to break off as another Messerschmitt manoeuvred for position on my tail. As I still had lots of speed from the dive I pulled up sharply and in a four-seconds burst at 30° astern, I saw cannon strikes on his fuselage behind the cockpit. I was forced to break off by a Spitfire attacking me from out of the sun, and had no time to finish this off."

In the late afternoon five 185 Squadron Spitfires were ordered off to patrol the north of the island, and were still up at 1710 when 16 more Spitfires took to the air, eight each from 1435 Flight and 126 Squadron. Three Ju88s of II/KG77 were intercepted at 18,000 feet as they approached Hal Far. The first two were attacked by several pilots and both went down, one in flames and the other trailing white smoke, which developed into a full fire before it hit the sea. There were no survivors from Uffz Fritz Rottenbecher's 4 Staffel aircraft (3Z+EM) or from 3Z+BP flown by Ltn Wolfgang Marzahl of 6 Staffel. One of the bombers was credited to Plt Offs Paul Baril (BR387/GL-W) and Jimmy Guthrie (BR321/GL-J) of 185 Squadron, shared jointly with two pilots of 126 Squadron, Sgts Alastair Tiddy and Nigel Park (BR345/MK-S). The latter fired a four-seconds burst and saw flames before being forced to break away as a Bf109 closed in on him. Guthrie reported:

> "We climbed to 22,000 feet south of Zonqor, and sighted three Ju88s coming in at about 18,000 feet. All Green Section dived towards these aircraft over Hal Far, but by the time we got near them, two had already been shot down. I delivered a short head-on attack on the remaining Ju88 closing to 50 yards, and then pulled left on a climbing turn. When I completed the turn, the Ju88 was going down in pieces. The Ju88 was already damaged when I attacked it."

Plt Off Baril thought the bomber fell into the sea off Delimara after he had seen his fire hitting the starboard wing, fuselage and tail. The second bomber fell to the combined attacks of five pilots of 126 Squadron – Flg Off Rip Jones, Plt Offs Jock Thompson, Freddie Thomas, Jerry Smith and Flt Sgt Gord Farquharson. It would seem that this bomber was the one that crashed in flames on a Dorset Regiment billet at Tas-Silc; one of the crew was found dead near the wreckage. Jerry Smith, who soon discovered that the cannons of his aircraft (MK-A) had not been loaded, then suffered a jammed machine-gun, noted:

> "Turned port into bombers. Fired from 200 yards closing at port 88 – a two or three-seconds burst and aircraft immediately burst into flames around port engine and front of fuselage. It turned to port and down. I turned into the middle Ju88 and fired a short burst and saw a trail of white smoke... observed the starboard 88 going down almost vertically in flames. Also saw four Spits chasing an 88 at deck level five miles south-east of Kalafrana, which trailed white smoke, turned to port and crashed into the sea."

Jerry Smith's aircraft suffered a hit in the glycol tank and had to force-land on return. The third Ju88 was attacked by his brother, Plt Off Rod Smith (MK-C):

> "Intercepted three escorted Ju88s heading west over Kalafrana Bay at the same height. We turned left into them and this time I was on the side farthest away and therefore last into them. One of the 109 escort came right down among us blazing away but we ignored him. As was common, most of our pilots attacked the nearest 88. The one on the left side of their formation, and a couple of them attacked the one in the centre. Both of them caught fire and started down in seconds. I flew across and opened fire at the port engine of the one on the far side, which no one else had attacked.
>
> "The port engine of 'my' 88 caught fire immediately, and I carried my aim into the port wing root and then the fuselage, and then the starboard engine, all of which also caught fire. The aircraft headed downwards but I kept firing for the full 12 seconds. Finally the engines came out, the wings fell off, and all the burning pieces fell like a shower of golden rain. I think that firing all my ammunition in one 12-seconds burst was an emotional reaction from being fired upon so often before, with rarely a chance to fire myself. I was amazed to find later that three [*sic*] of the crew got out. They must have been quick off the mark, perhaps put on their toes by the other two 88s going down seconds before. I hadn't noticed them among the big pieces that were coming off all the time."

Unbeknown to Rod Smith, this particular bomber was also under attack by other Spitfires – those flown by Sqn Ldr Lovell and Plt Off Mejor (EP140/V-P) of 1435

Flight, joined by Wg Cdr George Stainforth[88] (CO of the Beaufighter night fighter squadron) who had borrowed one of the unit's Spitfires and come along 'for the ride'. The Ju88 – 3Z+WP flown by Uffz Albert Führer – went down close to Kalafrana Bay and two of the crew baled out. The ASR unit commander, Flt Lt Crockett, quickly put to sea in seaplane tender *ST338* and within seven minutes had picked up Uffz Gustav Frick (the gunner) and four minutes later the badly wounded wireless operator Uffz Karl-Max Bauer, who would undoubtedly have been lost but for Crockett's prompt action. The other two members of the crew died. Of his part in this, his first combat, 43-year-old Wg Cdr Stainforth (a former Schneider Trophy pilot, and holder of the World Air Speed Record in 1931) reported:

"After climbing to about 16,000 feet approximately south of Kalafrana, CO (Sqn Ldr Lovell) turned and dived on a Ju88 which was then untouched, flying east, followed by the rest of the section. Several Me109s were about, but no other Ju88s. Got left 200-300 yards behind on the outside of the turn. A 109 turned in front of and below me allowing an easy quarter attack from close range. Did not see it go down as I went over the top of it and broke off to keep with my section. After the Spitfire in front (Sqn Ldr Lovell) attacked the Ju88, I saw two occupants bale out and the starboard engine began smoking. I made diving quarter attack on it (short burst), then did wide zig-zag to come back for second attack from astern and below. The Hun was flying level after turning north, smoke coming from the starboard engine, both engines running. Opened fire from 200 yards, kept the button pressed until passed a few feet over the top of it. Many strikes observed – fuselage burst into a mass of flames. Nobody else baled out. Did not watch or follow it down, but dived after a Spitfire chasing a 109 – Sqn Ldr Lovell – joined up eventually."

The battle had not quite finished as Sgt Nigel Park, having shared in shooting down one bomber, then claimed an escorting Messerschmitt. He fired a short burst from about 50 yards as it passed him in a turn and saw strikes right beside the cockpit; it veered away and was seen to go down. Many on the ground had witnessed the fighting above, including LAC Phil Chandler, who wrote in his diary:

"While having tea, three bombers came in and Spitfires and ack-ack engaged. Heard a cheer as one kite came down and, a few seconds later, another; but was too busy trying to pinch a bit of bread in the cook's absence to go out. Then came a third cheer! I went to the door of the dining hall and saw an 88 diving and on fire, right above. One of the crew baled out, but his parachute only half opened and he would be lucky to get away with his life. The machine hit some buildings on the other side of the bay and became a huge mass of flames. Finished my tea and was just in time to see one of two more parachutists hit the sea not far out. Watched them brought in. One was said to be about sixteen, and had a hole through his arm."

This would have been Uffz Bauer who, during subsequent interrogation, complained that in all his flights over Malta his aircraft had always been detailed to fly on the outside of the bombing formation and thus was the first to be attacked. His gunner, Uffz Frick, admitted that as a result of their manoeuvrability he reckoned the Macchis gave better close escort protection than did the Messerschmitts. Although he considered Italian pilots were not up to German standards generally, he said the Macchis had always afforded him good protection on such flights he had made with them. I/JG77 was again involved, Oblt Siegfried Freytag claiming two Spitfires but neither was granted as confirmed.

During the afternoon a section of four Spitfires from 603 Squadron was scrambled, led by Plt Off Dicks-Sherwood, to intercept an unidentified 'plot' that appeared on the radar screens. Finding a Z506B floatplane just above the surface of the sea about ten miles off the coast, and suspecting that it might be about to make a torpedo attack on the harbour, he opened fire but missed as the Cant took evasive action. His No.2, fellow-Rhodesian Sgt Bill Young, then opened fire and gained strikes on the port wing, following which the floatplane alighted on the sea without mishap. Control was informed of the incident and *HSL107* was despatched to the scene. It transpired that the floatplane, 13-139/MM45432 of 139^Squadriglia RST, had been hijacked by the crew[89] of a Malta-based Beaufort shot down in the previous day's strike against an Italian convoy off Sapienza, southern Greece. The crew had safely ditched and had been rescued from the sea by a Z506B. They were taken to the Greek harbour of Prevesa. Next morning they boarded another Z506B for a flight to Taranto and captivity, but managed to overpower the crew and force the pilot to divert to Malta. They were fortunate not to have been shot down by the Spitfires.

After about an hour *HSL107* arrived – to find all nine occupants sitting on the wings, enjoying brandy and wine! Subsequently the captured floatplane was taken in tow by the launch and eventually brought into St Paul's Bay, while Spitfires patrolled overhead to prevent it from being attacked by any 'snooper' in the vicinity. The unfortunate Italian crew now found themselves to be the prisoners. In their absence, they and the accompanying armed guard were tried by court martial and found guilty of carelessly allowing the enemy to capture their aircraft. The Cant was put to good use by its new owners.

The following morning (**29 July**), seven 249 Spitfires were scrambled at 0915 to intercept a sweep by an estimated 16 Bf109s and four MC202s, which came in after an earlier raid had turned back before reaching the island. After an initial skirmish, one fighter dived out of the sun on Sgt Beurling's Spitfire (BR301/UF-S), shooting off the cockpit canopy. Beurling immediately turned onto the tail of what he believed to be the aircraft that had just attacked him, and from 450 yards fired a one-second burst, which hit the engine of the Messerschmitt. At once it went down in flames into the sea 500 yards off Sliema Point, as his subsequent combat report revealed:

"As Tiger Blue 1, I attacked 15 Messerschmitts over Grand Harbour. Dogfighting ensued for 15-20 minutes. Made an attack on one e/a from port quarter below; gave a three-seconds burst cannon and machine-gun fire; large pieces of e/a came off, then e/a's gas tank exploded and the aircraft burned. E/a struck the sea one mile north of Grand Harbour."

His victim on this occasion was Uffz Karl-Heinz Witschke, flying Yellow 2 (13060) of 3/JG77, who had claimed his own third victory a day earlier. The action was witnessed by 126 Squadron's Plt Off Jerry Smith: "Pilot baled out but apparently his chute burned because he splashed in shortly after from several thousand feet."

It seems unlikely, however, that Witschke had been the pilot who attacked Beurling's aircraft, for two claims were submitted by Messerschmitt pilots, one by Oblt Geisshardt of 3/JG77 (his 86th victory), and the other by Obfw Rollwage of 5/JG53 (his 28th). One of these apparently related to Beurling and the other to another member of the 249 flight, Sgt Ernie Budd, who returned to Takali with a damaged aircraft (EP131/T-O) and crashed on landing, although he was unhurt. Budd reported shooting the fin and rudder off a second fighter, which he believed was another Messerschmitt, and this also fell into the sea. It seems likely that he had misidentified his victim, for Serg Domenico Manini baled out of his 378^Squadriglia Macchi about three miles south of Marsascala, from where he was picked up by a British minesweeper and taken to Malta.

The day's major activities concluded at around 1800, when seven Spitfires of 185 Squadron were scrambled due to the appearance of a possible hostile 'plot' on the radar screens. This turned out to be three delivery aircraft flying in from Gibraltar. 185 Squadron had endured a fairly quiet day:

"B Flight scrambled twice after Me109s but after dashing around the ozone, the Black Knight [Flt Lt Charney] failed to make contact with Joe Kesselring's band of buggers and nothing happened. Tomorrow being a stand-down, everybody staggered over to the sergeants' mess for a few noggins."

At 0755 on the morning of **30 July**, seven of 1435 Flight's Spitfires were scrambled, followed by 16 more from 249 and 603 Squadrons, to meet a reported fighter sweep believed to include approximately 20 Messerschmitts and six Macchis. In fact, there were three Ju88s present but these did not cross the coast, but the escort included 15 MC202s of 51°Stormo led by TenCol Remondino, as well as Bf109s. The Macchis were undertaking a simulated raid to confuse British radars.

1435 Flight reported being jumped by ten Messerschmitts at 26,000 feet ten miles north of Grand Harbour, but it would seem that the attackers may have included Macchis, for the Italian pilots claimed two Spitfires shot down, one by Remondino himself, and one jointly by Cap Bruno Tattanelli, Cap Egeo Pittoni, Ten Alberto Volpi, Ten Giuseppe Bonfiglio, Serg Magg Alcide Leoni and Serg Luigi Berna. Serg Magg Giovanni Gambari of 378^Squadriglia reported seeing two Spitfires crash in flames. Oblt Michalski also claimed a Spitfire at this time, his 40th victory. Only one Spitfire actually fell, 24-year-old Sgt Colin Wood (a New Zealander from Auckland) being killed when his aircraft (EP344) went into the sea off St Paul's Bay, as noted by Plt Off Mejor (EP209): "Got jumped at 26,000 feet by six 109s. Had dogfight for about one minute, then they left us. Wood's bought it. 88s turned back without making landfall."

Four Spitfires of 126 Squadron were despatched immediately to search for the missing pilot but nothing was sighted. Pilots of 603 Squadron reported sighting six Bf109s and six Macchis eight miles north of Zonqor Point. Sgt Noel Pashen:

"Tangled with 109s – turned into four and gave short burst when seat collapsed and broke. Blacked out and regained control completely at 500 feet. Thought my time had come. Must have hit at least two 109s, but no claims."

Flt Sgt Parkinson (BP989/4-N) later recorded:

"Scrambled about 8am. Flew to about 20,000 feet. Intercepted six 109s. I shot one down, hit him in the engine with my first burst, followed him down to about 500 feet and gave a burst from astern at about 50 yards. His port wing fell off and he fell in the sea."

Somewhat later, at 1109, seven 126 Squadron Spitfires were scrambled to join others from 249 and 603 Squadrons, as another fighter sweep approached at great height. As they climbed over Grand Harbour, two Messerschmitts dived out of the sun and hit the aircraft flown by Sgt Dave Ritchie, who promptly baled out and landed with nothing worse than a bruised arm. His assailants were almost certainly Staffelkapitän Oblt Freytag (his 64th victory) and Fw Pohl (10th) of 1/JG77, each of whom claimed a Spitfire shot down.

Shortly before 1600 at least six Axis fighters crossed the coast at great height, presumably on a reconnaissance sortie, but no contact was made by four 249

Squadron Spitfires that were up at the time. The Spitfires were actually escorting the captured Cant seaplane from Zonqor to Kalafrana, where it would be repaired, serviced and given new colours to serve the island as an air-sea rescue craft. Apparently Obfw Walter Brandt of 2/JG77 fired at a Spitfire but his claim was not allowed.

At 1000 on **31 July**, Plt Off Stenborg of 185 Squadron took off on an air test in BR321/GL-J. Warned of hostile aircraft in the vicinity, he encountered three Bf109s one of which he claimed shot down; he reported:

> "I heard Gondar [Control] inform the squadron which was airborne that the enemy was at 20,000 feet. I then lost height to 22,000 feet and while flying west saw three Me109s below, flying in a northerly direction. It was a perfect jump so I attacked. I opened fire at the 109 on the right who was lagging farthest behind at 400 yards closing to 50 yards – bits flew off the aircraft and it burst into flames. The remaining two 109s half-rolled and disappeared."

This latest claim raised Stenborg's total to ten, five of them during the month. Although Spitfires of 126 Squadron were sent after this small fighter formation, no further contact was made.

A large sweep occurred during the early afternoon, when an estimated 18 Messerschmitts from II/JG53 and I/JG77 were seen. Sixteen Spitfires of 185 and 603 Squadrons were up but had insufficient height to intercept, and were bounced. Four Spitfires of the former unit were hit. From a burning EP255 Sgt John 'Doc' Livingston baled out into the sea, the Canadian being picked up by *HSL128* within the hour; meanwhile Sgt Weaver succeeded in crash-landing his damaged aircraft (EP343) and survived unhurt. Not so fortunate was the pilot of another aircraft hit in this attack. Flg Off Tony Bruce was obliged to bale out of EP137 and despite an intensive search he was not found. Close behind 185 Squadron had come the 603 Squadron aircraft, Flt Sgt Parkinson recording:

> "Scramble at about 3pm. Climbed to about 15,000 feet. Two of my section had to land because of engine trouble. The CO and myself were left by ourselves. I was keeping watch behind when I saw six enemy aircraft, called up to the CO but he took no notice. I called about six times all told – the Messerschmitts were coming too close for comfort. I called up once more and broke up sun and dived to attack. The enemy aircraft were going so fast that I only had them in range for a second. Gave a long burst and saw strikes but no other results. The CO broke also when he saw me."

Of the two pilots who had suffered engine malfunctions during this sortie, Flg Off Newman made a successful landing, but Flt Sgt Ballantyne was not quite so fortunate. Having suffered engine failure when at 20,000 feet he attempted to glide back to Luqa, but overshot and damaged BR562, although he was not hurt. Oblt Michalski of 4/JG53 claimed two of the Spitfires shot down during this action, his 41st and 42nd victories, while Ltn Rüdiger Belling of 1/JG77 also reported shooting down a Spitfire, his first victory.

The final action of the month occurred shortly after 1800 when an estimated 27 fighters were plotted to the north of the island. Sixteen Spitfires, eight each from 126 Squadron and 1435 Flight, were sent to investigate and a number of skirmishes broke out some miles out from St Paul's Bay. Plt Off Jerry Smith noted:

> "Intercepted two squadrons of 109s about 20 miles west but couldn't get near them. While flying with Rip [Flg Off Ripley Jones] one intrepid beggar came up behind us, firing at Rip. I turned into him but he climbed quickly and fired from well out of range.

> When 15 miles off Sicily a squadron of 109s passed us going back; turned to chase them, but they stooged home."

Not all members of the unit were unsuccessful however, Flt Lt Bill Johnson (BR345/MK-S) claiming a Messerschmitt shot down, and Plt Off Jock Thompson a RE2001, although Italian fighters were apparently not engaged on this sweep. Johnson noted:

> "28,000 feet over Gozo, vectored north. Engaged 109s at 27,000 feet 15 miles north of St Paul's Bay. I got one. Thompson got a RE2001. Blue Section chased the rest back to Sicily."

* * *

In terms of aircraft losses honours were fairly even for the month, but actual pilot casualties in the RAF units had been relatively low, whilst those among Axis aircrew had been quite heavy. Axis bomber losses had been particularly severe, including at least 22 Ju88s and about half-a-dozen Italian types (13 were victims of the night fighter Beaufighters). The two carrier deliveries of Spitfires had certainly made good the attrition, but food and fuel remained the island's greatest problem. During the month Spitfire pilots had flown 1,780 sorties and had claimed 137 aircraft shot down. 38 Spitfires had been lost from which almost half the pilots had been saved. The AA guns were credited with a further eight victories. The PR Spitfires had chalked up a further 58 sorties without loss and continued to provide valuable information throughout the month. Belated recognition of the work carried out by the reconnaissance Spitfire pilots of 69 Squadron finally came with the award of a DFM to Sgt Leslie Colquhoun, who also received a commission. 249 Squadron's outstanding Canadian pilot, Sgt Screwball Beurling, received two DFMs and a commission; he was now the island's leading fighter pilot with 17 victories, 15 of which had been scored during July. Of the many stories that circulated around him, one of his contemporaries recalled:

> "Beurling, as a sergeant pilot, dressed very casually in khaki shorts, leather flying boots and Australian battle dress top, with New Zealand wings and carried his sergeant's stripes in his pocket. The day he was informed by his flight commander that he was to attend at the office of the AOC in Valetta, the following morning, to be awarded a commission in the field as a pilot officer, he advised his flight commander that he would be unable to attend because it was in fact his day off! Nonetheless, he did get his commission."

Fellow Canadian Bob Middlemiss, who received his commission at the same time as Beurling, added:

> "I arrived at the Wingco's office and sat outside the room on a chair, with just a beaded curtain dividing me and the office. I was dressed in my best blue uniform, shoes, buttons all polished and sparkling, but there was no sign of Beurling. Suddenly he arrived off the aerodrome, where he had been working with the airmen [groundcrews] on the guns of an aircraft. He was in his khaki shirt and shorts, sweaty, oily and dusty. He asked me if he could borrow my comb. He was not the least bit concerned about the interview. When he went into the office I could hear the conversation between him and the wing commander. Beurling told the Wingco he really did not want a commission, that the airmen would not look up to him and would have to salute him and such. Wing Commander Gracie replied that he was the type that the men looked up to and would be proud working for. Of course, he was commissioned. He was also granted a second Distinguished Flying Medal. He did not appear overly impressed, however, and

continued to live with the sergeant pilots."[90]

A belated DFM came the way of Flt Sgt Paddy Schade of 126 Squadron, with $13^1/_2$ victories the top-scoring Malta pilot until eclipsed by Beurling. He was also recommended for a Bar to the DFM at the same time, but this did not come through. He was now taken off operations pending his return to the UK[91]. 185 Squadron's Plt Off Gray Stenborg received a DFC. A DFM and a commission were also announced for 185 Squadron's Flt Sgt Don Reid, who had been killed on 22 July.

It was decided that the indefatigable Wg Cdr Jumbo Gracie – one of the unsung heroes of Malta – would now be replaced as OC Takali by Wg Cdr W.K. LeMay, who had recently arrived on the island. Gracie returned to the UK, but was not officially recognised for what he had achieved over the past few months, possibly having offended too many brass caps with his often officious and straight-talking attitude. At 31, overage for a fighter pilot, particularly one with poor eyesight and a damaged neck, he had nonetheless raised his score to 15 including three shared and five probables[92]. Even Beurling, the ultimate disregarder of rank and authority, commented:

> "Everybody felt like hell to see Wing Commander Gracie go back to England for a rest. He'd been Mr Malta and the dump wouldn't be like home without him."

Another to depart at the end of the month was 126 Squadron's Plt Off Junior Crist, who had been on the island since the end of March. Newly commissioned Plt Off Jack Rae[93] was also taken off operations at this time when his wounded leg became badly infected; he was returned to the UK for further treatment.

It is noteworthy that bombing raids had fallen away considerably during the second half of the month, only 19 attacks being made during which 160 tons of bombs were dropped, compared to more than double that tonnage during the first two weeks of July, when 390 tons had been directed at the island. Indeed, the bombers had increasingly been conspicuous by their absence, as the focus of the Axis effort became devoted to fighter sweeps. On the face of it, Air Vice-Marshal Park's new tactics would appear to have been instrumental in an unacceptable rate of attrition being forced on the Ju88 units. This would cause a resumption of effort by the Axis to force an air superiority battle between opposing fighters before the bombers could resume their offensive. The end of the month also marked the end of the Regia Aeronautica's latest offensive. All further operations by Italian fighters were suspended due to low serviceability caused by the problems that were being experienced with the Macchi 202.

Due to the surplus of Spitfires now on the island, it was decided to expand 1435 Flight to full squadron status, and to reform 229 Squadron, previously a Hurricane squadron that had served briefly on the island earlier in the year, from the personnel of 603 Squadron, which effectively disbanded. Sqn Ldr Bill Douglas was to remain in command while Flt Lt Peter Lovell took command of one flight.

CHAPTER VII

THE DECEPTIVE CALM

August – September 1942

The first day of the month was notable by its lack of aerial activity over Malta. It was not until three hours before midnight that the air raid alarms sounded in earnest on the approach of three BR20Ms that had set out to raid Luqa. A further small force – three Z1007bis – followed close on their tails. Beaufighters were up and the AA barrage was intense, but only minor damage was inflicted on the bombers and very little to Luqa. 185 Squadron received a new diarist:

> "And with the start of the month we get a new, albeit temporary scribe who, I fear, will lack greatly in literary style. Early in the morning, at 0610, Sgt Drew led a section of A Flight on a search for F/O Bruce before we heard he had arisen from deep, demanding a drink."

Bruce[94], shot down the previous day, eventually paddled ashore in his dinghy, exhausted after having covered 15 miles in 15 hours. He complained that although he saw searching Spitfires, including one which came within 800 yards of him, he had no fluorescent dye with which to attract them, nor a torch or whistle, without which he stood little chance of being seen or heard by aircraft or launch. He also reported that the hand paddles with which the dinghy was equipped were not suitable, and recommended that any sort of small paddle with a shaft would be preferable. The diarist continued:

> "Later, at 0930 after a hearty if not tasty breakfast in dispersal, P/O Guthrie led six of A Flight's valiants up towards a plot of 15-plus but nothing came of it. The rest of the morning was spent doing air tests. In the afternoon P/O Ogilvie led scrambles which made no contact with our friends from Sicily."

Three or four bombers plus fighter escort approached Malta at between 20-30,000 feet just after 1400 on the afternoon of **2 August**. Twenty-three Spitfires were up by the time the force reached the island, but only eight of 185 Squadron made contact. Four Bf109s were observed orbiting Gozo at 26,000 feet and these were engaged, Sgt Weaver (EP139) claiming one as probably destroyed:

> "I was Green 2 patrolling at 27,000 feet when I noticed a Me109 on the tail of Green 3. I gave the break and turned towards the enemy aircraft. Green 3 broke down and to the right. The enemy aircraft turned slightly my way and I got in a two-seconds burst from 200 yards, head-on. I noticed pieces flying off the starboard wing root and hits on the engine cowling and about the cockpit."

More Messerschmitts arrived and two Spitfires were lost during the skirmish, however. Plt Off Jimmy Guthrie, a 22-year-old Surrey man in BR362 crashed on the island midway between Zebbieh and Dwejra Lines and was killed, as was 21-year-old New Zealander Sgt Matt McLeod, whose BR321/GL-J was shot down into the sea. The diarist wrote:

> "They were well and truly bounced. I have to regretfully report that Guthrie was killed and McLeod is missing. Jimmy Guthrie was well liked by the Squadron and although new to us was very experienced, having done over 80 sweeps over France. We can ill-

afford this type of loss. P/O King led a search for Sgt McLeod but saw nothing. Then Sgts Mitchell and Reid went out and had another search but were still unable to find him. Mac was from NZ and although also new to our Squadron will be missed by the types for he was always smiling."

The jubilant Messerschmitt pilots accurately claimed two victories, one of which was the sixth victory for Ltn Karl Eberle of 2/JG77; the other was shot down by Oblt Michalski of 4/JG53 (his 43rd); a third was claimed by Oblt Jürgen Harder of 7 Staffel, but this was not confirmed.

Twenty-three Spitfires of 185, 229 and 1435 Squadrons were airborne by 1100 on **3 August**, to meet a fighter sweep of 27 Bf109s, but the Messerschmitts apparently avoided combat. However, Sgt Bill Knox-Williams of 1435 Squadron was bounced by one and shot down in EP331, baling out into the sea. He was rescued by *HSL107* and taken to hospital with superficial facial burns. On this occasion the pilots of I/JG77 overclaimed, Obfw Brandt (his 28th), Oblt Freytag (65th) and Obfw Georg Ludwig (26th) each a Spitfire shot down. In addition, Fw Pohl claimed another but this was not confirmed.

Four Spitfires of 229 Squadron were off early on the morning of **4 August**, to investigate 'hostiles' approaching the island, and two fighters identified as MC202s were seen east of Zonqor Point. Lt Zulu Swales attacked one, which reportedly smoked heavily, and was last seen flying low over the water. He claimed it as probably destroyed, but there is no apparent record of Italian fighter activity on this occasion. Soon after lunch eight Spitfires of 126 Squadron were scrambled and joined seven of 229 Squadron to challenge 15-plus Bf109s reported approaching. The former unit sighted six Messerschmitts and engaged them over St Paul's Bay, resulting in Sgt Baron Richardson being shot down in BR357. The Australian managed to bale out safely. Colin Parkinson of 229 Squadron noted: "I saw a Spit shot down today. It came down like a bat out of hell, pouring glycol, on fire. The pilot baled – it was the Baron Richardson, a friend of mine."

Pilots of 185 Squadron were given a break from operations, allowing some to let their hair down, as the diarist noted:

"Squadron was stood down, bars all over the island were busy. Those in Sliema in particular. F/Lt Charney had a slight altercation with numerous and sundry including the police, and returned to Birzebuggia at 0500 in a very bedraggled condition, while Killer Stenborg, upon perceiving that the Black Knight [Charney] had failed to follow his leap aboard the departing ferry boat in Sliema, shouted, 'Women and children first' and leaped overboard in full blue. With peak cap firmly clamped on his head he paddled ashore to the delight of the watching Maltese. Other types continued the other Malta pastimes of swimming and attempted seduction of women."

An estimated 20 Bf109s of II/JG53 in two formations approached the coast at 0840 next morning (**5 August**), to be met by eight Spitfires of 1435 Squadron. Oblt Siegfried Freytag claimed a Spitfire but this was not confirmed. Blue Section engaged three aircraft from 6 Staffel, one of which was shot down by Flt Sgt Pinney, while Green Section patrolled over a Catalina flyingboat in Kalafrana Bay to prevent it being strafed. Four of 229 Squadron led by Flt Lt Peter Lovell (EP339) were sent off to search for the downed German pilot but nothing was sighted. Of his combat, Pinney reported:

"My section was flying along in south-easterly direction when we were attacked by four 109s, which broke off this attack without firing and passed over our heads, splitting into pairs. I turned and saw another pair of 109s diving down towards us in a south-easterly direction, and completed my turn. I fired a short burst from head-on position, breaking off the attack at less than 50 yards, without observing strikes. On turning again, however, I saw a 109 with glycol pouring from it. This aircraft has been confirmed as destroyed."

Plt Off Mejor (EN980), leading the 1435 Squadron's Blue Section, noted:

"Water babies [Catalina] patrol! Four 109s tried to box us but my No.4 [Pinney] shot one down – the Staffel leader [sic]. Helluva flap in Sicily! My No.4 inexperienced. Did we laugh?"

Two hours later eight Bf109s were reported to have crossed the coast while others escorted a seaplane identified as a Do24. Four of 229 Squadron and eight of 126 Squadron were scrambled, four of the latter briefed to patrol over the Catalina in the bay. Red Section saw what they believed was a Do18 (sic) on the sea, some ten miles off St Paul's Bay, with a number of Bf109s orbiting. On the approach of the Spitfires, the seaplane took off and headed for Sicily and combat resulted. In fact, it would seem that the formation seen was actually seven 51°Stormo CT Macchis covering a Z506B searching for the German pilot, who had baled out into the sea south of Cape Scaramia. He was rescued unharmed[95]. The Italians reported sighting three Spitfires but no action ensued. The Macchis were back at 1745 when 11 aircraft of 51°Stormo escorted bombers over Malta. Messerschmitts were also present. Eight Spitfires of 229 Squadron had scrambled on their approach and these intercepted 15 fighters described as Messerschmitts and Reggianes, about 20 miles off Comino. Flt Sgt Irwin reported:

"I was flying Blue 3 to Lt Swales. We were flying due west about 15 miles west of Gozo at 20,000 feet. When Blue 4 reported e/a at 1400 – there were about 15 of them – we swung round to attack and I looked behind to see six Me109s attacking us from behind. Blue Section broke right and I climbed up steeply and lost contact with the rest of the section. I got mixed up in a 'do' with three or four 109s and while circling saw three new e/a enter the scrap from above. One of them attacked me. I skidded sharply to port and throttled back then when the e/a overshot, swung in behind, and fired a three-seconds burst from astern at 250 yards. I saw strikes on port wing, forward part of the fuselage and tail. The e/a streamed glycol and black smoke and dived away inverted. At that point I was attacked by his No.2 and was struck by an explosive shell in the starboard magazine. Three or four of my own bullets exploded and I went into a spin from which I was unable to recover until I was right on the water. The enemy aircraft attacked appeared to be a RE2001."

51°Stormo CT reported engaging two Spitfires south-west of Gozo and claimed both shot down, one by Ten Vittorio Bastogi and the other shared by M.llo Iannucci and Serg Magg Vittorio Iannilli.

Two relatively quiet days followed. In the early hours of **7 August**, a Hudson transport of 24 Squadron arrived from Gibraltar carrying amongst its passengers newly promoted Wg Cdr Peter Prosser Hanks DFC, and Sqn Ldr Bryan Wicks DFC. Both had fought in France in 1940. Hanks was to take command of the Luqa Spitfire Wing, while Wicks had been appointed to succeed the wounded Sqn Ldr Phil Winfield as CO of 126 Squadron.

8 August brought a resumption of fighter engagements, when seven Spitfires scrambled at 0830 to intercept a small formation of Bf109s of I/JG77; two of the Spitfires had to return early but the remaining five engaged the intruders. Plt Off

Beurling (EN373/T-T) fired at one as it headed northwards, but was jumped by two more. He claimed that he hit one in the glycol tank and engine with a two-and-a-half-seconds burst, and that it went straight into the sea. This was apparently confirmed by his section leader. Beurling's aircraft was then hit and the engine almost seized; having decided against baling out, he carried out a successful belly-landing in a ploughed, stone-walled field, as he later recalled:

> "As I came close in over the wall I put the left wing down to take up the bump and bellied down into the ground. The wing absorbed the wallop and stopped me cold. The far wall was too near for comfort. I climbed out, unhurt except for a superficial cut in one arm."

Flt Lt Frank Jones (BP869/T-K), who was leading Blue Section, also claimed a Bf109 shot down:

> "Six enemy aircraft passed overhead. We turned towards e/a and saw two more coming down on our tails. I told Blue Section to spiral down to draw e/a down. I saw e/a attacking Blue 2, Sgt Budd, and warned him. He broke in front of me followed by the e/a, which appeared in front of my nose at less than 15 yards, presenting his belly to me at point-blank range. I fired a burst of one second and then was forced to break as I was being fired at myself. E/a disappeared and was seen by my No.3 [Beurling] to be going down smoking and in obvious distress. I fired a short burst at close range at another Messerschmitt but saw no results."

Sgt Budd claimed damage to one more but his own aircraft (EP131/T-O) was also hit and damaged, and he sustained shoulder wounds. Despite his injuries, he succeeded in landing safely. A number of Spitfires of 1435 Squadron were scrambled at 1020 to aid 249 Squadron but Sgt Clarence Kelly, a New Zealander from Auckland, was reported missing in EP336. His leader, Flt Lt McLeod (V-P), reported:

> "Wavy Blue 1 (myself) and Blue 2 (Sgt Kelly) observed three Me109s pass below us at 10,000 feet. We were at 15,000 feet. We turned into the sun and attacked. I picked out the right hand one who was flying wide. I closed to 250 yards firing a four-seconds burst from dead astern. Strikes were observed. Then broke left firing head-on at one of the other two, both of whom had broken right into us. I pulled up and circled to the left, observing my No.2 doing the same. He was some distance behind me and in my opinion did not have an opportunity to fire at the one I had attacked as the other two delivered a head-on attack at him, or at least, were in a position to do so. The one I hit did not seem to do much of anything but stagger along. The two who had broken right continued climbing in a northerly direction after having passed through us. I then informed my No.2 to come home as this was his first engagement on operations, and my starboard cannon had jammed. After looking round for the other aircraft and observing none, I looked down and saw a plane hit the water. There was no parachute. I gave a 'Mayday', thinking it might have been my No.2."

The Luftwaffe reported that 20 Bf109s of II/JG53 and II/JG77 encountered an estimated 30 Spitfires, one of which Obfw Rollwage claimed shot down two miles north of Valetta as his 30th victim. Three more were claimed by Oblt Freytag (66th), Fw Pohl (11th) and StFw Helmut Gödert of 1/JG77.

In a bid to establish that Axis seaborne forces were not assembling for an invasion of Malta, pairs of Spitfires were now being despatched to reconnoitre the Sicilian coastline. One such pair flown by Plt Offs Ogilvie and Sherlock of 185 Squadron, departed Hal Far at about 1940. They flew at low level in order to avoid being detected by radar, and when the south-east corner of Sicily was reached, flew along the beach for about 20 minutes; no suspicious craft or invasion preparations were observed and they flew back to Hal Far in darkness, where a barely discernible flare path had been laid out for them. Notwithstanding this, both landed without undue mishap, as noted by the diarist: "The whole squadron stood out in the failing dark listening for the noise of their approach. Needless to say, with such an incomparable pair, they got away with it. Both undercarts were severely strained by the dusk landings."

At 0950 on **9 August**, a total of 22 Spitfires (eight/229 Squadron, eight/1435 Squadron, six/126 Squadron) were ordered off to challenge 19 plus Bf109s as they approached the island. Blue Section of 229 engaged three of the Messerschmitts over Filfla at 26,000 feet, one of which was credited to Plt Off Dicks-Sherwood. His No.2, Plt Off Hugh Reynolds, also reported seeing the Messerschmitt on fire but the Rhodesian's own combat report was not so conclusive:

"I was leading Blue Section. Putting my nose almost vertical I managed to give the leading enemy aircraft a two-seconds burst, beam attack. Saw strikes slightly forward of cockpit, pieces fell off and enemy aircraft went in northerly direction losing height and streaming glycol (other pilots of 229 Squadron also saw this and were of the opinion the Messerschmitt was destroyed)."

The 126 Squadron flight reported meeting four Bf109s over St Paul's Bay at 11,000 feet, Sgt Nigel Park (MK-U) claiming one of these shot down: "Scrap with four 109s. Got one. One hit me in port wing. Cunning bastard!"

Fifteen Spitfires were scrambled on the approach of a further fighter sweep at 1420, eight of 126 Squadron spotting a number of hostile aircraft but these were not engaged. However, Sgt Dave Ritchie's Spitfire (BR122/MK-O) was seen to break formation, turn on its back and go in a shallow dive into the sea; this was the second occasion in under two weeks that the Canadian had been shot down, and he was to spend all night in his dinghy before being rescued next day by *HSL107*. That evening, Flt Lt Hetherington and Plt Off Beurling were despatched to search the southern coastline of Sicily for signs of a reported MTB flotilla. Although nothing untoward was sighted on this occasion, packs of such Italian and German craft were indeed active and would cause havoc when let loose amongst an approaching convoy.

Flt Lt Coldbeck was briefed to fly a Spitfire PR sortie to Catania on the morning of **10 August**, and was instructed to drop a package as he passed over the airfield. This contained the personal belongings, including family letters, of the crew of the Cant seaplane captured two weeks earlier. The mission was successfully undertaken and the package was dropped from AB300 at a height of about 3,000 feet. 69 Squadron received a further aircraft (BR431) and pilot when Sgt Frank Gillions, another New Zealander, arrived from Gibraltar on posting to the unit.

Spitfires of 185 Squadron and 1435 Squadron scrambled to intercept a raid by Ju88s and II/JG53 Bf109s at 1025, attacking these over the island after they had bombed Luqa, where a Beaufighter was badly damaged, five others and two Spitfires less seriously so; an airman was killed and an ambulance destroyed. Flt Sgt Mahar of 185 Squadron had his aircraft (AB526) shot-up – possibly by Oblt Michalski of 4/JG53 (his 44th victory) – and crash-landed at Luqa. The diarist wrote:

"Action again today. B Flight led by the intrepid Black Knight [Flt Lt Charney] was well and truly bounced in a turn by some 109s they had already seen. F/Sgt Mahar insists there were at least 20 or 30 of them. Sgt Red Walker tried out his guns on an obliging Hun who posed momentarily as a target. However, he was a bit out of practice and the Hun went home. Johnny Sherlock had fun and games with a pair of 109s up north of Grand Harbour but his shooting eye was out, too, so he didn't get anything. F/Sgt Mahar went down to take a Hun off Johnny's tail but his port cannon fired just two shots and the starboard didn't fire at all. He used his machine-guns on him and then decided to go home. A dirty great Messerschmitt crept up his tail and let him have it. Eric got to Luqa only to have a bullet hole in his tyre and completely wrote off the kite on landing. However, he wasn't hurt, but I bet he looks behind the next time he comes home alone!"

Meanwhile, Flt Lt McLeod (V-J), Plt Off Lattimer and Flt Sgt Maclennan of 1435 Squadron each claimed a Messerschmitt shot down. One dogfight over Kalafrana Bay ended with Uffz Walter Schmidt's fighter (Yellow 9/7609) bursting into flames, from which the badly wounded 6/JG53 pilot baled out and landed in the sea close by. Within ten minutes the rescue tender *ST338* had reached him and he was soon wrapped in blankets, on his way to hospital – prompt action that undoubtedly saved his life. It would seem that Schmidt fell to Wally McLeod's shooting, as both Lattimer and Maclennan reported combats north of St Paul's Bay. McLeod recorded:

"I was Green 1, patrolling at 20,000 feet between Takali and Luqa. We observed the raid off St Paul's Bay and travelling east, cut in behind the bombers. My section singled out several Me109s behind, and attacked. I closed on the left-hand one, firing a four-seconds burst from 150 yards. Aircraft broke up and pilot baled out."

Of his first victory claim, fellow Canadian Ian Maclennan reported:

"I was Green 3, patrolling at 20,000 feet between Takali and Luqa. As the raid was going out we came down from behind on two Me109s at the rear of the formation. Green 1 (McLeod) took the left, which I observed to go down in flames, and I took the right. I opened fire at close range from slightly below gaining, then had four bursts dead astern. I broke sharply right as I was being bounced. When last seen, he was going down about 45° pouring heavy black smoke. Blue 1 (Lattimer) reports oil patch north of St Paul's Bay, half a mile offshore, as our attack finished and before he started his."

Lattimer's report is an example of how easy it was for pilots to double claim:

"After the main formation of enemy aircraft had left the island, with Blue 3. I attacked three Me109s who were heading north but turned south-west on observing us. I made a quarter to port head-on attack at one 109 on the left and gave him a two-seconds burst with cannon and machine-gun, opening fire at range 250 yards, and closing to follow around with deflection so that after observing strikes – cockpit, wing root and rear of cockpit – I spun to the right and recovered after losing some height. Gondar Control, a few minutes later, reported a parachute coming down five miles north-east of St Paul's Bay and requested Gondar Blue to investigate. He stated the victim to be a Hun and requested his captivity. This I consider to confirm my claim."

Two Spitfires of 126 Squadron followed at 1145 on a patrol over minesweepers in Grand Harbour, with two others patrolling over *HSL107* departing St Paul's Bay. A Ju88 was seen heading northwards, probably a straggler from the raid intercepted by 1435 Squadron, and Plt Off Jerry Smith (BR366) gave chase. He did not return. It seems likely that he caught the Junkers, for Fw Helmut Streubel's 3Z+ET of 9/KG77 failed to reach Sicily; possibly Smith's aircraft fell to return fire or was, in turn, intercepted by one of the Messerschmitts. It seems probable that he was shot down by pilots of I/JG77, who made three claims, one each by Obfw Brandt (his 29th victory), Ltn Rüdiger Belling (his second) or Fw Gerhard Häcker, his first. His brother Rod was amongst those who searched the sea in vain.

The end of the second Italian offensive against Malta coincided with preparations to run a further convoy through the Western Mediterranean. The arrival of only two damaged freighters in June had done little to alleviate the ultimate problem facing the defenders – starvation, both in terms of food and fuel. Hence, a large convoy comprising 13 heavily laden freighters and the American tanker *Ohio* had departed the Clyde in late July, heading for Gibraltar where a strong naval force, including four aircraft carriers, one of which – *Furious*[96] – carried 39 Spitfires for Malta (Operation Bellows), was being assembled to escort the convoy towards its destination. Among the pilots assembled aboard *Furious* was Grp Capt Walter Churchill DSO DFC, a Battle of France veteran with seven victories including three shared, who was on his way to Malta to take up a new appointment as deputy to the AOC, Air Vice-Marshal Park. Although he could have accepted passage to the island aboard a transport aircraft, he much preferred to ferry a Spitfire, as did Wg Cdr Arthur Donaldson DFC AFC (a former Whirlwind fighter-bomber pilot), who was to take up an appointment as Wing Commander Flying at Takali. Two further experienced pilots had joined the group as flight leaders, Flt Lt Eric 'Timber' Woods DFC (three victories including one probable) and Plt Off Bill Rolls DFM, a Battle of Britain veteran with a dozen victories to his credit including three probables.

The convoy and its escort finally sailed from Gibraltar at dawn on 10 August. Now, as the time approached midday on **11 August**, it was planned to despatch 38 Spitfires (one having developed a fault) in three flights of eight and two of seven. Churchill and Donaldson would lead the first two, Woods and Rolls the next two, and Flt Lt 'Dan' Magruder, a Scot, the fifth. The first flight began taking off at 1229, and included American[76] pilot of Greek ancestry, Sgt Nicholas Dimitrios Sintetos:

> "I took off in the first group of four Spitfires. Taking off from a carrier made for a tense feeling. All those other Spitfires awaiting their turn, and you hope your kite starts up all right and you don't pull a stupid thing to mess up an important operation. It all happens so fast, once you start up. When I hit the rise during take-off, I kind of bounced into the air and never even got a chance to use full throttle."

As the Spitfires took to the air, vigilant observers picked up the telltale blips on the screens of the Italian-manned German radar unit on Lampedusa, but despite immediate warning to Air HQ on Sicily, inexplicably, no action was taken. No fighters were scrambled, and all except one of the Spitfires completed the long flight without interference or undue mishap. The Spitfires were flown by:

Grp Capt W.M. Churchill, DSO DFC (flight leader)	Flt Sgt J.G. Sanderson RAAF (EP517)
Wg Cdr A.H. Donaldson DFC AFC (flight leader) (EP329)	Sgt W.R. Whitmore
	Sgt J. Tarbuck
Flt Lt E.N. Woods DFC (flight leader)	Sgt J.D. Vinall
Plt Off W.T. Rolls DFM (flight leader)	Sgt D.G. Guy
Flt Lt E.P.F.L.T. Magruder (flight leader)	Sgt J.M. Harrison
Flt Lt G.H.A. Wellum DFC	Sgt L.R. Gore
Flg Off H.F. Gedge	Sgt L.H. Swain
Flg Off P.A. Woodger (US)	Sgt E.H. Francis
Flg Off L.S. Nomis (US) (EP410)	Sgt C.H. Cornish
Flg Off. A.I. Lindsay RCAF	Sgt N.D. Sintetos RCAF (US)
Lt K.C Kuhlman SAAF	Sgt J.E. Mortimer RNZAF
Plt Off P.A.J. O'Brien (EP472)	Sgt R.J. Roe RNZAF
Plt Off R. Seed	Sgt J.A. Houlton RNZAF

Plt Off A.R.H. Maynard

Plt Off D.P. Pollock

Plt Off L. Cheek RCAF

Plt Off A.F. Roscoe RCAF (US)[97]

Plt Off R.B. Park RAAF

Flt Sgt E.T. Hiskens RAAF[98]

Sgt T.R.D. Kebbell RNZAF

Sgt L.P. Garvey RNZAF (EP685)

Sgt A.B. Stead RNZAF

Sgt J.F. Yeatman RNZAF

Sgt F.W. Clewley RAAF

As these operations were underway, the fleet oilers were refuelling destroyers and it was at this point, taking advantage of the general activity that the commander of *U-73* manoeuvred his submarine within range of the passing procession of major warships. Selecting the carrier *Eagle*, he put a salvo of four torpedoes into her port side. She at once took on a list to port, which rapidly became more pronounced as she capsized and sank within six minutes. One hundred and twenty-three of her crew were lost, 930 being saved by the prompt action of escorting destroyers. The sinking was witnessed by many of those on *Furious* including Paddy O'Brien:

> "The second section [of Spitfires] was quickly brought up on deck and the first two had taken off when suddenly *Eagle* was seen to be in trouble. She had been sailing parallel to us about one mile to starboard. Now she was stopped, smoke was pouring from her and she started to list to port. She was sinking rapidly. Planes could be seen slipping off the flight deck and men jumping into the sea. Destroyers were dashing about and depth charges going off. Pandemonium! As we watched helplessly *Eagle* turned over and sank all within ten minutes.
>
> "I shot down to my cabin and put on my Mae West. It certainly looked as if I might need it as our ship had been lagging behind the convoy to get room to manoeuvre for our take-offs. The other planes took off and joined up with the leaders, setting course for Malta. There seemed to be a new urgency as the next section was wheeled up on deck. Each group took about half an hour to organise, and I was in the last section. At least another hour and a half to go! It was not a nice feeling that there were subs around, having just seen how quickly an aircraft carrier could be sent to the bottom. I was naturally looking forward to getting airborne although I couldn't help feeling that I was running out on the navy. We did hear some sailors remark that they didn't have aeroplanes. We knew how they felt. At least in the air you have mostly yourself to blame for your misfortunes."

At 1347 *Furious* resumed despatch of her Spitfires, the final 22 aircraft going off by 1512. As the last flight of Spitfires became airborne, New Zealander Allen Stead discovered that his long-range tank was not feeding through. Initially, the pilots had been told that should they experience problems immediately following take-off, they were to bale out ahead of the nearest destroyer, which would pick them up if not too busy! This was greeted with so much adverse comment that it was agreed that should problems arise, a landing could be attempted on the nearest carrier. Stead favoured the latter option, and having carried out a low pass over the *Indomitable*, successfully landed at the second attempt. The navy pilots were reportedly delighted to receive a Spitfire, and were keen to fly it into combat when the opportunity arose. O'Brien was unaware of the drama:

> "In the next few minutes we had a visit from some enemy aircraft. They were flying at a great height and the guns of the fleet opened up. No bombs were dropped – probably reconnaissance planes having a good look. The third and fourth sections took off without incident and soon after I was being strapped in and wheeled onto the lift for the trip up to the flight deck. I got a shock to find there was no air pressure. Once again I

had visions of being stuck on the ship, but the groundcrew soon put things right. Air pressure is needed to operate the brakes, flaps and guns and I could not have taken off without it. When all the checks had been made the wing commander gave us the signal to start engines. With brakes on and chocks in front of the wheels we ran the engines up to full power. Two airmen straddling the tail to hold it down. The pitch control on my aircraft was very sluggish at first but settled down.

"The carrier turned into wind and our section leader P/O Rolls took off. I taxied a few feet forward and lined my aircraft to the right of a white line, which had been painted down the deck. As none of us had taken off carriers before, it was hoped this would help to keep us straight. I was given the green flag – opened up the throttle with brakes on, until the plane started to slip forward. Then full throttle and release brakes. The take-off was unexpectedly brief and I was off the end of the carrier in seconds. I made a climbing turn after my leader and adjusted the engine controls. The plane seemed very sluggish and I took this to be due to the extra weight of the 90-gallon long-range tank. Then I realised that I had not retracted the wheels. Having done this, and feeling a bit stupid, I switched to my long-range tank and circled around waiting for the rest of the section to join up."

Meanwhile, realising that the Axis were now fully aware of what was going on, Plt Off Bill Rolls decided not to lead his Spitfire flight over the planned route directly east until off Bizerta, then south-east to Malta, passing Pantelleria to the south – as he anticipated likely interception, particularly from the latter quarter. Instead he headed immediately south-west, which took the flight to the Algerian coast, making landfall at Cape Bougaroni, and passing south of Bône and Tunis. Leading his aircraft in a dive as they passed over the Tunisian coast out over the Gulf of Hammamet, Rolls thus avoided any reaction from the Vichy French. Of this part of the flight, O'Brien recalled:

"Some French fighters were spotted well below us but they did not try to intercept. We made our final course alteration at Hammamet with about an hour's flying time left. Shortly after leaving the coast my engine started to splutter. I quickly switched over to the main fuel tanks and it picked up immediately. Gave me a bit of a start. We had to keep a very sharp lookout from now on as the Italian base at Pantelleria came into view on our port side, and soon after Linosa and Lampedusa appeared. We hoped to avoid meeting up with enemy fighters, having no machine-guns and we did not want to jettison our long-range tanks."

The Spitfires reached their destination without further event, turning to approach the island from the south. O'Brien continued:

"Our aircraft followed each other around the circuit at Luqa and landed one after the other. My landing was one of the worst I had ever made. I blamed it on fatigue after a three-hour flight. My stomach was sore and my rear end most uncomfortable. I landed with a heck of a thump, fortunately without any damage."

Another of the new arrivals, 20-year-old Flg Off Leo Nomis, an American from Los Angeles of part-Irish, part-Sioux Indian ancestry, later commented:

"They should have awarded a medal for the mere arriving at Malta. I have never been to another place with such a visible atmosphere of doom, violence and toughness about it at first sight. Coming out from England as we did, the filth, flies, diseases and near starvation absolutely fascinated us, the more so because the interception missions – which were boundless, were not in the least deterred by these handicaps. The air war seemed more deadly here, the 109s more sinister."

Her task completed, *Furious* – with an escort of eight destroyers – turned back westwards and headed for Gibraltar to pick up further Spitfires for subsequent delivery, while the convoy continued its bloody and costly battle towards Malta[99].

With all the fighting away to the west, Malta had experienced a relatively uneventful day. Two more Spitfires, BP911 and BP883, both PRIVs, arrived at Luqa from the Middle East during the morning, including one flown by the legendary Flt Lt Adrian Warburton DSO DFC and Bar. This was Warburton's second tour at Malta, having flown Marylands and Beaufighters during his first stint on the island[100]. He was now promoted to Sqn Ldr to take command of the PR Spitfire Flight of 69 Squadron. His unannounced arrival and general attitude did not go down well with everybody, including Flt Lt Coldbeck who was in charge of the Spitfire Flight:

> "I was alone sitting on my office seat reflecting and attending to censoring letters and the programme for the morrow when I was surprised by a flight lieutenant walking in silently behind me in desert boots. I recognised him as the person I had seen 'holding court' in the bar at Luqa, in March, at the time I had first transferred myself and AB300 from Takali. Yes, it must be Flt Lt Warburton. I said, 'Just in?' He answered 'Yes'. Then he quickly reversed and disappeared. As on the first occasion, no names were exchanged. It was several days later that he appeared again – now wearing the rank badges of squadron leader.
>
> "I asked the new squadron leader, when I had the chance, if he would be flying with us and received an affirmative. I put him on the programme after enquiring if the sortie I offered would be convenient to him. That worked for a short time but very soon he began to ignore my programme and without reference to me he would take a Spitfire and head off in it. This played havoc with our schedule, trying to keep up with the requirements of AHQ with the very limited aircraft available. A pilot on my programme would go out to the dispersal and find his sortie and aircraft had disappeared. The ground crew would confirm that Sqn Ldr Warburton was flying it although the Form 700 would not have been signed. On his return, he would take a seat in the Intelligence Office to reveal then where he had been and the tremendous adventures he had endured to get his photographs. His voice travelled through the building, which provoked some of my pilots to feign sickness and move about with hand over mouth and clutching stomachs. Having started with the Intelligence Office, he would then telephone AHQ and if the AOC was not available, would talk in flamboyant terms to the SASO. Afterwards, he would transfer himself to 'my' chair and entertain any off-duty pilots with stories of his remarkable feats relating to his recent flying activity and history.
>
> "My office now being full to capacity, I could stand about or go elsewhere. The places he was talking about we had been servicing for six or seven months at least. He didn't move far from my office nor did he take any part in running the Flight except to undertake sorties which appealed to him and which it seemed to us gave him the best chance of a good story for the AOC. The Senior Air Staff would seek out the CO of 69 Squadron to pass on important information to his PRU people in the Flight. Unfortunately, that's where the information stayed and we were left in ignorance of quite relevant intelligence and instructions/orders."[101]

Three more PR Spitfires arrived shortly thereafter from Gibraltar. Although the aircraft – BR653, BR662 and BR665 – were retained for use with 69 Squadron, the pilots were not. Sqn Ldr Warburton was soon into his stride and flew a reconnaissance (in BP883) over Taranto to check on proceedings there, mainly to establish if vessels of the Italian fleet were at sea or preparing to depart to intercept the surviving ships of the convoy. He reported nothing amiss.

Over Malta during the mid-morning on **12 August**, Blue Section of 185 Squadron was scrambled, the four Spitfires led by newly promoted Capt Swales. The section was vectored towards a suspicious aircraft, reported about 60 miles north-east of Zonqor Point, but just then Plt Off Ogilvie (EP139) experienced a leaky oxygen valve, which caused him to run short, and he was forced to descend very rapidly. On reaching 14,000 feet, Ogilvie sighted a He111, an aircraft of 6/KG26, flying at about 4,000 feet below, in a north-westerly direction; he recalled:

> "I immediately went into attack after notifying Blue 1 of my position. I attacked from above, opening fire at about 200 yards, closing to point-blank range, with a five-seconds burst of cannon and machine-gun; saw strikes along fuselage. I finished my ammunition and broke off attack. The attack was continued by Blue 4 (Plt Off Sherlock). He found the Heinkel pouring black smoke from its port engine; he made attacks, firing short bursts, and saw e/a turn over on its back from about 3,000 feet. Swales then made port quarter attack from astern and finished nearly all his ammunition – saw strikes and e/a kept diving, then flew at water level, smoking badly. He followed for about 800 yards when e/a suddenly disappeared – he was convinced it had dived into the sea."

Plt Off Sherlock recalled a slightly different version of events:

> "It was one of those interceptions which worked out perfectly. Zulu [Swales] and Buzz attacked immediately and I pulled up and around in front of e/a, and fired at the perspex nose as the Heinkel was gliding down, smoking. I merely fired at a 'dead duck'. The Heinkel crashed into the sea and I could see no survivors."

The Heinkel was officially credited to Ogilvie, and was celebrated as 185 Squadron's 100th victory – all claimed in the defence of Malta.

The convoy making for Malta had come under sustained aerial attack and had suffered severe losses.The situation at first light on **13 August**, as a flight of Spitfires led by Wg Cdr Hanks appeared over the surviving vessels of the convoy, was that one freighter was well on its way towards Malta, two others plus the tanker *Ohio*, which had been damaged, were still making good progress. Far behind came three more freighters, one on its own way to the north and another hugging the Tunisian coastline. The remaining seven had been sunk or were in the throes of sinking. With the ships now in reach of Axis aircraft based in Sicily and Pantelleria, more aerial assaults were anticipated, with Ju88s from II/LG1 and 9/KG54 leading the way, followed by Ju87s of 102°Gruppo Tuff, escorted by MC202s of 51°Stormo CT. *Ohio*, with her 11,500 tons of kerosene and diesel oil fuels, was the obvious target.

From Malta sections of Beaufighters were dispatched to provide some protection, then a flight of four Spitfires from 1435 Squadron followed, these engaging the Italian Stukas. Sqn Ldr Tony Lovell promptly shot down the 209^Squadriglia aircraft flown by Serg Magg Guido Savini, the dive-bomber ditching in the sea with some difficulty. Savini and his gunner, 1°AvArm Nicola Patella, were both thrown out[102]. Claims were also made for Ju87s damaged by Plt Off Mejor (EP209) and Flt Sgt Pinney (two), but Flt Sgt Bob Buntine (EP197) failed to return. It was later admitted that gunners on the freighter *Dorset* had shot down the 24-year-old Australian's Spitfire in flames by mistake, the pilot being lost. Ten minutes later an unidentified tri-motor – believed to have been an SM84 – was encountered with an escort of six fighters, the bomber being claimed shot down by Pinney. This may possibly have been a Do24 from 6 Seenotstaffel, the crew of CH+EU reporting being attacked by a Spitfire but the flyingboat managed to alight safely at Marsala despite some damage. Of his part in this action, Mejor, who had earlier flown a dawn patrol, wrote:

> "Convoy patrol. Control ship had been sunk. We waited up sun but the swine came in down sun. Bags of flak. We dived through and I fired short bursts of one-second each at three Ju87s. Observed strikes on tail of one. I saw two Ju88s making for largest ship. Peeled off through flak to make head-on attack. I was hopelessly out of range but fired to scare 'em. It did. They dropped bombs far wide of target and turned away. I followed. Rear gunners poured tracer at me. I took poor view of it. Ran out of ammo."

There were several other actions reported at this time by the pilots of the Spitfires, which were now out in strength. At 0930, Wg Cdr Hanks led Plt Off Freddie Thomas and Sgt John Tanner of 126 Squadron on an escort, but Hanks had to return almost immediately with engine trouble. The remaining two carried on and near the convoy Thomas (AB465) claimed a Ju88 damaged, but Tanner (EP472) was shot down by a Bf109, probably that flown by Ltn Hans Märkstetter of 6/JG53 who claimed a Spitfire at about this time. The 22-year-old New Zealander from Wellington did not survive. Magg Duilio Fanali of 51°Stormo also claimed a Spitfire during this action, while during a reconnaissance over the Sicilian channel, Ten Adriano Visconti of 76^Squadriglia claimed two Spitfires shot down over the convoy. Four 229 Squadron aircraft went out at 1020, Flt Sgt Parkinson reporting:

> "Counted about nine [sic] merchant ships, one of which (Ohio) was leaking oil very badly and evidently in tow. One of the Beaus went in, the crew baled out but haven't been picked up yet."

His section leader, Flt Lt Northcott (X-L), saw two Ju88s, he and Flt Lt Magruder giving chase. Northcott closed to point-blank range and reported "masses of strikes", as did Magruder; black smoke was seen pouring from both engines and it was last seen rapidly losing height. They were jointly credited with the bomber's probable destruction, and this was apparently updated to confirmed by Y Service. However, it seems likely that this was an aircraft from 8/KG77 that returned to Comiso in a damaged condition.

Close behind the 229 Squadron quartet came another four from 126 Squadron, Wg Cdr Hanks flying his third sortie of the morning. He was accompanied by Sqn Ldr Bryan Wicks on his second sortie, with Plt Off Rod Smith and Flt Sgt Varey making up the section. They arrived just as a new attack commenced against the surviving ships of the convoy, at 1125, carried out by five SM79sil of 132°Gruppo Aut AS, led by Cap Ugo Rivoli, and escorted by 14 more 51°Stormo MC202s, again led by Magg Fanali. Those aboard the ships reported that the Spitfires became involved with the Macchis while the torpedo-bombers – estimated by them to be at least a dozen strong – swept in to attack, most releasing their missiles from long range due to the heavy AA. One was seen to be hit and crashed into the sea on fire, and a second was claimed by another destroyer, while others were believed to have been damaged. Again it would seem that the gunners were firing at aircraft under attack by fighters, for Rod Smith (AB465) recorded: "SM79 destroyed. Gave four-seconds burst. Starboard engine caught fire. Crashed in sea. It was over convoy at 800 feet. Mass of flames." Ten Guido Barani and his crew were lost in the missing bomber. Hanks (EP290) had initially fired at this aircraft, and had observed strikes before Smith had applied the *coup de grâce*.

The Spitfire pilots continued to report engagements. During a patrol begun at 1350, Flt Lt Watts (EP448/T-F) of 249 Squadron claimed damage to an aircraft identified as a BR20 – probably another Savoia, since the crews of two SM79s of

30°Gruppo reported that their aircraft were attacked by fighters, one of 55^Squadriglia being slightly damaged while the second, from 56^Squadriglia, escaped when attacked south of Pantelleria by an estimated five fighters. Another 56^Squadriglia machine was damaged by AA fire from a destroyer at 1250, the bomber landing on Pantelleria where it burst into flames and was destroyed. A further four of 249 Squadron's Spitfires had followed at 1400 to patrol over the convoy, but from this section Flt Sgt Tommy Parks[103] was obliged to bale out of BR246/T-J when hit by AA fire from the convoy's escorts. He came down in the sea, slightly wounded, and was picked up by a destroyer from which he eventually disembarked in Gibraltar! His unit was not immediately notified of his rescue and Parks had been posted missing for some time before details of his whereabouts were received at Malta.

Towards the end of the afternoon there were several more engagements. At 1705, Sqn Ldr Lovell of 1435 Squadron claimed an SM84 shot down, and two hours later Flt Sgt MacNamara and Sgt Jim Hawkins of the same unit destroyed another SM84. Flt Sgt Alan Scott (EN968/V-H) claimed what he thought was a Breda 88:

> "Raid came in with a Breda and six 109s and some Reggianes. Blew up the Breda when I got a three-seconds burst in his petrol tank. A mass of flames and he went straight into the drink. I flew through the wreckage. No survivors. While this was happening the ships were pooping off at everything they could find and flak clouds from them were highly dangerous from our point of view!"[104]

The Italians reported the loss of two of their reconnaissance aircraft during the afternoon, a Z1007bis of 59^Squadriglia flown by Ten Italo Masini that had departed Chinisia at 1355, and an SM79 (MM21544) of 58^Squadriglia, in the hands of Ten Bartolomeo Ferrante, which had lifted off from Castelvetrano at 1632; these undoubtedly fell to 1435 Squadron. Plt Off Mejor (EP714), flying with Flt Lt McLeod's section, was led to believe that he may have accounted for one of the bombers:

> "Patrol tanker *Ohio* and SS *Brisbane Star*. Both disabled. Eytie rescue boat flyingboat (like the one we captured) flying up and down, looking for stray Wops. Myself and No.2 did dummy attack to make sure his crosses were red. He panicked. We flew across him, waggling wings. Shook him! Mac [McLeod] went after a 109 low down on drink but could not catch him. Mac used bad language on R/T. Three 88s came in and dropped bombs. We chased them for short while. I fired three-seconds burst but saw no result. Pity! Nos.3 and 4 had squirt at one each. They did not claim – saw no result… Y Service thinks we got all three. Good show. Hope they all bought it."

This was not the case, however. McLeod (V-J) did nonetheless claim damage to the Bf109 he encountered, which may have been Fw Hugo Langer's aircraft (13190) of 2/JG77 that crashed at Pantelleria, killing the pilot. Obfw Brandt, also of 2 Staffel, claimed his 30th victory, another Spitfire. No Ju88 was lost in this action, although McLeod was credited with one probably destroyed and shared a second as damaged with Mejor, Sgt James Harrison and Sgt Wally Whitmore.

A little later, at 1740, three 249 Squadron aircraft met a lone reconnaissance Ju88 of 2(F)/122 at about 14,000 feet, some 15 miles east of Linosa, which Flt Lt Frank Jones (EP448/T-F) attacked at once; his head-on pass peppered the nose and wings, while Sgt Wynn, following in BR565/T-T, gained strikes on the fuselage; Plt Off Beurling (EP135/T-Z) then waded in and shot out the starboard engine; the Junkers (F6+KK) went down in flames. Uffz Hans-Joachim Schmiedgen and the observer were lost, but two others baled out and both were rescued from the sea. Fw Johann

Brenner, who was wounded, was picked up by a Fiat RS14 seaplane.

At 1800, two sections each of four Spitfires from 126 Squadron were patrolling over the convoy at 9,000 feet, when three Ju88s of LG1 were seen about three miles away, commencing their dives from out of the sun. Sqn Ldr Wicks immediately endeavoured to intercept but by the time he arrived the first had released its bombs and disappeared. The second failed to drop any bombs and climbed away but Wicks engaged the third – L1+BL flown by Uffz Gerhard Bohr – as it dived on *Ohio*:

> "I closed with it expending all my ammunition, opening fire at 200 yards, closing to 100 yards. I saw strikes on the starboard mainplane, and a piece dropped off. I then broke away. Red 3, who then attacked the Ju88, states that as I broke away, the starboard engine of the Ju88 started to smoke."

Red 3 was Plt Off Rolls (BP870), newly posted to the squadron, who added:

> "The CO dived down and fired at one of them. I saw smoke coming from it and went in and fired a two-seconds burst. I saw another Spit dive in front of me so I broke away and dived on a Ju88 from above, firing about three or four seconds of cannon and machine-gun. I saw strikes on the port engine and a cloud of black smoke came from it. The aircraft went in a gentle dive as I broke away. I made another attack from about 15° to line astern, and saw a pattern of strikes zig-zag along the fuselage. I ran out of ammo. By this time the 88 was pouring black smoke from both engines, and it dived vertically into the sea."

Sgt Tiddy (AB531), who was flying as Red 2, also claimed one of the bombers destroyed, as his subsequent report revealed:

> "Red 1 attacked one and I turned to port and attacked another, which was turning to port. I rapidly overhauled and commenced firing at 200 yards. The Ju88 was weaving violently. I observed strikes on the tail and a large piece fell off. I fired another burst and saw strikes on port engine, which instantly emitted dense white smoke. I pulled up and attacked again from starboard quarter and saw strikes along the fuselage. I turned for final attack. The Ju88 had stopped weaving, the return fire had ceased and the port engine had failed. It was losing height, gradually turning to port, white smoke still issuing from the engine, at about 1,500 feet. In view of the fact that it was losing height in the general direction of Linosa, and a large column of smoke arose from Linosa as I rejoined the section, I claim this as destroyed."

Finally on this frenetic day, at 1925, four more 126 Squadron aircraft – including Plt Off Mejor on his fourth flight of the day totalling almost seven hours – arrived over the ships, again led by Wg Cdr Hanks[105], where two Ju88s were reported attacking. Flg Off Rip Jones (BP992) engaged one and saw strikes on top of the fuselage near the gunner's position, but then all his guns jammed. He remained in the bomber's slipstream for a minute trying to get them to fire but was finally forced to abandon the attack.

A fourth Spitfire was lost during the day when Sgt Fred Clewley, a new Australian pilot in 185 Squadron, crashed EP292 on take-off from Hal Far. His vision had been impaired by a dust cloud formed as the leading aircraft took off. Temporarily blinded, he crashed into a stone-built aircraft dispersal pen. He suffered a badly lacerated chin and concussion, while his aircraft was deemed irreparable and was written off. During the late afternoon Sqn Ldr Warburton carried out a search between Sardinia and Cap Bon, his fifth Spitfire PR sortie in the two days he had been back on Malta. His other flights had ranged from Taranto to Messina and Palermo. Another PRIV arrived for the unit during the day (BR663), but two other recent arrivals – BP883 and BP915 – were now ferried to the Middle East, and would shortly be followed by BP908 and BP911.

Daybreak on **14 August** found the crippled tanker *Ohio* surrounded by a bevy of destroyers and minesweepers, crawling slowly towards Grand Harbour. One of the freighters also limped towards the island; three others had already reached the relative safety of the harbour. The price had been severe but at least some supplies had arrived. In the meantime, the Germans had turned their attention to the warships now returning to Gibraltar, leaving the Italians to deal with the convoy's stragglers. Three Z1007bis bombed the damaged freighter, but she again survived and reached Grand Harbour beneath an umbrella of Spitfires. At 0950 however, five Ju87s from 102°Gruppo B'aT led by Cap Antonio Cumbat took off from their base at Gela, escorted by 23 MC202s of 51°Stormo, led by TenCol Remondino. They approached *Ohio* at 1050 to find the tanker protected by Spitfires from 229 and 1435 Squadrons. Sqn Ldr Tony Lovell and his No.2, Sgt Shorty Philp, jointly attacked and shot down one Stuka, as Lovell reported:

> "As we arrived I saw one Ju87 diving and went for it, overtook it rapidly, opened fire at 300 yards and broke away at 30 yards. I saw strikes all over the engine and fuselage. White smoke poured from both sides. He lost height, smoke stopped and he did a steep turn to port and flew west, losing height. I turned back towards the convoy and saw the Ju87 crash into the sea. I claim half share with Sgt Philp."

Philp, a New Zealander from Wellington, added:

> "Blue 1 fired and smoke poured from the engine, and as I went in to fire enemy aircraft began to weave. I fired a four-seconds burst then broke. Looking back I saw the enemy aircraft turn sharply left, losing height, then crash into the sea. Turned and attacked another Ju87 flying north, and fired from about 250 yards range. Fired about two-seconds burst then had to break off engagement as I was being attacked from the rear by enemy fighter. Saw a few strikes on the Ju87 fuselage but no smoke or flames."

Flt Lt George Swannick (229 Squadron) claimed damage to a third. One Ju87 pilot managed to break through the fighter screen and placed a 500kg bomb alongside the tanker (which the Italians incorrectly identified as a small aircraft carrier). *Ohio*'s great bulk was flung forward, her screws twisted and her rudder smashed. Water gushed in through a great hole in her stern, and her plates began to buckle. But still she did not sink. The escorting Macchis belatedly came to the aid of their charges, Ten Giobatta Caracciolo Carafa, Ten Giuseppe Bonfiglio and Serg Magg Giuseppe Mirrione each claiming one Spitfire shot down, while Ten Italo D'Amico claimed one damaged. No Spitfires were actually lost, although Flg Off Nomis' aircraft was targeted:

> "In a skirmish over St Paul's Bay my machine was hit by fire from an Italian Reggiane [*sic*] and I nearly fell victim to the stories we had heard in England that the Italians were not really competent in air combat. This was not necessarily true at Malta and some of the Macchi pilots especially were experienced and dangerous adversaries."

In return, Flt Sgt Maclennan was able to shoot down Cap Egeo Pittoni's 20°Gruppo Macchi, which he incorrectly identified as an RE2001:

> "Started firing from 150 yards to 25 yards. Saw many strikes all along top of the aircraft. White smoke started pouring out; he turned very slowly to the left, nose slightly up. I closed in to 15 feet or less, firing all over the cockpit and pieces flew off

again. His nose dropped and he kept turning slowly to the left, going down, trailing thick white smoke. I claim this aircraft as destroyed as I think the pilot was dead."

In fact, Pittoni was later rescued from the sea by a Do24. Only one Ju87 had actually gone down, apparently the victim of Lovell and Philp – but this was flown by the 239^Squadriglia's commander, Cap Cumbat. He and his gunner, 1°AvArm Michele Cavallo, survived and were able to get into their dinghy. As Cavallo had been wounded in the right arm and chest, Cumbat decided to ditch his burning aircraft in the sea rather than bale out. Heading towards Pantelleria, he made a successful ditching, the undercart being torn off and the aircraft settling on its belly. Helping his wounded gunner into the dinghy, Cumbat examined the wound, which had been caused by a 20mm cannon shell. Whilst obviously painful, it was not bleeding profusely even though Cavallo's chest was torn and his right arm broken, but he soon lapsed into a semi-coma, causing Cumbat to fear that the wound or shock might be fatal.

Nothing was to be seen until about 1430 when Cumbat heard the sound of approaching aircraft engines, following which four Beaufighters appeared overhead. These spotted the dinghy and circled low; the pilots waved with Cumbat responding. Apparently the RAF crews thought they had found their missing compatriots from earlier in the day. While three Beaufighters departed, one remained overhead for an hour until suddenly attacked and shot-up by Spitfires that had mistaken it for a Ju88. Another Beaufighter was sent out to relieve the damaged aircraft, and continued orbiting the dinghy, covered by an escort of three Spitfires. By now the sun was setting, and the Italians' hopes of rescue began to recede, when over the horizon appeared a Do24 flyingboat, which was being escorted by six 51°Stormo Macchis. However, the fighters had just reached the limit of their range and turned back before they had sighted the Beaufighter. The crew of the Dornier had, however, seen this aircraft and realising that they were too late to escape, manoeuvred so as to make clear their intention to alight and execute a rescue. To the amazement of the watching Italians, the Beaufighter actually turned alongside the flyingboat and escorted it to their aid, the pilot having received instructions from Ops not to attack. Cumbat and Cavallo could not believe their luck, but the whole flight had been tracked by Ops on the radar screens. With the departure of the Macchis, the controller had sanctioned the safe conduct of the Dornier in the belief that it was the Beaufighter crew[106] which was about to be rescued, deciding that captivity was better than a possible lingering death at the mercy of the elements.

There occurred more Italian losses shortly thereafter. At 1515, four Spitfires of 126 Squadron that were escorting the captured Cant floatplane flown by Wg Cdr Jack Satchell, who was still searching for the missing Beaufighter crew, arrived on the scene. Spotting three fighters – identified as MC202s but in fact RE2001s – beneath them, Flt Lt Bill Johnson (BR311/MK-L) and Sgt Norm Marshall (BP860) undertook a perfect bounce, shooting all three down into the sea. Two fell to Johnson's fire – his fourth and fifth victories – the other to his Canadian No.2. They had shot down Magg Pier Giuseppe Scarpetta, OC 2°Gruppo Aut CT, Ten Giorgio Pocek and Sottoten Isidoro Disint. Pocek was later to be rescued by a Do24 of 6 Seenotstaffel, while Scarpetta – the second commanding officer to be lost by the unit in little more than a month, was later posthumously awarded the *Medaglia d'Oro*. In his report, Johnson recorded:

"I was leading Dumbell Yellow Section escorting the Cant out towards Linosa. Just north of Linosa I saw the enemy approaching. They immediately turned round and made off towards Pantelleria. I gave chase with my No.2 after telling Yellow 3 and 4 to stay with the Cant. The enemy made no evasive action until we were almost on top of them, and then the Macchis [*sic*] turned left. I attacked the centre one. They were in line astern. Attacked from port quarter and gave it a burst. I saw the hood come off and the pilot bale out [almost certainly Ten Pocek]. I saw my No.2 firing at the first Macchi [probably Magg Scarpetta], which went straight into the sea. I turned round into the third Macchi and gave it a burst, and saw strikes on the wings and fuselage. It turned away, streaming oil and climbing, so I climbed right up underneath him and gave him a burst, and he immediately rolled over and went into the sea. The pilot did not bale out."

Sgt Marshall added:

"My leader attacked the centre Macchi [*sic*]. I shot at the last one and saw hits on the port side of the fuselage. The first Macchi got on my tail and after much manoeuvring, I got in a long burst from astern to port quarter. He rolled over and went in. I saw the middle one's pilot bale out, the aircraft go in, and saw the last aircraft go in as well."

Meanwhile, of the other two Spitfires escorting Wg Cdr Satchell and his five-man crew in the Cant, one developed engine trouble and was obliged to return, leaving only an incensed Plt Off Rod Smith to provide protection for the vulnerable floatplane. Shortly after 1530, two sections of Spitfires, flying cover for *Ohio*, spotted the floatplane and Flg Off Newman led Flt Sgts de l'Ara, George Hogarth and Sgt Bob Lamont down into a diving attack. Fortunately for Satchell and his crew, the Spitfires suffered iced-up windscreens, which prevented an accurate attack being carried out, and the Cant was not hit.

During this traumatic period of time Malta had not remained entirely raid-free. At 1825, Spitfires of 249 Squadron were scrambled, the pilots seeing a trio of Bf109s over Hal Far, probably on a reconnaissance. Flt Sgt Ted Hiskens (EP706/T-L) claimed damage to one but Flt Sgt Hogarth (EP207) was shot down by Oblt Michalski of II/JG53, his 46th victory. The Canadian baled out safely into the sea, being rescued by *HSL128*. Flt Lt Crockett, OC the ASR unit, wrote:

"I saw one of our fighter boys bale out of his damaged Spitfire, informed Control, left base at 1902 hours in *HSL128*, picked him up safely three miles south-west of Benghaisa Point and was back at base at 1926 hours. The pilot, F/Sgt Hogarth, was unhurt – and he constituted *HSL128*'s half-century in pick-ups. Air Vice-Marshal Park, who was watching our score boards with great interest, sent us a signal of congratulations, which ended: '...hope *HSL128* will complete her century with Huns!'"

Although Hogarth landed in the sea, his aircraft came down in a field west of Qrendi, not far from a heavy gun site.

Statistically, Malta's fighter pilots had flown 414 sorties in support of the convoy – 389 by Spitfires, including 97 long-range sorties, and 25 by Beaufighters. At least 14 aircraft had been claimed shot down, with a further two probables and nine damaged being credited, for the loss of four Spitfires and one Beaufighter. Although only four merchantmen and *Ohio* had survived the gauntlet, more than enough by way of provisions – some 32,000 tons – proved sufficient to keep the garrison fed and armed into the autumn; moreover, the arrival of the tanker with her precious cargo for the aircraft was a major victory. Malta now had food, ammunition, fuel and Spitfires to continue the fight. The morning following the last ship's arrival in harbour, an emotional main front-page story in the *Times of Malta* declared:

"Malta feels humble in the presence in her harbours of the Mercantile Marine. If the feelings of the people could be expressed in simple action, Malta's George Cross would be nailed to the mast of every ship in harbour."

There occurred a curious sequel to the arrival of the surviving ships of the convoy, when Plt Off Mejor of 126 Squadron and others were invited to dinner by the grateful captain of the *Brisbane Star*, one of the vessels they had helped to protect. Mejor was amazed to discover that the captain, Capt David Macfarlane, was an uncle.

The success of the re-provisioning seemed to take the steam out of Axis activities from Sicily. Despite Rommel's desperate preparations to ready his forces for an offensive in North Africa before so much British strength built up as to make this impossible, efforts to neutralise Malta faded. The Italians continued to have problems with aircraft serviceability, particularly of their fighters, which was due to deteriorating quality control at the factories. In addition, it appeared that the Luftwaffe was taking the opportunity to send some of the long-serving aircrew of II/JG53, KüFlGr606 and KGr806 on extended leave. However, the need to get convoys across to Africa was never greater – particularly so in the case of tankers carrying fuel for the Afrika Korps' Panzers. It was to be against these targets that Malta's striking force was particularly active during the weeks that followed. Over the island itself, small-scale fighter penetrations proved to be the order of the day.

At 0645 on **15 August**, seven pilots of 1435 Squadron continued the search for their missing colleague, Flt Sgt Buntine. There were no sightings. They reported attacking a Z506B and an SM84, but made no claims. Eight more aircraft of 185 Squadron were scrambled at 0925, meeting four fighters identified as Bf109s, six miles east of Zonqor. Capt Swales (EP313) and Sgt Jimmy Tarbuck (EP410) claimed one shot down between them, but Tarbuck's aircraft was then hit. Among those watching the fight from the ground was Plt Off Paddy O'Brien, who recalled:

"We could hear and see some 109s mixing it up at about 20,000 feet. Suddenly some fire – a long burst and four short ones, and the next thing we saw was a Spit coming down at a hell of a rate, making bags of noise and with glycol pouring from it. It flattened out of its glide over the sea. It half-rolled and went straight down into the drink. Poor bugger, or so we thought, but a few seconds later a parachute appeared."

Tarbuck, a Liverpudlian, was picked up three miles south-west of Benghaisa Point by *HSL128*. He may have been accidentally shot down by his No.1. Five Spitfires of 229 Squadron had also been scrambled but had failed to make an interception. On returning from this sortie, Flt Sgt Ballantyne (BR169) collided with a stationary Spitfire (EP517) of 249 Squadron and although he was unhurt, both aircraft were damaged beyond repair.

No action was reported over Malta during the daylight hours of **16 August**, the only event of significance concerning a Beaufighter crew who sighted an aircraft identified as a Caproni 312 floatplane. The Beaufighter pilot fired two short bursts before it was observed to be a Red Cross aircraft, whereupon it was allowed to proceed without further hindrance. On the morning of **17 August**, a further batch of reinforcement Spitfires began arriving, having flown from the carrier *Furious*, which was making a second run from Gibraltar (Operation Baritone). To lead the 32 Spitfires on this occasion were Malta veterans, Flt Lt Halford, Flg Off McElroy and newly commissioned Plt Offs Evans and Parkinson, all of whom had been ferried to Gibraltar three days previously. The pilots were believed to have been (including the spare pilot):

Flt Lt J.R.S. Halford (flight leader)   Sgt R. Miller
Flg Off J.F. McElroy RCAF (flight leader)   Sgt J.G. McGill (BR482)
Plt Off K.W.S. Evans (flight leader)   Sgt E.F. Crosswell
Plt Off C.H. Parkinson RAAF (flight leader)   Sgt J.S. Jarrett
Plt Off J.R. Scott RCAF   Sgt J.M.W. Lloyd
Plt Off C. Taylor RCAF   Sgt F.G. Stewart
Plt Off J.D. Stevenson RCAF   Sgt B.C. Peters
Plt Off H.T. Nash RCAF (US)   Sgt F.W. Sharp
Plt Off I.F. Preston RCAF (US)   Sgt D.C. Eva
Flt Sgt M.W. Frith   Sgt P.M. Charron RCAF
Flt Sgt D.L. Rawson (Rhod)   Sgt A.O. MacLeod RCAF
Sgt P.A. Dixon (EP573)   Sgt L.J. McDougall RCAF (EP606)
Sgt W.J.A. Fleming (EP194)   Sgt J.F. Farrell RCAF (US)
Sgt D.G. Fuller   Sgt J.C. Sullivan RNZAF (EP152)
Sgt T. Wallace   Sgt A.B. Stead RNZAF
Sgt R.H. Saunders   Sgt D.D. MacLean RNZAF
                                                   Sgt R.B. Hendry RNZAF

Parkinson recalled:

> "Watched the first eight take off without mishap, the second crowd also. The third
> bunch were unlucky, one kite taking off, swerved, stalled one wing, and crashed over
> the side after knocking its tail off. Hit the water on its back and sank immediately."

This was Bill Fleming's Spitfire, which had struck a signal lamp in the port navigation
position as it swerved, and this hit one of the watching pilots, Rhodesian David
Rawson, breaking his arm. The 28-year-old Fleming from Londonderry was lost with
his aircraft. One of the spare pilots took over Rawson's aircraft for the flight to Malta.
Of the techniques required before take-off and subsequent flight to Malta, Philip
Dixon recounted:

> "The aircraft that were to fly to Malta had been stowed in the hangar deck before being
> taken up by means of a lift to the flight deck and ranged at the stern in batches of eight.
> The aircraft engines were started, warmed up and pilot checked; if anyone had any
> doubts about the serviceability of the aircraft, they got out and the aircraft would be
> pushed overboard complete with their kit, which in fact was only a haversack stowed
> behind the armour-plating in the fuselage. Because of the short deck, the engine would
> have to be opened up against the chocks and brakes so as to get as many revs on as
> possible before the aircraft would be allowed to move forward. During this revving up
> period, the aircraft would be subjected to considerable torque from the engine. In an
> effort to combat this, the aircraft was not lined up on the centre-line of the flight deck
> but pointed towards the ship's island; in addition to this, some right rudder was applied.
> Both these measures helped to combat the pull to the left exerted by the engine. Not
> only was this rather uncomfortable from the point of view of the pilot, who could see
> the deck on his left where he had to go, but he had to overcome the tendency to correct
> his line; he was in fact flying down the deck instead of allowing the engine to pull him
> round. This was probably the cause of the one fatal crash that took place on take-off.
> As *Furious* had a ramp towards the front of the flight deck, one had to apply slight
> pressure on the control column to change the angle; this again gave rise to difficulty to
> the one person who crashed.
>
> "As far as could be deduced, Sergeant Fleming, not having flown off a carrier
> before, tended to put on left rudder to straighten his run and, as he approached the ramp,
> he pulled hard back on the stick, creating two factors which tended to create a stall:

coarse rudder and backward pressure on the control column. It appears that he dropped his left wing, which caught a signal lamp just off the edge of the deck and cartwheeled into the water. At the time, I was in my aircraft between decks waiting to go onto the lift as the first of the next batch of aircraft to go up, and it was rather disconcerting to hear the engine noise of the aircraft going across the lift and then hearing the Tannoy announce, 'Do you hear there, do you hear there, crash on the port side'.

"After take-off we climbed to 20,000 feet, as instructed, and flew the mapped course. This took us round the north of Cap Bon and down to a point slightly south-west of Pantelleria and then on a more easterly course to Malta. We were told that if the weather was fine, and the weather would normally be fine, from the island of La Galite we should fly south-east over Tunis to Korba and then join our original track. This was to keep further away from Pantelleria. We had 90-gallon overload tanks on our Spitfires and these were to be dropped somewhere off the coast of Korba. For some reason or other, possibly because I was concentrating on making sure that I had sufficient fuel, I lost my formation and flew most of the way on my own, fortunately without incident. After I had crossed the coast near Korba I made a very brief transmission calling the base at Malta, giving my call-sign and asking for a homing. It was very reassuring to have an almost immediate response with a course to steer. As I followed this course, eventually a small bank of clouds appeared on the horizon, as it often did with Malta. I approached the island from the south and landed at Luqa. I got out from the aircraft, which was subjected to the usual very quick rearming and refuelling and it took off with another pilot."

Continued Parkinson:

"Two other kites [EP152 and EP606, flown by Sgts John Sullivan and Lawrence McDougall respectively] could not get their wheels up after taking off, so the pilots had baled out. They were picked up OK. My section got off the deck OK and set course for Malta. The trip was uneventful. Bags of fuel when we arrived. Had to orbit off the island while a raid was in progress. One of our section [Sgt John McGill in BR482] crashed at Luqa, and was badly burned."

Included in the party was the New Zealander Sgt Al Stead, who had landed his Spitfire on *Indomitable* when he experienced problems during the previous ferry. Of the 29 new arrivals, seven were immediately posted to 185 Squadron. The influx of reinforcement pilots allowed further releases of tour-expired men, and amongst those leaving the island at this time were Flt Lt Les Watts and Plt Off Ossie Linton of 249 Squadron, Flt Lt Geoff Northcott, Flg Off Eric Dicks-Sherwood, Plt Offs Paul Forster, Ray Smith (who had been diagnosed as suffering from hepatitis) and Len Webster of 229 Squadron, and Flg Off Reade Tilley DFC and Plt Off John Mejor of 126 Squadron.

*   *   *

Shortly before midday (on the same day), 15 Bf109s swept over the island to be met by an almost equal number of Spitfires (eight/126, six/185). The 126 Squadron flight failed to make contact, while two of the 185 Squadron aircraft patrolled over Grand Harbour and sighted nothing. EP546 force-landed on return and was badly damaged, though the pilot was unhurt. The other four, led by Plt Off Stenborg, engaged six Messerschmitts over Kalafrana. Sgt Weaver (BR374) immediately dived to attack and claimed two shot down, and Stenborg one more, but the New Zealander's aircraft (EP457) was also hit and he was forced to bale out, as he recalled:

"I was with an American sergeant [Weaver] flying at 31,000 feet. He saw

Messerschmitts, which I could not, so I told him to attack and I would follow, but as he went down for six Huns, three more followed him up. I shot one down from his tail at point-blank range, but the next minute a great chunk flew off my starboard wing. I heard explosions and the plane shook everywhere and black smoke poured into the cockpit. I began diving out of control at 27,000 feet. I tried to get the hood off, but it would not budge. I tried all ways, while the Spitfire fell 14,000 feet at over 400mph, and the cockpit filled with smoke. I thought I had had it. It was a horrible feeling. I was expecting the plane to blow up at any moment. But fortunately the hood came off, and I suddenly found myself thrown out. I had seen a German pilot open his parachute at that speed and his harness was ripped off by the force of sheer speed, so I waited for a while before pulling the ripcord in order to slow up, and then I pulled the cord and landed in the sea. I spent five minutes trying to get free from the parachute and get the dinghy working. That trip shook me to the teeth."

Stenborg came down three miles north-east of Delimara Point and was soon picked by *HSL128*, which was called out at 1226 with Flt Lt Crockett in charge. The rescue launch was back at base at 1245. Sgt Pashen (X-V) of 229 Squadron took part in a scramble during the day, only to have to return early when his oxygen mask blew off, taking with it one earpiece. The Australian had been down with Malta Dog since the beginning of the month.

A torrential rainstorm next day (**18 August**) effectively curtailed flying over the island for the next 24 hours, Takali in particular being badly flooded. After the latest delivery of Spitfires, the Air Ministry in London sent the following signal to the AOC Gibraltar, with a copy for Air Vice-Marshal Park at Malta:

"Now that 'Baritone' is completed it is intended to dispense with further carrier operations for these reinforcements and to make deliveries of Spitfires from Gibraltar to Malta by air carrying 170-gallon jettisonable tanks. Still air range is 1,380 land miles and therefore you will have to restrict despatches to days of favourable winds on the route or at the worst to days of average still air. Under these conditions the risk of occasionally failing to reach Malta and having to land in Tunisia is acceptable. It is considered that flights by single Spitfires are likely to give better results than formations led by twin-engine aircraft. Spitfire with full 170-gallon tank is slightly overloaded even without guns or ammunition but the carrying of Brownings and 200 rounds per gun is permissible and consequent reduction in range is negligible. You will therefore have to decide in consultation with Malta and taking into account the smoothness of the Gibraltar runway whether this light armament is essential or whether aircraft should proceed unarmed. Cannons and Brownings will be flown from Gibraltar to Malta by shuttle service as required.

"Technical instructions on fitting and use of 170-gallon tanks and on performance of aircraft so loaded follow separately. Certain additional training in navigation and in fuel economy is being carried out at home by 12 pilots out of the next batch of 32, but you should give them instruction at Gibraltar on petrol system of 170-gallon tanks and on most economical cruising speeds with that tank. The remainder of pilots should be flown in to Malta by shuttle service. Only one take-off, i.e. that for the delivery flight, is advisable when carrying the full 170-gallon tank, and in fact any non-essential flying with the tank even empty should be avoided as these tanks are easily damaged. Commencement of these delivery flights from Gibraltar to Malta is to await instructions from Air Ministry."

On the following day Park replied:

"Considered advisable for Spitfires carrying 170-gallon petrol tanks to be fitted with two Brownings and 350 rounds per gun but not to carry cannons. Better for Spitfires to proceed in pairs instead of singly or in big formations. Not requiring any reinforcements of Spitfires until about second week in September."

Despite the continuing bad weather, half a dozen Spitfires from 1435 Squadron undertook a sweep off the south-east coast of Sicily during the morning of **19 August**, and a repeat of this operation was carried out in the afternoon. On this occasion three of the five Spitfires of 126 Squadron were flown by Grp Capt Churchill, Wg Cdr Hanks and Sqn Ldr Wicks, but nothing of interest was seen on either sortie, although the pattern had been set for further such operations. Churchill should not have been flying on operations. He had very poor eyesight and carried a pair of binoculars in his cockpit to enable him to see more clearly! He had also been troubled by severe sinus problems when flying, which had grounded him for a considerable time. Apart from the fact that he was overage for a fighter pilot, being almost 35, he was a married man with two young sons. Obviously he had twisted the AOC's arm to some extent.

20 August was to herald a new era for Malta's fighter pilots – the first official offensive fighter sweep (codenamed Rodeo 1) over southern Sicily; the object was to draw enemy fighters into the air. Grp Capt Churchill (EP339) again led the Spitfires, equally drawn from 229 and 249 Squadrons, but the operation turned out to be something of an anti-climax, as Plt Off Beurling recounted:

> "We formed up south of the island and whisked across the water in three layers. We swept into Sicily over Cape Scaramia and took a look at each of the main enemy airfields at Comiso, Biscari and Gela. Not a Jerry stirred. Not a drop of flak was poured up at us. We rolled along, coming out over Cape Scaramia and beetled home. Nothing much to it, bar the pleasure of sticking your nose into the enemy's country for a change."

Although no sightings of enemy aircraft were reported by the Spitfire pilots, Uffz Otto Russ of 4/JG53 submitted a claim for a Spitfire shot down 25-30km east-north-east of Valetta. However, he received no confirmation and it was not awarded.

With a lull in Axis operations directed against Malta, the island's attention now turned to a convoy that had departed Messina bound for Benghazi. The convoy comprised a 7,800-ton tanker, a German steamer, two escorting Italian destroyers, two Italian torpedo boats and a small flak craft, and had been spotted off the toe of Italy by Plt Off Colquhoun in PR Spitfire BR431. A strike by Beauforts and Beaufighters from Malta was launched. For the loss of two Beauforts and one Beaufighter, one of the destroyers was damaged and returned to port. A further strike was launched next day (**21 August**) after Warburton and Colquhoun had re-located the convoy crossing the Gulf of Taranto to seek a safer route down the Greek coastline. On this occasion the tanker was severely damaged and was towed to safety and beached. One Beaufort and one Beaufighter were lost, but covering Beaufighters engaged and shot down a variety of escorting aircraft including a Ju52, a Ju88, two BR20s and what was incorrectly identified as a Piaggio P.32. Back at Malta the frustrated fighter pilots seethed with jealousy. They hoped for better things on **22 August**, when 15 Spitfires from 126 and 1435 Squadrons carried out a second offensive sweep over southern Sicily, followed by eight more from 229 and 249 Squadrons during the late afternoon. Once again, no Axis fighters were drawn up to the challenge, however.

Recent reconnaissance of Italian airfields revealed about 150 fighters – Bf109s, MC202s and RE2001s – at Gela, Biscari and Comiso, with in excess of 100 Ju88s being counted at Trapani. A further 50-plus Italian tri-motors were seen at Castelvetrano, together with about 50 more Macchis. It was now decided to really stir the hornet's nest by targeting Gela using the three Hurricanes armed with bombs, these to be flown by volunteer naval pilots. Hence, during the afternoon of **23 August**, the three bomb-laden fighters set out, escorted by eight Spitfires of 249 Squadron and four of 229, the formation again led by the irrepressible Grp Capt Churchill and Wg Cdr Donaldson (who had taken command of the Takali Wing, with Wg Cdr Thompson moving over to lead the Hal Far Wing). One Hurricane suffered engine trouble shortly before the area was reached, and the pilot had to jettison his two 250lb bombs and return to Malta. The other two found 10/10th cloud over Gela, so one dropped his bombs on a small collection of buildings north-east of the airfield, while the other bombed Biscari airfield. Results were unobserved. However, Italian reports suggest that four civilians were killed at Gela and three injured. The covering Spitfire pilots spotted two Bf109s but no contact was made. Whilst these pin-prick attacks were underway, the Spitfires hunted for likely targets but soon Donaldson experienced problems with his hydromatic propeller, and the sweep was aborted.

Beauforts from Malta were again engaged in a strike against a tanker located off Corfu, Sqn Ldr Warburton (BR431) accompanying the force to observe results. While flying at 10,000 feet off mainland Greece, he was jumped by a pair of CR42s, which managed to close range to 100 yards before he realised he was under attack and carried out evasive action. The biplanes continued to chase but Warburton easily outdistanced them, the Italian pilots having lost their advantage of surprise.

Malta continued to remain free of attack on **24 August**, although an unidentified plot appeared on the radar screens during the late afternoon. As a result, Plt Offs Beurling and Johnny Farmer of 249 Squadron were scrambled from Takali to intercept the suspected 'hostile', encountering instead a crippled Beaufort 40 miles east of Malta, a survivor of another strike against a small convoy that had been sighted leaving the Gulf of Taranto by Flt Lt Coldbeck of 69 Squadron (BR665). Trailing black smoke, the Beaufort was escorted by the two Spitfires back to Malta, where it successfully belly-landed.

While the action was taking place over the sea to the east of the island, Grp Capt Churchill and Wg Cdr Hanks (BR498/PP-H) led another Rodeo over southern Sicily but again the Spitfires, drawn from 126, 185 and 1435 Squadrons, failed to bring either German or Italian fighters into the air. Following the return of the Spitfires, a further ten of 229 Squadron were scrambled at 1640 from Takali to intercept another 'hostile' reported some 40 miles off Zonqor Point, as recorded by Plt Off Parkinson: "Red Section shot an unescorted Hun bomber down. They don't know what it was. Four of them had a squirt. It finally crashed into the sea in flames. They were given a quarter each destroyed." The four pilots – Flt Lt Magruder, Plt Off Tex Nash, Flt Sgt Ballantyne and Sgt Tim Brough – tentatively identified the victim as a He111 in Italian markings. Magruder reported:

> "Controller's interception, followed implicitly, was 100% accurate. I led section up sun and attacked from port quarter astern and above. Before I fired, the port side gunner fired at me. I gave a two-and-half-seconds burst; strikes on nose and port wing root. Second burst; strikes on intersection of fin and tail. Broke away starboard and up and circled round to cover rest of section while they went in to attack. When everyone had finished with enemy, he glided shallowly into the sea, with fire from port engine. No one seen to get out."

They had, in fact, despatched an SM82 transport (MM60611) of the 45°Stormo Trasporti, which had been flying from Benghazi to Lecce. Ten Francesco Zavattarelli and his crew were lost. Flying with top cover to Red Section was Sgt Pashen (X-V) whose run of misfortunes continued: "Passed out at 20,000 feet owing to hole in oxygen pipe – shaky do! However, lower section collected He111 [*sic*] at 12,000 feet."

Activity resumed over Malta on **25 August**. At 1130, ten Spitfires were scrambled by 249 Squadron when at least 30 Bf109s were reported approaching Grand Harbour. Three of these were spotted at 21,000 feet and two promptly turned into the sun and dived on the Spitfires, one getting on the tail of Plt Off Reg Round's aircraft (EN976/T-C), and shooting it down into the sea; the 28-year-old New Zealander from Canterbury was killed. Rod Smith recalled seeing the demise of his colleague:

"He was hit high up and slowly glided in swooping circles, throttled back or engine quit, into the sea off St Julian's Bay, where our mess was, and where we were swimming. I guess he was killed high up, poor chap."

185 Squadron had also scrambled eight of its aircraft, Red Section encountering nine Messerschmitts over St Paul's Bay. The ever-eager American Sgt Weaver (BR374) reported an engagement with one over Luqa, which he claimed probably destroyed. During this fighting, a stray bullet hit the ASR Cant 506B moored in Kalafrana Bay, and rendered it temporarily unserviceable.

Ten of 249 Squadron's Spitfires took off at 1745, together with nine from 229 Squadron, for another sweep over southern Sicily, when they were also to escort the three RNAS Hurricanes to raid Biscari. As they took off, one of 229's aircraft (EN829/X-U with Sgt Pashen aboard) suffered a burst tyre and was hit by a following aircraft (BR359) piloted by fellow Australian Sgt Wally Parks, which burst into flames. Neither pilot was hurt. Pashen wrote in his diary:

"On take-off my port tyre blew and I nearly collected the flight commander – then when I stopped on the runway another kite took off straight through me – God knows how I got away with it. Result – two aircraft written off, pilots unhurt."

When just under halfway to Biscari the Hurricanes were recalled owing to adverse weather conditions, the pilots being ordered to jettison their bombs in the sea. One experienced a hang-up, but the bomb fell off as Malta was approached on return and fell into the midst of a group of Maltese fishing boats! Fortunately, no one was hurt and an explanation and apology later accepted. Meanwhile, Wg Cdr Donaldson, the Spitfire leader, decided to carry out the sweep, but as the force headed northwards, 249 Squadron's Flt Sgt Micky Butler called out that his aircraft had suffered a malfunction of the hydromatic propeller, similar to that experienced by Donaldson two days previously, and that he was going to bale out. Sadly, before he was able to do so, his aircraft (EP695) dived vertically into the sea. The 21-year-old Canadian from Niagara Falls was killed instantly. Donaldson led his formation over Cape Passero to Comiso, then out again just east of Pozzallo. Two Bf109s were seen but they were too far away to engage.

During the day there were a number of command changes amongst the fighter units, Sqn Ldr New of 185 and Sqn Ldr Mitchell of 249 – at the end of their tours – relinquishing command of their respective units. 185 Squadron's new leader was to be its South African flight commander Capt Swales, now promoted to Major, while 249 Squadron welcomed newly promoted Sqn Ldr Timber Woods. In 126 Squadron, Woods' fellow-newcomer from *Furious*, the highly experienced Plt Off Bill Rolls, was promoted flight commander. 229 Squadron saw the departure of Flt Lt Peter Lovell[107], who left for the Middle East aboard a DC3.

Two of the RNAS Hurricanes set out for Biscari again just before midday on **26**

August, with a close escort provided by ten Spitfires from 185 Squadron, and high cover of 16 more from 126 and 1435 Squadrons. Over the target area the Hurricanes dived out of cloud and planted their bombs in the middle of the airfield from 6,000 feet, then dived down to strafe buildings, joined by two Spitfires of 185 Squadron. No aircraft were seen on the airfield, and one Hurricane was hit twice in the port wing by AA fire as it swept by at low level. An assemblage of 50 or so German soldiers was machine-gunned, the pilots believing they had inflicted considerable casualties.

While the sweep was in progress a substantial number of raiders approached Malta although none crossed the coast. Twenty Spitfires were scrambled but only ten of 229 Squadron sighted a pair of Messerschmitts, ten miles north-east of Comino at 27,000 feet, then six unidentified fighters at sea level. One section dived down to investigate and 21-year-old Twickenham man Sgt Cliff Cornish (BR496) was either shot down or misjudged his height, his aircraft crashing into the sea. Flg Off Dudley Newman (EP190), a 22-year-old from Chippenham, reported that he was orbiting the aircraft in the sea, but also failed to return. Neither survived. It seems that he was bounced by Ltn Schiess of Stab/JG53, who claimed a Spitfire shot down for his 22nd victory. His companion, Uffz Otto Russ of 4 Staffel, also claimed a Spitfire, although this was unconfirmed and therefore not allowed. This may have been the occasion described later by Flg Off Nomis:

"It was one of those brilliantly clear mornings that somehow stay in one's memory. The wind had been blowing hard during the night, and was continuing this day, with tremendous gusts causing long streamers of spray across the sea surface. At the time, I was still suffering the after effects of sand fly fever, and found myself to be quite weak when we got into the air. This fact, together with the turbulence, made it necessary for me to use both hands on the control column. We climbed to about 15,000 feet before we got bounced. I remember the moment before, retaining mentally the picture of the sky – a pale blue in the east, darker in the west, the whole air with an aura of brilliance, and the sea a dark blue below. Every detail of the island under us was absolutely clear.

"Then there wasn't time for anything but the 109s that we had observed above us. They hesitated not at all before they were on top of us. As usual in these circumstances, things became confused. I suddenly found myself with no wingman and no leader. I remember trying a ridiculously long-range deflection shot at one of the 109s. This proved to be prophetic, because I found out instantly that the system was jammed. Neither the cannons nor the machine-guns would fire. As I was contemplating what to do next, I racked the Spit upward to port and in one of those strange occurrences found myself practically in formation with a 'yellow-nose' who evidently had been coming up quite rapidly from below. We found ourselves almost locked together on a parallel course at the same speed and curving to the left in a climb.

"My first impulse was to turn away, but I had an instant realisation that this would be fatal. The 109 pilot had evidently resolved this also, because I could see him fanning his rudder in an attempt to slow down more quickly and drop behind or under me. Even then, at the verge of panic, I remember registering the extreme clarity and beauty of the scene, incongruous as it was – the enemy plane, the yellow nose etched perfectly against the dark blue of the sea below. I remember staring fascinated for a second at the number 24 [*sic*] on the 109's fuselage. I was slowing the Spit down to keep pace with him, and at the same time fighting the urge to panic. It was at this point, when our wingtips were literally together, that the brilliant idea struck me. I could make an appeal to chivalry.

"Our gazes at each other had never faltered since the beginning of the predicament. We could see only each other's eyes; he wore a mask, and I did too. So, in a motion which I considered should explain everything – he had a cockpit canopy but mine was open, so every movement must have been perfectly clear – I pointed dramatically down at the port wing cannon with a gloved finger, then raised the finger and drew it across my throat. This, I figured, would indicate that my guns were jammed and therefore mercy could be accorded me. Panic promotes foolish actions. Where in hell I got the idea of chivalry, especially at Malta and especially from a 'yellow-nose', I do not know. The gesture, however, did have an effect.

"The 109 pilot stared, it seemed almost incredulously, at me and then, in one lightning movement, went onto his back and did the most rapid split-S I ever saw. He was a miniature against the seascape by the time I could follow him with my eyes. I looked around, and found myself absolutely alone. The whole thing seemed like a dream. It was only when I was almost back to Takali that the truth of the farce hit me. I started to laugh, because I could suddenly picture the 109 pilot after he got home – telling the experience and saying that those Spitfire pilots must either be crazy or tougher than hell – they indicate by gestures what they are going to do to you before they shoot you down!"

On learning of the two missing aircraft, 1435 Squadron despatched eight more to carry out a search but nothing was sighted. Another was undertaken by five of 229 Squadron, and later by another section from 1435 Squadron, but again no sign of the missing pilots or the wreckage of their aircraft was seen.

The Luftwaffe was back during the morning of **27 August**, eight 126 Squadron Spitfires being scrambled after nine Bf109s over St Paul's Bay. Flg Off Wallace (EP332) and Flt Sgt Farquharson (BP992) each claimed one damaged. Greater things were afoot, however, for a major strike on the Sicilian airfields had been planned, following the lack of reaction during recent fighter incursions. Just before 1300, ten Spitfires from 185 Squadron headed for Comiso, led by Wg Cdr Thompson and Maj Swales, followed five minutes later by eight from 229 Squadron, led by Grp Capt Churchill and Wg Cdr Donaldson, bound for Biscari. Finally, Sqn Ldr Woods led off a further eight of 249 Squadron five minutes after the departure of 229 Squadron. Their target was Gela.

Crossing the coast south-east of Comiso at sea level, Thompson's formation had penetrated inland for about nine miles when eight Ju88s of II/KG77 were encountered, flying at heights between 50 and 500 feet. These had just taken off from the airfield, prior to forming up for a raid on Malta. All Spitfires attacked, and four of the bombers were claimed shot down, with three more probably destroyed, and the eighth damaged. Maj Swales (EP122) reported:

"I was leading Red Section. Crossed coast and turned slightly to starboard, following Sgt Weaver, who had sighted a Ju88. The rest of Red Section as well as Blue Section followed me. Weaver closed in on a Ju88 which was heading towards us and made an attack on the beam. I, who was about 800 yards behind Weaver, saw him firing and broke away to port making towards Comiso. As I approached the drome I saw a Ju88 at about 300 feet. Closing to line astern, firing in two bursts, closing all the time until cannon ammunition was finished. I saw strikes on the starboard side of fuselage and on starboard mainplane. E/a started to go down as soon as I got in line astern, and when I broke to port at 100 feet, he was still going down. On looking back I saw great clouds of smoke and flames coming up from the ground."

Swales then carried out a strafing attack on another Ju88 that was on the airfield, and saw many machine-gun strikes. He claimed this damaged. Sgt Weaver (BR374) recorded:

"We were going up the valley towards Comiso when I sighted several Ju88s at 100 feet. I reported these and attacked the last one. I fired a four-seconds cannon burst from 200 yards, noticing a small amount of smoke coming from the port engine. Closing in to 30 yards astern, I fired a further two-seconds burst cannon and machine-gun, noticing strikes on starboard fuselage and mainplane. I manoeuvred for a further attack when it flicked over on its back at about 50 feet, and burst into flames, exploding very violently. Immediately after seeing mine go in, I saw Red 3's (Lt Kuhlmann) Ju88 spin in about 500 yards south of mine, and blow up. I then proceeded to the aerodrome where I saw another Ju88 at 400 feet. I dived under him and pulled up behind, about 40 yards, firing the rest of my cannon. The starboard motor flamed up and he went into a steep dive to the right, burning badly. While attacking the second Ju88 I noticed four 109s taking off south to north. I dived into the starboard one and fired about five-seconds machine-gunfire, from 200 yards quarter astern. He crashed straight ahead into a field, north-east of the aerodrome."

Although forced to land, this 6/JG53 machine was only slightly damaged. Weaver was however credited with its destruction, also the destruction of one Ju88 and the second as probably destroyed. Lt Keith Kuhlmann (EP187) related:

"We turned to starboard and I saw Ju88s ahead and another three further to the right, all below 200 feet. Sgt Weaver attacked one Ju88 from astern and hit the port engine, causing it to smoke badly. I then took a two-seconds burst from 400 yards and saw it crash and burst into flames on the ground. I do not claim any share in this destroyed aircraft for I consider Sgt Weaver's attack responsible for its destruction. I then saw another Ju88 to port, and turned towards it. Range approximately 600 yards. The Ju88 turned to port and I was then able to close in to about 200 yards before opening fire. I broke to port at about 70 yards range and my last view of the enemy aircraft was as it dived down to port, with port engine streaming smoke. While firing I observed cannon strikes. No return fire except at the last moment. Sgt Weaver saw this aircraft strike the ground and burst into flames."

Sgt Len Reid (BR380/GL-R) also claimed a bomber shot down:

"I chased one up and down a valley, just over the tree tops. I was chasing him over the olive groves, in and out. He was doing everything possible to shake me off, but he didn't have the flying speed. I had a lot of trouble catching him. Another Ju88 shot in front of me, going in the opposite direction – I think somebody else was chasing him. Finally I closed in and gave it two good bursts, saw big red flashes on the back and starboard engine. It immediately went steeply down."

Flt Lt Charney (BR112/GL-X) was credited with a probable and a damaged while Wg Cdr Thompson (EP685/L) and Sgt Ken Mitchell (EP553) jointly reported probably destroying another, the latter recalling:

"We caught them taking off and forming up. I can still see my cannon shells going through the 88, which was below me, and exploding on the harsh, rocky terrain underneath."

185 Squadron suffered the loss of Flg Off Phil Woodger when the engine of his Spitfire was hit by light AA fire, the victim of the ground defence unit of Stab I/JG77. The American crash-landed EP200/GL-T near Marina di Ragusa. The aircraft made a near-perfect belly-landing and was relatively undamaged. Woodger was captured before he was able to carry out any demolition work on his machine.

Three Ju88s of 4 Staffel were, in fact, shot down and two others crash-landed. Oblt

Willi Köhl in 3Z+HM (140256) and Uffz Karl Diestler in 3Z+DM (8582) were killed with their respective crews, both aircraft crashing near Santa Croce. 3Z+GM (3633) flown by Fw Georg Mayr crashed nearby, the pilot and his crew surviving. A machine of 5 Staffel (8621) crash-landed near Pachino, Uffz Heinz Emanuel and two of his crew sustaining injuries, and a fifth bomber (140120) also of 5 Staffel crash-landed on the airfield, with a wounded crew member. On the airfield, an observer officer of II/LG1 was killed by the strafing Spitfires, but other casualties are not known. A Klemm 35 communications aircraft (KE+SR) of II/JG53 was destroyed on the ground and one of the new Bf109G-2s of the same unit damaged.

Of the 229 Squadron formation sent to attack Biscari, one aircraft had to return early, the remainder eventually crossing the Sicilian coast about six miles east of Gela at 300 feet. Red Section encountered what they took to be a Do217, which had just taken off from Biscari, and this was claimed probably destroyed by Wg Cdr Donaldson (BR529/AD) and Flt Sgt Ballantyne. It would seem that this aircraft was in fact a Ju88 (140738) of 8/KG77 that crash-landed at Gerbini, its crew unhurt. Donaldson reported:

"I saw a Do217 [sic] bomber about to take off and by the time he was in my sights he was airborne. I chased him for about 20 miles, caught up to 300 yards and opened fire from quarter starboard, closing to astern 100 yards. Strikes all along the fuselage and mainplanes. Black smoke from engine and enemy aircraft turned north, losing speed and height. Then sighted two Me109s so could not see if it actually crashed. It disappeared below a small hill. I was not able to see him hit the ground, but it was obvious that he was a dead duck."

Red Section then attacked buildings and two water tanks in a railway yard about eight miles north-west of Biscari. Meanwhile, Blue Section made a run south-west to north-east over Biscari, claiming the destruction of two Ju88s and damaging three unidentified twin-engined aircraft on the ground, as well as a hangar and other buildings. From this section Plt Off Parkinson (X-N) recounted:

"As we passed a large town, Vittoria, my leader fired at a tall building. The rest of the section fired also. In the distance on the right I could see a thick, black column of smoke coming from one of the dromes already attacked. I could hear the boys natter as they went in. At last our objective came into view. Biscari aerodrome. I could see a line of about six bombers on the deck, quite close together. Quarter of a mile from the drome my leader, Group Captain Churchill, was hit by flak, started to smoke, and then burst into flames, rolled on his back and crashed into the ground. Rather shook me!

"By this time the ground defences had started in earnest. I fired at the line of aircraft on the ground and set one on fire. Attacked the large hangar on the right. After passing over the drome I flew for about five minutes trying to dodge anti-aircraft fire, which was coming from every direction: the ground below, the hills all around. I could see a large black column of smoke coming from the drome. Finally managed to dodge into a valley where it was more or less safe. Saw a small train so fired a few rounds at it but didn't notice any strikes.

"As I flew across the coast I was fired at again by anti-aircraft. Fifteen miles off the coast of Sicily, I saw two 109s on the port and above. I looked to the other side and saw another 109 about to attack. I turned into the two and continued to turn. The single aircraft overshot and got in front of me. I shot him down in flames. The other two nearly collided with one another and flew off out of sight. Five miles off the coast of Malta I saw a dinghy so orbited until an aircraft came to relieve me. As I flew back to the coast I saw some aircraft in the distance to starboard. Flew over to investigate and saw that three were Spits and that the other two were Macchi 202s. They immediately broke and turned away too fast for me. I found out later that I had no ammunition left anyway."

Apart from that claimed destroyed by Parkinson, one more of the grounded bombers was claimed in flames by Sgt Eric Francis. Sgt Philip Dixon (EP691/X-A) reported strikes on three more, although his own aircraft was hit and slightly damaged. Dixon, who had arrived only ten days earlier, had been nominated to fly No.2 to Churchill, as he recalled:

"Following dispersal, Grp Capt Churchill singled me out and said: 'Right, keep close, and we'll be all right.' We reached Biscari. As we crossed the foremost boundary a shell hit his aircraft (EP339) under the port wing root and exploded. He pulled up to the right and over my head, and I did not see him again. In front of me was a line of Ju88s and I passed over them firing one long burst with my guns. At the end of the aerodrome I turned to the left and in front of me was a Do217, right on the deck and with black smoke coming from his exhausts as he pushed throttles through the gate. I fired at him, but found I only had machine-gun ammunition left. I followed him for a couple of minutes and fired again, but without results and turned again to resume my flight home.

"About halfway to the Sicilian coast there was an explosion in my right wing. It would appear that in my eagerness to fire as much ammunition at the 88s as possible, I had fired in one long burst and had over-heated the guns. The last round that remained in the cannon had gently cooked until this point and then exploded. However, no damage was done to the aircraft. On my return, I found a bullet hole in the side of the cockpit, on the left side. Further inspection showed an exit hole about the size of a half crown on the right hand side, and when we ran a rod between the two, we found that the bullet had passed between the control column and myself. It had not touched my thighs, my arm, my stomach or control column, having passed through a space of about nine inches by six inches."

Simultaneous with the attack on Biscari, the eight Spitfires of 249 Squadron dived on Gela airfield from 300 feet, Red and Blue Sections flying along the west and east dispersal pens respectively. During the strafing attack one Ju88 was claimed destroyed on the ground by Plt Off Bob Seed (EP708/T-U), and a MC202 by Sqn Ldr Woods (BP867/T-E). It was believed that three airmen seen working on the Macchi had been killed (in fact, one airman of 155°Gruppo CT was killed and two of 102°Gruppo wounded). Plt Off Williams (EP706/T-L) was credited with the probable destruction of a Ju87, apparently an aircraft of 102°Gruppo that was destroyed but not before three of the unit's ground personnel had managed to remove the 1,000kg bomb with which it was armed. Sgt Brydon (EP700/T-Q) was credited with probably destroying a Ju88 and Sgt Red Shewell (EP338/T-A) a Bf109, while another Messerschmitt was claimed damaged by Flt Lt Hetherington (BR373/T-N). Woods reported:

"We approached the aerodrome from the south-east corner and attacked four Macchi 202s parked on the perimeter. I saw strikes all along the fuselage and cockpit, then an explosion. I turned left at 0 feet and attacked a group of soldiers or airmen, killing or wounding them. There were no more suitable targets, so I set course for base. After crossing the Sicilian coast on our return, a very large column of black smoke was seen coming from the aerodrome. About five miles offshore from Gela, there was a two-masted schooner which Red 3 attacked."

Of his part in the operation, Plt Off Seed (Red 3) recalled:

"I saw a Ju88 parked outside a hangar on the north-west corner of the field. I opened fire at about 400 yards and gave a four-seconds burst. I saw many strikes and the aircraft caught fire. Several mechanics, who were working on the port engine on a ladder, fell to the ground. I turned to port and followed Red Leader out to sea over Gela town. About three miles out to sea I attacked a two-masted, motor-driven cutter of about 80 feet. I saw cannon and machine-gun strikes from the water line to the bridge. Tiger Blue 4, who was a distance behind, reported smoke coming from it."

Apart from the loss of Churchill and Woodger, the operation was considered a great success with claims submitted for four Ju88s, two Bf109s shot down, and a Do217, plus three more Ju88s, probably so, while six aircraft of various types were destroyed or badly damaged on the ground. Before he was shot down and killed Churchill had been seen firing at a Ju88 on the ground. So perished one of the RAF's more illustrious and senior fighter leaders. Despite his age and the problems he had recently suffered, he nonetheless, refused to be tied to his desk, and paid the price. Plt Off Beurling, who missed the sweep due to a bout of Malta Dog, was one of his many admirers: "When the war ends, our side should erect a monument over his grave to commemorate a daringly conceived and courageously led raid."

Seven Spitfires of 1435 Squadron patrolled ten miles off the Sicilian coast at 15,000 feet, to protect the squadrons on their return. No enemy aircraft were sighted. Two aircraft, acting as contact between the controller and the main body of the strike, crossed the Sicilian coast at 17,000 feet south of Ragusa and flew inland for 20 minutes, re-crossing the coast at the same point. Both aircraft strafed two small two-masted motor schooners south of Ragusa before returning home. *HSL128* was sent out after one of the RNAS Hurricane pilots spotted a body in the sea, which turned out to be a badly decomposed, unidentifiable Axis pilot. The corpse was weighted down to enable 'burial' at sea, but first it had to be shot to release the body gasses that prevented it from sinking.

Early on the morning of **28 August**, 69 Squadron's Flt Lt Coldbeck (BR663) sighted yet another small convoy – a single merchantman and two escorting destroyers or MTBs – about 100 miles north of Derna. A strike by Beauforts from Malta later sank the vessel, which was carrying 1,500 tons of fuel for the Luftwaffe in North Africa. A second steamer, also carrying fuel, was sighted and sunk by a 69 Squadron Baltimore.

229 Squadron's Sgt Pashen suffered another demoralising incident during the day. At 1625, seven Spitfires of 249 Squadron and nine of 229 Squadron were scrambled, but the Australian collided with another piloted by Plt Off Art Roscoe:

"Things were pretty quiet until we were sent up on a scramble early in the afternoon. On taxiing through the dust I managed to collect another kite and wipe it off. A very bad show and my first black in the air force. I was severely annoyed. This little effort delayed me in getting off the ground and I couldn't catch the boys."

Four fighters identified as MC202s were reported above the remaining reduced flight of 229 Squadron, and then four more below, Flt Lt Dan Magruder and Sgt Eric Francis attacking two of the latter, one of which Francis claimed damaged. He then experienced trouble with the hydromatic airscrew on his aircraft (BR488), tried to get back to Takali but had to crash-land on the Naxxar to Mosta road. He was thrown clear, but suffered multiple cuts and abrasions and was taken to hospital. On learning of Francis' difficulties Magruder, the flight leader, turned back to look for him but then disappeared, and when the remainder of the formation returned there was no sign of him or his aircraft (BP871). Records indicate that there was no Italian fighter activity on this date but Ltn Iring Englisch of 3/JG77 claimed a Spitfire for his third victory, so the opponents may well have been Messerschmitts, rather than Macchis.

The three RNAS Hurricanes carried out a nocturnal intruder patrol over Comiso aerodrome making a bombing run from north to south. They faced intense AA fire and the results of their attacks were not observed in their haste to get away. Despite the hot reception however, all three returned unscathed. Shortly before 0200, a lone Spitfire took off from Takali on an unauthorised flight, at the controls of which was one of 229 Squadron's Americans Flg Off Nomis. Intoxicated by the successes achieved by colleagues over Sicily during the past few days – and frustrated at his own inactivity – he had 'stolen' the Spitfire (EP691/X-A), intent on carrying out a lone sweep over Sicily. Of his misadventure, he recalled:

"The night was very bright with a full moon. The sortie was diverted about 20 minutes after becoming airborne, by a direct order over the R/T from fighter control to return immediately to Luqa – the only base then with an adequate night operations facility. Upon returning to Luqa, I was greeted – after I had alighted from the cockpit – by Wg Cdr [Stan] Grant, and informed that I was, to phrase it kindly, confined to quarters. I was returned to Takali the following morning, under escort, and was further informed that I was grounded and confined to quarters until told otherwise. Everyone at Takali, with the exception of the interrogators, regarded the incident as funny, and such was the state of mind and atmosphere at Malta in those days, no one (except the Inquiry Board) ever asked me why. I soon discovered that I was charged with conducting an unauthorised sortie (at night in a day fighter), unnecessary expenditure of ammunition – I had tested the guns over the sea because we had been having instances of cannon jamming – and unauthorised consumption of petrol. There were several other related charges, but the final upshot of the whole thing was that about three weeks later I received summary disciplinary action through HQ Mediterranean in the form of a transfer to the Middle East."[108]

On **29 August**, Plt Off Parkinson of 229 Squadron recorded in his diary:

"A Flight came down and took over our machines to do a sweep over Sicily. The CO, Bill Douglas, went with them. All came back OK. Another squadron was jumped and one of our machines was shot down. I think he got back OK. Another was shot down in the sea and I don't think he's been found yet."

Sgt John Vinall of 185 Squadron crash-landed on return with a damaged machine (EP196), but Plt Off Dennis Pollock of 1435 Squadron, who took part in a scramble at 1120, failed to return in BS160. He was not found in spite of *HSL128* being despatched to the area of battle; only an oil patch was to be seen. In the skirmish, when an estimated 15 Messerschmitts of II/JG53, including some of the new, more powerful G-2 sub type, were sighted north of St Paul's Bay, both Flt Lt McLeod (BR236/V-E) and Flt Sgt Scott (EP612/V-B) claimed Bf109s shot down. Plt Off Stewart and Sgt Wilson claimed probables, the latter also damaging one. It is not known who accounted for Pollock, but Fw Joachim Kölzsch of 4 Staffel was shot down and killed in White 10 (10489), one of the new aircraft.

The day marked a new era in the development and operational use of the Spitfire, when Wg Cdr Hanks flew the first Spitbomber (EP201), a standard fighter locally fitted with underwing bomb racks, enabling two 250lb bombs to be carried. The trials were successful. Air Vice-Marshal Park had approved the idea and later wrote:

"The reason I introduced the Spitbomber was that the enemy were ignoring our fighter sweeps over his aerodromes in the south of Sicily. I used Hurricane bombers at first and the enemy reacted by sending up his fighters to intercept. As a result of flying trials we found that the fitting of two 250lb bombs to the Spitfire slightly increased the take-off run, and slowed down the rate of climb by about 10%. There was practically no difference in speed at level flight. We designed the bomb gear so that there was no loss of performance when the bombs were dropped. Unlike the Hurricane bomb gear, our Spitfire throws away all external fittings with the exception of a steel rib which protrudes less than one inch from the wing."

Wg Cdrs Hanks and Donaldson were instrumental in testing the Spitfire bomber. Others soon followed including BR236 and BR368. Soon pilots were allowed to practice dive-bombing, amongst whom was Flt Lt Rolls:

"Our Wing Commander Flying had been experimenting trying out a Spitfire with a bomb under each wing. It was a bit of a 'Heath Robinson' arrangement and it was a 250lb bomb hooked onto a Beaufighter bomb rack. It operated by pulling a piece of string in the cockpit, which pulled out two pins holding the bombs in the rack. The danger was if the bomb got caught hooked up on one pin only because the bomb was likely to hit the ground when you landed."

Another of those selected was 229 Squadron's obviously less-enthusiastic Sgt Pashen, who recorded:

"I was selected to do Spit bombing practice. Unfortunately for myself I scored six out of eight hits on a small target (Filfla rock) and so am considered the bomber boy for Sicily – a shaky show."

The following morning (**30 August**), a 69 Squadron PR Spitfire achieved another sighting of a small convoy, as the Germans and Italians continued trying to get fuel across the Mediterranean to help the Afrika Korps in its push towards Egypt. On this occasion newly commissioned Plt Off Dalley, who had recently been awarded a DFM, was the reconnaissance pilot (in BR431), and on receipt of news of the sighting in the Gulf of Taranto, Beauforts and Beaufighters were despatched from Malta. As a result of the attack, a 5,000-ton tanker was set ablaze and drifted out of control while the escorting MTB was heavily damaged. Despite flak damage and skirmishes with escorting aircraft, all of the strike force returned safely to Malta. It was Flt Lt Coldbeck's turn (in BR665) to make a sighting next day (**31 August**), spotting a small tanker – one of two that had set out from Taranto – which was subsequently attacked and damaged. The second tanker was caught the following day and duly sank after being bombed by two 69 Squadron Wellingtons.

August had been altogether a quieter month for Malta's fighter pilots. The Spitfire Flight of 69 Squadron had, however, been as busy as usual and carried out 115 sorties (321 flying hours) during the month, the workload shared by Sqn Ldr Warburton, Flt Lt Coldbeck, Plt Offs Colquhoun and Dalley and newcomer Sgt Gillions. There were no losses, while many convoy sightings were achieved. What was not known to the pilots, or to very many of those on Malta, was that information gleaned from Ultra intercepts was in the main responsible for these successes. This takes nothing away from the determination and gallantry of the pilots involved in the long and potentially dangerous oversea flights to locate the convoys and to report on their actual positions.

September

September opened quietly for the defenders and there were no operations of any note on the first day, allowing Plt Off Williams of 249 Squadron, among others, to catch up on their letter writing to folks back home, including one to a girlfriend, Hilda, serving with the RCAF in Canada:

"I guess I'd better toss my hat in first to see if the coast is clear!! Gee! I sure have an awful bawling out to come from you, so in your next letter give me lick! Honestly, Hilda, accept my deepest apologies for not writing to you but I even found it difficult what to say in my letters back home. However, I have some spare time so here goes to let you know how everything is. I think I've been through the hottest weather I ever want to be in. Doggone it, the sun shines all day long with not a breath of air or a cloud in view in the sky. Honestly, it's terrible at times! I'd like to tell you all about flying, Hilda, but I'm afraid it's out of the question. Our mail is heavily censored. I certainly have been a lucky lad lately, in that I received my commission a few weeks back and, slap bang, after that comes the DFC – it shook me to the core!"

Action returned next day (**2 September**) when four of 249 took off at 1305 for an offensive reconnaissance over Sicily, passing inland west of Licata some 25 minutes later. Macchis from 51°Stormo were scrambled from Gela to intercept and near Cape Scalambria one of these, flown by Sottoten Emanuele De Seta, was spotted at 16,000 feet. The Spitfires were at the same height, so they split up and Flt Lt Hetherington (EP338/T-A) made a stern attack from 50 yards while Wg Cdr Donaldson (BR529/AD) fired several bursts from 200 yards, following which Plt Off Farmer (BR373/T-N) made a beam to stern attack, closing to within about ten yards. All three gained hits on De Seta's aircraft and the tail came off as the Macchi went down streaming coolant. The Italian pilot was able to bale out and was picked up safely from the sea.

There was little activity over Malta during the next few days, but on the morning of **5 September** an incoming plot caused six 249 Spitfires to be scrambled at 0855 followed ten minutes later by five of 185 Squadron; one of the former had to return early when the cockpit hood blew off. Four Bf109s were spotted over Grand Harbour at 25,000 feet, then six more at 32,000 feet; the latter were attacked by 249, Plt Offs Williams (BP867/T-E) and Ken Giddings (EP488/T-S) each claiming a damaged. Flt Lt Charney (BR375/GL-A) attacked another in a half-roll, then pulled up and got in a long burst; the fighter turned on its back and dived into the sea about a mile south-east of Kalafrana. Charney believed his victim to have been a Macchi but there seems little doubt that this was actually a Bf109G-2 of II/JG53, Ltn Hans-Volkmar Müller, the nine-victory ace being reported shot down in Black 6 (10510) by a Spitfire off Marsaxlokk Bay. He did not survive. Flying No.2 to Charney was new boy Sgt Johnny Houlton:

"The first scramble I flew on was uneventful; but on the second one Control had just reported twenty-plus bandits passing over the Hal Far area, when the R/T was completely jammed up as the Takali boys went into action to the north. Watching across Ken Charney's tail I saw him waggling his wings, then half-roll away down after a Macchi 202 which dived under him from head-on, so I went with him. The Macchi pilot pulled up again and turned in front of Ken, who got in a long burst to send the Macchi over on its back and into the sea. Back in the crew room Ken asked me what I had seen; then he quietly told me that another Macchi had made a head-on firing pass at me, which was why he had waggled his wings, being unable to warn me because of the R/T chatter. Thereafter I made a point of looking ahead much more often."

Spitfire pilots were starting to get a taste for the offensive forays over Sicily when orders arrived from London effectively curtailing such freelance operations. The following notice of explanation was issued by AHQ to all aircrew:

"In order to conserve Malta's stock of aviation petrol, the Air Ministry has ordered that offensive sweeps and attacks on enemy land objectives should not be undertaken except when they contribute to the success of attacks on shipping and its escorting air forces. Air Ministry has, however, given instructions for operational training to be re-introduced at Malta so long as it contributes to the success of offensive operations."

In spite of these clear instructions, later that morning Wg Cdr Donaldson led 19 Spitfires of 229 and 249 Squadrons on a wing sweep to southern Sicily – presumably under the guise of operational training – but only two fighters were seen about 30 miles off Zonqor Point, and these promptly fled. Apparently Donaldson received a mild rebuke from the AOC on his return for his complete disregard of the Air Ministry ruling.

Early on the morning of **6 September**, four pilots of 249 Squadron had been briefed to carry out a reconnaissance of Porto Empedocle, where two 25-ton twin-masted motor vessels were sighted. The Spitfires dropped down to sea level, one pilot gaining strikes on the hull and cabin of one of the vessels, which were, in fact, fishing boats. The other evaded the attack and made for harbour. There was little to report during the next two days, with only the occasional offensive reconnaissance sorties by small groups of high flying Bf109s causing alarm, although on the morning of **8 September**, two Messerschmitts of 3/JG77 bounced a section of 126 Squadron Spitfires and Oblt Geisshardt (his 87th victory) shot down Sgt Henry Roberts' Spitfire (AB531). The 23-year-old New Zealander from Wellington baled out and came down in the sea off Benghaisa Point. *HSL128* set out from Kalafrana before Roberts hit the sea, and he was in the water for only four minutes before being picked up! The delighted pilot commented to his rescuers as they fished him out: "A little bit sooner and you could have caught me on the deck and saved me getting wet at all!"

On **9 September** it was the turn of 185 Squadron to lose an aircraft and pilot, when seven Spitfires carried out a sweep over southern Sicily at 0930. Six Messerschmitts and a lone Macchi were spotted over Biscari airfield at 18,000 feet, the Italian fighter being attacked and claimed shot down by Capt Kuhlmann (EP122) after it was seen to be smoking badly as it dived vertically; in fact, the Macchi pilot got down safely, his aircraft having been hit by three cannon shells. Sgt Weaver then called up to say that he had shot down a Bf109 but that his aircraft was in trouble, and that he intended an attempted landing on the coast. He succeeded in belly-landing BR112/GL-X on the beach at Scoglitti. He had in fact been shot down by Ten Paolo Damiani of 352^Squadriglia, who had scrambled from Gela with two others on the approach of the Spitfires. The circumstances of the combat seem to have been contentious, for Plt Off Parkinson recorded in his diary:

"Claude Weaver DFM was shot down by Macchis, mainly through disobedience and over-confidence. Dived after a Macchi but was bounced by another two and shot down. Crash-landed in flames [*sic*]. He may be alright but I doubt it – kept firing his guns as he went down."

An airman of 185 Squadron, LAC Ken Cox, recalled the incident in more specific detail:

"Weaver's aircraft was hit in the cooling system over Sicily. This he reported to the CO over the R/T. He was told to fly as low as possible towards Malta, land in the sea, and the HSL would be sent out to pick him up. His reply was something like: 'You go to hell, they might not find me!' By this time he was over the sea; he turned back and landed on the beach, and a few minutes later waved to some of our aircraft that had escorted him in."

In fact, the extrovert young pilot from Oklahoma City survived unhurt to become a prisoner. His captors were well-aware who they had got, for the able operator of the Italian radio intercept service spoke good English and had followed the exchanges between Weaver and the controller at Malta as the combat progressed. Hence, Weaver was obviously very surprised to be greeted with, "Hello Claude, how are you?" by his captors (see Appendix IV). On losing its top-scoring pilot, 185's diarist wrote:

"On this occasion half-a-dozen Macchi 202s were run into and Keith Kuhlmann promptly shot one down. 'Weave' went down after others and the last we saw of him was sitting on the tail of a Macchi (or 109), which was going down almost vertically. The other Eyeties had put their noses down and beat a hasty retreat. As the flight made for home, 'Weave' called up on the R/T and told us that he was on fire and was going to land on the beach – he also mentioned something about stealing a rowing boat and coming back as soon as possible. He claimed an enemy aircraft destroyed. The Italian radio next day said that their 'chasers' had found a British aircraft on land and that the pilot, an American, had been taken prisoner. They also announced the loss of two Italian aircraft."

The following few days were relatively quiet for Malta's fighter pilots. Even the strike crews had run out of targets to attack. Earlier in the month Sqn Ldr Henry 'Butch' Baker, another Battle of Britain veteran with six victories including two shared and one probable, arrived from the Middle East to take command of 229 Squadron from Sqn Ldr Douglas, who was now tour-expired. Commented Plt Off Parkinson:

"We are going to lose our CO, Bill Douglas. Will be very sorry to see him go. He's been very good to me. We're to have a new one from the Middle East, 'Butch' Baker. Seems to be OK."

Sqn Ldr Douglas took the opportunity to write home to his wife:

"I'm writing this on the terrace at the rest camp, where I've been for the past five or six days having a simply glorious holiday. There are only two of us here at the moment – the doc and I – and we're having a grand laze – swimming, sailing, sunbathing and writing letters. It really is wizard here. We've got a very pleasant house, with the garden going down to the sea and the bathing is excellent. We've had a bit of rain this month, and the garden is really beautiful. The third crop of roses are out and there are all sorts of flowers whose names I don't know, but whose colours and perfumes are terrific. The scenery is rather like those highly coloured pictures one sees of Italian lakesides, only of course the mountains are lacking. I've absolutely forgotten all about the war here, and except for the occasional Spit flying round, there's nothing to remind me of it. The weather is more or less what it was like when we came here – a certain amount of cloud about, a cool breeze, and not the scorching heat we had in the summer months. I hope that I have another week here before I go, but I expect to get packed off at any minute now."

Another waiting to leave the island, although for different reasons, was Flg Off Nomis, who was currently down with sandfly fever and Malta Dog. He was convalescing at the mess in Mdina, prior to being posted to the Middle East. He recalled that Beurling often visited him:

"He would some to see me on the roof verandah and we would throw stones at the starving cats that hung incessantly about the morgue at the bottom of the terrace. He called this curious pastime deflection practice!"

During the morning of **11 September**, more reinforcements arrived in Sicily.

22°Gruppo Aut CT, the second unit to be equipped with the RE2001, arrived at San Pietro di Caltagirone from Sardinia to replace the recently departed 2°Gruppo Aut CT. The new arrivals had been specially trained for fighter-bomber activities, but would find few opportunities to operate in this rôle. Commanded by Cap Vittorio Minguzzi, the unit's three squadriglie were: 359^Squadriglia (Cap Germano La Ferla), 362^Squadriglia (Cap Leo Boselli) and 369^Squadriglia (Cap Giovanni Cervellin).

Five Spitfires of 185 Squadron were scrambled at 0800 on 13 September, but the anticipated raid did not materialise. Capt Kuhlmann was ordered to patrol over Hal Far and was then instructed to allow his new pilots some practice flying. In the course of a practice dogfight between Kuhlmann and Sgt Lawrence Swain, the latter got into a left-hand spin at 3,000 feet, was seen to pull out at 500 feet but then went into a right-hand spin; the Spitfire (BR374) crashed into a field near Safi and the 20-year-old from Essex was killed. The Luftwaffe at last returned to the skies over Malta early on **15 September**, when nine Spitfires of 249 Squadron were scrambled at 0825 to patrol over Zonqor Point at 21,000 feet. Three-quarters of an hour later, two Bf109s suddenly dived out of the sun and shot down Flt Sgt Bernard (Pedro) Peters' aircraft (BP867/T-E), which crashed into the sea with the loss of the 22-year-old pilot from West Wickham in Kent, who was reputed to have flown as a volunteer in the Spanish Civil War (hence the nickname). Plt Off Beurling later recalled:

"A bunch of Macchis [*sic*] tried to gang us. One of them caught him with a wild-eyed deflection shot, clear out of nowhere, and Pete never knew what hit him. He simply fell off the end of the line-abreast formation and dived into the sea from 20,000 feet. Another of the well-liked guys gone home!"

It would seem, however, that Peters was the victim of a Messerschmitt flown by Oblt Günther Hess of 6/JG53, who claimed a Spitfire at 0853 as his seventh victory. Plt Off John Sanderson (T-O) was on this operation: "20 Me109s and 10 Macchis in scattered sections. Got bounced quite a lot, but all missed. Chased four Macchis but must have missed. No result."

At 0955, four 229 Squadron Spitfires undertook a reconnaissance patrol when plots on Malta's radar screens showed aircraft approaching southern Italy from the south. These were, in fact, SM82 transports carrying captured survivors of the ill-fated British commando raid on Tobruk[109]. The Savoia transports were not intercepted by the Spitfires, however, which instead sighted what they believed to have been eight MC202s, flying in pairs off Cape Scalambria, although it seems probable they were Bf109s from I/JG77. Flt Lt Roscoe fired a one-second burst at one, which dived away trailing white smoke from its engine, but 20-year-old Canadian Plt Off John Scott (BR486) turned to attack, he was not seen again. Sgt George Turner became separated from the others and headed for home but 15 miles north of Gozo, when flying at 4,000 feet, he was attacked and shot-up, and had to force-land at Luqa. Two Spitfires of 249 Squadron were immediately despatched to search for Peters and Scott, and at 1215 a dinghy was sighted about 25 miles north of St Paul's Bay. A body was seen face up in the water nearby, dressed in white, but was not considered to be one of the missing pilots. During the day I/JG77's Obfw Georg Ludwig claimed a Spitfire (his 27th victory), as did Ltn Wilhelm Scheib for his 11th victory, and they were probably responsible for shooting down the two Spitfires. Later in the day, at 1810, Ltn Berres reported shooting down another Spitfire (his 13th victory), but his possible victim has not been identified.

During the early evening of **16 September**, nine of 249's aircraft were again on patrol when eight Bf109s were encountered at 1745. A series of dogfights ensued, Flt

Lt Hetherington and Plt Off Beurling being engaged for nearly an hour before the Messerschmitts broke away; Beurling's aircraft (EP706/T-L) received damage to its starboard wing and tail, while Hetherington (BR373/T-N) claimed one of their opponents damaged.

229 Squadron's Sgt Pashen, who had suffered a run of bad luck, followed by a long bout of illness, confided to his diary:

"Received a hell of a shaking-up after lunch when the CO told me in a round about way that he thought I didn't want to fly – in fact, inferred that I wasn't game. It nearly broke me up, as I have done nothing to deserve such a statement. Perhaps my run of bad luck in August was the cause of it – I don't know. But I intend having it out with my flight commander... Passed a troubled evening because of yesterday's happening and still feel bad about it. Maybe I'm taking it the wrong way and too much to heart, but a slur like that is nothing to laugh about. Another day off – so far I've put in five hours this month and the prospects aren't so good for too many more."

17 September proved to be the busiest day for some time. At 0845 ten Spitfires from 229 Squadron and eight of 126 Squadron were scrambled, pilots of the former unit spotting two aircraft identified as MC202s, going north at 23,000 feet. Flt Lt Roscoe fired a two-seconds burst at one as it turned into the sun, seeing pieces fly off its wings and fuselage. It seems likely that the Italian fighters were actually RE2001s from 2°Gruppo, for Serg Luigi Berna of 151^Squadriglia crashed at Gela on return and was killed, presumably as a result of this combat. Apparently other pilots of 2°Gruppo claimed two Spitfires shot down in this action. As the Spitfires retired, Flt Sgt Irwin saw two Bf109s and chased one down to sea level, firing a four-seconds burst and seeing thick grey smoke and one leg of the undercarriage come down, but was credited only with a damaged.

Meanwhile, Sqn Ldr Wicks led his eight aircraft after an estimated 15 Messerschmitts seen over Zonqor, but a further eight were then spotted below at about 18,000 feet, and these were engaged some 20 miles north-east of Grand Harbour. Plt Off Jock Thompson, a Scot from Dundee, reported shooting one down, but Sqn Ldr Wicks' aircraft was slightly damaged, possibly by Oblt Freytag who claimed a Spitfire as his 68th victory. Thompson's victim crashed into the sea and was undoubtedly Yellow 9 (10506), a G-2 of 3/JG77, from which a slightly wounded Uffz Fritz Schneider baled out. Thompson reported:

"Two Me109s tried to jump me from behind, so I broke to left. The 109s overshot on my starboard and did a steep climbing turn to starboard. I gave the rear 109 six or seven one-second bursts and saw a few strikes, at a range of about 350 yards. I then managed to close into range but could not get a burst in as he rolled on to his back and dived away. I followed him and gave him a one-second burst. He then went into a starboard steep turn, so I gave him two one-second bursts and saw something red fly back from the cockpit. He then flew straight and level and the pilot baled out. I orbited parachute and was jumped by two 109s but came home as I had no ammunition left."

Two pilots were detailed to search for the downed pilot, which they did successfully, and after about an hour saw *HSL128* arrive and pick him up. Sgt Houlton was on this scramble:

"Control advised that 109s were around Hal Far, so we went into a steep dive from 23,000 feet. Passing through 7,000 feet, and with no warning whatever, I was hit with the most excruciating and indescribable pain in the forehead, and was blinded by a glaring white light, as if I was looking into the sun. Punching myself in the forehead and screaming in agony, I wanted to die then and there; but the Spitfire literally retrieved the situation, without any help from myself. I had gone flying with a slight head cold and the sinus passage had blocked in the dive, causing tremendous internal pressure, which distorted the bone structure above my left eye. When I took both hands off the control column, the aircraft reared out of the dive and climbed up again. My vision cleared, and when I was back at about 11,000 feet the pain became bearable. Letting down slowly I returned to Hal Far to find l was stone-deaf in the left ear, which lasted for three days; and also had a sizeable lump on my forehead."[110]

Houlton had experienced a severe bout of sinusitis, which plagued a number of pilots including other recent arrivals Flt Lts Basil Friendship DFM and Geoff Wellum DFC[111], both of whom had been returned to the UK.

Shortly thereafter, three small formations of aircraft were reported approaching from the north, presumably also searching for the missing pilot. A total of 22 Spitfires were sent up to investigate, and at 1115 several Bf109s and Macchis were seen by the ten patrolling Spitfires of 229 Squadron, about ten miles north of Comino at 25,000 feet. These were engaged, Flt Sgt Irwin reporting attacking a Messerschmitt head-on, gaining strikes on its fuselage and a wing, following which one of its underwing radiators was seen to fall away. Irwin then attacked a Macchi from astern, seeing strikes on this also, and Sgt John Sidey claimed another Macchi damaged. However, Oblt Freytag of 1/JG77 caught Plt Off Johnny Farmer (his 68th victim) off guard and gained a number of telling strikes on his Spitfire (EP663), forcing him into a power dive with his controls shot to pieces. Following a desperate struggle, Farmer managed to bale out at an estimated 450mph but pulled the ripcord too soon; the jerk of the parachute opening dislocated his shoulders, broke an arm and gave him a slight rupture. He came down in the sea and, fortunately for him, was soon rescued by *HSL107*.

Following another quiet day, 69 Squadron's Sgt Frank Gillions was ordered to reconnoitre Sicilian harbours and the island of Lampedusa on the morning of **19 September**. Control received a message from him at 1033 but then silence. It later transpired that he had just photographed Castelvetrano and was on his way to Trapani when the engine of AB300 faltered, then started smoking heavily. Gillions headed for Malta but had to bale out near Agrigento, and was captured at gunpoint almost straight away. This was the first loss suffered by the reconnaissance Spitfires in 363 operational sorties following the arrival of the first aircraft – which happened to have been AB300 – in early March.

During the morning Flt Lt Rolls of 126 Squadron took off with his New Zealander No.2 Sgt Jack Mortimer, to fly an anti E-boat sweep off Sicily. Making landfall east of Cape Scalambria, they flew along the coast to Cape Passero and then towards Syracuse. Suddenly they spotted two white wakes in the sea ahead, which they assumed at first to be E-boats. Turning out to sea, they then swung in to make a head-on attack, as Rolls (BR383) recalled:

"I was coming in at about 1,500 yards when I saw the wake of one stop; and then saw it was a Do24 flyingboat about 15 feet above the water. I opened fire with cannon and machine-gun, and, at the same time, my No.2 opened up on the other, which was a Do18."

Rolls reported a red-orange glow within the Dornier he attacked before it disappeared in a white splash in front of him. Climbing to avoid the column of water, he turned to attack the second aircraft, which had reversed its direction and was taxiing fast for land. He fired a short burst into this, and then watched Mortimer attack again. More strikes were seen and pieces flew off. When they dived down to look for survivors, only two white disturbed patches were visible on the water, and both flyingboats were claimed destroyed. Next day it was noted that Axis aircraft were out over the area in force, and launches were also seen in the vicinity. Radio intercepts by the Y Service led to the view that the aircraft had possibly been carrying German staff officers for a conference in North Africa, though this has not been substantiated.

Another quiet period allowed Malta's fighter pilots to relax in the sunshine, swim in the warm waters and generally enjoy a break from operations. On **21 September**, the only excitement for the Spitfire pilots came when Sqn Ldr Warburton, on a special reconnaissance sortie at 1730 along the Sicilian coast between Marsala and Sciacca in cannon-armed Spitfire Vc of 1435 Squadron (EP140/V-P), encountered a Do24 at sea level off Agrigento. Making the best of the opportunity, he opened fire as he sped past and claimed some strikes on the flyingboat, KK+UM of 6 Seenotstaffel. Although damaged, it managed to put down safely at Marsala without injury to the crew. This quiet interlude was interrupted on **23 September**. Eight Spitfires of 126 Squadron were in the air when a fighter sweep was reported coming in from the north, an estimated 32 Messerschmitts from I/JG77 and II/JG53 approaching but not crossing the coast. Ten more Spitfires from 229 and 249 Squadrons were scrambled, but it was the 126 Squadron flight that encountered seven of the German fighters 30 miles north of Zonqor Point. Sgt Nick Sintetos claimed one damaged – possibly a Bf109G (14253) of I/JG77 that crash-landed at Comiso on return – but his fellow-countryman, 22-year-old Plt Off Ian Preston (BR383) was shot down. The Illinoisan was killed. He was possibly the victim of Ltn Wilhelm Scheib of 1/JG77 who claimed a Spitfire, although this was not confirmed and therefore not officially awarded.

Sgt Pashen of 229 Squadron, following days of enforced inactivity much to his chagrin, finally found his name down for operations on the morning of **24 September**:

> "Hooray! I'm flying again today and down to dawn readiness this morning. We were going on a sweep – then it was cancelled at the last minute. After a stand-by we were scrambled at about 1130, but my wheels kept dropping down and I had to return early. I'm now regarded as the jinx of the squadron and I'm beginning to believe it."

It turned out to be very quiet over Malta, the only event of interest occurring during a late evening patrol by 16 Spitfires drawn from 229 and 249 Squadrons, when Plt Off Beurling spotted an unidentified fighter 15 miles from Cape Scalambria, but this was not engaged. Earlier in the day, a reconnaissance Spitfire had reported a large freighter carrying a deck cargo of 27 trucks. She was hugging the coast ten miles north of Punto Stilo, with an escort of three destroyers and a small naval auxiliary. Despite a report of approaching bad weather, and the onset of darkness, the standby Beaufort flight was briefed to carry out an attack. On this occasion the freighter escaped.

Ten 249 Spitfires scrambled at 1120 on **25 September**, joining two others of 1435 Squadron to intercept a plot reported as 15 to 20 miles north-east of Grand Harbour. A dozen Messerschmitts were encountered orbiting 30 miles north-east of Zonqor Point, and attacked from up sun although only Plt Off Beurling (EP706/T-L) enjoyed any success:

> "As Tiger White 2, I attacked two Messerschmitts of a formation of 12, from starboard quarter above. Fired one-and-a-half seconds burst from 300 yards. Enemy aircraft disintegrated. Attacked No.2 aircraft from astern. Two-seconds burst, 350 yards. E/a emitted black smoke from engine with pieces coming off cowling, then glycol followed afterwards. Attacked third e/a five minutes later, six miles east of previous position, from port quarter, slightly above, 250-300 yards. Fired two-seconds burst. E/a

enveloped in flames, dived vertically, striking the sea. Enemy pilot was seen going down by parachute, and was fired upon by Messerschmitt, causing the parachute to stream."

Two of his victims appear to have been the new Bf109G-2s of I/JG77, Obfw Georg Ludwig of the Stab and an unidentified pilot of 1 Staffel (flying White 8/14260) both getting back to Sicily with badly damaged aircraft, the latter with a gaping hole just behind the cockpit, apparently caused by a cannon shell. The identity of the pilot seen to bale out is similarly not known, although Obfw Kurt Görbing (White 11/10551) of 2 Staffel was mortally injured, as Ltn Köhler recorded in his diary:

"Off the coast of Gozo everything goes wrong. I see four Spitfires through the fog over the island, and we turn back. Obfw Görbing from 2 Staffel was hit so hard that he made a forced-landing. He was so badly hurt that he died a little later."

The third aircraft attacked by Beurling had been firing at the Spitfire flown by Plt Off Budd, who was unhurt, although Plt Off Junior Moody's aircraft (EP136/T-P) was hit and he crash-landed at Takali. His victor was probably Ltn Berres of 1/JG77, who claimed a Spitfire as his 14th victory. 249 Squadron noted that the German fighter sweeps were getting bigger and tougher. Ltn Köhler recorded:

"We fight with 30 Spitfires south of Malta, but at high speed at 8,500 metres you easily get your flaps frozen. In spite of this, we outflew the Spitfires. Obfw Ludwig was hit in the engine, and I had problems with my guns. Again I had a Tommy behind me and I could see his cannons and cooler on the right side of his plane. Bad, bad situation. I could not go up, there were seven Tommies, so I pushed my stick forward and dived into a quick loop down to 4,000 metres. I looked around me. No enemies, thank God!"

At last 229 Squadron's Sgt Pashen saw some action:

"We just missed a scramble at five o'clock but then I got mixed up in it while on an air test – about 30 109s were over and one of our section passed them when coming back from Sicily. About 15 109s above – I hit one in port side – damaged."

During the morning of **26 September**, four Spitfires of 1435 Squadron carried out a reconnaissance of south-east Sicily, and when just south of Syracuse two Bf109s of 2/JG77 were seen at 20,000 feet. The Spitfires had height advantage and dived on these, Flt Lt McLeod (BR236/V-E) shooting down Ltn Karl Eberle's White 6 (a G-2, 10559). Despite suffering wounds, Eberle succeeded in baling out and was later rescued from the sea. A Messerschmitt was also claimed probably destroyed by Sgt Wilson, who may, however, have attacked the same aircraft as McLeod, as suggested by his subsequent report of the action:

"I half-rolled into one of them and closed to 150 yards, firing a two-seconds burst from dead astern, closing to 40 yards; saw his tailplane rudder disintegrate into about six large pieces. He half-rolled very sharply and went down vertically. I turned right but lost sight of him."

Eberle's companion, Ltn Konrad Fels, claimed a Spitfire as his seventh victory, although it was probably his leader's Messerschmitt that he saw fall into the sea rather than a Spitfire. A second Spitfire was claimed by Fw Pohl.

Before the month was out, a very experienced RAF fighter pilot arrived at Luqa aboard a Dakota from the Middle East. This was Sqn Ldr Mike Stephens[112] DSO DFC and Bar, whose last operational flight, some ten months earlier, resulted in him being shot down and wounded. On his release from hospital he had been employed in

278 SPITFIRES OVER MALTA

East Africa and Egypt on non-operational duties. He was about to find himself thrown in at the deep end.

September had proved the quietest month of the year with only 38 daytime alerts, and much-reduced night activity. Such action as there had been by the fighters was fairly evenly divided between defensive action against Axis fighter sweeps, and offensive operations over their opponent's bases. However, in clashes with the new Bf109G-2, the Spitfires had achieved much success, shooting down at least six during the month. Anti-shipping forces had remained very active, however, though not perhaps to quite the same degree as during August. The Spitfire Flight of 69 Squadron received a replacement for the missing Sgt Frank Gillions in the guise of Canadian Flg Off Tony Gubb, who arrived towards the end of the month in BP910, a month in which the PR unit had carried out 111 sorties occupying almost 182 flying hours.

CHAPTER VIII

THE FINAL ASSAULT

October 1942

Of this intensely frustrating and demoralising period for the Axis, Feldmarschall Kesselring was to write:

> "The way our convoys were being increasingly molested showed that freedom of movement in the Mediterranean could not be secured by merely defensive action. I could not reconcile myself to this slow ruination in idleness. It was clear to me by the middle of September that an effort must be made to ease our supply situation if only temporarily by an air operation against Malta. I knew the difficulties well enough; the island was fully capable of defending herself and had a substantially strengthened fighter force on hand.
>
> "The transfer of British fighter aircraft, taking off from aircraft carriers, was going on apace without our being able to do anything about it. Even though we were able to spot their approach by radar, our fighters always arrived on the scene too late; we just could not overcome the difficulties of getting fast aircraft into the area. It followed that as regards comparative strength, the scales had tipped against us, German-Italian formations being so much in demand to shield our convoys. Finally, the British had learnt the lesson of the first air battle of Malta; they had widened their base and achieved the highest degree of protection from bomber attack."

Nonetheless, in spite of this apparent air of despondency, Kesselring remained optimistic and confident about the outcome of such a clash, and showed admirable faith in his men:

> "The C-in-C Luftwaffe gave extensive support to the proposed operation; but still every requirement could not be fulfilled. The quality of the formations, however, made up for this to some extent. The fighter wing were old hands at taking on the British, and the bomber formations had years of operational experience. It was hardly possible, however, to place much reliance on the Italian bombers and fighters because their aircraft were obsolescent and the bomber crews had insufficient night operational training."

Indeed, the Axis air forces were now building up in preparation for a final all-out assault on Malta. There was no longer a question of a possible invasion – the pendulum had swung the other way, and the concern now was for the survival of the Afrika Korps. Despite all Rommel's successes of the summer, he was now stalled at Alamein, faced with a massively strong Allied line, and with British Eighth Army and the Western Desert Air Force rapidly outstripping him in numbers. He knew it was only a matter of time before the British launched their own offensive backed by devastating strength. It was absolutely vital, therefore, that the supply route across the Mediterranean be safeguarded from the depredations of Malta's submarines and aircraft, if a disaster was to be avoided.

Thus, it was around the end of September that Luftwaffe units had once again begun gathering on the Sicilian airfields. From North Africa, the Ju88s of Stab and I/KG54 returned, to join KGr806, which where then renumbered III/KG54. III/KG77 had moved to Crete during September for operations over Egypt, but this unit also now returned to join II Gruppe and KüFlGr606, which at this time became a new

I/KG77, II/LG1 also moved over from Crete to add further strength to the bomber force, and II/KG100 moved into Catania with He111s. The Germans also transferred to Comiso newly established I/Schlachtgeschwader 2, a fighter-bomber unit under the command of Hptm Johann-Georg Drescher (a former Staffelkapitän of 5/StG3) and equipped with bomb-carrying Bf109F, and formed with personnel drawn from the now defunct 10(Jabo)/JG27 and 10(Jabo)/JG53, including Fw Ernst Selzer who was nicknamed 'Amigo' as he had flown in the Spanish Civil War. Although the Regia Aeronautica della Sicilia looked powerful on paper – with nine squadriglie of MC202s and three of RE2001s to support three squadriglie of Z1007bis, four of SM79s, two of SM84bis, one with BR20Ms and two of Ju87s – the Italians would offer only limited support in the forthcoming battles. It was the Luftwaffe that would pose the most serious threat.

Having spent a busy time in southern Russia since June, I/JG53 and the balance of the Geschwader Stab also returned to Sicily. I Gruppe was now commanded by Oblt Friedrich-Karl Müller (103 victories). His three Staffeln were led by Ltn Hans Möller (20-plus victories), Ltn Erich Thomas, and Ltn Wolfgang Tonne, respectively. Tonne was an *Experte* of standing similar to his new Kommandeur, victor of 101 combats. Other high-scoring aces included Ltn Wilhelm Crinius (100), Ltn Fritz Dinger (48), Uffz Heinz Golinski (46), and Uffz Marian Mazurek (29). Additionally, the Bf109Gs of I/JG27 would fly into Pachino on 3 October. The Gruppe had been the most successful in the fighting in North Africa but had also suffered serious losses. The pilots were tired and demoralised, but there several notable *Experten* still serving with the Gruppe, including the Kommandeur, Hptm Ludwig Franzisket (37 victories), Ltn Karl von Lieres (24) and Ltn Hans Remmer (14). Formidable opponents indeed, who would sorely try Malta's defenders in the coming battle.

But Malta could boast its own array of experienced and successful fighter pilot/leaders in Wg Cdrs Prosser Hanks, Arthur Donaldson and John Thompson, while squadron commanders in the mould of Sqn Ldrs Timber Woods, Butch Baker, Bryan Wicks, Tony Lovell, Mike Stephens and Maj Zulu Swales were inspiring. The squadrons contained a sprinkling of aggressive and successful pilots including Screwball Beurling, Willie Williams and Mac McElroy of 249 Squadron; Bill Rolls, Rip Jones, Rod Smith, Gord Farquharson, Arthur Varey and Nigel Park of 126 Squadron; Wally McLeod, Charlie Lattimer, Wally Walton and Allan Scott of 1435; Art Roscoe, Eddie Glazebrook, Colin Parkinson, Jim Ballantyne and Ian Maclennan of 229 Squadron; and Ken Charney, Keith Kulhmann, Tubby Mahar and Len Reid of 185 Squadron. There were others. All of whom had proved themselves – some by simply surviving and thus gaining valuable experience.

October started off as September had finished – relatively quietly for Malta – but all on the island were aware that something was again brewing on Sicily. Shortly before 1000 on **1 October**, two Spitfires of 1435 Squadron on a reconnaissance south of Cape Scalambria spotted five RE2001s at 19,000 feet. Sqn Ldr Lovell and his No.2 Sgt Doug Eva dived on them and while three dived away, two climbed and circled once before making off towards Sicily. The Spitfires gave chase and Lovell (BS161/V-U) reported gaining strikes on one.

The next day (**2 October**) was marked by a minor historical event with the first operational use of bomb-carrying Spitfires – when six of 229 Squadron led by Wg Cdr Donaldson set out to raid Biscari aerodrome, covered by eight more Spitfires from 185 Squadron. One Spitbomber was obliged to return early but the others carried out their task. No aircraft were seen on the airfield, nor were any tangible results of the bombing observed, and all returned safely. Of this major event Sgt Pashen (X-V), one of the bombers, simply noted: "Two bombs dropped on Biscari". Whilst these and their escort were operating over Sicily, nine of 249 patrolled off the southern coast to cover the withdrawal. At 1005 two MC202s were sighted going south at 19,000 feet, then two sections each of four Bf109s were spotted. Sqn Ldr Woods (AR466/T-R) and Flt Sgt de l'Ara attacked one of the Macchis, the latter claiming strikes before it evaded and dived away.

Newly arrived Sqn Ldr Mike Stephens, who was attached to 249 as a supernumerary to gain experience of local conditions, made his first flight on **3 October** in one of the Hurricanes (BE397), before progressing to a Spitfire next day, a type he had not previously flown, but with in excess of 500 operational sorties under his belt, he was soon exhibiting his skill when engaged in dogfighting practice with Flg Off McElroy. He even carried out dive-bombing practice. Such was the calm before the storm that the defenders of Malta were able to relax to a degree. At Luqa, for example, an impromptu cricket match was arranged between an RAF team and gunners from the 59th LAA battery, the airmen emerging the victors.

The Luftwaffe put in an appearance during the morning of **4 October**, at least 20 Bf109Gs of I/JG77 approaching the coast, which only a few crossed. Sixteen Spitfires, drawn equally from 185 and 249 Squadrons, were airborne, Red Section of the latter encountering four of the intruders at 26,000 feet over Grand Harbour. Before these could be engaged, however, about a dozen more dived out of the sun, attacking in pairs. Sgt Irving Gass (EP700/T-Q), who was straggling, was shot down into the sea off Filfla; he did not survive. A second Spitfire was damaged; seriously wounded in the head, Flt Sgt George Hogarth struggled back to the island, only to crash-land in a field near Qrendi as he was approaching to land. The Spitfire (BR379/T-V) skidded into the only building around, where a number of airmen were sunning themselves; no one was hurt apart from the 21-year-old Canadian pilot from Winnipeg, who was further injured and rushed to hospital, where he died. *HSL128* was sent out to search for 20-year-old Sgt Murray Irving Gass from Somerset, but found only a Mae West and wreckage. One of the Spitfires – probably that of Irving Gass – was shot down by Ltn Hans-Joachim Gläss of 3/JG77 for his seventh victory, the other by Oblt Siegfried Freytag, but since it was not confirmed it was not allowed.

Another fighter sweep, estimated to number about two dozen, approached the coast at 23,000 feet during mid-morning on **6 October**, eight Spitfires of 1435 Squadron being ordered off to join three patrolling machines of 185 Squadron. Eight Bf109s of I/JG77 were spotted north-east of Zonqor Point, and the 1435 Squadron flight dived on these. They were seen however, and the Messerschmitts took violent evasive action to escape. Two more were then observed, one of these being attacked by Plt Off Lattimer (EN978/V-O) who claimed it damaged. The other German fighter turned on Sgt Philp's machine, which sustained slight damage. However, the German pilot was credited with its destruction. In fact, Spitfires were claimed by Ltn Berres (his 15th victory), Fw Gerhard Häcker (his second), and one unconfirmed by Oblt Freytag.

The next three days were relatively uneventful for Malta's Spitfire pilots, and no engagements were reported. Two of the PR pilots were despatched to check on the build-up of aircraft on Sicily's airfields, and on Pantelleria, the subsequent reports of Flg Off Tony Gubb and Plt Off Jo Dalley giving cause for some alarm when their photographs revealed the following:

Comiso	34 Ju88s, one He111, one Ju87, one medium-sized u/i aircraft, 41 fighters (mainly Bf109s).
Gela	14 Ju87s, 57 fighters including MC202s.

Biscari	33 fighters including MC202s.
Pachino	30 fighters – believed to be all Bf109s.
Catania	41 Ju88s, six He111s, four Dorniers, one Ju87, one SM84, two Z1007bis, two SM79s; two Ju52s, four Bf109s; 12 u/i fighters; three medium-sized u/i aircraft; three small u/i aircraft.
Gerbini	34 Ju88s, seven SM79s, three Dorniers, one He111, three small u/i aircraft; Gerbini satellite: Four Dorniers, one Ju52, two FW58s, three medium-sized u/i aircraft.
Trapani	21 Ju88s; 11 small u/i aircraft, three DFS230 gliders.
Sciacca	28 fighters, 27 SM79s/SM84s, 10 Ca310s, six Z1007bis.
Palermo	12 SM79s/SM84s, six Ca310s, three SM81s, six monoplanes; six CR42s, six u/i fighters, 18 medium-sized u/i aircraft.
Castelvetrano	23 Z1007bis, 10 SM79s/SM84s, 13 SM82s, three SM81s, three BR20s, one small u/i aircraft.
Pantelleria	Seven SM79s, one Ju87, six u/i fighters.

Such a formidable array of bombers and fighters assembled on the southern airfields could mean only one thing – Malta was soon going to be on the receiving end once again of a pounding from the air. But this time there was one major difference – there were in excess of 100 serviceable Spitfires available and many eager and fresh pilots to fly them. They did not have to wait long.

Two dozen Axis fighters approached Malta from the north shortly before 0800 on **10 October**, some of which crossed the coast. Eight Spitfires of 249 were airborne, one of which was flown by Sqn Ldr Stephens. Four Spitfires of 229 Squadron were also patrolling off the coast, but two of these were forced to return early; the remaining pair sighted about 17 fighters, including MC202s, some 18 miles north-east of Zonqor Point and were then attacked by a number of Messerschmitts. Plt Off Hugh Reynolds' aircraft was hit but he succeeded in reaching Takali, where he crash-landed. It seems likely that his attacker was Oblt Geisshardt of 3/JG77 who claimed a Spitfire shot down for his 88th victory. The Messerschmitts were driven away by three pilots of 249 Squadron, Sqn Ldr Stephens (EP140/V-P) opening his Malta account by claiming one damaged: "Met five or six 109s at 26,000 feet. Dived on one and got in a good squirt but had to break away as another was after me. Y Service picked up natter which may confirm."

At about this time, Plt Off Beurling was carrying out an air test on his newly serviced Spitfire (EP706/T-L), when Ops reported that two Bf109s had sneaked in at low level and were apparently searching for ground defences on the south side of the island. Beurling flew out to sea in a wide arc, sweeping back in close to Filfla, where the two Messerschmitts were seen at about 1,000 feet, flying in line abreast:

> "I dropped in on them. I went down and down, clean under the starboard fellow, and rolled up under him, giving him a quick burst into the engine. He pancaked right smack down on his belly on the island and flipped over onto his back. The other fellow tried to circle away, but I stayed with him. He turned out to sea, then whipped back across Filfla again. As he did I moved onto his starboard quarter and let him have it. The burst caught the gas tank and the ship blew up, complete with pilot."

These latest victories brought Beurling's Malta tally to 21 confirmed, plus another shared with two others, and his overall total to 23 and one shared[113].

At 1040 up to 50 aircraft including two Ju88s were reported approaching, some of which crossed over Gozo, where they were intercepted by Spitfires; the bombers jettisoned their bombs, some of these falling on the small Gozitan town of Sannat where 16 persons were killed and 60 injured. A total of 23 Spitfires were up but only 249 Squadron, joined by Wg Cdr Prosser Hanks, made contact, initially meeting a dozen Bf109s at 20,000 feet, 15 miles north of Gozo. Attacking head-on, one Messerschmitt was claimed shot down by newly commissioned Plt Off Sanderson (BR373/T-N) for his first victory, his own aircraft sustaining slight damage. He noted: "Gozo bombed. Intrepid! All-in dogfight with 12 Messerschmitts. One destroyed." Another was claimed shot down by Flg Off McElroy (EP708/T-U), who also damaged a second:

> "Attacked head-on; e/a dived to right so turned on their tails. Caught another climbing with two others in line astern. I attacked head-on from above quarter, fired a half-second burst, and observed cannon shells hit leading edge of e/a's wing. A large piece of wing blew off. I fired at other 109s, closing from 100 yards to 20 yards, but observed no strikes. I broke right on to another, 250 yards line astern, and fired a three-seconds cannon and machine-gun burst, observing hits on engine and wing roots; with heavy black smoke and pieces coming off the e/a half-rolled, so I followed it down and gained on him in the dive; the aircraft tried to pull out at 5,000 feet, so I closed to 200 yards and finished my cannon, observing strikes and glycol. I continued to attack with machine-guns down to 50 feet from the sea, 15 to 20 miles south of the Sicilian coast; e/a still diving towards sea, streaming glycol and black smoke."

Sqn Ldr Stephens (EP338/T-A) claimed a Bf109 as probably destroyed:

> "At 23,000 feet met 12 109s north of Gozo at slightly greater height. Think they must have been flown by skiers from their tactics. Three looped in line astern, I looped the other way and squirted each in turn. Wizard scrap, but I had no sight. Wish to God I'd had a bloody reflector sight. Squirted several and got one probable. Lumps off him and streams of glycol."

Sgt Stead (EP199/T-K) also claimed a probable. Two others were claimed damaged by Wg Cdr Hanks (BR498/PP-H) and Sqn Ldr Woods (AR466/T-R).

Six Ju88s, with an estimated 25 Messerschmitts and Macchis as escort, were then reported coming in from the north at 1600. Eight Spitfires of 229 Squadron, led by Wg Cdr Donaldson, encountered the bombers and a dozen fighters about 35 miles north of Gozo. As the Spitfires attempted to engage the bombers, the escort came to their aid, Sgt Sidey's aircraft being shot-up by what he believed was a Macchi, causing him to crash-land at Luqa on return; two other Spitfires sustained slight damage. Messerschmitts were claimed damaged by Wg Cdr Donaldson (BR529/AD) and Sgt Ron Miller, while Flt Lt Roscoe reported shooting one down:

> "I attacked No.4 of a section of four Me109s in line astern. After breaking off, I was attacked by the leader and he followed me down to 12,000 feet, about 20 miles north of St Paul's Bay. After levelling out, he overshot, which placed me in line astern at 30-75 yards. I gave a three-seconds burst and observed white and black smoke, strikes, and pieces fly off. He flopped over and dived down. I saw him hit the sea; then Sgt Miller also observed a kite go in the same spot, so it may be the same."

Uffz Horst Schlick of 1/JG77 claimed a Spitfire during this action, his sixth victory, although the identity of his victim remains a mystery[114]:

> "The first mission was intended to give me straightaway the opportunity to judge what Gustav 2 [the new Bf109G-2] was capable of. For some time a British fighter had been making his presence inconveniently felt by means of a particular tactic. He flew in the pack – not, however, just over the island, but hanging around the coast of Sicily. When

our pilot, already in the vicinity of our aerodrome, was feeling secure and relaxed, and no longer paying enough attention, then 'MacArthur', as we called him, would suddenly slam into him with the whole works – some had to pay with their life or just try to glide home [it is assumed that 'MacArthur' was in fact Beurling – ed.]

"Huka [StFw Helmut Huka], Gödert and I caught him, as he was again lurking at 6,000 metres. After a short air battle, I caught his *Kaczmarek* [his No.2] who baled out of the flaming Spitfire. Huka had attacked 'Mac' with the full works, but he didn't go down. A Do24, as a sea rescue aircraft, hauled the Tommy out and brought him to us. When the Tommy was brought in – he was an Oberleuntant [flight lieutenant] – he wanted to speak to his vanquisher right away. At first, I was shaking his hand – greetings and all that, even the Kommandeur came, but when he learned that I was 'only' a lower-ranking officer, he actually became a bit embarrassed. He wanted to know what number he was among those I had shot down. I said, 'the sixth,' and he answered just with an 'Oh!' We asked him about 'MacArthur', the commander of his flight. He was, we were told, an Oberst [wing commander] by the name of Whitehouse [*sic*]. He said that 'Mac' had shot down many of our Me109s and Ju88s. At this time, though, they were surprised that the Me109s did not dive away, but quickly climbed higher than the Spitfires. The Oberleutnant assumed a special flight of interceptors with souped-up engines had been sent to Sicily. When he was told that we had acquired new model 109s, he said laconically that they would not be of much help. What he meant, I did not know."

The increased activity in Malta's skies during the preceding few days was but a foretaste of what was to follow. Of the new blitz, LAC Metcalf at Takali wrote:

"Our boys knocked hells bells out of Jerry and even then we got three bashings at Takali, two at Luqa and one at Hal Far. For the first two raids I stayed on the runway but for the third (some killed) my nerves weren't up to much so I ran for the big hole! Most of the chaps were pretty shaky at supper and couldn't eat anything. I wonder what we'll be like if we have, say, a month of this?"

At the conclusion of the day's hard fighting, Lord Gort, the Governor, sent a message of congratulation to Air HQ, which read: "Well done. The Spitfires have produced a fine opening score." To which the AOC responded, continuing in the cricketing vein: "All ranks of RAF are grateful for your message of congratulations. Spitfires have won the toss and will keep up their hard hitting until the match is won."

At 0720 on the morning of **11 October**, nine Ju88s of I/KG54 escorted by 25 MC202s from 20° and 155°Gruppi and four Bf109s of I/JG77 approached the island, a few bombers crossing the coast to release bombs on Hal Far and Benghaisa Point. Nineteen Spitfires were scrambled (eight/1435, seven/126 and four/229). The first two units intercepted between 15-20 miles north-east of Grand Harbour, where the bombers were sighted at 25,000 feet, with their escorts 500 feet higher. 1435 Squadron climbed to attack, Plt Off Wally Walton (EP714/V-T) claiming damage to one Junkers, with Flt Sgt Hamilton (EP259/V-L) gaining strikes on a Messerschmitt.

126 Squadron then engaged the formation, which had descended to 18,000 feet, about 11 miles north of Zonqor, and several successful encounters were reported. Plt Off Jim Stevenson (EP209) shot down a 151^Squadriglia Macchi into the sea some 30 miles off Cape Scaramia, Sottoten Urbano Sciarra baling out of his stricken aircraft. A second Macchi was claimed damaged by Sgt Tiddy, Flt Sgt Varey claimed a Bf109 probably shot down and a second damaged, and Sgt Jack Yeatman another damaged. Others managed to reach the bombers, Sgt Marshall gaining strikes on one, which he claimed destroyed, and Flg Off Rod Smith (EP330) shooting down Uffz

Hermann Müller's aircraft (B3+YL), as he later recalled:

> "First Hun of Blitz. One of nine Ju88s at 18,000 feet north-east of Grand Harbour. I
> gave two six-seconds bursts from 250 yards and the port engine and wing caught fire;
> aircraft exploded and fell into sea. One of crew baled out and picked up."

The Macchi pilots returned to submit claims for four Spitfires shot down, M.llo
Pasquale Bartolucci and Serg Dante Testera each reporting that their victims had gone
into the sea. The latter shared a second with Ten Gustavo Castellano, and M.llo Ennio
Tarantola claimed another shot down in flames. Apart from the loss of Sciarra, Serg
Magg Angelo Cerri returned with his aircraft damaged in its port wing. One more
Spitfire was claimed by the crew of Uffz Woas' Ju88. The two squadrons involved
suffered no losses, although one Spitfire of each unit was damaged. Ltn Köhler of
I/JG77 noted in his diary:

> "Escort Ju88s towards Hal Far. We went straight into battle with enemy aircraft. A Ju88
> was shot down on the spot, then two Spitfires, one Macchi and a Me109 went down in
> flames. We were higher up, so we could not attack from all angles."

Immediately following this fight, *HSL128* was sent out to search for survivors from
the Axis aircraft; only Uffz Günther Grams, the W/Op in the Ju88 shot down by Rod
Smith, was recovered having been sighted ten miles north of Grand Harbour by a 126
Squadron pilot. LAC Chandler noted in his diary:

> "The air raids were resumed today. This morning, after breakfast, the camp siren went.
> Thinking it was before 0730 hours, I took no notice even when the ack-ack started. But
> the whistle and crash of bombs on Hal Far soon changed my attitude. I was definitely
> shaken. Plot was six 88s and about 85 fighters. Later on there was a plot of 40, which
> did not come in. After the first do, *HSL128* brought in a Jerry with a broken leg."

The remains of a German dinghy were also sighted but the three other crewmembers,
one of whom had also been seen to bale out, were not found. The missing Italian
fighter pilot (Sciarra) had been observed by members of his unit to be climbing into
his dinghy, but subsequent searches by Regia Aeronautica rescue aircraft failed to
locate him, either. Uffz Grams later told his interrogation officer:

> "I was the W/T operator of a Ju88 which took part in an attack on Malta, consisting of
> nine Ju88s escorted by some 40 fighters including Me109s. The bombing target was
> aircraft at Hal Far, but when at 15,000 feet, north-east of Grand Harbour, we were
> intercepted by Spitfires. At this time the nine Ju88s were flying in vic formation. While
> our fighter cover of Me109s above were being engaged by numbers of Spitfires, one
> lone but obviously experienced Spitfire [pilot] climbed up behind the bombers and
> picked off our aircraft, delivering first an attack from level with and astern of our Ju88's
> port engine, putting it out of action, and then making a second and similar attack on the
> starboard engine, after which our Ju88 broke formation and the Spitfire, its task
> accomplished, broke down and away. I was the only one able to bale out."

On Malta there was little damage from the opening attack – some buildings and motor
transport had been hit at Hal Far but there were no casualties. Amongst those
watching from the ground was 185 Squadron's Plt Off O'Brien, who was suffering
from Malta Dog:

> "The alert was sounded about 8am this morning and we went up on the roof when the
> guns started firing. As we've been having only fighter sweeps for the past two months
> they've been firing only 'pointers'. However this morning we saw them fire 'the real

McCoy' and then we saw the bombs going down on Hal Far. It looked as if they had pranged it but we were quite surprised and relieved to find it undamaged. Looks as if Jerry has started his blitzing again – well here's hoping he has!"

Shortly after 1000 the next raid approached, comprising six Ju88s and an estimated 65 fighters. Twenty Spitfires were ordered off (eight/185, six/229, four/1435, two/126), the 229 Squadron flight making initial contact 15 miles north of Comino; but it became entangled with the top cover Messerschmitts, Flt Lt Roscoe claiming a probable, and Sgt Miller one damaged. Minutes later the 185 Squadron aircraft engaged the same formation, which had now reached Luqa. They were similarly held at bay by the escort, and one Spitfire suffered slight damage. The 1435 Squadron quartet attacked next, Sqn Ldr Lovell claiming one damaged and Plt Off Walton (EP717/V-D) a probable, as he reported:

"I was Red 3 and climbed to 16,000 feet and saw some little jobs west of us, down sun and about two miles away. I dived towards them. Red 1 (S/L Lovell) followed me on two Me109s, which turned to the right ahead. Another 109 got on Red 1's tail and I turned on him. He started to climb, turning left. I followed giving him all my ammunition. White smoke poured out from him and he turned on his back and dived down."

Finally, the 126 Squadron pair spotted the bombers just after they had released their bombs over Takali, but were engaged by four Bf109s orbiting over Gozo at 17,000 feet, which were providing withdrawal cover. The bombing caused negligible damage and no casualties.

The third attack of the day began soon after 1330 with the approach of seven more Ju88s – believed to have been from II/LG1 – and the usual large escort. This time 28 Spitfires were scrambled (eight from each of 185, 229 and 1435 Squadrons, and four of 126 Squadron). The latter section made the initial contact ten miles north of the island, where they were bounced by Messerschmitts as they prepared to attack the bombers. One Spitfire (EP550 of 229 Squadron) was damaged, and crash-landed although the pilot survived unhurt. Just before this raid developed Wg Cdr Donaldson had been practicing dive-bombing, using Filfla as the target. Flying 249 Squadron's BR254/T-S, he was able to join up with 229 Squadron Spitfires as they took off, and led them into a head-on attack on the bombers, personally claiming one shot down; he also claimed strikes on a Messerschmitt, while Flt Sgt Ballantyne claimed to have shot down one of these. It is possible that one or both had hit an aircraft of I/JG77 (14250), which crash-landed at Comiso on return due to combat damage. The pilot was unhurt. Meanwhile, Plt Off Nash claimed damage to what he believed was a Macchi.

As the bombers reached their target, releasing bombs on Takali and Rabat, where a number of civilian casualties were sustained, Flt Lt McLeod led the 1435 Squadron flight to engage the top cover Messerschmitts, as AA bursts appeared amidst the bomber formation. Three of the German fighters were claimed damaged in this initial attack by McLeod (BR236/V-E), Flt Sgt Maclennan (EP203/V-G) and Sgt Knox-Williams (EN978/V-O). The Spitfires broke away, but re-engaged after the Ju88s had dropped their bombs. They again encountered the escort, three more being damaged by McLeod (whose own aircraft suffered some damage), Maclennan and Sgt Jack Jarrett; the latter's aircraft (EP727/V-N) also sustained damage in return, and he had to crash-land at Takali, suffering slight injuries. Sgt Tom Kebbell's EP138/V-K was also hit although he was able to land safely. McLeod reported:

"I was leading Red Section, Blue Section also being with me, when six Ju88s and numerous fighters were seen below us going south. I led my section into attack, going after the fighters and leaving the bombers open for Blue Section, who came down after me. Blue Section failed to engage at that time. I jumped four to six 109s and fired at one from point-blank range, firing a two to three-seconds burst only breaking away in time to miss him. Strikes and pieces were observed but due to the undue attention of many other 109s, failed to observe 109 go in. After numerous dogfights with yellow-nosed 109s operating against me in pairs with great determination, I closed to 300 yards on one from astern and fired a short burst. Glycol was observed coming from the 109, which dived down and was subsequently lost in cloud haze and a dirty windscreen after a bit of a chase, leaving him about 25 miles north of Grand Harbour. After several more encounters I returned to base. I claim two 109s damaged pending further evidence."

Meanwhile, four pilots of 185 Squadron patrolling north of St Paul's Bay at 21,000 feet saw a single Ju88 and many fighters over Takali. The Spitfires dived on these and engaged RE2001s near Comino, Plt Off Bob Park claiming one damaged. Pilots from I/JG77 claimed two Spitfires, one by Uffz Schlick near Valetta (his seventh victory), the other by Oblt Freytag for his 69th victory. Hptm Bär, the Kommandeur of I Gruppe, also claimed a Spitfire but this was unconfirmed, but another was credited to Ltn Schiess of Stab/JG53. Of his victory, Horst Schlick wrote:

"We took off for Valetta. Here we met a squadron of Spitfires and one of them broke away to port and I followed him along the coast. We went down to just a few metres above the water. Suddenly, his right wing hit the water and he splashed into the sea. We were cruising around at about 9,000 metres when my concentration slipped. I heard a Spitfire behind me, before I saw it. I heard his shots and my port flap was hit. I had to run. I speeded up and got away from the Tommy. I must have done 750-780kph. My aircraft collapsed on landing but I was OK."

The fourth raid proved a rather larger affair, 16 Ju88s taking part on this occasion, escorted by 17 bomb-carrying RE2001s of 22°Gruppo Aut CT and 25 MC202s (twenty/155°Gruppo, five/20°Gruppo), led by Magg Fanali. Their main target was the radar station at Salina Bay, but the bombs fell harmlessly in the Mellieha Ridge area. Just before 1700, as this raid was being plotted, 25 Spitfires were scrambled (nine/126, eight/185, eight/229), Wg Cdr Hanks (BR498/PP-H) leading the 126 Squadron formation to engage a large number of fighters north of Comino at 27,000 feet. Hanks attacked first, claiming a Bf109 which he reported crashed into the sea off the Sicilian coast, and later damaged a second as he headed back towards Malta. His victim was possibly White 2 (10485) of 4/JG53 in which Ltn Ewald Schumacher was killed. Sqn Ldr Wicks and Flg Off Wallace each claimed a Macchi damaged, while Flt Lt Rolls (MK-Q) claimed two RE2001s:

"I came up under one fighter and delivered one two-seconds burst, observing pieces fall away from the enemy aircraft. The Reggiane then went over on its back and went down. After being in a dogfight with several aircraft I picked out one for attack and dived from 24,000 feet to 4,000 feet towards Sicily; when only 15-20 miles from the Sicilian coast I gave it a burst of two seconds and saw glycol stream from it."

He later recalled that the pilot of the second Reggiane had baled out, adding:

"Then I saw him flip the aircraft over. He came out and eventually his parachute opened ... I circled him as I saw him get in his dinghy... He waved to me as I circled him, but I did not wave back."

Two Bf109s then attacked Rolls' Spitfire, gaining a strike on his engine, which started to falter. Although some 30 miles out to sea, by carefully nursing his aircraft and with a slice of good luck he was able to get back to Luqa and land safely. However, 20-year-old New Zealander Sgt David MacLean from Wellington was shot down into the sea in BR183 and killed; Sgt Nigel Park's MK-M was attacked by a succession of fighters and was damaged. Unable to defend himself as his guns had jammed, Park nonetheless got back to Takali.

Soon after this interception 229 Squadron attacked and split up a formation of 30 fighters some 14 miles north of Gozo, Flt Lt Glazebrook and Flt Sgt Ballantyne each claiming a Macchi shot down. The controller then called in 185 Squadron and Wg Cdr Thompson (EP122/JM-T) led them to attack fighters between St Paul's Bay and Comino, where three Bf109s were claimed shot down, one each by Thompson, Sgt Les Gore (BR375/GL-A) and Plt Off Len Reid (EP186), who reported:

"Attacked a large number of 109s flying in formation at 20,000 feet. Dived down on them from 24,000 feet and upon breaking up under last two to port, gave one a long burst. It broke up and crashed into sea."

The Italians reported meeting 25 Spitfires north of Gozo, where M.llo Remo Zedda and M.llo Cesare Ferrazza of 360^Squadriglia, and Serg Ferdinando Zanardi of 351^Squadriglia, each claimed one shot down, which they believed fell in flames. Others claimed four probables and no less than 21 damaged. Losses included M.llo Romano Pesavento's Reggiane of 369^Squadriglia, who was shot down and killed after bombing – presumably a victim of Flt Lt Rolls – and Serg Paolo Pedretti of 353^Squadriglia, who force-landed his damaged Macchi near Gerbini on return. Cap Italo D'Amico's 151^Squadriglia Macchi was slightly damaged. It seems that the Messerschmitts present included aircraft from the recently arrived I/JG27, Uffz Walter Timmermann's White 7 crashing on Gozo with the death of the pilot – presumably a victim of 185 Squadron.

Soon after these late afternoon actions had ceased – and with the onset of dusk – the Luftwaffe launched the strongest bomber formation of the day. Thirty Ju88s from I and III/KG54 and III/KG77 approached at 1745, attacking Hal Far and Luqa. Bombs fell at Tarxien and Qormi, where a number of homes were destroyed and civilian casualties suffered. At Luqa, a Beaufighter and a Beaufort were damaged beyond repair. Five Spitfires of 229 Squadron and four of 1435 were airborne at the time of the attack, the latter quartet sighting 15 bombers when they were at 20,000 feet and 20 miles north of St Paul's Bay. Flt Lt Wally McLeod (BS161/V-U) led the Spitfires in for a highly successful attack during which he claimed two Ju88s shot down. Two more were claimed by Flt Sgt Maclennan (EP717/V-D), while Sgt Tom Kebbell (AB264/V-Z) claimed another; the fourth member of the flight, Sgt Ronnie Roe (AR470/V-Q), gained hits on two more, while Maclennan damaged yet another; afterwards he reported:

"I climbed and delivered a stern attack, diving down and opening fire from about 100 yards. Return crossfire was inaccurate. Strikes were observed on the fuselage, also white sheets of flame and pieces flew off, then aircraft caught fire. As I broke off, I observed three parachutes come out. I then attacked another Ju88 over the island from very close range and saw strikes, on wing, also on fuselage. I broke upwards and lost him. Attacked another approximately south-east of the island, this time attacking from astern and above. Flak and return fire was fairly intense and accurate, both of which hit me, I got strikes all over the fuselage and port engine cowling flew off. I broke away, attacked again but was out of ammunition. The Ju88's port engine caught fire and it spread rapidly and the Ju88 went down into sea, flaming."

Half an hour later the 229 Squadron pilots saw nine Ju88s, about 15 miles north of Grand Harbour, coming south at between 12,000-15,000 feet. Wg Cdr Donaldson led them in a head-on attack, personally claiming one probably destroyed. Two others were claimed damaged by Flt Sgt Ballantyne and Plt Off Nash, with Plt Off Parkinson (EP691/X-A) probably destroying another:

"I could see the ack-ack going up and the search lights. Decided to wait off Zonqor Point to try and catch an odd bomber on the way home. I was lucky. I caught a glimpse of one at 10,000 feet, about 2,000 feet below. Dived in to attack; was fired at by rear gunner who I put out of action with my first burst. Made about two more attacks and finally the Ju88 caught fire. Followed it down to about 1,000 feet where I lost sight of it while trying to manoeuvre for another attack. It probably dived into the sea."

Although two of the attacking Spitfires were claimed shot down by bombers' gunners, the raiders had indeed been hard hit during these interceptions. Two failed to return and two more were seriously damaged. One of the latter was Uffz Johann Schmitt's B3+JK of 2/KG54, the pilot recalling:

"We approached the island at 7,000 metres and while heading towards the harbour area, my radio operator cried out 'Fighters! Fighters!' Three Spitfires, flying at higher altitude, dived and opened fire on my aircraft, killing the observer [Uffz Hermann Schulte-Rebbelmund] in his seat on my right, and wounding the radio operator. As the engines were running rough, I did an emergency dive, released the bombs and turned back towards Sicily with one of the engines on fire. When some 300 metres away from Catania airfield, the gunner [Uffz Walter Wutz), who was uninjured, jumped out of the aircraft. I stopped the engine to prevent the fire from spreading and crash-landed in a field. Luckily I escaped with injuries to my head and legs only. Italian civilians took the radio operator and me out of the aircraft and we were driven to hospital at Catania; my radio operator [Uffz Franz Vanis) died whilst being operated upon. I was the sole survivor."

I/KG54 was hardest hit. Apart from B3+JK, 2 Staffel's B3+DB captained by Ltn Hans Scheller failed to return, he and his crew being reported missing. Ltn Günther Wittenberg and his 3 Staffel crew aboard B3+DL also failed to return; B3+MH of 1 Staffel piloted by Oblt Karl Palliardi returned seriously damaged and with the observer, Uffz Hörst Lenz, dead. Two Ju88s from 9 Staffel (B3+CT and B3+GR) collided in mid-air near Comiso on return, following which CT crashed, killing Fw Wilhelm Ohrt, though Ltn Wittkausky was able to safely land GR at the airfield. It is not known if one or both of these aircraft had been damaged in combat. Additionally, a Ju88 of III/KG77 returned badly damaged although without crew casualties. I/JG77's Ltn Kölher noted cynically:

"Another flight. The sky was full of Spitfires, but we got home safely, only because the Ju88s did a great job keeping the enemy away!"

All was not yet over, however, for with darkness came the night bombers. For very little return, two were shot down by a Beaufighter crew, a Ju88 of 7/KG77 and a He111 of 7/KG100. Both fell into the sea.

The first raid on the morning of **12 October** arrived soon after 0620. Eight Spitfires of 185 Squadron and four more from 229 Squadron met the first wave of Ju88s from III/KG54, the former intercepting before the raiders reached the island, Capt Kuhlmann (EP187) claiming one of the escorting Messerschmitts destroyed –

believed to have been aircraft from I/JG27 – and Sgt Vinall (EP139) one Ju88 damaged. The 229 Squadron section engaged the same wave, and one Ju88 was seen to jettison its bombs when attacked. Flt Lt Glazebrook claimed one Ju88 probable and Flt Sgt Ballantyne one damaged. Despite interception, some bombers reached Takali and Luqa and bombed, and several aircraft were damaged at the latter airfield. Ten of 249 Squadron engaged as the bombers departed, Sqn Ldr Woods (AR466/T-R) claiming a Ju88 destroyed before attacking an escorting Bf109, which he claimed damaged. Sgt Stead (EP199/T-K) attacked and damaged a second. The latter then reported shooting down another Messerschmitt which Sqn Ldr Stephens (AB377/T-E) had already attacked. Stephens meanwhile engaged another of the escort, also claiming this shot down. Finding himself alone following the action, he attempted to join up with a second Spitfire but was bounced by a lone Bf109. The engine of his Spitfire seized after being hit:

"After my engine cut I had plenty of time to transmit for a fix before baling out. I spent a long time in the water floundering around, as the air bottle in my dinghy was flat, but eventually managed to climb aboard and finish inflating it with bellows. I had a grandstand view of quite a number of combats during which I saw four aircraft shot down. I was quite confident throughout that I should be picked up by our ASR service, which was quite magnificent. Eventually, I was rescued by a seaplane tender [ST280], since all the ASR boats were already out. There was quite a swell and I was as sick as a dog after I had been picked up."

Meanwhile, surviving Ju88s of the second wave swept in to bomb Hal Far, where one Spitfire was burnt out. One more Spitfire and two Hurricanes were slightly damaged. This formation had already suffered heavily from attacks by six of 126 Squadron north of Grand Harbour – one Ju88 had been hit and had turned for Sicily, while four were claimed shot down. Escorting 51°Stormo Macchi pilots reported seeing many parachutes over the target, and one Italian pilot claimed a Spitfire damaged, but their attacks did not appear to deter the Spitfires from going for the bombers. However, 22-year-old Sqn Ldr Bryan Wicks from Totnes in Devon – the CO in BR377 – failed to return. The two Spitfires flown by Stephens and Wicks were probably victims of Hptm Ludwig Franzisket, Kommandeur of I/JG27, who claimed his 39th victory, and Oblt Jost Schlang of 2 Staffel. Flt Lt Rolls (flying Wg Cdr Hanks' aircraft BR498/PP-H) claimed one Ju88, Sgt Park (BR311/MK-L) two more, and Flt Sgt Carl Long yet another. Rolls noted:

"I saw one of the Ju88s I had fired at diving down and I put a final burst into it and it almost fell to pieces. I followed to 4,000 feet and thought I saw two bale out. I did not see what happened to the others I had hit, I was too busy getting out of the mass of aircraft flying around. I saw Ju88s burning and going down all over the place. I had reached the outside of the mêlée when I saw a Spitfire going down. I flew up to it and saw it was my CO. He was injured by the looks of it. I watched him bale out and saw his chute open. After what seemed ages he hit the water and his Mae West was supporting him, but there was no sign of life. I circled him but got no response. I gave five fixes but was attacked by RE200ls from 2,000 feet. I called up the HSL and directed it to the parachute in the waters."

Long added:

"I picked out the outside starboard Ju88 and gave him three quick bursts of cannon fire of about two seconds each, opening at approximately 250 yards and closing to almost zero yards. I saw flashes and the top engine cowling fell away. I went directly over the top of it and broke away to port. I saw the Ju88 was dropping behind the others and diving slightly. I turned towards it and saw the Ju88's dive increasing and flames from his starboard wing. Before I could get within range his starboard wing fell away and he went straight down into the sea."

Four of 1435 Squadron then joined the fight. Sgt Knox-Williams (EN978/V-O), Plt Offs Stewart and Lattimer shared one Ju88 damaged, but were then attacked by Bf109s. Two Spitfires were hit and damaged, including that flown by Knox-Williams, with Plt Off Pip Owen (BP873/V-Y) claiming one of the attackers damaged.

8 Staffel of KG54 lost four of its bombers during the raid including B3+KS in which Ltn Ingo Menny and his crew were lost apart from one. Aboard this aircraft as an observer was the Gruppenkommandeur, Maj Kurt Stein, who was among those killed. B3+FT flown by Uffz Max Zettelmaier, also failed to return, though two crewmembers survived to be taken prisoner. A third total loss was M7+DR in which Obgfr Rudolf Pauli and his crew were killed; finally, Fw Hans Hertz's M7+GS crash-landed back at base with three crew wounded, one of whom later died. *HSL128* was sent out to search for Sqn Ldr Wicks but instead located an empty German dinghy. Fifteen minutes later Zettelmaier, the pilot of B3+FT, was found in the water. Then two more Luftwaffe airmen, Uffz Otto Kobszinowski (W/Op in Zettelmaier's aircraft) and Uffz Gerhard Lang (W/Op in Menny's aircraft) were picked up during the next 20 minutes, but Wicks was not found.

The raiders were back at 0910, seven Ju88s from III/KG54 and a dozen MC202s crossing the coast. Bf109s from both I/JG77 and I/JG53 provided indirect escort. Bombs fell on Luqa, where some aircraft were damaged, and at Takali. The formation was intercepted on the way in – about 30 miles north of Gozo – by eight of 229 Squadron led by Wg Cdr Donaldson (BR529/AD), who shared in the destruction of a Ju88 with Plt Off Reynolds; the pilot of the bomber was seen to bale out. A second bomber was claimed damaged by Flt Lt Glazebrook. Plt Off Parkinson (X-O) recorded:

"The whole [Takali] Wing intercepted a mixture of Ju88s and Breda 205s [*sic*] about halfway to Sicily. We dived into attack from beam astern. I picked out a Breda, fired, only my machine-guns worked. Cannons were u/s. Came back to drome disgusted."

He and Plt Off Nash each claimed a bomber damaged, and Flt Sgt Ballantyne claimed an MC202 destroyed. In return, the Macchi pilots claimed one Spitfire shot down and five damaged during two attacks. Meanwhile, nine Spitfires from 249 engaged the indirect escort comprising Bf109s from II/JG53, stepped from 21,000 to 30,000 feet. Flg Off McElroy (AR488/T-S) reported: "I got my sights on one and let him have it fair and square, and then engaged another. But the Jerries had had enough and they broke off and headed for home." He was credited with shooting down one Messerschmitt, but his own aircraft also sustained damage. A probable was claimed by Flt Sgt Hiskens (EP135/T-Z); both Plt Off Sanderson (BP869/T-K) and Sgt Stead (EP199/T-K) reported damaging two others. Hiskens also engaged a Ju88, which he and Flt Sgt de l'Ara (EP338/T-A) jointly claimed probably destroyed. Four of 126 Squadron attacked the remaining bombers 15 miles north of Gozo, Plt Off Bazelgette and Flt Sgt Bush each claiming one damaged. Flg Off Wallace reported:

"I picked out the leading Ju88 and gave him a two to three-seconds burst of cannon and machine-gunfire on the nose, and then I had to break away. One minute later, Red Section also intercepted the enemy, but found only five Ju88s. Owing to this confirmation and the vulnerability of the nose of the Ju88 (containing the pilot and observer), I claim one Ju88 destroyed."

Two of 126 Squadron then attacked the same formation north-west of Filfla after they had dropped their bombs. Sgt Park (BR311/MK-L) claimed one Ju88. His leader Flt Lt Rolls (BR498/PP-H) claimed two MC202s, apparently both later confirmed by Y Service:

> "At first I thought they had not seen me because they made no attempt to take avoiding action, or so I thought, and when we were in range to open fire they suddenly pulled up in the steepest climb I had ever seen an aircraft do from straight and level flight. I knew that when they had height they would half-roll down on us, which they did, but before they started to turn over for the roll, I did a steep turn and as they came down we were behind them. It was easy. We were nicely in position and I fired at one of a pair and it blew up. I followed the other one who had turned round by now and was trying to get on my tail."

Just off Gozo he made further attacks and reported gaining strikes on another Macchi. On return to Luqa he was advised that two Macchis had been reported down in the sea off Gozo, but no such losses were actually suffered. 1435 Squadron spotted the second wave – six Ju88s and close escort (a dozen MC202s of 153°Gruppo) with Bf109s as indirect escort, 15 miles north of Grand Harbour, and these were attacked at 20,000 feet just after they had crossed the coast. Flt Sgt Maclennan (EP203/V-G) claimed one Messerschmitt shot down, but Sgt Kebbell (BR368/V-I) was shot down by another over St Julian's and baled out. He landed safely in Valetta with slight bruises; his Spitfire fell into Spinola Bay. Takali was attacked by the Ju88s, where eight of 185 Squadron intercepted, but were held at bay by Bf109s and Sgt John Vinall (EP139) was shot down into the sea and killed. The body of the 22-year-old from Beckenham was later washed ashore at Dingli. The two Spitfires were probably the victims of Ltn Hans Röhrig of 3/JG53, who claimed his 57th victory, and Obfw Brandt of 2/JG77, whose victory was not confirmed. Wg Cdr Thompson (EP122/JM-T) claimed one Messerschmitt damaged and Plt Off Len Reid (EP186) reported damage to a Ju88: "Climbed to 15,000 feet over the island. Six 88s reported to starboard. Attacked and dived on one at 10,000 feet; observed strikes and left it smoking."

Flg Off Rod Smith of 126 Squadron was not on duty and watched the battle from the roof of a house in St Julian's, and witnessed the demise of Sgt Kebbell's aircraft:

> "We had access to the roof of the third floor. On the north-west corner of this roof there was a small stone flat-roofed square structure. Its roof afforded a view of the whole bay. On this day some action was taking place high up and a little to the south-west. Rip Jones and I climbed onto this small structure to get a better look. We saw a parachute high up to the south-east, and we became aware of the roar of an aircraft in a very fast dive. It was not whining, so its constant speed unit was obviously still controlling the propeller revolutions within the limits, but the roar was increasing so relentlessly it indicated distress. We suddenly spotted a diving Spitfire seven or eight thousand feet up to the south-east, streaming flame and smoke. It kept a perfectly straight course and an unchanging attitude, but its dive was about 30 degrees off the vertical and it appeared to be coming absolutely straight at us.
>
> "For a second or two I considered rushing down below but I realised I wouldn't get far enough to make any difference. Rip and I just stood staring upwards, mesmerized by the sight of the oncoming aircraft and its ever-increasing roar. After a few more seconds we noticed that we could see slightly more of its underside than its top. It

began to look as if it was going to pass over us, and it did, roaring incredibly by then. It hit almost dead in the centre of the bay with an enormous splash. It left a yellowy-green patch on the surface, which lasted a surprisingly long time. I turned to Rip and said, 'You'll never see another sight like that as long as you live', or something like that. This so amused him he kept repeating it to others the rest of the day. I remember our being told that the pilot had baled out and that the parachute we had seen was his."

Eight Ju88s approached the island at midday, covered by ten MC 202s of 51°Stormo and 20 Bf109s from I/JG77 and II/JG53. The bombers were intercepted south of Sicily by 15 Spitfires (eight/249, seven/229) all led by Wg Cdr Donaldson (BR529/AD), who reported:

"I was leading 229 Squadron with 249 Squadron as high escort... I sighted eight Ju88s escorted by 30-plus fighters, five miles south of Gela, coming south... made a head-on attack on leading Ju88. No hits were observed. I broke upwards and did a stall turn and turned into a Ju88, which I singled out. I made an astern attack from 200 to 80 yards. Port engine smoked and burst into flames. Aircraft dived vertically and crashed into the sea in flames."

Sqn Ldr Woods led 249 Squadron into a diving attack on the bombers, two of which were claimed shot down by Flg Off McElroy (AR488/T-S) and Flt Sgt Hiskens (EP135/T-Z); a third was claimed probably destroyed by Flt Sgt de l'Ara (EP338/T-A), who damaged a second, while both Woods (AR466/T-R) and Plt Off Joe Lowery (EP706/T-L) reported strikes on the aircraft they attacked. By this time the escorting Macchis and Messerschmitts had joined the action, as Donaldson's report revealed:

"I then saw a Messerschmitt and got on his tail. I fired a two-seconds burst and he burst into flames and crashed vertically into the sea. No parachute. This was witnessed by Plt Off Sanderson [of 249]. I was then attacked by an unseen aircraft and hit in rear fuselage by one bullet."

Woods also reported shooting down a Messerschmitt, whereas Plt Off Sanderson (EP340/T-M) claimed a probable and Plt Off Yates (EP199/T-K) a damaged. Pilots of 229 Squadron claimed one bomber and probably a second, plus two Bf109s, one of which was claimed by Plt Off Parkinson (EP691/X-A):

"Long before we were within range the bombers started to panic. I closed to within a few yards firing head-on; could see shell bursts all over him. Put front gunner out of action. Both engines were smoking. Went into a spiral dive. In the meantime I was attacked by three 109s. One overshot me so I turned into him and gave him a burst, which hit the engine and pilot. The 109 went down in a series of wide barrel rolls, burning and smoking. Crashed into sea."

Parkinson shared the probable destruction of the Ju88 with Plt Off Nash, while Flt Lt Glazebrook reported shooting down another bomber. The second Messerschmitt fell to Flt Sgt Ballantyne, who also claimed one damaged. The survivors turned back. It seems that several of the combats with 'Messerschmitts' were, in fact, with MC202s, two of which were damaged in this engagement, Ten Agostino Cigala Fulgosi suffering a leg wound after he and Ten Plinio Sironi had claimed a Spitfire shot down. A second Spitfire was claimed by Magg Fanali and several other pilots. In all, the two Spitfire squadrons claimed four bombers and four fighters shot down, two bombers and one fighter probably shot down, and two bombers and three fighters damaged in this engagement, all without loss. The action inspired Wg Cdr Donaldson to write:

"It was the most spectacular sight I have ever seen. The whole sky was filled with enemy aircraft in severe trouble! I saw three flaming Ju88s and another three flaming Messerschmitts, and counted no less than ten parachutes descending slowly, three of them from the Junkers I had shot down."

At that stage six of 1435 Squadron led by Flt Lt McLeod joined the fight about 40 miles north of Grand Harbour, attacking seven Bf109s seen flying at 25,000 feet. McLeod described the action thus:

"I closed to point-blank range on the right Me109, breaking upwards after the attack. Strikes were observed, but he tried to get on the tail of my No.2 who was, at this time, in front of him. I attacked again, from astern, 200 yards, observing several explosions of cannon on the port wing root. The 109 flicked over on to its back and then straightened out. I closed in again, firing from 250 yards, observing strikes behind the cockpit, and pieces fly off. The 109 flicked on to its back and went straight down. I broke as his friends were attacking me and after a few turns to shake them off, saw a large green patch directly below, where an aircraft had gone in. The one I attacked was, I believe, the leader of the formation, as he rocked his wings after my section attacked and the other 109s formated on him."

Although two more Messerschmitts were claimed damaged by Flt Sgt Maclennan and Sgt Roe, Sgt Knox-Williams' EN978/V-O was severely damaged after the Australian thought he had destroyed another. He was the victim of either Oblt Michalski of Stab II/JG53 (his 47th victory), or Oblt Ernst-Albrecht Schultz of 5 Staffel (his 20th). He baled out and, as soon as it was safe to do so, Sub Lt(A) Reg Elliott took off in Hurricane BN110 to search for him. He was sighted about 12 miles north-east of Grand Harbour, and *HSL100* was directed to pick him up. The launch, making its first rescue, had to be towed back due to faulty engines.

The fourth raid of the day came in at 1445 and lasted 15 minutes. Radar plots and ground observation indicated up to 45 fighters approaching from Sicily and, in fact, the raid comprised ten MC202s of 51°Stormo, 13 of 153°Gruppo and eight Bf109s of II/JG53 escorting 13 RE2001 fighter-bombers of 22°Gruppo. The Italians reported being attacked by 15-20 Spitfires, ten miles out from Malta, and claimed two probables and nine damaged. Twenty-three Spitfires were airborne (nine/126, six/229, eight/185), Wg Cdr Hanks (BR498/PP-H) leading four of 126 Squadron to engage many Messerschmitts at 23,000 feet:

"I saw 18 enemy aircraft (mostly Me109s) in three vics of six aircraft in close formation at 23,000 feet. I dived to attack the right-hand section and immediately saw four of six 109s on our tails. I gave the order to break right and, as I broke, went into a violent spin and recovered at 20,000 feet. I weaved around preparatory to climbing up and saw one 109 at 15,000 feet going towards Sicily. I dived to attack, opening fire from 250 yards closing to point-blank range, giving approximately four-seconds burst (port cannon u/s), and observed strikes on the fuselage and cockpit followed by thick smoke and flames. The enemy aircraft went through cloud shedding pieces and burning fiercely."

The rest of the formation turned back. One Macchi of 51°Stormo was also hit by a cannon shell in the port wing during this engagement.

At about 1530, an estimated 57 aircraft approached, including five Ju88s. It is believed that both I/JG27 and I/JG77 provided escort. The bombers were intercepted halfway to Malta, initially by eight of 1435 Squadron led by Sqn Ldr Lovell (AR470/V-Q), who recalled:

"While closing in rapidly on the starboard bomber I fired a two-seconds burst from a range of 300 to 50 yards and large pieces flew off, and flames came from the starboard engine. I then broke away sharply. P/O Walton and F/Sgt Scott witnessed the aircraft on fire."

The unit's other claims were a Ju88 probably destroyed by Plt Off Walton (EP140/V-P) and Sgt Hawkins (EP259/V-L), while Flt Sgt Scott (EP203/V-G) claimed a Ju88 shot down, a Bf109 probable and a second as damaged:

"We climbed as high as we could to get above the bombers, saw them coming in, three large boxes escorted by lots of 109s above which meant we had to come in from the sun and so try to avoid them if possible. The idea was to dive down on the leaders and try and knock them out of the sky because, if you knocked the leader down so that the 'Gruppenfuehrer' wasn't barking out commands to the rest of the squadron, they would be lost to know what to do – well, that was the idea. We did this, we dived down, I took No.1, and my No.2 took third in the line and so on. I managed to get one and then immediately dived down to the sea because with only four Spitfires the best plan was to run away to fight another day. The one I got went straight down into the ground. Looking back I saw that there were more falling to the ground so we'd all done our job fairly well and we did actually turn the Germans round. They started to weave. Getting down to the ground on the way home, unfortunately four 109s spotted me and attacked – but the Spit could out-turn any 109 and I managed to out-turn them all and very luckily shoot one down. That was enough, they turned tail, I turned back to Malta but blow me down if another two didn't turn after me and we got into a mêlée and very fortunately I got my third."

These successes were claimed for the loss of Flt Sgt Ron Stevenson, a 26-year-old married man from Ilford, who failed to return in EP209/V-B. Eight of 229 Squadron then arrived and attacked the escort, Sgt Ron Miller claiming what he thought was a Macchi, and a second as damaged, with strikes observed on two Messerschmitts attacked by Sqn Ldr Baker and Flt Lt Roscoe, as the latter recalled:

"After our initial attack on the escorting fighters, a 109 made a quarter attack on me from slightly above. The first thing I felt was a blow to my right shoulder – no pain at all. I immediately and instinctively broke hard right, realising what a fool I was not to have watched my tail properly. At the time the Spit was in good shape, just minus a few minor bits and pieces with the engine running fine. The 20mm shell passed through me, through the lower instrument panel and out, missing the petrol tank in front of me. As the 109 was still on my tail, and I felt disinclined to engage in a prolonged dogfight, I risked a mid-air collision by pulling the throttle all the way back kicking on a 'yard' of right rudder. The sudden deceleration of my aircraft forced the 109 to detour around me to port. It was at this point that we exchanged glances in passing. As the 109 went by I applied full power and left rudder, and from almost point-blank range and dead astern I let him have it. He went down immediately[113].

"I headed directly for Malta as I only now began to realise that I had been badly hit. The Spitfire was flying OK and the engine purring. About halfway to the island I was bounced again by a lone 109. He must have been on his way back to Sicily, and below me as I had been watching my tail above and behind as best I could, but I never saw him until I was hit. Another wild break, a few turns and he was gone. Now, however, I was in real trouble. I had been hit in the engine and cooling system. All the engine instruments I had left went off the clock, smoke came pouring out of the engine room accompanied by strange clanking noises and lots of vibration. As I crossed the coast I decided to try and bale out. A crash-landing in the countryside was not recommended, too much rock and stone. I released the Sutton harness, rolled the Spit over on her back, and pushed the stick forward. Nothing, I didn't budge! I righted the aircraft and continued on towards Takali. The unproductive manoeuvre had cost me altitude and I was so low that I was doubtful I'd ever get there. But the good old reliable Merlin kept chugging along on a few cylinders, spewing smoke, keeping the badly mauled Spitfire barely flying. The last thing I remember was praying, cursing and hoping until, at the edge of the field, I hit the top of a blast pen – and arrived!"

Despite the danger of exploding ammunition and petrol tanks, two medical orderlies – LAC Cliff Jenkins and AC1 George Poppleton – ran to the wreckage of Roscoe's aircraft (BR464) and succeeded in extricating the semi-conscious pilot, who was then rushed to hospital. His rescuers were each awarded the BEM for their actions.

During these latter engagements, the 51°Stormo Macchi pilots had claimed a further two victories against the ten Spitfires they reported meeting – one by Serg Magg Giovanni Gambari, the other shared by Magg Fanali and Serg Ferruccio Serafini; the unit suffered no loss. It is probable that Bf109s from 2/JG27 were again involved, Ltn von Lieres claiming his 26th victory north of St Paul's Bay during the late afternoon, Fw Paul Becker claiming another Spitfire north of Gozo. It would seem that two of the Messerschmitt claims related to the shooting down of Roscoe's Spitfire. Moreover, either Roscoe or Scott had shot down Ltn Wilhelm Scheib's White 12 (10579) of 1/JG77, which failed to return from this mission. A colleague, Uffz Schlick, later wrote:

"Ltn Scheib was attacked by Spitfires and went into the sea in flames. The oil burned for a long time before it disappeared. Ltn Scheib was a good example for all of us and a good mate. When the memorial service was held, Flieger Lukas was absent. He could not take it. He was one of his best friends."

Conclusion of action at dusk indicated a considerable victory for the defenders, who had claimed 27 'confirmed' victories (13 Ju88s, 11 Bf109s, three MC202s), plus 12 probables and many damaged, for the loss of seven Spitfires (three pilots killed, one seriously wounded) and six more damaged. OKW reported 15 victories for the Axis – seven and four probables in the air for the Luftwaffe, and four by the Regia Aeronautica. Additionally, returning Ju88 crews claimed two aircraft destroyed on the ground.

II/JG53 lost three Bf109s totally destroyed during the day with two pilots killed and one injured. Gfr Georg Gunkel of 4 Staffel (White 10/10535) and Uffz Paul Ströhla of 5 Staffel (Black 7/10498) both fell to fighters and their aircraft crashed into the sea, although both were seen to bale out. Oblt Franz Schiess and Ltn Wolfgang Dreifke of StabStaffel flew a search mission for these pilots during which they clashed with Spitfires. Dreifke was reported to have run out of fuel and baled out of Black 2 (14249) near Noto Modica. He was injured when he hit the ground.

In addition to the four Ju88s of 8/KG54 listed as lost in action, 7/KG54 also lost M7+FR to fighters, Ltn Fritz Öhlmann and his crew being killed, and 9/KG54 reported two aircraft damaged – B3+ES aboard which the gunner was wounded, and M7+FT which crash-landed on return, all members of Uffz Ulrich Scuber's crew being wounded or injured. The other main bomber unit involved in the raids, KG77, similarly reported severe casualties: Uffz Franz Jaeger's 3Z+BH of 1 Staffel crash-landed on return, killing three of the crew, while Uffz Willi Schael's 3Z+GK of 2 Staffel failed to return. Two of 7 Staffel's aircraft were written-off when Oblt Albert Paetz crashed his damaged machine at Gerbini, during which he sustained injuries and his observer was killed. The gunner had baled out over the sea and was lost. Fw Karl Fellhöfer's damaged aircraft crashed at Comiso, three crewmembers having been wounded. Finally, 9 Staffel suffered a loss when Obfw Kurt Wöhl crash-landed his damaged bomber at Comiso, killing himself and one other; two others were injured. To complete this disastrous day for the bomber force, II/LG1 had two of its aircraft damaged in action, one of which crash-landed near Cape Passero.

At 0635 on the morning of **13 October**, eight Spitfires of 185 Squadron and eight of 249 were scrambled as seven Ju88s of II/LG1, under an umbrella of 30 Bf109s from I/JG77, approached the island. 185 Squadron tangled with the escort, Maj Swales (EP685) and Plt Off Tony Maynard (EP343) each claiming a Messerschmitt damaged, and Flt Lt Charney (BR375/GL-A) one probably shot down. Two Spitfires were slightly damaged and may have been the victims of Hptm Bär of I/JG77, who claimed two shot down, one at 0658 five miles south of the Sicilian coast, and another 17 minutes later north of Marsaxlokk Bay. These two victories raised the Gruppenkommandeur's score to 115. Oblt Freytag also claimed one during the early morning action, his 70th victory. Meanwhile, Flt Lt Hetherington (AR466/T-R) led 249 to engage the bombers, then three miles north of St Paul's Bay. Plt Off Beurling (BR173/T-D) reported:

"As Tiger Red 3, I attacked eight [*sic*] Ju88s, taking a straggler from slightly above to the right with a two-seconds burst of cannon and machine-guns. Pieces came off the starboard wing. I broke away to port and down and saw one Messerschmitt closing in from port above. I broke left and then turned onto him [and from] 50 yards astern fired one-and-a-half-seconds burst of cannon and machine-guns. Enemy aircraft burst into flames. A second Messerschmitt came down from starboard quarter above. As enemy aircraft pulled out ahead at 250-300 yards, I gave him a four-seconds burst with machine-guns; observed no strikes but pilot baled out. At this time I saw first e/a strike the sea."

Plt Off Seed (AR488/T-S) claimed another Messerschmitt as damaged and also one of the bombers as probably destroyed, and others were damaged by Hetherington, Plt Off Giddings (EP338/T-A) and Sgt Shewell (EP135/T-Z). Despite the attention of the Spitfires, some of the bombers reached Luqa and released their loads; two civilians were killed. As they sped northwards, Beurling was able to get on the tail of one, catching it about eight miles north of Zonqor:

"I attacked a Ju88 from starboard quarter above, 300 yards, with cannon and machine-guns, two-seconds burst, and observed strikes on roots of starboard wing, and black, oily smoke poured out. I gave it the remainder of my ammunition into the fuselage. Enemy aircraft did a diving turn to the right, striking the sea."

This was probably Fw Anton Wilfer's L1+KP, which was shot down over Valetta and crashed into the sea just off the coast. Meanwhile, Plt Off Yates force-landed his damaged Spitfire (EN954) at Takali, skidding into the building housing the squadron armoury, but he escaped unhurt. Eight of 1435 Squadron and two of 185 Squadron intercepted the remaining bombers as they headed north, catching them at 13,000 feet. Plt Off Walton (EP140/V-P) claimed one shot down, and Plt Off Pinney (BR591/V-R) reported damage to another, before probably destroying a Bf109. Both 185 Squadron pilots claimed, Plt Off Maynard and Flt Sgt Mahar (EP696) each gained strikes on bombers they attacked. Two RNAS Hurricanes went out at 0730, searching for survivors. The Luftwaffe also sent one Do24 under fighter escort. Four of 126 Squadron scrambled to intercept the latter but nothing was seen.

During mid-morning six Ju88s of III/KG77 escorted by 28 MC202s of 153°Gruppo and 36 Bf109s of I/JG77 approached. Sixteen Spitfires of 126 and 1435

Squadrons scrambled and attacked halfway to Malta, led by Wg Cdr Hanks (BR498/PP-H). 1435 Squadron went after the bombers, but were able only to claim one shot down by Sgt Hawkins (EP259/V-L) before the escort intervened, although Hanks claimed one damaged, as did Sgt Freddy Sharp (EN968/V-H); Flt Sgt Scott (EP612/V-B) and Sgt Eva (EP714/V-T) claimed strikes on two apiece. In the subsequent tussle with the escort, Scott claimed a Messerschmitt shot down and Eva damaged a second. The pilots of 126 Squadron meanwhile had directly engaged the escort, Wt Off Farquharson (BP992) claiming a probable and Plt Off Thompson a damaged.

The Italian fighter pilots reported seeing one Ju88 being shot down by Spitfires and two men bale out, one falling into the sea between Comino and Gozo. This was undoubtedly Ltn Gustav Duvenhörst's 3Z+ET of 9/KG77, which failed to return. The Macchi pilots also claimed one Spitfire probably destroyed and two damaged, and Ltn Berres of Stab I/JG77 claimed another; 3 Staffelkapitän Oblt Geisshardt scored his 89th victory. A third Spitfire was claimed by Gfr Hans Jacobi of 2 Staffel but this was not confirmed. One 126 Squadron aircraft was badly damaged, although the pilot landed safely. The remaining bombers raided Luqa, bombs falling on the Safi dispersal area. AA gunners claimed damage to one raider. Following this attack seven of 249 Squadron were scrambled to meet the next incursion, but this turned out to be an ASR search for the missing KG77 crew. During a lull, an RNAS Hurricane also looked for the three Spitfire pilots lost the previous day, but while unidentified wreckage was seen 15 miles east of Grand Harbour, no dinghies were found.

Six Ju88s, 25 MC202s of 51°Stormo and 40 Bf109s of I/JG77 and II/JG53 approached in the early afternoon. Their adversaries on this occasion were Spitfires from both 185 and 229 Squadrons. Eight of 185 Squadron intercepted 25 miles north of Zonqor Point, but the top cover Messerschmitts shot down Sgt Alex MacLeod (EP316), who was killed, and damaged a second. Eight of 229 Squadron then intercepted the bombers off Kalafrana Bay as they were flying north-west at 20,000 feet, and attacked before they could release their bombs. Sgt Miller claimed one Ju88 damaged, with Sqn Ldr Baker and Flt Sgt Des Bye each claiming a Bf109 damaged. Two Spitfires were hit, Bye crash-landing BR293 at Takali. Plt Off George Turner's aircraft was also hit and crash-landed. Both pilots survived uninjured. They were probably the victims of Oblt Michalski of Stab II/JG53 and Fw Paczia of 6 Staffel, who both claimed. Bombs fell near Luqa, causing little damage, although two soldiers were wounded. Two of 185 Squadron and eight of 126 Squadron pursued as the bombers departed and engaged them between 12,000-17,000 feet, north of Zonqor Point. Maj Swales (EP685) of 185 Squadron recorded:

> "When we reached a position roughly south-west of Benghaisa Point, I led Blue 3 in on the bombers, making an attack from beam to line astern. I fired a two-seconds burst and observed strikes on a Ju88's starboard engine and mainplane. First white smoke then black smoke started coming from this engine. I broke off and climbed away as the Me109s were attacking. The smoking Junkers was falling back from the formation, so I attacked it again, firing from beam to quarter. I observed two strikes on the right side of the fuselage. I broke again and attacked again, going from quarter to line astern, giving about a one-and-half-seconds burst, but saw no results."

Swales was credited with shooting down this aircraft, but it was also attacked by 126 Squadron's Flt Sgt Varey and seems almost certainly to have been the II/LG1 machine which crash-landed at Comiso, badly damaged. Flg Off Rip Jones of 126 Squadron claimed an escorting Messerschmitt shot down and Wt Off Farquharson (BP992) a probable. Flg Off Rod Smith (EP573) shot down a Macchi:

"Prosser Hanks was leading 126 Squadron and we got into position a couple of thousand feet above the 88s over Luqa, heading the opposite way. Prosser tried to half-roll down to come in behind them but he wasn't high enough above them for that. He came down through them and wound up under them, too low to shoot. His aircraft was badly riddled by return fire. I was sure we weren't high enough above the 88s to half-roll down to them without coming out below them, so I did a half-spiral down to the left and though I found myself level with them I was behind them, now heading north-west as they were, but considerably out of range. I was faced with the prospect of trying to overhaul them from a position directly underneath their escort, not a safe tactic.

"I suddenly saw a Macchi 202 not far below me to my right, heading east for some reason, and I decided to attack it. I made a half spiral down to the right and attacked it from the starboard quarter, firing a three-seconds burst with slight deflection from about 250 yards. Strikes appeared on his engine, and it began to stream smoke. I fired another three-seconds burst and got more strikes on it. It went into a very tight and almost vertical spiral dive towards the mouth of Sliema Bay. As it neared the water I could tell that one or more of its guns were firing because, before it made its own great splash, a pattern of little splashes had appeared on the surface, which exactly matched its tight spiralling. It was the fifth enemy aircraft I destroyed, and I realised with some satisfaction, I must admit, that I had become an ace."

He had in fact shot down an aircraft of 352^Squadriglia flown by M.llo Maurizio Iannucci, who was killed. Other pilots in the Italian formation reported that the missing pilot had shot down a Spitfire before his demise, and they claimed damage to five more.

Eight Spitfires of 249 Squadron were scrambled shortly thereafter when a further seven Ju88s were detected, covered by no fewer than 30 MC202s from 51°Stormo and 153°Gruppo, with 42 Bf109s from I/JG77 and II/JG53 providing indirect support. There was apparently thick fog out to sea, as Ltn Köhler of 3/JG77 wrote:

"A squadron of Spitfires was hiding in the fog and they came at us. I was so surprised I forgot to fire my guns. I didn't know what to do! And I was so far behind the others that I was of little use anyway. But I saw Uffz Franck have a shot. We found 30 Spitfires waiting over Gozo and Valetta. We had our guardian angels that day and went home."

Although he does not mention a specific combat, Köhler was officially credited with shooting down a Spitfire, his 14th victory, while Uffz Hans Franck got his first. Uffz Hans Hempfling was also credited with his first, with Fw Pohl claiming his 12th. That made four victories for 3 Staffel. Another was credited to Ltn Hans-Jürgen von Möller of Stab II/JG53, raising his score to 11. The bombers were intercepted 20 miles north of Gozo, but only Sqn Ldr Stephens (EP338/T-A), leading four of the Spitfires, was able to make a positive claim:

"We saw Ju88s and escorting fighters among AA bursts, flying south near Filfla. I dived after them through AA and they turned east. I attacked one Ju88, hitting the starboard engine, which began to smoke nicely, but then disengaged as the Macchis were after me. This Ju88 was seen from Qrendi strip by the squadron adjutant to be diving from about 1,000 feet with his starboard engine in flames. I then attacked two more Ju88s and was closing in on them when I was warned to break, which I immediately did and a 109 flashed by."

Sgt Stead (BP869/T-K) reported inflicting damage on a second bomber but was chased away by the escort, four of which were claimed shot down by Sqn Ldr Woods' flight, two by Woods (AR466/T-R) himself (both Bf109s), a Macchi by Flt Sgt Hiskens (EP135/T-Z) and the other by Flg Off McElroy (EP340/T-M), who identified his victim as an RE2001. Stephens also engaged a Macchi:

"I then attacked a MC202, observing strikes on starboard side of the engine. Plt Off Nash of 229 Squadron watched these attacks and saw the aircraft crash and the pilot bale out after I was forced to break away."

The same aircraft was also attacked by Flt Sgt de l'Ara (BR565/T-T), who was credited with a share in its destruction. Eight of 229 Squadron joined the battle after bombs had fallen on Qrendi, Plt Off Nash claiming a Ju88 shot down, Plt Off Parkinson (EP691/X-A) a probable and Wg Cdr Donaldson reporting strikes on a third. Donaldson's Spitfire (BR529/AD) was then hit and damaged, and he was forced to crash-land at Takali. Flt Sgt Ballantyne, whose aircraft had been shot-up by a Bf109 did likewise, while Sgt Miller's aircraft suffered a hole in one wing. As the Axis force headed homewards eight of 1435 Squadron pursued, Sgt Whitmore (EN968/V-H) claiming a bomber about eight miles north of Zonqor Point, and Flt Lt McLeod (BR236/V-E) a Macchi; two others were claimed damaged by Sgts Philp (EP612/V-B) and Knox-Williams (EP714/V-T), but one of the unit's Spitfires was slightly damaged. During the fight 153°Gruppo lost two MC202s, Cap Enzo Radini and Ten Felice Mezzetti both being reported missing. Radini had baled out badly burned and was later picked up six miles south-east of Delimara by *HSL128*.

With the close of hostilities for the daylight hours, the Luftwaffe issued a communiqué that implied it had been another successful day for its air force:

"Raids on bases on the island of Malta once again resulted in large-scale destruction and fires. German fighters shot down thirteen British fighters without loss in heavy air fighting. One of our bombers was lost."

Communiqués are not always entirely accurate, however. At least two Ju88s failed to return and only one Spitfire was actually shot down, although half a dozen more crash-landed; several others had sustained minor damage. Although attacks against Malta were to continue unabated for several more days, already the mini blitz was effectively over from the German point of view, for the Axis command had now accepted that it was failing in its intended aim. Feldmarschall Kesselring later revealed:

"The assault in the middle of October had not been the success we hoped for; I broke it off on the third day because, especially in view of the expected landings [the Anglo-American landings in Vichy-controlled North-West Africa], our losses were too high. The surprise had not come off, and neither had our bomber attacks against their air bases. Instead, the battle had to be fought against enemy fighters in the air and their bomb-proof shelters on the ground."

During the preceding three days the Luftwaffe had lost at least 16 Ju88s and two He111s, the latter during night raids, with a further nine Ju88s written off in crashes or crash-landings on returning to Sicily; 68 aircrew had been lost, a crippling rate of attrition to the fairly small forces involved. The Spitfire pilots owed much of their current success to the skills of the various fighter controllers. They played an instrumental part in the successes achieved. Plt Off Philip Dixon of 229 Squadron recalled:

"It was remarkable how on many occasions the controllers were able to interpret their plots to such a high degree that they could differentiate between an ordinary fighter formation and a fighter-bomber formation. The information that we were given by the controllers was, of course, invaluable and very reassuring, both from the point of knowing where your enemy was coming from, and what he was using in the way of aircraft; further it was also heartening to know that you would probably be plotted if you had to force-land in the sea."

At least eight Ju88s with a high escort of some 40 fighters stepped up to 28,000 feet approached soon after 0700 on the morning of **14 October**, the majority crossing the coast. Twenty-nine Spitfires (nine/126, eight/185, eight/249, four/229) were airborne to meet the raid, the first engagements occurring at 0720. Wg Cdr Donaldson led a head-on attack and saw strikes on one bomber, but was attacked from astern by a Bf109. Bullets smashed the cockpit and engine, splinters hitting him in the face, body, arms and legs; two fingers of his shattered left hand were severed, and blood was splashed all around the cockpit. Reluctant to bale out – as the sight of all the blood led him to believe he might pass out and drown – he managed to control his Spitfire (BR130/S) in a glide back to Takali with his good hand, and to effect a highly creditable belly-landing. Even before the aircraft stopped, a fire tender was alongside and he was dragged free and rushed to hospital. From here he despatched a message to Takali, requesting that somebody look into the cockpit of his aircraft to see if they could find his wedding ring.

Led by Sqn Ldr Woods, 249 Squadron intercepted the bombers over Grand Harbour, carrying out a stern attack as they headed for Takali, but only Woods (AR466/T-R) and Flt Sgt de l'Ara (BR565/T-T) were able to make claims, for a probable and two damaged respectively. Plt Off Sanderson (AR488/T-S) noted: "Large party of Messerschmitts kept us very busy. Hottest fight yet. Hit in wing."

Wg Cdr Thompson (EP122/JM-T) was at the head of the Hal Far Spitfires which engaged the escort. He claimed one damaged in the subsequent skirmish, and two others were damaged by Plt Offs Reid (EP521) and O'Brien (BR375/GL-A), who wrote:

"We sighted them above St Paul's Bay and turned for them. Some silly buggers in Spits jumped us from the sun and we all broke up. Sods! I went with the Wingco and we joined the dogfight around the bombers, which were going out. I climbed up sun to try and pounce something and entered a dogfight about 20 miles out. A 109 pooped at me and I broke. Then I saw some tracer over my port wing and I broke again. Quite a flap! Had a duel with a 109. He attacked and I turned into him. He squirted head-on and hit me with one shot. I turned after him and spun, firing off my guns by mistake. Got real scared as I saw the tracer (my own) and felt the kite shuddering like hell (3,000 feet only). I squirted at him more in anger than in hope, and missed (range 400 yards plus). He made another attack on me and I got around onto his tail and squirted again (four-five seconds). I saw strikes on his fuselage around the cockpit and some thick black smoke. He didn't stay to play any more but headed off home. I did not follow. I felt bloody relieved to see him go. This was my first really hectic dogfight and I was rather shaken! A near thing. Came back with four bullet holes."

Bombs fell on Takali, doing little damage but temporarily rendering the airfield unserviceable. There were two civilian casualties. Eight of 126 Squadron pursued the departing raiders, but top cover Messerschmitts attacked them. Flt Lt Rolls (BR498/PP-H) dived the formation to port and went for the bombers head-on:

"I saw my cannon shells hit the leading aircraft; its port engine blew up and the aircraft went down. The others had also opened up at the other bombers and although it was only a couple of seconds firing, several of the bombers had been hit and the formation broke up in chaos. We pulled up above the formation and attacked the fighters, which were in a turn and broken formation. I soon ran out of ammunition and went down on the deck to see what had happened and I saw a Spitfire hit the water and a couple of Ju88s were floating half submerged. I could see above me two other Ju88s smoking and coming down."

Sgt Park (MK-A), having shot down another bomber, added:

"I was jumped by two Me109s. I turned quickly to avoid their attack, which was on my rear starboard quarter, and after a couple of turns, got onto a 109's tail. I closed in without opening fire to about 100 yards when he changed his turn and I gave him a three-seconds burst from dead astern. He went into a steep dive straight into the sea. I circled the spot but there was no sign of any crew."

Two more bombers were claimed damaged by Flt Sgt Bush and Sgt Reynolds Hendry while Flg Off Wallace reported shooting down a Messerschmitt. Rolls had seen a Spitfire (AR489 flown by Flt Sgt Carl Long) striking the sea, shot down by either Oblt Michalski of Stab II/JG53 (his 48th victory), Obfw Brandt of 2/JG77 (his 31st), or Ltn Berres of I/JG77, his 17th victory. Two other Spitfires were damaged. The downed pilot was spotted in his dinghy – 12 miles out from Kalafrana – by one of the searching RNAS Hurricane pilots, Sub Lt(A) Ernie Pratt, and was soon picked up by ST280.

The bombers returned shortly after 1000, when seven Ju88s of I/KG54 approached, escorted by 45 Bf109s of I and II/JG53, I/JG77 and I/JG27, and 29 MC202s of 51°Stormo, the latter led by TenCol Remondino. Eight Spitfires of 1435 Squadron initially intercepted 20 miles north of Grand Harbour, three Ju88s being claimed damaged by Flt Lt McLeod (BR236/V-E), Flt Sgt Maclennan and Sgt Whitmore (EP322). McLeod then pursued the raiders across the island and claimed one shot down after it had released its bombs. Sgt Bill Knox-Williams, a 26-year-old Australian from New South Wales (AR470/V-Q) and New Zealander Sgt Ronnie Roe (EP203/V-G) were both lost. It was third time unlucky for the Australian, having survived two previous bale-outs since arriving at Malta. Another Spitfire was damaged, and only Whitmore was able to claim strikes on a Messerschmitt in return. The Italians reported that one bomber was seriously damaged in the initial attack, and was escorted back to Sicily by two of their number. Wg Cdr Thompson (EP122/JM-T) meanwhile led eight of 185 Squadron to intercept the bombers over Kalafrana, but could not prevent an attack on Hal Far and Safi, though little damage resulted. Thompson noted:

"I dived vertically on two 88s and attacked the starboard one. I opened fire with my cannons and machine-guns at 200 yards closing to 50 yards, and saw cannon strikes, which caused the enemy aircraft to burst into flames in the middle of the fuselage. Confirmed by ground observation from Luqa."

Three others were claimed damaged by Flg Off Len Cheek (EP696), Capt Kuhlmann (EP712) and Sgt Jimmy Tarbuck (AB532), Cheek also claiming a probable. The Spitfires pursued the attackers out to sea and engaged the escorts in a series of dogfights, during which one Spitfire was slightly damaged. In return Kuhlmann claimed a Messerschmitt shot down and a second damaged, with Tarbuck claiming another damaged. Plt Off Reid (EP722) was also successful:

"Climbed to 20,000 feet out from the island – again broken up by Me109s. Saw three

109s diving on Spits below, gave the last one a good burst from quarter astern and it hit the sea. After breaking away got in a burst at Ju88 from below. Observed strikes under belly."

Eight of 229 Squadron also intercepted the raiders as Hal Far was attacked. Sgt Brough claimed one Ju88 shot down in a head-on attack, and another was damaged jointly by Flt Lt Glazebrook and Plt Off Nash, with strikes on two others reported by Flt Sgt Martin Lundy. The escorting fighters attacked and Nash's EN979 was shot down into the sea. The Texan got out with a fractured upper jaw and other facial injuries, and was soon picked up by *HSL128*. Plt Off Dixon's AR471 was also badly shot-up but he got down safely, although his aircraft was deemed to be irreparable:

"We had gone in after some 88s and I had seen two 109s attacking us from above and to the left. I turned into them as they started firing and then veered off. By this time I was on my own so bearing in mind the adage never fly straight, I was gently weaving, watching out on each side and to the rear my attention was caught by the sight of one of the 88s in the bomber formation being set on fire, and I must have relaxed my attention for a moment. The next thing I knew there was a bang from the rear of the aircraft, a smell of cordite and I felt a sting above my flying boot."

On his return to Takali, Dixon found that his aircraft had holes in each tailplane, obviously caused by cannon shells, one of which had then exploded in the fuselage, while the other passed straight through, also holing the starboard wing. The control cables and trimming-gear wires were also severely damaged. One of the Messerschmitts was claimed probably destroyed by Sgt Eric Francis but several claims were made in return by the Axis pilots, Fw Paul Becker of I/JG27 recording his third victory north of Valetta, Ltn Hans Röhrig of 3/JG53 his 58th, and Ltn Hans Esser of Stab II/JG53, his first; probables were awarded to Ltn Englisch (2/JG77) and Uffz Wolf Focke of Stab I/JG77. The Italians claimed two Spitfires were shot down during the initial engagements by Serg Magg Giuseppe Mirrione and M.llo Ennio Tarantola. Three more were claimed damaged, although Tarantola's aircraft suffered serious damage and he subsequently baled out near the Sicilian coast. Later, two more Spitfires were claimed by Serg Luigi Santuccio and Serg Ferruccio Serafini.

During a brief lull three Beaufighters departed Luqa to locate and attack a German freighter and a large Italian MTB that a reconnaissance Spitfire pilot had sighted south of Malta a little earlier. Sqn Ldr Warburton accompanied the strike force in BR665 to observe results. The vessels were seen some 25 miles off Homs under an escort of MC202s. The Beaufighters attacked and one was shot down in flames and a second hit, ditching a short distance away. Seeing the crew scramble into their dinghy, Warburton circled the MTB in an effort to guide it to the downed airmen. In so doing his Spitfire was fired on – not surprisingly – and was also attacked by six of the escorting Macchis. Having succeeded in evading one persistent fighter which got on his tail four times, he noted that the MTB's captain had apparently understood the Spitfire's actions, for the craft now headed for the dinghy, and the Beaufighter crew was picked up. For this completely unselfish act, Warburton was awarded a second Bar to his DFC.

Malta's defences were meantime girding themselves for the next onslaught and 22 Spitfires were up to meet the next raid, at 1310, when at least seven Ju88s approached, accompanied by the usual strong escort. Seven 126 Squadron aircraft intercepted initially at 20,000 feet, 15 miles north-east of Zonqor Point. Flt Sgt Bush was able to claim damage to one of the bombers, but his friend and colleague Sgt Park (MK-A) found that his guns had apparently frozen, and he was forced to dive away to a lower altitude. Here, the warmer air seemed to resolve the problem and he was able to attack a Bf109 at 10,000 feet, which he claimed to have shot down – the second time the New Zealander had claimed three in one day.

Meanwhile, Sqn Ldr Stephens led eight 229 Squadron Spitfires to engage the raiders before they could reach the coast. Attacking at 17,000 feet, they reported encountering Ju88s and many fighters. Flt Lt Parkinson (X-V) claimed a Macchi and Stephens damaged a bomber before claiming an RE2001 shot down:

"Met nine Ju88s with fighter escort of about 60 Me109s, Macchi 202s and RE2001s. Led the boys in head-on attack and damaged one Ju88, then chased an RE2001 back to Sicily. My cannons weren't working, but blew him up from about 60 yards with my machine-guns. Shot-up by 109 on my way home."

Two of the Spitfires sustained minor damage during this engagement. Flt Lt Hetherington (AR466/T-R) now led an attack by seven Spitfires from 249 Squadron, catching the bombers just south of Zonqor Point, and personally claimed one probably destroyed. Two more were damaged by Plt Off Giddings (EP338/T-A) and Sgt Brydon (BR254/T-S) before Messerschmitts from I and II/JG53 intervened. In the ensuing series of dogfights, Giddings claimed one shot down, Sgt Wynn (BR373/T-N) a probable and Plt Off Williams (EP340/T-M) two damaged. But it was Plt Off Beurling (BR173/T-D) who once again stole the show however, though this time at a cost:

"As the action opened I spotted five fighters pulling up high, as if to get ready to dive on Giddy and Hether. I called into the mike and we soared up to 24,000 feet, just as the five Messerschmitts got there. The Messerschmitts promptly peeled off and dived and away we went, right among the bombers. We each picked a Ju88. I took the one on the starboard rear position of the V and gave him a two-seconds burst from starboard. He burst into flames and we went headlong toward the sea. As I nabbed the bomber, Hether came whipping just under me, diving away from eight Messerschmitts on his tail. I went down in a hurry with them, right past my flamer, and lashed into the leading Hun, just as he was going to let Hether have it. As I passed the burning bomber the rear gunner took a shot at me, peppering the port side of my fuselage and the port wing. I picked up about 30 bullet holes, I guess. Explosive bullets were snapping through the cockpit and one nicked the left middle finger of my throttle hand. Another stabbed my left forearm.

"I'd picked up two Messerschmitts on my own tail and still had Hether to worry about. I took a long shot from about 450 yards from above and to port. I got the bastard in the engine and he dove for the sea, streaming smoke and shedding pieces. One of the Messerschmitts on my tail riddled my port wing like a sieve and put a couple of bullets through the perspex hood, right over my head, while the other blasted my starboard wing full of holes. A call for help came over the R/T. My own position was right above Kalafrana, so I rolled over and had a look down, to see a swell mêlée going on below. I went down vertically, hitting almost 600mph in my riddled crate and at 14,000 feet pulled up under a Messerschmitt, just as he was all set to pot Willie the Kid. I gave the Hun a two-seconds burst and blew his whole left wing off at the root. He flicked over, and that was that. Just as I shot Willie's pal down, another Messerschmitt nailed me from behind. He got me right in the belly of the Spit. A chunk of cannon shell smashed into my right heel. Another went between my left arm and body, nicking me in the elbow and ribs. Shrapnel spattered into my left leg. The controls were blasted to bits. I threw the hood away and tried to get out, but the spin was forcing me back into the seat.

The engine was streaming flame by this time, but somehow I managed to wriggle my way out of the cockpit and out onto the port wing, from which I could bale into the inside of the spin. At about 1,000 feet I managed to slip off."

Plt Off Seed had seen Beurling's predicament and followed him down. Now, as Seed circled the wounded pilot who was struggling to get into his dinghy, he called control and requested that a rescue launch be sent out immediately. Within 20 minutes *HSL128* had arrived, and Flt Sgt Head – the coxswain – was subsequently able to record another side of Beurling's rebellious and obstinate character:

"Immediately on gaining the deck of the launch he was very, very concerned with the fact that he could not find his bible. This small volume was quickly located and handed to him whereupon he became more composed, and explained that it had been given to him by his mother and under no circumstances would he fly without it. In the launch on the way back to base he told the crew that he would be flying again that afternoon but it was obvious to the crew that this would not be so. Beurling has a nasty dull blue closed wound in the heel which indicated a possible bullet lodged deep in the flesh."

A piece of cannon shell had indeed penetrated Beurling's right heel, and this effectively ended his participation in Malta's defence. Although not the easiest of men to live and fly alongside, the Canadian's outward fearlessness and undeniable success had proved an inspiration to other pilots, and he was hero-worshipped by many of the ground personnel. His three final claims had raised his personal total to 29 and one shared, all but two whilst flying with 249 from the island.

One Messerschmitt of I/JG53 was damaged in this action, the wounded Obfw Josef Ederer crash-landing his 2 Staffel machine (Black 1/7619) at San Pietro, where another I Gruppe aircraft (7080) was damaged when it was rammed by a landing Macchi. Three II Gruppe aircraft were reported to have been damaged in landing accidents at Comiso, an aircraft (10554) having suffered combat damage. Spitfires were claimed by Obfw Riker of 4/JG53 and Ltn von Lieres of 2/JG27 (his 26th).

A successful early interception of the afternoon raid caused the majority of the eight Ju88s involved to jettison their bombs before reaching the coast. However, the Spitfire pilots overclaimed wildly on this occasion. As the bombers approached, escorted by no fewer than 44 Bf109s and 31 MC202s – the latter drawn from 51°Stormo and 153°Gruppo – ten 126 Squadron pilots, with Wg Cdr Hanks leading, were the first to attack shortly after 1630. No less than five of the bombers were initially claimed shot down, including one by Flg Off Rod Smith (AR471):

"We made a head-on attack and slightly to the right, then turned right and attacked from the stern. Many 109s were also observed in the vicinity. I flew across and attacked the left-hand, rear Ju88 from astern at 250 yards range. I gave two six-seconds bursts and the port engine and wing caught fire. The Ju88 dived to the port and I saw it crash into the sea."

A second was claimed by Plt Off Thompson:

"I chose the port Ju88 which was in a left-hand turn jettisoning its bombs. I came underneath him and chased him out to sea. He was doing half steep turns to left and right. I was able to draw in to 100 feet underneath him and delivered a starboard quarter attack, giving him a full one-and-a-half-seconds burst, and observed strikes on the underside of the fuselage, wing root and starboard engine; he rolled onto his back in a clockwise half-roll downwards, and I was about to follow him when I hit his slipstream and blacked out. When I recovered control I saw the Ju88 going straight down into the sea."

Another was claimed by Sgt Marshall:

> "With a steep turn to port I found myself within 50 yards of a Ju88 which was turning
> to port. Closing to 30 yards, I opened fire, seeing strikes on the port engine and cockpit
> and large pieces fly off the cockpit and engine. I saw the Ju88 dive into the sea just short
> of Grand Harbour. As I turned away I saw a Me109 hit the sea off St Paul's Bay."

Two more Ju88s were credited to Sgt Phil Charron and Flt Sgt Varey, the latter
claiming a second as probably destroyed and a third damaged. Sgt Tiddy also claimed
a probable. In all, it was believed that damage – at the least – had been inflicted on all
eight bombers, with five, possibly seven, shot down. As 126 Squadron was attacking
from astern in this manner, seven more Spitfires from 229 Squadron struck the same
formation head-on over Mosta. Sgt Ron Miller claimed one bomber shot down and
one damaged, with others claimed damaged by Plt Off Fred Johnson and Sqn Ldr
Stephens, who noted:

> "Climbed up to 20,000 feet with the boys and loitered around up sun and waited for
> them to come in. Dived between them and their escort, head-on – and did they scatter!
> Jettisoned their bombs in the sea and beat it. Chased one halfway home, one cannon
> jammed."

The scattered survivors now turned out to sea, at which point they were pursued and
engaged by a further eight aircraft from 185 Squadron, Flt Sgt Mahar (EP722)
claiming yet another bomber shot down north of Grand Harbour, and Sgt Geoff Guy
one damaged. AA gunners also engaged as the force reached the coast, and were
credited with sharing in the destruction of one Ju88. Several of the Spitfire pilots had
become engaged with the escorts, Wt Off Farquharson of 126 Squadron claiming a
Messerschmitt shot down. Guy claimed one probably destroyed and Wg Cdr Hanks
(BR498/PP-H) a Macchi damaged. One of II/JG53's Messerschmitts limped back to
base badly damaged, though the pilot was unhurt.

On this occasion no Spitfires were lost, although Macchi pilot, M.llo Cesare
Ferrazza, reported shooting down one that he believed had crashed into Salina Bay.
The aircraft attacked may well have been a returning 69 Squadron photo-
reconnaissance Spitfire (BP910), since Flg Off Tony Gubb reported being attacked by
a MC202 but had evaded by throwing his aircraft into a steep turn, a tactic which
allowed him to escape without suffering any damage. No fewer than four Spitfires[116]
were claimed by I/JG77 in this action, one by Hptm Bär (his 116th) the
Gruppenkommandeur, and others by Oblt Freytag (71st), Obfw Brandt (two, his 31st
and 32nd), but claims submitted by Ltn Bruno Koltoff, Uffz Heinz Wiefels, Obfw
Georg Ludwig and Stabs-StFw Helmut Gödert were not confirmed.

In a final analysis of the claims, squadron intelligence officers concurred that
seven Ju88s had been shot down and an eighth probably so. The attacking bomber
force had been estimated at ten strong and it was thought that although two had
escaped, both had suffered damage. Despite all the claims for Ju88s, records suggest
that only one failed to return from operations over Malta during the day – Ltn Hasso
Holst's B3+AA of I/KG54, which was reported shot down into the sea off the coast.
Two more Ju88s crash-landed on return to Sicily, one 3 Staffel aircraft coming down
at Pachino, near Syracuse, and M7+JT of 9/KG54 bellied-in near Pozzalo, Fw Georg
Thiel being killed. After dark a Beaufighter shot down yet another raider, on this
occasion a He111 of II/KG100, on board which was the Gruppenkommandeur, who
was among those killed.

Six Ju88s swept in to bomb Luqa during the morning of **15 October**. Although 28

Spitfires were airborne, they failed to intercept the raiders prior to their arrival over the island. Sqn Ldr Lovell led eight of 1435 Squadron to engage over Kalafrana Bay as the bombers were pulling out of their dives. Plt Off Walton (EP140/V-P) claimed one shot down, with Flt Sgt Scott (BP873/V-Y) claiming an escorting Messerschmitt. Eight more Spitfires from 249 Squadron, that had been ordered to patrol north of Zonqor Point, were attacked by escorting Bf109s before the bombers were sighted. These were driven off however, Sgt Wynn (BR373/T-N) claiming one shot down. The bombers were then seen coming away from Kalafrana, Plt Off Moody (EP135/T-Z) claiming one, Plt Off Williams (EP340/T-M) reporting a probable, and Plt Off Giddings (T-N) a damaged.

As the raiders fled out to sea they were pursued by four 229 Squadron aircraft, which forced them down to 3,000 feet. Five miles out, a number of 1435 Squadron Spitfires joined the chase. Sqn Ldr Stephens kept after two of the bombers for 35 minutes, finally managing to claim one shot down, but he was then attacked by six Bf109s. Although able to claim one of these also, his own aircraft (BR562/X-R) was hit and badly damaged. He escaped at low level, passing through the Grand Harbour barrage to crash-land at Takali:

"Attacked Ju88s over Kalafrana. Chiselled one from the formation and I chased him north from Zonqor. Had to leave him when I was attacked by a 109, but then found another flying north at sea level. Chased him, passed him and did a head-on to point-blank range. He dived into the sea. I was then attacked by six 109s from both sides and had to fight my way home, turning into each attack as it developed. I shot down one 109 but then two others, which I'd hoped had been Spits coming out to help me, joined in, and the seven of them chased me to within ten miles of Grand Harbour. With my R/T u/s, I really thought I'd had it this time. Guardian Angel working overtime!"

One of the 229 Squadron pilots, Sgt Pashen (X-V), claimed damage to a fighter he identified as an RE2001. Flt Lt Rip Jones led eight 126 Squadron Spitfires to join the fray, but these were bounced by a number of Messerschmitts north of Zonqor Point and four of the Spitfires were hit. Wt Off Farquharson baled out of BR176 into the sea, with a splinter wound in his heel. Flt Sgt Varey recorded:

"I was very lucky in a dogfight right over the island at 25,000 feet. Shells hit my aircraft and stopped my engine. Fortunately, I was able to glide down and land all right, only to find two cannon shells embedded in the armour-plating behind my seat."

The other two Spitfires suffered only minor damage. Before he was hit, Varey had been able to claim one of the attackers shot down, as did Flt Lt Jones. It seems likely that both had actually fired at the same aircraft – one of II/JG53's new Bf109G-2s (10484) flown by none other than the Gruppenkommandeur, Hptm Gerhard Michalski, who was shot down into the sea off Marsaxlokk Bay on his 500th operational sortie. He managed to bale out and scramble into his dinghy, to await his fate. Two more Messerschmitts were claimed damaged by Plt Off Thompson and Sgt Charron.

Soon after 1000, eight Ju88s and eight bomb-carrying Bf109s – from the newly formed I/ SchG2 – were escorted towards the island by 25 MC202s, with more Messerschmitts as high cover. The presence of intercepting Spitfires caused the bombers to turn back before reaching Malta. However, the Jabo were engaged out to sea by seven Spitfires from 1435 and eight from 249. Several were seen to jettison their bombs as they crossed the coast, one or two falling on Mellieha where a civilian was killed and two injured. Before the Spitfires could engage though, those from 249

Squadron were bounced by escorting Messerschmitts. Sgt Red Brydon had his leg shattered by a cannon shell, which penetrated the cockpit of his aircraft (BR254/T-S). In great pain, he managed to bale out into the sea. The aircraft (EP135/T-Z) flown by Plt Off Moody was also hit although he got back to Takali, where he crash-landed. Sgt Wynn (BR373/T-N) claimed strikes on one of the Messerschmitts and it seems likely that his victim was one of the fighter-bombers, for such an aircraft crash-landed at Comiso on return. The 1435 Squadron pilots engaged six Messerschmitts 20 miles north of Comiso but no claims were made, although Plt Off Lattimer's Spitfire (BR591/V-R) was damaged in the skirmish.

Meanwhile, Wg Cdr Hanks (BR498/PP-H) had led four 126 Squadron Spitfires to the north of Zonqor, where two Bf109s were seen at 4,000 feet, with a third at sea level. These were from 2/JG53 engaged in the search for Hptm Michalski, while at the same time acting as escorts to the ASR Do24s of 6 Seenotstaffel. The Messerschmitts were chased northwards for 15 miles or so, Flg Off Rod Smith going after the one flying at the lower level. As he closed on this another attacked him from behind, but was shot down in turn by Hanks. This was Fw Gerhard Stockmann of 2/JG53, who was wounded and baled out of Black 2 (7542), coming down in the sea south of Sicily. Flt Sgt Varey reported strikes on another and Smith was able to nurse his damaged Spitfire (BR471) back towards Malta where he baled out opposite the Sliema Point Battery; a launch promptly put out and picked him up. Of his experience, he later recalled:

> "For some reason I glanced down at my left wing and happened to see a small bullet hole in it just a few feet from me. I assumed I had picked it up earlier, when we were sparring with the 109s high up. I then fired a few more rounds over the top of the 109 in front of me, but still he would not turn. I looked again at the bullet hole in my left wing, and saw a second one about a foot from it. It took a long second for me to realise that there must be a 109 behind. I broke violently to the left and upwards. In an instant, things began to happen. Exploding balls of fire making sharp cracking bangs appeared on the left side of my engine. The aircraft shook as if poked from behind by long metal rods. The cockpit filled with the smell of cordite. The engine oil pressure dropped to nothing. The oil temperature shot upwards. But the engine kept going without missing a beat. Over my left shoulder I saw the yellow nose of a 109 about 100 yards behind me and closing in. Puffs of smoke were billowing from its guns and being blown back over it. It came so close it almost touched me as it passed behind.
>
> "As soon as I was pointing back to Malta, I straightened out and climbed at full power. We had been told that if a Rolls-Royce Merlin engine ever lost its oil pressure you should flog it, not nurse it. To my great relief I reached 600 feet and then 1,000 feet. The engine kept delivering full power. I marvelled how it could do this with no oil pressure. I switched the R/T over to emergency and called 'Mayday! Mayday! Mayday!' Immediately, the Malta controller responded. 'Keep transmitting', he said, 'we've got you!' Soon I was at 2,000 feet and Malta looked closer. To my wonderment and admiration the engine kept going till I reached 3,800 feet and was almost at the coast of Malta. By then, acrid smoke was pouring through the cockpit and the power was failing. I baled out and was rescued from the sea. I could never ask for greater luck than I had on that October morning when two bullets, timed and spaced by chance, gently warned me not to linger."

During the morning's actions two victories were claimed by 3/JG77's Staffelkapitän, Oblt Geisshardt, raising his score to 91, and two more by Oblt Freytag, Staffelkapitän of 1/JG77, whose tally now stood at 74. Both the downed German pilots were safely rescued by the crew of Obfw Pundt's Do24, Hptm Michalski's liferaft being sighted first but then, having become airborne again, Fw Stockmann's liferaft was seen, as recalled by the Dornier's commander, Oblt Kühne:

"We of course risked a second landing to pick up the wingman. It, too, was successful. But we were unable to take off again at first and for reasons of safety we taxied for several hours with the two pilots on board until we reached calmer water. Then we risked taking off again. The whole time the fighters from Comiso covered us in relays, for they knew that we had the two downed pilots on board."

From the other direction *HSL128*, during its first call-out of the morning, found Wt Off Farquharson about three miles off Zonqor Point, and the injured Canadian was back on land by 0818. *HSL128* was called out again at 1019 and on this occasion found its second Canadian of the day, Sgt Brydon, who had been clinging to his partially inflated dinghy for an hour about ten miles off Delimara Point, as noted by the launch's skipper Flt Lt Crockett:

"He looked rather like a giant spider with the various lines and strings in his dinghy and parachute tangled all round himself in his efforts to get in. He was very cheerful about it all, though he had a broken leg, while we made him as comfortable as possible on the way back to Kalafrana through rather rough seas."

Midday found the island's radar screens alive with 'blips' as about 50 fighters approached from the north. Patrolling Spitfire pilots reported that they appeared to be escorting ASR aircraft; nonetheless eight 185 Squadron aircraft engaged four aircraft – identified as MC202s – found orbiting at 4,000 feet about 35 miles east of Malta, with a pair of Bf109s circling above. Maj Swales ordered his section to attack the Macchis, two being claimed shot down by Flt Lt Charney (AB532) and Flt Sgt Mahar (EP722); two others were damaged by Swales (EP122) and Sgt Leo Garvey (EP521). At higher level eight Spitfires of 229 Squadron provided cover but although several Messerschmitts were seen at the same height, no contact was made. However, at this point another aircraft dived on them and opened fire. Flt Lt Glazebrook immediately fired back, gaining strikes on the engine of what he took to be the attacker, before realising it was a Spitfire – none other than that flown by Wg Cdr Thompson! The latter recalled a "hell of a bang" as four Spitfires flew over the top of his formation, and his engine began to smoke; he had to crash-land at Hal Far, and on inspection one shell was found to have hit his engine, with a second entering the fuselage just behind the cockpit.

The eight 1435 Squadron aircraft were still airborne as an estimated 30 more fighters, about seven of them carrying bombs, then swept in. Seven more 249 Squadron aircraft and eight from 126 Squadron were scrambled to meet this new threat, the former unit encountering the Jabo five miles north of St Paul's Bay at 20,000 feet. Four were seen to jettison their bombs immediately and turn away, but the remaining three were harried as they attempted to attack Takali, all their missiles falling wide of the target; no claims were submitted however. The other two units both engaged in indecisive encounters, but an attempted attack on five more Jabo seen over Filfla was thwarted by further misidentification, as Sgt Tiger Park recorded later: "We were just going in on 109 bombers when we were jumped by four Spitfires." On this occasion no damage was inflicted.

249 Squadron scrambled seven Spitfires to meet a further fighter-bomber raid just after midday, meeting the raiders five miles off St Paul's Bay at 20,000 feet. Four jettisoned their bombs immediately and turned away, but the remaining three were harried as they attempted to attack Takali, their bombs falling wide of the target; no

claims were submitted however. Six Ju88s were back mid-afternoon, escorted by 30 Bf109s of I/JG53 and 31 Macchis of 51°Stormo and 153°Gruppo. Sqn Ldr Woods led 249 in a head-on interception off Kalafrana as the formation approached from north-east of Zonqor, when once again bombs were seen to be jettisoned into the sea. Woods reported:

> "I sighted ten [sic] Ju88s with about 30 fighter escort at about 19,000 feet, flying south. We turned towards them and I led my section down in a quarter head-on attack. I opened fire at about 400 yards, firing cannon and machine-guns. I saw strikes on the leader and his No.2, who was echeloned to port of him. I turned to starboard and came underneath another Ju88 and opened fire at about 100 yards and saw strikes on the belly. I received no return fire but was forced to break off and down as a Messerschmitt was attacking me from the stern. I found myself in the middle of about 20 Messerschmitts, one of which broke to port and up, right in front of me. I opened fire at about 100 yards, gave it a two-seconds burst and saw no strikes but the engine started to smoke and then burst into flames. At this point I stalled and spun down. I came out of my spin behind and below the bombers and climbed up after them, four of which jettisoned their bombs into the sea. Two Ju88s were smoking badly from both engines and four Spitfires were attacking the remainder from all angles and, as I climbed up, I saw strikes on practically all the bombers. The bombers started to dive down and I dived down on one who was straggling, and opened fire at about 200 yards; both cannons jammed but I exhausted my machine-guns, closing to point-blank range and silencing the rear gunner."

Although he had seen strikes on four of the Ju88s he had attacked, Woods was credited with one damaged only, in addition to the destruction of a Bf109. Sgt Stead (EP338/T-A) claimed a Messerschmitt probably destroyed, having earlier attacked a Ju88 in conjunction with Plt Off Yates (AR488/T-S), which was also credited as probably destroyed. Another probable was claimed by Plt Off Sanderson (EP448/T-F). Flg Off McElroy (BR373/T-N) reported shooting another into the sea and claimed a second bomber as damaged, as did Wt Off Pete Carter (BP869/T-K). The escorting Messerschmitts attempted to come to the rescue of their charges, Uffz Marian Mazurek of 1/JG53 shooting down the Spitfire flown by Flt Sgt Ted Hiskens (EP340/T-M) for his 30th victory, the action confirmed by his wingman, Uffz Heinz Loch; the German ace reported:

> "Before the Ju88s were able to drop bombs, they were attacked by six to eight Spitfires. I followed them immediately and fired my machine-guns from a far distance. I managed to place myself in a good shooting position behind a Spitfire. As I came closer I started to fire with all my weapons out of a left turning. After that the plane tumbled down without control and hit the sea 15 kilometres from Valetta and sank."

The 21-year-old Australian from Queensland was killed. McElroy's aircraft was also badly shot-up and he was slightly wounded in one leg by shrapnel. With the aircraft diving out of control and the cockpit full of smoke, he decided it was time to jump but then discovered that the hood was jammed shut. Struggling to regain control, he managed to level out and reach Takali, where he crash-landed the Spitfire without further injury.

Other units now engaged, 185 Squadron encountering three escorted Ju88s diving from 13,000 feet over Delimara, Flg Off Cheek (EP696) claiming one shot down. Sgt Tarbuck (AB532) claimed damage to a Bf109, but two of the unit's Spitfires suffered slight damage in return. Eight 229 Squadron Spitfires also intercepted bombers over

Kalafrana, one being claimed damaged by Flt Lt Glazebrook, and Sgt Francis reported strikes on a Macchi. Leading the Italian fighters, Magg Luigi Borgogno claimed one Spitfire shot down and a second probably so, his pilots reporting strikes on seven more. From this attack one Ju88 of 3/KG77 – 3Z+CL flown by Uffz Herbert Gröss – failed to return, probably shot down by McElroy of 249 Squadron and Cheek of 185 Squadron. A 4 Staffel aircraft returned to Comiso badly shot-up by Spitfires and crash-landed. During this raid AA gunners claimed to have hit one of the bombers that was then believed to have been shot down by a Spitfire. This may have been L1+DN of 5/LG1, which was reported damaged by flak over Luqa; one of the gunners, Obgfr Robert Becker, baled out, landing in the grounds of a technical school near Birkirkara to become a prisoner. As the raid receded three Spitfires lifted off from Luqa for the short hop to Hal Far. AVM Park, literally on a flying visit, was accompanied by Wg Cdr Thompson and Plt Off Len Reid.

With the conclusion of daylight operations II Fliegerkorps issued another brief communiqué, which purported to show that Malta and its defences had really taken a pounding:

> "With 14 Ju88s and 98 Me109s we attacked the airfield of Luqa. Many good hits were observed. Black, stinking smoke rose skywards. This was followed by two attacks on Ta Venezia [Takali] that destroyed most of the landing ground. During a later strike we managed to shoot down seven enemy fighters and probably six more."

Eight Ju88s from I/KG54 with the usual large escort approached early in the morning of **16 October**, 23 Spitfires from 126, 185 and 1435 Squadrons intercepting about 15 miles north of Zonqor. A number of bombers were seen to jettison their bombs into the sea as the Spitfires closed in. One claim was submitted by Flt Lt Rolls (BR498/PP-H) of 126 Squadron who, of his 16th victory, recorded:

> "The bombers started a shallow dive and I gave the order for a head-on attack. I chose the leader of the formation and gave a three-seconds burst and hit the starboard engine. He immediately started to smoke and he did a steep turn to port, glycol coming from the engine. The rest followed him and jettisoned bombs in St Paul's Bay. The last I saw of the leader he was going down very steeply. The whole action was seen from the shore and F/O Shipard and F/O Gray [both night fighter pilots] and several others who were on Balluta Buildings saw this Ju88 crash into the sea, about ten miles east of Grand Harbour."

Other claims were submitted by 185 Squadron pilots Capt Kulhmann (EP187) and Plt Off Reid (EP343), who were awarded probables, and one damaged by Plt Off O'Brien. The latter wrote in the Squadron diary:

> "A Flight scrambled for a 70-plus and intercepted them just north of Grand Harbour. We dived on the 88s that were about 5,000 feet below and forced them to jettison their bombs in the sea. They turned round and fled for home. Sgt Gore (BR109] shot a 109 off the Wingco's tail and damaged it. We were travelling at such a hell of a speed that we nearly all blacked out and got split up. Sgt Tarbuck [AB532] also damaged a 109 but did not claim."

Of his claim for a probable, Reid reported:

> "I was flying Red 3. Climbed to 21,000 feet out from Grand Harbour. A party of Ju88s was reported below us. I followed W/Cdr Thompson (Red 1) down on to the bombers about 5,000 feet below. Made an attack on one as it was going in towards the island but as we were going at a terrific speed observed no results. The 88s then turned left and I

was able to pull round on to another. Opening up at about 200 yards from almost line astern, I closed right in to about 50 feet. Saw my cannon and my guns striking top of 88 which, when I left, was smoking badly and rapidly losing height, about five miles off Grand Harbour."

Another claim for a bomber damaged was made by 1435 Squadron's Sgt Harrison (EP140/V-P). One of the bombers was piloted by Uffz Woas, whose gunners reported shooting down a Spitfire, their second such claim within the last few days. One or two bombers did get through though, bombs falling on Sliema and St Julian's causing some damage to property and injuring 13 civilians. On this occasion the escorting Messerschmitts attacked with great determination and inflicted severe casualties: Flg Off Ed Wallace (BP992), the 6'6" tall, 26-year-old Canadian from Toronto who had been serving with 126 Squadron since the early summer, and Sgt Willy Wilson (EP718/V-S) of 1435 Squadron were both shot down and killed, while Sgt Whitmore of 1435 Squadron was slightly injured when he crash-landed his damaged aircraft (BP873/V-Y) at Hal Far. Flt Sgt Maclennan's aircraft (BP860/V-X) was also hit but he was able to land safely. One of these Spitfires fell to the sharp-shooting Uffz Mazurek of 1/JG53, witnessed by Ltn Hans Röhrig of 3 Staffel, some ten miles north of Valetta. Of his 31st kill, the victorious pilot recorded:

"After the Ju88s bombed they were attacked by eight Spitfires. Coming out of the sun and doing a left turn I attacked one Spitfire. The plane lost parts of the motor and cockpit. It went down in a black smoke trail which then disappeared as the Spitfire went vertically down into the sea."

A second Spitfire was claimed by Ltn Fritz Dinger of 4/JG53 but this was not allowed since it was not seen to crash. In return for these losses, Sgt Park (MK-J) of 126 Squadron claimed one of the Messerschmitts shot down:

"We were at about 12,000 feet, 12 miles north of Grand Harbour, when my No.2 was jumped by three Me109s. I called to him to break, which he did, and as the leading 109 turned towards me I took a two-seconds burst at him from 250 yards to 150 yards. I saw strikes, one on his motor and one on the wing root. I turned into the other two, which made off. Capt Kuhlmann of 185 Squadron followed the one I had damaged and saw it go into the sea, 12 miles north of Zonqor. He later phoned through confirmation."

It seems likely that Kuhlmann actually saw one of the missing Spitfires crash. Flt Lt McLeod (EP541) and Plt Off Pip Owen (EP332) of 1435 Squadron each claimed a Messerschmitt damaged, Owen also claiming a second as probably destroyed. A Bf109 fighter-bomber of I/SchG2 crash-landed at Comiso on return, and an aircraft (7084) of 1/JG53 crash-landed at San Pietro, both of which may have been involved in one of these combats. Throughout the engagement 249 Squadron patrolled up sun, 20 miles north-east of Zonqor, in order to intercept high cover but saw nothing. Flt Lt Crockett and his crew carried out searches in *ST338*, going six miles south-west of Delimara Point where an aircraft was seen to fall. Only wreckage could be found, however.

There was a short lull before raiders again approached, but these proved to be only three Bf109s, which crossed the coast presumably on reconnaissance. Spitfires of 229 Squadron patrolled between Kalafrana and Zonqor, but saw nothing. A further Axis formation then followed, but appeared to be making a sea search and did not approach the island. Hardly had this plot disappeared from the radar screens when about 60 aircraft were detected coming in from the north, which included at least seven Ju88s, preceded by a large fighter sweep. 185 Squadron Spitfires were still on the ground, being refuelled, as noted by Plt Off O'Brien:

"As we were refuelling the crafty Hun sent over some 88s and caught us in our pens. A very comical sight was the Wingco and Keith [Kuhlmann] with their heads tucked under a dirty bit of netting, hiding from the crackerjacks like a couple of ostriches!"

Six 1435 Squadron Spitfires engaged first, encountering nine Bf109s some ten miles north of Zonqor but without decisive results. The bombers meanwhile penetrated the defensive screen and attempted to dive-bomb Hal Far, being intercepted near Kalafrana by eight aircraft of 229 Squadron. Sqn Ldr Stephens noted:

"My R/T packed up but I tagged along and met nine Ju88s over Grand Harbour with an escort of 30-40 Me109s. Head-on attack, followed by stern attack. Both cannons and one machine-gun u/s, but squirted him from 100 yards with remaining three machine-guns. Then attacked by two 109s. Got a squirt in at each and they at me – everybody happy. A very inconclusive show!"

Flt Sgt Ballantyne and Plt Off Reynolds reported strikes on two of the Ju88s before a swarm of Messerschmitts fell upon them. Sgt Francis claimed one of these shot down, but Flt Sgt Lundy's BP989 was hard hit and the pilot baled out into the sea opposite the Blue Grotto, from where he was soon rescued by Maltese fishermen, having suffered only minor injuries. Reynolds' Spitfire (BP860/V-X) was also badly shot-up by the Messerschmitts, though he managed to carry out a creditable landing. His misfortune had been witnessed by Plt Off Dixon:

"I saw a Spitfire approaching. He rocked his wings and he drew alongside me at about 200 yards off to my left. As I looked further left and craned round hard behind, I saw a 109 coming up behind him. I shouted 'Break!' into my microphone but as I did so a whole series of flashes appeared around the cockpit of the other aircraft; I had never seen anything like it before. The propeller stopped and the aircraft literally seemed to stand still or stop in the air. It fell away and began to spiral down.

"I, by this time, had pulled up and left to try and get over and round back onto the tail of the 109, but he pushed his nose down and got away. I saw the other aircraft spiralling down below me and gave a 'Mayday' signal in case he went into the sea. I then lost sight of him and continued to weave my way round the sky and gradually made my way back to Takali where I landed. I was quite convinced that whoever had been in the aircraft had either been killed or crashed into the sea. It transpired that the other pilot was Hugh Reynolds. The flashes I had seen had not, in fact, gone through the cockpit but into the back of the engine, fortunately missing the petrol tanks. However, he managed to spiral down and made a forced landing without an engine, at Luqa, completely unhurt. We celebrated that evening with orange juice!"

Reynolds was possibly the latest victim of Uffz Mazurek of 1/JG53, who claimed his second victory of the morning at about this time, while flying White 11:

"After dropping bombs the Ju88s were attacked by eight to ten Spitfires. After the attack I noticed two other Spitfires above the fighter group. I managed to go up into the sun unnoticed and placed myself behind the enemy. From a close distance I fired with all my weapons at the left plane. It went down showing a dark smoke trail, turning again and again and burned when it hit the sea three km south of Hal Far."

From the details of Mazurek's and Dixon's accounts, it seems very likely that the former had indeed attacked Reynolds' aircraft, but after watching it spiral down had then seen Lundy's stricken machine hit the sea.

Meanwhile, Sqn Ldr Woods led six 249 Squadron Spitfires against the small formation of Ju88s and their escorts near Hal Far. One of the bombers was claimed shot down by Flt Sgt de l'Ara (BR565/T-T) and two others were damaged by Woods (AR466/T-R) and Flg Off McElroy (EP132/T-J). The escorting Messerschmitts of I/JG53 then attacked, inflicting damage to Woods' aircraft and shooting down that flown by Wt Off Pete Carter (EP338/T-A), who was killed. The South African-born American pilot's victor may have been Fw Heinz Golinski of 3 Staffel, who was seen by other JG53 pilots to shoot down one Spitfire before being shot down by another. Golinski (Yellow 1/10582), victor of 46 combats in Russia, was killed and may have fallen to Plt Off Joe Lowery (EP201/V-F), the American claiming one of the attackers. Alternatively he may have been shot down by Flt Lt McLeod, who spotted a lone Messerschmitt at 15,000 feet over Luqa as 1435 Squadron trickled back to their airfield. He reported shooting this down three miles north of Hal Far before being attacked by another, causing him to crash-land EP541/V-Q at Luqa on return. The subsequent I/JG53 casualty report noted:

"During an attack on a bomber formation Uffz Golinski got on the tail of a Spitfire and shot it down. At 2,500 metres the *Rotte* [pair] was attacked from above left out of the sun by a Spitfire. The Spitfire fired a brief burst at Golinski then half-rolled and dove away. The right undercarriage leg of Golinski's machine came down and pieces flew from the right wing. Golinski then went straight down and crashed."[117]

In addition to the Spitfires credited to Mazurek and Golinski, two more were claimed by Obfw Ehrenberger and Uffz Hans Feyerlein of 6/JG53 but they were awarded probables only. Three Hurricanes flown by the RNAS pilots made searches for the various missing pilots and covered an area six miles north of Grand Harbour and one mile west of Filfla. All that was spotted, however, were Spitfires of 229 Squadron orbiting oil patches off Kalafrana, where Flt Sgt Lundy was waiting to be picked up. As Sub Lt(A) Ernie Pratt approached in his Hurricane (BE110), a Spitfire broke away from the formation and attacked his aircraft. His starboard wing was damaged before he was able to evade, and before his assailant realised his mistake.

At about 1300, 35 Bf109s, including a number of Jabo, undertook a hit-and-run attack that saw bombs fall harmlessly near Luqa and Mellieha. Patrolling Spitfires of 126 and 185 Squadrons sighted six Messerschmitts near Comino but were unable to intercept. The bombers were back three hours later. Seven Ju88s of KG77 accompanied by 42 MC202s and 40 Bf109s from I/JG27 and I/JG77, including at least six Jabo, crossed the coast in six waves. The Spitfires were late in making contact on this occasion and, consequently, Luqa was bombed, where a Beaufighter was damaged beyond repair, and a second suffering from blast effects. Takali was also attacked by the Jabo, the airfield being rendered temporarily unserviceable. Two civilians working on the airfield were injured.

Seven 1435 Squadron Spitfires then attacked the Ju88s and 20 escorting fighters – incorrectly identified as RE2001s – two miles north of St Paul's Bay. Three bombers were claimed damaged by Plt Off Walton (EP140/V-P), Sgts Eva and David Fuller, one Spitfire being hit in return. Flt Lt Hetherington (BR565/T-T) then led his eight 249 Squadron Spitfires in a head-on attack just after the bombers had crossed the coast on their way home, claiming one damaged as did Plt Off Budd (EP459/X-P). Plt Off Williams (AR488/T-S) was more successful and believed he had shot down one, while Sgt Wynn (BR177/T-E) claimed a probable. For the second day running Flg Off McElroy was obliged to crash-land at Takali, having been bounced by a Bf109 before he could reach the bombers. In return, Plt Off Sanderson (EP132/T-J) claimed a

Messerschmitt shot down.

Seven more Spitfires, from 229 Squadron, also attacked head-on at about the same time, Sgt Miller gaining strikes on two, one of which he considered probably destroyed, but his own aircraft was considerably damaged by return fire. Flt Lt Parkinson (X-V) claimed damage to another:

"We made head-on attacks on about seven Ju88s. I very nearly collided with one on my right side. Saw strikes along wings, both engines and cockpit. Starboard engine cowling came off."

While this attack was under way ten more Spitfires from 126 Squadron swept in from the flanks, catching the bombers over the island. Sgt Phil Charron claimed one shot down, with two others damaged by Sgts Tiddy and Henry Roberts. Assessment of the three-squadron attack reached the conclusion that, of the eight Ju88s believed to have comprised the formation (there were actually seven), two had been shot down, two probably so, and the remaining four all damaged. In fact Fw Rolf Pester's 3Z+HH failed to return, a second Junkers crash-landed on arrival at Comiso after suffering severe damage, and was destroyed, and a third returned with one engine shot out (possibly by Parkinson). Some of the 126 Squadron pilots became engaged with the escorts, Sgt Marshall claiming a Bf109 probably shot down, while Sgt Tiddy claimed one damaged and Flt Lt Jones a Macchi damaged. As the attackers departed Flt Lt Crockett again set out in *ST338* as two men had been sighted in the sea five miles south-east of Delimara Point. Both were located and picked up. They were Uffz Anton Wallenberger (observer) and Uffz Otmar Wehner (gunner), who had baled out of Pester's blazing I/KG77 bomber; both were suffering from burns.

The Italian pilots reported engaging 12-15 Spitfires and claimed four shot down, Serg Dante Testera being credited with two of these, the third being shared by Ten Giuseppe Bonfiglio and Cap Giovanni Franchini. The fourth was credited jointly to Ten Italo D'Amico, Ten Beniamino Spadaro and M.llo Ferruccio Vignoli. Luftwaffe fighter pilots were credited with four Spitfires shot down during the evening mission, one of them by Ltn Hans Remmer of I/JG27, his 14th victory. The others were awarded to Oblt Freytag – Nos. 75 and 76 – and Obfw Brandt, raising his score to 33. With the four Regia Aeronautica claims and that made by the KG54 Ju88 crew, this gave a total of 13 for the day against an actual loss of four Spitfires shot down, five crash-landed and three damaged.

The defenders had noticed that Axis tactics had changed during the day. Many formations were now attacking on a wide front and approaching from several directions simultaneously. While some raids had thereby got through, they had failed to inflict much damage on the airfields. As daylight faded, Air Vice-Marshal Park despatched a message to the Spitfire squadrons:

"Grand work fighter boys. Your magnificent fighting in the last five days is being watched not only in Malta but by the RAF on other fronts as well, as well as by our Russian allies. Although heavily outnumbered last May, the Malta Spitfires came out on top and I am confident that you will win the second Battle of Malta. Some of the enemy bomber squadrons have already shown they cannot take it. Keep it up and in a few days the other German bombers will throw in the sponge. Replacement pilots and Spitfires are on the way but there is still some stiff fighting to finish the job. Good luck to you and good shooting."

The AOC did not forget the hard-working maintenance personnel either and sent congratulations to them, but added:

"Your part in the present Battle for Malta greatly appreciated but serviceability of Spitfires continues to fall. You can and must get it up again. Where you have worked hard you must work harder and faster. Give the fighter boys Spitfires and they will drive the Hun out of the sky."

But behind the façade of morale-boosting messages to the squadrons and groundcrews, Park was a worried man and informed the Air Ministry accordingly:

"For the last important operation Pedestal [the supply convoy in August] Malta's Spitfire strength was 163 of which 120 were serviceable. When the present battle began October 10 we had 141 Spitfires of which 113 were serviceable. The last five days' intensive fighting has reduced total strength to 119 of which 55 are serviceable. In addition to the absolute losses of 22 Spitfires in the last five days a further 20 are beyond our capacity to repair before the end of October making a total wastage of 42. If the enemy maintains his present scale of attack for another week we shall not be in a position to put up any effective fighter defence owing to lack of serviceable Spitfires. Therefore the 12 Spitfires promised by the end of October are totally inadequate as previously reported. The foregoing figures do not take into account our losses of aircraft on the ground which have been negligible but will increase in proportion as our fighter effort decreases."

Daylight on **17 October** brought a resumption of the attacks after a fairly quiet night. At 0645, some 50 raiders were plotted approaching, including seven Ju88s, the formation flying at between 18,000 and 31,000 feet. Five 249 Spitfires were airborne when the bombers approached the island, but their task was to search for the high-flying Messerschmitt escort. Two were sighted at 25,000 feet orbiting ten miles east of Zonqor Point but these avoided combat. Meanwhile, Sqn Ldr Lovell led four 1435 Squadron aircraft in a head-on attack on the four leading bombers, 12 miles north-east of Zonqor Point. Lovell (EP612/V-B) gained strikes on one, but did not make a claim as it was then attacked and shot down by another Spitfire. The victor was from 126 Squadron, eight more Spitfires from this unit being led into the attack by Wg Cdr Hanks (BR498/PP-H). As Flt Lt Rip Jones closed rapidly on the leading Junkers, he was either hit by return fire or misjudged his speed, for EP341 collided head-on with Maj Heinrich Paepcke's 3Z+AC. The Kommandeur of II/KG77 and the 27-year-old former US Navy pilot from New York were both killed instantly, though three other members of the German crew were seen to bale out. Returning bomber crews reported that the Spitfire pilot appeared to have deliberately rammed the bomber, KG77 subsequently being credited with a 'ramming' victory as the Spitfire had been seen to go down.

    Three more claims for bombers destroyed were submitted by Hanks, Plt Offs Thompson and Jim Stevenson; meanwhile, Flt Sgt Varey and Sgt Yeatman claimed two more probably destroyed; Varey also claimed one of the escorting Messerschmitts shot down, but one Spitfire suffered slight damage. Two further bombers were actually shot down during 126 Squadron's attack, both machines of 6 Staffel. Ltn Franz Köchling and his crew were lost in 3Z+KP, although the other crew survived their crash and were later rescued by Axis ASR craft. The remaining bombers jettisoned their bombs in the sea and turned back. The raiders were spotted leaving by eight patrolling 185 Squadron pilots, who were at 21,000 feet over Kalafrana Bay, but they were too far off to intercept. However, three fighters identified as MC202s were seen below and one of these was claimed damaged by Flt Lt Charney (AB532). Two Spitfires were claimed shot down in this action, Ltn Berres getting his 17th victory, though Ltn Konrad Fels' claim was not allowed.

During the remainder of the morning Spitfire patrols were constantly alerted as small groups of aircraft appeared over the sea south of Sicily, but all were apparently seeking the missing crews and none approached or were engaged. The midday raid was precisely ten minutes late, but when it did appear it comprised eight Ju88s of II/LG1, nine Jabo Bf109s from I/JG27 and a heavy escort provided by 41 Bf109s and 31 MC202s. Again the Spitfires were late getting off and by the time they had intercepted, the attacking force had reached the Comino-St Paul's Bay area. Despite vigorous attempts to intercept all the diverse groups of attackers, the Jabo could not be prevented from raiding Takali. Little damage was sustained however, although bombs also fell on Mosta where three civilians were killed and six injured. The Junkers released their bombs in the Birkirkara area, where several houses were demolished or damaged. AA gunners reported gaining strikes on one Ju88 and two Bf109s.

Two Ju88s were claimed shot down by the Spitfire pilots, one by Sgt Tiddy of 126 Squadron and the other by Plt Off Giddings (AR488/T-S) of 249 Squadron and it seems that both fell. L1+YC crashed into the sea off Valetta. On board was the Gruppenkommandeur, Maj Gerhard Kollewe, who baled out with the rest of the crew but was lost, as was the observer. From the second bomber, Ltn Ottokar Fritscher's L1+CP of 5 Staffel, there were no survivors. It crashed into the sea about 12 miles south-east of Sicily. Italian pilots had watched as the pilot desperately struggled in vain to keep the aircraft flying on one engine and the other belched flames. The gunner in an aircraft of 4 Staffel was wounded over Luqa. Other claims were made for a Ju88 probable by Plt Off Seed (BP866/T-Q) of 249 Squadron, with Flt Lt Charney (EP467), Plt Off Bob Park (EP187) and Plt Off Harry Smith – all of 185 Squadron – each reporting strikes on aircraft attacked, Park claiming damage to two bombers.

The escorting Messerschmitt and Macchi pilots were doing their utmost to frustrate the Spitfires, one being claimed by Ten Italo D'Amico of 51°Stormo CT. However, it seems likely that pilots of I/JG77 were responsible for the casualties inflicted, Hptm Bär claiming a Spitfire for his 117th victory, Oblt Freytag two more (75th and 76th) and Obfw Brandt one (his 34th). Sgt Ron Miller of 229 Squadron was shot down in BP955/X-A and two 185 Squadron aircraft and one of 126 Squadron were damaged, Sgt Leo Garvey (EP521/GL-F) of the former unit crashing when his engine cut as he approached to land. Fortunately, Wg Cdr Thompson and Flg Off Alec Lindsay were on the scene in seconds, and were able to extricate Garvey from the blazing wreck before he was seriously burned. Three Messerschmitts were claimed shot down in this fight, one each by Flt Lt Hetherington (BR565/T-T) and Plt Off Giddings (AR488/T-S) of 249 Squadron, and the other by Flt Lt Parkinson (X-V) of 229 Squadron. Plt Off Ernie Budd (EP201/V-F) claimed a probable and Plt Off Park one damaged. Parkinson recalled:

"CO's kite u/s. Led squadron. Some of the boys had the twitch. I had a hard job to keep them together. Someone spoilt my interception of Ju88 by breaking down across the squadron. Managed to get them all together again and dove to attack. 109s shadowed us all the way in. Attacked bombers and fighter escort. I shot a 109 down. Pilot baled out. Hell of a mix up for a minute or two. Sky was full of blokes who had baled out. Saw various aircraft in flames and diving into sea. Came back to drome to land. Just approaching the runway when a stick of bombs fell just near drome. I saw three 109s going like bats out of hell. Pulled wheels and flaps up, closed hood and chased them out to sea. Couldn't catch them. Saw Dusty Miller in his chute so decided to orbit. Three 109s attacked me from 3,000 feet. I broke into them and gave one a squirt but I missed. They buggered off anyhow, which was the main thing. Dusty landed in the drink. I saw rescue launch so directed it to him. Escorted launch for a while and landed with ten gallons of petrol."

On landing, Parkinson discovered that sadly it was not Sgt Ron Miller – the 22-year-old from Leeds who had shown such a fine fighting spirit during the last few days – in the launch, but a German airman. *HSL128* had been ordered out to pick up survivors from a Ju88, three of whom had been seen to bale out as the aircraft crashed seven miles east of Delimara Point. This was Maj Paepcke's bomber from the earlier raid. At first, only an empty dinghy had been found, but then Obgfr Erwin Seibt was spotted in the water, and five minutes later Obfw Walter Borner. Flt Lt Crockett wrote:

"Neither of the men was helpful or seemed to care about the locality of the third member of their crew who had been seen to bale out. I searched, rather hopelessly in the heavy swell, for almost an hour without result. Then I got my deckhand, Merralls, who spoke German fluently to question the two survivors again as to where the third man should have landed but they were dull and apathetic, their morale sunk very low compared to the men we had rescued at the beginning of the week. Obstinately, I decided we would carry on searching for a while longer before reporting two survivors only to HQ. An hour and a quarter after picking up the second man we spotted the head of the last member of the German crew bobbing about in the swell. His name was Fw Ewald Futterknecht and we landed him back with the others at Kalafrana at 0948 hours."

HSL107 was called out shortly after midday and located two more German airmen, both survivors from Maj Kollewe's aircraft. On being pulled aboard, the W/Op, Obfw Martin Assum, claimed that a Spitfire had swooped on the defenceless airmen in the sea and machine-gunned Kollewe and the observer (Fw Bernhard Mahler) both of whom had been killed.

A number of Bf109s were seen during the early afternoon, obviously searching for the missing aircrew, but no contact was made with patrolling Spitfires. Ltn Köhler of I/JG77 was one of those involved:

"Major Kollewe was shot down. As long as the Tommies have orders not to attack our seenots [rescue aircraft] we respect them by keeping away from their speedboats [rescue launches]. Kollewe's Ju88 was hit hard and he tried to land on the sea but misjudged and went in."

The three RNAS Hurricanes also undertook searches – Sub Lts(A) Elliott, White and Pratt patrolled a semi-circular area from St Paul's Bay to Kalafrana, six to ten miles out to sea. One pilot saw the launch rescue the two survivors of Kollewe's crew ten miles north-west of Delimara, then Elliott (BN408) directed the vessel to a parachute in the sea three miles east of Zonqor Point, but no survivor was seen.

During mid-afternoon about 60 Bf109s, including at least ten Jabo, approached from several directions at great height. Some crossed the coast and bombs fell in the St Paul's Bay area without causing any damage. Thirty Spitfires were in the air and a flight from 1435 Squadron was bounced out of the sun, about 15 miles north of Comino: EP259 was badly shot-up, although Plt Off Stewart was able to get back to base and crash-land. 249 Squadron was also bounced, but on this occasion the seven Spitfires avoided any damage. 185 Squadron was over the island in two sections, the topmost being attacked by a pair of Bf109s. Wg Cdr Thompson's EP343 was hit and the hydraulic system was damaged but he, too, managed to reach base where he was obliged to put the aircraft down on its belly. A second Spitfire, flown by Capt

Kuhlmann, received some damage to one wingtip during this action. Oblt Schiess of Stab/JG53 claimed one Spitfire (his 24th victory) and Uffz Erich Juhls of 2 Staffel another for his 10th; Ltn Berres of Stab I/JG77 claimed his second of the day.

It was now the turn of the ASR unit to receive Air Vice-Marshal Park's plaudits:

> "The AOC sends personal congratulations to the Air/Sea Rescue Unit on their fine achievements during the recent Battle of Malta when they made 36 trips and rescued 12 British and 16 enemy pilots [aircrew]. All pilots and aircrews are grateful for your efficient Air/Sea Rescue Service."

Indeed, to date since the beginning of the year, the unit had rescued more than 100 airmen of whom about 40 were Germans or Italians; ten bodies had also been recovered from the sea. Under cover of darkness two of Malta's biplane torpedo-bombers, a Swordfish and an Albacore, were sent out to search for a damaged Italian freighter off the Tunisian coast, the pilots Sub Lt(A)s Elliott and Pratt respectively. As FAA pilots, they were doing the job for which they were trained – helping the RAF to locate downed aircrew in RAF Hurricanes was voluntary. On this occasion Elliott, who was to release flares to assist with the attack, had to return early with a malfunctioning engine and, although, Pratt released his torpedo in bad light, he failed to observe any result of his attack.

Despite Feldmarshall Kesselring's suspension of the bombing assault, the island was not yet spared further attack. Just as the end of daylight bombing raids on England in September 1940 had brought several weeks of fighter sweeps and pin-prick fighter-bomber attacks – designed to draw up the British fighters for destruction in the air – this now became the pattern for Malta:

> "A sense of pointlessness concerning their Malta missions began to spread among the bomber crews, and also among the fighter pilots – as early as September Kesselring had found that the airmen of the units that had been based on Sicily for a long time were tired of constantly flying over the water and something akin to 'Malta sickness' was beginning to spread."[118]

The early hours of **18 October** saw the welcome arrival from Gibraltar of a Hudson carrying six replacement fighter pilots, the first of approximately eight dozen who would arrive during the next few days, as promised by the AOC. Those aboard the aircraft, FH307 of 24 Squadron, included Flt Lt Blair White, a Battle of Britain veteran with three victories including one probable. The same Hudson would return the following week with a further five pilots, but the majority of those waiting at Gibraltar would be ferried to Malta by two Liberators of the newly established 511 Transport Squadron, while another batch were to fly their Spitfires from the deck of the carrier *Furious*.

The first raid came in at 0640, eight Spitfires of 126 Squadron and eight of 185 Squadron scrambling to meet approximately 50 fighters that approached at 0700. They were reportedly escorting seven Italian bombers, which had apparently turned back 15 miles north of Zonqor Point. This was probably the occasion referred to by Hptm Heinz Wittmeyer, a staff officer with II Fliegerkorps:

> "While the Luftwaffe was still mounting attacks on Malta, I called Obstlt von Maltzahn and told him that I would like to fly with the Geschwader again. He replied, 'Great, Heinz, then you can come along on our next mission.' As it turned out I was only to fly one mission with the Geschwaderstab – escort for an Italian bomber group. The mission took an unexpected turn: instead of going to Malta the Italian bombers flew into the area south of the island and there, under no pressure from the enemy, dropped their

bombs into the sea. We were speechless. Later, Italian radio broadcast praiseworthy and commendatory words about the efforts of their bomber crews; we in the Geschwaderstab had a great laugh about it."

Six Messerschmitts bounced the 185 Squadron flight five miles north-east of Grand Harbour, although these were evaded. Plt Off Reid (EP722) reported: "Jumped by several 109s. Broke left and was able to get in a good squirt at one from a quarter line astern from above. Observed strikes and flashes over top of cockpit and engine." The Messerschmitt attacked by Reid had been lining up to shoot at the Spitfire flown by Plt Off O'Brien, who later noted in his diary: "Some 109s came up sun of us and around behind us. Someone gave a break and I went to the left. A 109 came right up my tail but I turned in time. Len Reid took a squirt at it and claimed a damaged." A dozen Messerschmitts in two separate groups were encountered by the 126 Squadron pilots five miles east of Zonqor Point, Sgt Mortimer claiming one shot down. This was possibly Uffz Heinrich Frankenberger's G-2 (10554) of 4/JG53, which crashed in the sea off Cape Scaramia. The injured pilot was rescued by Axis ASR craft. Meanwhile, Sgt Park's EP345/MK-X had been badly shot-up, the New Zealander crash-landing on return and suffering slight injuries.

Thirty-five Messerschmitts, including a number of Jabo, raided mid-morning and bombs dropped on Takali without causing damage or casualties. The attack was over before interception could be achieved, but eight Bf109s were seen by pilots of 229 Squadron – and another four by 1435 Squadron. None could be engaged, however. Within 20 minutes another 15 fighters swept in to attack Luqa, again with little effect. At 1355 an estimated 20 Messerschmitts were reported, six of 229 Squadron and three of 126 Squadron being scrambled. Fifteen minutes later, the latter trio were bounced by six Messerschmitts four miles south-west of Comino but evaded these. A few minutes afterwards, a lone Bf109 was seen at 7,000 feet over Gozo flying northwards, and Sgt Tiddy dived from 10,000 feet to shoot it down into the sea off Dahlet Qorrot. The pilot was seen to bale out and this was undoubtedly the aircraft flown by Uffz Karl Könning of 3/JG27, who failed to return. At around the same time the 229 Squadron pilots spotted two more Bf109s heading west at 23,000 feet, about two miles south of Gozo, although only Sqn Ldr Stephens was quick enough to get in a burst at one, claiming some damage: "Patrolled south of Gozo as a pair. Attacked by two 109s and chased them up into the sun. Damaged one. My No.2 pissed off and left me. Chased two 109s but was attacked by another pair – inconclusive."

Up to 75 fighters, Jabo included, crossed the coast in small groups at great height between 1545 and 1700. A number of bombs fell on Luqa, where a Wellington was slightly damaged, and in the Gharghur area. Although 38 Spitfires were airborne only two of 1435 Squadron were able to get near enough to engage, Flt Sgt Hamilton (AB264/V-Z) claiming strikes on one Messerschmitt. As the Spitfires returned to land, Plt Off Jim Stevenson's EP332 of 126 Squadron went out of control and crashed into a field south-west of Gharghur. The 29-year-old Canadian pilot from Winnipeg was killed.

Fifteen-plus Bf109s and Jabo attacked Hal Far between 0625 and 0652 on the morning of 19 October, two Hurricanes being slightly damaged. Eight of 1435 Squadron scrambled and saw six Messerschmitts over Kalafrana at 0635. They dived on these from 10,000 feet, Flt Sgt Scott (EP203/V-G) claiming one damaged. This may have been the occasion when Scott had an amazing experience:

"I'd used all my ammunition up and was returning to Malta on my own – we always got split up after a dogfight – when I was attacked by two 109s, and obviously with no ammunition I was in a bit of a hole and all I could do was to use the Spitfire in its defensive rôle to keep out-turning them as they came down – you could only watch one fighter at a time and as he came down firing, I out-turned him and managed to keep him in front of me and watch for the other one to come down afterwards. By keeping one in front and not firing they soon found that I was obviously out of ammunition and they kept attacking. I kept one in front, the other one came down, I out-turned him and so on, until literally we were in a stalemate. Fortunately for me I was close to Malta and they were quite a way from their base in Sicily and were obviously going to run out of fuel if they messed about any more. So then a most remarkable thing happened – they both flew away and then came back in a sort of sideways motion and formated on me at quite a distance. I was pretty nervous, thinking they might come close, but they just formated on me and, as we flew along, waggled their wings. And then they peeled off and flew back to Sicily and I, most gratefully, to Malta."

Three hours later 15 MC202s of 51°Stormo, 23 of 153°Gruppo and 19 Bf109s escorted three RE2001 fighter-bombers to attack the Gharghur area. Twenty-three Spitfires were airborne. At 0948, 1435 Squadron saw five fighters identified as RE2001s over St Paul's Bay at 20,000 feet and dived to attack, Plt Off Walton (BR236/V-E) claiming one probable. This was most likely Serg Ferruccio Serafini's Macchi, which was damaged, the pilot being wounded in both hands. None of the Reggianes was hit. Macchi pilots claimed one Spitfire probably shot down and one damaged.

Some 20 fighters crossed the coast during the early part of the afternoon and Attard was bombed. Eight 185 Squadron Spitfires intercepted, Capt Kuhlmann (EP722) and Sgt Jimmy Gunstone (EP471) each claiming a Messerschmitt damaged, but Kuhlmann's Spitfire was also damaged and he crash-landed on return to Hal Far. The next two raids were not intercepted despite large numbers of Spitfires being airborne, although little damage was caused at Luqa and Mosta where a few bombs fell.

This somewhat frustrating day was to end with better success for the defenders when, at dusk, 40 unescorted Ju88s from II/LG1 and III/KG77 approached the island in two formations. It was still light enough, however, for a standing patrol of three 249 Spitfires to spot the KG77 aircraft 25 miles out to sea, as they approached from the west. The Spitfires were joined by two Beaufighter night fighters, whereupon a number of bombers jettisoned their loads and turned back. Meanwhile, Flt Sgt de l'Ara (EP201/V-F) led his section to intercept the other formation, which was encountered 15 miles east of Malta and again bombs were jettisoned, as de l'Ara recorded:

"Whenever I manoeuvred my section nearly within range of a bomber in these groups, they would jettison their bombs and dive into cloud. I was vectored onto one bomber, which I recognised as a Ju88, about 400 yards ahead, and crossing my starboard bows. I brought my section round behind it. The top gunner fired at me at about 200 yards but I had closed to about 150 yards and fired a three or four-seconds burst at the port motor. The engine gave a flash, caught fire and streamed a considerable amount of black smoke. The gunner stopped firing and I noticed a glow inside the cockpit, then I broke right to avoid ramming. Immediately I broke, my No.2 [Sgt Stead] opened fire from astern. The e/a turned slightly to the right, then flicked over and spun into cloud."

Among those watching from the ground was a Beaufighter pilot, who related:

"The Ju88s are still in formation and are just starting to open up and dive on the drome now. One has been hit, a Spit got him and one engine is on fire. Two of the crew have baled out. Christ, here come the bombs also. The Ju88 that was hit has just hit the ground and blown up about a mile from here. Three of the crew are coming down in parachutes."

Another eyewitness wrote:

"... about a hundred feet from the deck she [the crippled Ju88] levelled out, crashing 500 yards away. I think that it was the pilot's unlucky day for his chute never opened and I remember him flashing past my eyes to disappear in a cloud of dust 50 yards distant."

Only three bombers had in fact crossed the coast and it was one of these, 3Z+GS flown by Uffz Gerhard Demuth, which fell to de l'Ara and Sgt Stead (EP520/T-V), although it seems that Plt Off Sanderson (EP199/T-K) also participated in this action, since he noted: "Many Ju88s around. Fired at one in the dark. We got two between us. Ju88 destroyed. Night landing."

A second Ju88, an aircraft of II/LG1, was pursued north-eastwards by one of the Beaufighters which shot it down into the sea. The crew was later rescued by *HSL128*. Bombs fell near Luqa and Hal Far but caused no material damage.

The morning of **20 October** brought with it heavy rain and further sporadic raids but few interceptions. Indeed, the only one of note occurred shortly after 1100 when 15 fighters raided Safi strip and Luqa under cloud cover, four bombs were dropped. Eight 1435 Squadron Spitfires were scrambled, but Red Section was jumped by four Bf109s from 20,000 feet and one Spitfire was slightly damaged.

By night, for the first time in weeks, no alerts were sounded. The mini blitz was clearly at an end, and a rush of congratulatory messages followed. From GOC Troops, Malta to AOC:

"On what appears to be the conclusion of the first phase of the renewed enemy air offensive on Malta, all ranks of the Army send their heartiest congratulations to their comrades of the Royal Air Force on their magnificent achievement."

To which Air Vice-Marshal Park replied:

"All ranks of RAF Malta greatly appreciate your messages of congratulation of the recent success of our fighter defences. We are very grateful for the assistance of our comrades in the Army in keeping our aerodromes working at high pressure. The Spitfire squadrons are especially grateful for the helpful co-operation of the AA batteries in the engaging and breaking up of enemy formations that crossed our coast. In spite of the evening bombing of our aerodromes in the past ten days, we have carried out more attacks on his shipping than during the previous ten days."

Park backed up the latter statement with a signal to the RNAS at Hal Far:

"Grand work. Congratulations on your brilliantly successful attacks on enemy convoy on the night 19/20 October. This will teach the Hun to try and put Malta aerodromes out of action as attempted in his recent blitz."

Heavy rain rendered Takali unserviceable for the second consecutive day (**21 October**), but fighter incursions continued unabated. At 0703, 15-plus Messerschmitts were reported over at 20,000 feet, Jabo bombing Safi and Gudja without effect. Eight of 1435 Squadron encountered four over Kalafrana at 6,000 feet and Flt Sgt Scott (EP621/V-N) claimed one probable. Two hours later an estimated 35 German and Italian fighters attacked Luqa and Safi, two-dozen MC202s of 51°Stormo and three 22°Gruppo RE2001s taking part. Eight of 126 and eight of 1435 Squadrons were airborne, the latter engaging a similar number of Macchis at 23,000 feet over St Paul's Bay. Plt Off Walton (EP209) claimed one shot down, while 126 Squadron's Sgt Marshall claimed two Bf109s probably destroyed. At Safi strip a Beaufighter was damaged. Three further raids between 1125 and 1600 were not intercepted. A Beaufighter crew shot down a BR20 during the night.

Fifteen fighters, including some Jabo, crossed the coast at a great height at 0715 on **22 October**, and, taking advantage of cloud cover, dropped bombs in the Birkirkara and Hamrun areas. Some damage resulted and there were several civilian casualties. Patrolling Spitfires did not make contact on this occasion. At least ten Messerschmitts, two dozen Macchis and three RE2001 fighter-bombers raided Takali just before 1000, bombs falling in the Mosta area causing little damage. Sixteen Spitfires of 249 and 1435 Squadrons were airborne, Red Section of 1435 climbing to 25,000 feet over Comino to be bounced by two MC202s, one of which Flt Lt McLeod (BS161/V-U) claimed shot down. The eight 249 Squadron aircraft then met 14 fighters at 24,000 feet north of Grand Harbour, following these in a dive, with the result that Flt Lt McElroy (EP708/T-U) and Plt Off Lowery (EP201/V-F) jointly claimed a Bf109 shot down while Plt Off Sanderson (EP199/T-K) identified his victim as a MC202. A Messerschmitt was claimed probably destroyed by Sqn Ldr Woods (BR529/AD), who claimed a second damaged, as did Sgt Stead (EP520/T-V), who also reported strikes on a Macchi. It seems that either Sanderson or McLeod had attacked Ten Mario Mazzoleni's Macchi, causing severe damage. It crash-landed near Marina di Ragusa on return. Italian pilots claimed damage to three of the Spitfires.

Twenty-five fighters raided all three airfields at 1130. There were no interceptions by eight patrolling Spitfires of 126 Squadron, although Bofors gunners claimed one of the raiders shot down. The raiders were back just after 1500, an estimated 60 German and Italian fighters, including 30 MC202s of 51°Stormo and three bomb-carrying RE2001s, approached the coast with about half crossing in cloud cover. Bombs were dropped at Luqa. Two dozen Spitfires from 126, 229 and 1435 Squadrons scrambled, the latter unit engaging MC202s and RE2001s north of St Paul's Bay, where the Jabo were seen to jettison their bombs into the sea. Plt Off Walton (EP612/V-B) and Flt Sgt Bob Brown (V-A) each claimed two Macchis damaged, and the Italian pilots claimed five Spitfires hit in return.

Next day (**23 October**) saw a continuation of the fighter-bomber raids, which achieved negligible success. About 35 Bf109s approached Malta in two swift raids, the first just after 0630. Bombs fell in St Paul's Bay and near Mosta and Mtarfa. Bofors gunners put up an intense barrage and claimed two low-level raiders shot down, and indeed Black 12 (10524) of 5/JG53 crashed near Mgarr, Uffz Herbert Wagner being killed. A section of 185 Squadron intercepted Bf109s diving on Dingli and Sgt Ray Saunders (EP467), on only his second operational flight from Malta, claimed one shot down. It would seem that his victim was Obgfr Rudolf Hagen of 4/JG53, who baled out of White 8 (10479) into the sea off Gozo. He was picked up by a rescue craft and made a prisoner. Flt Lt Charney (EP471) claimed a second as damaged. However, Flg Off Alec Lindsay's Spitfire (EP685) was hit and was seen to dive from 20,000 feet, minus its tail unit, to crash into a field near Dingli. The pilot was killed. Initially it was assumed that he had been shot down by Messerschmitts, but later it transpired that his was the second fighter claimed shot down by the Bofors batteries.

The raiders were back just after 1000, 30 fighters strafing and bombing Takali but the bombs again fell wide, mostly into Mosta where houses were damaged and one civilian injured. Sixteen Spitfires were airborne, and eight of 229 Squadron intercepted about a dozen Messerschmitts over Dingli without success although Sgt Marshall of 126 Squadron encountered five more over St Paul's Bay at 23,000 feet, and claimed strikes on two. Afternoon incursions were not intercepted.

The opposing fighters clashed over Malta on **24 October**, with rather more severity than of late. An early attack on Takali damaged a Spitfire and wounded three airmen; one of the raiders was believed to have been brought down by small-arms fire. No interceptions were made. Shortly after lunchtime 15 fighters and Jabo again attacked Takali but all bombs missed their intended targets. Eight Spitfires of 185 Squadron were scrambled and Black Section spotted ten Bf109s diving over Dingli, but were unable to catch them. Minutes later, this section was bounced by other Messerschmitts and Sgt Ray Saunders – who had made his first kill the day before – was shot down and killed, EP467 crashing into a field near Rabat.

During the late afternoon at least 40 Messerschmitts and Macchis approached, these being intercepted about 25 miles north of the island at 1610 by seven Spitfires of 249 Squadron. Attacking head-on, Plt Off Giddings (BR565/T-T) claimed one Macchi shot down and a second probably so. Plt Off Williams (EP520/T-V) reported shooting down a Messerschmitt, possibly an aircraft of 6/JG53 from which the pilot was rescued by an Axis ASR craft; Giddings reported:

> "I attacked one gaggle of Macchis in line astern, when the last three rolled onto their backs and dived down. I fired at No.3 aircraft of the remainder with cannon and machine-guns for about three seconds. Glycol poured from it and there was a violent explosion around the cockpit and the fuselage broke up. I then fired a long burst at the No.4 of the formation and saw a thick stream of glycol pour from it. At that moment I was forced to break away and aileron-turned down to 2,000 feet. In my dive I saw an e/a streaming black smoke crash into the sea. This was probably the one claimed by Tiger Blue 1 [Williams]."

A section of 126 Squadron spotted two Macchis over Filfla at 20,000 feet but they were unable to close. However, seven 229 Squadron aircraft engaged eight Bf109s five miles south of Kalafrana, climbing to attack them when they were themselves attacked from the sun. Sgt Bud Milligan's EP716 was hit and the American pilot was wounded in the leg. He crash-landed on return. Plt Off Sandy Goodyear, a new arrival, was also attacked. His aircraft (EN955) suffered a hole through one wing, but he managed to return safely. Sqn Ldr Stephens noted:

> "Climbed laboriously up to 26,000 feet. Hood froze open – bloody uncomfortable! Bounced by four 109s who shot Milligan down (slight injuries) and shot Goodyear up (no injuries). We broke into them in the nick of time! No luck though."

A Spitfire was claimed shot down by Obfw Rollwage of 5/JG53, his 30th victory, and Ltn Hans-Jürgen von Möller of Stab II/JG53 claimed a second shortly after, although this was not allowed.

Two fighter-bomber raids on Takali were the main features of **25 October**, on the first of which a Bf109 Jabo had a wing shot off by Bofors gunners and spun into the ground in flames, Oblt Richard Eckhardt being killed in White 14 (8349). Spitfires of 126 and 229 Squadrons engaged other raiders, newly promoted Flt Lt Rod Smith (BR311/MK-L) of the former unit reporting: "Bounced four 109s from 24,000 feet; four-seconds burst – flash from cockpit and pieces off – dived into sea – confirmed by rest of section and Y Service." There is little doubt that Smith's victim was another I/SchG2 machine, Uffz Willi Diepensiefen's White 16 (13124) being shot down into the sea with the loss of the pilot. Flt Lt Colin Parkinson of 229 Squadron attacked another: "Had a squirt at a 109 ... hit him in the wings, cannon fire – he got away."

For Jabo pilot Uffz Werner Zirus it was his first operational flight:

"I took off from Comiso in my Bf109F-4 'White 12' carrying a 250kg bomb under the belly [sometimes the Jabo carried four 50kg bombs slung under the wings]. The Messerschmitts climbed to 3,000 metres. From that altitude, one can see Malta. We know that we have been spotted by the radars. At 7,000 metres over Gozo, we learn the arrival of 'Indians' (enemy fighters). Then, diving over Luqa at 700kph, we drop our bombs at a height of 1,500 metres before flying to the north. Enemy fighters try to catch me but I escape by flying very low over the sea. At 1717, after 52 minutes in the air, I landed at Comiso."

At 1435 a total of 15 MC202s from 153°Gruppo escorted three RE2001s to Takali, whilst ten 51°Stormo Macchis undertook a sweep as indirect support. An hour later both units reported engagements with Spitfires. Serg Ferruccio Serafini of 51°Stormo claimed one shot down, and four of the unit's other pilots – Ten Manlio Biccolini, Sottoten Plinio Sironi, Serg Magg Giovanni Gambari and Serg Magg Paolo Pedretti – shared a second with Ten Gianni Rossini of 153°Gruppo. Cap Riccardo Roveda, the 51°Stormo formation leader, claimed a third as a probable. Among the units engaging the Italians was B Flight of 126 Squadron, led by Flt Lt Rolls, who also reported meeting Messerschmitts. Rolls' own aircraft (BR345/MK-S) was hit during the engagement but he got down safely. On landing, however, he discovered that highly successful New Zealander Sgt Nigel Park from Auckland was missing in BR311/MK-L:

"I was told by one of the pilots that he had seen Parky's aircraft hit the sea and he thought he had seen a parachute coming from it. Someone else had seen a Spitfire crash into the sea, but that it went down with the pilot still in it. I hastily rang the ASR and they told me they had the information but it would take some time to get there and it would be getting dark soon. I rang Operations to ask permission to go out and search for Parky or to protect him if he was in his dinghy... we took off to that area which we searched for almost an hour and as it was getting dark, we had to return to base and leave it to the ASR."

Park, just 21 years old, who had fully lived up to his nickname of 'Tiger', was not located and it seems likely that he went down with his aircraft. It was, however, believed that he had accounted for a Messerschmitt before he fell, and he was awarded a victory accordingly. Bill Rolls personally made the appropriate entry in the New Zealander's logbook to raise his total to ten and one shared. This was possibly another aircraft from I/SchG2 that was shot down in to the sea, its unidentified pilot being rescued by a Do24 from Sicily. The remaining Jabo escaped with only slight damage to Uffz Werner Zirus' aircraft, inflicted by AA fire. Messerschmitts of II/JG53 were also involved in this action, Ltn Alfred Hammer of 4 Staffel claiming one Spitfire shot down – his first victory after flying 306 sorties and being engaged in 80 combats over the island since 12 December, 1941[118]. Whether he or the Italians – or both – were responsible for Park's demise is not known.

During the day the first two of the promised one dozen long-range Spitfires arrived safely at Malta following a five-and-a-quarter-hour flight direct from Gibraltar, the aircraft flown by Flt Lt John Burgess and Flt Sgt Les Pow RCAF. Each one was fitted with a 170-gallon jettisonable slipper tank beneath the belly, together with an extra 29-gallon tank in the rear fuselage, plus a larger than normal oil tank[120]. The Air Ministry was accordingly advised of their safe arrival:

"First two Spitfires with 170-gallon tanks reached Malta. Tanks not jettisoned and have been returned with extra oil tanks by Liberator. Five more Spitfires awaiting favourable weather for despatch [they in fact departed 31 October]. Briefing of these regarding engine control only required slight modification as result of experience hours flying. On landing both had 13 gallons oil and 43 and 47 gallons petrol respectively. Long-range tanks were gained in first flight. Take-off presented no difficulty and run was under 800 yards."

Meanwhile, in response to the AOC's plea for more Spitfires, *Furious* was on its way from Gibraltar with the final carrier-borne reinforcements for the island. In the meantime, on the night of **25/26 October**, two Liberators from newly formed 511 Transport Squadron, arrived from Gibraltar, carrying a total of 47 replacement fighter pilots including three more Americans – Plt Off Gardner Kelly and Sgts George Warcup and Willie Wendt, all three members of the RCAF.

An estimated 35 Axis aircraft approached the island at 0655 on **26 October**. About half the force turned back upon being intercepted, the rest attacking Takali without tangible result. Three Spitfires of 249 Squadron engaged six Bf109s about 20 miles south of Scalambria, but were themselves bounced by four more, which were evaded. Eight 1435 Squadron aircraft, led by newly arrived Flt Lt Blair White, were jumped by six more Messerschmitts 25 miles north of St Paul's Bay but evaded with minor damage only to Flt Sgt Hamilton's EP140/V-P. A second section from this unit intercepted seven Messerschmitts going south over St Paul's Bay, and Plt Off Maclennan (BR591/V-R) claimed one shot down.

A further 35 Messerschmitts approached on a sweep just after 1030, the first wave being intercepted 25 miles out to sea by eight 126 Squadron aircraft. After breaking up the main formation of Jabo, Flt Lt Rolls (BR345/MK-S) and his No.2 patrolled off Filfla at 16,000 feet, seeing a pair of Bf109s diving down over Luqa, which they pursued. At 8,000 feet one turned to starboard and he fired. It went down pouring black smoke from the side of the engine. At 4,000 feet he fired again, hitting the starboard wing with cannon fire, whereupon it went into a vertical dive at 2,000 feet. At this point he overshot and pulled up, firing at a second Messerschmitt with machine-guns only. Initially he claimed only a probable, but this was later upgraded to destroyed when the crash of a machine in the vicinity of his combat was reported – his 17th and last victory. Of his action, Rolls later wrote:

"I picked out one on the wing and with my first burst of cannon, blew it out of the sky and within a couple of seconds was turning into a second one. I started to fire at it and was so intent on hitting it, that I did not see one behind me. I managed to lose it."

He may well have been attacked by Obfw Rollwage of II/JG53, who claimed a Spitfire some ten miles north of Valetta at this time as his 31st victory. An afternoon raid by almost 40 Messerschmitts, including six Jabo, was engaged initially by eight Spitfires of 1435 Squadron, Plt Off Walton (EP188/V-G) claiming one shot down north of St Paul's Bay. This was possibly an aircraft of I/SchG2 from which the pilot baled out, and who was later rescued from the sea by Axis ASR craft. Sqn Ldr Lovell (EN980/V-W) chased the fighter-bombers across the island, attacking and claiming damage to one as they dived, with bombs falling harmlessly near Birzebbuga.

During a lull between the raids, two Hurricanes were sent out, finding a body in a partially inflated dinghy eight to ten miles north of Gozo. *HSL100* was called out to investigate and eventually located a downed live German airman in his dinghy.

The fighter-bombers were back early on the morning of **27 October**, continuing their series of largely ineffective raids. At 0700, 24 fighters and Jabo crossed the coast and bombs fell near Takali. Eight 249 Squadron Spitfires engaged and two raiders were claimed damaged over Dingli by Sqn Ldr Woods (BR529/AD) and Plt Off Moody (AR466/T-R), Woods believing his victim would have difficulty in getting back to Sicily. This was most likely Fw Horst Rösser of 2/JG53, whose aircraft (10612) crashed into the sea off Comiso. At 1015 six Jabo escorted by about 60 Bf109s and MC202s attacked Luqa, where one Spitfire was damaged on the ground. Eight of 126 Squadron and eight of 229 Squadron attempted to intercept without success, and Bofors gunners claimed one Messerschmitt probably shot down into the sea. There followed another engagement during the afternoon when three Spitfires from 249 Squadron encountered yet another fighter-bomber raid, during which Flt Lt McElroy (T-O) claimed one damaged. However, on this occasion, an escorting fighter attacked the Spitfire (T-D) flown by Sgt Greg Cameron RCAF, a new pilot, who was slightly wounded in the head. Despite his injury, he was able to land his damaged aircraft at Takali[121].

Several days of relative quiet were to follow, during which there were a number of changes amongst the Luftwaffe units in Sicily. I/JG27 returned to Africa, having claimed seven Spitfires over Malta for the loss of two of its Bf109Gs. Next day III/JG53 arrived from the Desert once again in order to release I/JG77, which was to move to the battlefront. Here it was planned that the whole of JG77 should replace the tired and depleted Gruppen of JG27. The Ju88s of KG54 and KG77 were also withdrawn from operations against Malta and assigned to convoy escort duties.

The reinforcements for Malta arrived on **29 October**, 29 Spitfires reaching the island safely from *Furious*. Three of the original 32 Spitfires loaded on board were found to be unserviceable and were therefore returned to Gibraltar with the carrier. Their arrival at Malta did not pass unnoticed and between 1000 and 1120 more than 40 Bf109s were reported to be airborne in an effort to intercept the delivery aircraft, about half of these crossing the coast. AA guns opened fire and 27 Spitfires were scrambled, but no engagements were reported and all the delivery aircraft landed safely. However, two of the Spitfires ordered to provide cover crashed on take-off, including AR488/T-S flown by Plt Off Giddings. His aircraft collided with a truck which had just delivered building materials to Takali; Giddings broke his wrist and several small bones in his arm but Emanuel Grech, one of the Maltese labourers unloading the lorry, was killed instantly and another, Michael Zerafa, was seriously injured. Sgt Wally Parks of 229 Squadron was also not so fortunate. A wing of his Spitfire (EP329) struck a steamroller and crashed sideways into a dispersal pen. The 20-year-old Australian from New South Wales sustained severe injuries to face and head, also breaking his left arm and leg. He failed to regain consciousness and died about 30 minutes later. The Spitfires were led by four Malta veterans who had been flown to Gibraltar for the task:

Plt Off H.G. Reynolds (flight leader)	Plt Off D.A. Piggott RNZAF
Plt Off E.L. Mahar RAAF (flight leader)	Plt Off N.D. Harrison RNZAF
Plt Off K.R. Mitchell RAAF (flight leader)	Sgt A. Williams
Flt Sgt C.F. Bush (flight leader)	Sgt C.D. Leeming
Flt Lt R.E. Atkinson[122]	Sgt J.D. Thorogood
Flg Off H.A. Knight (SA)	Sgt D.W. Goodwin RCAF
Flg Off H.A. Crafts RNZAF[123] (EP404)	Sgt J.N. Miller RCAF
Plt Off J.A.N. Dawkins	Sgt W.A. Laing RCAF
Plt Off J.T. Murchison RCAF	Sgt C.F.J. Harwood RCAF
Plt Off E.G. Lapp RCAF	Sgt J.D. Billing RCAF
Plt Off J.R. Mowbray RCAF	Sgt R.M. Zobell RCAF
Plt Off M.J. Reid RCAF	Sgt R.A.G. Nadon RCAF

Plt Off W.B. Randall RCAF   Sgt F.R. Vance RCAF (US)
Plt Off A.F. Eckert RCAF (US)   Sgt B.W. Dunning RCAF (US)
                                           Sgt M.J. Costello RNZAF

One of the flight leaders, Joe Bush remembered:

> "Three other pilots and I were to lead 30 [*sic*] Spits off the carrier. The take-off near
> Algiers was similar to my previous trip from the *Eagle*. Two enemy aircraft tried to
> intercept us but were way below us… On returning to Malta I found that my friend
> Tiger Park had been killed – hitting a 109 head-on. Bill Rolls, our flight commander,
> had informed us that he had recommended us both for a DFM. I had been a Flight
> Sergeant for nearly a year and was therefore shortly due to become a Warrant Officer –
> however, I was awarded a commission."

With no action for Malta's defenders for 48 hours, the end of the twenty-ninth month
of the siege allowed stock to be taken. Although losses of Spitfires had been high,
pilot casualties had not. Moreover new arrivals both from *Furious* and the Hudsons
from Gibraltar were about to allow numbers of time-expired old hands, together with
some of the wounded, to be given a welcome rest. The defenders were in good heart.
October's claims by Spitfires were assessed at 126 confirmed (49 Ju88s, 58 Bf109s,
17 MC202s, two RE2001s), 62 probables (31 Ju88s, 26 Bf109s, three MC202s, two
RE2001s) and 162 damaged (67 Ju88s, 72 Bf109s, 18 MC202s, two RE2001s, three
BR20s). The guns were credited with a respectable eight destroyed and one probable.

Five more long-range Spitfire fighters arrived safely from Gibraltar round about
midday on **31 October**, proving just how reliable the 170-gallon belly tanks were.
One of these, AR561, was flown by former American Eagle Squadron pilot Flg Off
John Lynch Jr., who was destined for much success in the coming months. During the
evening, 24 tour-expired or wounded fighter pilots including Wg Cdr Donaldson and
Plt Off Beurling, together with ten civilians (including two young children), who were
to be evacuated, boarded a Liberator transport – AL516 of 511 Squadron – bound for
the UK via Gibraltar. The aircraft had arrived from Alexandria carrying, amongst
others, Sqn Ldr Tommy Smart DFC, who was to take command of 229 Squadron, and
Sqn Ldr Jack Urwin-Mann DFC, the new CO of 126 Squadron. After refuelling, the
Liberator took off at 0300, arriving over Gibraltar in the midst of a violent storm, low
on fuel. The pilot overshot the runway landing two-thirds along its length. Because
the runway terminated in the sea, he opened the throttles in an attempt to go round
again. With insufficient speed the aircraft stalled, flopped into the sea about 100 yards
off the runway, broke its back and sank like a stone. Although the pilot and his
navigator were injured in the crash, the whole crew escaped, but not all the passengers
were so fortunate, many being trapped in the rear half of the fuselage when it broke
away. Of the ten civilians aboard, eight were drowned or died of injuries – including
the children – and the survivors were both injured.

Four of the fighter pilots were drowned – Flt Lt Eddie Glazebrook DFC and Plt
Off John Williams DFC, together with fellow-Canadians Flt Sgt Rip Mutch and Sgt
Rupert Davey. Additionally, Flt Lt Erik Hetherington DFC was seen conscious and
apparently not in difficulties when rescuers arrived. He suggested they help others
first, but seconds later he died, presumably from internal injuries. Despite his
wounded foot encased in plaster, Beurling managed to get out and was picked up from
the sea. Wt Off Gord Farquharson, also with a foot in a cast, saved himself by clinging
to the broken leg of another pilot who had managed to seize a piece of floating
wreckage. The American Flt Lt Art Roscoe remembered:

> "As dawn was breaking I went aft to the waist gun position where there were two

gunners at the wide open ports. Beurling came aft and joined me. The gunners produced a thermos of hot coffee and we stayed there for the rest of the flight. As we crossed the end of the runway on final approach we could see out of the gun ports that we were way too high, and as yards and yards of runway went by we felt sure the pilot would go round again for another approach. He didn't however, and the wheels touched down hard somewhere near the end of the runway. Power was applied and the big plane struggled to get airborne again but it was too late now to go round again. The gunners yelled at us to brace for a crash-landing, and I grabbed on to something solid. With an almighty whack the Liberator hit the water, and the deceleration was so sudden we were thrown into the corner of the compartment, suffering minor cuts and bruises.

"My arm was in a sling and all this jostling didn't make it feel any better. The aircraft had stopped now and was fast filling with water; we were up to our waist in water in no time. Flt Sgt [Desmond] Bye of 229 Squadron appeared in the waist compartment, bleeding badly from head cuts. I found a loose life raft, inflated it, and helped Bye out of the gun port and into the raft. I exited the aircraft myself at this time. Beurling was in the water near me and offered to help me, with my arm being in a sling, but I told him I was OK and he swam off toward shore. I was a good swimmer but didn't trust my bad arm. The aircraft had settled to the bottom of the shallow bay, resting on the extended undercarriage, with the wing just awash. I climbed onto the wing and tried to help others up. Some of those in the water were all right, others dying or already dead. The army put rafts out from shore and soon we were all taken off, drenched and cold, many suffering from shock."

Beurling, leg encased in plaster, had a remarkable escape:

"The pilot began to pour coal in a hurry to all his throttles. The big ship jumped to it and picked up speed. When we went, into the clear, off the end of the runway, we must have been making close to a hundred, and chances are we might have been OK if we'd taken our climb easy. We stalled at 40 feet and dived into the sea. As we stalled, I flung open an escape door right by my back seat, and just as we hit the water, before the big wallop hit us, I dived out. Two or three others followed right behind me. But at least half our passenger list was trapped in the cabin. Then, perhaps half a minute after the impact, the ship broke apart. The first person I saw was Art Roscoe, hanging onto a chunk of wreckage. His fractured collarbone made swimming impossible.

"The crew had broken out of the cockpit and a couple of rubber dinghies had floated out. Half a dozen survivors who couldn't swim were loaded into the life rafts. I hung around, looking for people to help, trying to find Hether and Willie and Rip Mutch, but couldn't see a sign of any of them. They, with Eddie Glazebrook and eight or nine others, had been trapped in the ship, or killed by the impact of the blow when we hit the water. A bunch of army lads on the beach had seen us whisk over their heads and into the water, only 200 yards offshore, and plunged in, swimming out to help. Somebody yelled: 'Better get ashore, if you can make it!' and I started dog-paddling in, the best I could do with a cast-encased foot. As soon as the people on the shore saw the clubfoot they grabbed me and shoved me onto a stretcher. I kept saying: 'I'm OK. Get somebody else', but I might as well have been yelling in the middle of the desert. First thing I knew the stretcher was being hoicked into an ambulance and I was on my way to hospital and bed."

Another survivor was Wg Cdr Donaldson:

"The passengers were all in the bomb bay... sitting on parachutes or anything comfortable they could find. Next to me was a beautiful Maltese girl called Bella [Mrs Ashton]; she had a son of about one year with her and she was going home to join her husband, a FAA pilot. I can remember a loud noise as we hit the sea. We were all thrown forward, not being strapped in and everything was chaos. In no time we hit the seabed. I can remember seeing above me there was a small crack, which looked lighter; this turned out to be where the aircraft had broken its back. I simply fought my way up through the broken hull to the surface … there seemed to be literally hundreds of men swimming out to the position of the wreck and soon someone got hold of me and pulled me towards the shore."

Flt Sgt Arthur Varey recounted:

"There were a lot of us in the bomb bay. I was temporarily knocked out and vaguely remember scrambling through the torn fuselage and swimming valiantly to the shore, only realizing afterwards that I was in full uniform with my belt and ammunition strapped round my waist. I recall that Screwball Beurling was alongside me, and I did not realise until we got ashore that he had one leg in plaster."

Flt Sgt Joe Bush, having just led a flight of Spitfires from *Furious*, was among those returning:

"I happened to be asleep on the luggage and was awakened by the 'bang' to find water rising inside the fuselage. I was wondering how to get out – we had entered through the bomb doors – when a member of the crew bubbled up and we found an emergency hatch. We knocked it out and climbed out of the wreck. The Liberator had almost sunk and the top of the wings and fuselage were the only bits showing. People on shore swam out with life rafts and we were pulled ashore and taken to hospital. They tried to pull the Lib ashore later but its back broke and all the luggage floated into Spanish waters. I lost my logbook, flying jacket, parachute, revolver, flying boots and personal items – I had nothing left! After a day in hospital for checks, I returned to the UK in a Hudson."

Other survivors included Flg Offs Al Yates and Fred Johnson, Plt Offs Mac Barbour, Johnny Farmer, John Pinney, Freddie Thomas[123], Ken Mitchell, Len Reid and Tubby Mahar, Flt Sgt Les Pow and Sgt Fred Clewley. They were the lucky ones. As he lay in bed in hospital, Beurling reflected on his fortunate escape and the fate of his friends:

"Gradually the news began to come through, 15 people dead or missing. All the male civilians had been killed. One of the Maltese women had been killed in the crash and the Englishwoman had died on the way to hospital. Both babies were drowned. By nightfall the bad news was almost all in. I lay abed that night and looked out the window on the lights of Gibraltar. So this was how it had to end. You fly and you fight and you live for the minute, and you team up with guys who know nothing about you and about whom you know nothing. All you know is that the other guy is full of guts and does the job. Then the break comes and you all fly away together, each to go his own way at the journey's end, but each with something to share with the others that none of you will ever forget. Then this… I'd never go roaring up to 28,000 feet again with Hether, both of us proud as hell that we could beat any team in 249 to get up where the Jerries were. I'd never wipe another Hun off Willie's tail, or bawl him out for cruising around watching a flamer spiral down. There wasn't any Hether. And there wasn't any Willie."

* * *

During the month, with the end of the mini blitz, a plethora of awards were announced for Malta's fighter pilots, including DSOs for Wg Cdr Hanks DFC, Wg Cdr Donaldson DFC AFC, Sqn Ldr Lovell DFC, and rather surprisingly, for Plt Off Beurling DFC DFM. The latter award evinced some sharp comment, not everyone considering that the award of a medal normally associated with outstanding leadership was appropriate in Beurling's case. Possibly, the AOC decided to recommend this award for inspiration rather than leadership.

A third DFC was announced for Sqn Ldr Stephens DFC, with Bars to DFCs for Wg Cdr Thompson DFC, Sqn Ldr Woods DFC and Flt Lt McLeod DFC; DFCs were awarded to Flt Lts Hetherington, Glazebrook, Rolls DFM, Parkinson, Roscoe, Rod Smith and McElroy, with a DFM for fellow Canadian Plt Off Maclennan. 249 Squadron's Flt Sgt de l'Ara received an immediate DFM in recognition of his leadership against the Ju88 raid on 19 October. DFMs were also awarded to Flt Sgts Ballantyne, Varey and Scott; later a DFM was gazetted for the deceased Sgt Park. DFCs were later gazetted for the South African pair, Maj Swales and Capt Kuhlmann, and also for 185 Squadron's Flt Lt Charney and Plt Off Len Reid. 1435 Squadron's Plt Off Walton also received a DFC and was promoted to flight commander. Flt Lt Crockett, the commander of the ASR Marine Unit subsequently received an MBE in recognition of his and his unit's achievements, while the three RNAS pilots – Sub Lts(A) Elliott, White and Pratt – who assisted the ASR launches each received a DSC in recognition of their services in that respect and also for their night operations.

CHAPTER IX

THE BATTLE IS WON

November – December 1942

1 November was marked by a single scramble by four Spitfires of 1435 Squadron at 1205 to investigate a raid, which did not materialise. But as Rhodesian Plt Off Russell Wright's aircraft (EP138/V-K) became airborne, his engine failed and he was fatally injured when attempting to carry out a crash-landing. Flt Lt Rod Smith, who witnessed the incident, later recalled:

> "I was on readiness when poor Wright was killed. 126 Squadron's dispersal was at the west end of the east-west runway at Luqa, and 1435's was at the other end of it. Once in a while the two squadrons would be scrambled at the same time, and the aircraft of each would have to pass those of the other while taking off in opposite directions in clouds of dust. Wright had just got airborne, heading west, and was barely past the west end of the east-west runway when his engine gave a cough and quit cold. He was in a hopeless position because there was a rocky steep-sided terraced ravine off the west end of the runway, and the plots in it were tiny and surrounded by low stone fences. He had no choice but to glide straight ahead into the ravine. He went out of sight from where I was standing. There was a sickening crunch and a column of thick black smoke appeared above the edge of the ravine."

During an afternoon sweep by Messerschmitts from 9/JG53, Oblt Franz Götz claimed a Spitfire about six miles north of Gozo but this was not confirmed. Shortly thereafter, III/JG53 flew to Bari on the mainland to re-equip with the new Messerschmitt Bf109G-4. Oblt Jürgen Harder of 7 Staffel took the opportunity to write home:

> "Today my first letter from Europe. Finally escaped this less than pleasant theatre of war. The flight over and the subsequent trip here went very smoothly. I spent a day on Crete, then a day at Taranto, and the rest here in the nice city of Bari. The last weeks over there were a little too much. But now happily everything is over and soon we will have new tasks. It will be three or four days before my Staffel ferries twelve new aircraft to Comiso. I'll stay here until then. Then we have to wait for the ground personnel and then we can return to Malta. We have new aircraft, faster and more powerfully armed, and are now superior to the Tommy in every respect. At the moment our theatre Malta is less dangerous than Africa."

Five days later Harder added in a letter from San Pietro:

> "Finally back in business, a new aircraft, the whole gang together and Africa far away to the south. Our new base is 20km from Comiso on a small plateau amid olive groves and vineyards. It does the eyes good to finally see green again as well as streets, houses and people."

On **2 November** at 1340, up to two dozen fighters and Jabo crossed the coast at great height and although four Spitfires of 249 Squadron were up, no sightings were made. A number of Spitfires of 185 and 229 Squadrons were on a training flight however, and four of these were bounced by Bf109s diving from 28,000 feet but there were no casualties. Bombs were dropped on Luqa by a single Jabo flown by Uffz Werner Zirus although a second would-be raider was shot down by ground fire from RAF defences. The Messerschmitt – Yellow 3 (10045) of I/SchG2 – blew up and crashed near

Kirkop. Its pilot, Obfw Joachim Schanina, was killed. Just over two hours later another fighter sweep approached the coast but only six crossed. 126 and 229 Squadrons each had eight aircraft in the air but failed to make contact. Five more from 249 Squadron were bounced from out of the sun by two Messerschmitts, Sgt Bill Weir's EP448/T-F sustaining some damage and the pilot suffering slight wounds; he crash-landed at Takali on return. His assailant was clearly Ltn Fritz Dinger of 4/JG53, who claimed a Spitfire shot down for his 49th victory.

At 1335 on **3 November**, seven Spitfires of 185 Squadron were scrambled on the approach of a Jabo raid directed at Luqa, EP138 crashing on take-off. The others intercepted a trio of what was thought to be MC202s as they turned away to the east. Chasing these down to 10,000 feet, Sgt Gunstone claimed to have shot down one into the sea seven miles north of Grand Harbour. No Italian losses were recorded, but Fw Hermann Hertel of I/SchG2 was shot down. He was later rescued by a Do24 from 6 Seenotstaffel. Another Jabo strike – directed against Hal Far two hours later – destroyed a Spitfire (EP697) in its blast pen. Seven civilians were killed and 19 injured when a bomb fell on Zebbug, and on the same day a delayed-action bomb exploded in Lija, killing five more[125]. Although seven Spitfires were airborne, they failed to make contact. It was 1435 Squadron which was sent off again on **5 November**, four Spitfires engaging an equal number of Bf109s during the middle of the afternoon, one of which was claimed damaged by Flt Lt John Burgess (V-A) north of St Paul's Bay. Over Malta on **6 November**, five Spitfires of 229 Squadron were sent off at 1025 but were bounced by Bf109s, which slightly damaged Flt Sgt George Edwards' aircraft. Two of 126 Squadron's aircraft, one flown by Flt Lt Rod Smith, fought an estimated 12-15 Messerschmitts at 22,000 feet over Grand Harbour for 25 minutes, albeit without obvious result. Next day, feeling ill, Smith reported sick and was hospitalised for a month.

Luqa saw the arrival of the final batch of five long-range Spitfires from Gibraltar, making a total of twelve such deliveries of Spitfire Vcs, although PR IVs were frequently flying directly from Gibraltar. Although the long-range tank had proved effective, the requirement would soon no longer exist following the imminent Allied invasion of North-West Africa. On the down side, 22-year-old Australian Flt Sgt Bill Irwin of 229 Squadron, a married man who had performed well during the past weeks, found himself facing a court martial, accused of theft. He was found guilty, demoted to AC2 and imprisoned for four months[126].

185 Squadron lost the services of one of its new Canadian pilots next day (**8 November**), when Sgt Charlie Harwood was badly injured in a flying accident at Hal Far in EP609, and was rushed to hospital. He would survive his injuries. A scramble by Blue Section of 249 Squadron on **9 November** resulted in the interception of a PRU Baltimore. While the intensity now eased for Malta's fighter pilots, the Spitfire reconnaissance pilots of 69 Squadron were called upon to provide continuous daytime surveillance of not only Sicilian ports and airfields, but also those along the North African coastline – and suffered a number of losses as a consequence. Following the Anglo-American landings in North-West Africa on **10 November**, 69 Squadron's Spitfires were sent to carry out reconnaissance sorties of Sicilian ports to establish if any Axis naval forces were preparing to put to sea, Flt Lt Harry Coldbeck departing at 1344 in BS367. He failed to return. Other pilots, however, reported as many as 115 aircraft – including Ju52s, Ju90s, Ju87s, giant Me323s and Bf109s – on the Tunisian landing ground at El Aouina, and called in a strike by Malta-based Beaufighters. Many Ju52s were also sighted on Sicilian airfields, these being prepared to transport troops to Tunisia to reinforce the Afrika Korps. It transpired that the missing

Coldbeck, on his 153rd operational sortie from Malta, had been shot down by AA fire but survived to be taken prisoner. Having successfully photographed Taranto and Messina, he had headed for Augusta:

"On my way past Mount Etna, I was climbing again, for there were three cruisers there which had been confirmed in Augusta on previous thrice-daily sorties. They had moved over from Navarino in Greece where we had been watching them. Once again my altimeter began to unwind as I descended below the first layer of cloud, looking for a hole to observe the three cruisers. Another layer of cloud over the harbour saw me south of Augusta looking north through a hole in that cloud layer and my luck was in, for the moment. There were the three cruisers; I was free to go home. I had just rounded out, at 4,000 feet, and my speed was approximately 400mph. There was a loud crunching noise from the rear of the aircraft and the nose went violently down as in a bunt. Simultaneously, I had a glimpse of the windscreen distorting in front of me before I lost consciousness. I came to, outside the aircraft, falling freely through the air. I looked down as I felt the air rushing past my ears. My helmet had gone and there was a swirling turbulent circle of sea below where, presumably, the Spitfire had gone in. I looked down again and found the rip-cord misplaced down my body and although there didn't seem to be any urgency, I pulled it and the parachute opened with a jerk and I was in the sea."

After some time, by which time dusk was beginning to settle in, a small vessel appeared:

"It pulled in alongside me and strong arms reached down and began lifting me up towards the deck and I, oddly, reached behind me and pulled the dinghy up too! They lay me down on the deck alongside the wheelhouse, which was illuminated inside with electric lights. I had not been there very long before a sleek launch pulled alongside and I was transferred to this other vessel. Once on board, I was laid down on a stretcher this time. The only crew personnel of whom I was aware, was the coxswain, a medical man and a naval padre who asked me, in English, if I was a Roman Catholic. The medical naval man tied up my bleeding face and head and we then left the vicinity of the steamer and presumably set course for the Augusta harbour heads. At the quayside steps I was unshipped on the stretcher and loaded like a tray of buns, into the waiting ambulance. The vehicle started up and we motored a short distance then stopped again. I lay there in the stationary ambulance for what seemed in excess of half an hour. I do not remember whether I was covered but I was still in my wet uniform with my teeth chattering. I was laid before an assembly of officers mainly Italian navy, at a long table, with a central figure, whom I later learned, was the admiral in command at Augusta. He chaired proceedings and led most of the questions in English. The admiral said the marine artillery had shot me down."

Thus, for the New Zealander, began a long spell of imprisonment.

Due to the critical situation in North Africa, II/JG53 was again called upon to fly escort missions for the formations of transports bound for Africa, the Gruppe suffering two casualties on 10 November while thus employed. One of these was Obfw Herbert Rollwage, who had for long been a scourge of Malta's Spitfire pilots. Following engine failure he was forced to belly-land his new Bf109G-2 (105000) on the island of Koufonisi, and was injured. The increasing amount of air traffic between Sicily and the German air bases at Tunis now began to offer many opportunities for interception by the Malta-based fighters, a floatplane identified as a He115 being shot down by the Beaufighters off Cap Bon on **11 November** to start the ball rolling. Next day (**12 November**), Sqn Ldr Warburton was off at 0605 in BS364 to carry out a photo-recce of the Tunis-Bizerta area, where he spotted Ju52s taking off from the landing ground, but was then engaged by two Bf109s. These were evaded with no damage to his aircraft. Following Warburton's return to Malta, Flg Off Tony Gubb (BR663) set out at 1115 on a shipping search off Cap Bon. At a lower level he observed 14 Bf109s – aircraft from III/JG53 that were transferring from Sicily to Tunis – and one of these, piloted by Uffz Fritz Döht of 7 Staffel, pulled up into a steep climb and attacked the Spitfire from beneath. The German pilot fired one burst, following which his Messerschmitt stalled, spun and crashed into the sea. The Canadian returned to Malta, excitedly claiming one Bf109 destroyed "by evasive action." Another formation of transports were intercepted by Malta's Beaufighters during the afternoon, five SM75s being shot down. A further interception of a large force of transports on **13 November** brought claims for the Beaufighters for four Ju52s, two SM81s and a Do24 shot down, with a further six transports claimed probably destroyed. Malta's Spitfire pilots could only twiddle their thumbs in the hope that some trade would come their way. They did not have to wait long.

On the morning of **14 November**, 126 Squadron was instructed to carry out a sweep between Sicily and Tunis, during which various Axis aircraft were encountered. The New Zealand pair Plt Off Dave Piggot (EP205) and Sgt Reynolds Hendry (AR497) jointly claimed a BR20, Hendry also claiming a Ju90 as probably destroyed, and fellow New Zealander Sgt Jack Mortimer (EP573) damaged a Bf109. The Squadron then became embroiled in a dogfight with Bf110s of III/ZG26 that were escorting a formation of Ju52s, and Plt Off Jesse Hibbert (EP433/V-N) shot down 3U+CD (4501) crewed by Obfw Richard Schaal and Gfr Paul Thurn of 9 Staffel, but 24-year-old Canadian Flg Off George Davidson (EP310) was shot down by other Bf110s in return. Beaufighters also accounted for a Z.501 flyingboat, an SM75 and a Ju88 for the loss of two of their own. Wg Cdr Hanks (AB526) led the sweep:

> "Cap Bon patrol. SM79 [*sic*] shot down by No.2. 35-40 transports intercepted, escorted by Me110s. One Me110 destroyed by Blue 2, several damaged. One Spit lost. Own cannons u/s."

Four Spitfires from 185 Squadron carried out a bombing strike on Lampedusa in the morning, Flt Lt Ron Atkinson and Flg Off Henry Withy forming one pair, and Canadian Sgts Jerry Billing and Al Laing the other, as Billing recorded:

> "After the bombing effort, no one being too interested, we tooled off west of Linosa for the Ju52 train. These trains carried gasoline. If shot down, a huge fire followed. Off to my left I spotted a couple of enemy boats. I reported them, and Atkinson says, 'OK, let's get them. Line astern.' Great, I thought. This leaves me tail-end charlie. They pressed on the attack. I gained altitude and veered off to starboard, leaving me in a much better position as this angle gave me sufficient time to rake both boats thoroughly. As I passed over the last boat, I swear I'd hit it, I was so low. We banked and climbed sharply to port, positioning ourselves for another attack. That's when I engaged the Macchis flying high cover, which Laing never saw.
>
> "The Macchis were flying in a loose gaggle, no similarity for defensive cover. I was climbing at full throttle as fast as I could. I pulled the nose of the Spitfire up easily, while the other Macchis had seen me and began to turn. I easily turned behind the second Macchi and closed to about 150 yards and opened fire. I took only one good burst and I was obliged to get the hell out because of the other Macchis. Laing called me, and I thought he said, 'What are they?' so I immediately said, 'They're Macchis,

I'm sure of the nose, tail and wings. Al, they're Macchis all right.' Al must have wrenched himself with disgust, as his aircraft twisted a bit, and he said to me, 'For Christ's sake, Billing, where are they? Where? Where?' I took off pieces of one and got a squirt in on the second before fuel forced us to turn back. I made no claims for these attacks. No one was free to view them, everyone concentrating on the bloody boats.

"We flew back at about 50 feet over the water, towards Malta, joining up with Withy and Atkinson. Near our destination it became quite hazy. Laing was on the extreme left, Atkinson, Withy, then myself all flying abreast formation. I checked my fuel and it read ten gallons. I called the leader, Atkinson, and said, 'I can't see the island yet. How about a fix from Gondar?' It became damned thick now, and Laing was barely visible. We received a course, which I set, and I dropped down to a few feet above the water, hoping I could increase my visibility. I looked back to my left and saw Malta. I called and said we had passed the island."

All four landed safely, albeit with near-empty fuel tanks. In the early afternoon 126 Squadron was out again over the same area, this time joined by 1435 Squadron, and on this occasion two transport aircraft were intercepted by the latter unit, Flt Lt Maclennan (EP519/V-U) shooting down one, which he identified as an SM82, and Plt Off John Kirkman (BR376/V-V) and Sgt Kebbell (EP444/V-B) claimed a Fiat G.18. These aircraft were in fact an SM75 (MM60416 flown by Cap Rodolfo Segreti) and a Fiat G.12 (MM60683 flown by Cap Adamo Vigo) respectively, both of which failed to return. The Spitfires had been vectored to the area following a R/T report by 69 Squadron's Plt Off Dalley (BR653), who had spotted 24 transports in sections of four off Tunis. Dalley then continued to carry out his allotted task, a reconnaissance to Decimomannu airfield in Sardinia, but encountered six MC202s that attempted to intercept him:

"The leader opened up at what must have been 500 yards. I put on full right rudder, banging my head violently against the left hood blister. White streaks were observed passing over my port wing. Immediately the two aircraft had passed overhead – the second of which did not fire – I went into a steep climbing turn towards the other four aircraft, the leader of which was roughly 200 yards away and firing. He followed me round but was unable to obtain sufficient deflection to hit my aircraft. I maintained the tight climbing turn and experienced no difficulty in out-climbing and out-turning them, and escaped in cloud cover."

Although Dalley managed to escape on this occasion, 69 Squadron suffered the loss of two more Spitfires next morning (**15 November**). New arrival Plt Off Frank Jemmett (BS359) was ordered to cover Catania, Naples and Messina, but nothing more was heard of the 20-year-old Canadian from Ontario after he took off. In the other direction, Sqn Ldr Warburton departed to photograph the Tunisian airfields. He, too, failed to return. However, he was more fortunate. Over Bizerta he was attacked by Bf109s from both above and below, and his aircraft (BR646) was damaged, possibly by aircraft from III/JG53. Managing to evade, his engine continued to run for a further 25 minutes before it seized up, whereupon he force-landed at Bône airfield, which had been recently captured by Allied forces. Of the interception and subsequent arrival at Bône, a reporter[127] later wrote:

"Warburton hurriedly darted into a bank of clouds. Coming out at the other side he saw the sinister silhouettes of three more 109s heading for him. Swiftly he turned into the clouds again. 'There seemed to be no future in that sort of situation,' he said afterwards, 'so I flew as fast as I could in a very startled aircraft.' His oil tank was punctured. He knew he could not keep flying for long. But down below the British and Americans were getting stuck in after the North African landings. Any strange aircraft zooming out of the sky was likely to be blown to pieces. His engine kept running and he made a good landing at Bône, a Tunisian airfield that had just been taken over by Britain's 1st Army. The reception they gave him, though suspicious, was not actively hostile. His Spitfire was unserviceable."

A squadron of Spitfires had recently arrived at the airfield (111 Squadron), which was being held by British paratroops. Germans were still in the area. Warburton realised he had quickly to make arrangements to move on and soon made contact with the local French governor, Admiral Villeneuve, who agreed to give him a lift to Algiers Maison Blanche airfield in his personal Caudron Goeland (F-BACK). From there he gained a lift in a Halifax bomber that was about to depart for Gibraltar.

Although patrols were maintained every day by the Spitfires at Malta, little trade came their way although losses continued. At 1025 on the 15th, three Beaufighters had been ordered to fly to Malta on detachment from the Western Desert, but all three failed to arrive. During the afternoon four Spitfires from 249 carried out a search for them, but from this operation Sgt John Roberts, a 21-year-old Welshman from Rhosilanerchrugog, failed to return. It was assumed that his aircraft (EP199/T-K) had crashed into the sea although the cause of its loss was undetermined. 249 Squadron moved from Takali to a new strip at Qrendi on **18 November**, and was among those units which began taking the war to the enemy, Spitbombers carrying out a series of raids directed initially against the airfields at Gela and Comiso. They were soon to be joined at Qrendi by 229 Squadron.

126 Squadron was called upon to provide air cover on **19 November** for a convoy approaching Malta, which cost the lives of two of its pilots in unknown circumstances. Plt Offs Gardner Kelly and John Hodges had departed at 0655 and sometime later the latter returned on his own, having suffered oxygen supply problems. Kelly, an American from Sioux City, Iowa, failed to return but his body was later recovered from the sea following a bale out from BP952/MK-F. There were no reports of enemy aircraft in the area. Shortly after, a single Spitfire from the relief patrol landed at Takali, its pilot reporting that New Zealander Sgt Henry Roberts was seen to bale out of EP260. Again, there were no reports of enemy action. It is not known if one or both pilots had experienced oxygen failure, although that seems unlikely since both had baled out, or if they had suffered engine malfunctions, or if they had been shot down by friendly fire from the ships they had set out to escort. 185 Squadron also lost a pilot when 18-year-old Australian Plt Off Bob Park[128] was drowned after he had baled out of EP823 during a convoy patrol; Sgt Jerry Billing was flying as his No.2:

"We took off and stayed low level for quite a while, then set up a square search for the supposed convoy. I happened to glance at Park's aircraft when at the same instant his canopy flew off. He pulled up sharply and leapt out. I heard nothing on the R/T nor saw any other aircraft. Being about 400-500 feet, he dropped quickly and struck the water without his chute opening. Surely he must have been shot down, I thought, but there were no aircraft about. I set up a low cruise and circled, calling 'Mayday' on the R/T. Finally, after what seemed like hours, I was instructed to return to base, but I insisted that I was OK and that my fuel reading was good. In the distance I saw the approaching rescue launch, and I led them to his body. When I arrived back at Hal Far I was told by my erk that the fuel put in was the full amount that the aircraft held. I must have been flying on fumes."

Park's body was later recovered from the sea and interred in Capuccini Cemetery. The cause of his loss was not determined, but one source suggested his aircraft had been damaged in action; Oblt Jürgen Harder of 7/JG53 was credited with shooting down a Spitfire during the day and may have accounted for the Australian teenager, or one of the other two losses.

The following day (**20 November**) Spitfires from 229 Squadron carried out a submarine search, locating one, which Sgt Sandy Goodyear (X-B) attacked, claiming some damage following a strafing pass. Sgt Billing of 185 Squadron flew his second sortie from Malta, as No.2 to Flt Lt Charney:

"We were scrambled after 12-plus 109s. There were four of us in line abreast battle formation. It became typical: a mêlée that lasts some four to five minutes, then half-roll and go home. Very brief, leaving one wondering: Where did they all go? One moment all hell broke loose, the next instant bright blue empty skies, sometimes broken by the sound of fire of an enemy aircraft up your ass. I was unable to get into position for a shot; however, Charney claimed [one damaged] on the sortie."

Malta's Beaufighters claimed further victories when they shot down two Caproni 314s on convoy patrol, then accounted for a He115 the following day, and a Z506B, two Ju52s and three SM82s on the 22nd. These successes were followed by a Z506B, a He115 and an SM75 next day, and three Ju52s and a BV222 six-engined flyingboat on the 24th. Two Beaufighters were lost during the course of these actions, one shot down by a destroyer and the other falling to return fire from a Ju52. In the meantime, Sqn Ldr Warburton had obviously made an impression on those in authority at Gibraltar:

"Gibraltar was rocked. The young man with the unruly fair hair had dropped out of the clouds and no one had told the security wallahs that he was arriving. He was dirty. Several days' growth of beard sprouted from his chin. He carried a German pistol. Tucked in one of his flying boots was a sinister-looking commando knife. For a while anyway, the security wallahs felt they were justified in regarding him as a suspicious character. But the young man had a winning smile and a persuasive manner. With their help he was at last able to convince Gibraltar that he really was a RAF squadron leader. And while they were still under the spell of his charm he asked if they would, please, lend him a Spitfire. Nearly a week before he had left Malta. Now he wanted to get back. It was hard to refuse this young man anything. Gibraltar gave him a Spitfire."[128]

Thus equipped, Warburton set out for Malta in ER647, a cannon-armed Spitfire Vc, calling in at Maison Blanche to top up his fuel tanks before heading for Bône, but specifically to collect the film from his damaged PR Spitfire. One magazine had been destroyed by a cannon shell but the other was salvageable. At Bône he renewed his brief friendship with the CO of the Spitfire squadron, Sqn Ldr Tony Bartley DFC (111 Squadron). It was rumoured that he managed to fly a sortie with the squadron before helping the pilots to enjoy the local wine that evening. Taking off at 0750 next morning (**21 November**), he set out on the final leg of his flight:

"Off Cap Bon, not far from the spot where he had been attacked, he spotted a Ju88. The pilot appeared to be not very wide-awake. 'He seemed to take no notice of me,' Warby said. Before the pilot was aware that he had a Spitfire on his tail he was attacked. An early blast from Warby's guns set the Ju88's port engine on fire and soon the bomber fell blazing into the sea. The Ju88 had a companion. Warburton spotted it sneaking up on him and opened fire. But his ammunition ran out. Although damaged, it was able to slip away through the clouds."[130]

Warburton's return was welcomed and unexpected – he had been posted as missing, and his father advised accordingly. Few at Luqa had any idea that he was safe. While away, notification of his promotion to wing commander had been received. In his absence several new pilots had arrived on posting to 69 Squadron including Flg Off Laurie Philpotts RCAF, Plt Off John Frazer RAAF, and Sgts David Howard and Keith Durbridge. Within 1435 Squadron, Flt Lt Blair White was promoted to command 185 Squadron, Maj Swales being rested.

There occurred another loss during the day when Flt Sgt Martin Lundy, a 28-year-old from Bolton, crashed near Naxxar when his Spitfire EN954 spun off during an upward roll; the 229 Squadron pilot was killed. Sqn Ldr Woods led the first raid by three Spitbombers from 249 Squadron, at 1450 on **22 November**, covered by seven more; four bombs were seen to explode on the runway at Gela and two others among aircraft dispersal pens. Wg Cdr Hanks also led six Spitbombers to Comiso, with Sqn Ldr Lovell leading the top cover. 185 Squadron lost Plt Off Tony Maynard, a 22-year-old Yorkshireman, who was killed when EP696 was shot down.

Next day (**23 November**), Wg Cdr Warburton had another tussle with Messerschmitts when flying an early morning reconnaissance along the Tunisian coastline in BR426, on this occasion three JG53 aircraft catching him temporarily off guard. He was chased westwards for many miles, eventually landing at Souk el Arba in Morocco, with just three bullet holes in his aircraft. Once refuelled and replenished, he made his way back to Malta via Bône, where he landed to see his friends in 111 Squadron. 229 Squadron lost another pilot when Sgt Tom Wallace was obliged to bale out of EP832 while on patrol. He was seen climbing into his dinghy but was not found despite exhaustive air and sea searches. His loss was believed due to engine failure.

Three 249 Squadron Spitbombers again led by Sqn Ldr Woods returned to bomb Gela on **24 November**, although two returned early when the target was found to be obscured by thick cloud. During the afternoon of **25 November**, Woods again led six Spitbombers back to Gela and all bombs were seen to explode within the aerodrome perimeters. Wg Cdr Stan Grant (Wing Commander Flying Takali) led the escort although no enemy aircraft were sighted. Later, Wg Cdr Hanks led three Spitbombers again to attack Gela with Sqn Ldr Lovell leading top cover, but defenders were airborne on this occasion and three Bf109s and two MC202s were sighted, but it was a FW190 that intercepted and shot down Flt Lt John Burgess' aircraft (BR236/V-E), which crashed in flames into the sea just offshore. Burgess was promptly picked up to become a prisoner for the duration. II/JG2, equipped with FW190s, was staging through Sicily en route to Tunisia, and it was Obfw Kurt Goltzsch of 4 Staffel who was responsible for shooting down Burgess. Before being handed over to the Italians, Burgess was entertained by pilots of II/JG2 at San Pietro. Meanwhile, on returning from the sortie, Flt Lt Ron Atkinson had experienced undercarriage trouble when landing EP471 at Takali and crash-landed, but survived uninjured. Earlier in the day four Spitfires of 249 Squadron had taken off for a weather patrol and intercepted two Bf109s about six miles off the Sicilian coast, one of which Flt Lt Seed (EP708/T-U) claimed to have damaged. This may have been an aircraft of 9/JG53 flown by Ltn Gerd Böttcher, who was on his way to Tunisia from Sicily. On arrival at Bizerta his aircraft crashed and he was killed.

During a patrol on **28 November** by a section of 229 Squadron Spitfires, Flt Sgt George Edwards became separated and lost. The Canadian was last heard from when apparently flying on a reciprocal course and presumably eventually had to ditch EP520 in the Mediterranean, losing his life in the process. Wg Cdr Tommy Thompson (EP122/JM-T) led four 185 Squadron Spitfires to carry out a lunchtime dive-bombing attack on Gela, while eight more squadron aircraft flew cover on the run-up to the target. The Spitfires climbed right up to the cloud base of 12,000 feet, before peeling off to dive at the target. Sgt Houlton (BR375/GL-A), having released his bombs, was on his way back to Malta when he heard a radio transmission:

"A faint call from Control reported bandits at 10,000 feet in the area and, as I shot out low over the coast I saw eight Ju52 aircraft in close formation below me, heading for North Africa. Calling a sighting report to the leader to come and give me a hand, I attacked in turn each of the three aircraft on the left of the formation, starting with the rear one. As the 20mm guns fired only one round, I had to do the best I could with the four machine-guns and was surprised by the amount of return fire from the formation. At least some of the aircraft had upper gun turrets, and it also appeared that some irate passengers were using automatic weapons through the windows. The first Ju52 dropped below the formation and turned towards Sicily, and the next two were still descending steeply towards the sea when the Me109 escort came diving down, and I ducked into a handy cloud. The return fire had taken some effect. There was a bullet through the mirror above the windscreen, and an oil line in the engine had been grazed, causing oil to flow back over the cowling and the cockpit cover."

Sgt Billing (EP520) also attacked the Ju52s:

"I spotted three Ju52s in close formation passing slightly under my starboard wing. I called 'Tally-ho!' but no one responded, so I simply continued the attack. I gave him a quick squirt and saw it flaming from the starboard engine. After firing at the first Ju52 I pulled up vertically, half-rolled to starboard and pulled through with a 90° roll, placing me in a terrific quarter astern attack. Bags of time to settle the pipper on the wing root of the second Ju52. I called to the CO and said: 'Come on, there is some fun back here.' Pulling up to starboard and entering some low clouds, I rolled back to port and was ordered by the CO to get back to the formation. I broke out of the clouds again and saw no more of the Ju52s."

On landing, both Billing and Houlton were admonished by Sqn Ldr White for breaking formation. Houlton was clearly unhappy:

"Back at Hal Far I was astounded when the leader said he had heard my radio call and had sighted the transports; but that our task had been to drop bombs, not to go chasing after enemy aircraft. My response to that made it clear that I was unlikely to succeed as a career diplomat!"

Billing added:

"The CO was most upset, as was Wg Cdr Thompson. A Battle of Britain veteran with the DFC. He was not too keen now, burnt out in my estimation. He really gave Houlton and me hell about dragging behind."

Some time later Sgt Houlton was called in to explain to the AOC:

"Sir Keith Park later questioned me on the incident and it seemed that, while Malta radar had picked up the fighter escort at 10,000 feet, the transport formation at low level had not been detected. About one week later a telephone call from HQ advised that the Y Service had confirmed at least one Ju52 crashing into the sea."

German records show that three Ju52s from KGzbV.11, flying from Reggio to Bizerta, were shot down as a result of fighter action during the day, but it seems that P-38s of the US 14th Fighter Group operating from Algeria reported shooting down six Ju52s near Bizerta, one pilot alone claiming four. Presumably these were part of the same formation.

At 0730 on **29 November**, five Spitbombers from 249 Squadron and four escorts set out to raid Comiso where light and inaccurate flak was encountered. Just before midday six Spitbombers with two escorting fighters set out to attack Gela. Over the target Sgt Willie Wendt's aircraft (BR293/T-M) was hit by flak. Although it was last seen going down under control and other pilots believed a crash-landing was a possibility, he in fact baled out at 7,000 feet and was captured, the third American Spitfire pilot to be captured in Sicily (see Appendix V). A second Spitfire was also hit but fellow-American Plt Off Moody managed to return to Qrendi safely. Eight Spitfires of 185 Squadron followed on a fighter-bomber sweep over Gela, meeting some MC202s. Sgt Gunstone claimed one damaged but had his own aircraft shot-up in the exchange. Next day (**30 November**), 69 Squadron's Flg Off Tony Gubb failed to return from an afternoon reconnaissance, but news was later received that he had landed at Benina. He made his way back to Malta next morning.

During the month, 69 Squadron's Spitfire pilots had flown 159 ops totalling 301 flying hours. Flt Lt Colquhoun logged 24 sorties, closely followed by Wg Cdr Warburton and Plt Off Dalley[131] each with 23, while newcomers Sgt Durbridge, Flg Off Gubb and Plt Off John Frazer[132] notched up 16, 15 and 12 sorties respectively. But the cost to the PR unit had been high with two pilots missing (one killed, one POW) and three aircraft lost.

December

December saw a continuation of the trend set in November, with Spitbomber attacks against Sicilian airfields, escorts to Beaufighters and shipping protection. On the morning of **1 December**, six 249 Spitbombers led by Flt Lt Seed (BR373/T-N) took off to carry out an attack on Biscari airfield, closely escorted by four more led by Plt Off Sanderson (EP833/T-F). Bombs were seen to burst near buildings and aircraft pens. Gela airfield was again targeted during the afternoon, Sqn Ldr Woods (EP343/T-P) leading six Spitbombers while four others acted as close escort, and a further eight from 229 Squadron flew top cover. Bf109s of I/JG53 engaged the top cover, Ltn Wilhelm Crinius of 3 Staffel claiming two Spitfires shot down for his 101st and 102nd victories. One of these was Canadian Plt Off John Mowbray, a 23-year-old from Ontario, who was killed when his aircraft (EN972) was seen to ditch off the coast. Nonetheless, the fighter-bombers took the Gela defences by surprise and several aircraft were damaged on the ground during the attack, with three personnel killed and five wounded.

On the morning of **6 December**, four Spitfire pilots from 185 Squadron – Flt Sgt Red Walker (EP844), Sgt Houlton (EP791), Sgt Reg Bolland (EP722), and Sgt Billing (EP313) – were briefed to fly an armed reconnaissance over Lampedusa and Linosa, departing at 0725. Houlton wrote:

"Our briefing from HQ advised that no Allied aircraft would be anywhere near Lampedusa, and that we should be on the lookout for enemy aircraft from the island. But what began as an interesting patrol ended in a kind of personal nightmare. The patrol went as planned as we turned and dived in wide line abreast over the aerodrome, where only a couple of twin-engined Italian aircraft were to be seen on the ground. As we crossed out very fast at 200 feet a violent barrage of light flak chased us. I glanced ahead and saw a single-engined aircraft with floats, flying low to my left, visible in the bright glare of the sun off the water, and about 500 yards away. Giving a quick call to the section leader, I turned in and down, opening fire at 200 yards. For once both cannons fired, pounding into the sea ahead of the target, while the pattern from the four machine-guns was churning the surface slightly behind it; so I pulled through to hit the wing root, cockpit and engine area with the machine-guns. Simultaneously I glimpsed a roundel on the fuselage and recognised the target as a Hurricane, with long-range fuel tanks under each wing, which I had mistaken for floats.

"I broke away and screamed over the R/T to the other pilots who were turning into attacking positions. From start to finish the sighting and attack were over in about six seconds; then began 45 minutes of the ultimate form of self torture for any fighter pilot. The Hurricane was well riddled in the wing root and lower cockpit area, a sizable chunk of the wing leading edge was missing and the pilot's airspeed was down to 120mph as he nursed the aircraft along, right down to sea level. I realised the Hurricane came from the small RNAS unit at Hal Far, which operated anti-shipping Swordfish and also possessed a couple of Hurricanes.

"Malta appeared out of the haze after what felt like several lifetimes. The Hurricane pilot lowered his wheels and landed straight in at Hal Far, slithering round to the right and stopping in a great cloud of dust on the edge of the field. By the time I completed a circuit and landed, the ambulance was disappearing towards the camp hospital, which screwed my anxiety level right off the clock again. I arrived at the hospital breathless and knocking at the knees to find the naval lieutenant pilot unhurt, which testifies to the benevolence of both our guardian angels on duty that day. He had been returning from a courier flight to the Middle East. To relieve the boredom of just stooging over hundreds of miles of ocean, he had detoured to Lampedusa to strafe shipping in the harbour beside the aerodrome. Pulling out from his last attack, the wing of his Hurricane had hit a schooner, and he just staggered away amongst a storm of flak when we arrived on his back. He said his worst moment was when the tyre of his starboard wheel had been blown apart beneath his right foot, and he had no idea he was being attacked by a fighter until I pulled up alongside him.

"The lieutenant very decently said that he had asked for trouble by attacking the harbour without orders; and we both had enormous strips ripped off us by the authorities, in my case for 'bloody awful' aircraft recognition. A check on my aircraft showed that the 20mm guns were, in fact, incorrectly harmonised well above the machine-guns, which had been the best of good luck for both of us."[133]

Strangely, another of those who participated in this patrol, Sgt Billing provides a different – and probably slightly erroneous – account:

"Red Walker, Twitch Bolland, John Houlton and myself were flying low level, Walker leading just above the water, when Bolland screamed: 'Break port, Jerry.' I stood on the rudder and pulled as hard as I could. The old Spit was juddering madly. Looking back, I could see bullet splashes just inside and below me. I pulled through a 360° turn, gaining height, and rolled inverted to see Twitch was shooting hell out of a Hurricane. The poor chap had mistaken us for Me109s and attacked. At the dispersal I thanked Twitch for saving me, however, he was not feeling well about the whole episode."

The Hurricane pilot, Sub Lt(A) Ernie Pratt in Hurricane BE110, one of the air-sea rescue heroes of recent times, was fortunate to have survived this encounter[134]. It would seem that the bullet splashes Billing had seen were from one of the Spitfires (probably that flown by Bolland) attacking the Hurricane, and not from the Hurricane itself.

Four Spitfires from 185 Squadron were scrambled around 1600 on **7 December**, to intercept a Ju88 off Filfla and this was claimed damaged by Sgt Geoff Guy (BR295), but the 27-year-old Dorset man failed to return, and may have been the victim of return fire, although Bf109s were around, as Sgt Billing was soon to discover:

"Geoff Guy called to say that he had gotten the bastard. We heard no further R/T from him. Geoff was never seen again. From the haze above we were bounced by four 109s. A great hassle followed, with everyone split up to fight alone. Things looked OK until I was bounced by two 109s, a third closing in from the opposite side. He fired, striking my engine. There was a great bang, smoke and fire. Time to go. I immediately pulled hard, jettisoned everything and went over the side. There was no one around on my way down. A few feet above the water I released the chute harness, this being the best procedure not to become tangled in the shrouds. My dinghy inflated OK and I was picked up by an air/sea rescue launch about 30 minutes later. No injuries except to my pride."

His victor was probably Obfw Anton Hafner of 4/JG51, operating from Bizerta. Four 1435 Squadron aircraft had taken off five minutes later on a convoy patrol, and these saw the damaged Ju88 jettisoning a torpedo, and gave chase at zero feet, Sqn Ldr Lovell (EP653/V-F) getting in several bursts before the bomber, 1T+HS of 8/KG26, crashed into the sea in flames. Ltn Werner Herz and his crew were killed.

During the day Sgts Noel Pashen and John Sidey were instructed to fly their Spitfires, fitted with long-range tanks, to Gambut. Both pilots had been ill and were considered unfit for further operations at Malta. Pashen[135] (flying PR Spitfire BP910) wrote:

"Sighted twice by formations of our own fighters and evaded interception both times – once they were coming into attack. Became lost in two electrical storms and landed at LG140 – flew too far inland. Sidey crashed at Mersa Matruh with u/s hydraulics. Managed crafty look at pyramids en route. Eventually reached Kilo 8 next day."

There followed a period of relative inactivity although patrols and sweeps were maintained, but this dramatically changed on **11 December**, when eight 249 Spitfires led by Wg Cdr Grant (EP622/T-P), which were escorting six Beaufighters on an offensive patrol of the Pantelleria-Lampion-Kirkennah area, encountered a formation of 32 Ju52s of KGzbV.1 near Lampion. The lumbering troop transports were flying at sea level, with an escort of three Bf110s of III/ZG26 and two Ju88s some 1,500 feet above them; a lone four-engined aircraft was also seen. The Beaufighters went for the transports, claiming five shot down and three damaged for the loss of one of their own, while the Spitfires tackled the escort. There was an element of double-claiming since four Bf110s were reported shot down, Sqn Ldr Woods (AR559/T-W) and Flg Off Lynch (EP833/T-F) claiming one apiece, Woods also sharing a Ju88 with Flt Sgts Jack Hughes (EP177/T-E) and Morrie Costello (AB535/T-Z). Another Bf110 was shared by Grant and Plt Off Bill Locke (EP132/T-J), and a similar claim was made by Flt Lt Seed (EP728/T-S) and Plt Off Bill Cleverly (BR373/T-N). The Spitfires then attacked the transports, Grant and Seed each claiming one, Lynch a probable, Seed and Costello each one damaged. Seed's aircraft was slightly damaged by a Bf110 though he was able to return safely.

In return, Fw Heinrich Ulrich of 9/ZG26 claimed a 'Hurricane' shot down, and was probably responsible for the damage to Seed's Spitfire. At least two Ju52/3ms of 2 Staffel (1Z+6K and 1Z+DK) were lost. In addition, Bf110 3U+ZR (5156) flown by Fw Hermann Breitenbach of 7 Staffel crashed into the sea with the loss of pilot and gunner (Gfr Günther Reinecke). Obfw Willy Reater and his gunner (Obfw Helmut Schön) of 9 Staffel were also killed when their aircraft (3480) crashed on Pantelleria;

the third Bf110 was also believed to have crashed on the island, although the crew apparently survived.

A Wellington that arrived at Malta from Gibraltar during the hours of darkness carried among its passengers Flt Sgt Les Taylor, a former pilot of 165 Squadron, who had been waiting a couple of months at Gibraltar to ferry a Spitfire to the island. Having at last arrived, he was posted to 229 Squadron. To help pass away the time when off duty or on readiness, pilots devised various pastimes. Sgt Billing recalled:

"A sport which all pilots enjoyed on the island was to be able to have a .38 pistol and to pretty well shoot at will. This sport, of course, carried on into the mess and quarters until at one time it wasn't odd to have pilot after pilot shooting behind over his head in sport as something to do. On one occasion I was rooming with Rastus Sinclair. Old Sinc never appreciated the small long-tailed lizards that plagued the island. They are harmless creatures and it is not uncommon to see them in the quarters, the mess hall or in homes. Each afternoon we would rest. Our beds were covered with a large shawl-type mosquito netting secured at the ceiling then flowing down over the entire bed.

"I hooked up a string to Sinclair's netting and ran it along the wall over to my side of the room. As we entered the room I told Sinc that I had seen a bloody lizard in the room that day. He immediately took his .38 pistol and put it beside the pillow. As we lay down, I grabbed the string and gave a jerk. Sinc jumped up horizontally and sat bolt upright. Of course, seeing me lying in my bed undisturbed, he said, 'rotten bastard lizards', and began to search for it. I saw him nearing the string and I departed from my bed but quick, Sinc in close pursuit. I thought I'd fool him and double-back into our room. He guessed my move and trapped me as I entered the room. He fired his gun almost point blank as I ducked to the floor. The bullet barely missed my head and lodged itself into the wall, just below a mounted goat's head that I had acquired and hung as a decoration."

On another occasion Billing received a caution for his boisterous behaviour:

"I was stopped by a Maltese called Manuel who tried to sell me an old-fashioned Colt – I don't think it would even fire. Getting quite cheesed off with the conversation, I took out my small Italian automatic and aimed it at him. He got quite scared and started to turn towards the dispersal, so I fired a couple of rounds into the sky. My Jesus, the change of pace was terrific. On entering the dispersal room I was greeted by the Wingco and he started lecturing me on firing at people and thought perhaps he would have to take our guns away from us. I was brassed off with this as we were going to fly in approximately 20 minutes, so why the hell couldn't he leave us alone?"

Four 249 Squadron Spitfires flew an armed reconnaissance at 1550 on **13 December**, meeting ten Bf109s and three Ju88s over Pantelleria at 1,000 feet. Flg Off Lynch (EP833/T-F) and Plt Off Stead (AB535/T-Z) claimed to have damaged one of the bombers between them and, in fact, a Ju88 (142147) of II/KG30 was lost when returning from an attack on Malta. The crew survived, so were presumably rescued by an Axis craft from Sicily or Pantelleria. A late morning convoy patrol led by Wg Cdr Grant ended when Sgt Ginger Bage was obliged to bale out of EP557 owing to engine trouble; he was soon rescued from the sea, none the worse for the dunking. AR466/T-R force-landed on return and was written-off, though the pilot was not hurt. 69 Squadron's Plt Off Frazer (BR424) had a narrow escape during an afternoon sortie to Palermo, Trapani and Augusta when intercepted by a Bf109. The Australian from New South Wales later reported:

"I heard a short burst of cannon fire and on looking out of port blister saw a 109 pass about 50 feet under my port wing, in a dive. I next saw it reappear about 1,000 feet below from behind my starboard wing, still diving and turning to starboard. I headed out to sea at full throttle. Aircraft not damaged."

Next day (**14 December**), 249 again provided cover for a single Beaufighter on a reconnassiance over Lampedusa, where at 1040 a Ju88 of II/KG30 was seen to the south-west of the island. The bomber was promptly shot down by the combined attacks of Flg Off Lynch (EP140/T-M), Plt Off Stead (BR373/T-N) and Sgt Bill Stark (EP706/T-L), the survivors observed getting into a dinghy. At 1305 four Spitfires set out again to escort a single Beaufighter on another mission to the same area, meeting another Ju88 of II/KG30 west of Lampedusa. The Beaufighter, flown by Wg Cdr Buck Buchanan[136], was joined by Sqn Ldr Woods and Flt Lt Seed (EP708/T-U) in making stern attacks on the bomber until it caught fire and spun into the sea. One of the bombers was 4D+DM (140431) of 4 Staffel, flown by Oblt Karl Rauhmacher, the other 4D+EN (140386) flown by Ltn Walter Klauser of 5 Staffel; there were no survivors from either machine.

The Beaufighter escorts continued on **15 December**, four Spitfires from 126 Squadron departing at 1135 to patrol over Lampedusa, where, at 1325, a formation of transports – estimated as 15 in number and identified as Ju52s – with top cover of fighters were seen north of the island. These were in fact nine SM81s of 18°Stormo Trasporti, that had departed Sciacca aerodrome in Sicily and were headed for Lampedusa, covered by five MC202s from 153°Gruppo CT. As the Beaufighters went after the transports, claiming one destroyed, one probable and a damaged, the Spitfires held off the escort. Plt Off Yeatman (MK-S) claimed a fighter probably destroyed, believing it to have been a Bf109. The Italians admitted the loss of two SM81s (MM2071 and MM20516) shot down in flames, from which there were no survivors, but claimed two Beaufighters and five Spitfires in the engagement. There were no RAF losses.

Eleven Spitfires, led by Sqn Ldr Woods, and five Beaufighters set out on offensive reconnaissance off the Tunisian coast at 1100 next day (**16 December**). A flight of three twin-engined aircraft was seen and as the Spitfires closed, they were fired upon, Flt Lt Seed's aircraft (EP708/T-U) sustaining damage[137]. Seed returned the fire but broke away on recognising the bombers as Bostons (*sic*) – they were in fact Marauders of 14 Squadron – which then identified themselves by firing the colours of the day. By then, however, it was too late for the aircraft – FK367/CX-J – fired at by Seed, which crashed into the sea 15 miles off Benghazi with the loss of four of the crew. The Australian pilot, Sgt Len Einsaar RAAF, was rescued by an ASR launch after two hours in the sea, as were two others[138]. Seed, meanwhile, belly-landed his damaged Spitfire on returning to Luqa.

69 Squadron's Sgt David Howard (BR424) had a narrow escape during a morning PR sortie covering Sfax, Lampedusa and Tunis. When over Sousse he experienced heavy flak and one burst off his starboard wing upturned his aircraft, but he was able to regain control and made a safe return to Luqa.

For the second consecutive day bad weather prevented much activity, although the Beaufighters and Spitfires continued regular patrols between Sicily and Africa. Four Beaufighters and six Spitfires of 249 Squadron took off at 0800 on **17 December**, on a sweep, and at the same time four 1435 Squadron Spitfires were scrambled to intercept six Ju52s, three of which were claimed shot down, two by Flt Lt Walton (AR561/V-J) and one by Sgt Kebbell (EP519/V-U), Walton also claiming a probable, but Sgt Jimmy Harrison (EN980/V-W), a 22-year-old from Kent, failed to return. His body was later recovered from the sea by *HSL107*.

Two Ju52s were actually lost, one machine (5046) from KGrzbV.600 flown by Uffz Wolfgang Lange, crashing into the sea with the loss of the crew; the other – 5157 from IV/KGzbV.1 – carried out an emergency landing. A third Ju52, flown by Uffz Josef Aichinger, was apparently shot down by German flak on reaching Trapani, and all four members of the crew were killed. It is not known if this machine had been part of the formation attacked by 1435 Squadron. Meanwhile the 249 Squadron pilots proceeded with their sweep, one Spitfire returning early with technical trouble. At 1020, two Ju88s were seen east of Cape Passero. These were from Erg/LG1 operating out of Catania – L1+RV (140189) of 11 Staffel flown by Obfw Gerhard Meyer-Döhner and L1+DW (8612) of 12 Staffel (Ltn Dieter Hahn) – their destination Castel Benito (Libya). All aircraft attacked, Flg Off Lynch (EP343/T-P) and Flt Sgt Costello (EP131/T-O) sharing one with a Beaufighter pilot (Flt Sgt Pien), Lynch and Plt Off Locke (EP140/T-M) then sharing the second with another Beaufighter pilot (Sqn Ldr Rankin). Both Ju88s crashed into the sea. There were no survivors.

During the afternoon Sqn Ldr Woods led four Spitbombers from 249 Squadron to Lampedusa where the landing ground was bombed. Light inaccurate flak was experienced over the target. This raid was followed by a strafing attack by six Spitfires of 1435 Squadron. About eight aircraft were sighted on the ground, Sqn Ldr Lovell (EP619/V-I) claiming to have destroyed an SM79, Wg Cdr Hanks (BR498/PP-H) probably getting a second and also damaging one, and Flt Sgt Ken Ilsley (EP444/V-B) hitting a Bf109. Two more transports were claimed damaged, by Sgts Freddy Sharp (EP717/V-D) and Gordon Bray (EP519/V-U), but Plt Off Tom Sullivan (BR376/V-V) failed to return. He was rescued from the sea by an Italian craft and taken prisoner. It seems that the aircraft targeted were in fact the seven surviving SM81s from the formation attacked in the air two days earlier, and five of these (including MM20258, MM20259, MM20596 and MM20644) were destroyed during the strafe. From Malta *HSL128* also effected another successful rescue during the day, picking up 1435 Squadron's Sgt Dave Fuller, who had baled out some 40 miles out to sea, presumably due to engine malfunction.

At 0600 on **18 December**, Sgt David Howard of 69 Squadron took off from Malta at 0830 in Spitfire BR426 to photograph the Taranto and Augusta area; he did not return. It seems probable he was shot down by Uffz Jens Bahnsen of 8/JG53, who claimed a Spitfire (his eighth victory) at 0941 some 20 miles north-west of Valetta. An intensive search was carried out, Sgt Garvey (GL-U) of 185 Squadron being among those who spotted Howard's body in his dinghy. Having survived a life-threatening incident two days earlier, Howard's luck had run out. Four 249 Spitfires escorted two Beaufighters on an offensive reconnaissance at 0840 on **19 December**; soon after 1100 a Do24 and a Ju88 were seen near Delimara at between 500 feet and 1,000 feet, and at once Sqn Ldr Woods (EP728/T-S) shot down the flyingboat, as he noted: "Offensive recce – east of Malta. Dornier 24 destroyed. Hit in elevators by return fire. OK."

The crew of the flyingboat – KK+UP (0011) from 6 Seenotstaffel – survived and were later themselves rescued. The Dornier's gunner claimed the attacking Spitfire shot down. Meanwhile, Plt Off Locke (EP186/T-K) and Flt Sgt Hughes (BR373/T-N) engaged the Ju88 – 1T+AD (140432) of Stab III/KG26 commanded by the Gruppenkommandeur Major Horst Kayser – and shot this down with assistance from the Beaufighter leader, Wg Cdr Buchanan. Prior to its destruction, the bomber's gunner, Obgfr Werner Schmuck, had hit the second Beaufighter as it attacked, which crashed into the sea with the loss of the crew (the Beaufighter pilot was Belgian Sgt Henri Pien, who had shared in shooting down a Ju88 with 249 Squadron two days earlier). Flt Sgt Costello (EP825/T-Z) crashed on landing at Qrendi on returning from this sortie although he was unhurt.

With Christmas approaching, Wg Cdr Warburton suddenly departed Malta at the controls of a battered, but recently repaired Wellington bomber that had been struck off charge following a bombing raid on Luqa many months before. It had been made flyable by groundcrews of 69 Squadron at Warburton's instruction in preparation for this special flight – to Cairo and back with a load of Christmas booze and other goodies. It has to be assumed that the AOC and Luqa's OC had turned a blind eye to these events, unless, of course, they had furnished Warburton with their own shopping lists.

On **23 December**, two Spitfires from 126 Squadron, on an armed reconnaissance, encountered six Ju88s covering a destroyer in the Gulf of Hammamet. They went in to attack and Flt Lt Jack Long (AB526/MK-P) claimed one shot down and damaged a second, with new pilot Sgt Allen Hunter (AR497/MK-E) also damaging one. Both returned safely. While practice flying over St Paul's Bay, four Spitfires of 1435 Squadron were vectored on to two Bf109s, which were subsequently chased to within 30 miles of Sicily, Sgts Sharp (AR561/V-J) and Laurie McDougall (EP833/T-F) jointly claiming one damaged. Sqn Ldr White led a bombing attack by four Spitfires of 185 Squadron on Lampedusa, as noted by the diarist:

> "Four intrepid types of B Flight under the CO made a bombing attack on Lampedusa. Eight 250lb bombs were duly dropped but wispy cloud made observations of results difficult, although two hits were seen on the aerodrome. There was some flak and Sgt [Al] Laing got a piece in his radiator, which fortunately was not serious."

185 Squadron later scrambled a section when four Bf109s were reported approaching, following which Flt Sgt Bob McLaren's aircraft developed a glycol leak and he carried out a belly-landing on return. The 22-year-old Canadian from Ontario was unhurt.

On Christmas Eve (**24 December**) eight Spitfires from 249 Squadron carried out a patrol between Lampedusa and Pantelleria, Flt Lt Seed returning early with engine trouble. Although the ORB states 'no sighting', Sandy Sanderson (T-F) noted in his logbook:

> "Searched Lampedusa area. Shared Me110 with Jimmy. Good party. Huns gave us a little sneak raid for Xmas! Nice types."

Next day – **Christmas Day** – Sqn Ldr Woods of 249 Squadron led Plt Off Locke, Flt Sgts Costello and Hughes on an offensive patrol over southern Sicily, sighting two locomotives about 20 miles inland. Both were strafed and many strikes were seen, followed by much steam. Both were claimed probably destroyed. 249 Squadron's fighter-bombers returned to Lampedusa on **26 December**, where Flt Lt Seed (T-T) saw his two bombs explode between two aircraft. Four Spitfires from 185 Squadron were scrambled at 1430 to intercept six Bf109s, Flg Off Cheek claiming damage to one. There occurred another scramble at 1235 next day (**27 December**), four Spitfires from 229 Squadron intercepting a Bf109G on a weather reconnaissance, Plt Off Arthur Chaplin, a South African from Johannesburg, shooting down Uffz Ludwig Laue of 7/JG53 over Gozo, whose White 7 (16023) crashed into the sea with the loss of the pilot. One of the escorting Messerschmitt pilots Oblt Wilfried Pufahl claimed a Spitfire in return, for his tenth victory, but there were no losses. Four Spitfires from 249 Squadron again escorted four Beaufighters on **29 December**, carrying out a sweep of the Gulf of Hammamet. At 1529, a Ju88 of II/KG54 was seen near

Pantelleria and was shot down by the Beaufighter leader (Wg Cdr Buchanan) before the Spitfires could engage. Plt Off Locke crash-landed EP728/T-S on return but was unhurt. Another Spitfire, EP313 of 185 Squadron, was badly damaged when it taxied into a vehicle. On the last day of the year (**31 December**) Wg Cdr Mike Stephens led six 185 Squadron Spitfires to bomb Lampedusa airfield once again:

> "But the only result observed was two strikes – in the sea! Cloud made accurate observation difficult, so the last day of the old year passed without seeing any enemy aircraft."

How different from the start of 1942 and the subsequent twelve months. The tide had really turned.

* * *

Conclusion

The defence of Malta was not just about swirling dogfights in the blue Mediterranean sky between Spitfires, Messerschmitts and Macchis; the task of the defenders was to repel the incessant bombing attacks and to prevent an Axis invasion of the island. In this they succeeded notably, and it was in part the high attrition amongst Kesselring's bomber force that led to the cessation of attacks following the October blitz – as had happened in 1940 during the Battle of Britain. By the end of 1942 the German air force had become overstretched with too many fronts to support. Each time the Luftwaffe appeared to be achieving aerial supremacy, the greater demands of other fronts led to dispersion elsewhere, while the Regia Aeronautica lacked suitable aircraft for such a task.

Malta's survival as a base for interdiction of Axis supplies played a major part in aiding the success of British operations in North Africa, whilst the need to maintain substantial air forces in Sicily denied Rommel the reinforcements he desperately required to counter the RAF's Desert Air Force. Once the Allies had landed in French North Africa in November 1942, many of Sicily's air units were diverted to this new theatre of war. Malta was saved and the siege was lifted. There can be no doubt that the Spitfires and their pilots played a major rôle in the successes achieved. Allied forces continued to build up at Malta and six months later, in July 1943, the island was pivotal in the invasion of Sicily – a turning point in the Mediterranean theatre of war*. By the eve of the invasion no fewer than 23 Spitfire fighter squadrons were based at Malta and Gozo (where an airstrip had been hurriedly constructed to house three squadrons of USAAF Spitfires), plus two Spitfire reconnaissance units, totalling some 400 aircraft.

The statistics

But the cost had been high – 102 Spitfires pilots lost their lives in 1942 defending the skies of Malta, 45 from Britain, 20 Canadians, 12 New Zealanders, 10 Australians, 10 Americans, three Rhodesians, one South African, and one Frenchman in the RCAF. Some 600 victories were claimed by the Spitfire pilots during this period (see Appendix II), with many more probables. Plt Off Screwball Beurling emerged as the top-scorer by far with $26^1/_2$ victories, while Flt Sgt Paddy Schade was credited with $13^1/_2$, and Flt Lt Wally McLeod, Plt Off Ray Hesselyn and Plt Off Slim Yarra each notched up a dozen; 31 others achieved acedom while flying from Malta (see Appendix III).

German records reveal in excess of 250 total losses of aircraft, with a further 30 severely damaged and written off. Almost two-thirds of these were Ju88s. In the brief

October blitz two bomber Gruppenkommandeurs had been lost. At least 70 Bf109s were shot down and some 45 Messerschmitt pilots lost their lives. In return, Luftwaffe fighter pilots' claims approached the 400 mark, with Hptm Gerhard Michalski of II/JG53 heading the list with 26 victories, closely followed by Oblt Siegfried Freytag of I/JG77 with 24, and Obfw Herbert Rollwage of 5/JG53 with 20. Fourteen others claimed five or more. The fighter pilots of the Regia Aeronautica saw only limited action and were credited with far fewer victories, although claims on occasion were extremely high. Between May and July alone, over 100 Spitfires were claimed shot down by Italian pilots, the final total being in excess of 150. Cap Furio Doglio Niclot was credited with nine (three shared), M.llo Ennio Tarantola with eight (three shared) and Ten Agostino Celentano with five. At least 60 MC202s and RE2001s were lost on operations and 39 Italian fighter pilots killed. Other losses included 24 tri-motors (mainly Z1007bis, SM84, SM79 bombers/torpedo-bombers; and at least five transports); four Ju87s, three Z506Bs including one hijacked, and one RS14.

* For an account of Malta's Spitfires during the first six months of 1943 leading up to and including the invasion of Sicily in July 1943, see the authors' *Spitfires over Sicily*.

APPENDIX I

ROLL OF HONOUR

Spitfire Pilots Killed Malta 1942

10/3/42	Plt Off Kenric Newton Lathrop MURRAY RAAF	249 Sqn	Spitfire AB343
17/3/42	Flt Sgt Ian Maxwell CORMACK	249 Sqn	Spitfire AB330
18/3/42	Plt Off Harold Mitchell FOX	249 Sqn	Spitfire AB334
20/3/42	Plt Off Douglas Cecil LEGGO (Rhod)	249 Sqn	Spitfire AB337
21/3/42	Flg Off John Charles Mortimer BOOTH	249 Sqn	on ground
	Plt Off James Joseph GUERIN RAAF	249 Sqn	on ground
2/4/42	Plt Off Winston McCARTHY RCAF	126 Sqn	Spitfire BP844
20/4/42	Plt Off Hiram Aldine PUTNAM RCAF (US)	126 Sqn	Spitfire AB336
	Plt Off George Albert Jack RYCKMAN RCAF	126 Sqn	Spitfire BP969
21/4/42	Plt Off Stanley Frederick BROOKER RCAF	126 Sqn	Spitfire BP977
22/4/42	Plt Off Gordon MURRAY RCAF (US)	603 Sqn	Spitfire BP970
	Plt Off Frank James JEMMETT (died in hospital)	126 Sqn	Spitfire BR180
25/4/42	Plt Off Kenneth William PAWSON	601 Sqn	Spitfire BP973
26/4/42	Plt Off Walter Ephrain CRIPPS RCAF	601 Sqn	Spitfire BR125
4/5/42	Flt Lt Norman Carter MACQUEEN DFC	249 Sqn	Spitfire BR226
9/5/42	Plt Off Harold Ashton MILBURN	249 Sqn	Spitfire BP845
	Plt Off Gordon Russell TWEEDALE DFM RAAF	185 Sqn	Spitfire BR248
	Flt Lt John Walter BUCKSTONE	603 Sqn	Spitfire BP872
	Flt Lt Raymond Harold Charles SLY RAAF	USS *Wasp*	Spitfire BR348
10/5/42	Plt Off George Maxwell BRIGGS RAAF	601 Sqn	Spitfire BR282
12/5/42	Plt Off Herbert Robert MITCHELL RNZAF	603 Sqn	Spitfire BR127
	Sgt Charles Edward GRAYSMARK	601 Sqn	Spitfire BR196
14/5/42	Plt Off John Livingstone BOYD DFM RAAF	185 Sqn	Spitfire BR349
	Sgt Colin Vernon FINLAY	185 Sqn	Spitfire BR291
	Flt Sgt Harold Joseph FOX RCAF (US)	249 Sqn	Spitfire BR878
17/5/42	Plt Off Peter Alfred NASH DFC	249 Sqn	Spitfire BP951
20/5/42	Sgt Frank Stanley HOWARD (Rhod) (wounded 17/5/42)	601 Sqn	Spitfire BR344
25/5/42	Plt Off Walter Alexander CALDWELL RNZAF	601 Sqn	Spitfire BR354
1/6/42	Plt Off Andrew Albert McNAUGHTON RCAF	185 Sqn	Spitfire BP950
8/6/42	Flg Off Leslie George BARLOW (SA)	603 Sqn	Spitfire BR231
15/6/42	Sgt Jack Nock McCONNELL RNZAF	601 Sqn	Spitfire BR306
26/6/42	Flt Sgt Maurice Ernest TOMKINS	249 Sqn	Spitfire BR382
2/7/42	Plt Off John HURST DFC	603 Sqn	Spitfire BR184
	Plt Off Harry KELLY (US)	249 Sqn	Spitfire BR356
6/7/42	Flt Sgt Edwin DeWitt MOYE RCAF (US)	185 Sqn	Spitfire BP979
7/7/42	Flt Sgt Peter Clifford TERRY	185 Sqn	Spitfire BR317
	Flt Sgt Haydn HAGGAS	185 Sqn	Spitfire BR283
8/7/42	Flg Off Neville Stuart KING	603 Sqn	Spitfire BR198
	Flg Off John SMITH	249 Sqn	Spitfire BR233
	Plt Off John Carlton GILBERT	249 Sqn	Spitfire BR227
9/7/42	Flg Off Guy André LEVY-DESPAS RCAF (French)	603 Sqn	Spitfire BP957
	Plt Off John Longton HICKS	126 Sqn	Spitfire BR355
10/7/42	Flt Sgt Bernard Walter REYNOLDS RCAF	126 Sqn	Spitfire BR244
11/7/42	Plt Off Charles Benn RAMSAY RCAF	249 Sqn	Spitfire BR111
12/7/42	Flg Off Owen William Hugh BERKELEY-HILL	249 Sqn	Spitfire BR324
19/7/42	Flt Sgt Joseph Edward OTIS RCAF (US)	126 Sqn	Spitfire BP861
20/7/42	Plt Off Hugh Robert RUSSEL RCAF	185 Sqn	Spitfire BR117
22/7/42	Plt Off Donald George REID DFM RCAF	185 Sqn	Spitfire BR203
	Plt Off Joseph Hubert Roger PARADIS RCAF	249 Sqn	Spitfire BR128
23/7/42	Flg Off David William KENT	185 Sqn	Hurricane Z2825
28/7/42	Sgt Donald Frank HUBBARD	1435 Sqn	Spitfire EP189
30/7/42	Sgt Colin Lethbridge WOOD RNZAF	1435 Sqn	Spitfire EP344
2/8/42	Plt Off James William GUTHRIE	185 Sqn	Spitfire BR362
	Sgt Matthew Leonard McLEOD RNZAF	185 Sqn	Spitfire BR321

Date	Name	Squadron	Aircraft
8/8/42	Sgt Clarence Lloyd KELLY RNZAF	1435 Sqn	Spitfire EP336
10/8/42	Plt Off Jerrold Alpine SMITH RCAF	126 Sqn	Spitfire BR366
13/8/42	Flt Sgt Robert Athol BUNTINE RAAF	1435 Sqn	Spitfire EP197
	Flt Sgt John Harold TANNER RNZAF	126 Sqn	Spitfire EP472
25/8/42	Flg Off Reginald Pearson ROUND RNZAF	249 Sqn	Spitfire EN976
	Flt Sgt Basil BUTLER RCAF	249 Sqn	Spitfire EP695
26/8/42	Flg Off Dudley Gerald NEWMAN	229 Sqn	Spitfire EP190
	Sgt Clifford Harry CORNISH	229 Sqn	Spitfire BR496
27/8/42	Grp Capt Walter Myers CHURCHILL DSO DFC	Takali Wing	Spitfire EP339
28/8/42	Flt Lt Ernest Pendleton Francis Louis Tarcisius MAGRUDER	229 Sqn	Spitfire BP871
29/8/42	Plt Off Dennis Patrick POLLOCK	1435 Sqn	Spitfire BS160
13/9/42	Flt Sgt Lawrence Harold SWAIN	185 Sqn	Spitfire BR374
15/9/42	Flt Sgt Bernard Charles PETERS	249 Sqn	Spitfire BP867
	Plt Off John Richard SCOTT RCAF	229 Sqn	Spitfire BR486
23/9/42	Plt Off Ian Fraser PRESTON RCAF (US)	126 Sqn	Spitfire BR383
4/10/42	Flt Sgt Murray IRVING GASS	249 Sqn	Spitfire EP700
	Flt Sgt George Alexander HOGARTH RCAF	249 Sqn	Spitfire BR379
11/10/42	Flt Sgt David Derek MacLEAN RNZAF	126 Sqn	Spitfire BR183
12/10/42	Sqn Ldr Bryan John WICKS DFC	126 Sqn	Spitfire BR377
	Sgt John Douglas VINALL	185 Sqn	Spitfire EP139
	Flt Sgt Ronald Alfred STEVENSON	1435 Sqn	Spitfire EP209
13/10/42	Flt Sgt Alexander Owen MacLEOD RCAF	185 Sqn	Spitfire EP316
14/10/42	Flt Sgt William Bedlington KNOX-WILLIAMS RAAF	1435 Sqn	Spitfire AR470
	Sgt Ronald John ROE RNZAF	1435 Sqn	Spitfire EP203
15/10/42	Wt Off Edwin Tytler HISKENS RAAF	249 Sqn	Spitfire EP340
16/10/42	Flg Off Edward Wilson WALLACE RCAF	126 Sqn	Spitfire BP992
	Wt Off Peter CARTER RCAF (US)	249 Sqn	Spitfire EP338
	Sgt William Renton WILSON	1435 Sqn	Spitfire EP718
17/10/42	Flt Lt Ripley Ogden JONES (US)	126 Sqn	Spitfire EP341
	Flt Sgt Ronald MILLER	229 Sqn	Spitfire BP955
18/10/42	Flg Off James Douglas STEVENSON RCAF	126 Sqn	Spitfire EP332
23/10/42	Flg Off Alec Ian LINDSAY	185 Sqn	Spitfire EP685
24/10/42	Sgt Raymond Harold SAUNDERS	185 Sqn	Spitfire EP467
25/10/42	Plt Off Nigel Manfred PARK DFM RNZAF	126 Sqn	Spitfire BR311
29/10/42	Flt Sgt Walter PARKS RAAF	229 Sqn	Spitfire EP329
1/11/42	Plt Off Russell Albert WRIGHT (Rhod)	1435 Sqn	Spitfire EP138
15/11/42	Plt Off Francis Charles Martineau JEMMETT RCAF	69 Sqn	PR Spitfire BS359
	Sgt John Edward ROBERTS	249 Sqn	Spitfire EP199
19/11/42	Plt Off Gardner Hill KELLY RCAF (US)	126 Sqn	Spitfire BP952
	Sgt Henry ROBERTS RNZAF	126 Sqn	Spitfire EP260
	Plt Off Robert Bruce PARK RAAF	185 Sqn	Spitfire EP823
21/11/42	Flt Sgt Martin Aloysius LUNDY	229 Sqn	Spitfire EN954
22/11/42	Plt Off Anthony Richard Hutton MAYNARD	185 Sqn	Spitfire EP696
23/11/42	Sgt Thomas WALLACE	229 Sqn	Spitfire EP832
28/11/42	Flt Sgt George Sydney EDWARDS RCAF	229 Sqn	Spitfire AB520
1/12/42	Flg Off John Roy MOWBRAY RCAF	249 Sqn	Spitfire EN972
7/12/42	Sgt Daniel Geoffrey GUY	185 Sqn	Spitfire BR295
17/12/42	Sgt James Martin HARRISON	1435 Sqn	Spitfire EN980
18/12/42	Sgt David Trevor HOWARD	69 Sqn	PR Spifire BR426

Spitfire pilots killed in the Liberator crash at Gibraltar

31/10/42	Flt Lt Erik Lawson HETHERINGTON DFC	249 Sqn
	Plt Off John William WILLIAMS DFC RCAF	249 Sqn
	Flt Lt Edwin Herbert GLAZEBROOK DFC RCAF	229 Sqn
	Flt Sgt Charles Edward MUTCH RCAF	249 Sqn
	Sgt Rupert Henry DAVEY RCAF	126 Sqn

Spitfire pilots killed on ferry flights to Malta

9/5/42	Sgt Robert Donald SHERRINGTON RCAF	USS *Wasp*	Spitfire BP972?
	Flt Sgt Charles Napoleon VALIQUET RCAF	USS *Wasp*	Spitfire BP965?
	Flt Sgt John Vaughan ROUNSEFELL RCAF	USS *Wasp*	Spitfire BP971?
3/6/42	Flg Off James Howard MENARY	HMS *Eagle*	Spitfire BR322
	Plt Off David Francis ROULEAU RCAF	HMS *Eagle*	Spitfire BR358
	Flt Sgt Hugh Douglas Kingsley MacPHERSON RCAF	HMS *Eagle*	Spitfire BR308
	Flt Sgt Thomas Francis BEAUMONT	HMS *Eagle*	Spitfire BR313
21/7/42	Sgt Lewis EVANS	HMS *Eagle*	Spitfire EP703?
17/8/42	Sgt William Joseph Alexander FLEMING	HMS *Furious*	Spitfire EP194

APPENDIX II

COMBAT CLAIMS

10/3/42	Flt Lt P.W.E. Heppell	249 Sqn AB262	Bf109
	Plt Off P.A. Nash	249 Sqn AB335	Bf109 probable
	Plt Off J.A. Plagis (Rhod)	249 Sqn AB346	Bf109 probable
11/3/42	Sqn Ldr S.B. Grant	249 Sqn AB262	Bf109 probable
14/3/42	Flt Lt N.C. Macqueen	249 Sqn	Bf109
15/3/42	Flt Lt W.C. Connell RCAF	249 Sqn AB346	Ju88
17/3/42	Sgt V.P. Brennan RAAF	249 Sqn AB346	Bf109
18/3/42	Flt Lt N.C. Macqueen	249 Sqn	Bf109
	Plt Off R.A. Sergeant	249 Sqn AB336	Bf109 probable
20/3/42	Flt Lt R.W. McNair RCAF	249 Sqn AB341	Bf109
22/3/42	Flt Lt N.C. Macqueen	249 Sqn	Bf109
23/3/42	Flt Lt H.A.S. Johnston	126 Sqn	Ju88
	Flt Lt N.C. Macqueen ⎫	249 Sqn	
	Plt Off R.A. Sergeant ⎬	249 Sqn AB344	Ju88
	2 Hurricane pilots ⎭	185 Sqn	
	Plt Off M.A. Graves	126 Sqn	Ju88
24/3/42	Plt Off J.E. Peck (US)	126 Sqn	Bf109
	Plt Off D.W. McLeod (US)	126 Sqn	Bf109
	Flt Lt H.A.S. Johnston	126 Sqn	Ju87 probable
25/3/42	Sqn Ldr S.B. Grant	249 Sqn	Ju87, Bf109
	Plt Off J.A. Plagis (Rhod)	249 Sqn BP850	Ju87, Ju87 probable
	Plt Off P.A. Nash	249 Sqn AB264	Ju87
	Plt Off D.W. McLeod (US)	126 Sqn	Bf109
26/3/42	Sgt V.P. Brennan RAAF ⎫	249 Sqn AB335	
	Flt Lt W.C. Connell RCAF ⎬	249 Sqn GN-L	Ju88
	Flt Lt R.W. McNair RCAF ⎭	249 Sqn AB264	
	Flt Lt W.C. Connell RCAF	249 Sqn GN-L	Ju87
	Flg Off G.A.F. Buchanan (Rhod) ⎫	249 Sqn GN-L	
	Flt Lt W.C. Connell RCAF ⎬	249 Sqn	Ju88
	Flt Lt R.W. McNair RCAF ⎭	249 Sqn AB264	
	Flt Lt H.A.S. Johnston	126 Sqn BP850	Ju87, Ju87 probable
28/3/42	Sqn Ldr S.B. Grant ⎫	249 Sqn	
	Flg Off N.W. Lee ⎬	249 Sqn	Ju88 probable
	Plt Off J.A. Plagis (Rhod) ⎥	249 Sqn AB346	
	Plt Off P.A. Nash ⎭	249 Sqn AB335	
30/3/42	Flt Lt N.C. Macqueen ⎫	249 Sqn	Ju88 probable
	Flg Off W.R. Daddo-Langlois ⎭	249 Sqn AB337	
1/4/42	Plt Off J.A. Plagis (Rhod)	249 Sqn AB335	Bf109, Ju88
	Plt Off J.A. Plagis (Rhod) ⎫	249 Sqn AB335	
	2 Hurricane pilots ⎭	185 Sqn	Ju88 probable
	Plt Off P.A. Nash	249 Sqn GN-Z	Ju88
	Plt Off J.A. Plagis (Rhod)	249 Sqn AB335	Bf109

	Sgt R.B. Hesselyn RNZAF	249 Sqn	Bf109
	Plt Off P.A. Nash	249 Sqn BP844	Ju87
	Plt Off J.A. Plagis (Rhod)	249 Sqn AB335	Ju87
	Sgt R.B. Hesselyn RNZAF	249 Sqn	Ju87
	Sqn Ldr S.B. Grant	249 Sqn	Ju87 probable
	Flg Off G.A.F. Buchanan (Rhod)	249 Sqn AB451	Ju87 probable
2/4/42	Sqn Ldr E.J. Gracie	126 Sqn	Ju88 probable
	Plt Off M.A. Graves	126 Sqn	Ju88 probable
4/4/42	Flt Lt N.C. Macqueen	249 Sqn	Ju88
5/4/42	Plt Off J.H. Bisley RAAF	126 Sqn	Ju87, Ju88
	Plt Off H.A. Putnam (US)	126 Sqn	Ju88
	Flt Lt H.A.S. Johnston	126 Sqn	Bf109
8/4/42	Plt Off J.G. West RNZAF	249 Sqn	Bf109
	Flt Lt P.W.E. Heppell	249 Sqn	Ju88
	Flt Lt P.W.E. Heppell⎤	249 Sqn	
	Flg Off R. West ⎬	249 Sqn	Ju88
	2 Hurricane pilots ⎦	185 Sqn	
	Plt Off D.W. Kelly	249 Sqn	Ju88
	Flg Off R. West	249 Sqn	Bf109
10/4/42	Flt Lt N.C. Macqueen⎤	249 Sqn	
	Flg Off N.W. Lee ⎬	249 Sqn	Ju88
	AA Command ⎦		
	Flg Off G.A.F. Buchanan (Rhod)	249 Sqn BP844	Bf109
	Flg Off N.W. Lee	249 Sqn	Ju88 probable
	Plt Off P.A. Nash	249 Sqn GN-X	Bf109, Ju87 probable
14/4/42	Flt Lt N.C. Macqueen⎤	249 Sqn	Bf109
	Plt Off R.A. Sergeant⎦	249 Sqn AB340	
20/4/42	Sgt J.L. Tayleur	249 Sqn BR465	Ju87 probable
	Flg Off W.R. Daddo-Langlois	249 Sqn GN-C	Bf109
	Flt Lt R.W. McNair RCAF	249 Sqn GN-K	Bf109
	Flg Off R. West	249 Sqn	Ju87
	Flg Off G.A.F. Buchanan (Rhod)	249 Sqn 1-W	Bf109
	Sgt R.B. Hesselyn RNZAF	249 Sqn BR192	Bf109
	Flt Lt N.C. Macqueen	249 Sqn	Ju88
	Plt Off R.A. Sergeant	249 Sqn 1-L	Ju88
	Flt Sgt V.P. Brennan RAAF	249 Sqn BR192	Bf109, Ju88
	Flt Lt R.W. McNair RCAF	249 Sqn GN-K	Bf109 probable, Ju88 probable
21/4/42	Sqn Ldr S.B. Grant ⎤	249 Sqn	Ju88
	Plt Off J.A. Plagis (Rhod)⎦	249 Sqn AB263	
	Sqn Ldr E.J. Gracie	126 Sqn BR125	2 Ju88s
	Sgt A.P. Goldsmith RAAF	126 Sqn BP964	Bf109
	Plt Off J.A. Plagis (Rhod)	249 Sqn AB263	Bf109 probable
	Sgt R.B. Hesselyn RNZAF	249 Sqn	Ju87, Bf109
	Flg Off G.A.F. Buchanan (Rhod)	249 Sqn BP966	Ju87
	Sqn Ldr J.D. Bisdee	601 Sqn BP964	Ju88
	Flt Sgt V.P. Brennan RAAF	249 Sqn BR192	Ju88 probable
	Flt Lt N.C. Macqueen	249 Sqn	Bf109
	Flg Off G.A.F. Buchanan (Rhod)	249 Sqn BP966	Ju88
22/4/42	Flt Lt R.W. McNair RCAF ⎤	249 Sqn BP968	
	Plt Off W.E. Cripps RCAF ⎬	601 Sqn BP969	Ju88
	Plt Off W.J.E. Hagger (Rhod)⎮	601 Sqn BP975	
	Sgt L.F. Webster ⎦	603 Sqn BP973	
	Flt Sgt J. Hurst	603 Sqn	Bf109
	Flt Lt A.R.H. Barton	126 Sqn BR120	Ju87, Ju87 probable
	Plt Off J. Bailey	126 Sqn BR125	Ju88 probable
23/4/42	Sqn Ldr E.J. Gracie⎤	126 Sqn BR120	Ju87
	Flt Sgt P.A. Schade⎦	126 Sqn BP850	
	Flt Sgt P.A. Schade	126 Sqn BP850	Ju87
24/4/42	Flt Lt H.A.S. Johnston	126 Sqn	Ju88 probable
	Sgt E.A. Crist RCAF	126 Sqn BP850	Ju88 probable
	Flt Lt A.R.H. Barton⎤	126 Sqn BP973	Ju88
	Sgt W.H.L. Milner ⎦	126 Sqn BR176	

	Flt Lt D.W. Barnham	601 Sqn BP975	Ju87
	Sgt E.A. Crist RCAF	126 Sqn BP850	Ju87 probable
25/4/42	Plt Off K.W. Pawson	601 Sqn BP973	2 Ju87 probable (also FTR)
	Sgt V.P. Brennan RAAF	249 Sqn 2-E	Bf109, Ju88
	Flt Lt W.A. Douglas	603 Sqn BP962	Ju88
26/4/42	Sgt R.B. Hesselyn RNZAF	249 Sqn	Ju87
28/4/42	Plt Off R.F. Tilley RCAF (US)	126 Sqn BR185	Bf109
29/4/42	Sgt E.A. Crist RCAF	126 Sqn BR190	Ju88
	Plt Off J.E. Peck (US)	126 Sqn BR116	Bf109 probable
30/4/42	Flt Sgt J. Hurst	603 Sqn	Ju88
	Flt Lt A.R.H. Barton	126 Sqn	Bf109 probable
1/5/42	Flt Lt N.C. Macqueen ⎫ Plt Off L.W. Watts ⎭	249 Sqn 249 Sqn BP962	Bf109
	Sqn Ldr D. Douglas-Hamilton ⎫ Plt Off H.R. Mitchell RNZAF ⎭	603 Sqn 603 Sqn	Bf109
3/5/42	Plt Off P.A. Nash	249 Sqn BR184	Bf109
	Plt Off J.W. Slade	603 Sqn	Bf109
4/5/42	Flt Sgt V.P. Brennan RAAF	249 Sqn BR190	Bf109
8/5/42	Plt Off R.F. Tilley RCAF (US)	126 Sqn	2 Bf109
	Plt Off J.G. Mejor	126 Sqn	Bf109
9/5/42	Flg Off A.C.W. Holland ⎫ Flt Lt J.W. Buckstone ⎬ Plt Off H.R. Mitchell RNZAF ⎭	603 Sqn 603 Sqn BP872 603 Sqn	Bf109 (also FTR)
	Flt Lt L.V. Sanders	603 Sqn	Bf109
	Plt Off P.A. Nash	249 Sqn BR108	Bf109, Bf109 probable
	Flg Off G.A.F. Buchanan (Rhod)	249 Sqn C-15	Bf109 probable
	Plt Off C.E. Broad	185 Sqn BR294	Ju87 probable
	Flt Lt K.A. Lawrence (NZ)	185 Sqn	Ju87
	Plt Off P. Wigley	185 Sqn BR306	Ju87 probable
	Plt Off P.A. Nash	249 Sqn BR108	Ju87 probable
	Flt Sgt P.A. Schade	126 Sqn	2 Z1007
	Sgt A.B. Goldsmith RAAF	126 Sqn BP871	Z1007
	Plt Off J.H. Bisley RAAF	126 Sqn	MC202
	Plt Off G.M. Briggs RAAF	601 Sqn	Bf109
	Flt Lt W.A. Douglas	603 Sqn	Bf109
10/5/42	2/Lt A. Bartleman SAAF	601 Sqn 4-A	2 Ju87 probable
	Sgt J.W. McConnell RNZAF	601 Sqn	Ju87
	Sgt V.P. Brennan RAAF	249 Sqn 3-U	Ju87
	Plt Off P.A. Nash	249 Sqn BR108	2 Ju87
	Plt Off J.A. Plagis (Rhod)	249 Sqn 3-N	Ju87
	Flg Off N.W. Lee	249 Sqn	Ju87 probable
	Flt Sgt J. Hurst	603 Sqn	Ju87
	Flt Lt W.A. Douglas	603 Sqn	Ju87 probable
	Flt Sgt P.A. Schade	126 Sqn	Ju88
	Plt Off J. Bailey	126 Sqn	Ju87
	Flt Lt A.R.H. Barton	126 Sqn	Bf109
	Sgt A.B. Goldsmith RAAF	126 Sqn BP871	Bf109
	Sgt W.H.L. Milner	126 Sqn	Bf109 probable
	Flt Lt J.E. Peck (US)	126 Sqn	Ju87
	Plt Off J.G. Mejor	126 Sqn BP850	Ju88 probable
	Plt Off M.A. Graves	126 Sqn BP877	Ju88, Ju87 probable
	Sgt J.L. Boyd RAAF	185 Sqn BR350	Ju88 probable
	Plt Off J.I. McKay RCAF	185 Sqn BR306	Ju88
	Flt Lt K.A. Lawrence (NZ)	185 Sqn	Ju88
	Flt Sgt W.G. Dodd RCAF	185 Sqn BR291	Ju87
	Plt Off C.E. Broad	185 Sqn BR294	Ju88
	Sqn Ldr S.B. Grant	249 Sqn	Ju88
	Flg Off G.A.F. Buchanan (Rhod)	249 Sqn BR170	Ju88 probable
	Sgt R.B. Hesselyn RNZAF	249 Sqn	Bf109 probable
	Sqn Ldr J.D. Bisdee	601 Sqn	Z1007
	Sgt F.W. Farfan	601 Sqn	Z1007 probable
	Plt Off W.A. Caldwell RNZAF	601 Sqn 4-H	MC202
	Flt Sgt W.H.L. Milner	126 Sqn	Bf109 probable

	Plt Off R.F. Tilley RCAF (US)	126 Sqn	Bf109 probable
	Flg Off R.A. Mitchell	603 Sqn	Ju87
	Flt Lt W.A. Douglas ⎱	603 Sqn BP964	Ju87
	Plt Off J.W. Forster ⎰	603 Sqn	
	Sgt A.B. Goldsmith RAAF	126 Sqn BP877	2 Bf109
	Plt Off L.W. Watts	249 Sqn BP989	Bf109
	Plt Off E.L. Hetherington	249 Sqn	Bf109 probable
11/5/42	Plt Off J.A. Plagis (Rhod)	249 Sqn 3-N	MC202
	Plt Off P.A. Nash	249 Sqn BR107	Bf109
	Sgt V.B. Brennan RAAF	249 Sqn 3-N	Bf109
	Flt Sgt J.W. Williams RCAF	249 Sqn	Ju88 probable
	Flt Lt A.R.H. Barton	126 Sqn	Bf109 probable
	Flt Sgt R.J. Sim RNZAF ⎤	185 Sqn	
	Flt Lt W.A. Douglas ⎥	603 Sqn BP964	Bf109
	Plt Off R.R. Barnfather ⎥	603 Sqn BP991	
	Plt Off J.W. Forster ⎦	603 Sqn	
	Sqn Ldr J.D. Bisdee	601 Sqn	Bf109 probable
	Plt Off D.E. Booth (US)	601 Sqn	Bf109 probable
12/5/42	Sgt R.B. Hesselyn RNZAF	249 Sqn	Bf109
	Flt Lt R. West	249 Sqn	Ju88 probable
	Sgt J.W. Yarra RAAF	185 Sqn GL-K	Ju88 probable
	Plt Off M.A. Graves	126 Sqn BP877	Ju88 probable
	Sgt J.W. McConnell RNZAF	601 Sqn	MC202 probable
	Plt Off E.S. Dicks-Sherwood (Rhod)	603 Sqn	SM84
	Flt Lt L.V. Sanders ⎱	603 Sqn	SM84
	Flg Off R.A. Mitchell ⎰	603 Sqn	
13/5/42	Sgt R.B. Hesselyn RNZAF	249 Sqn	2 Bf109
14/5/42	Flt Lt R. West	249 Sqn	Ju88
	Sgt R.B. Hesselyn RNZAF	249 Sqn	Ju88
	Sgt A.B. Goldsmith RAAF	126 Sqn BR290	Bf109
	Plt Off R.F. Tilley RCAF (US)	126 Sqn	Bf109
	Sgt J.L. Boyd RAAF	185 Sqn BR349	Bf109
	Flt Lt J.P. Winfield	185 Sqn	Bf109 probable
	Flt Sgt D.W. Ferraby	185 Sqn	MC202 probable
	Flt Lt D.W. Barnham ⎱	601 Sqn 1-U	Ju88
	Plt Off M.R.B. Ingham RNZAF ⎰	601 Sqn	
	Flt Sgt J. Hurst	603 Sqn	Ju88
	Flt Lt L.V. Sanders ⎱	603 Sqn	Ju88
	Flg Off R.A. Mitchell ⎰	603 Sqn	
	Plt Off E.S. Dicks-Sherwood (Rhod) ⎱	603 Sqn	Ju88
	Sgt A.B. Goldsmith RAAF ⎰	126 Sqn BR290	
	Flg Off G.A.F. Buchanan (Rhod)	249 Sqn BR107	Bf109 probable
	Flt Sgt H.J. Fox (US)	249 Sqn BP878	Bf109 (also FTR)
	Flt Lt D.W. Barnham	601 Sqn 1-U	Ju88, Bf109 probable
	Sqn Ldr A.R.H. Barton	126 Sqn	Bf109, Bf109 probable
	Plt Off R.F. Tilley RCAF (US)	126 Sqn	Bf109
15/5/42	Plt Off L.A. Verrall RNZAF	249 Sqn	MC202
	Sgt J.W. Yarra RAAF	185 Sqn GL-K	2 MC202
	Sqn Ldr D. Douglas-Hamilton	603 Sqn	Bf109
	Flt Sgt W.R. Irwin RAAF	603 Sqn	Bf109 probable
16/5/42	Flg Off C.M. Hone ⎱	601 Sqn	Z1007 probable
	Plt Off W.J.E. Hagger (Rhod) ⎰	601 Sqn	
	Sgt J.W. McConnell RNZAF	601 Sqn	MC202 probable
	Flg Off G.A.F. Buchanan (Rhod)	249 Sqn BR107	MC202
	Plt Off P.A. Nash ⎤	249 Sqn BR195	Bf109 (249 Sqn's 100th Malta victory)
	Plt Off J.A. Plagis (Rhod) ⎦	249 Sqn BR176	
	Flt Lt L.V. Sanders	603 Sqn	Bf109 probable
	Flt Sgt J. Hurst	603 Sqn	Bf109 probable
17/5/42	Flg Off G.A.F. Buchanan (Rhod)	249 Sqn BR107	Ju88
	Flt Sgt T. Parks RCAF	249 Sqn	Do24T
	Flt Lt J.P. Winfield	126 Sqn	Bf109
	Plt Off P.A. Nash	249 Sqn BP951	Bf109 (also FTR)

	Plt Off L.A. Verrall RNZAF	249 Sqn	Bf109
	Plt Off L.G. Barlow (SA) ⎫	603 Sqn	Do24
	Flt Sgt J. Hurst ⎬	603 Sqn	
	Plt Off M.H. Le Bas	601 Sqn	RE2001 probable
	Plt Off A.R. Boyle	601 Sqn	RE2001 probable
	Plt Off W.A. Caldwell RNZAF	601 Sqn BR306	Bf109
18/5/42	Flt Lt R. West	249 Sqn	RE2001
	Flt Sgt V.B. Brennan RAAF	249 Sqn	RE2001
	Sgt J.C. Gilbert	249 Sqn	RE2001
	Plt Off T.W. Scott RAAF	601 Sqn	Bf109
	Sgt J.W. Yarra RAAF	185 Sqn GL-K	Bf109, Bf109 probable
	Flt Lt J.E. Peck (US)	126 Sqn	Bf109, Bf109 probable
	Plt Off R.O. Jones (US)	126 Sqn	Bf109
	Plt Off J.H. Bisley RAAF	126 Sqn	Bf109
	Sgt J.C. Gilbert	249 Sqn	Bf109
	Sgt J.C. Gray	249 Sqn	Bf109 probable
	Flt Lt J.E. Peck (US) ⎫	126 Sqn	Bf109
	Plt Off R.O. Jones (US) ⎭	126 Sqn	
19/5/42	Plt Off W.A. Caldwell RNZAF	601 Sqn BR344	Z1007
21/5/42	Plt Off J.F. Lambert RCAF	185 Sqn GL-C	Bf109
22/5/42	Flt Lt R.W. McNair RCAF	249 Sqn BR170	Bf109
	Flt Sgt W.G. Dodd RCAF	185 Sqn BR294	Bf109
	Plt Off C.E. Broad	185 Sqn BR126	Bf109 probable
23/5/42	Plt Off R.F. Tilley RCAF (US)	126 Sqn	MC202
	Plt Off R.O. Jones (US)	126 Sqn	Z1007 probable
	Flt Sgt P.A. Schade	126 Sqn	Bf109, Bf109 probable
	Sgt J.W. McConnell RNZAF	601 Sqn	RE2001
	Sgt J.W.L. Innes	601 Sqn	RE2001
24/5/42	Plt Off J.R.S. Halford ⎫	185 Sqn GL-B	Ju88
	Plt Off N.J. Ogilvie RCAF ⎭	185 Sqn GL-C	
	Plt Off L.G. Barlow (SA)	603 Sqn	MC202
	Plt Off E.S. Dicks-Sherwood (Rhod)	603 Sqn	MC202
25/5/42	Flt Lt R. West	249 Sqn	RE2001
	Flt Lt R.W. McNair RCAF	249 Sqn BR109	Bf109 probable
	Plt Off M.A. Graves	126 Sqn	Z1007 probable
	Sgt A.B. Goldsmith RAAF	126 Sqn BR290	Z1007 probable
26/5/42	Flg Off R.A. Mitchell	603 Sqn	RE2001
	Plt Off L.G. Barlow (SA)	603 Sqn	RE2001
28/5/42	Flt Sgt P.A. Schade	126 Sqn	Bf109 probable
30/5/42	Flt Sgt D.W. Ferraby ⎫	185 Sqn BP876	
	Plt Off W.J. Johnson ⎬	126 Sqn	
	Plt Off A.B. Goldsmith RAAF ⎬	126 Sqn	SM84
	Flt Sgt W.H.L. Milner ⎭	126 Sqn	
	Plt Off A.B. Goldsmith	126 Sqn	RE2001 probable
1/6/42	Flt Sgt J.W. Yarra RAAF	185 Sqn GL-K	Bf109
2/6/42	Flt Sgt D.G. Reid RCAF	185 Sqn BR353	RE2001 probable
	2/Lt A. Bartleman SAAF	601 Sqn BR125	RE2001 (claimed as MC202)
3/6/42	Flg Off J.H. Menary ⎫	HMS *Eagle* BR322	FW58 (both lost)
	Plt Off D.F. Rouleau RCAF ⎭	HMS *Eagle* BR358	
6/6/42	Flt Sgt H. Haggas ⎫	185 Sqn	Ju88
	Flt Sgt J.E. MacNamara RCAF ⎭	185 Sqn	
	Flt Lt P.B. Lucas ⎫	249 Sqn BR109	Ju88
	Plt Off F.E. Jones RCAF ⎭	249 Sqn BR246	
	Plt Off O.M. Linton RCAF ⎫	249 Sqn BR111	Ju88
	Flt Sgt B. Butler RCAF ⎭	249 Sqn BR377	
	Wt Off C.B. Ramsay RCAF	249 Sqn BR387	RE2001
	Sgt J.C. Gilbert	249 Sqn BR119	RE2001
	Plt Off N.S. King	603 Sqn	RE2001 probable
	Flg Off R.A. Mitchell	603 Sqn	RE2001 probable
	Flg Off W.R. Daddo-Langlois	249 Sqn BR107	RE2001
	Plt Off F.E. Jones RCAF	249 Sqn BR246	RE2001
	Flt Lt J.A. Plagis (Rhod)	185 Sqn BR321	2 RE2001

	Flt Sgt D.G. Reid RCAF	185 Sqn BR375	RE2001
	Plt Off J.F. Lambert RCAF ⎤	185 Sqn	
	Flt Sgt W.G. Dodd RCAF ⎬	185 Sqn BR294	Z506B
	Sgt H. Russel RCAF ⎦	185 Sqn	
7/6/42	Flt Lt J.A. Plagis (Rhod)	185 Sqn BR321	Bf109
	Flt Sgt D.G. Reid RCAF	185 Sqn BR375	Bf109 probable
9/6/42	Plt Off M.A. Graves	126 Sqn MK-E	Bf109
	Flt Sgt K.W.S. Evans	126 Sqn BP992	RE2001 probable
10/6/42	Flt Sgt J.C. Gray	249 Sqn T-W	MC202
	Wt Off C.B. Ramsay RCAF	249 Sqn BR170	Bf109 probable
	Sqn Ldr S.B. Grant	249 Sqn BR170	RE2001
	Flt Lt R.W. McNair RCAF	249 Sqn BR107	Bf109
	Plt Off W.R.P. Sewell RCAF	601 Sqn	MC202
11/6/42	Plt Off J.H. Bisley RAAF	126 Sqn	Bf109
15/6/42	Plt Off A.B. Goldsmith RAAF	126 Sqn MK-J	RS14, MC200 probable
	Flt Sgt K.W.S. Evans ⎤	126 Sqn BR496	SM84
	Plt Off A.B. Goldsmith RAAF⎦	126 Sqn MK-J	
	Flt Lt J.P. Winfield	126 Sqn	SM84 (claimed as BR20)
	Plt Off M.R.B. Ingram RNZAF ⎤	601 Sqn UF-M	Ju87
	Sgt G. Allen-Rowlandson ⎦	601 Sqn BR360	
	2/Lt A. Bartleman SAAF	601 Sqn UF-G	Ju87
	Plt Off C.R. Scollan RCAF	601 Sqn	Ju87 probable
	Plt Off J.A. Smith RCAF	601 Sqn BR175	Ju87 probable
	Flt Sgt P.A. Schade	126 Sqn	Bf109
	Flt Lt J. Bailey ⎤	126 Sqn	
	Flt Lt A.C. Rowe RNZAF ⎬	126 Sqn	Z506B
	Plt Off F.D. Thomas ⎥	126 Sqn	
	Plt Off E.W. Wallace RCAF ⎦	126 Sqn	
	Plt Off J.A. Smith RCAF	601 Sqn BR381	Ju88
	Flt Lt R. West	185 Sqn	Bf109, Ju88 probable
	Flt Sgt R.J. Sim RNZAF	185 Sqn BR126	Ju88
	Plt Off G. Stenborg RNZAF	185 Sqn BR375	Bf109
	Plt Off C.E. Broad	185 Sqn BR380	Bf109
	Plt Off M.R.B. Ingram RNZAF	601 Sqn UF-G	Ju88
	Flt Lt P.B. Lucas ⎤	249 Sqn BR377	Ju88
	Plt Off L.W. Watts ⎦	249 Sqn BR254	
	Plt Off O.M. Linton RCAF ⎤	249 Sqn BR111	Ju88
	Plt Off F.E. Jones RCAF ⎦	249 Sqn BR119	
16/6/42	Plt Off A.B. Goldsmith RAAF	126 Sqn 1-D	Bf109
	Flt Sgt J.W. Yarra RAAF	185 Sqn GL-J	Bf109
21/6/42	Flt Sgt J.W. Yarra RAAF	185 Sqn BR387	2 Bf109
	Flt Sgt R.J. Sim RNZAF	185 Sqn GL-D	Bf109
22/6/42	Flt Sgt D.G. Reid RCAF	185 Sqn BR126	Bf109
23/6/42	Plt Off H.W. McLeod RCAF	603 Sqn X-B	MC202
	Plt Off D.G. Newman ⎤	603 Sqn	
	Plt Off R.G. Smith ⎬	603 Sqn BR128	Z1007
	Flt Sgt C.H. Parkinson RAAF⎦	603 Sqn X-N	
25/6/42	Plt Off O.W.H. Berkeley-Hill	249 Sqn	Bf109 probable
	Plt Off C.H. Lattimer RNZAF	249 Sqn BR108	Bf109, Bf109 probable
26/6/42	Plt Off J.H. Curry RCAF (US)	601 Sqn BR301	MC202
	Flt Sgt P.A. Schade	126 Sqn MK-B	MC202
	Plt Off A.A. Glen	603 Sqn	Bf109
	Flt Lt R. West	185 Sqn GL-J	RE2001
27/6/42	Wt Off J.D. Rae RNZAF	249 Sqn BR377	RE2001, RE2001 probable
	Flt Sgt R.G. Middlemiss RCAF	249 Sqn BR184	RE2001
	Plt Off L.A. Verrall RNZAF	249 Sqn BR295	RE2001
1/7/42	Flt Lt J.R.S. Halford	185 Sqn BR387	Bf109
	Flt Sgt D.G. Reid RCAF	185 Sqn BR294	Bf109
	Plt Off J.R. Sherlock RCAF	185 Sqn BP876	Bf109 probable
	Flt Sgt J.H. Ballantyne RCAF	603 Sqn BR367	MC202 (claimed as Bf109)
	Flg Off R.A. Mitchell	603 Sqn	MC202 probable
	Plt Off J. Hurst	603 Sqn	SM84 probable
	Flt Sgt C.H. Parkinson RAAF	603 Sqn BR184	RE2001

	Plt Off M.A. Graves	126 Sqn MK-P	Bf109
2/7/42	Flt Sgt D.G. Reid RCAF	185 Sqn BR294	Bf109
	Flt Sgt T. Parks RCAF	249 Sqn BR379	Bf109
	Sqn Ldr P.B. Lucas	249 Sqn BR324	Bf109 probable
	Flg Off N.S. King	603 Sqn BR345	MC202 probable
	Plt Off E.H. Glazebrook RCAF	603 Sqn BR365	
	Plt Off R.G. Smith	603 Sqn	
	Plt Off D.G. Newman	603 Sqn	Z1007 probable
	Sgt K.R. Mitchell RAAF)	603 Sqn	
	Flt Sgt C.S.G. de Nancrède RCAF	249 Sqn	
	Flt Lt W.R. Daddo-Langlois	249 Sqn BR170	Ju88
	Flt Sgt R.G. Middlemiss RCAF	249 Sqn BR295	Bf109
	Flg Off J.R. Stoop	185 Sqn BP979	MC202
	Sgt H. Haggas	185 Sqn BR387	MC202
3/7/42	Sgt D.K. Parker	185 Sqn BP979	Bf109
4/7/42	Sqn Ldr P.B. Lucas	249 Sqn BR324	SM84
	Plt Off J.D. Rae RNZAF	249 Sqn BR233	SM84
	Flt Lt W.R. Daddo-Langlois	249 Sqn BR170	SM84
	Flt Sgt R.G. Middlemiss RCAF	249 Sqn BR295	
	Plt Off R.G. Smith	603 Sqn BP990	Bf109
	Plt Off M.A. Graves	126 Sqn MK-P	Z1007 probable
	Plt Off J.F. McElroy RCAF	249 Sqn BR111	RE2001 probable
5/7/42	Flt Sgt J.W. Yarra RAAF	185 Sqn BR387	Ju88, Bf109 probable
	Plt Off G. Stenborg RNZAF	185 Sqn BR380	2 Bf109
	Flt Sgt P.A. Schade	126 Sqn MK-H	Bf109
	Flt Sgt K.W.S. Evans	126 Sqn BR122	Bf109, Bf109 probable
	Flt Lt J.E. Peck RCAF (US)	126 Sqn	Bf109 probable
	Plt Off J.G. Mejor	126 Sqn BR244	Bf109 probable
6/7/42	Sgt G.F. Beurling (Can)	249 Sqn BR323	2 MC202
	Flt Lt N.W. Lee	249 Sqn BR379	MC202
	Plt Off A.A. Glen	603 Sqn	Ju88
	Plt Off G. Carlet RCAF (FF)	603 Sqn BP957	Ju88
	Flt Sgt W.R. Irwin RAAF	603 Sqn	Bf109 probable
	Sqn Ldr W.G. New	185 Sqn BR321	Ju88 probable
	Flg Off K.L. Charney	185 Sqn BR380	Bf109
	Flt Sgt W.G. Dodd RCAF	185 Sqn BR303	Bf109
	Sgt A. Drew	185 Sqn BR119	Ju88
	Flt Sgt D.G. Reid RCAF	185 Sqn BR317	Bf109 probable
	Plt Off J.H. Bisley RAAF	126 Sqn	
	Flg Off D.H. Smith RAAF	126 Sqn BP873	Z1007
	Flt Sgt G.H.T. Farquharson RCAF	126 Sqn	
	2/Lt C.J.O. Swales SAAF	603 Sqn BP873	
	Sqn Ldr J.P. Winfield	126 Sqn	Z1007 probable
	Plt Off G. Carlet RCAF (FF)	126 Sqn BP957	MC202
	Sqn D. Douglas-Hamilton	603 Sqn	MC202 probable
	Flt Lt J. Bailey	126 Sqn	MC202 probable
	Plt Off A.A. Glen	603 Sqn	Ju88, Bf109
	Plt Off G. Carlet RCAF (FF)	603 Sqn BP957	Ju88
	Flt Sgt W.R. Irwin RAAF	603 Sqn	
	Sgt G.F. Beurling (Can)	249 Sqn BR323	Bf109
	Flt Sgt W.G. Dodd RCAF	185 Sqn BR303	Bf109
7/7/42	Plt Off V.P. Brennan RAAF	249 Sqn AB526	Bf109
	Plt Off O.M. Linton RCAF	249 Sqn BR324	Bf109
	Flt Sgt E.L. Mahar RAAF	185 Sqn BR292	Bf109
	Plt Off J.F. McElroy RCAF	249 Sqn BR301	MC202
	Flt Sgt P.A. Schade	126 Sqn MK-G	2 Bf109
	Plt Off J.L. Hicks	126 Sqn	Bf109
	Plt Off J.G. Mejor	126 Sqn MK-R	Bf109
	Plt Off J.D. Rae RNZAF	249 Sqn BR323	Bf109
	Flt Sgt J.W. Yarra RAAF	185 Sqn BR387	2 RE2001
8/7/42	Flg Off D.H. Smith RAAF	126 Sqn BR122	Bf109
	Flt Sgt C.F. Bush	126 Sqn	Bf109
	Flt Sgt J.W. Williams RCAF	249 Sqn BR111	Bf109

	Plt Off R.B. Hesselyn RNZAF	249 Sqn AB526	Bf109
	Sgt G.F. Beurling (Can)	249 Sqn BR128	Bf109
	Plt Off R.B. Hesselyn RNZAF	249 Sqn AB526	Bf109
	Plt Off J.W. Williams RCAF	249 Sqn BR111	Ju88
	Sgt G.F. Beurling (Can)	249 Sqn BR128	Bf109 probable
	Flt Sgt W.G. Dodd RCAF	185 Sqn AB469	Bf109
9/7/42	Plt Off R.F. Tilley RCAF (US)	126 Sqn	Bf109
	Flt Sgt K.W.S. Evans	126 Sqn BR244	MC202
	Plt Off J.D. Rae RNZAF	249 Sqn BR323	MC202 probable
	Plt Off J.F. McElroy RCAF⎱	249 Sqn BR301	Ju88
	Plt Off J.D. Rae RNZAF ⎰	249 Sqn BR323	
	Plt Off R.F. Tilley RCAF (US)	126 Sqn	Ju88
	Plt Off J.G. Mejor	126 Sqn MK-F	Ju88
	Flt Lt R.A. Mitchell	603 Sqn	Ju88
	Flg Off H.W. McLeod RCAF	603 Sqn 4-N	Ju88 probable
	Flg Off G.W. Northcott RCAF	603 Sqn X-N	Bf109 probable
	Flt Sgt P.A. Schade	126 Sqn MK-N	2 Bf109
	Plt Off G. Stenborg RNZAF	126 Sqn BR109	2 Bf109
	Flt Sgt C.H. Parkinson RAAF	603 Sqn BR464	Bf109
10/7/42	Plt Off C.H. Lattimer RNZAF	249 Sqn BR128	MC202
	Sgt G.F. Beurling (Can)	249 Sqn BR323	Bf109
	Plt Off E.S. Dicks-Sherwood (Rhod)	603 Sqn	Ju88
	Flg Off D.H. Smith RAAF	126 Sqn BR366	Ju88
	Flt Lt J.W. Slade	126 Sqn	MC202 (claimed as Bf109)
	Sgt G.F. Beurling (Can)	249 Sqn BR323	MC202
	Plt Off J.W. Williams RCAF	249 Sqn BR324	Bf109
	Flt Lt R.A. Mitchell	603 Sqn	MC202
	Flt Sgt W.H.L. Milner	126 Sqn	Bf109
	Flt Sgt C.F. Bush	126 Sqn	Bf109
	Plt Off J.A. Smith RCAF	126 Sqn	Ju88
	Flg Off R.O. Jones (US)	126 Sqn	Ju88
11/7/42	Plt Off A.S. Yates RAAF ⎱	249 Sqn BR301	Bf109
	Wt Off C.B. Ramsay RCAF⎰	249 Sqn BR111	
	Flt Lt W.R. Daddo-Langlois	249 Sqn BR565	Bf109
	Sqn Ldr J.P. Winfield⎱	126 Sqn	Ju88
	Plt Off J.G. Mejor ⎰	126 Sqn MK-P	
	Flt Sgt G.H.T. Farquharson RCAF	126 Sqn	RE2001 (claimed as MC202)
	Plt Off F.E. Jones RCAF	249 Sqn	Bf109
	Flt Sgt P.A. Schade	126 Sqn MK-K	Bf109
	Plt Off J.W. Yarra RAAF	185 Sqn BR305	Bf109
12/7/42	Flt Sgt R.J. Sim RNZAF	185 Sqn BR321	Bf109
	Sgt G.F. Beurling (Can)	249 Sqn BR565	RE2001
	Flg Off E.L. Hetherington	249 Sqn	RE2001
	Sgt G.F. Beurling (Can)	249 Sqn BR565	2 RE2001
	Flt Lt K.L. Charney	185 Sqn BR368	MC202
13/7/42	Flt Sgt A.W. Varey	126 Sqn	Ju88
	Plt Off G.W. Northcott RCAF	603 Sqn X-N	Ju88
	Flt Sgt K.W.S. Evans	126 Sqn BP992	MC202
	Sqn Ldr J.P. Winfield	126 Sqn	MC202 probable
	Plt Off J.D. Rae RNZAF	249 Sqn BR323	MC202 (claimed as RE2001)
	Plt Off J.F. McElroy RCAF	249 Sqn BR301	Bf109
	Flt Sgt W.R. Irwin RAAF	603 Sqn	Ju88
	Flt Sgt C.H. Parkinson RAAF	603 Sqn GL-T	Bf109 probable
	Flt Sgt R.H. Brown RCAF	603 Sqn	Bf109 probable
14/7/42	Flg Off D.H. Smith RAAF	126 Sqn BP992	Ju88
	Flg Off R.O. Jones (US)	126 Sqn	Ju88
	Flt Sgt J.E. MacNamara RCAF	185 Sqn BR460	Ju88 probable
	Plt Off R.F. Tilley RCAF (US)	126 Sqn	Bf109 probable
	Flt Sgt C.H. Parkinson RAAF	603 Sqn EP200	Bf109
15/7/42	Sgt A. Richardson RAAF	126 Sqn	Bf109
17/7/42	Flt Lt J.R.S. Halford	185 Sqn BR321	Bf109

	Flt Sgt D.G. Reid RCAF	185 Sqn BR380	Bf109
	Sgt C. Weaver RCAF (US)	185 Sqn BR292	Bf109
	Flg Off H.W. McLeod RCAF	603 Sqn	Bf109
18/7/42	Plt Off J.A. Smith RCAF ⎫	126 Sqn BR176	Ju88 probable
	Plt Off R.I.A. Smith RCAF⎭	126 Sqn BP952	
	Flt Lt W.J. Johnson	126 Sqn BR311	Bf109 probable
20/7/42	Sgt D.K. Parker	185 Sqn BR387	Bf109
	Flt Sgt W.R. Irwin RAAF	603 Sqn	Bf109 probable
21/7/42	Flt Sgt A.W. Varey	126 Sqn	Bf109 probable
22/7/42	Flt Sgt D.G. Reid RCAF	185 Sqn BR203	Bf109 probable (also FTR)
	Sgt C. Weaver RCAF (US)	185 Sqn EP122	2 Bf109
23/7/42	Sqn Ldr R.A. Mitchell	249 Sqn BR301	Ju88
	Sgt G.F. Beurling (Can)	249 Sqn EP135	RE2001
	Flt Lt J.R.S. Halford	1435 Flt	Bf109
	Flt Lt L.W. Watts ⎫	249 Sqn BR373	Bf109 probable
	Plt Off J.F. McElroy RCAF⎭	249 Sqn EN976	
	Plt Off B.C. Downs (US)	126 Sqn	Bf109 probable
	Sgt C. Weaver RCAF (US)	185 Sqn EP122	2 Bf109
24/7/42	Plt Off C.H. Lattimer RNZAF	1435 Flt	Bf109
	Flt Lt H.W. McLeod RCAF	1435 Flt EP209	Bf109 probable
	Sgt C.L. Baxter RAAF	1435 Flt	Bf109 probable
	Plt Off R.I.A. Smith RCAF	126 Sqn BR122	Ju88
	Plt Off J.A. Smith RCAF	126 Sqn MK-A	Ju88
	Plt Off J.W. Guthrie	185 Sqn EP200	Ju88
	Sgt L.S. Reid RAAF	185 Sqn AB526	Ju88
	Sgt C. Weaver RCAF (US)⎫	185 Sqn EP122	Ju88
	Sgt A. Drew ⎭	185 Sqn EP139	
25/7/42	Plt Off E.H. Glazebrook RCAF	603 Sqn	MC202
26/7/42	Flt Lt W.J. Johnson	126 Sqn MK-W	Ju88 probable
	Flg Off R.O. Jones (US)	126 Sqn	Ju88
27/7/42	Sgt G.F. Beurling (Can)	249 Sqn BR301	2 MC202, Bf109
	Sgt N.G. Brydon RCAF	249 Sqn EP196	Bf109
	Plt Off J.W. Williams RCAF	249 Sqn EN976	Bf109
	Plt Off J.W. Guthrie	185 Sqn AB526	Bf109
	Flt Lt W.J. Johnson	126 Sqn MK-W	2 Ju88
	Flt Sgt A.W. Varey	126 Sqn	Ju88
	Flt Sgt K.W.S. Evans⎫	126 Sqn AB531	
	Flt Lt W.J. Johnson ⎬	126 Sqn MK-W	Ju88
	Sgt C.F. Bush ⎭	126 Sqn	
	Flt Sgt K.W.S. Evans	126 Sqn AB531	Bf109
	Plt Off B.C. Downs (US)	126 Sqn	Bf109
	Plt Off J.W. Williams RCAF	249 Sqn EN976	Bf109
	Sgt G.F. Beurling (Can)	249 Sqn BR301	Bf109
	Flt Sgt K.W.S. Evans	126 Sqn AB531	Bf109, Bf109 probable
	Plt Off J.D. Rae RNZAF	249 Sqn BR323	Bf109 probable
28/7/42	Sqn Ldr R.A. Mitchell	249 Sqn BR373	Ju88 probable
	Plt Off J.D. Rae RNZAF ⎫	249 Sqn BR323	Ju88 probable
	Sgt M Irving Gass	249 Sqn EP196	
	Flt Sgt T. Parks RCAF	249 Sqn EP131	Bf109 probable
	Plt Off J.W.P. Baril RCAF⎫	185 Sqn BR387	
	Plt Off J.W. Guthrie ⎬	185 Sqn BR321	Ju88
	Sgt A.J. Tiddy (SA) ⎪	126 Sqn	
	Sgt N.M. Park RNZAF ⎭	126 Sqn BR345	
	Flg Off R.O. Jones (US) ⎫	126 Sqn	
	Plt Off W.L. Thompson ⎪	126 Sqn	
	Plt Off F.D. Thomas ⎬	126 Sqn	Ju88
	Plt Off J.A. Smith RCAF ⎪	126 Sqn MK-A	
	Flt Sgt G.H.T. Farquharson RCAF⎭	126 Sqn	
	Plt Off R.I.A. Smith RCAF⎫	126 Sqn MK-L	
	Sqn Ldr A.D.J. Lovell ⎬	1435 Sqn EP140	Ju88
	Plt Off J.G. Mejor ⎪	1435 Sqn	
	Wg Cdr G.H. Stainforth ⎭	89 Sqn	
	Sgt N.M. Park RNZAF	126 Sqn	Bf109

29/7/42	Sgt G.F. Beurling (Can)	249 Sqn BR301	Bf109
	Sgt E.A. Budd	249 Sqn EP131	MC202 (claimed as Bf109)
30/7/42	Flt Sgt C.H. Parkinson RAAF	603 Sqn BP989	Bf109
31/7/42	Plt Off G. Stenborg RNZAF	185 Sqn BR321	Bf109
	Flt Lt W.J. Johnson	126 Sqn BR345	Bf109
	Plt Off W.L. Thompson	126 Sqn	RE2001
2/8/42	Sgt C. Weaver RCAF (US)	185 Sqn EP139	Bf109 probable
4/8/42	Capt C.J.O. Swales SAAF	229 Sqn	Bf109 probable
5/8/42	Flt Sgt J.A.H. Pinney RCAF	1435 Sqn	Bf109
8/8/42	Plt Off G.F. Beurling (Can)	249 Sqn EN373	Bf109
	Flt Lt F.E. Jones RCAF	249 Sqn BP869	Bf109
9/8/42	Plt Off E.S. Dicks-Sherwood (Rhod)	229 Sqn	Bf109
10/8/42	Flt Lt H.W. McLeod RCAF	1435 Sqn V-J	Bf109
	Plt Off C.H. Lattimer RNZAF	1435 Sqn	Bf109
	Flt Sgt I.R. Maclennan RCAF	1435 Sqn	Bf109
	Plt Off J.A. Smith RCAF	126 Sqn BR366	Ju88 (also FTR)
12/8/42	Plt Off N.J. Ogilvie RCAF	185 Sqn EP139	He111 (185's 100th victory)
13/8/42	Sqn Ldr A.D.J. Lovell	1435 Sqn	Ju87, SM84
	Flt Sgt J.A.H. Pinney RCAF	1435 Sqn	SM84
	Flt Lt G.W. Northott RCAF ⎱	229 Sqn X-L	Ju88
	Flt Lt E.P.F.L.T. Magruder ⎰	229 Sqn	
	Plt Off R.I.A. Smith RCAF	126 Sqn AB465	SM79
	Flt Sgt J.E. MacNamara RCAF ⎱	1435 Sqn	SM84
	Sgt R. Hawkins ⎰	1435 Sqn	
	Flt Sgt A.H. Scott	1435 Sqn V-H	SM84 (claimed as Breda 88)
	Flt Lt H.W. McLeod RCAF	1435 Sqn V-J	Ju88 probable
	Flt Lt F.E. Jones RCAF ⎱	249 Sqn EP448	
	Plt Off G.F. Beurling (Can) ⎬	249 Sqn EP135	Ju88
	Sgt V.H. Wynn RCAF (US) ⎰	249 Sqn BR565	
	Sqn Ldr B.J. Wicks ⎱	126 Sqn	Ju88
	Plt Off W.T.E. Rolls ⎰	126 Sqn	
	Sgt A.J. Tiddy (SA)	126 Sqn	Ju88
14/8/42	Sqn Ldr A.D.J. Lovell ⎱	1435 Sqn	Ju87
	Sgt G. Philp RNZAF ⎰	1435 Sqn	
	Flt Sgt I.R. Maclennan RCAF	1435 Sqn	MC202
	Flt Lt W.J. Johnson	126 Sqn BR311	2 RE2001
	Sgt N. Marshall RCAF	126 Sqn BP860	RE2001 (claimed as MC202)
15/8/42	Capt C.J.O. Swales SAAF ⎱	185 Sqn EP313	Bf109
	Sgt J. Tarbuck ⎰	185 Sqn EP410	
17/8/42	Sgt C. Weaver RCAF (US)	185 Sqn BR374	2 Bf109
	Plt Off G. Stenborg RNZAF	185 Sqn EP457	Bf109
24/8/42	Flt Lt E.P.F.L.T. Magruder ⎫	229 Sqn	
	Plt Off H.T. Nash (US) ⎬	229 Sqn	SM82 (claimed as He111)
	Flt Sgt J.H. Ballantyne RCAF ⎪	229 Sqn	
	Sgt E.T. Brough RNZAF ⎭	229 Sqn	
25/8/42	Sgt C. Weaver RCAF (US)	185 Sqn BR374	Bf109 probable
27/8/42	Maj C.J.O. Swales SAAF	185 Sqn EP122	Ju88
	Sgt C. Weaver RCAF (US)	185 Sqn BR374	Ju88, Bf109, Ju88 probable
	Lt K.C. Kuhlmann SAAF	185 Sqn EP187	Ju88
	Sgt L.S. Reid RAAF	185 Sqn BR380	Ju88
	Flt Lt K.L. Charney	185 Sqn BR112	Ju88 probable
	Wg Cdr J.M. Thompson ⎱	Hal Far Wing EP685	Ju88 probable
	Sgt K.R. Mitchell RAAF ⎰	185 Sqn EP553	
	Wg Cdr A.H. Donaldson ⎱	Takali Wing BR529	Ju88 probable (claimed as Do217)
	Flt Sgt J.H. Ballantyne RCAF ⎰	229 Sqn	
	Plt Off C.H. Parkinson RAAF	229 Sqn X-N	Bf109
29/8/42	Flt Lt H.W. McLeod RCAF	1435 Sqn BR236	Bf109
	Flt Sgt A.H. Scott	1435 Sqn EP612	Bf109
	Plt Off A.R. Stewart	1435 Sqn	Bf109 probable

Date	Pilot	Squadron/Aircraft	Claim
	Sgt W.R. Wilson	1435 Sqn	Bf109 probable
2/9/42	Wg Cdr A.H. Donaldson ⎫	Takali Wing BR529	
	Flt Lt E.L. Hetherington ⎬	249 Sqn EP338	MC202
	Plt Off J.G.W. Farmer ⎭	249 Sqn BR373	
5/9/42	Flt Lt K.L. Charney	185 Sqn BR375	Bf109G-2 (claimed as MC202)
9/9/42	Capt K.L. Kuhlmann SAAF	185 Sqn EP122	MC202
	Sgt C. Weaver RCAF (US)	185 Sqn BR112	Bf109 (also FTR – POW)
17/9/42	Plt Off W.L. Thompson	126 Sqn	Bf109G-2
	Flg Off A.F. Roscoe (US)	229 Sqn	RE2001 probable (claimed as MC202)
19/9/42	Flt Lt W.T.E. Rolls	126 Sqn BR383	Do24
	Sgt J.E. Mortimer RNZAF	126 Sqn	Do18
25/9/42	Plt Off G.F. Beurling (Can)	249 Sqn EP706	3 Bf109G-2
26/9/42	Flt Lt H.W. McLeod RCAF	1435 Sqn BR236	Bf109G-2
	Sgt W.R. Wilson	1435 Sqn	Bf109 probable
10/10/42	Plt Off G.F. Beurling (Can)	249 Sqn EP706	2 Bf109
	Plt Off J.G. Sanderson RAAF	249 Sqn BR373	Bf109
	Flg Off J.F. McElroy RCAF	249 Sqn EP708	Bf109
	Sqn Ldr M.M. Stephens	249 Sqn EP338	Bf109 probable
	Sgt A.B. Stead RNZAF	249 Sqn EP199	Bf109 probable
	Flt Lt A.F. Roscoe (US)	229 Sqn	Bf109
11/10/42	Plt Off J.D. Stevenson RCAF	126 Sqn EP209	MC202
	Flt Sgt A.W. Varey	126 Sqn	Bf109 probable
	Flg Off R.I.A. Smith RCAF	126 Sqn EP330	Ju88
	Sgt N. Marshall RCAF	126 Sqn	Ju88
	Flt Lt A.F. Roscoe (US)	229 Sqn	Bf109 probable
	Plt Off W.C. Walton	1435 Sqn EP717	Bf109 probable
	Wg Cdr A.H. Donaldson	Takali Wing BR254	Ju88, Ju88 probable
	Flt Sgt J.H. Ballantyne RCAF	229 Sqn	Bf109
	Wg Cdr P.P. Hanks	Luqa Wing BR498	Bf109
	Flt Lt W.T.E. Rolls	126 Sqn MK-O	2 RE2001
	Flt Lt E.H. Glazebrook RCAF	229 Sqn	MC202
	Wg Cdr J.M. Thompson	Hal Far Wing EP122	Bf109
	Sgt L.R. Gore	185 Sqn BR375	Bf109
	Plt Off L.S. Reid RAAF	185 Sqn EP186	Bf109
	Flt Lt H.W. McLeod RCAF	1435 Sqn BS161	2 Ju88
	Flt Sgt I.R. Maclennan RCAF	1435 Sqn EP717	2 Ju88
	Sgt T.R.D. Kebbell RNZAF	1435 Sqn AB264	Ju88
	Flt Sgt J.H. Ballantyne RCAF	229 Sqn	MC202
	Plt Off C.H. Parkinson RAAF	229 Sqn EP691	Ju88 probable
12/10/42	Capt K.L. Kuhlmann SAAF	185 Sqn EP187	Bf109
	Flt Lt E.H. Glazebrook RCAF	229 Sqn	Ju88 probable
	Sqn Ldr E.N. Woods	249 Sqn AR466	Ju88
	Sqn Ldr M.M. Stephens ⎫	249 Sqn AB377	Bf109
	Sgt A.B. Stead RNZAF ⎭	249 Sqn EP199	
	Sqn Ldr M.M. Stephens	249 Sqn AB377	Bf109
	Flt Lt W.T.E. Rolls	126 Sqn BR498	Ju88
	Sgt N.M. Park RNZAF	126 Sqn BR311	2 Ju88
	Flt Sgt C.A. Long	126 Sqn	Ju88
	Wg Cdr A.H. Donaldson ⎫	Takali Wing BR529	Ju88
	Plt Off H.G. Reynolds RCAF ⎭	229 Sqn	
	Flt Sgt J.H. Ballantyne RCAF	229 Sqn	MC202
	Flg Off J.F. McElroy RCAF	249 Sqn AR488	Bf109
	Flt Sgt E.T. Hiskens RAAF	249 Sqn EP135	Bf109 probable
	Flt Sgt L.G.C. de l'Ara ⎫	249 Sqn EP338	Ju88 probable
	Flt Sgt E.T. Hiskens RAAF ⎭	249 Sqn EP139	
	Flg Off E.W. Wallace RCAF	126 Sqn	Ju88
	Sgt N.M. Park RNZAF	126 Sqn BR311	Ju88
	Flt Lt W.T.E. Rolls	126 Sqn BR498	2 MC202
	Flt Sgt I.R. Maclennan RCAF	1435 Sqn EP203	Bf109
	Wg Cdr A.H. Donaldson	Takali Wing BR529	Ju88, Bf109
	Flg Off J.F. McElroy RCAF	249 Sqn AR488	Ju88

	Flt Sgt E.T. Hiskens RAAF	249 Sqn EP135	Ju88
	Flt Sgt L.G.C. de l'Ara	249 Sqn EP338	Ju88 probable
	Sqn Ldr E.N. Woods	249 Sqn AR466	Bf109
	Plt Off J.G. Sanderson RAAF	249 Sqn EP340	Bf109 probable
	Plt Off C.H. Parkinson RAAF	229 Sqn EP691	Bf109
	Flt Sgt J.H. Ballantyne RCAF	229 Sqn	Bf109
	Flt Lt E.H. Glazebrook RCAF	229 Sqn	Ju88
	Plt Off C.H. Parkinson RAAF ⎫	229 Sqn EP691	Ju88 probable
	Plt Off H.T. Nash (US) ⎭	229 Sqn	
	Flt Lt H.W. McLeod RCAF	1435 Sqn AR420	Bf109
	Sgt W.B. Knox-Williams RAAF	1435 Sqn EN978	Bf109 probable
	Wg Cdr P.P. Hanks	Luqa Wing BR498	Bf109
	Sqn Ldr A.D.J. Lovell	1435 Sqn AR470	Ju88
	Plt Off W.C. Walton ⎫	1435 Sqn EP140	Ju88 probable
	Sgt R. Hawkins ⎭		
	Flt Sgt A.H. Scott	1435 Sqn EP203	Ju88, Bf109 probable
	Sgt R. Miller	229 Sqn	MC202
13/10/42	Flt Lt K.L. Charney	185 Sqn BR375	Bf109 probable
	Plt Off G.F. Beurling (Can)	249 Sqn BR173	2 Bf109, Ju88
	Plt Off R. Seed	249 Sqn AR488	Ju88 probable
	Plt Off W.C. Walton	1435 Sqn EP140	Ju88
	Plt Off J.A.H. Pinney RCAF	1435 Sqn BR591	Bf109 probable
	Sgt R. Hawkins	1435 Sqn EP259	Ju88
	Flt Sgt A.H. Scott	1435 Sqn EP612	Bf109
	Wt Off G.H.T. Farquharson RCAF	126 Sqn BP992	Bf109 probable
	Maj C.J.O. Swales SAAF ⎫	185 Sqn EP685	Ju88
	Flt Sgt A.W. Varey ⎭	126 Sqn	
	Flg Off R.O. Jones (US)	126 Sqn	Bf109
	Wt Off G.H.T. Farquharson RCAF	126 Sqn BP992	Bf109 probable
	Flg Off R.I.A. Smith RCAF	126 Sqn EP573	MC202
	Sqn Ldr M.M. Stephens	249 Sqn EP338	Ju88, Bf109
	Sqn Ldr E.N. Woods	249 Sqn AR466	2 Bf109
	Flg Off J.F. McElroy RCAF	249 Sqn EP340	MC202 (claimed as RE2001)
	Flt Sgt E.T. Hiskens RAAF	249 Sqn EP135	MC202
	Sqn Ldr M.M. Stephens ⎫	249 Sqn EP338	MC202
	Flt Sgt L.G.C. de l'Ara ⎭	249 Sqn BR565	
	Plt Off H.T. Nash (US)	229 Sqn	Ju88
	Sqn Ldr M.M. Stephens	229 Sqn EP338	MC202
	Plt Off C.H. Parkinson RAAF	229 Sqn EP691	Ju88 probable
	Sgt W.T. Whitmore	1435 Sqn EN968	Ju88
	Flt Lt H.W. McLeod RCAF	1435 Sqn BR236	MC202
14/10/42	Sqn Ldr E.N. Woods	249 Sqn AR466	Ju88 probable
	Flt Lt W.T.E. Rolls	126 Sqn BR498	Ju88
	Sgt N.M. Park RNZAF	126 Sqn MK-A	Ju88, Bf109
	Flg Off E.W. Wallace RCAF	126 Sqn	Bf109
	Flt Lt H.W. McLeod RCAF	1435 Sqn BR236	Ju88
	Wg Cdr J.M. Thompson	Hal Far Wing EP122	Ju88
	Flg Off L. Cheek	185 Sqn EP696	Ju88 probable
	Capt K.L. Kuhlmann SAAF	185 Sqn EP712	Bf109
	Plt Off L.S. Reid RAAF	185 Sqn EP722	Bf109
	Sgt E.T. Brough RNZAF	229 Sqn	Ju88
	Sgt E.H. Francis	229 Sqn	Bf109 probable
	Sgt N.M. Park RNZAF	126 Sqn MK-A	Bf109
	Sqn Ldr M.M. Stephens	229 Sqn	RE2001
	Flt Lt C.H. Parkinson RAAF	229 Sqn X-V	MC202
	Flt Lt E.L. Hetherington	249 Sqn AR466	Ju88 probable
	Plt Off K.C.M. Giddings	249 Sqn EP338	Bf109
	Sgt V.H. Wynn RCAF (US)	249 Sqn BR373	Bf109 probable
	Plt Off G.F. Beurling (Can)	249 Sqn BR173	Ju88, 2 Bf109
	Flg Off R.I.A. Smith RCAF	126 Sqn AR471	Ju88
	Plt Off W.L. Thompson	126 Sqn	Ju88
	Sgt N. Marshall RCAF	126 Sqn	Ju88

	Sgt P.M. Charron RCAF	126 Sqn	Ju88
	Flt Sgt A.W. Varey	126 Sqn	Ju88, Ju88 probable
	Sgt A.J. Tiddy (SA)	126 Sqn	Ju88 probable
	Sgt R. Miller	229 Sqn	Ju88
	Flt Sgt E.L. Mahar RAAF	185 Sqn EP722	Ju88
	Wt Off G.H.T. Farquharson RCAF	126 Sqn	Bf109
	Sgt D.G. Guy	185 Sqn	Bf109 probable
15/10/42	Plt Off W.C. Walton	1435 Sqn EP140	Ju88
	Flt Sgt A.H. Scott	1435 Sqn BP873	Bf109
	Sgt V.H. Wynn RCAF (US)	249 Sqn BR373	Bf109
	Plt Off V.K. Moody RCAF (US)	249 Sqn EP135	Ju88
	Plt Off J.W. Williams RCAF	249 Sqn EP340	Ju88 probable
	Sqn Ldr M.M. Stephens	229 Sqn BR562	Ju88
	Flt Lt R.O. Jones (US)	126 Sqn	Bf109
	Flt Sgt A.W. Varey	126 Sqn	Bf109
	Wg Cdr P.P. Hanks	Luqa Wing BR498	Bf109
	Flt Lt K.L. Charney	185 Sqn AB532	MC202
	Flt Sgt E.L. Mahar RAAF	185 Sqn EP722	MC202
	Sqn Ldr E.N. Woods	249 Sqn	Bf109
	Sgt A.B. Stead RNZAF	249 Sqn EP338	Bf109 probable
	Plt Off A.S. Yates RAAF ⎱	249 Sqn AR488	Ju88 probable
	Sgt A.B. Stead RNZAF ⎰	249 Sqn EP338	
	Plt Off J.G. Sanderson RAAF	249 Sqn EP448	Ju88 probable
	Flg Off J.F. McElroy RCAF	249 Sqn BR373	Ju88
	Flg Off L. Cheek	185 Sqn BR498	Ju88
16/10/42	Flt Lt W.T.E. Rolls	126 Sqn BR498	Ju88
	Capt K.L. Kuhlmann SAAF	185 Sqn EP187	Ju88 probable
	Plt Off L.S. Reid RAAF	185 Sqn EP343	Ju88 probable
	Sgt N.M. Park RNZAF	126 Sqn MK-J	Bf109
	Plt Off A.D. Owen	1435 Sqn EP332	Bf109 probable
	Sgt E.H. Francis	229 Sqn	Bf109
	Flt Sgt L.G.C. de l'Ara	249 Sqn BR565	Ju88
	Plt Off J.L. Lowery RCAF (US)	249 Sqn EP201	Bf109
	Flt Lt H.W. McLeod RCAF	1435 Sqn EP541	Bf109
	Plt Off J.W. Williams RCAF	249 Sqn AR488	Ju88
	Sgt V.H. Wynn RCAF (US)	249 Sqn	Ju88 probable
	Plt Off J.G. Sanderson RAAF	249 Sqn EP132	Bf109
	Sgt R. Miller	229 Sqn	Ju88
	Sgt P.M. Charron RCAF	126 Sqn	Ju88
	Sgt N. Marshall RCAF	126 Sqn	Bf109 probable
17/10/42	Flt Lt R.O. Jones (US)	126 Sqn EP341	Ju88 (by collision, also KiA)
	Wg Cdr P.P. Hanks	Luqa Wing BR498	Ju88
	Plt Off W.L. Thompson	126 Sqn	Ju88
	Plt Off J.D. Stevenson RCAF	126 Sqn	Ju88
	Flt Sgt A.W. Varey	126 Sqn	Ju88 probable, Bf109
	Sgt J.F. Yeatman RNZAF	126 Sqn	Ju88 probable
	Sgt A.J. Tiddy (SA)	126 Sqn	Ju88
	Plt Off K.C.M. Giddings	249 Sqn AR488	Ju88, Bf109
	Plt Off R. Seed	249 Sqn BP866	Ju88 probable
	Flt Lt E.L. Hetherington	249 Sqn BR565	Bf109
	Flt Lt C.H. Parkinson RAAF	229 Sqn X-V	Bf109
	Plt Off E.A. Budd	249 Sqn EP201	Bf109 probable
18/10/42	Sgt J.E. Mortimer RNZAF	126 Sqn	Bf109
	Sgt A.J. Tiddy (SA)	126 Sqn	Bf109
19/10/42	Plt Off W.C. Walton	1435 Sqn BR236	MC202 probable (claimed as RE2001)
	Flt Sgt L.G.C. de l'Ara ⎱	249 Sqn EP201	
	Sgt A.B. Stead RNZAF ⎬	249 Sqn EP520	Ju88
	Plt Off J.G. Sanderson RAAF ⎰	249 Sqn EP199	
21/10/42	Flt Sgt A.H. Scott	1435 Sqn EP621	Bf109 probable
	Plt Off W.C. Walton	1435 Sqn EP209	MC202
	Sgt N. Marshall RCAF	126 Sqn	2 Bf109 probables

22/10/42	Flt Lt H.W. McLeod RCAF	1435 Sqn BS161	MC202
	Flt Lt J.F. McElroy RCAF ⎫	249 Sqn EP708	Bf109
	Plt Off J.L. Lowery RCAF (US)⎭	249 Sqn EP201	
	Plt Off J.G. Sanderson RAAF	249 Sqn EP199	MC202
	Sqn Ldr E.N. Woods	249 Sqn BR529	Bf109 probable
23/10/42	Sgt R.H. Saunders	185 Sqn EP467	Bf109
24/10/42	Plt Off K.C.M. Giddings	249 Sqn BR565	MC202, MC202 probable
	Plt Off J.W. Williams RCAF	249 Sqn EP520	Bf109
25/10/42	Flt Lt R.I.A. Smith RCAF	126 Sqn BR311	Bf109
	Sgt N.M. Park RNZAF	126 Sqn BR311	Bf109 (also FTR)
26/10/42	Plt Off I.R. Maclennan RCAF	1435 Sqn BR591	Bf109
	Flt Lt W.T.E. Rolls	126 Sqn BR345	Bf109
	Plt Off W.C. Walton	1435 Sqn EP188	Bf109
27/10/42	Sqn Ldr E.N. Woods	249 Sqn BR529	Bf109 probable
3/11/42	Sgt T.J. Gunstone	185 Sqn	Bf109
12/11/42	Flg Off A.W. Gubb RCAF	69 Sqn BR663	Bf109 (by evasive action)
14/11/42	Plt Off D.A. Piggot RNZAF⎫	126 Sqn EP205	BR20
	Sgt R.B. Hendry RNZAF ⎭	126 Sqn AR497	
	Plt Off W.J. Hibbert	126 Sqn EP433	Bf110
	Sgt R.B. Hendry RNZAF	126 Sqn AR497	Ju90 probable
	Flt Lt I.R. Maclennan RCAF	1435 Sqn EP519	SM75 (claimed as SM82)
	Plt Off J.N. Kirkman ⎫	1435 Sqn BR376	Fiat G.12 (claimed as Fiat G.18)
	Sgt T.R.D. Kebbell RNZAF⎭	1435 Sqn EP444	
21/11/42	Sqn Ldr A. Warburton	69 Sqn ER647	Ju88
7/12/42	Sqn Ldr A.D.J. Lovell	1435 Sqn EP653	Ju88
11/12/42	Sqn Ldr E.N. Woods	249 Sqn AR559	Bf110
	Flg Off J.J. Lynch (US)	249 Sqn EP833	Bf110, Ju52 probable
	Wg Cdr S.B. Grant ⎫	Takali Wing EP622	Bf110
	Plt Off W.J. Locke RCAF⎭	249 Sqn EP132	
	Flt Lt R. Seed ⎫	249 Sqn EP728	Bf110
	Plt Off W.J. Cleverly⎭	249 Sqn BR373	
	Sqn Ldr E.N. Woods ⎫	249 Sqn AR559	
	Flt Sgt J.C. Hughes RCAF ⎬	249 Sqn EP177	Ju88
	Flt Sgt M.J. Costello RNZAF⎭	249 Sqn AB535	
	Wg Cdr S.B. Grant	Takali Wing EP622	Ju52
	Flt Lt R. Seed	249 Sqn EP728	Ju52
14/12/42	Flg Off J.J. Lynch (US) ⎫	249 Sqn EP140	
	Plt Off A.B. Stead RNZAF⎭	249 Sqn BR373	Ju88
	Sgt W.J.B. Stark	249 Sqn EP706	
	Sqn Ldr E.N. Woods⎫	249 Sqn AR559	
	Flt Lt R. Seed ⎬	249 Sqn EP708	Ju88
	Beaufighter ⎭	272 Sqn	
15/12/42	Plt Off J.F. Yeatman RNZAF	126 Sqn MK-S	MC202 probable (claimed as Bf109)
17/12/42	Flt Lt W.C. Walton	1435 Sqn AR561	2 Ju52
	Sgt T.R.D. Kebbell RNZAF	1435 Sqn EP519	Ju52
	Flg Off J.J. Lynch (US) ⎫	249 Sqn EP343	
	Flt Sgt M.J. Costello RNZAF⎬	249 Sqn EP131	Ju88
	Beaufighter ⎭	272 Sqn	
	Flg Off J.J. Lynch (US) ⎫	249 Sqn EP343	
	Plt Off W.J. Locke RCAF⎭	249 Sqn EP140	Ju88
	Beaufighter	272 Sqn	
19/12/42	Sqn Ldr E.N. Woods	249 Sqn EP728	Do24
	Plt Off W.J. Locke RCAF ⎫	249 Sqn EP186	
	Flt Sgt J.C. Hughes RCAF⎬	249 Sqn BR373	Ju88
	Beaufighter ⎭	272 Sqn	
23/12/42	Flt Lt J.H. Long RCAF	126 Sqn AB526	Ju88
24/12/42	Plt Off J.G. Sanderson RAAF⎫	249 Sqn T-F	Bf110
	Unknown pilot ⎭	249 Sqn	
27/12/42	Plt Off A.R. Chaplin (SA)	229 Sqn	Bf109G

APPENDIX III

SPITFIRE ACES – MALTA 1942

		Malta Claims	Total WWII
†Plt Off G.F. Beurling DSO DFC DFM+	249 Sqn	26^1/$_3$	30^1/$_3$
†Flt Sgt P.A. Schade DFM	126 Sqn	13^1/$_2$	13^1/$_3$ + 3^1/$_3$ V-1s
†Flt Lt H.W. McLeod RCAF DFC+	603/1435 Sqns	12	20
Plt Off R.B. Hesselyn RNZAF DFM+	249 Sqn	12	21^1/$_2$
†Plt Off J.W. Yarra RAAF DFM	185 Sqn	12	12
Flt Lt J.A. Plagis DFC+ (Rhod)	249/185 Sqns	11	15
†Flt Sgt C. Weaver III RCAF (US) DFM	185 Sqn	10^1/$_2$	12^1/$_2$
†Sgt N.M. Park RNZAF DFM	126 Sqn	10^1/$_4$	10^1/$_4$
†Plt Off V.P. Brennan RAAF DFC DFM	249 Sqn	10	10
Plt Off A.P. Goldsmith RAAF DFC DFM	126 Sqn	9^3/$_4$	13^3/$_4$
†Plt Off P.A. Nash DFC	249 Sqn	9^1/$_2$	11^1/$_3$
Flt Lt W.T.E. Rolls DFC DFM	126 Sqn	8^1/$_2$	17
Flt Lt C.H. Parkinson RAAF DFC	603/229 Sqns	8^1/$_2$	8^1/$_2$
Flt Lt J.F. McElroy RCAF DFC	249 Sqn	8	11^1/$_2$
Plt Off R.F. Tilley RCAF (US) DFC	601/126 Sqns	8	8
Flt Lt R.W. McNair RCAF DFC	249 Sqn	7^3/$_4$	15^3/$_4$
†Sqn Ldr E.N. Woods DFC+	249 Sqn	7^2/$_3$	10^2/$_3$
†Flt Lt R.O. Jones (US)	126 Sqn	7^1/$_2$ + ^{1}/$_5$	7^1/$_2$ + ^{1}/$_5$
†Flt Lt N.C. Macqueen DFC	249 Sqn	7^1/$_2$	7^1/$_2$
†Flt Lt R. West DFC+	249/185 Sqns	7^1/$_4$	7^1/$_4$
Flg Off G.A.F. Buchanan DFC (Rhod)	249 Sqn	7	7^1/$_2$
†Plt Off G. Stenborg RNZAF DFC	185 Sqn	7	14^1/$_3$
†Plt Off J.W. Williams RCAF DFC	249 Sqn	7	7
Flt Lt I.R. Maclennan RCAF DFM	1435 Sqn	7	7
Sqn Ldr M.M. Stephens DSO DFC++	249/229 Sqns	7	22
Flt Lt R.I.A. Smith RCAF DFC	126 Sqn	6^1/$_4$	13^1/$_2$
Wg Cdr S.B. Grant DFC	249 Sqn/Takali Wg	6	7
†Sqn Ldr R.A. Mitchell DFC	603/249 Sqns	6	6
Flt Lt W.C. Walton DFC	1435 Sqn	6	6
Plt Off J.H.E. Bisley RAAF DFC	126 Sqn	5^1/$_2$	6^1/$_2$
Flt Sgt A.W. Varey DFM	126 Sqn	5^1/$_2$	5^1/$_2$
Sqn Ldr W.J. Johnson DFC	126 Sqn	5^1/$_3$ + ^{1}/$_4$	6^1/$_3$ + ^{1}/$_4$
Flt Sgt W.G. Dodd RCAF	185 Sqn	5^1/$_3$	6^2/$_3$
†Flt Sgt J.H. Ballantyne RCAF DFM	603/229 Sqns	5^1/$_4$	5^1/$_4$
†Flt Sgt D.G. Reid RCAF DFM	185 Sqn	5	5
Flt Sgt K.W.S. Evans DFM	126 Sqn	5	5
Flt Sgt A.H. Scott DFM	126 Sqn	5	5

† indicates pilot was killed at Malta or later during the war, the exception being Plt Off Screwball Beurling who was killed shortly after the end of the war.

APPENDIX IV

SGT CLAUDE WEAVER III DFM RCAF 185 SQUADRON

On his return to the UK, arriving at Hendon by air on 16 October 1943, Claude Weaver DFM was interviewed by MI.9 the same day. His subsequent report stated:

"On 9 September 1942 I was pilot of a Spitfire engaged over Sicily. I was hit by anti-aircraft fire [*sic*] and force-landed on the beach at Comiso. My aircraft was damaged, but I was immediately arrested by Carabinieri and did not have time to destroy it. I was very thoroughly searched on the spot and my compass (a small round one), aids box and food pack were taken. I spent five days living in the joint German-Italian officers' mess at Comiso. I was not interrogated, even informally. The treatment was good. On 14 September I was taken to the interrogation centre at Camp 50, Poggio. I was given five days' solitary confinement. I was given a straightforward interrogation two or three times by an Italian officer and for a time an Australian RAF Sergeant shared my cell. I suspected him from the start, as in talking about shows and women it appeared that he had seen no shows in England subsequent to 1937, and he used the expression 'preservative' instead of 'preventative'. He got nothing out of me. Before leaving Poggio I filled in a genuine Red Cross form."

[Nonetheless, an Italian interrogation report apparently stated that Weaver was "very loquacious and confided a little secret." This may have had something to do with the Spitfire's IFF equipment, which Weaver did not have time to destroy. It was the second such complete set captured by the Italians, the first being removed from a Blenheim (Z7508) shot down near Crotone the previous year.]

"I was drastically searched. All my clothes were removed and my person was examined in detail. I left Chieti about the middle of March 1943 for Campo 49 (Fontanellato), ten miles north-west of Parma with about 40 others, including four officers of the USAF. Three of us made an abortive attempt to jump the train on the way. After three months at Campo 49 I managed by special request to get myself sent back with other Americans to Chieti. I arrived back there about the middle of June.

"First attempt to escape: From Chieti. I tried to get out through the wire in March 1943, but was hung up and after half an hour discovered, I was severely beaten up by the sentries, one of them breaking his rifle over me. I was given 30 days in cells as punishment. Parcels were smuggled in to my cell. Second attempt to escape: From Campo 49 (Fontanellato). I attempted with Sergeant W. Wendt, USA of No. 249 Squadron RAF to escape through the camp sewer. We got some distance down the pipe, but then found that the contents had caked and blocked the exit, so that we had to come back. We were not discovered.

"Lt-Colonel Rideout and I escaped from Chieti early on the morning of 17 September 1943. By that time the Germans had entered the camp. The Senior British Officer had given the all clear, and the Italian guards had largely deserted. We went over two layers of wire and a 16-foot wall. We were challenged once from one of the raised sentry boxes (I think by a German), but we pretended to be drunk, called out 'Amigo' and were not fired at. We wore British battle dress, and little blue skull-caps. We were posing as Spanish workmen. Our passes had been forged by Lt Goldingham and the photographs used on them had been taken by the Italians at Campo 21. We were wearing blue battle dress tunics when photographed, but we pared the photographs down to show only part of the collar. The passes were over-stamped BRERNO-INTRETA. In addition, we each had a tracing from a silk map obtained in the camp, and homemade compasses. We intended making for the Eighth Army on the east side of Italy.

"We covered 17 miles southward across country on the morning of 17 September. On the evening of 17 September we reached Fara San Martino, which we found full of European civilian internees. We were given 100 lire by a Russian woman. Two Italian youths wanted to attach themselves to us, in the hope of reaching the Allied armies with our assistance. We decided that the assistance should be mutual. We left Fara on the evening of 17 September and were guided over fields by the two youths to an electrified railway station, where we caught a train at 0400 hours on the morning of 18 September. On the train we exchanged clothes with some Italians, who were glad of our warmer battle dresses. We left the train at Villa San Maria at 1300 hours on 18 September, and at 0200 hours, reached Agnone, where we slept in straw stacks outside the town. On 19 September we walked all day to San Ellena. On 20 September we by-passed Campbasso, where we learned that German staff were installed, and walked to near Riccia. On 21 September we went on to Motta (north of Volturno). At this point we decided to push on without our guides. At 1400 hours on 23 September we had reached a position just east of Lucera from where we could see Foggia. We heard that Foggia was still in German hands. We had acquired by now shepherds' crooks, floppy hats, and a great growth of beard. At noon on 24 September we reached Melfi, where we heard that the Allied Forces were at La Capiscola, some 20 miles distant. We decided to push on, but between Melfi and Rionero I sprained my ankle. We saw some Germans patrolling along a railway track. I struggled along for about three miles and we reached Rionero and broke into an empty house.

"Lt-Colonel Rideout went out to scrounge for food and then started off through the German lines to get help for me. He was back within 12 hours, bringing with him a mule which he had obtained from two Canadian engineers. I rode on the mule into La Capiscola on 25 September with Rideout from whom I then parted. I was taken to Eighth Army Headquarters. I was interrogated by several Intelligence and Staff officers on General Montgomery's staff. On 27 September I was flown to Malta where I was interrogated and taken before Air Vice-Marshal Park. I was kept in Malta about a week in a rest camp and was then allowed to rejoin my squadron, where I did some practice flying. On 6 October I received instructions to return to the UK. I was four days in Algiers where I was interrogated by Major Holder and Colonel Hunter (Combined Allied HQ and POW Centre). I flew to

UK in a Fortress, leaving Algiers on 14 October."

Wt Off Weaver received a Mention in Despatches for his escape. He also received his commission and after a brief rest was posted to 403RCAF Squadron at Kenley. He was soon back in action, claiming a Bf109 destroyed on 30 December 1943. A FW190 followed on 21 January 1944, but he was then shot down on 28 January by a FW190 (believed to have been flown by German ace Fw Gerhard Vogt of 6/JG26, his 18th victory). Apparently alive when captured, he died from his wounds two hours later. He was still only 20 years of age. His DFC was gazetted in March 1944.

APPENDIX V

SGT WILLIE WENDT RCAF 249 SQUADRON

From the confines of his holding camp Willie Wendt wrote to his mother on 5 December 1942:

"My good luck has finally come to an end, temporarily at least. I was forced to bale out over Sicily. Did not even have time to let the boys know I was OK. If I had it would have saved all of you a lot of needless worry. I am temporarily in a quarantine camp not far from Rome. I will be here two weeks and then go to a permanent camp where I will be able to receive mail. The food is edible. We can get extra stuff from the Red Cross. I am well, uninjured and getting along as well as could be expected. I can take it until I get another chance to dish it out. I still hope to get a crack at the Japs."

Along with other prisoners, Wendt made his way to Allied lines following the Italian armistice in September 1943. On his return to the UK he was interviewed by officers of MI.9:

"I took off from Malta on 30 November 1942 in a fighter-bomber to bomb Biscari. After having reached my objective and dropped my bombs, I developed trouble as I came out of my dive. My engine caught fire and I was compelled to bale out. I came down about five kilometres west of Mt Calvo. I slashed my chute to the best of my ability, hid it under some trees, and started to walk in a westerly direction. I saw a man and a boy in a cart, and rode along with them for about half an hour. When their route turned away from the direction in which I wanted to travel, I got off and approached a woman standing outside a house, asking her for a drink. She gave me some food and wine. I was just finishing my meal when three Carabinieri and a civilian came to the house and rounded me up. I was kept in the house till about 1900 hours and then sent to Gela aerodrome. I was at Gela until 2 December. I was then moved by car to Catania, and then by rail to Poggio Marteno (40 kilometres north-east of Rome). This was a sort of Interrogation Camp. I was left in solitary confinement for about five days, and then put in with other airmen. The interrogation was not pressed. On about 18 December I was moved to Chieti (Campo 21).

"I escaped with Captain Borradaile [in September 1943] and the details of my escape are the same as his. I left Captain Borradaile on the first evening and joined up with Captain McFall and Captain Collingwood. We slept for about three hours in a field and on the night of 25 September stayed in a house, moving on 26 September to another house and reaching Villa Magna on 27 September, where we stayed with some people until 5 October. On 4 October we made contact with some parachutists who told us that there was an evacuation scheme in hand for any stragglers to be taken off by the Navy from the mouth of the River Foro (south of Francavilla). We made our way there on 5 October and waited until 9 October. The parachutists had a beach party here and signalled each night, but no boats appeared. On the fifth night (9 October) a German boat appeared and opened up with a machine-gun. In the confusion we got separated from Captain McFall. Captain Collingwood and I carried on to Giullano Teatino, where we stayed in a house until 17 October. On 17 October I left Captain Collingwood, as he wished to remain, and I moved on my own. My route was via Orsogna to Castel Frentano, where I stayed in a farmhouse three kilometres south of Castel Frentano until 26 October, then in another house nearby, returning to the first house on 29 October and staying till 1 November.

"My route was now across the Sangra River to Gissi. I made contact with our troops at the bend of the road near Capello on 6 November. I was sent by truck with a German prisoner to Capello, from where I hitch-hiked to San Salvo. On 7 November, I reached Bari, staying here with the Prisoner of War Commission till 10 November. I moved on 10 November to Taranto. I stayed at an aerodrome with some friends on 13 November, got a lift on 14 November to Algiers, and on 15 November to Rabat. I left Rabat on 17 November, reaching UK on 18 November."

Following his return to the UK Sgt Wendt was repatriated to Canada on special leave. He returned to the UK 30/1/44 and rejoined 421RCAF Squadron, the unit from which he had been posted to Malta, before receiving his commission and joining 19 Squadron on Mustangs. On his return to operations, his flew under the name of 'William Harvey' in case he was recaptured. Sadly, he was shot down by flak on 7 June 1944 and crashed on farmland near La Chappelle Brestoy, where he was killed. The local farmer managed to retrieve part of his parachute on which was written in ink: 'Wee Willie' and '5987' (possibly mis-transcribed by the Investigating Officer since this number was assumed to be the last four digits of his Service No.J/39857) and also a drawing of a dice. The Germans removed the body for burial in the Communal Cemetery at Eturqueraye.

APPENDIX VI

AMERICAN SPITFIRE PILOTS AT MALTA 1942

(† killed at Malta)

† Plt Off Hiram Aldine **Putnam** RCAF (J/15079) known as 'Tex'; from Clarkwood, Texas; b.4/11/12; enlisted RCAF Ontario 14/9/40; posted to UK 8/5/41; 133 (Eagle) Squadron UK; arrived Malta aboard Sunderland 16/2/42; 126 Squadron Malta (claims 1-0-0); killed in action 21/4/42.

Plt Off Richard E. **McHan** RAF (100991) known as 'Sandy'; 121 (Eagle) Squadron UK; arrived Malta 16/2/42 aboard Sunderland; MNFU/249/126 Squadrons Malta; shot down and wounded 3/7/42; † Died 26/12/75 California USA.

Plt Off/Flt Lt James Elvidge **Peck** DFC RAF (103471) b. 1921; from Berkeley, California; 121 (Eagle) Squadron UK; HMS *Eagle* to Malta 21/3/42; 126 Squadron Malta (3¹/₂-3-9) DFC; transferred to USAF, 52ndFG (claims 1-0-1); † killed in flying accident (P-38) 11/4/44 (Captain).

Plt Off Donald William **McLeod** RAF (103466); from Boston; 121 (Eagle) Squadron UK; HMS *Eagle* to Malta 21/3/42; 126 Squadron Malta (claims 2-0-0); shot down injured 24/3/42; transferred to USAF; Major 83rdFS 78thFG (claims 2-0-2); shot down, evaded 10/6/44; US DFC. † Died 10/46 Connecticut USA.

Plt Off/Flg Off Reade Franklin **Tilley** DFC RCAF (J/15011) from Clearwater, Florida, b.15/3/18; enlisted RCAF 10/6/40 Hamilton; posted to UK 6/3/42; 121 (Eagle) Squadron UK (claims 0-1-0); USS *Wasp* to Malta 20/4/42; 601/126 Squadrons Malta (claims 7-2-6); transferred to USAF 13/10/42 (Major, non operational). Retired as Colonel.

Flt Sgt Arthur Bernard **Cleaveland** RCAF (R/67504), known as 'Artie', from Springfield, Ohio b.14/10/18; 601 Squadron UK; USS *Wasp* to Malta 20/4/42; 601 Squadron Malta (claims 0-0-1); transferred to USAF 13/12/42 (2/Lt) 66thFS North Africa (5-0-0: 5 Ju52s in one sortie 18/4/43 flying P-40F); 1/Lt May 1943. US DFC, US Silver Star. Rejoined USAF 1949, Capt. † Died 15/4/51 in Washington.

Plt Off Douglas E. **Booth** RAF from New York known as 'Tiger'; 121 (Eagle) Squadron UK; USS *Wasp* to Malta 20/4/42; 126 Squadron Malta (claims 0-2-0); shot down and crash-landed 15/5/42, unhurt; transferred to USAF 9/9/42 4thFG (335thFS) no claims; 12th RCD 9/43. US DFC.

† Plt Off Gordon **Murray** RCAF (J/7232); possibly Scot living in USA; enlisted RCAF 9/11/40 Niagara Falls; posted to UK 21/9/41; ex-603 Squadron UK; USS *Wasp* to Malta 20/4/42; 603 Squadron Malta; killed in action 22/4/42.

Plt Off Fred **Almos** RAF; 121 (Eagle) Squadron UK; USS *Wasp* to Malta 20/4/42; 249/126 Squadrons Malta (no claims). Posted away.

Sgt Salvador Bassi **Walcott** RCAF (R/79006) known as 'Bud'; US citizen b.24/12/19; enlisted RCAF 28/12/40 Montreal; posted to UK 11/11/41; 603 Squadron UK; USS *Wasp* to Malta 20/4/42 but landed at Setif Constantine, Algeria; interned by Vichy; released 11/42 and back to UK; transferred to USAF 8/12/42; 346thFS, 350thFG North Africa (2/Lt); believed with 31stFG (307thFS) Italy 1944 (2/Lt-Lt: Air Medal and Oak Leaf Cluster); † killed in helicopter flying accident 1950s.

Plt Off Bruce C. **Downs** RAF; 121 (Eagle) Squadron UK; USS *Wasp* to Malta 8/5/42; 126 Squadron

Malta (claims 1-1-1); transferred to USAF 9/42; 4thFG. No claims.

† Flg Off/Flt Lt Ripley Ogden **Jones** RAF (100520); known as 'Rip'; from Cooperstown, New York (b.10/4/15). USN pilot before joining RAF; 611 Squadron UK; USS *Wasp* to Malta 8/5/42; 126 Squadron Malta (claims 7¹/₂-1-3); killed in action 17/10/42.

Flt Sgt Merriwell William **Vineyard** RCAF (R/86179) known as 'Tex'; from Bells, Texas, b.21/9/20; enlisted RCAF 19/12/40 Winnipeg; posted to UK 14/9/41; USS *Wasp* to Malta 8/5/42. 185 Squadron Malta (0-0-1); commissioned 7/7/42 (J/15736); transferred US Navy 9/11/42. VF-2 (F6F-3) 1944 (claims 6-0-0); US DFC, US Silver Star. Remained in USN postwar (Capt 1963).

Sgt Leroy Joseph **Morsheimer** RCAF (R/79171) b 28/9/18; enlisted RCAF 21/2/41 Montreal; posted to UK 11/11/41; 611 Squadron UK; USS *Wasp* to Malta 8/5/42, but not retained due to operational inexperience; transferred to USAF 30/11/42, 346thFS, 350thFG North Africa (1/Lt).

Flt Sgt/Plt Off Basil Wilfred **Andrews** RCAF (R/74315) from Chicago (b.7/11/17); enlisted RCAF 21/10/40 Ottawa. Posted UK 14/8/41. USS *Wasp* to Malta 8/5/42; 185 Squadron Malta (claims 0-0-1); commissioned (J/15739); † killed in flying accident UK 30/10/42.

† Sgt Edwin DeWitt **Moye** RCAF (R/67913) known as 'Cactus' or 'Alabama', from Mobile, Alabama, b.17/3/17; enlisted RCAF 27/10/40 Ontario; posted to UK 17/9/41; USS *Wasp* to Malta 8/5/42; 185 Squadron Malta; killed in action 6/7/42.

† Flt Sgt Harold Joseph **Fox** RCAF (R/78316) known as 'Bud'; from New York City (b. 6/7/13); enlisted RCAF 19/10/40; posted to UK 27/8/41; USS *Wasp* to Malta 8/5/42; 249 Squadron Malta (claims 1-0-0); killed in action 14/5/42.

Plt Off John Harvey **Curry** RCAF (C/2645) known as 'Crash'; from Dallas, Texas b.12/8/15; enlisted RCAF 27/8/40 Ottawa; posted to UK 20/11/41; 137/601 Squadrons UK; HMS *Eagle* to Malta 3/6/42; 601 Squadron Malta (claims 1-0-0); 601 Squadron Western Desert (claims 6¹/₃-2-4) DFC. CO 80 Squadron 1943-44 (OBE); Repatriated to Canada 26/7/44, No.1 Flying Instructor School.

† Plt Off Harry **Kelly** RAF (108639); from Texas; HMS *Eagle* to Malta 9/6/42; 249 Squadron Malta, killed in action 2/7/42.

Plt Off Ernest Warner **Spradley** RCAF (J/15328); known as 'Tex'; born Texas 7/8/18; enlisted RCAF 20/7/40; posted to UK 29/5/41; HMS *Eagle* to Malta 9/6/42; 249 Squadron Malta (claims 0-0-¹/₃); to ME; transferred to USAF 13/2/43.

Plt Off Vincent Kenneth **Moody** RCAF (J/15362); known as 'Junior'; born 18/12/19 Taunton, Massachusetts of Nova Scotian parents; enlisted RCAF 23/10/40 Halifax, Nova Scotia; posted to UK 3/8/41; 118 Squadron UK (claims 0-¹/₂-1); HMS *Eagle* to Malta 15/7/42; 249 Squadron Malta (claims 1-0-2); 610 Squadron UK (claims 1-0-1); 610 Squadron UK (claims 1-0-1); 131 Squadron (Flight Commander) UK; † killed in action 12/6/44 (DFC 1/44).

Plt Off Joseph Lee **Lowery** RCAF (R/93011); known as 'Smokey Joe'; enlisted RCAF 5/2/41 Toronto; graduated as pilot but then deserted from RCAF 11/8/41; reached UK and presumably joined RAF; 242 Squadron UK; HMS *Eagle* to Malta 15/7/42; 249 Squadron Malta (claims 1¹/₂-0-1); transferred to USAF (formally discharged from RCAF 21/3/44).

Flt Sgt Daniel James **Hartney** RCAF (R/70719); known as 'Danny'; from Drinkwater, Saskatchewan, but apparently US citizen (b.17/12/19); enlisted RCAF 13/9/40 Regina. Posted to UK 14/8/41; HMS *Eagle* to Malta 15/7/42; 185 Squadron Malta; injured flying accident 19/7/42; † died from Infantile Paralysis (Polio) 3/1/43 on board hospital ship *HTL6* en route for UK; buried at sea.

Sgt Claude **Weaver** III DFM RCAF (R/83374) known as 'Weave'; from Oklahoma City, b. 18/8/22; 403 RCAF Squadron UK. HMS *Eagle* to Malta 15/7/42; 185 Squadron Malta (claims 10¹/₂-3-0); POW 9/9/42, Sicily. Following Italian capitulation escaped from POW camp 9/43 and arrived allied lines riding a donkey, dressed as a goatherd (see Appendix V). Returned to UK; 403 RCAF Squadron (claims 2-0-0); † POW: died from wounds received in action 28/1/44. Received DFC.

† Sgt Joseph Edward **Otis** RCAF (R/82872); known as Joe; b.1/1/22; enlisted RCAF 11/2/41 Ottawa; posted to UK 1/11/41; 406 RCAF Squadron UK; HMS *Eagle* to Malta 15/7/42; killed in action 19/7/42.

Flt Sgt Vasseure H. **Wynn** RCAF (R/95640); known as 'Georgia' although from Oklahoma, b.11/10/17; enlisted RCAF 4/3/41 Ottawa; posted to UK 12/12/41; HMS *Eagle* to Malta 15/7/42; 249 Squadron Malta (claims 1¹/₃-2-2); wounded by Bf109 20/7/42; commissioned 5/11/42 (J/16127); transferred USAF 6/43 4thFG (claims 2¹/₂-0-0, plus 2 on ground); POW 13/4/44 (Capt); Korea 1951 27thFEW Major (claims 0-0-1). Two US DFCs (WW2), US DFC (Korea).

† Wt Off Peter **Carter** RCAF (R/87697); American citizen born in South Africa (b.16/8/17); enlisted RCAF 8/1/41 Vancouver; posted to UK 2/11/41; HMS *Eagle* to Malta 21/7/42; 249 Squadron Malta (claims 0-0-1); killed in action 16/10/42.

Sgt Herbert Percival **Milligan** RCAF (R/79317) known as 'Bud'; possibly from Idaho, b. 3/1/18; enlisted RCAF 28/3/41 Montreal; posted to UK 6/1/42; HMS *Eagle* to Malta 21/7/42; 603/229 Squadron Malta (claims 0-1-0); wounded 24/10/42; commissioned 24/3/44 (J/45892); released from RCAF 3/4/45.

Flg Off Phillip Alexander **Woodger** RAF (62290); US citizen; known as 'Woody'; 79 Squadron UK; HMS *Furious* to Malta 11/8/42; 185 Squadron Malta; POW Sicily 27/8/42.

Plt Off/Flt Lt Arthur Ford **Roscoe** DFC RAF (100530); known as 'Art'; born Chicago 12/4/21; 71 (Eagle) Squadron UK (claims 1-2-0); HMS *Furious* to Malta 11/8/42; 229 Squadron Malta (claims 1-2-2); shot down wounded 12/10/42; survived crash of Liberator at Gibraltar 31/10/42; 165 Squadron UK; 229 Squadron Malta (1943), 242 Squadron Sicily, CO 232 Squadron Corsica.

Plt Off/Flg Off Leo S. **Nomis** RAF; Los Angeles, California, b. 9/3/22; part Irish, part Sioux Indian; enlisted RAF Ottawa 1941; known to his Eagle Squadron friends as 'Chief'; 71 Eagle Squadron UK (claims 1/2-0-1); HMS *Furious* to Malta 11/8/42: 229 Squadron Malta (no claims); posted to ME 9/42; 92 Squadron (claims 2-0-0); transferred to USAF 3/43; 57thFG 1943; returned to USA as instructor, 50thFG, 53rdFG (Capt). Volunteered to join the embryonic Israeli Air Force 1948; flew Czech-built Bf109Gs, known as Avia S-199s with 101 Squadron. On return to USA flew with Air National Guard until 1956. Real Estate until retired in 1982. Author of *The Desert Hawks* with Brian Cull, published 1998. † Died 2000.

Sgt Nicholas Demetrius **Sintetos** RCAF (R/82804) US citizen of Greek origin, known as 'Nick'; b.10/11/20; enlisted RCAF 3/2/41 Ottawa; posted to UK 7/1/42; 121 (Eagle) Squadron UK; HMS *Furious* to Malta 11/8/42; 126 Squadron Malta (claims 0-0-1); transferred to USAF 12/12/42.

† Plt Off Ian Fraser **Preston** RCAF (J/15388); from Glencoe, Illinois, b.10/2/20; enlisted RCAF 9/4/41 Toronto; posted to UK 8/12/41; HMS *Furious* to Malta 17/8/42; 126 Squadron Malta; killed in action 23/9/42.

Plt Off Herbert Temple **Nash** RAF (121440) US citizen from Texas, known as 'Tex'; 121 (Eagle) Squadron UK; HMS *Furious* to Malta 17/8/42; 229 Squadron Malta (claims 1 3/4-0-4); shot down and wounded/injured 14/10/42.

Flt Sgt James Francis **Farrell** RCAF (R/79164) from Jersey City, New Jersey, b. 14/5/18; enlisted RCAF 20/2/41 Montreal; posted to UK 25/10/41; HMS *Furious* to Malta 17/8/42; 229 Squadron Malta; UK late 1942; commissioned 24/11/43(J/44106); repatriated to Canada 6/43; commissioned 29/11/43 (J/39857); posted to UK 2/44; 602 Squadron 1944 (Flg Off); repatriated to Canada 2/8/45; Mention in Desptaches 1/1/46.

Flt Sgt William David **Wendt** RCAF (R/100092) known as 'Wee Willie'; from Little Falls, Minnesota, b. 6/5/16; enlisted 20/3/41; posted to UK 23/11/41; 421RCAF Squadron UK; believe arrived Malta aboard Liberator 26/10/42; 249 Squadron Malta; POW 29/11/42 Sicily; following Italian capitulation escaped Italian POW camp 9/43 and made his way to Allied lines (see Appendix IV) Returned to UK; commissioned; † killed in action 7/6/44 (19 Squadron).

† Plt Off Gardner Hill **Kelly** RCAF (J/15375) from Sioux City, Iowa (b.24/3/21); enlisted RCAF 11/1/41 Toronto; posted to UK 19/11/41; 165 Squadron UK; commissioned 6/7/42; believe arrived Malta aboard Liberator 26/10/42; 126 Squadron Malta, killed in action 19/11/42.

Sgt George Charles **Warcup** RCAF (R/90478) known as 'Shorty'; possibly Canadian-born, living in USA, b.11/12/14; enlisted RCAF 22/3/41 Ontario; posted to UK 7/1/42; 406 RCAF Squadron UK; believe arrived Malta aboard Liberator 26/10/42; 185 Squadron Malta; commissioned 22/12/43 (J/42787); released RCAF 23/1/45.

Flt Sgt Fred Renshaw **Vance** RCAF (R/80721) known as 'Freddie'; from Washington DC (son of Capt Deane Vance MC USN) b.19/1/18; enlisted RCAF 4/11/40; posted to UK 14/10/41; 121 (Eagle) Squadron UK (claims 0-0-2). HMS *Furious* to Malta 29/10/42; 185 Squadron Malta. To Middle East, 112 Squadron (claims 1-0-0); † killed in action 13/7/43 Sicily.

Plt Off Albert Fremont **Eckert** RCAF (J/15344) b. 27/12/18; known as 'Al'; enlisted RCAF 11/9/40 Vancouver; posted to UK 8/8/41; 131 Squadron UK (claims 1 1/4-0-0); commissioned 20/4/42; HMS *Furious* to Malta 29/10/42; 185 Squadron Malta. Transferred to USAF 26/4/43.

Sgt Boyd Whitford **Dunning** RCAF (R/79272) b.19/10/18; enlisted RCAF 14/3/41 Montreal; posted to UK 7/1/42; HMS *Furious* to Malta 29/10/42; 185 Squadron Malta; commissioned (J/19678) 26/1/44; repatriated to Canada 3/12/44.

Flg Off/Sqn Ldr John Joseph **Lynch** Jr DFC & Bar RAF (103470); known as 'JJ'; from Alhambra, California; 71 (Eagle) Squadron UK (claims 1-0-0); flew long-range Spitfire to Malta 31/10/42; 249 Squadron Malta 1942/43 (claims 12-1-1½); CO 249 Squadron 1943; transferred to USAF (non operational); † killed in flying accident (F-84G) 9/3/56 (Lt Colonel).

APPENDIX VII

SPITBOMBERS

Notes from Malta on the Operational Use of the Spitfire Bomber
RAF Tactical Committee Report No.33

In the latter part of 1942, the Spitfire Vc was modified in Malta to take two 250lb bombs slung directly underneath the two outboard cannons. The reason for the introduction of this weapon was that during the preceding summer the enemy was ignoring our fighter sweeps over airfields in Southern Sicily. Hurricane bombers had been used, and the enemy reacted by sending his fighters up to intercept. The Hurricane had not the same good performance as the Spitfire and made co-operation difficult, especially after the bombs had been dropped.

Flying Characteristics of the Spitfire Vc Bomber
The modification to the Spitfire resulted in the aircraft being rather heavy during and immediately after the take-off, the take-off run being lengthened by about 150 yards. The best climbing speed was 160 IAS at 2,600 revs. The time taken to 18,000 feet at plus 4 boost was approximately 20 minutes, but above 18,000 feet the rate of climb dropped off considerably. There was practically no difference in the speed in level flight, and in the dive the speed was increased owing to the higher wing loading. The aircraft handled quite normally, and aerobatics were carried out with bombs attached and all controls responded normally. One bomb could be dropped at a time, and hardly any difference was noticed in the trim except at very high speeds.

Approach
Approach was made to the target at 18,000 feet to 20,000 feet, and it was found advisable to put the nose down and gain a little speed as the target was reached.

Bombing
The original method adopted in Malta was to approach directly over the target, execute a 180° stall turn, losing all possible speed, and diving vertically on to the target. This method was extremely accurate, but it was found impracticable because of turning back into the flak. Bombs were released at 10,000-12,000 feet. However, over targets where no heavy flak was expected this was found the best method, care being taken not to dive down into the light flak area.

The method subsequently adopted was for the bombers to fly in vics of three aircraft, closing into close formation near the target. Approach was made with the target to one side, usually so that it was between the cannon and the wing tip. When the target re-appeared behind the trailing edge, the bombers turned on to the target in a dive of about 75°. They commenced pulling out at about 13,000 feet. The perimeter of the airfield could usually be seen on each side of the nose at this height, and bombs were dropped by order from the leader when the near edge of the airfield was crossed. When the bombs were released, each aircraft jumped upward a few feet, although no reaction was felt when bombs were dropped in a vertical dive. Only very slight allowances had to be made for wind.

The bomb gear was designed so that there was no loss of performance once the bombs were dropped. Unlike the Hurricane bomb gear, the Spitfire (as modified by Malta) threw away all external bomb fittings, with the exception of a steel rib protruding less than one inch from the wing.

Tactics used by No.249 Squadron
The Officer Commanding No.249 Squadron, Qrendi, [Squadron Leader E.N. Woods] states that the best

results were ultimately obtained by using the following tactics: Six Spitfire bombers, each with 2 x 250lb GP bombs with stick attachments, flew in two vics of three escorted by four fighters in pairs, line abreast. They climbed to 20,000 feet to cross the Sicilian coast. Before approaching the target the bombers formed echelon starboard, and then started a gentle dive, attaining 220 IAS [318mph True] at about 18,000 feet. The bomber leader flew over the target until it appeared behind the trailing edge of his port main plane near the wing root. He then half-rolled to the left on his back and dived down vertically, followed by his section, which were then echeloned to port. The leader of the second section carried out a like manoeuvre with his section in line astern of the first. The resultant dive was 80-90°. The bombs were released at 10,000 feet, the reflector sight being used as a bombsight. On releasing the bombs the IAS was found to be about 450mph [about 515mph True], thus enabling the aircraft to be pulled out at 8,000 feet, or above the light flak.

Before starting the dive it was found advisable to wind back the rudder bias, and trim the aircraft considerably nose heavy. It was impossible to trim the aircraft during the dive, as both hands were needed on the control column. During the dive, the bomber's acceleration was much greater than that of the fighters, which were compelled to open their throttles fully to maintain their position. After bombing, the bombers continued their dive to ground level when out of the light flak area, and re-formed in line abreast. The enemy ground defence greatly underestimated the speed of our aircraft, and the flak was usually found to be some distance behind. In these bombing attacks, none of the targets was more than 15 miles from the coast.

OC 249 Squadron observes that the bomb fittings did not impede the performance of the aircraft as a fighter in any way. With bombs on, the aircraft was somewhat sluggish at low speeds, but fully aerobatic. In some cases landings were made with one bomb on. A much greater accuracy was obtained by the Spitfire bombers than that which our pilots had observed while escorting Bostons over France. The AOC Malta states that some squadrons preferred to break away in a climbing turn so as to rejoin the Spitfire escort. Other squadrons preferred to get away in a gentle dive under cover of the fighter escort.[139]

APPENDIX VIII

SPITFIRES BELIEVED TO HAVE OPERATED AT MALTA 1942

Serial No.	Mode/date of arrival	Aircraft fate/Pilot fate
AB262/GN-B	*Eagle* 7/3/42	DBR ground 7/4/42: Air raid.
AB263	*Eagle* 21/3/42	DBR ground 22/4/42: Air raid.
AB264/GN-H	*Eagle* 7/3/42	249 Sqn. 1435 Sqn 10/42. To USAF.
AB329	*Eagle* 7/3/42	SOC 6/5/42.
AB330/GN-C	*Eagle* 7/3/42	Lost 17/3/42 (acc): Sgt I.M. Cormack 249 Sqn – killed.
AB331	*Eagle* 7/3/42	DBR ground 21/3/42: Air raid.
AB332	*Eagle* 7/3/42	249 Sqn.
AB333	*Eagle* 21/3/42	SOC 5/42.
AB334/GN-J	*Eagle* 7/3/42	Shot down by Bf109 18/3/42: Plt Off H. Fox 249 Sqn – KiA.
AB335/GN-F	*Eagle* 7/3/42	Shot down by Bf109 2/4/42: Plt Off D.W. McLeod 126 Sqn – baled out, injured.
AB336	*Eagle* 7/3/42	Shot down by Bf109 20/4/42: Plt Off H.A. Putnam 126 Sqn – KiA.
AB337/GN-A	*Eagle* 7/3/42	Shot down by Bf109 20/3/42: Plt Off D.C. Leggo 249 Sqn – KiA.
AB338	*Eagle* 7/3/42	DBR ground 6/4/42: Air raid.
AB340	*Eagle* 21/3/42	DBR crash-landing (acc) 6/5/42: Flt Sgt A. Otto 603 Sqn – injured.
AB341/GN-E	*Eagle* 7/3/42	DBR ground 28/4/42: Air raid.
AB342	*Eagle* 21/3/42	Shot down by Bf109 14/4/42; Plt Of D.W. Kelly 249 Sqn – baled out, injured.
AB343	*Eagle* 7/3/42	Shot down by Bf109 10/3/42: Plt Off K.L. Murray 249 Sqn – KiA.
AB344 GN-M	*Eagle* 7/3/42	Shot down by Bf109 20/4/42: Flt Lt H.A.S. Johnston 126 Sqn – baled out.
AB346/GN-K	*Eagle* 7/3/42	Shot down by own AA 8/4/42: Flt Lt P.W.E. Heppell 249 Sqn – baled out, injured.
AB347	*Eagle* 3/42	DBR ground 12/4/42: Air raid.

AB348	*Eagle* 3/42	DBR ground 28/4/42: Air raid.
AB377/T-E		Shot down by Bf109 12/10/42: Sqn Ldr M.M. Stephens 249 Sqn – baled out, rescued.
AB418	*Eagle* 29/3/42	DBR on ground 3/4/42: Air raid.
AB419	*Eagle* 29/3/42	DBR on ground 3/4/42: Air raid.
AB420	*Eagle* 29/3/42	DBR on ground 3/4/42: Air raid.
AB454	*Eagle* 29/3/42	DBR on ground 6/4/42: Air raid.
AB451/GN-T	*Eagle* 3/42	DBR on ground 4/42: Air raid.
AB464		126 Sqn 9/42.
AB465	*Eagle* 29/3/42	126 Sqn/249 Sqn: Shot down 6/1/43.
AB469	4-6/42	Shot down by Bf109 14/7/42: Flg Off J.R. Stoop 185 Sqn – baled out, rescued.
AB500	*Eagle* 29/3/42	Shot down by Bf109 7/7/42: Flt Sgt D.W. Ferraby 185 Sqn – baled out.
AB526		Crash-landed by Bf109 10/8/42: Flt Sgt E.L. Mahar 185 Sqn unhurt; 126 Sqn MK-P: FTR 28/1/43.
AB531		Shot down by Bf109 8/9/42: Sgt H. Roberts 126 Sqn – baled out, rescued.
AB532		185 Sqn 10/42: To USAF SOC 31/8/44.
AB535/T-Z		249 Sqn 11/42.
AB536		126 Sqn 11/42: FTR 10/8/43.
AR466/T-R	7-8/42	249 Sqn 10/42. Force-landed 13/12/42, pilot unhurt.
AR470/V-Q	7-8/42	Shot down by Bf109 14/10/42: Sgt W.B. Knox-Williams 1435 Sqn – KiA.
AR471	7-8/42	DBR by Bf109 14/10/42: Plt Off P.A. Dixon 229 Sqn unhurt.
AR488/T-S	7-8/42	DBR 29/10/42: hit truck while taxiing.
AR489		Shot down by Bf109 14/10/42: Flt Sgt C.A. Long 126 Sqn – baled out, rescued.

12 long-range Spitfires Gibraltar to Malta 25/10/42 (two), 31/10/42 (five), 6/11/42 (five).

AR464 Gib-Malta 10-11/42	249 Sqn/126 Sqn DBR 11/1/43.
AR496 Gib-Malta 10-11/42	1435 Sqn: DBR 16/12/43.
AR497 Gib-Malta 10-11/42	126 Sqn MK-E 12/42; 74 OTU SOC 13/9/45.
AR551 Gib-Malta 10-11/42	126 Sqn/1435 Sqn.
AR556 Gib-Malta 10-11/42	1435 Sqn V-C. Lost 18/3/43.
AR557 Gib-Malta 10-11/42	126 Sqn.
AR559 Gib-Malta 10-11/42	249 Sqn T-W 11/42. Lost 24/2/43.
AR560 Gib-Malta 10-11/42	JM-T: Wg Cdr J.M. Thompson's personal aircraft. Became DS: Wg Cdr W.G.G. Duncan-Smith's personal aircraft: 1435 Sqn. Lost 29/6/43.
AR561 Gib-Malta 31/10/42	Flown by Flg Off J.J.Lynch; to 1435 Sqn V-J: Lost 30/1/43.
AR565 Gib-Malta 10-11/42	229 Sqn X-C. Lost 3/3/43.
AR595 Gib-Malta 10-11/42	126 Sqn/1435 Sqn.
AR596 Gib-Malta 10-11/42	249 Sqn. Lost 30/2/44.

BP844/GN-W	*Eagle* 21/3/42	Shot down by Bf109 2/4/42: Plt Off W. McCarthy 126 Sqn – KiA.
BP845	*Eagle* 3/42	Shot down by Bf109 9/5/42: Plt Off H.A. Milburn 249 Sqn – KiA.
BP846	*Eagle* 21/3/42	DBR 25/3/42: Crash-landing. SOC 2/5/42.
BP849	*Eagle* 3/42	DBR ground 21/4/42: Air raid.
BP850/F	*Eagle* 21/3/42	Crash-landed 24/4/42: Sgt E.A. Crist 249 Sqn unhurt.
BP860/V-X		126 Sqn 8/42; 1435 Sqn 10/42: damaged by Bf109 11/10/42: Sgt G. Philp 1435 Sqn unhurt; force-landed by Bf109 16/10/42: Flt Sgt I.R. Maclennan 1435 Sqn unhurt; shot-up by Bf109 16/10/42: Plt Off H.G.Reynolds force-landed unhurt. To USAF.
BP861		Damaged by Bf109 19/7/42: Sgt J.E. Otis 126 Sqn crashed – KiA.
BP866/X-Q		126 Sqn/229 Sqn/1435 Sqn/185 Sqn.
BP867/T-E		Damaged by Bf109 20/7/42: Sgt V.H. Wynn 249 Sqn – wounded. Shot down by Bf109 15/9/42: Flt Sgt B. Peters 249 Sqn – KiA.
BP868/GN-N	*Wasp* 20/4/42	249 Sqn. Malta. SOC 24/6/43.
BP869	5/42	Crash-landed by MC202: Flt Sgt B.W. Reynolds 126 Sqn – unhurt; T-K 249 Sqn 7/42-10/42. Lost 20/3/43.

BP870	*Eagle* 9/5/42	126 Sqn 8/42. Lost 10/1/43.
BP871	*Eagle* 9/5/42	601 Sqn UF-R; to 603 Sqn 7/42. Shot down by Bf109 28/8/42: Flt Lt E.P.F.L.T. Magruder 229 Sqn – KiA.
BP872	*Eagle* 9/5/42	Shot down by Bf109 9/5/42: Flt Lt J.W. Buckstone 603 Sqn – KiA
BP873	5-6/42	126 Sqn 7/42. 1435 Sqn V-Y.Crash-landed by Bf109 16/10/42: Sgt W.T. Whitmore 1435 Sqn slightly injured.
BP874	*Wasp* 20/4/42	DBR ground 21/4/42: Air raid
BP875	5/42	Shot down by MC202 10/6/42: Plt Off J.W.L. Innes 601 Sqn – baled out, unhurt.
BP876	*Eagle* 18/5/42	Overturned on landing Hal Far 2/7/42; Flt Sgt D.J. Reid 185 Sqn unhurt.
BP877	*Eagle* 5/42	Shot down by Ju88 return fire 12/5/42: Plt Off M.A. Graves 126 Sqn – baled out, unhurt.
BP878	5/42	Shot down by Bf109 14/5/42: Flt Sgt H.J. Fox 249 Sqn – KiA
BP950	5/42	Shot down by Bf109 1/6/42: Plt Off A.A. McNaughton 185 Sqn – KiA
BP951	5/42	Shot down by Bf109 17/5/42: Plt Off P.A. Nash DFC 249 Sqn – KiA
BP952/MK-F	5/42	Damaged bomb crater 17/5/42: 126 Sqn: FTR convoy patrol 19/11/42: Plt Off G.H. Kelly – killed.
BP953	*Eagle* 9/5/42	Shot down 12/5/42: Plt Off D.E. Llewellyn 126 Sqn – baled out, unhurt.
BP954/1-D	*Wasp* 20/4/42	Shot down by Bf109 21/4/42: Sqn Ldr J.D. Bisdee 601 Sqn – baled out, unhurt.
BP955/X-A	*Wasp* 20/4/42	Shot down by Bf109 17/10/42: Sgt R. Miller 229 – KiA.
BP956	*Wasp* 20/4/42	DBR ground 20/4/42: Air raid
BP957	*Wasp* 20/4/42	Shot down by Bf109 9/7/42: Plt Off G. Levy-Despas 603 Sqn – KiA
BP958	*Wasp* 20/4/42	Landed Algeria 20/4/42: Sgt B.S. Walcott interned by Vichy French.
BP960	*Wasp* 9/5/42	Shot down by own AA 10/5/42: Sgt G.R. Dickson 601 Sqn – baled out, injured.
BP961	*Wasp* 20/4/42	603 Sqn. 249 Sqn. DBR 24/3/43.
BP962/2-R	*Wasp* 20/4/42	Shot down by Bf109 1/5/42: Flt Sgt J.A. Rae 603 Sqn, baled out, wounded.
BP963	*Wasp* 20/4/42	DBR ground 21/4/42: Air raid
BP964/1-X	*Wasp* 20/4/42	Air collision with BP991 11/5/42: Flt Lt W.A. Douglas 603 Sqn – baled out, unhurt.
BP965	*Wasp* 9/5/42	Probably shot down en route to Malta by Bf109 9/5/42: Flt Sgt C.N. Valiquet – KiA.
BP966/2-L	*Wasp* 20/4/42	DBR on ground: Air raid 12/7/42 603 Sqn.
BP967	*Wasp* 20/4/42	DBR ground 28/4/42: Air raid
BP968/2-N	*Wasp* 20/4/42	DBR ground 28/4/42: Air raid
BP969/1-R	*Wasp* 20/4/42	Shot down by Bf109 20/4/42: Sgt G.A.J. Ryckman – KiA
BP970	*Wasp* 20/4/42	Shot down by Bf109 22/4/42: Plt Off G. Murray – KiA.
BP971	*Wasp* 9/5/42	Probably shot down en route to Malta 9/5/42: Flt Sgt J.V.Rounsefell – KiA.
BP972		Possibly lost 9/5/42: Sgt R.D. Sherrington crashed on take-off from *Wasp* – killed.
BP973/2-J	*Wasp* 20/4/42	Shot down by Bf109 25/4/42: Plt Off K.W. Pawson 601 Sqn – KiA.
BP974	*Wasp* 20/4/42	DBR ground 21/4/42: Air raid.
BP975/1-K	*Wasp* 20/4/42	601 Sqn/249 Sqn T-T 7/42. To USAF.
BP976/1-O	*Wasp* 20/4/42	Crash-landed DBR 21/4/42: Flt Lt D.W. Barnham 601 Sqn unhurt.
BP977	*Wasp* 20/4/42	Shot down by Bf109 21/4/42: Plt Off S.F. Brooker 126 Sqn – KiA.
BP979	*Wasp*	Shot down by Bf109 6/7/42: Flt Sgt E.D. Moye 185 Sqn – KiA
BP980	*Wasp* 9/5/42	Crash-landed, DBR by Bf109 10/5/43: Plt Off R. Noble 185 Sqn – wounded.
BP982	*Wasp* 20/4/42	601 Sqn.
BP983	*Wasp*	249 Sqn. 601 Sqn to ME 6/42. DBR 17/11/43.
BP989/4-N	*Wasp* 9/5/42	249 Sqn 7/42; 229 Sqn: Shot down by Bf109 16/10/42: Flt Sgt M.A. Lundy 229 Sqn – baled out, rescued.
BP990/4-O	*Wasp* 9/5/42	Shot down by Ju88 7/7/42: Flt Sgt C.S.G. de Nancrède 249 Sqn baled out – rescued.

BP991/4-W	*Wasp* 9/5/42	Air collision with BP964 11/5/42: Plt Off R.R.Barnfather 603 Sqn unhurt.
BP992	5/42	Crash-landed by Bf109 14/7/42: Flg Off D.H. Smith 126 Sqn – wounded. Shot down by Bf109 16/10/42: Flg Off E.W. Wallace 126 Sqn – KiA.
BP993	5/42	Shot down by Bf109 19/5/42: Plt Off N.R. Fowlow 603 Sqn – baled out, rescued unhurt.
BR106	5/42	249 Sqn. DBR on ground 18/5/42: Air raid.
BR107/C-22	*Eagle* 3/6/42	Damaged by Bf109 12/6/42: Flg Off R. Daddo-Langlois 249 Sqn unhurt. 185 Sqn. Lost 4/2/43.
BR108/C-20	*Eagle* 5/42	249 Sqn. Shot down by Bf109 8/7/42: Flt Lt L.V. Sanders 603 Sqn – ditched, injured.
BR109/C-30	*Eagle* 18/5/42	Crash-landed by MC202 6/6/42: Plt Off J. Sherlock 185 Sqn unhurt; Lost 20/3/43.
BR110	*Wasp* 9/5/42	249 Sqn.
BR111/C-18	*Eagle* 18/5/42	249 Sqn T-M: Shot down by Bf109 11/7/42: Wt Off C.B. Ramsay 249 Sqn – KiA.
BR112/GL-X	*Eagle* 6/42	Crash-landed by Bf109 21/6/42; Flt Sgt P.L. Terry 185 Sqn – unhurt. Shot down by MC202 9/9/42: Sgt C. Weaver DFM crash-landed Sicily – POW.
BR114		601 Sqn. To ME 6/42.
BR115	*Eagle* 18/5/42	Crash-landed by Bf109 7/7/42: Plt Off E.W. Wallace 126 Sqn – slightly wounded.
BR116/1-V	*Wasp* 20/4/42	Shot down by Bf109 6/5/42: Flt Lt H.A.S. Johnston 126 Sqn – baled out, burned.
BR117/2-X	*Wasp* 20/4/42	Shot down by Bf109 20/7/42: Sgt H.R. Russel 185 Sqn – KiA.
BR119/1-C	*Wasp* 20/4/42	185 Sqn 7/42. 249 Sqn.
BR120/2-T	*Wasp* 20/4/42	DBR on ground: Air raid SOC 6/5/42.
BR121		DBR on ground: Air raid SOC 29/6/42.
BR122/2-O	*Wasp* 20/4/42	Shot down by Bf109 9/8/42: Sgt D. Ritchie 126 Sqn MK-O – baled out, rescued.
BR123	*Wasp* 20/4/42	DBR on ground: Air raid SOC 21/5/42.
BR124/2-U	*Wasp* 20/4/42	DBR on ground 28/4/42: Air raid.
BR125/1-P	*Wasp* 20/4/42	Shot down by Bf109 26/4/42: Plt Off W.E. Cripps 601 Sqn – KiA.
BR126/3-X	*Wasp* 18/5/42	Became GL-O. DBR belly-landed, glycol leak 15/6/42: Flt Sgt R.J. Sim 185 Sqn unhurt.
BR127	*Wasp* 20/4/42	Shot down by Bf109 12/5/42: Plt Off H.R. Mitchell 603 Sqn – KiA.
BR128/3-W	*Wasp* 9/5/42	Shot down by Bf109 22/7/42: Plt Off J.P.R. Paradis 249 Sqn – KiA.
BR129	*Wasp* 20/4/42	DBR ground 22/4/42: Air raid.
BR130/2-H	*Wasp* 20/4/42	Damaged by Bf109 14/7/42: Sgt G.F. Beurling 249 Sqn – slightly wounded. Crash-landed by Bf109 14/10/42: Wg Cdr A.H. Donaldson wounded.
BR131		249 Sqn. Lost 9/4/43.
BR133		601 Sqn to ME 6/42. SOC 8/3/44.
BR134		601 Sqn to ME 6/42.
BR135		249 Sqn. 601 Sqn to ME 6/42.
BR136/C	4/42	Collided on ground with BR350 (damaged) 12/5/42; 601 Sqn to ME 6/42. Lost 2/4/43.
BR137	4/42	Shot down by Ju88 return fire or Bf109 12/5/42: Flt Sgt W.C. Conway – baled out.
BR161		229 Sqn 8/42; 1435 Sqn. Lost 3/3/43.
BR163	*Eagle* 18/5/42	Shot down by Bf109 16/6/42: Flt Sgt M.W. Vineyard 185 Sqn – baled out.
BR165/C-23	*Eagle* 18/5/42	Shot down in error by own AA 7/7/42: Flt Sgt T. Parks 249 Sqn – baled out, slightly injured.
BR166/3-T	5-6/42	185 Sqn 7/42. 249 Sqn. Lost 19/9/44.
BR169		DBR 15/8/42: ground collision with EP517.
BR170/C-25	*Eagle* 18/5/42	Became T-B. Crash-landed by Bf109 18/7/42: Plt Off C.H. Lattimer 249 Sqn – slightly wounded.
BR173/T-D	7-8/42	Shot down by Bf109 14/10/42: Plt Off G.F. Beurling 249 Sqn – baled out, wounded, rescued.

BR175/C-31	*Eagle* 18/5/42	Became UF-Z; 601 Sqn to ME late 6/42
BR176/1-N	*Wasp* 20/4/42	Became MK-Q 126 Sqn 7/42; shot down by Bf109 15/10/42: Wt Off G.H. Farquharson 126 Sqn baled out – slightly wounded.
BR177/T-E		249 Sqn. To 74 OTU. Lost 21/6/44.
BR179		Malta: SOC 26/6/42.
BR180	*Wasp* 20/4/42	DBR (acc) 22/4/42: Plt Off O.R. Linton 249 Sqn unhurt.
BR182	*Wasp* 20/4/42	SOC 29/6/42.
BR183/2-D	*Wasp* 20/4/42	Force-landed by Bf109 8/7/42: Plt Off F. Johnson 126 Sqn – wounded. Shot down by Bf109 11/10/42: Sgt D.D. Maclean – KiA
BR184/2-C	*Wasp* 20/4/42	Became X-C. Shot down by Bf109 2/7/42; Plt Off J. Hurst 603 Sqn – KiA.
BR185/2-Q	*Wasp* 20/4/42	DBR heavy landing 1/5/42: Plt Off J.E. Peck 126 Sqn – unhurt.
BR187/1-O	*Wasp* 20/4/42	Crash-landed by Bf109 4/5/42: Sgt J.W. McConnell 601 Sqn unhurt.
BR188	*Wasp* 20/4/42	DBR ground 22/4/42: Air raid.
BR190/2-A	*Wasp* 20/4/42	SOC 13/5/42.
BR192/2-W	*Wasp* 20/4/42	601 Sqn to ME 6/42.
BR194	*Wasp* 20/4/42	185 Sqn/249 Sqn. DBR 14/5/43.
BR196	5/42	Shot down by Bf109 12/5/42: Sgt Graysmark 601 Sqn – DoW.
BR198	*Wasp* 20/4/42	Shot down by Bf109 8/7/42: Flg Off N.S. King 603 Sqn – KiA.
BR199	*Wasp* 20/4/42	DBR crash-landed 26/4/42: Plt Off R.W. James 249 Sqn – wounded.
BR203/1-F	*Wasp* 20/4/42	249 Sqn T-X. Shot down by Bf109 22/7/42: Flt Sgt D.G. Reid DFM 185 Sqn – KiA.
BR204	*Wasp* 20/4/42	DBR ground 22/4/42: Air raid.
BR226	*Wasp* 20/4/42	Shot down by Bf109 4/5/42: Flt Lt N.C. Macqueen DFC 249 Sqn – KiA.
BR227/T-T	*Wasp* 20/4/42	Shot down by Bf109 8/7/42: Flt Sgt J.C. Gilbert 249 Sqn – KiA.
BR229	5/42	DBR Crash-landed by Bf109 15/5/42: Plt Off D.E. Booth 126 Sqn unhurt.
BR230	*Eagle* 3/6/42	Shot down by Bf109 16/6/42: Flt Sgt J.E. MacNamara 185 Sqn – baled out.
BR231	*Eagle* 3/6/42	Shot down by Bf109 8/6/42: Plt Off L.G. Barlow 603 Sqn – KiA.
BR232	*Eagle* 3/6/42	601 Sqn to ME 6/42: Lost 6/7/42.
BR233/T-Q	5-6/42	Shot down by Bf109 8/7/42: Flg Off J. Smith 249 Sqn – KiA.
BR236/V-E	1435 Sqn 8/42	Used for Spitbomber trials 9/42. Shot down by FW190 24/11/42: Flt Lt J.B.H. Burgess 1435 Sqn – POW.
BR242/MK-A	5-6/42	Shot down by Bf109 13/7/42: Sgt V. Wille 126 Sqn – baled out, wounded.
BR244	5/42	Shot down by Bf109 10/7/42: Flt Sgt B.W. Reynolds 126 Sqn – KiA.
BR246/C-40	*Eagle* 3/6/42	Crash-landed by MC202 6/7/42: Plt Off A.S. Yates 249 Sqn T-J, unhurt; shot down by own ships' AA 13/8/42: Flt Sgt T. Parks 249 Sqn – baled out, rescued.
BR248	*Wasp* 9/5/42	Shot down by Bf109 9/5/42: Flt Sgt G.R. Tweedale 185 Sqn – KiA.
BR251/4-S	*Wasp* 9/5/42	249 Sqn T-E; Shot down by Bf109 7/7/42: Flt Sgt R.G. Middlemiss 249 Sqn baled out, wounded.
BR254/T-G	5/42	249 Sqn T-G; later T-S 10/42; shot down by Bf109 15/10/42: Sgt N.G. Brydon – baled out, wounded, rescued.
BR282	9/5/42	Shot down by Bf109 10/5/42: Plt Off M. Briggs 601 Sqn – KiA.
BR283		Shot down by Bf109 7/7/42: Flt Sgt H. Haggas – KiA.
BR285	5/42	Shot down by RE2001 2/6/42: Plt Off J.R.S. Halford 185 Sqn – ditched, rescued.
BR291/GL-H	5/42	Shot down by Bf109 17/5/42: Sgt C.V. Finlay 185 Sqn – KiA.
BR293	*Eagle* 6/42	185 Sqn 6/42; 229 Sqn 10/42. Shot down by Bf109, crash-landed: Sgt D.A. Bye 229 Sqn unhurt; Shot down by AA 29/11/42: Sgt W.D. Wendt 249 Sqn T-M – baled out, POW.
BR294 /GL-E	*Wasp* 9/5/42	Crashed on landing 2/7/42: Flt Sgt D.G. Reid 185 Sqn unhurt.
BR295/C-39	*Eagle* 3/6/42	249 Sqn T-H; belly-landed out of fuel 8/7/42; 185 Sqn 10/42. Shot down by Ju88 7/12/42: Sgt D.G. Guy 185 Sqn – KiA.
BR300	*Wasp* 9/5/42	DBR 29/7/42: undershot on landing, 249 Sqn pilot unhurt.
BR301/UF-S	*Wasp* 9/5/42	601 Sqn; to 249 Sqn 7/42. Damaged by Bf109 29/7/42: Plt Off G.F. Beurling 249 Sqn unhurt.

BR303	5-6/42	185 Sqn 7/42. Shot down by Bf109 28/7/42: Flt Sgt R.H. Brown 126 Sqn – baled out, rescued.
BR305/GL-N	5-6/42	Crashed on air test 19/7/42: Sgt D.J. Hartney 185 Sqn – injured.
BR306/3-D	*Wasp* 9/5/42	Shot down by MC202 15/6/42: Sgt J.W. McConnell 601 Sqn – KiA.
BR308	*Eagle* 3/6/42	Shot down en route Malta 3/6/42: Flt Sgt H.D.K. Macpherson – KiA.
BR311/MK-L	5-6/42	Shot down by Bf109 25/10/42: Sgt N.M. Park 126 Sqn – KiA.
BR312/C-42	*Eagle* 3/6/42	Crash-landed by Bf109 8/6/42: Flt Sgt B. Butler 603 Sqn – slightly injured.
BR313	*Eagle* 3/6/42	Shot down by Bf109 en route Malta 3/6/42: Flt Sgt T.F. Beaumont – KiA.
BR315/GL-T	*Eagle* 6/42	Crash-landed by Bf109 21/6/42: Flt Sgt W.C. Conway 185 Sqn – injured.
BR316		DBR on ground 27/7/42: Air raid. 249 Sqn.
BR317	5-6/42	Shot down by Bf109 7/7/42: Flt Sgt P.L. Terry 185 Sqn – KiA.
BR320/X-K	5/42	Shot down by Bf109 29/6/42: Plt Off C.A.Mc. Barbour 603 Sqn – baled out, rescued.
BR321/GL-J	5/42	Shot down by Bf109 2/8/42: Sgt M. McLeod 185 Sqn – KiA.
BR322	*Eagle* 3/6/42	Shot down by Bf109 en route Malta 3/6/42: Flg Off J.H. Menary – KiA.
BR323/T-S	5-6/42	Shot down by Bf109 18/7/42: Wt Off C.B. McLean 249 Sqn – baled out burned, rescued.
BR324/T-R	5-6/42	Shot down by Bf109 12/7/42: Plt Off O.W.H. Berkeley-Hill 249 Sqn – KiA.
BR344/3-M	*Wasp* 9/5/42	Crash-landed DBR by Bf109 17/5/42 Sgt F.S. Howard – DoW. 601 Sqn to ME: 6/42.
BR345/3-Z	*Wasp* 9/5/42	603 Sqn X-A. Force-landed by MC202 2/7/42: Flg Off N.S. King 603 Sqn unhurt; Damaged by MC202 6/7/42: Flg Off H.W. McLeod 603 Sqn unhurt. 126 Sqn MK-S 7-10/42. Lost 20/3/43.
BR346	5/42	Crash-landed DBR by Bf109 12/5/42: Flt Sgt C.R. Bush 126 Sqn – wounded.
BR347/T-Z	5-6/42	Crash-landed by Ju88: Flg Off E. L. Hetherington 249 Sqn unhurt; crash-landed 11/7/42: Flt Sgt L.G.C. de l'Ara 249 Sqn – slightly injured.
BR348	*Wasp* 9/5/42	Crashed 9/5/42: Flt Lt R.C. Sly USS *Wasp* – KiA.
BR349/C	5/42	Shot down by Bf109 14/5/42: Sgt J.L. Boyd DFM 185 Sqn – KiA.
BR350/3-J	*Wasp* 9/5/42	Collided on ground with BR136 12/5/42 – DBR.
BR352	5/42	DBR by Bf109 18/5/42: Sgt J.W. McConnell 601 Sqn – slightly wounded.
BR353/GL-D	5/42	Shot down by Bf109 15/6/42: Plt Off P.W. Baril 185 Sqn – baled out, rescued.
BR354	*Eagle* 18/5/42	Shot down by RE2001 25/5/42: Plt Off W.A. Caldwell 601 Sqn – killed.
BR355		Shot down by Bf109 9/7/42: Plt Off J.L. Hicks 126 Sqn – KiA.
BR356	5-6/42	Shot down by Bf109 2/7/42: Plt Off H. Kelly 249 Sqn – KiA.
BR357		Shot down by Bf109 4/8/42: Sgt A. Richardson 126 Sqn – baled out, rescued.
BR358	*Eagle* 3/6/42	Shot down by Bf109 en route to Malta 3/6/42: Plt Off D.F. Rouleau – KiA.
BR359		DBR 25/8/42: Hit EN829 on take-off: Sgt W. Parks 229 Sqn unhurt.
BR360/S	5-6/42	Lost, fuel shortage 15/6/42: Sgt G. Allen-Rowlandson 601 Sqn – baled out, rescued.
BR362	5-6/42	Crash-landed by Bf109 23/6/42: Flt Sgt J.E. MacNamara 185 Sqn – unhurt. Shot down by Bf109 2/8/42: Plt Off J.W. Guthrie 185 Sqn – KiA.
BR364	*Eagle* 6/42	Shot down by Bf109 9/7/42: Flt Sgt J.H. Ballantyne 603 Sqn – baled out, rescued.
BR365	5-6/42	Crash-landed by Bf109 2/7/42: Plt Off E.H. Glazebrook 603 Sqn unhurt.
BR366/MK-P	5-6/42	Shot down by Bf109 10/8/42: Plt off J.A. Smith 126 Sqn – KiA.

BR367/X-O	5-6/42	Shot down by Bf109 2/7/42: Flt Sgt J.H. Ballantyne 603 Sqn baled out – rescued.
BR368	5-6/42	185 Sqn 7/42: Used for Spitbomber trials 9/42; 1435 Sqn V-I 10/42: shot down 12/10/42, Sgt T.R.D. Kebbell – baled out, rescued.
BR373/T-N	7-8/42	Crash-landed by Bf109 15/10/42: Flg Off J.F. McElroy 249 Sqn – wounded. Lost 8/2/43.
BR374		Crashed (acc) 13/9/42: Sgt L.H. Swain 185 Sqn – killed.
BR375/GL-A	5-6/42	185 Sqn 11/42.
BR376	*Eagle* 9/6/42	185 Sqn Damaged by Bf109 2/7/42; 1435 Sqn 10/42 V-V: shot down by AA 17/12/42: Plt Off T.G. Sullivan – POW.
BR377/C-41	*Eagle* 3/6/42	249 Sqn T-K 7/42; crash-landed by MC202 2/7/42: Flt Sgt C.S.G. de Nancrède unhurt. 126 Sqn 10/42. Shot down by Bf109 12/10/42: Sqn Ldr B.J. Wicks 126 Sqn – KiA.
BR379/T-V	5-6/42	Shot down by Bf109 4/10/42: Flt Sgt G.A. Hogarth 249 Sqn – DoW.
BR380/GL-R	*Eagle* 9/6/42	Crash-landed by Bf109 1/7/42; Flg Off K.L. Charney 185 Sqn unhurt.
BR381	*Eagle* 9/6/42	Shot down by Ju88 15/6/42: Plt Off J.A. Smith 601 Sqn – baled out, rescued.
BR382	*Eagle* 9/6/42	Crashed, damaged by Bf109 26/6/42: Flt Sgt M.E. Tomkins 249 Sqn – DoW.
BR383/MK-O	7-8/42	Shot down by Bf109 23/9/42: Plt Off I.F. Preston 126 Sqn – KiA.
BR385	*Eagle* 6/42	Shot down by Bf109 23/6/42: Flg Off R.R. Mitchell 603 Sqn – baled out, rescued.
BR387/GL-W	*Eagle* 6/42	Crash-landed by Bf109 2/7/42: Plt Off N.J. Ogilvie 185 Sqn – unhurt.
BR388	*Eagle* 9/6/42	Crash-landed on arrival Malta 9/6/42: Plt Off J.F. McElroy – unhurt.
BR460		Shot down by Bf109 20/7/42: Flt Lt J.F. Lambert 185 Sqn – baled out rescued.
BR461		1435 Sqn.
BR463		249 Sqn. DBR 7/1/43.
BR464/X-S	5-6/42	Damaged on ground: Air raid 10/7/42 603 Sqn. Shot down by Bf109 12/10/42: Flt Lt A.F. Roscoe 229 Sqn crash-landed – badly wounded.
BR465/MK-X	*Eagle* 9/6/42	Shot down by Bf109 3/7/42: Flg Off R.E. McHan 126 Sqn – baled out, wounded.
BR471		Shot down by Bf109 15/10/42: Flg Off R.I.A. Smith 126 Sqn – baled out, rescued.
BR482	*Furious* 17/8/42	Crashed on arrival Malta ex-*Furious* 17/8/42: Sgt J.G. McGill badly burned.
BR486		Shot down by Bf109 15/9/42: Plt Off J.R. Scott 229 Sqn – KiA.
BR488		Crash-landed (acc) 28/8/42: Sgt E.H. Francis 229 Sqn unhurt.
BR496		Shot down by Bf109 26/8/42: Sgt C.H. Cornish 229 Sqn – KiA.
BR498/PP-H		Wg Cdr P. Prosser Hanks' personal aircraft.
BR529/AD	7-8/42	Wg Cdr A.H. Donaldson's personal aircraft; force-landed by Bf109 13/10/42: Wg Cdr Donaldson unhurt; damaged by Bf109 27/10/42: Sgt G.D.A.T. Cameron 249 Sqn – slightly wounded.
BR534		126 Sqn/185 Sqn. Lost 1/3/43.
BR562/X-R	*Eagle* 7/42	Crashed on landing 31/7/42: Flt Sgt J.H. Ballantyne 603 Sqn unhurt; crash-landed by Bf109 15/10/42: Sqn Ldr M.T. Stephens 229 Sqn unhurt. Lost 17/1/43.
BR564	5-6/42	Lost 3/7/42 (acc): Plt Off F.D. Thomas 126 Sqn baled out, rescued.
BR565/T-T	5-6/42	249 Sqn 7/42.
BR566	5-6/42	Shot down by Bf109 7/7/42: Sgt R. Davey 126 Sqn baled out – rescued.
BR591/V-R		Damaged by Bf109 15/10/42: Plt Off C.H. Lattimer 1425 Sqn unhurt.
BS160	7-8/42	Shot down by Bf109 29/8/42: Plt Off D.P. Pollock 1435 Sqn – KiA.
BS161/V-U	7-8/42	Crash-landed by Bf109 11/10/42; Flt Lt H.W. McLeod 1435 Sqn unhurt. To USAF.

EN829/X-U	7-8/42	DBR 25/8/42. Hit from behind on take-off by BR359: Sgt N.L. Pashen 229 Sqn unhurt.
EN954	7-8/42	Force-landed by Bf109 13/10/42 DBR: Plt Off A.S. Yates 249 Sqn unhurt; crashed (acc) 22/11/42: Flt Sgt M.A. Lundy 229 Sqn – killed.
EN955/X-A	7-8/42	229 Sqn 10/42.
EN968/V-H	*Eagle* 15/7/42	1435 Sqn 10/42.
EN972	*Eagle* 15/7/42	Shot down by Bf109 1/12/42: Plt Off J.R. Mowbray 249 Sqn – KiA.
EN973/T-T	*Eagle* 7/42	Crash-landed by Bf109 8/8/42: Plt Off G.F. Beurling 249 Sqn – slightly injured.
EN976/T-C	7-8/42	Shot down by Bf109 25/8/42: Plt Off R. Round 249 Sqn – KiA.
EN978/V-O	7-8/42	Shot down by Bf109 12/10/42: Sgt W.B. Knox-Williams 1435 Sqn – baled out, rescued.
EN979	7-8/42	Shot down by Bf109 14/10/42: Plt Off H.T. Nash 229 Sqn – baled out, injured.
EN980/V-W	*Eagle* 7/42	185 Sqn 8/42. 1435 Sqn 12/42. Shot down by return fire from Ju52 17/12/42:Sgt J.M. Harrison 1435 Sqn – KiA.
EP117	*Eagle* 15/7/42	Damaged in take-off accident, did not reach Malta: Sgt W.B. Knox-Williams unhurt.
EP122/JM-T	*Eagle* 21/7/42	185 Sqn. Wg Cdr J.M. Thompson's personal aircraft 10/42. Lost 27/3/43.
EP131/T-O	*Eagle* 7/42	Damaged by Bf109 29/7/42: Sgt E.A. Budd 249 Sqn unhurt; damaged by Bf109 8/8/42: Sgt E.A. Budd 249 Sqn wounded. Lost 9/4/43.
EP132/T-J	7-8/42	249 Sqn 10/42.
EP135/T-Z	7-8/42	249 Sqn 10/42. Crash-landed 15/10/42.
EP136/T-P	7-8/42	Crash-landed by Bf109 25/9/42: Plt Off V.K. Moody 249 Sqn unhurt.
EP137	*Eagle* 21/7/42	Shot down by Bf109 31/7/42: Flg Off E.A.G.C. Bruce – baled out, rescued.
EP138/V-K	7-8/42	Crashed on landing 1/11/42: Plt Off R.A. Wright 1435 Sqn – killed.
EP139	*Eagle* 21/7/42	Shot down by Bf109 12/10/42: Sgt J.D. Vinall 185 Sqn – KiA.
EP140/V-P	*Eagle* 15/7/42	1435 Sqn; to 249 Sqn 11/42 T-M. DBR 3/3/43.
EP152	*Furious* 17/8/42	Abandoned following take-off *Furious* 17/8/42: Sg L.J. McDougall rescued.
EP186/T-K	7-8/42	229 Sqn 10/42; 249 Sqn 12/42.
EP187	*Eagle* 21/7/42	185 Sqn 8/42-10/42.
EP188/V-G	7-8/42	1435 Sqn 10/42. Lost 30/4/43.
EP189	*Eagle* 7/42	Shot down by Bf109 28/7/42: Sgt D.F. Hubbard 126 Sqn – KiA.
EP190	7-8/42	Shot down by Bf109 26/8/42: Flg Off D.G. Newman 229 Sqn – KiA.
EP194	*Furious* 17/8/42	Crashed overside on take-off *Furious* 17/8/42: Sgt W.J.A. Fleming killed.
EP196/T-M	*Eagle* 15/7/42	Damaged by Bf109 29/8/42: Sgt J.D. Vinall 185 Sqn unhurt; to 249 Sqn.
EP197	*Furious* 11/8/42	Shot down by own ships' AA 13/8/42: Sgt R.A. Buntine 126 Sqn – KiA.
EP199/T-K	7-8/42	Lost (acc) 15/11/42: Sgt J. Roberts 249 Sqn – killed.
EP200/GL-T	*Eagle* 21/7/42	Shot down by AA fire 27/8/42: Flg Off P.A. Woodger 185 Sqn – POW.
EP201/V-F	*Eagle* 7/42	First experimental Spitbomber 9/42. 249 Sqn T-L 10/42.
EP203/V-G	7-8/42	Shot down by Bf109 14/10/42: Sgt R.J. Roe 1435 Sqn – KiA.
EP205/MK-Y		126 Sqn 11/42-12/42. Lost 12/7/44.
EP207	*Eagle* 7/42	Shot down by Bf109 14/8/42: Flt Sgt G. Hogarth 249 Sqn – baled out, rescued.
EP209	*Eagle* 21/7/42	126 Sqn 8/42; 1435 Sqn V-B: Shot down by Bf109 12/10/42: Flt Sgt R.A. Stevenson 1435 Sqn – KiA.
EP255	*Eagle* 7/42	Shot down by Bf109 31/7/42: Sgt J.G. Livingston – baled out, rescued.
EP259/V-L	7-8/42	Damaged by Bf109 17/10/42: Plt Off A.R. Stewart 1435 Sqn unhurt.

EP257		1435 Sqn. To 249 Sqn.
EP260		FTR convoy patrol 19/11/42: Sgt H. Roberts 126 Sqn – killed.
EP286		1435 Sqn.
EP290	*Furious* 11/8/42	1435 Sqn. To 126 Sqn.
EP292	*Eagle* 7/42	Crashed on take-off 13/8/42: Sgt F.W. Clewley 185 Sqn – injured.
EP297	*Eagle* 7/42	DBR by Bf109 27/7/42: Sgt N.G. Brydon 249 Sqn unhurt.
EP305		229 Sqn. Lost 26/8/43.
EP306		249 Sqn. 185 Sqn.
EP310		Shot down by Bf110 14/11/42: Flg Off G. Davidson 126 Sqn – KiA.
EP313	*Eagle* 7/42	185 Sqn 8/42-12/42. Hit vehicle while taxiing 29/12/42. DBR.
EP316	*Eagle* 7/42	Shot down by Bf109 13/10/42: Sgt A.O. MacLeod 185 Sqn – KiA.
EP329	*Furious* 11/8/42	Crashed on take-off 29/10/42: Sgt W. Parks 229 Sqn – DoW.
EP330	7-8/42	126 Sqn 10/42.
EP331	*Eagle* 7/42	Shot down by Bf109 3/8/42: Sgt W.B. Knox-Williams 1435 Sqn – baled out, rescued.
EP332	7-8/42	Crashed on landing 18/10/42: Plt Off J.D. Stevenson 126 Sqn – killed.
EP336	*Eagle* 7/42	Shot down by Bf109 8/8/42: Sgt C.L. Kelly 1435 Sqn – KiA.
EP338/T-A	7-8/42	Shot down by Bf109 16/10/42: Wt Off P. Carter 249 Sqn – KiA.
EP339	*Furious* 11/8/42	Grp Capt W.M. Churchill's personal aircraft: shot down by AA 27/8/42: Grp Capt Churchill – KiA.
EP340/T-M	7-8/42	Shot down by Bf109 15/10/42: Flt Sgt E.T. Hiskens 249 Sqn – KiA.
EP341	7-8/42	Flt Lt R.O. Jones 126 Sqn – collided with Ju88 17/10/42 – KiA.
EP343/T-P	*Eagle* 7/42	Damaged by Bf109, belly-landed 17/10/42: Wg Cdr J.M. Thompson unhurt. Lost 31/8/44.
EP344	*Eagle* 7/42	Shot down by Bf109 30/7/42: Sgt C.L. Wood – KiA.
EP345/MK-X	7-8/42	Damaged by Bf109, crash-landed 18/10/42: Sgt N.M. Park 126 Sqn – slightly injured.
EP365		249 Sqn.
EP404	*Furious* 29/10/42	1435 Sqn.
EP410	*Furious* 11/8/42	Shot down, possibly by Spitfire, 15/8/42: Sgt J. Tarbuck 185 Sqn – baled out, rescued.
EP433/V-N		1435 Sqn 11/42.
EP436/V-S		1435 Sqn.
EP444/V-B	*Furious* 29/10/42	1435 Sqn 11/42: (Flg Off H.C. Crafts flew this aircraft when he shot down a Ju88 on 11/10/42 while at Gibraltar, waiting to fly to Malta). Lost 19/7/43.
EP448/T-F	*Furious* 11/8/42	Crash-landed by Bf109 2/11/42: Sgt W.B. Weir 249 Sqn – injured.
EP457	*Furious* 11/8/42	Shot down by Bf109 17/8/42: Plt Off G. Stenborg 185 Sqn – baled out, rescued.
EP459/X-P	7-8/42	229 Sqn 10/42.
EP460		229 Sqn. Lost 17/1/43.
EP467	7-8/42	Shot down by Bf109 24/10/42: Sgt R. Saunders 185 Sqn – KiA.
EP471	7-8/42	185 Sqn 10/42. Lost 3/3/43.
EP472	*Furious* 11/8/42	126 Sqn 8/42. Shot down by Bf109 13/8/42: Sgt R.H. Tanner 126 Sqn – KiA.
EP473		185 Sqn. Lost 8/2/43.
EP517	*Furious* 11/8/42	DBR 15/8/42: ground collision with BR169.
EP519/V-U		1435 Sqn 11/42. Lost 11/3/43.
EP520/T-V	7-8/42	249 Sqn 10/42. 185 Sqn. To USAF.
EP521/GL-F	7-8/42	DBR (acc) crash-landed 17/10/42: Sgt L. Garvey 185 Sqn – badly burned.
EP541/V-Q	7-8/42	Crash-landed by Bf109 16/10/42: Flt Lt H.W. McLeod 1435 Sqn unhurt.
EP546	7-8/42	126 Sqn. Force-landed 17/8/42 DBR.
EP550	7-8/42	229 Sqn. Crash-landed by Bf109 11/10/42: pilot unhurt.
EP553	7-8/42	185 Sqn 8/42.
EP554	7-8/42	185 Sqn. Lost 6/5/43.
EP557		Lost (acc) 13/12/42: Sgt N. Bage 249 Sqn – baled out, rescued.
EP567		126 Sqn. Lost 7/4/43.
EP571		185 Sqn. Lost 20/5/43.

EP573	*Furious* 17/8/42	126 Sqn 10/42.
EP606	*Furious* 17/8/42	Abandoned following take-off *Furious* 17/8/42: Sgt J.C. Sullivan rescued.
EP609		Crashed in overshoot Hal Far 8/11/42: Sgt C.F.J. Harwood 185 Sqn – injured.
EP612/V-B	*Furious* 8/42	1435 Sqn 8/42-10/42. Lost 24/11/43.
EP619/V-I		1435 Sqn 12/42.
EP621/V-N	7-8/42	1435 Sqn 10/42. SOC 1/9/43.
EP622/T-P		249 Sqn 12/42.
EP641		229 Sqn. Lost 15/2/43.
EP647		126 Sqn.
EP652		185 Sqn.
EP653/V-F		1435 Sqn 12/42.
EP654		185 Sqn.
EP663	7-8/42	Shot down by Bf109 17/9/42: Plt Off J.G.W. Farmer 249 Sqn – baled out, injured.
EP669		229 Sqn. DBR 29/4/43.
EP685/GL-L	*Furious* 11/8/42	Shot down in error by own AA 23/10/42: Flg Off A.I. Lindsay 185 Sqn – killed.
EP691/X-A	7-8/42	229 Sqn 8/42.
EP695	7-8/42	Lost (acc) 25/8/42: Sgt B. Butler 249 Sqn – killed.
EP696	7-8/42	Shot down by Bf109 22/11/42: Plt Off A.R. Maynard 185 Sqn – KiA.
EP697		DBR on ground 3/11/42: Air raid.
EP698		229 Sqn.
EP700/T-Q	7-8/42	Shot down by Bf109 4/10/42: Sgt M. Irving Gass 249 Sqn – KiA.
EP701		185 Sqn. Lost 19/1/43.
EP702		DBR 16/4/43.
EP703	21/7/42	Possibly lost on take-off *Eagle* 21/7/42: Sgt L. Evans – killed.
EP706/T-L	*Eagle* 7/42	249 Sqn 8/42. Lost 3/3/43.
EP708/T-U	7-8/42	249 Sqn 8/42-10/42. Damaged by return fire from Marauder attacked in error, belly-landed: Flt Lt R. Seed 249 Sqn unhurt.
EP709		229 Sqn. Lost 12/5/43.
EP711		185 Sqn.
EP712	7-8/42	185 Sqn 10/42.
EP714 /V-T	*Furious* 11/8/42	1435 Sqn 8/42-10/42.
EP716	*Eagle* 21/7/42	229 Sqn. Lost 11/4/43.
EP717/V-D	7-8/42	1435 Sqn 10/42. Lost 3/3/43.
EP718/V-S	7-8/42	Shot down by Bf109 16/10/42: Sgt W.R. Wilson 1435 Sqn – KiA.
EP722	7-8/42	185 Sqn 10/42. DBR 13/4/44.
EP724		Lost Gib-Malta 14/11/42.
EP725		229 Sqn. Lost 26/8/43.
EP727/V-N	7-8/42	Crash-landed by Bf109 11/10/42: Sgt J.S. Jarrett 1435 Sqn unhurt.
EP728/T-S		Crash-landed 29/12/42: Plt Off W.J. Locke 249 Sqn unhurt. To USAF.
EP790		229 Sqn.
EP791	*Furious* 29/10/42	185 Sqn 12/42. To USAF.
EP812		1435 Sqn.
EP818		126 Sqn.
EP820		229 Sqn.
EP823	*Furious* 29/10/42	FTR convoy patrol 19/11/42 – possibly shot down by Bf109: Plt Off R.B. Park 185 Sqn – killed.
EP825/T-Z	*Furious* 29/10/42	Crashed on landing 19/12/42: Flt Sgt M.J. Costello 249 Sqn unhurt.
EP828		126 Sqn.
EP829		249 Sqn.
EP832	*Furious* 29/10/42	Crashed (acc) 23/11/42: Sgt T. Wallace 229 Sqn – killed.
EP833/T-F	*Furious* 29/10/42	249 Sqn 12/42. 1435 Sqn. Lost 11/5/43.
EP834		229 Sqn.
EP835		Malta. To USAF.
EP839		185 Sqn.
EP842		229 Sqn. Lost 21/5/43.
EP843		Malta.
EP844	*Furious* 29/10/42	185 Sqn 12/42.

EP887	229 Sqn.
EP905	1435 Sqn.
EP915	1435 Sqn. Lost 17/2/43.
ER647	Gib-Malta via Bone 21/11/42 flown by Sqn Ldr A. Warburton. 126 Sqn MK-J. To USAF.

PR Spitfire IVs

AB300	Gib-Malta 7/3/42 flown by Plt Off H.G. Coldbeck: shot down by AA 9/9/42: Sgt F.R. Gillions POW.
BP885	Gib-Malta 2/4/42 flown by Sgt L. Colquhoun.
BP908	Gib-Malta 5/42: flown to ME 14/8/42 by Plt Off G.H.E. Maloney.
BP915	Gib-Malta 6/42 flown by Sgt J.O. Dalley: flown to ME 13/8/42 by Plt Off W.S. Bracken.
BR431	Gib-Malta 8/42 flown by Sgt F.R. Gillions. To ME.
BP911	ME-Malta 11/8/42 flown by Flt Lt A. Warburton: flown to ME 15/8/42 by Sgt A.G.D. Terret.
BP883	ME-Malta 11/8/42 flown by Flt Lt Day: flown to ME by Plt Off M.G. Brown.
BR665	Gib-Malta 12/8/42 flown by Plt Off W.S. Bracken. To ME.
BR653	Gib-Malta 12/8/42 flown by Sgt A.G.D. Terret. SOC 6/5/43.
BR662	Gib-Malta 12/8/42 flown by Plt Off M.G. Brown.
BR663	Gib-Malta 13/8/42 flown by Plt Off G.H.E. Maloney. Lost 4/4/43.
BP910	Gib-Malta 9/42 flown by Flg Off A.W. Gubb; flown to ME 7/12/42 by Sgt N.L. Pashen.
BR424	Gib-Malta 8/11/42 flown by Sgt D.T. Howard. Lost 29/1/43.
BR426	Gib-Malta 8/11/42 flown by Sgt K. Durbridge. Shot down by Bf109 18/12/42: Sgt D.T. Howard – died of wounds/exposure.
BR646	Gib-Malta 8/11/42: damaged by Bf109s 15/11/42: Sqn Ldr A. Warburton force-landed. DBR.
BR647	Gib-Malta 13/11/42 – failed to arrive.
BS359	Gib-Malta 13/11/42 flown by Plt Off F.C.M. Jemmett: FTR 13/11/42: Plt Off F.C.M. Jemmett – KiA.
BS364	Gib-Malta 13/11/42 flown by Flg Off L.E. Philpotts.
BS367	Gib-Malta 13/11/42 flown by Plt Off J.A. Frazer: shot down by AA 13/11/42: Flt Lt H.G. Coldbeck POW.

Please note: While every effort has been made to ensure accuracy with the above listings, it should be emphasised that there are no official lists from which to extract information. Therefore, it is inevitable that some inaccuracies may occur. Any additional information/amendments would be welcomed by the authors.

CHAPTER FOOTNOTES

1 Sqn Ldr Stan Turner, a colourful and forceful character, had seen much action in France in 1940.

2 Plt Off Jeff West had won his DFM with 616 Squadron, and had frequently flown as No.2 to Wg Cdr Douglas Bader the previous year.

3 This verse was published in the *Times of Malta*; the cutting was affixed in the logbook of Flt Sgt Paddy Schade DFM, 126 Squadron.

4 Figures vary as to how many crated Spitfires arrived at Gibraltar; one source implies 16, another 17, but the authors believe 18 to be the correct number. Fifteen were actually flown to Malta and two others were returned to Gibraltar as unserviceable. In addition, one had been cannibalised at Gibraltar to provide spares for the others (see *Spitfire at War Volume 3* by Dr Alfred Price.)

5 Sgts Irving Gass and Fox would join a later ferry flight to Malta, where both lost their lives.

6 Sqn Ldr Stan Grant had seen action during the Battle of Britain; credited with 4 victories.

7 Ioannis Agorastos Plagis was born in Hartley, Southern Rhodesia in March 1919 of Greek parents. Having failed to join the Royal Rhodesian Air Force due to his nationality, he travelled to England and was accepted by the RAF, where his first name was westernised to John.

8 Extracted from *Spitfire at War Volume 3*.

9 Sgt Cyril Bush flew to Malta from the USS *Wasp* on 9 May 1942 and joined 126 Squadron.

10 The 15 Spitfires were AB262, 264, AB329-332, AB334-338, AB341, AB343, AB344 and AB346. Of these, Plt Off Peter Nash flew AB336 to Malta, Plt Off John Plagis AB343, Flt Sgt David Ferraby AB331 and Flt Sgt Paul Brennan AB344.

11 Extracted from *The Air Battle of Malta*: HMSO 1944.

12 See *Raiders Passed* by Charles E. Grech.

13 Hagar Qim, the site of a prehistoric settlement.

14 George Lord – see *Battle over Malta* by Tony Rogers.

15 Stan Fraser – *ibid*.

16 Howard Bell – *ibid*.

17 Translated for the authors by Sonja Stammwitz.

18 Sqn Ldr Gracie, a 30-year-old former Battle of Britain pilot with some ten victories to his credit including probables and shares, was known for his aggressiveness and intolerance – just the type of leader required at Malta.

19 Plt Off Don McLeod's one claim to fame, up until his arrival at Malta, was that he was the only person to have been shot down while 'flying' a Link trainer! Apparently, when at FTS, a German aircraft strafed the airfield and shot the training device off its pedestal while McLeod was inside. He was unhurt.

20 Flt Lt Barton had at least five victories to his credit; Sgts Ryckman and Crist each had one victory under their belts from fighting over Northern France.

21 See *Hell Island* by Dan McCaffery.

22 69 Squadron at Luqa was currently operating PR Mosquito W4063, which had been shanghaied by the AOC when it landed at Malta en route for the Middle East. It had been slightly damaged in an air raid but was again flying by the end of March.

23 Paudrick Schade was born in Singapore of Dutch father and Irish mother. His mother later remarried an officer in the Royal Navy, also based at Singapore. When WWII broke out Paudrick joined the Malayan Volunteer Air Force and trained as a pilot. Showing promise, he was sent to Canada to complete his training, where he was attached to the RCAF, although retaining his Malaya insignia. Having completed his training, he was posted to the UK, where he joined the RAF and was sent to a fighter OTU. On graduating he initially joined 501 Squadron in early 1941, then was posted to 54 Squadron, from where he volunteered for service at Malta. By coincidence, 8/JG53 had on its strength at this time the successful Fw Hans Schade, but the two were not destined to meet in the air as the 13-victory ace German pilot was shot down and killed on 1 April, the day after Paddy Schade's arrival.

24 Miss May Agius to the *Times of Malta*.

25 In his book *A Thorn in Rommel's Side*, Laddie Lucas credits Sqn Ldr Colin Davis, Command HQ dentist as the originator.

26 Unidentified airman whose diary survives and is located in the NWMA archives.

27 See *Battle over Malta*.

28 Only 47 of the 52 Spitfires were fully serviceable and it is believed that the aircraft allocated to Plt Off G.P.B. Davies, Sgts R. Buckley RCAF, and R.H. Brown RCAF of 603 Squadron were among those that were unserviceable and remained aboard the carrier, and that they were returned to Gibraltar together with the pilots.

29 Brian Cull had the pleasure of visiting Archie Bartleman on his farm in the Orange Free State in the mid-70s, when researching *Malta: The Spitfire Year 1942*. During his two-week stay on the Bartleman

homestead, before driving up to Rhodesia (now Zimbabwe), many enjoyable hours were spent in the company of Archie and his charming wife Freda and their beautiful daughter Doreen.

30 Sgt Salvador Walcott, known as Bud, crash-landed his Spitfire BP958 at Setif Constantine on the Algerian coast and was taken prisoner by Vichy French troops. He later told RAF interrogators that he did this 'due to enemy action' but when he transferred to the USAF in December 1942, following his release, and joined the 346th FS, 350th FG, he related that after taking off from the *Wasp* he was unable to retract his undercarriage. Since there was a danger of the engine overheating, and it was too far to fly to Gibraltar, he opted to fly to Algeria. He was imprisoned by the French at Sidi Bel-Abbes in Laghout Internment Camp. He attempted an escape with another RAF pilot in July 1942, but both were re-captured. He was eventually released following the Allied landings in November 1942 and was back in the UK by 24 November. Commissioned, he served with the 346thFS for a year in North Africa. Sadly, he was killed in a helicopter crash in the 1950s. Information provided by Lt Col Dow USAF Ret'd.

31 Although Sqn Ldr Bisdee was combat experienced, most of the remaing 45 pilots on this ferry were not, and that included Sqn Ldr Douglas-Hamilton. Exceptions included Flt Lt Denis Barnham of 601 and Flt Sgt Jack Rae of 603; the latter had been credited with one destroyed, four probables and two damaged with 485 Squadron.

32 Of Belgian father and Scottish mother, John Mejor had been born in Antwerp, Belgium in 1921. When his father died prematurely, the family moved to Liverpool, where John was educated. He joined the RAF in 1940.

33 In his logbook Junior Tayleur wrote: "Spent between 20 April and 13 June in 90th General Hospital, Mtarfa, where they tried unsuccessfully to remove 150 perspex splinters from my eyes." On 8 July he was flown aboard a Whitley to Gibraltar, and on 13 July reached the UK. In a similar incident to which Tayleur was wounded, another 249 Squadron pilot, Flt Lt James Nicholson, had been awarded a Victoria Cross during the Battle of Britain, the only such award made to a fighter pilot in WWII. Tayleur's only reward was much pain and discomfort, and he later returned to operations, but not to Malta.

34 Chuck MacLean in his 1957 novel *The Heavens Are Not Too High*, loosely based on his own experiences, identified Wg Cdr Jumbo Gracie as 'Wing Commander Pongo Baker'. Whilst his book is fiction, it is obvious that he was referring to Gracie's actual lecture at Takali.

35 Sgt Gordon Bolton joined 213 Squadron in the Western Desert and was killed in action on 3 July 1942.

36 See *Raiders Passed* by Charles B. Grech.

37 See *Hell Island*.

38 We are indebted to Dan McCaffery for permitting use of this paragraph, slightly edited, from his book *Hell Island*.

39 Flt Lt Nip Heppell later returned to Malta during his second tour.

40 Flt Lt Johnston eventually made a good recovery from his burns and did not lose his eyesight, as feared. As soon as he was fit to travel he was flown back to the UK.

41 American Sgt Leroy Morsheimer, due to his lack of combat experience, was not destined to remain on the island.

42 Plt Off Gunn later became a successful night fighter pilot.

43 According to Sgt Ron Hind, he and possibly a few other pilots, were conveyed to Malta aboard HMS *Welshman*.

44 Colin Bell was later commissioned and lost his life on 11/9/44 when his Spitfire of 127 Squadron was shot down by flak near Flushing.

45 In 1943, by then commissioned Reg Dickson was flying Spitfires with 129 Squadron. In July he was shot down over France but successfully evaded capture and returned to the UK. In the summer of 1944, still with 129 Squadron though by then flying Mustangs, he shot down two V-1 flying bombs and damaged a FW190.

46 See *Hell Island*.

47 *Ibid*.

48 Pilots of 4°Stormo claimed three Spitfires, one apiece by Serg Teresio Martinoli, Ten Mario Massa (strangely identified as a Defiant), and a third jointly by the missing Cap Dagasso, Ten Emanuele Annoni, Sottoten Leo Boselle and Serg Massimo Salvatore; the other three were credited to 2°Gruppo pilots Ten Remo Cazzolli, M.llo Olindo Simionato and the third jointly to Cap Roberto Fassi and M.llo Antonio Patriarca.

49 25-year-old Herbert 'Bert' Mitchell, who hailed from near Havelock in New Zealand, was killed. Prior to being posted to Malta he had flown more than 100 sorties with 41 Squadron, but had seen little combat.

50 See *Hell Island*.

51 *Ibid*.

52 The CW20 was the original prototype of what was later to become the C-46 Commando transport. It had been sold to Britain and, fitted with 24 seats and long-range tanks, was in use by BOAC as G-AGDI *St Louis*, and had begun flying a regular night service between Gibraltar and Malta.

53 It is believed that the Spitfires on this ferry flight from *Eagle* carried the painted letter C, followed by two digits, painted on the fuselage, to assist the groundstaff and pilots at Malta, similar to the number/letter combination of earlier deliveries of Spitfires.

54 M.llo Giovanni Durli, the engineer, who died of his wounds, was subsequently awarded the *Medaglia d'Oro* posthumously.

55 See *The Air Battle for Malta* by Lord James Douglas-Hamilton.

56 Flt Lt Ron West returned to the UK soon thereafter and was posted to 131 Squadron before joining 610 Squadron as a flight commander. On 23 May 1944 he was critically injured when he attempted to belly land his Spitfire, fitted with a slipper tank, on the metal PSP surface at the airfield.

57 Flt Lt Denis Barnham later wrote of his time at Malta, his depression and general feelings in his excellent book *One Man's Window* – probably the best and most moving personal memoir to come out of this period at Malta.

58 It is believed that Plt Off Tommy Scott later remustered on bombers and was KiA in 1944.

59 Artie Cleaveland was one of the many American pilots in the RAF/RCAF who later transferred to the USAF. By early 1943 he was flying P-40s with the 66thFS (57thFG) in Tunisia, and participated in the action which became known as the Palm Sunday Massacre (18/4/43), when 59 Ju52s flying from Tunisia to Sicily were shot down/force-landed by the P-40 pilots. 1/Lt Cleaveland was credited with five of the transports shot down, thereby becoming an ace in a day. He did not add to his score.

60 See *Hell Island*.

61 Guy Carlet had survived an accidental shoot-down by one of his colleagues a few months earlier when serving with 504 Squadron. While practicing dogfighting, his colleague erroneously pressed the gun button instead of the gun camera button. Carlet survived unscathed the resulting crash-landing.

62 See *Malta: The Spitfire Year 1942* by Chris Shores and Brian Cull with Nico Malizia for detailed accounts of the sea operations.

63 See *Hell Island*.

64 *Ibid.*

65 Sqn Ldr Lovell had some 15 victories at this stage including probables and shares.

66 The Spitfires ferried to Aboukir are believed to have included BP983, BR114, BR133, BR134, BR135, BR136/3-C, BR175, BR192, BR232, and BR344/3-M; Plt Off Cyril Hone flew Spitfire/D, the first leg to LG07 taking 4 hours 30 minutes; LG07 to LG13, 20 minutes; and finally from LG13 to Aboukir, one hour.

67 Following a rest, Flt Lt Barnham instructed at 57 OTU before finally returning to operations at the end of 1944, when he became a flight commander in 126 Squadron. Of those Malta veterans from 601 squadron who went to the Middle East, Plt Off Crash Curry soon distinguished himself.

68 Flt Lt Hugh Parry returned to operations and was shot down and taken prisoner on 24/9/43 while flying with 41 Squadron.

69 Laddie Lucas' father had died when he was still at junior school.

70 See *Hell Island*.

71 Wg Cdr Thompson had some ten victories to his credit including probables and shares.

72 Plt Off James Guthrie, a Surrey man, had one victory to his credit form his service with 54 Squadron.

73 Flt Lt Basil Friendship had distinguished himself in France in 1940, when he claimed nine victories including shares and probables, and was one of the few to receive a DFM and bar.

74 It is not clear if Köhler meant that he and his No.2 had fired at each other, or that their aircraft had touched each other.

75 This extract was taken from a novel written by Charles MacLean and published in 1957 under the title *The Heavens Are Not Too High*. It was apparently based on his own experiences but written in the third person; this has been changed to first person.

76 Sqn Ldr Laddie Lucas later flew a third tour and commanded a Mosquito intruder squadron. He was awarded a DSO and Bar to add to his DFC.

77 Wg Cdr Douglas-Hamilton also flew another tour and commanded a PR Mosquito squadron. He was killed in an accident on return from an operational sortie.

78 Flt Lt Sandy Sanders was killed in a flying accident on his return to the UK.

79 Pals Paul Brennan and Ray Hesselyn went on to achieve further success, but Brennan was killed in a flying accident in Australia and Hesselyn was shot down and taken prisoner. Both were awarded a DFC.

80 Bill 'Dusty' Miller was later posted to 486 Squadron flying Tempests and, during the summer of 1944, accounted for seven V-1 flying bombs and was awarded a DFC.

81 The 'Fighter pilot's paradise', which Malta at this time promised to be, did not suit everyone's temperament. Plt Off Barnfather, after a rest and recovery period, soon found himself back on an

operational squadron, and flew a full tour with 232 Squadron in Italy and Corsica in 1943-1944. Many fighter pilots struggled to find themselves at the start of their careers, even those who went on to achieve greatness. One prime example was Luftwaffe ace Major Klaus Mietusch, who had fought over Malta with 7/JG26 in 1941 before having a successful run in Russia. When he was eventually killed in action with US P-51s in September 1944, he had been shot down ten times, wounded on four occasions and had raised his score to 75. But earlier, he had confessed to a newspaper reporter: "I was a decidedly unskilled, poor fighter pilot, since I could not shoot. Everything happened too fast. When I had the enemy in front of me, everything turned red. The rush of blood clouded my reason, and my cone of fire lay below or above the target, but not on it. My motto became, bore in, until the enemy is as large as a barn door in your sights. When the situation becomes critical, there is usually only one correct reaction out of a hundred possibilities. Then you fight as though in a trance. The lightning swiftness of the necessary reactions does not permit calm deliberation. The situation requires immediate action. You grasp only fragments of the swirling, lightning-swift images. Later you can sometimes remember one thing or another; these are painful recollections if the situation was not grasped properly, and happier if you did the one and only correct thing."

82 Although Danny Hartney did recover from his injuries and was back flying by November, he then contracted Infantile Paralysis (poliomyelitis) to which he succumbed on 3 January 1943. He died aboard hospital ship *HTL6* en route to the UK and was buried at sea.

83 Nothing much is known about Sgt Ian Forrester's time at Malta, although he was posted to 1435 Squadron. By mid-1944 he had been commissioned and was flying Typhoons with 266 Squadron in the UK. He was killed in action on 28/7/44.

84 Of these departing pilots, Bob Sim and Slim Yarra were both later killed in action.

85 Magg Callieri had earned this nickname during his air force academy days when he had killed and eaten a cat for a bet! Other prominent Sicily-based Regia Aeronautica fighter leaders of the period were allotted radio codenames, thus: TenCol Aldo Remondino: 'Torino' (his home city); Magg Duilio Fanali: 'Roma' (his home city); Cap Luigi Borgogno: 'Borgo'; Cap Riccardo Roveda: 'Rovi'; Cap Furio Doglio Niclot: 'Furio'; Cap Riccardo Spagnolini: 'Pante' (Panther); Cap Carlo Miani: 'Tigre'; Cap Bruno Tattanelli: 'Leo' (Lion); Cap Vincenzo Sant' Andrea: 'Marte' (Mars).

86 Sqn Ldr Phil Winfield was flown back to the UK for treatment but, tragically, while convalescing at a nursing home was killed when it was hit by a bomb a few months later, on 25/10/42, during a hit-and-run raid by FW190s.

87 See *Hell Island.*

88 Wg Cdr Stainforth was killed in a flying accident in September 1942.

89 The crew of the Beaufort were Lt Ted Strever SAAF (pilot), Plt Off Bill Dunsmore (navigator), Sgt John Wilkinson RNZAF (W/Op), and Sgt Ray Brown RNZAF (gunner). For their achievement, both officers would receive the DFC, both NCOs the DFM. The unfortunate Italian crew comprised Ten Mastrodicasa (the pilot who had rescued the Beaufort crew the day before), M.llo Alessandro Chifari (co-pilot), Serg Treno Lossi (engineer), AvScMarc Antonio Schisano (W/Op), and Vice-Brigadiere (Police Sergeant) Giulio Scarciella.

90 See *Hell Island.*

91 Paddy Schade was commissioned on his return to the UK, where he became a flying instructor before returning to operations. Posted to 91 Squadron he shot down four flying bombs (one shared) in July 1944, but was then killed when his Spitfire collided with a Tempest while pursuing another on 31/7/44.

92 Wg Cdr Gracie returned to operations in late 1943 as CO of 169 Squadron flying Mosquitoes, but on 15/2/44 his aircraft was shot down over Germany and he was killed together with his radar operator.

93 Jack Rae returned to ops and ran his score to 22 including probables and shared, for which he received a DFC and Bar, but on 22/8/43 he became a POW when his Spitfire crashed in France.

94 Tony Bruce later flew with 92 Squadron in Sicily before joining 417RCAF Squadron as a flight commander in Italy. By early 1944 he was back in the UK serving with 161 Squadron flying Lysanders to France on special operations.

95 If, as implied by Plt Off John Mejor, the rescued pilot was indeed the Staffel leader, this would have been Oblt Günther Hess.

96 While *Furious* had joined *Ark Royal* in ferrying Hurricanes to Malta on four occasions in 1941, and had carried others to West Africa that year, she had never before launched Spitfires. Consequently, early in August she had slipped out into the Irish Sea from Greenock with a couple of Spitfires aboard for a trial launch. With her went three experienced fighter pilots, Grp Capt Walter Churchill DSO DFC, Flt Lt Eric 'Timber' Woods DFC and Plt Off Bill Rolls DFM.

After inspecting the ship, they had been concerned as to the prospects, for about one third the way along the deck from the point at which the first of a flight of eight Spitfires would have to take-off, there was a ramp. At the ship's forward end the flight deck ended some way short of the bow, which had originally incorporated a separate, lower flying-off deck at that level. This consequently greatly restricted the potential for an aircraft to 'sink' in front of the carrier as it left the flight deck. Woods elected to make the initial try. The usual wooden wedges were inserted to hold the flaps open, but chocks were also placed under the undercarriage wheels, and a number of sailors held down the tail with a rope while the pilot ran up the engine to maximum revs. The sudden release of the rope and chocks allowed a certain degree of 'catapult' effect, and the Spitfire shot forward but had hardly any real speed up to when it met the ramp. Woods literally had to bounce it off the end of the deck to stay in the air, but as he flew away to land ashore, Grp Capt Churchill had to advise the carrier's captain that such a take-off would probably be beyond the capabilities of the average relatively inexperienced pilot likely to be making the flight. At that point Rolls recalled having recently flown a Spitfire fitted with a new hydromatic propeller, which had offered a considerably shorter take-off run and better climb performance. He suggested that fitting these would probably make all the difference to a take-off from *Furious*. On return to Greenock the necessary arrangements were made at high speed, 40 Spitfires being loaded aboard together with 40 of the new propellers (and some 100 groundcrew to fit them) as the vessel sailed for Gibraltar. A volunteer was called for to make a test launch with an aircraft fitted with the new propeller, the *quid pro quo* being that he would then land ashore at Prestwick, and thereby miss the forthcoming operation. As there were no takers, an Australian sergeant was delegated for the task; the take-off proved quite easy and the ship set off southwards, the assembled pilots then being advised by Grp Capt Churchill of their destination.

97 Plt Off Art Roscoe, an American from Chicago, had three victories while flying with 71 Eagle Squadron, but only one had been confirmed.

98 Flt Sgt Ted Hiskens had claimed two FW190s damaged while flying with 129 Squadron in the UK.

99 The defending Sea Hurricanes, Fulmars and Martlets aboard the carriers *Eagle*, *Victorious* and *Indomitable*, together with the escort's guns, had gallantly repelled raid after raid but could not prevent the loss of nine of the 13 merchantmen. In two days' fighting, the Fleet Air Arm pilots claimed 39 Axis aircraft shot down and several more probables for the loss of seven Sea Hurricanes, four Fulmars and two Martlets.

100 Adrian Warburton was a legendary and charismatic figure, well known on Malta and by the Maltese. He had initially arrived at Malta in November 1940 as co-pilot of a Maryland reconnaissance aircraft.

101 See *The Maltese Spitfire* by Harry Coldbeck.

102 Savini was a non-swimmer, but on coming to the surface found that the aircraft's dinghy had released directly under his backside, and was able to climb into it at once. Thrown further away, Patella was fortunately a strong swimmer, although he was not able to see the dinghy due to the heavy sea. Overhead, watching the drama below, were the crew of another Ju87, whose pilot, Serg Giulio Campari, circled and dropped his own aircraft's dinghy, but this was carried away by the current. Somewhat later another Ju87 appeared. On sighting this aircraft, Savini fired off a signal rocket without it being sighted by the searching aircraft. Patella did see this, however, and with the last of his strength succeeded in swimming over to the dinghy and climbed aboard. Just before sunset, they spotted a head of red hair floating in the sea, which turned out to belong to Flt Sgt Ron McFarlane, the observer of a downed Beaufighter. The Italians pulled him aboard and for the next 60 hours they drifted at the mercy of the currents and the elements until finally the crew of a searching Do24 sighted them and executed a rescue.

103 Thurne Parks, known as Tommy, was a tough character from Oshawa, Ontario, who had had a number of scrapes with authority, dating back to his departure from Canada, as recalled by his close friend, John Sherlock: "Tommy was a tough hard-nosed kid who didn't know how to step backwards. Tommy took exception at the food served to the sergeant pilots on board the ship taking him and others to the UK from Canada, and he led a rebellion against the ship's company whom, I believe, were Polish. As a result, this was classed as mutiny and Tommy spent the rest of the trip in the brig, and he ended up at the OTU as a corporal pilot! He actually joined the RAF squadron as a corporal but the RAF CO had this rectified in short order."

104 See *Hurricane and Spitfire Pilots at War* by Terence Kelly.

105 Wg Cdr Prosser Hanks had flown four convoy protection sorties during the day, totalling in excess of seven hours flying over the sea, cooped up in an uncomfortable cockpit and under the threat of action at almost any time.

106 It transpired that the Beaufighter pilot, Plt Off David Jay DFC, an American in the RCAF, had been lost when the aircraft was shot down, but his Scottish observer, Flt Sgt Ron McFarlane, was rescued by the same Do24 that had picked up the Italian crew of the Ju87, Serg Magg Savini and 1°AvArm Patella.

107 Flt Lt Peter Lovell was posted to 74 Squadron in December 1942, and later still with 112 Squadron. He received a DFC in 1945.

108 Leo Nomis added: "For some curious reason (considering the wretched living and operating conditions at Malta) a transfer to a Western Desert unit was considered being sent to a 'punishment' squadron! So, by October, I was packed off to Egypt, flying out in a Dakota and, as it turned out, the 'punishment' squadron I was posted to in the Western Desert was the prestigious and high-scoring 92

Squadron, of the Desert Air Force's 244 Spitfire Wing." With 92 Squadron he shot down two Bf109s and later transferred to the USAF, but was employed as an instructor in the USA much to his chagrin. Although not Jewish, in 1948 he volunteered to fly S.199s (Czech-built Messerschmitt Bf109Gs) and PR Spitfires for the Israelis in the War of Independence. See *The Desert Hawks* by Leo Nomis and Brian Cull.

109 Another survivor of this operation who had been fortunate to be rescued by a Royal Navy destroyer when the AA cruiser *Coventry* was sunk, was Wg Cdr Stan Turner DFC, late of Malta, who had been aboard the cruiser as RAF Liaison Officer.

110 Sgt John Houlton continued: "Three days later I flew again, to find I was blacking out in quite moderate turns. By this time I had lost over a stone and a half in weight, while the insect bites had become a suppurating mass on my arms, legs, face and ears. Ken Charney chased me off to see the young Medical Officer, who refused to look me over outside his morning sick parade hours. I reckon he was on borrowed time anyway, for Ken made some phone calls and the MO was told to pack his bags for Cairo via the next submarine. Meanwhile, an ambulance took me to Mtarfa Military Hospital where I promptly acquired a case of tonsillitis, three days before my twentieth birthday."

111 Flt Lt Geoffrey Wellum had served with 92 Squadron during the Battle of Britain.

112 Sqn Ldr Mike Stephens had, at this time, some 15 victories to his credit, two of which had been claimed in 1941 whilst flying Hurricanes with the Turkish Air Force.

113 There would appear to be a problem with the date of these claims, since there is no record of a Messerschmitt crashing on the island on this date, nor any German losses.

114 One German source records Uffz Schlick's sixth victory as having occurred on 3 October, another on 10 October, but on neither day is there any record of a British pilot, or other member of an aircrew, being shot down and rescued by a Do24 to become a prisoner.

115 In a similar action during the Battle of Britain, Flt Lt James Nicholson of 249 Squadron had won a Victoria Cross.

116 According to one German source, a further seven Spitfires were claimed by pilots of I/JG77 on this date, 14 October, by Oblt Siegfried Freytag (his 72nd and second for the day), two by Fw Otto Pohl (his 13th and 14th), and one apiece by Ltn Hans-Joachim Gläss (his eighth), Ltn Konrad Fels (also his eighth), Oblt Hesse (first) and Ltn Rüdiger Belling (third).

117 A posthumous award of the Ritterkreuz to Uffz Golinski was announced during the following month.

118 See Jochen Prien's excellent JG53 history, from which this paragraph is extracted verbatim.

119 Ltn Alfred Hammer went on to raise his score to 26 by the end of the war.

120 On 5 September, The Air Ministry had informed AOC Park: "The trials of the Spitfire with the 170-gallon tank are now complete. Range is somewhat short for reasonable safety between Gibraltar and Malta and consequently 30-gallon internal tank is also being provided. The 170-gallon and 30-gallon tanks together with extra oil tank and necessary accessories are expected to begin arriving in Gibraltar during the first week in October. Precise date of commencement of despatch of aircraft and also rate of despatch are dependent on situation generally."

The first two of a dozen such long-range Spitfires departed on 25 October, followed by five more on 31 October and the final five on 6 November. A special team of assemblers and technicians had been flown out from the UK to Gibraltar to ensure accurate fitting of the tanks, this team also required to assemble and prepare the large numbers of Spitfires arriving by sea in readiness for the invasion of North-West Africa, planned for early November.

121 Sgt Cameron was flown back to the UK for treatment. Having been commissioned, he later returned to operations with 401 RCAF Squadron and was credited with six victories including one probable, for which he received a DFC.

122 Flt Lt Ron Atkinson had been badly burned around the face and hands as a result of an air collision while flying with 152 Squadron in the UK, but, on recovery, this did not deter him from volunteering for service at Malta.

123 Flg Off Howard Crafts had recently shot down a Ju88 while operating from Gibraltar.

124 Following his return to the UK, Plt Off Freddie Thomas joined 91 Squadron and was killed in an air collison on 6/12/43.

125 These were the last civilians to be killed by bombs at Malta in 1942. The next and final raid in which casualties occurred was on the night of 20 July 1943, when six were killed and 19 wounded in Sliema, Floriana and Valetta.

126 Bill Irwin, upon release from prison, re-offended and was imprisoned for a further six months, deprived of his flying badge and returned to Australia, where he was dishonourably discharged from the RAAF. Sadly, this troubled man died in 1948, presumably by his own hand.

127 Roy Nash of the *Star* (see *Carve Malta on My Heart* by Frederick Galea).

128 Plt Off Bob Park's young sister had been drowned at sea, and his father, a doctor, had died shortly before war broke out. His grief-stricken mother, Joanna, was a voluntary nurse in Australia. She

managed to visit her son's grave after the war (in 1948) when she generously donated £1,000 to the welfare of the Maltese people. She told a reporter: "I would not have Robert's body brought home for burial. I am proud that he should be buried in the island he died to save. I have spoken to many Maltese. They are fine people and I know they appreciate Robert's sacrifice. Nothing I can do for Malta will be too much."

129 As recorded by Roy Nash of the *Star*.

130 *Ibid*.

131 On his return to the UK, Plt Off Jo Dalley retrained as a fighter pilot and, during the V-1 blitz on England in the summer of 1944 shot down two of the flying bombs.

132 Plt Off John Frazer failed to return from a PR sortie on 11 January 1943.

133 See John Houlton's *Spitfire Strikes*.

134 Sub Lt Ernie Pratt DSC was killed in an accident a few weeks later, when Spitfire EP701 that he was flying crashed off the coast.

135 Despite his problems at Malta, Noel Pashen later received a commission and flew a full tour of ops in Italy.

136 Wg Cdr Buck Buchanan was another in the Adrian Warburton mould, and had increased his tally to 13 before he was eventually shot down by flak. Although seen in his dinghy, he succumbed to exposure and dehydration.

137 The damage to Flt Lt Seed's Spitfire was inflicted by Sgt Carr, the gunner aboard Flg Off F.F. Brown's Marauder.

138 Those killed in this tragic incident were Sgts Tom Exell RAAF, Ralph Ploskin, Alan Watts and Percy Cockington RAAF; the other two survivors were Sgt Dixon (broken ankle) and Sgt Willocks (burns). The three Marauders were returning from a mine-laying sortie to Tunis harbour, where Einsaar's aircraft had been hit by flak. After being shot down by Flt Lt Seed, three of the crew had managed to get into the dinghy. Len Einsaar had been separated from his navigator (Tom Exell) by a sea of flames, so he dived under the flames to rescue him, but Exell was so badly injured that he died in Einsaar's arms shortly afterwards. Len Einsaar, a 6'4" former policeman, had represented Australia as an oarsman in the 1936 Berlin Olympics. He was awarded the DFM for his performance. His aircraft was again shot down four months later, he and his crew being taken prisoner.

139 Extracted from *Spitfire: The Documentary History* by Dr Alfred Price.

SELECT BIBLIOGRAPHY

249 at War: Brian Cull (Grub Street 1997)
249 at Malta: Brian Cull and Frederick Galea (Wise Owl 2004)
Spitfires over Sicily: Brian Cull and Nicola Malizia with Frederick Galea (Grub Street 2000)
Malta: The Spitfire Year: Christopher Shores and Brian Cull with Nicola Malizia (Grub Street 1991)
The Desert Hawks: Leo Nomis and Brian Cull (Grub Street 1998)
Call-Out: Frederick Galea (Malta at War Publications 2002)
Lest We Forget: John Agius MBE and Frederick Galea (Malta Aviation Museum Foundation 1999)
Carve Malta on My Heart: Frederick Galea (Bieb Bieb 2004)
Buck McNair: Norman Franks (Grub Street 2001)
Those Other Eagles: Christopher Shores (Grub Street 2004)
Fighters over Tunisia: Christopher Shores, Hans Ring & Bill Hess (Spearman 1975)
Tattered Battlements: Tim Johnston DFC (Kimber 1985)
Kiwi Spitfire Ace: Jack Rae DFC (Grub Street 2002)
Five Up: Laddie Lucas DSO DFC (Sidgwick & Jackson 1978)
Out of the Blue: Laddie Lucas DSO DFC (Hutchinson 1995)
A Thorn in Rommel's Side: Laddie Lucas DSO DFC (Stanley Paul 1992)
Malta Spitfire: George Beurling DSO DFC DFM and Leslie Roberts (OUP Canada 1943)
Spitfires over Malta: Paul Brennan DFC and Ray Hesselyn DFM with Henry Bateson (Jarrolds 1943)
The Maltese Spitfire: Harry Coldbeck DFC (Airlife 1997)
The Air Battle for Malta: Lord James Douglas-Hamilton (Mainstream 1981)
Crash Sites in Malta: Anthony Rogers (Sutton 2000)
One Man's Window: Denis Barnham (Kimber 1956)
Jagdgeschwader 53: Volume 2: Dr Jochen Prien & Gerhard Stemmer (Schiffer)
Jagdgeschwader 77: Volume 3: Dr Jochen Prien & Gerhard Stemmer (Schiffer)
The Greatest Squadron of Them All, Volume 2: David Ross (Grub Street 2003)
Against all Odds: Lex McAulay (Hutchinson Australia 1989)
Hell Island: Dan McCaffery (James Lorimer, Toronto 1998)
Raiders Passed: Charles B. Grech (Midsea books 1998)
Spitfire Strikes: John Houlton DFC (Kimber)
Spitfire: A Documentary History: Alfred Price (Ian Allan)
Hurricane and Spitfire Pilots at War: Terence Kelly (Kimber 1986)
Warburton's War: Tony Spooner DSO DFC (Kimber 1987)
Spitfire Attack: Bill Rolls DFC DFM (Kimber 1987)
A Knave among Knights in their Spitfires: Jerry Billing
When Malta Stood Alone: Joseph Micallef (self published Malta 1981)

Diaries/journals/logbooks including: Grp Capt Mike Stephens DSO DFC; Sqn Ldr John Lynch DFC, Flt Lt Tim Goldsmith DFC RAAF; Wg Cdr Timber Woods DFC; Grp Capt Prosser Hanks DSO DFC; Plt Off Peter Nash DFC; Flt Lt Colin Parkinson DFC RAAF; Flt Lt Noel Pashen RAAF; Sqn Ldr Paddy O'Brien; Flt Lt Joe Bush; Sqn Ldr Rod Smith DFC RCAF; Plt Off Jerry Smith RCAF; Flt Lt Paddy Schade DFM; Sqn Ldr W.J. 'Johnny' Johnson DFC; Wg Cdr Laddie Lucas DSO DFC; Flt Lt Raoul Daddo-Langlois; Wg Cdr Lord David Douglas-Hamilton; Flt Lt John Sanderson RAAF; Sqn Ldr John Mejor DFC.

PERSONNEL INDEX

Wilfer, Fw Anton II/LG1 297
Willenbrink, Uffz Egbert II/JG53 200
Witschke, Uffz Karl-Heinz 3/JG77 214, 230, 233
Wittenberg, Ltn Günther 2/KG54 289
Wittkausky, Ltn 9/KG54 289
Wittmeyer, Hptm Heinz II FK HQ 319
Woas, Uffz I/KG54 285, 312
Wöhl, Obfw Kurt 9/KG77 297
Würzer, Fw Christoph 9/StG3 43
Wutz, Uffz Walter 2/KG54 289

Zellot, Ltn Walter 1/JG53 63, 70
Zettelmaier, Uffz Max 8/KG54 291
Zimmer, Oblt Josef 7/KG77 228
Zirus, Uffz Werner 3/SchG2 325, 332

Regia Aeronautica

Ambrosio, Ten Giovanni 378^Squadriglia CT 153, 203
Antonelli, Ten Francesco 60^Squadriglia BT 195
Arco, Sottoten Luigi 170^Squadriglia RM 102
Argenton, Cap Alberto 91^Squadriglia CT 128

Baraldi, Ten Giuseppe 152^Squadriglia CT 154
Barani, Ten Guido 278^Squadriglia Aut AS 249
Bartolozzi, Ten Giulio 150^Squadriglia CT 147
Bartolucci, M.llo Pasquale 360^Squadriglia CT 157, 285
Bastogi, Ten Vittorio 351^Squadriglia CT 159, 240
Berna, Serg Luigi 151^Squadriglia CT 234, 274
Bianchi, M.llo Pietro 352^Squadriglia CT 186
Biccolini, Ten Manlio 378^Squadriglia CT 198, 325
Boerci, 1°AvMot Enrico 209^Squadriglia B'aT 164
Bonannini, AvScArm Piero 170^Squadriglia RM 102
Bonfiglio, Ten Giuseppe 351^Squadriglia CT 153, 159, 234, 252, 315
Bonuti, Ten Ado 97^Squadriglia CT 96
Borgogno, Cap Luigi 352^Squadriglia CT 177, 179, 311
Boselli, Cap Leo 362^Squadriglia CT 273
Buvoli, M.llo Aldo 360^Squadriglia CT 172
Brugnera, Ten Paolo di Porcella Guacella 352^Squadriglia CT 203

Callieri, Magg Gino 20°Gruppo CT 177, 222
Carafa, Ten Giobatta Caracciolo 360^Squadriglia CT 159, 180, 252
Carnielli, Ten Antonio 144^Squadriglia RM 163
Castellano, Ten Gustavo 351^Squadriglia CT 285
Cavallo, 1°AvArm Michele 239^Squadriglia B'aT 253
Cazzolli, Ten Remo 152^Squadriglia CT 133
Celentano, Ten Agostino 150^Squadriglia CT 130, 159, 349
Cenni, Cap Giuseppe 102°Gruppo B'aT 164
Ceoletta, Serg Magg Giambattista 90^Squadriglia CT 60
Cerri, Serg Magg Angelo 351^Squadriglia CT 157, 159, 285
Cervellin, Cap Giovanni 369^Squadriglia CT 273
Cesaro, Serg Magg Elio 152^Squadriglia CT 205
Cherubini, Ten Fabrizio 353^Squadriglia CT 195
Chierici, Ten Ennio 151^Squadriglia CT 183
Converso, Serg Magg Gastone 102°Gruppo B'aT 164
Cristiani, Serg Magg Romolo 14^Squadriglia BT 185
Cumbat, Cap Antonio 239^Squadriglia B'aT 252, 253
Cusmano, Sottoten Ugo 288^Squadriglia RM 165

Dagasso, Cap Roberto 97^Squadriglia CT 96, 113

Dal Ponte, Serg Giovanni 210^Squadriglia BT 105
Damiani, Ten Paolo 352^Squadriglia CT 271
Damiani, M.llo Rinaldo 97^Squadriglia CT 125, 129
D'Amico, Ten Italo 151^Squadriglia CT 208, 225, 252, 288, 315, 317
Del Fabbro, Serg Magg Giovanni 378^Squadriglia CT 154, 172, 203
De Merich, Ten Arnaldo 152^Squadriglia CT 153, 154
De Seta, Sottoten Emanuele 353^Squadriglia CT 270
Di Bert, Serg Cesare 150^Squadriglia CT 181, 186
Di Pauli, Serg Magg Bruno 151^Squadriglia CT 222
Disint, Sottoten Isidoro 150^Squadriglia CT 253
Doglio Niclot, Cap Furio 151^Squadriglia CT 177, 182, 183, 188, 189, 194, 202, 203, 205, 208, 209, 225, 227, 228, 349
Dose, Sottoten Dante 352^Squadriglia CT 203
Dringoli, Serg Giovanni 150^Squadriglia CT 147, 148, 158, 159
Durli, M.llo Giovanni 210^Squadriglia BT 139

Fabbri, M.llo Dino 239^Squadriglia CT 141
Falcone, Sottoten Nicola 211^Squadriglia BT 137
Fanali, Magg Duilio 155°Gruppo CT 146, 147, 165, 181, 249, 287, 293, 296
Fassi, Cap Roberto 150^Squadriglia CT 94, 144
Ferrante, Ten Bartolomeo 58^Squadriglia BT 250
Ferri, Antonio 211^Squadriglia BT 112, 113
Ferrazza, M.llo Cesare 360^Squadriglia CT 180, 288, 306
Fischer, Sottoten Vincenzo 84^Squadriglia CT 135
Franchini, Ten/Cap Giovanni 351^Squadriglia CT 181, 315
Frigerio, Ten Jacopo 97^Squadriglia CT 128
Fulgosi, Ten Agostino Cigala 51°Stormo CT 293

Gallo, Ten Michele 151^Squadriglia CT 189
Gambari, Serg Magg Giovanni 378^Squadriglia CT 234, 296, 325
Gamberini, M.llo Gino 209^Squadriglia B'aT 165
Gasperoni, Ten Giorgio 358^Squadriglia CT 139, 141
Gaucci, M.llo Roberto 360^Squadriglia CT 165
Gelli, Serg Magg Falerio 378^Squadriglia CT 227
Geminiani, Serg Magg Aldo 152^Squadriglia CT 154
Giannella, Ten Luigi 97^Squadriglia CT 96, 105
Giovannini, Sottoten Adolfo 353^Squadriglia CT 191
Giudici, Serg Spiridione 353^Squadriglia CT 186
Gon, Cap Aldo 53^Squadriglia CT 87
Grillo, Sottoten Carlo 150^Squadriglia CT 130
Grosso, AvScMot Luigi 239^Squadriglia B'aT 165
Guerci, Serg Magg Mario 73^Squadriglia CT 128
Guiducci, Cap Giovanni 90^Squadriglia CT 60

Iannilli, Serg Magg Vittorio 353^Squadriglia CT 240
Iannucci, M.llo Maurizio 352^Squadriglia CT 198, 203, 240, 299

Jellici, M.llo Luigi 150^Squadriglia CT 148, 180, 186

La Ferla, Cap Germano 359^Squadriglia CT 273
Leoni, Serg Magg Alcide 351^Squadriglia CT 234
Longano, Sottoten Nicola 360^Squadriglia CT 180
Longo, Sottoten Rosario 151^Squadriglia CT 208
Lucchini, Cap Franco 10°Gruppo CT 42, 105, 128

Malagola, Serg Willy 360^Squadriglia CT 180, 182
Malosso, Ten Ettore 151^Squadriglia CT 191
Manini, Serg Domenico 378^Squadriglia CT 233
Marchetti, M.llo Antonio 239^Squadriglia B'aT 165